Praise for *The Longest War*

"*The Longest War* is ambitious both in scope and aims . . . you need to understand al-Qaida, and Bergen, with this detailed, serious, scrupulously fair, perceptive, and sometimes startling work has made a significant contribution to us doing exactly that."

—Jason Burke, *The Guardian*

"*The Longest War* is by far the best and most comprehensive book on the conflict so far."

—Christina Lamb, *Sunday Times*

"A grippingly important work that belongs on the shelf alongside *The Looming Tower* and *Ghost Wars*."

—*The Daily Beast*

"*The Longest War* is his history of a daunting subject that succeeds where other books have failed. That's because the author was one of the few people onto al-Qaeda years before the instant experts cropped up. And he is still there watching, long after most of those so-called experts packed it in and moved on."

—Colin Freeze, *The Globe and Mail*

"For years, I tried to read every new novel about how 9/11 affected our lives. Some were very thoughtful, but I always came away unsatisfied, feeling that the authors had worked hard but had somehow fallen short. As I read the stunning first section of Peter L. Bergen's new book on the war between the United States and al-Qaeda, I realized I had been looking in the wrong genre. None of the novels were as effective or moving as *The Longest War*, which is a history of our time. . . . *The Longest War* is one of the most important accounts on the subject to appear in years. But be warned: You will read it and weep."

—Thomas E. Ricks, *The New York Times Book Review*

"A revelatory, pull-no-punches history of the War on Terror, from before 9/11 to the present day. . . . One of the deepest and most disturbing investigations of one of the defining issues of our era."

—*Kirkus*, starred review

"Drawing on vast firsthand knowledge of the region and mining a huge stock of primary and secondary material, including his own interviews with combatants, the book's depth of detail and breadth of insight make it one of the more useful analysis of the ongoing conflict."

—*Publishers Weekly*, starred review

"In *The Longest War* Bergen attempts to provide us with an overarching narrative of the first ten years of the epic struggle that resulted from the 9/11 attacks, and he does an admirable job of it."

—Christian Caryl, *The Washington Monthly*

"[A] readable and well-reported appraisal"

—*The Economist*

"*The Longest War* is a useful synopsis of the struggle we've come to call the war on terror, and he chronicles it with the keen eye of an experienced journalist and on-the-ground observer. Bergen, who actually has interviewed bin Laden and is the author of two books on him, gives a particularly good view of al-Qaeda's operative behavior—it's much more bureaucratic than you might imagine—as well as a gripping re-creation of what went wrong at Tora Bora, the last opportunity the U.S. had to apprehend or kill bin Laden."

—*Los Angeles Times*

"When the War on Terror is consigned to the history books, one name will dominate as the steady, clear-eyed chronicler of that period. Peter Bergen was among the first to note the rise of al-Qaeda, and he is still on the case. *The Longest War* is a vital and essential account of the central conflict of our times."

—Lawrence Wright, author of *The Looming Tower: Al-Qaeda and the Road to 9/11*

"Peter Bergen has long since established himself as America's most authoritative and insightful analyst on Osama bin Laden and al-Qaeda, and time and again has given the nation an unblinking glimpse into the mind of the enemy. Now, with *The Longest War*, he has performed perhaps his greatest public service with what is certainly the finest comprehensive history of the war on terror yet written. Weaving together the wars in Iraq, Afghanistan, and the broader anti-terror campaigns of Bush and Obama, he does something nearly impossible. He explains how we got here from 9/11."

—James Risen, author of *State of War: The Secret History of the CIA and the Bush Administration*

"Peter Bergen has produced a masterful definitive assessment of al-Qaeda and America since September 11—rich with new details, elevated by careful analysis, and quickened by riveting characters and stories. This is essential reading."

—Steve Coll, two-time Pulitzer Prize–winning author of *Ghost Wars* and *The Bin Ladens*

"Peter Bergen's *The Longest War* is indispensable history. Authoritative and ambitious, it provides a damning account of the fitful fight against Islamic terrorism that every American should read."

—Jane Mayer, author of *The Dark Side: How the War on Terror Turned Into a War on American Ideals*

Also by Peter L. Bergen

The Osama bin Laden I Know
Holy War, Inc.

The Longest War

The Enduring Conflict between America and al-Qaeda

October 2011

Peter L. Bergen

To Dan,
with best wishes
Peter Bergen

Free Press
New York London Toronto Sydney

For Tresha with all my love.

Free Press
A Division of Simon & Schuster, Inc.
1230 Avenue of the Americas
New York, NY 10020

First Free Press trade paperback edition June 2011

FREE PRESS and colophon are trademarks of Simon & Schuster, Inc.

For information about special discounts for bulk purchases, please contact Simon & Schuster Special Sales at 1-866-506-1949 or business@simonandschuster.com

The Simon & Schuster Speakers Bureau can bring authors to your live event. For more information or to book an event contact the Simon & Schuster Speakers Bureau at 1-866-248-3049 or visit our website at www.simonspeakers.com.

Designed by Carla Jayne Jones

Manufactured in the United States of America

3 5 7 9 10 8 6 4

Library of Congress Cataloging-in-Publication Data

Bergen, Peter L.
The longest war : the enduring conflict between America and al-Qaeda / Peter L. Bergen. — 1st Free Press hbk. ed.
p. cm.
Includes bibliographical references and index.
1. War on Terrorism, 2001–2009. 2. Terrorism—United States—Prevention. 3. Terrorism—Prevention. 4. Iraq War, 2003- 5. Qaida (Organization) I. Title.
HV6432.B46 2011
909.83'1—dc22 2010015268

ISBN 978-0-7432-7893-5
ISBN 978-0-7432-7894-2 (pbk)
ISBN 978-1-4391-6059-6 (ebook)

Contents

Maps

Afghanistan and Pakistan

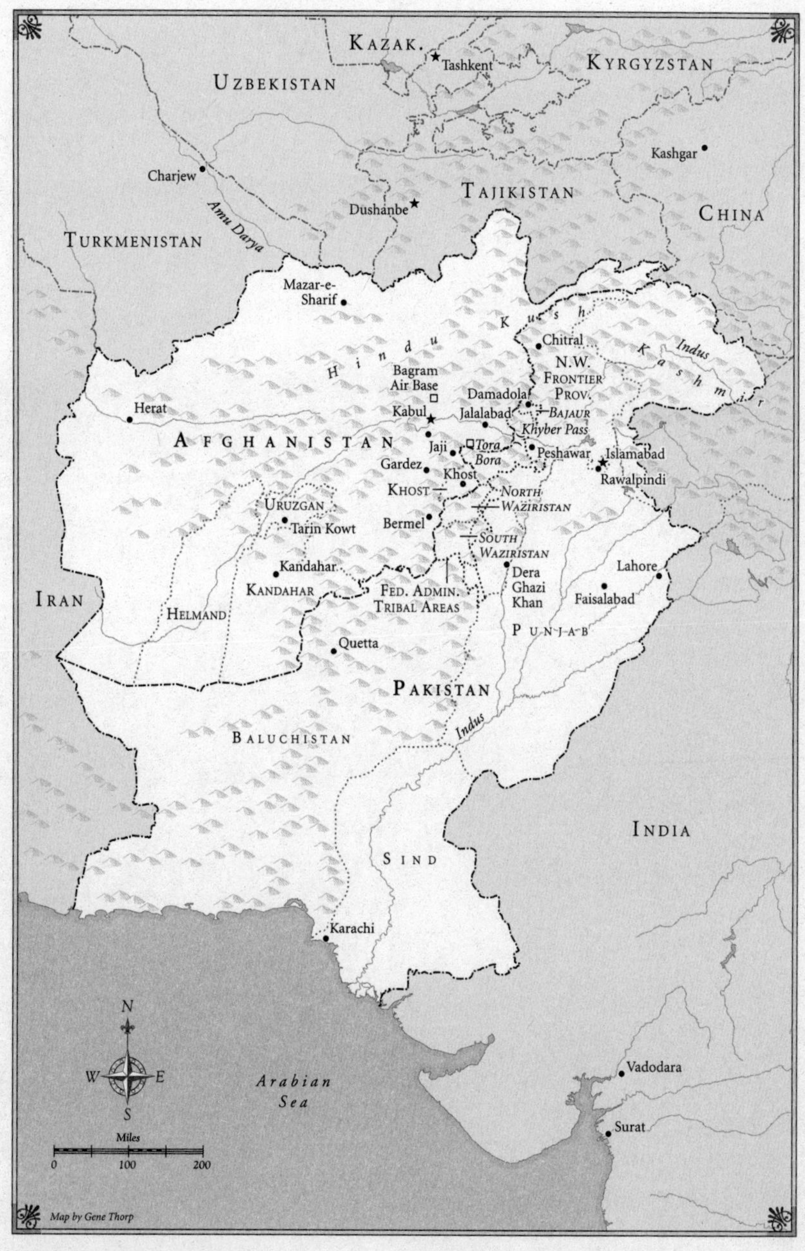

Kazak.
Tashkent
Kyrgyzstan
Uzbekistan
Kashgar
Charjew
Tajikistan
Dushanbe
China
Amu Darya
Turkmenistan
Mazar-e-Sharif
Hindu Kush
Chitral
Indus
Kashmir
N.W. Frontier Prov.
Bagram Air Base
Damadola
Herat
Kabul
Jalalabad
Bajaur
Khyber Pass
Afghanistan
Jaji
Tora Bora
Peshawar
Islamabad
Gardez
Khost
Rawalpindi
Khost
North Waziristan
Uruzgan
Tarin Kowt
Bermel
South Waziristan
Kandahar
Lahore
Dera Ghazi Khan
Iran
Kandahar
Fed. Admin. Tribal Areas
Faisalabad
Helmand
Punjab
Quetta
Pakistan
Indus
Baluchistan
India
Sind
Karachi
N
W
E
S
Arabian Sea
Vadodara
Surat
Miles
0
100
200
Map by Gene Thorp

Iraq and the wider Middle East

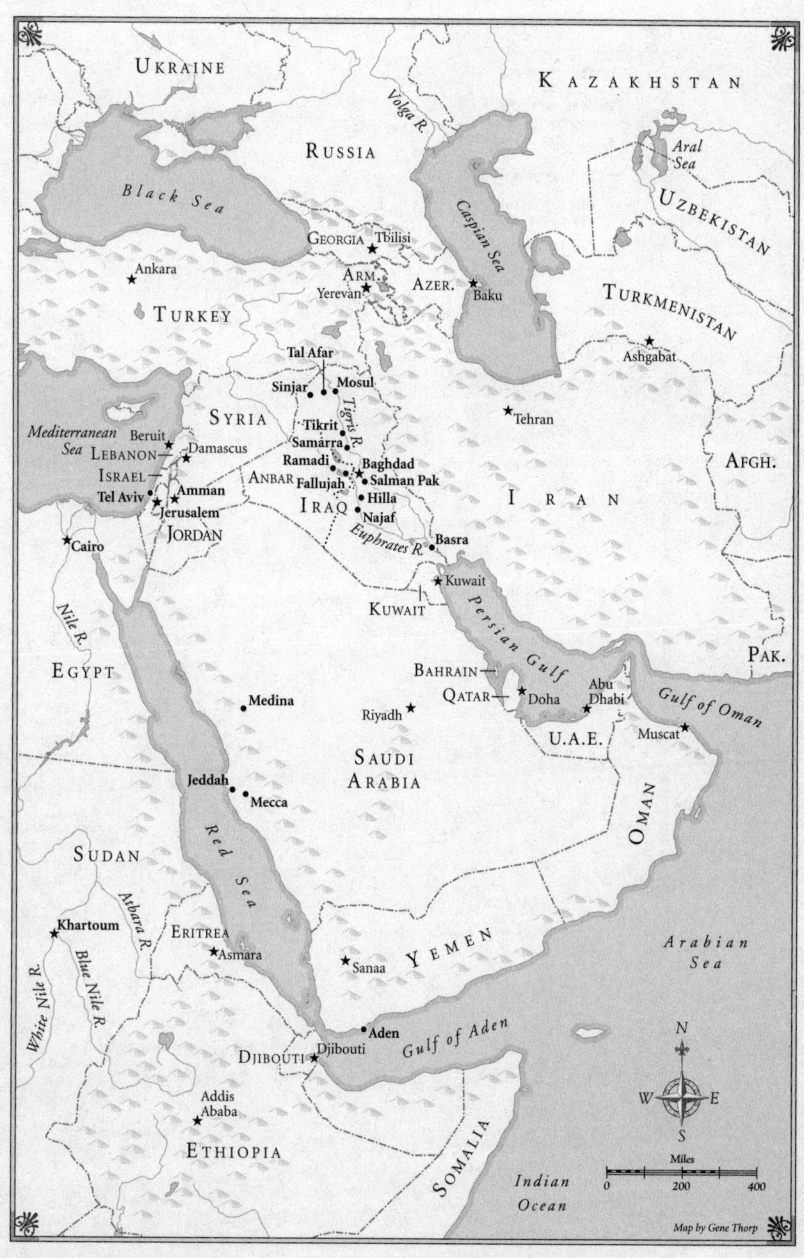

Significant events by al-Qaeda, its affiliates, or those inspired by its ideas.
Attack
Serious plot
Jihadist terrorist campaign
Terrorist group
Iceland
Planes plot 2006
Norway
Sweden
Finland
Oslo 2010
Russia
Manchester 2009
London 2005
Ire.
U.K.
Neth.
Den.
Fertilizer plot 2004
Amsterdam 2004
Atlantic Ocean
Moscow 2002 2010
Bel.
France
Ger.
Pol.
Bel.
Ramstein Air Base 2007
Munich 2006
Madrid 2004
Port.
Aus.
Ukraine
Hung.
Barcelona 2008
Spain
Rom.
Casablanca 2003
Italy
Beslan 2004
Algiers 2007
Bulg.
Black Sea
Morocco
Al-Qaeda in the Islamic Maghreb
Tun.
Greece
Istanbul 2003
Geo.
Arm.
Azer.
Casp. Sea
Turkey
Mediterranean Sea
Djerba 2002
Algeria
Syria
Iraq Campaign begins 2003
Amman 2005
Al-Qaeda in Iraq
Libya
Taba 2004
Jordan
Iraq
Iran
Mali
Egypt
Sharm el-Sheikh 2005
Saudi Arabia Campaign begins 2003
Burkina Faso
Niger
U.A.E.
Saudi Arabia
Chad
Al-Qaeda in the Arabian Peninsula
Nigeria
Erit.
Sudan
Yemen
Limburg 2002
Djib.
Cameroon
C.A.R.
Ethipoia
Gabon
Rep. of Congo
Somalia
Uganda
Kampala 2010
Al-Shabab
Somalia Ongoing campaign
Atlantic Ocean
Congo
Kenya
Mombasa 2002
Tanzania
Angola

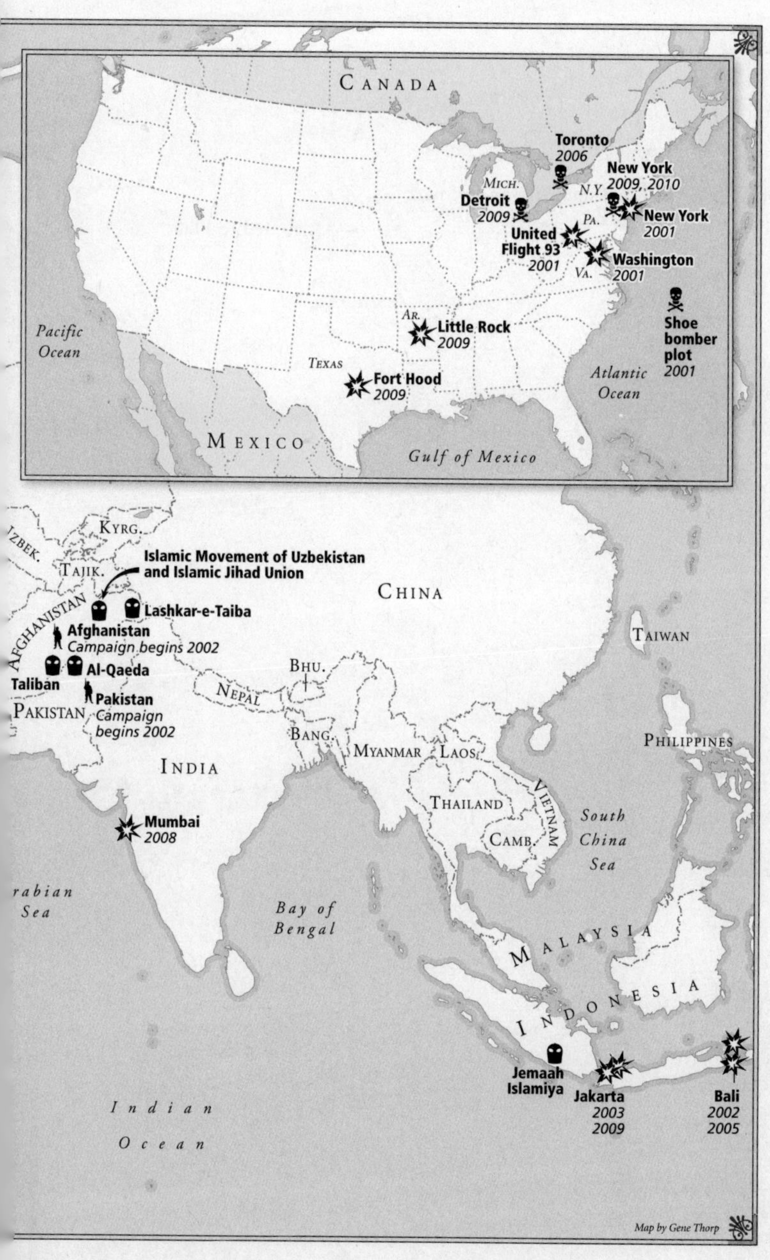

Canada
Toronto
2006
New York
2009, 2010
Mich.
N.Y.
Detroit
2009
New York
2001
Pa.
United
Flight 93
2001
Washington
2001
Va.
Shoe
bomber
plot
2001
Pacific
Ocean
Ar.
Little Rock
2009
Texas
Fort Hood
2009
Atlantic
Ocean
Mexico
Gulf of Mexico
Kyrg.
Uzbek.
Tajik.
Islamic Movement of Uzbekistan
and Islamic Jihad Union
China
Afghanistan
Lashkar-e-Taiba
Afghanistan
Campaign begins 2002
Taiwan
Al-Qaeda
Taliban
Bhu.
Nepal
Pakistan
Pakistan
Campaign
begins 2002
Bang.
Philippines
Myanmar
Laos
India
Vietnam
Thailand
Mumbai
2008
South
China
Sea
Camb.
rabian
Sea
Bay of
Bengal
Malaysia
Indonesia
Jemaah
Islamiya
Jakarta
2003
2009
Bali
2002
2005
Indian
Ocean
Map by Gene Thorp

Only the dead have seen the end of war.

—Attributed to Plato

Author's Note

The goal of this book is to tell a history of the "war on terror" in one volume. The organizing principle of this history is to examine not only the actions and strategies of the United States and its key allies, but also those of al-Qaeda and its allies, such as the Taliban. Most histories of the war on terror have been written largely from the American perspective, while this book folds into the narrative the perspective of al-Qaeda and allied jihadist groups. Just as histories of World War II told only from the point of view of Franklin Roosevelt would make little sense, so do we benefit from a better understanding of Osama bin Laden and his followers.

This is not, of course, to suggest a moral equivalence between al-Qaeda and the United States. Yet as we look back it is clear that each side has made a set of symbiotic strategic errors that has helped the other. Luckily, those of the United States have not been as profound as al-Qaeda's, although they certainly have been significant—from ceding the moral high ground with Guantánamo and coercive interrogations; to invading Iraq, which gave a new lease on life to the jihadist movement; to almost losing the Afghan War.

Yet al-Qaeda has made even more profound strategic errors. The attack on September 11, 2001, itself caused the collapse of the Taliban regime and the destruction of al-Qaeda's safe haven in Afghanistan, where it had once ruled with impunity as a kind of shadow government within the Taliban regime. Later, in Iraq, al-Qaeda's ruthless campaign of terror obliterated the support it had first enjoyed there, and so also severely damaged its "brand" around the Muslim world.

This book is first a narrative history of the "war on terror," based upon a synthesis of all the available open-source materials, together with my own interviewing and reporting during the course of more than a dozen visits to Afghanistan and Pakistan and other reporting trips to countries that have played a role in the narrative, such as Iraq, Egypt, Saudi Arabia, Jordan, Indonesia, Russia, Uzbekistan, the United Kingdom, and Italy. During those trips I have interviewed people from all sides of this war including: failed suicide bombers; leading Western counterterrorism and national security officials; members of the Taliban; the family and friends of Osama bin Laden; top American military officers; victims of American "extraordinary renditions" who have been taken by CIA officials to countries where they were then tortured; leading members of al-Qaeda, including bin Laden, and former militants who have turned against bin Laden's terrorist organization.

The book also aspires to provide an analytical net assessment of the "war on terror": to see what conclusions might now be drawn about what al-Qaeda and its allied groups accomplished in the first decade of the twenty-first century and where the United States and her partners have succeeded and failed in their wars with the militants.

Al-Qaeda and America face each other in a conflict in which no short-term resolution appears possible. Al-Qaeda's *jihad* has failed to achieve its central aims. Bin Laden's primary goal was always regime change in the Middle East, sweeping away the governments from Cairo to Riyadh with Taliban-style rule. He wanted Western troops and influence out of the region and believed that attacking the "far enemy," the United States, would cause the U.S.-backed Arab regimes—the "near enemy"—to crumble. For all his leadership skills and charisma, however, bin Laden accomplished the exact opposite of what he intended. A decade after the September 11 attacks, his last remaining safe havens in the Hindu Kush were under attack, U.S. soldiers patrolled Afghanistan and Iraq, and he was dead.

Above all, this is a mark of the weakness of his leadership. Osama bin Laden has proved an inspiring figure to many in the global jihadist movement; but he has overreached, failed to appeal to any wider constituency, and failed to build a secure and effective operational base after the loss of Afghanistan. Though it survives intact and dangerous, al-Qaeda is hemmed in, weakened and limited in its operations. Its ability to force a decisive change in America's Middle East policy is close to zero, even though it remains capable of dealing lethal blows around the world; like a snake backed into a corner, a weakened al-Qaeda is still dangerous.

Events since the launch of the "war on terror" have become deeply politicized: the debate about whether bin Laden could have been killed at the battle of Tora Bora in the winter of 2001; the putative linkages between al-Qaeda and Saddam Hussein, which were an important rationale for the war in Iraq; whether the American effort in Afghanistan was shortchanged because of the Iraqi conflict; the efficacy of coercive interrogations of al-Qaeda detainees and of military commissions to try militants held at Guantánamo; the scale of the threat to the West posed by al-Qaeda and its affiliates; the extent to which President Bush's "surge" of troops into Iraq in 2007 or other factors brought a measure of stability there; and whether President Obama had committed his presidency to a war in South Asia that would replicate the failures of Vietnam. This history aims to provide an assessment of these and other issues that have not received enough objective analysis.

This is also a book about the power of ideas. We are a highly ideological species with a deep need for ideas that help us to narrate and make sense of an often senseless world. For bin Laden and his followers, the world is explained by the idea that Islam is under assault by the West, in particular the United States, and that only by attacking America will this state of affairs ever be reversed. For its part, the Bush administration believed deeply that al-Qaeda and its supposed ally Saddam Hussein posed an existential threat to America and conflated that big idea with smaller fixations, such as its opposition to "nation building," all of which contributed to the problems the United States has since faced in Afghanistan, Iraq, and the Muslim world overall.

The book is divided into two parts. The first, titled "Hubris," traces al-Qaeda's miscalculations, and in particular its profound misunderstanding of the likely American response to 9/11, while also interweaving the strategic missteps of the United States from its initial anemic efforts in Afghanistan to its counterproductive invasion of Iraq. Part II, "Nemesis?" traces how the American government and military learned from their mistakes in Iraq and, later, Afghanistan and have since regained the initiative against al-Qaeda and its allies. At the same time, bin Laden and his followers severely damaged themselves with their actions in the Muslim world, from Indonesia to Iraq. Yet the West has snatched defeat from the jaws of victory a number of times already in this long war, and the jihadist militants have proven surprisingly resilient despite the wide range of forces arrayed against them.

Part I

Hubris

As a general rule, the easiest way to achieve complete strategic surprise is to commit an act that makes no sense or is even self-destructive.

—maxim once displayed on the desk of Robert Gates, U.S. secretary of defense in the administrations of Presidents George W. Bush and Barack Obama

No one loves armed missionaries.

—Maximilien Robespierre

Chapter 1

Holy Tuesday

At 2:30 A.M. on August 29, 2001, the lead hijacker Mohammed Atta called Ramzi Binalshibh, his al-Qaeda handler, telling him he had a riddle that he was trying to solve: "Two sticks, a dash and a cake with a stick down—what is it?" Binalshibh thought for a while and suddenly realized that the two sticks were the number 11, and a cake with a stick down was a 9, and that Atta was telling him the attacks would happen in two weeks, on 11/9. That date is known as 9/11 in the United States.

Binalshibh, a slight, intensely religious Yemeni who had volunteered to be one of the hijackers, was turned down for an American visa. As a consolation prize for not becoming a "martyr," Binalshibh took control of the coordination of al-Qaeda's plans for the attacks on America from his apartment in Hamburg, Germany. Atta communicated by email from the United States with Binalshibh, apprising him of the progress of the plot. In his email messages, Atta posed as a university student writing to his girlfriend "Jenny." Atta used an innocuous code to alert Binalshibh that the plot was nearing completion: "The first semester commences in three weeks. . . . Nineteen certificates for private education and four exams." The nineteen "certificates" referred to the nineteen al-Qaeda hijackers and the four "exams" to the four targets of the soon-to-be-hijacked planes.

On September 5, Binalshibh left Germany for Pakistan, where he dispatched a messenger to Afghanistan to warn Osama bin Laden about the exact timing and scope of the attacks. Expecting some kind of American reprisal for the coming assaults on Washington and New York, likely in the form of cruise missile attacks like those President Clinton had ordered following al-Qaeda's 1998 bombings of two U.S. embassies in Africa, all of the organization's camps and residential compounds were put on high alert in the days before 9/11. A Yemeni living at al-Qaeda's al-Farouq training camp in Afghanistan recalled that the trainers at the facility said, "If anyone wanted to leave, we were free to leave. There might be problems and there might be bombings." In Kandahar, the southern Afghan city that served as the de facto capital of the Taliban, bin Laden urged his followers to evacuate to safer locations in early September.

Earlier that summer the scuttlebutt around the al-Qaeda campfires was that a large anti-American attack was imminent. Feroz Ali Abbasi, a British militant of Ugandan descent who was eager to conduct terrorist operations against Jews and Americans, remembered "this information being commonly known amongst everybody in the training camps and guesthouses." Even "American Taliban" John Walker Lindh heard an instructor at his camp tell a group of trainees that bin Laden had dispatched dozens of suicide operatives for attacks against the United States and Israel.

In mid-June 2001 bin Laden and his top military commander, Mohammed Atef, also dropped broad hints that a major attack was in the works, during a meeting they held in Kandahar with Bakr Atyani, a correspondent for the Middle East Broadcasting Corporation. Atef said that "in the next few weeks we will carry out a big surprise and we will strike or attack American and Israeli interests." Atyani asked bin Laden, "Would you please confirm that?" The al-Qaeda leader responded only with one of his slight, enigmatic smiles. The report about al-Qaeda's plans for an anti-American attack was subsequently picked up by the *Washington Post* on June 23. For those who cared to look during the summer of 2001, al-Qaeda's plans to wreak havoc on the United States were an open secret.

But the timing, targets, and scale of the operation was information that was tightly held, confined only to the top leaders of al-Qaeda and the pilots of the planes to be hijacked. Ayman al-Zawahiri, the leader of the Egyptian Jihad group, first learned of the details of the operation in June 2001, and that was only after his organization had formally contracted its alliance with al-Qaeda. Bin Laden even kept his spokesman in Afghanistan, Suleiman Abu Ghaith, in the dark. A former high school teacher from Kuwait, Abu Ghaith learned about the attacks on Washington and New York from media reports.

Similarly, the "muscle" hijackers on the four planes, whose primary role was to restrain the passengers on the flights, knew that they were volunteering for a suicide mission in the United States, but only at the final stage of the operation were they told their targets. Before they journeyed to the United States, the hijackers videotaped suicide "wills," which al-Qaeda's video production arm would release over the coming years to milk the 9/11 tragedy repeatedly.

In the final run-up to the attacks, Binalshibh made a last call to Ziad Jarrah, a onetime Lebanese party boy who had moved to Hamburg in 1996 and had fallen in there with the zealots in al-Qaeda's local cell. Despite his increasing militancy, Jarrah continued to date a pretty Turkish dentistry student he had met in Germany. Now Jarrah was in the States to train as a pilot-hijacker, but in the summer of 2001 Binalshibh was concerned that personality clashes between Jarrah and the lead hijacker, Mohammed Atta, a dour misogynist known as "the Ayatollah," might endanger the entire operation. Binalshibh asked Jarrah, "How do you feel?" He replied, "My heart is at ease, and I feel that the operation will, Inshallah [God willing] be carried out." Jarrah would soon crash United Airlines Flight 93 into a Pennsylvania field, killing everyone on board.

Bin Laden was more optimistic than other al-Qaeda leaders that what they termed the "Holy Tuesday" operation would result in mass American casualties. Drawing on the experience he had working in his father's construction company, one of the largest in the Middle East, bin Laden calculated that the impacts of the crashes of the two planes into the World Trade Center towers would take out three or four floors of each building and would then cause intense fires fed by the jet fuel inside each of the hijacked aircraft, which were both headed to the West Coast on full tanks. As bin Laden explained to a fawning Saudi supporter who visited him a few weeks after 9/11, those white-hot fires would then in turn collapse all the floors above their points of impact. "This is all that we had hoped for," bin Laden told his Saudi guest.

Ali Hamza al-Bahlul, a Yemeni who made propaganda videos for bin Laden, hooked up a satellite receiver for the al-Qaeda leader so he could watch live coverage of the attacks, but Bahlul had trouble finding a satisfactory video signal in the mountainous terrain of Afghanistan. And so as their workday on

Tuesday, September 11, finished, eight and a half time zones ahead of Manhattan, bin Laden and some fifty other members of al-Qaeda gathered around radios to listen as the attacks unfolded.

When the news of the first plane to hit the World Trade Center was broadcast on the BBC's Arabic service, it was around 5:30 P.M. local time. Bin Laden's followers exploded with joy at the news, shouting and crying, "Allah Akbar! God is great!" Their leader, knowing there were more attacks to come, urged them, "Be patient!"

Ramzi Binalshibh was in Pakistan watching the attacks live on television with a group of others from al-Qaeda. Knowing how the plot was to unfold, Binalshibh could not contain his own excitement: "Our brother Marwan [one of the pilots] was violently ramming the plane into the Trade Center in an unbelievable manner! We were watching live and praying: 'God! Aim! Aim! Aim!'" Binalshibh remembers the elation of his colleagues: "They all chanted 'Allah Akbar!' and bowed to Allah in gratitude and they all wept."

But shrewder members of al-Qaeda and the Taliban felt otherwise. They realized that the 9/11 attacks might not be the stunning victory that al-Qaeda and many in the West took them to be at the time, and might in fact more resemble a kamikaze operation that would decimate their ranks. Vahid Mojdeh, a Taliban Foreign Ministry official, immediately understood that the game was up: "I was listening to BBC radio broadcasting news that several buildings in the States are burning and planes have crashed into those buildings, and it said that al-Qaeda is behind the attack. As soon as I heard the news, I realized that the Taliban were going to be terminated."

Abu Walid al-Masri, an Egyptian who was an early bin Laden associate in Afghanistan, explains that in the years before 9/11, bin Laden became increasingly deluded that America was weak. "He believed that the United States was much weaker than some of those around him thought," Masri remembered. "As evidence he referred to what happened to the United States in Beirut when the bombing of the Marines' base led them to flee from Lebanon."

Bin Laden's belief that the United States was a "paper tiger" was based not only on the American withdrawal from Lebanon in 1983 following the Marine barracks attack there, which killed 241 American servicemen, but also the withdrawal of U.S. forces from Somalia a decade later, following the "Black Hawk Down" incident, and the American pullout from the quagmire of Vietnam in the 1970s. Masri was not convinced by this paper-tiger narrative, though a number of bin Laden's acolytes were: "Some young Saudi followers confirmed to bin Laden his delusions from the gist of the experiences they had gained from their visits to the United States, namely, that the country was falling and could bear only few strikes." Bin Laden came to believe implicitly in his own analysis that the United States was as weak as the Soviet Union once was.

There were others in al-Qaeda's inner circle who worried that large-scale attacks on American targets were unwise. Saif al-Adel, a senior Egyptian military commander, and Abu Hafs the Mauritanian, a religious adviser, opposed the attacks because they feared the American response or were worried that the operation would alienate the Taliban leader Mullah Omar. Abu Hafs the Mauritanian was also concerned that killing American civilians could not be justified on religious grounds.

Other militants also warned bin Laden that attacking the United States would be counterproductive. Noman Benotman, a leader of the Libyan Islamic Fighting Group, an organization that occasionally aligned itself with al-Qaeda, traveled from London in the summer of 2000 to meet with the group's leaders in Kandahar. He told them bluntly that attacking America would be disastrous. "We made a clear-cut request for him to stop his campaign against the United States because it was going to lead to nowhere," Benotman recalled, "but they laughed when I told them that America would attack the whole region if they launched another attack against it." Benotman's warning should have carried some weight because he had known bin Laden since they were both fighting the communists in Afghanistan.

By early September 2001, al-Qaeda was at the height of its power; the group and its Taliban allies were on the verge of taking over Afghanistan entirely. Yet the curtain raiser for the 9/11 attacks had gone virtually unnoticed in the West; this was the assassination on September 9 of Ahmad Shah Massoud, the leader of the coalition of anti-Taliban groups known as the Northern Alliance, which was the only force that stood in the way of the Taliban's total victory in Afghanistan.

Bin Laden was well aware that key Taliban officials, such as the foreign minister, Wakil Muttawakil, wanted to rein him in because he was complicating the Taliban's desperate and ultimately ill-fated quest for international recognition of their government. The Taliban put bin Laden on notice to stop his terrorist plotting and stop giving incendiary anti-American interviews on television networks such as CNN and Al Jazeera. At one point Mullah Omar, their strange, reclusive, one-eyed leader, even visited the al-Qaeda leader to tell him to leave Afghanistan. Bin Laden responded, "Sheikh, if you give in to infidel governments, your decision will be against Islam." This argument was persuasive to Mullah Omar, a hyperdevout Muslim who had anointed himself "Commander of the Faithful" when he assumed total control of the Taliban movement in 1996.

Bin Laden agreed to desist from plotting terror attacks and from his media campaign and he pledged a religious oath of obedience to Mullah Omar, in exchange for the continued shelter that the Taliban offered his organization. Bin Laden would not honor those pledges and he did not clue in Mullah Omar about his plans for attacking America. But he calculated that there was one gift he could give the Taliban that might temper any anger they might have about his coming attacks on the United States: the head of Ahmad Shah Massoud.

Massoud, an intense, wiry warrior permanently dressed in fatigues, his gaunt face framed by a wispy beard, was one of the great guerrilla commanders of the late twentieth century. He had successfully resisted multiple Soviet offensives against his forces in northern Afghanistan during the 1980s and had taken Kabul from the communists in 1992. Four years later, as the black-turbaned Taliban appeared in force outside the capital, Massoud withdrew his forces to his bases in the north, where he continued to lead an intense resistance to the movement of religious warriors.

Much of Afghanistan's history over the past three decades, and even the events of 9/11 itself, were in some senses reflective of the ideological and military struggles between bin Laden and Massoud. Not only was there the personal enmity between the two men going back to the 1980s, but they were also both representative of the ideological civil war that was taking place in the Muslim world between those like bin Laden, who wanted to install Taliban-style theocracies from Indonesia to Morocco, and those like Massoud, who espoused a more moderate form of Islamism and an orientation to the West.

By the summer of 2001 the Taliban and their al-Qaeda allies had rolled Massoud's Northern Alliance back to a small patch of northeastern Afghanistan, where his army, now down to one working helicopter, was on life support. At this point bin Laden knew that killing its charismatic leader would be the coup de grace for the Northern Alliance, and indeed it nearly proved to be.

Al-Qaeda planned the Massoud hit with great care, tasking for the job two Tunisian-Belgian volunteers who disguised themselves as TV journalists eager to interview the heroic Massoud. The "journalists," who had been hanging around his headquarters for weeks to secure the interview with the storied Afghan military commander, finally got their chance to speak with him on September 9. They set up their gear, saying they were interested in asking Massoud why he had earlier declared that bin Laden was a murderer who should be expelled from Afghanistan. As their videotape appeared to be rolling, one of the men asked the first question: "Sir, what is the state of Islam in Afghanistan?" Then one of them detonated a bomb hidden in the camera, killing himself and mortally wounding Massoud.

Feroz Ali Abbasi, the British-Ugandan militant living in one of al-Qaeda's training camps, remembers that he heard about the Massoud assassination on the radio. "When this happened I thought that at last the Taliban were going to take the whole of Afghanistan. Massoud was crucial to the Northern Alliance." That assessment was shared by one of Massoud's closest confidants, Dr. Abdullah, who worried that the Northern Alliance was finished: "When I heard about the assassination, I was one hundred percent sure that the resistance would be over in a matter of days."

Northern Alliance commanders kept Massoud's death a secret for as long as possible, knowing that the news of their beloved leader's assassination would undermine the morale of their troops. Indeed, absent the 9/11 attacks, the Taliban would have likely taken over Afghanistan permanently.

Whatever the intensity of the internal debates within al-Qaeda about the wisdom of attacking the United States, and despite the fierce private criticism leveled at bin Laden by senior Taliban officials, the only person whose opinion really mattered in Afghanistan following the 9/11 attacks was Mullah Omar, the "Commander of the Faithful" who stood by his Saudi "guest" both publicly and privately. Ten days after the assaults on Washington and New York, the Voice of America radio network interviewed Mullah Omar. When the interviewer asked if bin Laden would be handed over to the United States, the Taliban leader put the issue in the most cosmic of terms: "We cannot do that. If we did, it means we are not Muslims; that Islam is finished."

As it became obvious that the United States was readying an attack on Afghanistan, bin Laden attempted to stiffen Mullah Omar's resolve with a letter written on an al-Qaeda computer on October 3, four days before the American bombing campaign against the Taliban began. In the letter, bin Laden explained, "A U.S. campaign against Afghanistan will cause great long-term economic burdens which will force America to resort to the former Soviet Union's only option: withdrawal from Afghanistan, disintegration, and contraction."

Even if he indeed received this letter, its arguments do not seem to have been especially persuasive to Mullah Omar. He told a group of his companions a few days before the American bombing campaign began, "You may consider me weak or scared, but I have to send my family to Pakistan." Up until this point, Taliban officials thought that even if Mullah Omar lacked other good qualities, at least he was both pious and courageous. But now he was showing the first sign of weakness.

On October 7, the day that the American aerial bombardment began, Faraj Ismail, an Egyptian journalist, interviewed Mullah Omar in Kandahar. The cleric naïvely assured him that bin Laden had no role in the 9/11 attacks: "I have control over Afghanistan. I'm sure he didn't do it." The Taliban leader also invoked the canard that 9/11 was a Zionist plot, based on "the absence on the same day of the incident of 4,000 Jews who worked in the World Trade Centre."

That night American bombs began falling on Taliban targets in Afghanistan, the beginning of a campaign that would destroy Mullah Omar's incompetent and brutal regime.

It was the opening salvo of a long war, a war that has already lasted longer than any conflict in American history. In 2006 the Pentagon even enshrined the concept of "the long war" into its Quadrennial Defense Review, its blueprint for military planning, while al-Qaeda's leaders and their allies fervently believe that their struggle with the United States and her allies could last for generations. Burning with the conviction that they have God on their side, members of al-Qaeda are generally not deterrable in the conventional sense, and their very relative weakness makes them far more willing to take on the United States than conventional state antagonists, who have good reason to fear American retaliation.

Chapter 2

Explaining 9/11

When people see a strong horse and a weak horse, by nature, they will like the strong horse.

—Osama bin Laden explaining the purpose of the 9/11 attacks

Khaled Batarfi was bin Laden's closest buddy when they were teenagers living in the coastal city of Jeddah, Saudi Arabia. They met in 1973, when bin Laden was sixteen, three years older than Batarfi. The Musharifa district, where the two friends grew up, is a typical upper-middle-class Jeddah neighborhood dotted with white-walled villas and anchored by the small mosque in which they offered their daily prayers. Next door to the mosque was a scruffy playground where the two played soccer after school. The young Osama was so pious that the neighborhood kids didn't swear or tell off-color jokes in his presence. Bin Laden even scolded Batarfi for wearing shorts to play soccer; he said they were immodest.

As a teenager bin Laden fasted twice a week in imitation of the Prophet Mohammed, and when a group of friends assembled at his house it was to chant religious songs about Palestine. Batarfi says his solemn friend would often say, "Unless we, the new generation, change and become stronger and more educated and more dedicated, we will never reclaim Palestine."

Alia Ghanem, bin Laden's Syrian mother, remembers her son fusing his religiosity with politics in his early teens: "He was frustrated about the situation in Palestine in particular and the Arab and Muslim world in general. He thought Muslim youths were too busy having fun to care about what they should do to propagate Islam and bring back the old glories of the Muslim nation."

Woven deep into the fabric of bin Laden's religious zeal was the fact that his family owed a good deal of its fortune and standing in society to its role for decades as the principal contractor renovating and expanding the holy sites of Mecca and Medina. One of the largest public works projects in the history of the modern Middle East, it had begun under his revered father, Mohammed, in the 1950s and continued under his admired older brother Salem.

While a student at the relatively progressive Al-Thagr High School in Jeddah, bin Laden fell under the spell of a charismatic Syrian physical education teacher who organized after-school Koran reading sessions and who may have inducted the teenager into the Muslim Brotherhood, a pan-Islamic movement that seeks to further Islamicize the Muslim world. Jamal Khalifa, bin Laden's classmate at King Abdul Aziz University in Jeddah, remembers that his college friend was religiously conservative already and wouldn't listen to music or watch television.

Bin Laden came of age as a deep religious current was sweeping through the Muslim world. The *Sahwa,* or Awakening, began swirling after the devastating and unexpected defeat of Egypt by Israel in the 1967 war, which called into question the then reigning orthodoxies of Arab nationalism and socialism. And this current was given an intellectual architecture by the Egyptian writer Sayyid Qutb, who claimed that much of the Middle East was living in a state of pagan ignorance, and that the way forward for Muslims besieged by the Western ideologies of socialism, capitalism, and secularism was an Islam that informed every aspect of life. Jamal Khalifa says Qutb made a profound impact on his generation of fundamentalists because he explained that true Islam was more than just observing the traditional tenets of the religion; it should penetrate all facets of the believer's life.

This Islamic awakening peaked in 1979—the first year of a new century on the Muslim calendar—with a series of seismic events that would profoundly influence bin Laden and other future members of al-Qaeda: the overthrow of the Shah of Iran by the fundamentalist cleric Ayatollah Khomeini, which demonstrated that an American-backed dictator could actually be eliminated by a group of religious revolutionaries; the armed takeover of Islam's holy of holies, the mosque in Mecca, by Saudi militants protesting the supposed impiety of the Saudi regime, later a central theme of bin Laden's; Egyptian President Anwar Sadat's historic peace agreement with Israel, which Islamist militants saw as a sacrilegious stab in the back; and finally the Soviet Union's invasion of Afghanistan.

It was a thrilling time to be a deeply committed Muslim, as the 22-year-old bin Laden then was. At the time there wasn't much remarkable about him; a priggish young man working in his family business, studying economics at university, married, with a couple of toddlers running around the house. He was admired by friends and family alike for his piety, although a good number of them found his religiosity a bit much, even by the conservative standards of 1970s Saudi Arabia.

But this would all change with the Soviet invasion of Afghanistan in late December 1979. It was the first time since World War II that a non-Muslim power had invaded and occupied a Muslim nation. For bin Laden it was the most transformative event of his life, uncoupling him from his tranquil domestic life of work and family in Saudi Arabia, and launching him into what would become a full-time job helping the Afghan resistance. His experiences in Afghanistan during the 1980s turned the pious, shy rich kid into a leader of men who fought the Soviets himself, and, at least in his own mind and those of his followers, he came to believe that he had helped to defeat the communist superpower.

A key to this transformation was bin Laden's relationship with the charismatic Palestinian cleric Abdullah Azzam. Azzam was the critical force both ideologically and organizationally for the recruitment of thousands of Muslims from around the world to engage in some way in the Afghan struggle against the Soviets. And Azzam would become bin Laden's mentor, the first and most important of a series of father figures that he would find to replace his own father, Mohammed bin Laden, who had died in a plane crash in Saudi Arabia when the future al-Qaeda leader was only ten.

The influence of bin Laden's revered father—a busy man who sired an impressive fifty-four children and also managed a business empire, and whom Osama rarely saw when he was alive—may have also helped to shape his desire to become a *mujahid*, or holy warrior. Bin Laden told Pakistani journalist Hamid Mir, "My father was very keen that one of his sons should fight against the enemies of Islam. So I am the one son who is acting according to the wishes of his father." Whether or not his father really wanted one of his sons to be a holy warrior is beside the larger point, which is that bin Laden increasingly fused together his own religious zealotry with the reverence and admiration that he felt for his father, and grafted it on to his self-conception as a heroic warrior defending Islam. Bin Laden was well aware that as one of the most junior of his father's twenty-five sons, he was unlikely to follow in his father's footsteps at the helm of the family business. But he could do something else of which his father would have approved: fight the enemies of Islam.

Together with his mentor Azzam, bin Laden founded the Services Office in 1984, an organization based in the western Pakistani city of Peshawar that was dedicated to placing Arab volunteers either with relief organizations serving the Afghan refugees who had flooded into Pakistan after the Soviet invasion of their country, or with the Afghan factions fighting the communists on the front lines.

That same year, Azzam, a true religious scholar (unlike his younger protégé) with a doctorate in Islamic jurisprudence from Al-Azhar University in Cairo, issued an influential *fatwa* that was to provide the ideological underpinnings for the recruitment of Muslims from around the globe to the Afghan jihad. The fatwa ruled that to expel foreign aggressors from Islamic lands was a *fard ayn*, or a compulsory duty for all Muslims. In effect Azzam was saying that every individual Muslim had a religious *obligation* to fight in some way in the Afghan war. The radical call to arms would help ignite the first truly global jihadist movement, inspiring men from Algeria to Brooklyn to travel to Pakistan and Afghanistan to wage jihad against the Soviets.

In all this bin Laden played only a financial role, helping to subsidize the operations of the Services Office, which served as the logistical hub for those who answered Azzam's call to arms. Faraj Ismail covered the Afghan jihad for the Saudi newspaper *Muslimoon* during the mid-1980s. He remembered that the shy Saudi rich kid exhibited no leadership charisma and was instead totally overshadowed by Azzam. "The relationship between bin Laden and Azzam was the relationship of a student to a professor," Ismail recalled.

In 1984 bin Laden for the first time ventured into Afghanistan, an experience that transformed his life. He told a journalist, "I feel so guilty for listening to my friends and those that I love to not come here [to Afghanistan] and stay home for reasons of safety, and I feel that this delay of four years requires my own martyrdom in the name of God." Bin Laden now began spending most of his time on the Afghan front lines, particularly with Jalaluddin Haqqani, a Pashtun commander based in Khost, in eastern Afghanistan.

From 1986 on, bin Laden's close relationship with his mentor Azzam would gradually fray as the young Saudi militant became preoccupied with personally fighting the Soviets rather than simply supporting the activities of the Afghan mujahideen, which was what Azzam saw as the most pressing task for the Arab volunteers. Abdullah Anas, Azzam's son-in-law and also a close friend of bin Laden, says that the future al-Qaeda leader, fast approaching the age of thirty, was now starting to assert his independence from the charismatic Azzam.

Khaled Batarfi, bin Laden's childhood friend, continued to see bin Laden when he returned home to Saudi Arabia, but noticed that his old soccer buddy had changed: "He became more assertive, less shy." Jamal Khalifa also noticed that his close friend, who had once enjoyed the give-and-take of a real discussion, would now no longer tolerate disagreement with his own views.

The Afghan war changed bin Laden. The humble, young, monosyllabic millionaire with the open checkbook who had first visited Pakistan in the early 1980s would, by the middle of the decade, launch an ambitious plan to confront the Soviets directly inside Afghanistan with a group of Arabs under his command. That cadre of Arabs would provide the nucleus of al-Qaeda.

Seeking martyrdom, in 1986 bin Laden established a base for several dozen Arab fighters close to a Soviet garrison inside eastern Afghanistan, located in Jaji, about ten miles from the Pakistani border. With the zeal of a fanatic, bin Laden told a journalist that he hoped his new base would draw heavy Soviet firepower: "God willing, we want [our base] to be the first thing that the enemy faces. Its place as the first camp visible to the enemy means that they will focus their bombardments on us in an extreme manner."

Jamal Khalifa was not impressed by his friend's plans to set up a military operation right next door to a Soviet military post. Khalifa knew that bin Laden had absolutely no military experience, and he was also concerned that his friend was sending idealistic young Arabs to the Afghan front lines on kamikaze missions. He confronted bin Laden inside his base in 1986. "I told him, 'Every drop of blood bleeds here in this place; God will ask you about it in the hereafter. Everybody is saying this is wrong, so Osama, please leave the place right now.' Everybody was hearing our argument, our voices become hard." The two friends rarely spoke again.

From the Jaji base, bin Laden fought near suicidal battles over three weeks with the Soviets during the spring of 1987. Esam Deraz, an Egyptian filmmaker who covered the battles in Jaji, explains that they were the making of bin Laden. "I was near him in the battle, many months, and he was really brave. . . . [bin Laden] fought in this battle like a private."

Bin Laden's stand against the Russians at the battle of Jaji was lionized in the mainstream Arab press, turning him into an authentic war hero. A 1988 article published in the Saudi magazine *Al-Majallah* featured bin Laden, who was quoted saying, "We sometimes spent the whole day in the trenches or in the caves until our ears could no longer bear the sound of the explosions around us." Bin Laden told the reporter from *Al-Majallah*, "It was God alone who protected us from the Russians during their offensive last year. . . . We depend completely on God in all matters." By the late 1980s, bin Laden already saw himself as an instrument of God's will in an epic struggle against the enemies of Islam.

Jaji was bin Laden's first brush with publicity and over time the shy millionaire would increasingly come to embrace the spotlight. But the battle of Jaji was only a morale booster for the scores of Arabs then fighting in Afghanistan. It was not a battle of any importance in the larger war against the Soviets.

Bin Laden's decision to found his own military force made no strategic sense and would be part of his pattern of strategic overreach that would culminate in al-Qaeda's attacks on 9/11. Informed estimates of the total number of Afghan mujahideen fighting the Soviets ranged up to 175,000. By contrast, the largest number of Arabs fighting the Soviets inside Afghanistan at any given moment amounted to no more than several hundred. To assemble those fighters in one force did not make much sense from a military standpoint. Indeed, despite bin Laden's subsequent hyperventilating rhetoric, his "Afghan Arabs" had no meaningful impact on the conduct of the war, which was won with the blood of the Afghans and the billions of dollars and riyals of the United States and Saudi Arabia.

Abdullah Azzam was opposed to the idea of a separate Arab military force because he envisioned Arabs seeded throughout all of the Afghan militias functioning as morale boosters who could simultaneously teach the Afghans about true Islam, aid them with education and medicine, and bring news of the Afghan jihad to wealthy donors in the Middle East. A single Arab military force would end this effort, and in any event could have no impact on the conduct of the war. Bin Laden saw matters differently. He believed that an

Arab military force would stand its ground against Soviet attacks because his recruits were more than willing to martyr themselves.

Bin Laden's military ambitions and personality evolved in tandem. He became more assertive, to the point that he ignored the advice of many of his old friends about the folly of setting up his own military force. That decision would also precipitate an irrevocable (but carefully concealed) split with his onetime mentor, Abdullah Azzam.

During the mid-1980s, bin Laden had been careful to distance himself from the more radical Arab elements in Pakistan who wanted to overthrow the ruling regimes of the Middle East. In 1987, when King Fahd of Saudi Arabia traveled to Britain on a state visit, he was presented a medal in the form of a cross by Queen Elizabeth II. In the hothouse radical atmosphere of Peshawar, some militants said that by accepting the crosslike decoration, King Fahd was no longer a Muslim. Bin Laden was having none of this, telling the militants, "For God's sake, don't discuss this subject; concentrate on your mission." And bin Laden continued to maintain cordial relations with the Saudi government. Prince Turki al-Faisal, the director of Saudi intelligence, met bin Laden on a number of occasions in Pakistan during the anti-Soviet jihad and remembered him as "a gentle, enthusiastic young man of few words who didn't raise his voice while talking."

It was not an accident that bin Laden's split from Azzam began around the time of his first meeting with the Egyptian doctor Ayman al-Zawahiri, in 1986. Zawahiri nurtured a far more radical interpretation of jihad than Azzam's vision of rolling back non-Muslims who had invaded Islamic lands, as the Soviets had in Afghanistan. The Egyptian doctor was a revolutionary who wanted regime change across the Middle East, something that Azzam would have no part of, as this was to engage in *fitna:* sowing discord within the Muslim community. Azzam did not approve of intra-Muslim violence. But Zawahiri gradually won over bin Laden to his more expansive view of jihad. Faraj Ismail, the Egyptian journalist who covered the war against the Soviets, recalls that it was Zawahiri "who got Osama to focus not only on the Afghan jihad, but regime change in the Arab world."

Osama Rushdi, a member of the militant Egyptian Islamic Group who had been jailed with Zawahiri in the early 1980s in Cairo, a few years later was living in Peshawar. There, he says, Zawahiri, a prickly intellectual, increasingly adopted the doctrine of *takfir* (declaring other Muslims to be apostates). Rushdi remembers that Zawahiri even told people not to pray with Azzam, "and that is a grave thing in Islam, because in Islam it is correct to pray with any Muslim." The conflict between Azzam and the Islamist militants in Peshawar may have signed his death warrant. He was assassinated there by unknown assailants on November 24, 1989.

A year earlier, Salem bin Laden, Osama's oldest brother, had died in a plane crash in San Antonio, Texas. Within a year Osama bin Laden had lost both his most important mentor and the brother who headed the bin Laden clan. They were perhaps the only two people in the world who might have been able to pull him back from the project he was just beginning: the establishment of al-Qaeda as an armed jihadist group with large ambitions. A relative lamented, "If Salem had still been around no one would be writing books about Osama bin Laden. Salem had a volcanic temper. . . . Salem would have grabbed Osama by the lapels and taken him back to Saudi Arabia."

The minutes of al-Qaeda's founding meetings did not mention the United States as an enemy but rather described the group's goals in the broadest and vaguest of terms: "to lift the word of God, to make His religion victorious." The minutes did note that the "work" of al-Qaeda commenced on September 10, 1988. Almost exactly thirteen years later the organization carried out the 9/11 attacks, inflicting more direct damage on the United States during a morning than the Soviet Union had done during decades of the Cold War.

So what had changed in the meantime? Or to put it another way: Where did bin Laden's anti-Americanism stem from? It was far from predictable that bin Laden would turn against the United States; several of his half brothers and sisters maintained vacation homes in the States and had substantial business interests there, while about a quarter of Osama's fifty-three siblings had studied there at some point. And in 1979, when he was twenty-two, bin Laden himself traveled to the United States with his wife Najwa and their two infant sons. On the two-week trip the bin Ladens visited Los Angeles and Indiana. His wife recalled that the visit was uneventful: "My husband and I did not hate America, yet we did not love it."

Over the course of the 1980s, bin Laden's indifference to the United States would gradually harden into hostility because of its support for Israel. The al-Qaeda leader explained that he made a speech in 1986 urging Muslims to boycott American products because "the Americans take our money and give it to the Jews so they can kill our children with it in Palestine." Bin Laden stopped drinking Pepsi and Coca-Cola and his son Omar recalls that his father refused to let his kids consume American soft drinks. (They would drink them anyway, behind his back.)

Bin Laden's anti-Americanism, hardly uncommon in the Muslim world, blossomed into full-blown hatred, springing, famously, from the rejection of his offer to deploy his army of veterans from the Afghan anti-Soviet jihad to defend the Saudi kingdom following Saddam Hussein's invasion of neighboring Kuwait in August 1990. The head of Saudi intelligence, Prince Turki, recalled bin Laden's offer of his men to help defeat Saddam's army, which was then the fourth largest in the world: "He changed from a calm, peaceful and gentle man interested in helping Muslims into a person who believed that he would be able to amass and command an army to liberate Kuwait. It revealed his arrogance."

Bin Laden's offer was summarily dismissed by the royal family and instead the Saudis sought the protection of Uncle Sam. Five hundred thousand American soldiers, including a number of women, soon arrived on Arabian soil, a force that bin Laden took to be "infidels" trespassing on the holy land. Omar bin Laden remembers his father ranting, "Women! Defending Saudi men!" The contemporaneous fatwas of the firebrand Saudi clerics Salman al-Awdah and Safar al-Hawali also had an important impact on bin Laden. Awdah and Hawali were among the first Saudi clerics to issue cassette tapes of sermons railing against the U.S. presence in Saudi Arabia.

By now bin Laden had become something of a thorn in the side of the absolute Saudi monarchy, not only because of his defiant stance against the American presence in the kingdom but also because he kept trying to insert himself into the affairs of neighboring Yemen. For bin Laden the first order of business as the Afghan jihad wound down was to dislodge the socialist government of southern Yemen, which had ruled over the bin Ladens' ancestral land since 1967, when the British protectorate of Aden was replaced by a government that aligned itself with the Soviets. As he had in Afghanistan, bin Laden envisaged raising his own jihadist army to help overthrow the socialist Yemeni government. Abu Musab al-Suri, a Syrian militant close to bin Laden, recalled that during this period, "Osama's main passion was the jihad in South Yemen."

As the Saudi government soured on bin Laden, he decided to flee his homeland in the spring of 1991. Abu Jandal, a Yemeni who became the al-Qaeda leader's chief bodyguard in Afghanistan, says that his boss was given a passport to leave the country because of his connections with members of the royal family so that he could travel to Pakistan to liquidate his investments there. The passport was given on the condition that bin Laden would then return to Saudi Arabia and live there under house arrest. Instead the al-Qaeda leader traveled to Pakistan, never to return to his native land.

Around the same time that bin Laden went back to Pakistan, increasing pressure was being exerted on the Pakistani government by a number of Middle Eastern states to expel the hundreds of Arab militants then living in the country, particularly in Peshawar. Bin Laden decided to pull his group out of Pakistan, sending a Sudanese member of al-Qaeda to find suitable property to purchase in Sudan so that he and other members of his organization could settle there. By 1992, bin Laden and his men had sold their properties in Peshawar and moved their operations to Sudan.

It was in Sudan that al-Qaeda's plans to attack American targets first matured. The presence of U.S. soldiers in Saudi Arabia continued to anger bin Laden deeply. In 1992, he gathered together his followers to tell them, "We cannot let the American army stay in the Gulf area and take our oil, take our money. We have to fight them." And in December 1992, following the arrival of American troops in Somalia as part of a humanitarian mission to help starving Somalis, bin Laden became even more adamant, saying, "The Americans have now come to the Horn of Africa, and we have to stop the head of the snake."

Al-Qaeda saw the arrival of those troops—just two years after the United States had based hundreds of thousands of soldiers in Saudi Arabia—as part of a larger American strategy to colonize ever greater chunks of the Muslim world. In late December 1992, an al-Qaeda affiliate bombed two hotels in Yemen housing U.S. soldiers in transit to Somalia. The bombs killed a tourist but no Americans. It seems to have been the first attack against an American target by al-Qaeda or one of its affiliates anywhere in the world.

Bin Laden also sent his men from Sudan to Somalia to explore ways that al-Qaeda could kill Americans there. In 1993, one of bin Laden's military commanders, Mohammed Atef, traveled to Somalia to determine how best to attack U.S. forces, later reporting back to bin Laden in Sudan. On October 3 and 4, 1993, eighteen American soldiers were killed and two U.S. helicopters were brought down by rocket-propelled grenades in an intense firefight in Mogadishu during a botched mission to try to snatch a Somali warlord. At least five hundred Somalis were also killed. Somalis trained by Arab veterans of the war against the Soviets in Afghanistan had been taught that the most effective way to shoot down a helicopter with a rocket-propelled grenade was to hit the vulnerable tail rotor. Within a week of the Mogadishu battle, the United States announced plans for its pullout.

Given the fog of war, it remains unclear who exactly brought down the American helicopter in Mogadishu. But what is clear is that by 1993, half a decade after its founding, al-Qaeda now conceived its central mission to be attacking American targets. That year al-Qaeda started five years of planning to launch major attacks on U.S. targets in Africa, which resulted in the August 1998 bombings of the American embassies in Kenya and Tanzania. Bin Laden took a strong interest in the details of those plots. Ali Mohamed, an Egyptian member of al-Qaeda, was dispatched by bin Laden to the Kenyan capital, Nairobi, in late 1993 to conduct surveillance of the U.S. embassy. Ali Mohamed then traveled to Khartoum, "where my surveillance files and photographs were reviewed by Osama bin Laden." After looking over the pictures of the embassy, bin Laden, who had spent years working in his family's construction business, pointed out the best place to position a truck bomb.

In 1996 the Sudanese government came under increasing pressure from the governments of the United States and Saudi Arabia to expel bin Laden and his small army of militants. Prince Turki, the head of Saudi intelligence at the time, recalled that the Saudi government had been carefully monitoring bin Laden's training camps in Sudan, where he was "recruiting persons from different parts of the Islamic world, from Algeria to Egypt, from East Asia to Somalia, to get them trained at these camps. It was an unacceptable activity."

In mid-May 1996, under intense pressure from the Sudanese government, bin Laden left for Afghanistan, an exile—or in Arabic, a *hijra*—that the hyper-religious al-Qaeda leader no doubt interpreted as a distant echo of the *hijra* that the Prophet Mohammed had himself made fourteen centuries earlier to escape the pagans of Mecca and to build up his perfect Islamic society in the nearby town of Medina. Bin Laden would even come to refer to Afghanistan as the Medina of the new age.

Bin Laden's fifteen-year-old son Omar was the only family member to travel in the small jet that flew the al-Qaeda leader from Sudan to Afghanistan (the rest of bin Laden's family and other members of al-Qaeda would follow months later). Omar recalls that the expulsion from Sudan "hugely embittered" his father, who blamed it largely on the American government.

Underlining that bitterness, bin Laden's first public statement that he was at war with the United States was issued on August 23, 1996, three months after his expulsion from Sudan. It was titled "Declaration of war against the Americans occupying the land of the two holy places [Saudi Arabia]," the text of which was published within a few days in the pan-Arab newspaper *Al-Quds al-Arabi.* In the declaration, bin Laden mentioned that one of his gripes against the United States was the hounding of his group out of Sudan.

Al-Qaeda was now officially at war with the United States, although only a handful of Americans were aware of this yet.

As we have seen, one of the intellectual architects of that war was Sayyid Qutb, a nebbishy Egyptian writer with a Hitler mustache who arrived in the placid town of Greeley, Colorado, in 1949 to attend college. A priggish intellectual, Qutb found the United States to be racist and sexually promiscuous, an experience that left him with a lifelong contempt for the West. One evening, the puritanical Qutb went to a dance at a local church hall, where the pastor was playing the big-band hit "Baby, It's Cold Outside." The idea of a house of worship playing a secular love song crystallized Qutb's sense that Americans were deeply corrupt and interested only in self-gratification.

On his return to Egypt, Qutb joined the Muslim Brotherhood. He was arrested in 1954 for supposedly plotting revolution and was then subjected to the most dreadful tortures. Writing from his prison cell, Qutb argued that Egypt's secular nationalist government was presiding over a country mired in a state of pre-Islamic barbarity known as *jahiliyyah* and, by implication, that the government should be overthrown. Qutb's jail-cell manifesto, *Milestones,* would become the primer for jihadist movements around the Muslim world. In it he insisted that jihad should be conducted offensively against the enemies of Islam. Qutb wrote, "As to the persons who attempt to defend the concept of Islamic jihad by interpreting it in the narrow sense of the current concept of defensive war . . . they lack understanding of the nature of Islam and its primary aim." In other words, fighting preemptive wars against Islam's enemies is the very essence of the Islamic project.

What was truly revolutionary was Qutb's insistence that Islam's enemies included Muslim governments that did not implement true *sharia* law. Qutb wanted secular Middle Eastern governments excommunicated from the Muslim community. That process of declaring other Muslims to be apostates, *takfir*, would become a key al-Qaeda doctrine.

Qutb was executed in 1966, but he would profoundly influence the young Ayman al-Zawahiri, who set up a jihadist cell when he was only fifteen dedicated to the Qutbian theory that Egyptian government officials were apostates from Islam and therefore deserved death. In Zawahiri's autobiography he repeatedly cited Qutb, saying that he "was the spark that ignited the Islamic revolution against the enemies of Islam at home and abroad." And Qutb's brother, Mohamed, the keeper of his brother's flame after his death, occasionally gave lectures at King Abdul Aziz University in Jeddah in the late 1970s, which bin Laden would attend.

Qutb's claim that Muslim rulers who presided over countries in what he considered to be the state of pagan ignorance known as *jahiliyyah* were effectively non-Muslims provided the intellectual underpinning for the assassination of Egyptian President Anwar Sadat in 1981. Sadat had signed Egypt's peace agreement with Israel two years earlier, thus effectively signing his own death warrant, too. In 1981, Zawahiri was arrested for his alleged role in Sadat's assassination, then imprisoned and tortured by Egyptian authorities just as Qutb had been, an experience that further radicalized him.

Sprung from jail, Zawahiri moved to Pakistan in 1986, where he eventually met bin Laden. For bin Laden, the slightly older, cerebral Zawahiri presented an intriguing figure, someone far more experienced politically than himself. For Zawahiri, bin Laden also presented an interesting opportunity: someone who was on his way to becoming a genuine war hero in the jihad against the Soviets and whose deep pockets were well-known. They would go on to embark on a marriage of convenience that would have hellish consequences.

The conventional view of al-Qaeda's war on America is that Zawahiri has really been the brains of the operation; a Machiavellian strategist like Karl Rove to bin Laden's George W. Bush, an analysis that appeared in myriad post-9/11 accounts. But this analysis misses the fact that in making the most important strategic shift in al-Qaeda's history—identifying the United States as its Main Enemy—bin Laden dismissed Zawahiri's obsessive, single focus on overthrowing the Egyptian government, and for years kept him in the dark about al-Qaeda's plans for the 9/11 attacks on America.

Certainly when bin Laden first met Zawahiri in 1986, the slightly older Egyptian militant, who had recently served three years in Egypt's notorious prisons for his jihadist activities, was far more of a hardened revolutionary than the shy son of a Saudi billionaire. Zawahiri already firmly believed that most of the modern Middle East had turned away from true Islam and that the correct response was to overthrow the "near enemy" Arab regimes run by their "apostate" rulers.

Bin Laden took the next step, urging Zawahiri to see that the root of the problem was not simply the Arab "near enemy" regimes, but the "far enemy," the United States, which propped up the status quo in the Middle East, a shift in strategy that took place when al-Qaeda was based in Sudan in the early 1990s. The al-Qaeda leader lectured to his followers there about the necessity of attacking the United States, without which the "near enemy" regimes could not survive. Noman Benotman, the Libyan militant who knew both of al-Qaeda's leaders, recalled that, "Osama influenced Zawahiri with his idea: Forget about the 'near enemy'; the main enemy is the Americans." The intense Syrian jihadist intellectual Abu Musab al-Suri explains that bin Laden came to this strategic analysis because "Sheikh Osama had studied the collapse of the Soviet Union and of the dictator governments in Warsaw Pact countries and, as had happened in East Germany, Romania, Poland and other countries; he was convinced that with the fall of the United States, all the components of the existing Arab and Islamic regimes would fall as well."

Conceptualizing the United States as the Main Enemy was also useful for bin Laden because it was a big enough idea that it could unite several militant Islamist organizations with purely local agendas, such as Zawahiri's Egyptian Jihad group, under al-Qaeda's banner as the standard-bearer of Global Holy War. And it had a further benefit in that it blamed America rather than the jihadist organizations themselves for their failures from Algeria to Egypt to mobilize genuine mass movements capable of toppling the authoritarian regimes in the Middle East.

When Zawahiri first arrived in Taliban-controlled Afghanistan in 1997, following a six-month spell in a Russian jail, his relations with bin Laden were on a quite different footing than they had been a decade earlier. Bin Laden was emerging as something of a global celebrity, the *emir* or prince of jihad, while Zawahiri was the penniless leader of a relatively small Egyptian terrorist group, not especially well liked or well regarded even by his own followers. It was now bin Laden who took Zawahiri under his wing. And even then the al-Qaeda leader kept Zawahiri at some distance. It was only in the summer of 2001 that the al-Qaeda leader disclosed to Zawahiri the details of the coming attacks on Washington and New York, and that was only after Zawahiri's Jihad group had formally merged with al-Qaeda in June. This merger was "more like the assimilation" of Zawahiri's organization into al-Qaeda, according to Feroz Abbasi, the British-Ugandan militant training in al-Qaeda's camps at the time.

Bin Laden exercised near-total control over al-Qaeda, whose members had to swear a religious oath personally to him, so ensuring blind loyalty.

Khalid Sheikh Mohammed, the 9/11 operational commander, outlined the dictatorial powers that bin Laden exercised over his organization: "If the Shura council at al-Qaeda, the highest authority in the organization, had a majority of 98 percent on a resolution and it is opposed by bin Laden, he has the right to cancel the resolution." Bin Laden's son Omar recalls that the men who worked for al-Qaeda had a habit of requesting permission before they spoke with their leader, saying, "Dear prince: May I speak?" Even Zawahiri would ask the al-Qaeda leader for leave to speak.

Before the 9/11 attacks, bin Laden was consolidating more power as the unquestioned, absolute leader of al-Qaeda. To his followers he was truly an extraordinarily charismatic man, someone who they knew had given up a life of luxury as the scion of one of Saudi Arabia's wealthiest families to live a life of danger and poverty in the cause of jihad. The way bin Laden lived his life was attractive to his followers. He had rejected all the comforts of the modern era, sleeping on the floor, eating little, a man of disarming personal modesty who displayed an almost freakish religiosity. The fact that he modeled his life of jihad on the life of the Prophet Mohammed was also not lost on them.

Several of his followers have described their first encounter with the al-Qaeda leader as an intense spiritual experience, and when they explain their feelings for him it is with *love*. Abu Jandal, a Yemeni who became one of his bodyguards, described his first meeting with bin Laden in 1997 as "beautiful" and said he came to look on him "as a father." Shadi Abdalla, a Jordanian who was also one of bin Laden's bodyguards, explained his boss's attraction: "A very charismatic person who could persuade people simply by his way of talking. One could say that he 'seduced' many young men."

Bin Laden's appeal was especially strong for militant Muslims living in the West. Nizar Trabelsi, a Tunisian who was a professional soccer player in Germany, traveled to Afghanistan in 2000. When he first met with the al-Qaeda leader in Kandahar, he remembers, "I was so impressed when I saw him that I didn't dare to speak to him. He asked me questions about my family and realizing that I felt uneasy he tried to cheer me up." And Mohammed Abdullah Warsame, a Canadian citizen of Somali descent living in Minneapolis who attended al-Qaeda training camps in Afghanistan, sat next to bin Laden during a meal and found him to be "very inspirational."

The special awe that his followers had for the al-Qaeda leader struck John Miller, an ABC News correspondent who interviewed bin Laden in 1998.

Miller is one of the few outsiders to have spent several days in and around the al-Qaeda organization when it was based in Afghanistan in the late 1990s. He recalled bin Laden's "charismatic aura or a scent . . . either you have it or you don't. They spoke of him with godlike reverence and they talked with great excitement about the Sheikh."

Bin Laden carefully tended his public image as "the Sheikh," a heroic warrior-monk who was not only fearless on the battlefield but could also recite the entire Koran from memory and wrote his own poetry. When he invited the Al Jazeera correspondent Ahmed Zaidan to attend the wedding of his son Muhammad in Afghanistan in January 2001, bin Laden read a poem of his own composition celebrating al-Qaeda's recent bombing of the USS *Cole* in Yemen. The hundreds of guests at the marriage feast cheered him on with chants of "Allah Akbar!" as he declaimed his poem, a performance that was videotaped for Al Jazeera by Zaidan. Later, when bin Laden and Zaidan were alone, the al-Qaeda leader told him, "Ahmed, I don't think my delivery was good." Zaidan recalls, "He's very much caring about public relations, very much caring how he would appear on the TV. And he said, 'I didn't like it. I'm going to deliver it again.'" Bin Laden repeated his performance and then watched both versions on tape, saying afterwards, "No, no. The first one was better."

Like many of history's most effective leaders, bin Laden told a simple story about the world that is easy to grasp, even for those of his followers from Jakarta to London who had not had a chance to sit at his feet. In bin Laden's telling there is a global conspiracy by the West and its puppet allies in the Muslim world to destroy true Islam, a conspiracy that is led by the United States. This single narrative purports to explain all the problems of the Muslim world; for Muslims in the United Kingdom the real problems that many of them face are not caused by simple British racial discrimination but by the fact they are Muslim; the long-running war between Russia and the Chechens is not a centuries-old imperialist land grab by the Russians, but is rather a war against Islam; and the American attack on Saddam Hussein in 2003 wasn't because he seemed to be flouting multiple United Nations resolutions aimed at disarming his supposed stockpiles of weapons of mass destruction, but rather it was a plot by America to take over a great Arab nation.

This narrative is silent, of course, about the well-documented cases when the United States had provided large-scale help to Muslims, such as belatedly and finally halting the Serb massacres of Bosnians in the mid-1990s and providing massive aid to the hundreds of thousands of Indonesians made homeless by the 2004 tsunami. Bin Laden is never one to let facts get in the way of his narrative of American-led Muslim humiliation.

Al-Qaeda's leader and his followers are strongly motivated by the belief that the Muslim world has been collectively humiliated for decades, and in particular by Western powers. Three weeks after 9/11, as the United States began launching airstrikes against Taliban positions, a video of bin Laden sitting on a rocky outcrop was broadcast on Al Jazeera. On the tape, he said, "What America is tasting now is something insignificant compared to what we have tasted for scores of years. The Islamic world has been tasting this humiliation and this degradation for 80 years."

In his first public statement following 9/11, bin Laden emphasized the "humiliation" that the Muslim world had felt for much of the past century and the negative effect of Western policies in the Middle East. For bin Laden, the 1916 Sykes-Picot Agreement, the secret plan to carve up the disintegrating Ottoman Empire between the French and British, has the same resonance that the 1919 Treaty of Versailles did for Hitler. It must be avenged and reversed. In mid-February 2003, a month before the U.S.-led invasion of Iraq, bin Laden railed on an audiotape posted to jihadist websites against "a new Sykes-Picot Agreement, the Bush-Blair axis."

By bin Laden's own account, it was U.S. foreign policy in the Muslim world that was the reason al-Qaeda is attacking America. In all the tens of thousands of words that bin Laden uttered on the public record, there were some significant omissions: he did not rail against the pernicious effects of Hollywood movies, or against the pornography protected by the U.S. Constitution. Nor did he inveigh against the drug and alcohol culture of the West, or its tolerance for homosexuals. Judging by his silence, bin Laden cared little about such cultural issues. What he condemned the United States for is simple—its policies in the Middle East: its wars in Iraq and Afghanistan; its support for regimes, such as Egypt and Saudi Arabia, that bin Laden regards as apostates from Islam; and its support for Israel.

Crucially, bin Laden blamed not just the U.S. government for its supposed campaign against Islam but also ordinary American citizens. In an interview a few weeks after 9/11 he explained: "The American people should remember that they pay taxes to their government, they elect their president, their government manufacture arms and gives them to Israel and Israel uses them to massacre Palestinians." Bin Laden claimed this makes them legitimate targets for his campaign of violence, citing a doctrine of Koranically sanctioned reciprocity to justify killing ordinary Americans: "Allah legislated the permission. . . . Whoever kills our civilians then we have the right to kill theirs."

There is sufficient truth to aspects of bin Laden's critique of American foreign policy for it to have real traction around the Muslim world. To cite three obvious examples: first, the U.S. government's largely reflexive and unqualified support for Israel at the expense of the Palestinian people; second, the obvious American hypocrisy when it comes to promoting "democracy," while also embracing the absolute monarchy of the Saudis; and third, of course, the U.S. invasion of Iraq.

Bin Laden's master narrative of a war on Islam led by America that must be avenged is embraced by a significant minority in the Islamic world. A Gallup poll in ten Muslim countries conducted in 2005 and 2006 found that 7 percent of Muslims said the 9/11 attacks were "completely justified." Or to put it another way, given the 1.2 billion Muslims in the world, around 100 million Muslims wholeheartedly endorsed bin Laden's rationale for the 9/11 attacks and the need for Islamic revenge on the United States.

In discussions of the "root causes" of Islamist terrorism, there is often little discussion of *Islam*. That is suprising because in the minutes of al-Qaeda's first meetings in 1988 the group's mission statement was explicitly religious: "Al-Qaeda is basically an organized Islamic faction; its goal will be to lift the word of God, to make His religion victorious." Similarly, bin Laden was quite clear about the religious nature of his war in his post-9/11 interview with Al Jazeera: "This war is fundamentally religious. . . . Under no circumstances should we forget this enmity between us and the infidels, for the enmity is based on creed." Living in societies that are largely postreligious, many Westerners find it hard to understand how someone might really believe in a war sanctioned by God, yet four centuries ago most European wars were fought over issues of religion.

Members of al-Qaeda view themselves as part of a vanguard defending true Islam. Bin Laden based justification of his war on a corpus of Muslim beliefs and he found enough ammunition in the Koran to give his war Islamic legitimacy, often invoking the "Sword" verses of the holy book, which can be interpreted as urging attacks on infidels who won't submit and convert to Islam. The Koranic verse 9:5 speaks for itself: "Once the Sacred Months are past (and they refuse to make peace), you may kill the idol worshipers when you encounter them, punish them, and resist every move they make. If they repent and observe the Prayers and give the obligatory alms-giving you shall let them go." That verse was quoted approvingly by bin Laden in his 1996 declaration of war against the United States and again in a statement he made seven years later in the run-up to the Iraq War.

Traditional Islamic theology recognizes five pillars of faith: the daily prayers, fasting during Ramadan, charitable donations, the profession of faith that there is only one God and his Prophet is Mohammed, and the pilgrimage to Mecca. But bin Laden claimed that jihad is an additional pillar of the faith: "No other priority except faith, could be considered before [jihad]."

The standard interpretation of jihad down the centuries is religiously sanctioned warfare. And this is hardly surprising; the Prophet Mohammed was not only a religious figure but also an able military commander. Mohammed took part in some two dozen military campaigns and he revolutionized the conduct of war in the Arab world with the concept of jihad and martyrdom in the service of Islam. Religiously sanctioned warfare is a constant theme of the Koran and in the model life of the Prophet.

It is not surprising, therefore, that bin Laden, who styled himself after the Prophet, tapped into this tradition. One of his Afghan training camps was named *Al-Badr*, after one of the Prophet Mohammed's most famous battles, and the guesthouse that bin Laden established for Arab volunteers in Peshawar, Pakistan, in the mid-1980s was known as the *Beit al-Ansar*, the House of Supporters, after those who helped the Prophet when he fled his native Mecca for Medina in 622.

Bin Laden was not, of course, a religious scholar, and so when on May 26, 1998, he held a press conference in Afghanistan to announce that he had formed "the International Islamic Front to do jihad against the Crusaders and Jews," also present were the sons of the Egyptian cleric Omar Abdel Rahman, "the Blind Sheikh." They distributed small cards to the journalists attending the conference, on which was printed their father's "will," which Rahman had supposedly written while serving a life sentence in an American prison for his role as the inciter of terrorist plots in New York in the mid-1990s.

The cleric's will read, "Extract the most violent revenge. . . . Cut off all relations with [the Americans, Christians, and Jews], tear them to pieces, destroy their economies, burn their corporations, destroy their peace, sink their ships, shoot down their planes and kill them on air, sea, and land." Sheikh

Rahman's will/fatwa seems to be the first time that a Muslim cleric had given his religious sanction to attacks on American aviation, shipping, and economic targets. The fatwa, with its exhortations to "shoot down their planes," "burn their corporations," and "sink their ships," would turn out to be a slowly ticking time bomb that would explode on October 12, 2000, when a suicide attack blew a hole the size of a small house in the USS *Cole* in Yemen, and it would explode again with even greater ferocity on 9/11.

To understand the significance of Sheikh Rahman's will/fatwa, it is crucial to understand the spiritual authority that its author exercises over al-Qaeda. Al-Qaeda may have been led by bin Laden and his deputy Ayman al-Zawahiri, but neither of them has any standing as a religious authority, while Sheikh Rahman has a doctorate in Islamic jurisprudence from Al-Azhar University in Cairo, the Harvard of Sunni Islamic thought. Indeed, Sheikh Rahman has long been the spiritual guide of Egypt's Jihad Group, members of which occupy senior leadership positions in al-Qaeda.

Al-Qaeda's leaders wanted to exact revenge on the United States for the imprisonment of their spiritual guide; at the same time, Sheikh Rahman gave his followers his spiritual sanction for terrorist attacks on American civilians. His fatwas are the nearest equivalent that al-Qaeda has to an ex cathedra statement from the pope. Sheikh Rahman, for the first time in al-Qaeda's history, ruled that it was permissible, and even desirable, to carry out attacks against American planes and corporations—not coincidentally, exactly the type of attacks that took place on 9/11. Indeed, up until 9/11 al-Qaeda had confined its attacks to American governmental and military targets. With Sheikh Rahman's fatwa, al-Qaeda now had clerical cover for its plans to kill American civilians.

As a result, the 9/11 hijackers saw themselves as taking part in a heroic religious war. When a number of the key plotters based in Hamburg, Germany, moved into a dingy, modern apartment block on Marienstrasse, they grandiloquently referred to it as *Dar al-Ansar*, or the Abode of the Supporters. The 9/11 conspirators also awarded themselves *kunya*s, Islamic honorific names, which often referred to figures from Islam's heroic early history. The lead hijacker, the dour Egyptian Mohammed Atta, was known as Abu Abdul Rahman, after an Egyptian who was told by the Prophet that he would go to Paradise.

The certainty that Paradise awaits those "martyred" in the defense of Islam is something that has long pervaded Muslim thought. In his August 1996 declaration of war against the United States, bin Laden approvingly quoted a *hadith*, a saying attributed to the Prophet: "The martyr has a guarantee from God . . . [He] marries him to seventy-two of the pure virgins of paradise." Al-Qaeda took the idea of martyrdom, which had traditionally been death in battle, and applied it to suicide operations against civilian targets, a serious leap of faith since suicide is a grave sin in Islam punishable by eternal torment in hell. (From a theological perspective, engaging in one of al-Qaeda's "martyrdom" operations that kills civilians is quite risky, because what if Allah chooses to see the operation as a simple suicide compounded by the murder of many innocents?)

In luggage that Atta left in a car at Boston's Logan Airport on the morning of 9/11, authorities discovered an Arabic document titled "Manual for a Raid," which used the Koranic word *ghazwah* for raid, demonstrating that the hijackers firmly believed that commandeering passenger jets and killing everyone on board was all in the great religious tradition of the heroic battles fought by the Prophet. In the manual, the hijackers were urged to invoke God as they entered the aircraft and were told they "will be with your heavenly brides soon." The manual mentions the "martyrs'" ascension into heaven twelve times, underlining that the hijackers were religious fanatics aflame with the belief that they were doing God's will and would shortly be in Paradise.

Making the elementary point that al-Qaeda's jihad is literally a holy war that has something to do with Islam is not to imply that Muslims are inherently more violent than the adherents of any other religion. Christianity has, of course, been used as the justification for any number of crusades, pogroms, wars, and imperial adventures in Christ's name. And it was from Christian countries that the monstrous secular political religions of Nazism and communism arose; in their relatively brief tenancies on the planet, these two arguably created more human misery than any of the other creeds that had preceded them.

Of course, not all of al-Qaeda's terrorists are religious fanatics. Some seem to be more in the game because they think it is a blast. Typical of this group is the 9/11 operational commander Khalid Sheikh Mohammed (KSM). KSM is a burly Pakistani born in Kuwait, who earned a degree in engineering from North Carolina Agricultural and Technical State University. In the mid-1990s, KSM lived in the Philippines, where he consorted with a number of girlfriends—unusual behavior for a committed jihadist militant. KSM's taste for terrorist theatrics could be seen in his initial scheme for al-Qaeda's attacks on the United States, which involved hijacking ten planes, nine of which were to be flown into buildings on both the west and east coasts. The tenth plane was to be hijacked to an American airport, and after all the adult male passengers had been killed, KSM would himself emerge from the plane to deliver to the assembled media a speech blasting American support for Israel. Tellingly, KSM cast himself as the superhero of his terror-snuff movie, a jihadist James Bond. Bin Laden ordered KSM's grandiose plans to be scaled back, but entrusted him with the overall execution of the attacks on Washington and New York.

But even those Islamist terrorists like KSM who get a kick out of planning epic terrorist operations share a deep and aggrieved sense with their more religiously motivated cadre that the Muslim-Arab world is under siege. All around the region a host of authoritarian kleptocracies have held on to power for decades. Those Middle Eastern authoritarian governments have been an important factor in incubating jihadist militants. Sayyid Qutb, the Lenin of the militant jihadist movement, and later Ayman al-Zawahiri were radicalized by their time in the jails of Cairo. And al-Qaeda draws many of its men from closed societies that are intolerant of dissent. In al-Qaeda's training camps in Afghanistan before the fall of the Taliban, according to KSM, 70 percent of the recruits were Saudi, 20 percent from Yemen, and the final 10 percent from elsewhere.

After the 9/11 attacks it became commonplace to say that bin Laden had only latched on to the issue of Israel and Palestine belatedly, as if saying this would somehow reduce the importance of the Palestinian issue as a rationale for al-Qaeda's attacks. Nothing could be further from the truth, as even the most casual reading of bin Laden's statements demonstrates. The al-Qaeda leader's first public declaration that he was at war with the United States was issued on August 23, 1996, and he was quite clear about where he stood on the issue of Palestine: "I feel still the pain of [the loss of] Al-Quds in my internal organs." Al-Quds—the name is Arabic for Jerusalem—is the site of the Al-Aqsa Mosque, the third-holiest place of pilgrimage in Islam, and which was annexed to Israel in 1967. Bin Laden went on to say that he felt the loss of Jerusalem "like a burning fire in my intestines."

Bin Laden also had a strong personal connection to Jerusalem's Al-Aqsa Mosque, since his father Mohammed's construction company was responsible for its restoration during the 1960s. And bin Laden relished telling interviewers that his father would pray at all three of Islam's holiest sites in one day. Pakistani journalist Hamid Mir recalls the al-Qaeda leader telling him it "was a routine of his father, once or twice in a month; he used to offer his morning prayers in Medina, afternoon prayers in Mecca, and then the evening prayers in Jerusalem, because he had a plane."

In 1982 the Israelis invaded Lebanon, an event that received wide coverage in the Arab world at a time when bin Laden was already quite politicized. Years later he would recall his hatred for the Americans, whom he blamed for Israel's policies: "The event that affected me personally began in 1982 when America gave the Israelis the green light to invade Lebanon. . . . I cannot forget those unbearable scenes of blood and severed limbs. . . . They produced an intense rejection of tyranny and a strong resolve to punish the oppressors."

And so in May 1998, when bin Laden held his first and only press conference to announce the formation of his "World Islamic Front," he said it was formed "to do jihad against the Crusaders and Jews."

Al-Qaeda's first videotape production, which was posted to the Internet in June 2001, focused heavily on the Israeli-Palestinian conflict. On the videotape bin Laden said, "Jews are free in Jerusalem to rape weak Muslim women and to imprison those young cubs who stand up to them." He then made the connection explicit between the suffering of the Palestinians and supposed American complicity, saying, "The American government is an agent that represents Israel inside America. Look at sensitive departments like the Defense Department or the State Department, or sensitive security departments like the CIA and others; you find that Jews have the first word in the American government."

Bin Laden was also a pathological anti-Semite. He told the Pakistani journalist Hamid Mir that one of his wives had a baby girl after 9/11 named Safia. Mir asked him, "Why Safia?" Bin Laden replied, "I gave her name of Safia who killed a Jew spy in the days of Holy Prophet. . . . She will kill enemies of Islam like Safia of the Prophet's time."

The very basis of al-Qaeda's campaign of murder against Americans and their allies derives, then, in part from U.S. support for the Jewish state. So intense were bin Laden's feelings about the Palestinian issue that he wrote two letters to Khalid Sheikh Mohammed, the operational commander of 9/11, urging him to move the attacks on Washington and New York forward to June or July 2001 to coincide with a planned visit to the White House by the right-wing Israeli politician Ariel Sharon.

What is striking about the accounts of those who knew him, whether they are close family members or mere acquaintances, is that bin Laden was a retiring, even shy man who was polite and deferential in his dealings with others and quick to forgive failings in his followers. Even his critics within the jihadist movement describe a humble man who led by example and abjured every material comfort for a life dedicated to defending his conception of Islam. So given this consistent portrait of him, why did bin Laden mastermind 9/11? After all, it was hardly the act of a humble or empathetic person. For that we must return to where we began with bin Laden: religion.

Bin Laden firmly believed that he was an instrument of God's will, as was made clear in the videotape he released after his near-death experience at the battle of Tora Bora in eastern Afghanistan in December 2001, in which he said, "I am just a poor slave of God. If I live or die, the war will continue." Arguably no man has been closer to the Saudi militant than Jamal Khalifa, who was his best friend at university. Bin Laden encouraged Khalifa to marry his half sister Shaikha, to whom he was close, as she is the other particularly religiously observant member of his family. Khalifa explains the key to understanding bin Laden: "Especially when you come to a religious issue—Osama is very sensitive and he really likes to implement Islam. And he's very much at the same time afraid that if he does not, God will punish him."

For bin Laden, not to defend Islam from what he believed to be its most important enemy, the United States, would therefore have been to disobey God; an unimaginable act for him.

The depth of feeling that burned inside bin Laden about his holy war could be seen during the January 10, 2001, wedding ceremony of his son Muhammad, where one of his youngest sons, then aged eight, made a short speech captured on video in which he declaimed, "I stand for a jihad against the infidels today and shall do so until eternity. Jihad is in my mind, heart and blood. No fear, no intimidation can ever take this feeling out of my mind." Indoctrinating his eight-year-old boy to believe that holy war is what gives meaning to his young life says much about how the al-Qaeda leader viewed the world.

Bin Laden's fanaticism burned so hot that he was even prepared to sacrifice his own kids in the service of his jihad. About a year before 9/11, bin Laden gave a lecture about "the joy of martyrdom" to a group of al-Qaeda fighters, after which he excitedly gathered a number of his sons around him, saying, "My sons, there is a paper on the wall of the mosque. This paper is for men who volunteer to be suicide bombers. Those who want to give their lives for Islam must add their names to the list." Omar bin Laden recalled, "That's when one of my youngest brothers, one too young to comprehend the concept of life and death, got to his feet, nodded reverently in my father's direction, and took off running for the mosque."

A further component of the al-Qaeda leader's thinking is explained by the Libyan Noman Benotman, who says that, based on his dealings with bin Laden and others in al-Qaeda stretching back decades, they have an ultrafundamentalist view of who has "immunity" from being killed during the course of a holy war. "They believe the only way to get immunity to your life is to be a Muslim," says Benotman. Bin Laden firmly believed that all non-Muslims are fair game in his jihad.

This helps explain the seeming paradox that the mastermind of 9/11 was described by so many of his family, friends, and acquaintances as a humble, empathetic, if religiously zealous man: because they are, of course, all Muslims, whom bin Laden generally treated with respect, a respect that he would not accord to non-Muslims. He took to heart the Koranic injunction, "O ye who believe! Take not the Jews and the Christians for your friends." And he went a significant step further when he said, "Every Muslim, from the moment they realize the distinction in their hearts, hates Americans, hates Jews, and hates Christians. This is part of our belief and our religion."

It was this blinding hatred and thirst for revenge that propelled forward bin Laden's plans to attack the United States.

Chapter 3

Blinking Red

This was the exchange between John Miller, the ABC News correspondent who had interviewed bin Laden in Afghanistan in May 1998, and ABC anchor Peter Jennings at 10:29 A.M. on September 11, 2001.

MILLER: The north tower seems to be coming down.
JENNINGS: Oh, my God.
MILLER: The second—the second tower.
JENNINGS: (A very long pause.) It's hard to put it into words, and maybe one doesn't need to. Both trade towers, where thousands of people work, on this day, Tuesday, have now been attacked and destroyed with thousands of people either in them or in the immediate area adjacent to them.

CIA analyst Gina Bennett knew who was responsible as soon as the second plane hit the World Trade Center. In August 1993, while working at the Bureau of Intelligence and Research, the small intelligence shop inside the State Department, Bennett had authored a paper that was the first warning of the threat posed by a man named "Osama Bin Ladin," who was "enabling hundreds of jihadists and training even more" in Afghanistan, Pakistan, Sudan, and Yemen. She also fingered him as the possible sponsor of the bombing of the World Trade Center on February 26, 1993, an attack that killed six and was the first time that a group of Islamist terrorists had struck in the United States. Bennett wrote an analytic assessment that same year noting that bin Laden had "established an organization called al-Qa'ida in the 1980s." This was many years before the name of bin Laden's terrorist group became public and was a term that was then unknown even to many of the foot soldiers in his training camps.

On the morning of September 11, 2001, Bennett was doing "something very typical, vomiting with morning sickness." She was three months pregnant with her fourth child, something that she had yet to tell her coworkers about, and was at her desk at the Counterterrorist Center (CTC) at the CIA. As something close to panic set in, Agency managers told everyone to evacuate—everyone, that is, but those in the CTC who would remain in the building doing their jobs; after all, there was no one group in the government who knew more about the source of the 9/11 threat.

Bennett and her colleagues tracking al-Qaeda were well aware that the CIA was a potential target. During the mid-1990s, Abdul Hakim Murad, an al-Qaeda associate, had developed a plan to fly a plane into CIA headquarters. The CTC officials also knew that one of the hijacked jets was heading toward Washington, D.C. (it was the plane that would eventually crash into the Pentagon). One of Bennett's most valued colleagues, Barbara Sude, a precise, careful analyst with a doctorate from Princeton in medieval Arabic thought, was at her desk. Only a month earlier the memo that Sude had coauthored warning "Bin Ladin Determined to Strike in U.S." had been briefed to President Bush at his ranch in Texas.

Sude knew that the CIA was a likely target but remained in the CTC offices on the ground floor of the Agency, preparing to write the avalanche of reports about al-Qaeda she knew were likely to fill her coming days. Chuckling, she remembers, "I told my boss, well, let me go to the restroom first before I have to write in case I get trapped in the rubble. I didn't want to not have gone to the bathroom beforehand." Sude recalls the moment the World Trade Center towers started collapsing: "I will never forget when my colleague comes up, his face ashen." But there wasn't much time to focus on anything but the task at hand: "Policy-maker appetite became insatiable for everything about al-Qaeda.... They didn't know as much as they realized they needed to know."

Like Gina Bennett, FBI Special Agent Daniel Coleman had also been tracking Islamist terrorists since the 1993 bombing of the Trade Center. And three years later he became the first official from the Bureau to be attached to a small, new CIA unit dedicated to tracking bin Laden. Walking around the streets of lower Manhattan near his FBI office, Coleman, a portly gentleman in his early fifties, wearing glasses and a tan raincoat, might have been mistaken for an auditor at one of the big banks. But Coleman, who comes from a long line of New York City cops going back to his great-grandfather, knew more about al-Qaeda from the inside than anyone else in government. "I'm the kind of guy who gets into the back room of everything, reads everything, and tries to remember everything," Coleman explained. As a result of a highly retentive memory and the fact that he had spent many, many hours debriefing the first defectors from al-Qaeda—Jamal al-Fadl, L'Houssaine Kherchtou, and Ali Mohamed—Coleman had an encyclopedic understanding of the terrorist organization. In December 1995, Coleman had even opened the first counterterrorism case against an obscure Saudi financier of terrorism named Osama bin Laden.

On the morning of September 11, 2001, Coleman was at his office at 26 Federal Plaza, a block away from the Trade Center. When the first plane crashed, Coleman hoped it was an accident, "but after the second building got hit I thought, 'Oh God almighty!' I was pretty certain who had done it." Coleman rushed down Broadway toward the Trade Center, looking to interview witnesses, when "all of a sudden this cyclone comes up the street and I hear this noise and it was the loudest noise I have ever heard in my life, and I'm like, okay, what was that? It was incomprehensible. I didn't know what it was, all these papers. This cloud was coming." This was the debris cloud from the South Tower imploding and collapsing, the first building to do so, at 9:59 A.M.

Almost immediately an important clue was found near the Trade Center. Someone picked up a passport that had fallen to the street shortly after the first hijacked plane, American Airlines Flight 11, had crashed into the twin towers. It was turned in to the FBI that day. The passport belonged to Satam al-Suqami, a Saudi law student, who had entered the United States a few months earlier and who would turn out to be one of the hijackers. Coleman remembers that Suqami's passport was only partially burnt and smelled strongly of kerosene.

Analysts at the CIA quickly realized with something close to horror that two men they had previously tagged as al-Qaeda associates, Nawaf al-Hazmi and Khalid al-Mihdhar, were on American Airlines Flight 77, which had crashed into the Pentagon shortly after 9:30 A.M. Barbara Sude recalls that Mihdhar's name "came up right away."

Bennett, Coleman, and Sude, who had put themselves into harm's way on September 11, were three of perhaps a few dozen U.S. government officials who understood the true scope of the al-Qaeda threat before it materialized so spectacularly in New York and Washington. Most of those officials were concentrated at the CIA or at the New York field office of the FBI, which had been investigating Islamist extremists since the early 1990s, or were part of the small counterterrorism group at the National Security Council. Otherwise, much of the rest of the government, including almost all of the top national security officials in the Bush administration, had no idea about the true scale of the al-Qaeda threat until they were evacuating their offices on the morning of 9/11.

After the 9/11 attacks no Bush administration official took responsibility, apologized, resigned, or was fired for what was the gravest national security failure in American history. The first and only official to offer an apology was counterterrorism coordinator Richard Clarke, who, when he appeared as a private citizen in 2004 before the 9/11 Commission, opened his remarks by addressing the families of victims sitting in the audience, saying, "Your government failed you. . . . And I failed you."

In contrast, following Pearl Harbor, to which 9/11 has often been compared, Admiral Husband Kimmel, the commander of the Pacific Fleet, who had been warned of a possible Japanese attack, was immediately relieved of his command and demoted; a year later he retired. The Roosevelt administration also quickly investigated what had happened at Pearl Harbor. Within seven weeks of the attacks, the Roberts Commission, which had been appointed by President Roosevelt, issued its first congressional report. It was one of *nine* official inquiries into Pearl Harbor convened in the middle of World War II. By contrast, the Bush administration thwarted congressional efforts to investigate 9/11, and only reluctantly acceded to an investigative commission more than a year after the attacks, following intense public pressure from the victims' families. Vice President Dick Cheney claimed improbably in May 2002 that he wanted to avoid the "circus atmosphere" that would come with establishing a separate investigatory body.

Once it was set up, the 9/11 Commission largely focused on the structural failures of agencies within the U.S. government. The commission was a bipartisan panel, and by examining the very real problems of particular government institutions it was able largely to skirt the wider policy failures of the Clinton and Bush administrations' handling of the al-Qaeda threat, subjects that were politically too hot to handle.

What does the historical record tell us about the culpability of the two American administrations sitting in the White House in the years before 9/11 in failing to counter the gathering al-Qaeda threat? In the winter of 2001, Richard Shultz, an American historian of Special Forces, was tasked by the Pentagon to find out why elite counterterrorism units, such as Delta Force, were not deployed to hit al-Qaeda before 9/11; after all, that was supposed to be their main mission. In a public version of his report, published under the apt title "Showstoppers," Shultz found that the "great reluctance in the Pentagon"—as General Peter Schoomaker, their commanding officer put it—to deploy Special Operations Forces arose from several factors. First, terrorism was generally seen as a crime until 9/11, and so the Pentagon saw terrorism as something that fell under the purview of the CIA and found it convenient to assume (wrongly) that the military did not have the statutory authority to engage in fighting terrorism.

A second key "showstopper" was the tendency by the Department of Defense to recommend "big footprint" operations involving as many as several hundred soldiers to take on al-Qaeda in Afghanistan. That made those operations nonstarters for President Clinton, who was looking for small-unit insertions, not mini-invasions of Afghanistan. Michael Scheuer, then the head of the bin Laden unit at the CIA, recalls that "Clinton wanted a rapier and they brought him a battle axe."

Finally, the Pentagon demanded high-quality "actionable intelligence" before launching an operation, which simply didn't exist in Taliban-controlled Afghanistan. Special Operations boss Schoomaker recalled: "Special Operations were never given the mission. It was very, very frustrating. It was like having a brand-new Ferrari in the garage and nobody wants to race it because you might dent the fender."

Given the reluctance of the Pentagon to send in Special Operations Forces, and the generally imperfect intelligence about bin Laden's location, what other options were available to policy makers? One option was to tighten the diplomatic noose around the Taliban and so increase their costs for sheltering al-Qaeda. After the embassy bombings in Africa in 1998, Michael Sheehan, the U.S. ambassador for counterterrorism, an intense, wiry former Special

Forces officer given wide latitude by his boss Secretary of State Madeleine Albright, put the Taliban on notice that they would be held responsible for future al-Qaeda attacks. And in 1999 the Clinton administration slapped sanctions on the Taliban and the United Nations followed suit.

As concerns about a possible terrorist attack during the turn of the millennium were gripping Clinton's national security team, Sheehan dispatched a strongly worded cable to Taliban leaders that said they would "be held fully accountable" for another attack by al-Qaeda. Sometime in January 2000, Sheehan followed that up with a forty-five-minute phone call with the Taliban foreign minister Wakil Muttawakil in which he read him an unambiguous statement from Clinton: "We will hold the Taliban leadership responsible for any attacks against US interests by al-Qaeda or any of its affiliated groups." Muttawakil, who was privately one of bin Laden's most bitter critics inside the Taliban movement, stuck to his talking points that the al-Qaeda leader was under the control of the Taliban and there was no proof that he was involved in terrorism.

The international community's pressure and sanctions on the Taliban did ratchet up the pressure on them, according to al-Qaeda insider Abu Walid al-Masri, who later wrote that a "nucleus of opposition" to bin Laden developed among senior leaders of the Taliban who urged that bin Laden be expelled. Taliban officials also told bin Laden to cease his international terrorist plotting in early 1999. Obviously, the al-Qaeda leader did not pay much heed to any of this.

The deeper problem the United States had in attacking al-Qaeda in Afghanistan before 9/11 was not simply the result of imperfect intelligence about the country, the reluctance of the military to take action, and the lack of political will to go to war against terrorists that had characterized American administrations for decades; rather, it was that policy makers in the Clinton and Bush administrations didn't have any overarching strategy for Afghanistan. This was the legacy of many years of American neglect of the festering problems in the country. After the brilliant success of the covert U.S. operation to arm the Afghan mujahideen that had helped to destroy the Soviet Union, the George H. W. Bush administration closed the U.S. embassy in Kabul in 1989. This turned out to be a grave error, as from that day forward the United States was largely flying blind in Afghanistan (the embassy only reopened after the fall of the Taliban). And as the Cold War receded into history, aid to Afghanistan, one of the poorest countries on the planet, was effectively zeroed out, dropping to only $2 million a year in Clinton's first term.

Both Bill Clinton and George W. Bush failed to see bin Laden as a political challenge. They both had hoped to end the al-Qaeda problem by decapitating its leader through cruise missile strikes or by using CIA assets on the ground. Of course, that would have left the training camps and al-Qaeda's organization in place even if the decapitation effort had succeeded. And instead of using the leader of the Northern Alliance, Ahmad Shah Massoud, as a strategic partner to defeat both al-Qaeda and the Taliban, the United States saw him only as someone who might be helpful in eliminating bin Laden.

There were some American officials who did see the larger strategic picture. Five days into the new Bush administration, on January 25, 2001, Richard Clarke wrote National Security Advisor Condoleezza Rice that a cabinet-level review of al-Qaeda policy was "urgently" needed. Attached to the memo was a paper titled "Strategy for Eliminating the Threat from the Jihadist Networks of al Qida." In the memo Clarke suggested arming Predator drones with Hellfire missiles to take out the group's leaders, giving "massive" support to Massoud's Northern Alliance, destroying terrorist training camps and Taliban command-and-control facilities using U.S. Special Forces, and expanding a deal with Afghanistan's northern neighbor, Uzbekistan, to allow U.S. assets like the Predator drones to be based there. But Rice seemed content to let her deputy Stephen Hadley move ahead at a businesslike but not urgent pace with an al-Qaeda policy review and otherwise do nothing. (The strategy that Clarke had outlined in the memo to Rice was essentially the same one that President Bush finally adopted after 9/11.)

With the exception of Clarke and CIA director George Tenet and the latter's deputy John McLaughlin, senior Bush administration officials consistently underestimated the urgent threat posed by bin Laden and al-Qaeda, who simply did not fit their worldview of what constituted a serious threat. A Nexis database search of all the newspapers, magazines, and TV transcripts of Rice's statements and writings from the mid-1990s until 9/11 shows that she never mentioned al-Qaeda publicly, and only referred to the threat from bin Laden during a 2000 interview with a Detroit radio station. Perhaps sensitive to this fact, when Rice testified before the 9/11 Commission in 2004, she said, "I, myself, had written for an introduction to a volume on bioterrorism done at Stanford that I thought that we wanted not to wake up one day and find that Osama bin Laden had succeeded on our soil."

The book that Rice referred to her in her testimony, *The New Terror: Facing the Threat of Biological and Chemical Weapons*, was published by Stanford in 1999. *The New Terror* has no mention of al-Qaeda or bin Laden either by Rice or any of its other contributors. It's no wonder that when Clarke first briefed Rice on al-Qaeda, "her facial expression gave me the impression that she had never heard the term before."

For other key members of Bush's national security team, the al-Qaeda threat also barely registered. A Nexis database search of all of Deputy Defense Secretary Paul Wolfowitz's pre-9/11 statements and writings shows he never mentioned al-Qaeda, and referred to bin Laden only once, in the context of the Saudi exile's supposed links to Saddam Hussein, testifying before a congressional committee in 1998 that there were "suspect connections between the Iraqis and this Osama bin Laden fellow." Indeed, during the summer of 2001, Wolfowitz enraged CIA officials, some of whom were frantic with worry, by pooh-poohing the flood of warnings pouring in by asking whether bin Laden was simply "trying to study U.S. reactions."

A Nexis search for anything that President Bush or Vice President Cheney might have written or said about the threat posed by al-Qaeda and bin Laden similarly comes up empty before 9/11. Of the thirty-three "principals" meetings of cabinet members held by the Bush administration before the attacks on Washington and New York, only one was about terrorism, although almost immediately after assuming office Bush convened his cabinet on February 5, 2001, to discuss the supposedly pressing issue of Iraq. The first cabinet-level meeting about the threat posed by al-Qaeda took place on September 4, 2001.

The fact that the Bush administration was strangely somnambulant about the al-Qaeda threat is puzzling. It was not as if they did not have enough information or warning about the threat posed by al-Qaeda; quite the opposite; President Bush was being regularly briefed about the terrorist group. Bush administration officials, of course, deny that they didn't take the threat urgently enough, but there is no debating that in their public utterances, private meetings, and actions, the al-Qaeda threat barely registered. The real question then, in the face of all this information about the threat, is why did the most experienced national security team in memory underestimate the problem?

The short answer: They just didn't get it. Key members of the Bush team had cut their teeth during the Cold War. Rice was a Soviet specialist at the National Security Council under President George H.W. Bush. Wolfowitz had worked on the "Team B" efforts at the Pentagon in the 1970s which concluded, wrongly, that the Soviet military threat was much larger than supposed. And Cheney and Defense Secretary Donald Rumsfeld had served as White House chief of staff and secretary of defense respectively during the Ford administration. Their views about the importance of state-based threats remained frozen in a Cold War mind-set. The quip that after the French Revolution the restored Bourbon monarchs came back to power having "learned nothing and forgotten nothing" applied equally well to the Bush national security team, who assumed office as if the 1990s and the gathering threat from al-Qaeda simply hadn't happened.

This was compounded by a self-confidence bordering on arrogance typified by the nickname Bush's foreign policy advisers accorded themselves during the 2000 election campaign. They dubbed themselves "the Vulcans," after the Roman god of fire and metal. Initially this was something of a joke, but as the campaign went on the Bush national security team became known in all seriousness as the Vulcans. The Vulcans, who prided themselves on their hard-nosed appreciation of the harsh realities of the national security realm, would go on to preside over the most devastating national security failure in American history.

To admit that al-Qaeda was the number-one threat to American security would then make it difficult, if not impossible, to argue that missile defense ought to be, as it was for the pre-9/11 Bush administration, a key national security imperative. Antiballistic missile systems, of course, do nothing to stop terrorists. To admit that nonstate terrorists were the primary danger to the nation, it then became impossible to argue, as many in the administration did, that a rogue state, Iraq, was the number-one danger. In a nutshell, bin Laden and al-Qaeda were politically and ideologically inconvenient to square with the Bush worldview.

The inattention of the Bush administration to the al-Qaeda threat had results: Bush stood down the force of submarines and ships stationed in the Arabian Sea that were capable of launching cruise missile strikes into Afghanistan and had been put in place by Clinton. And shortly before 9/11, Attorney General John Ashcroft turned down FBI requests for some four hundred additional counterterrorism personnel. Ashcroft also released a statement about the Justice Department's top ten priorities in May 2001. Terrorism wasn't one of them. Neither Rice nor her deputy Hadley got the squabbling Pentagon and CIA to fly Predator drones equipped with Hellfire missiles over Afghanistan. An unarmed Predator had filmed bin Laden at his farm near Kandahar late in the Clinton administration. The issue between the Agency and the Pentagon was, in part, cost: Predator drones cost $3 million each.

Michael Sheehan, then the Ambassador for Counterterrorism, recalls that Richard Clarke "was pounding on the [CIA and Department of Defense] to more quickly develop—and use—the armed Predator, which was being tested, in Nevada, at the time. And both of them were dragging their feet in terms of money, and they also were uncomfortable with the use of the armed Predator. Can you imagine that now? Back then they were very slow to develop the capability, very slow in testing, they had lawyers wrapping them up in knots, and Clarke was apoplectic over it, because he wanted to introduce this asset into the Afghan theater."

In Nevada in June 2001 the CIA had built a replica of bin Laden's four-room villa at Tarnak Farms where he was living outside of Kandahar. A Predator drone equipped with a missile obliterated the replica house in tests that the Agency conducted with the Air Force. National Security Council official Roger Cressey recalls that even this wasn't enough to get the CIA and Pentagon to move forward with the armed Predator. "I was at the meeting at the Agency afterwards, the data they got they said was inconclusive as to whether or not there was enough lethality in the explosion or the shrapnel to ensure that everybody inside would have been killed. Now, I'm looking at the video, this big fucking explosion packed in there, and I'm like, 'I can't believe anybody would have survived that.' . . . And that played into the Agency's real fear of—There's only one thing worse than not being allowed to do it; it's doing it and fucking it up. And then it becomes exposed, they get the shit kicked out of them on the Hill, and then they get the shit kicked out of them in the international community."

The armed Predator would fly only after 9/11.

The Bush administration's handling of the October 12, 2000, attack on the USS *Cole* in the Yemeni port city of Aden by al-Qaeda suicide bombers, an operation that killed seventeen American sailors and threatened to sink the billion-dollar destroyer, was especially puzzling. Following the *Cole* attack, the Clinton administration, in office for only three more months, sat on its hands. This was despite the fact that according to Ali Soufan, the lead FBI agent on the *Cole* case, within three weeks, "We knew one hundred percent that it was bin Laden." On December 21 the CIA made a presentation to the key national security officials in the Clinton cabinet that there was a "preliminary judgment" that al-Qaeda aided the *Cole* attack. In not responding to the *Cole* bombing in the waning days of his presidency, Clinton may not have wanted to complicate his legacy-building attempt to broker peace between the Israelis and Palestinians with an attack on a Muslim country. And the inaction on the *Cole* may have also reflected simple exhaustion at the end of the second term of the lame-duck Clinton administration.

Bin Laden certainly expected *some* retaliation for the attack on the *Cole*, after having only narrowly escaped the U.S. cruise missile strikes that had rained down on his training camps in eastern Afghanistan in August 1998. On September 27, 2000, two weeks before the *Cole* attack, bin Laden told a group of al-Qaeda members about the "possibility of a missile attack by the infidels" on their training camps. Around the time of the *Cole* bombing, the al-Qaeda leader evacuated everyone from his compound at Kandahar airport and split up from his senior advisers Mohammed Atef and Ayman al-Zawahiri so that all three would not be killed together in the event of a retaliatory American strike. But bin Laden's precautions were unnecessary; the United States never retaliated for the *Cole* attack.

By the time the Bush administration was sworn into office in January 2001, it was obvious that al-Qaeda was responsible for the *Cole* bombing. On February 9, Vice President Cheney was briefed that the attack was the work of bin Laden's men. At the end of March, Clarke's deputy Roger Cressey wrote the deputy national security advisor, Stephen Hadley, an email saying, "We know all we need to about who did the attack to make a policy decision." Cressey recalls that by the spring of 2001 "there was no disagreement about who was culpable. And yet there was no enthusiasm, no interest in doing anything about it, because it didn't happen on their watch."

In June 2001, al-Qaeda released a propaganda videotape strongly implying its responsibility for the *Cole* operation and calling for more anti-American attacks, something that Clarke pointed out to Rice in an email. If the Bush administration needed a casus belli, here it was broadcast around the world. The attack on the *Cole* was an act of war, plain and simple, and it merited an American military response. As we have seen, Michael Sheehan, the ambassador for counterterrorism under Clinton, had told Taliban leaders in early 2000 that they would be held responsible for future attacks against American targets because they were harboring al-Qaeda. Responding to the *Cole* attack by launching cruise missile strikes at key Taliban government buildings and military installations would have been relatively easy to do and might have put some pressure on the Taliban to expel bin Laden. Instead, the Bush administration did nothing.

Stephen Hadley says the lack of response to the *Cole* was largely due to the fact that the Clinton administration's cruise missile strikes against al-Qaeda's Afghan camps in 1998 were "inadequate, ineffective responses" and the Bush team "wanted a much more robust response to al-Qaeda generally, rather than just a response to the *Cole*. And that's what we set about trying to develop, in the first 6–9 months up to 9/11."

Ali Soufan, the FBI agent leading the *Cole* investigation, later interrogated a number of detainees held at Guantánamo, including Salim Hamdan, bin Laden's driver. Soufan says the lack of American response to the *Cole* bombing came up often during his interrogations: "Not only Hamdan—a lot of other people said the same thing: 'You want to know who is responsible for 9/11, you're responsible for 9/11, you didn't retaliate after the *Cole* and it emboldened bin Laden so he felt that we are untouchables.'"

The feckless response to the *Cole* attack was a bipartisan failure, but one that reflects especially poorly on the Bush administration. When members of the 9/11 Commission asked Bush about the lack of response to the *Cole* bombing, he said that he wasn't aware of the Clinton administration's warnings to the Taliban, warnings that his own ambassador to Pakistan, William B. Milam, had renewed in June 2001 when he told his Taliban counterpart that the Afghan government would be held responsible for attacks against American targets by al-Qaeda.

During the summer of 2001, CIA director George Tenet told the 9/11 Commission that the American intelligence "system was blinking red" because of a series of credible intelligence reports about al-Qaeda's plans for attacks on American targets. Below is a representative sampling of the threat reporting that was distributed to Bush officials, which gathered intensity during the spring and reached a crescendo during that summer.

CIA, "Bin Ladin Planning Multiple Operations," April 20
CIA, "Bin Ladin Attacks May Be Imminent," June 23
CIA, "Planning for Bin Ladin Attacks Continues, Despite Delays," July 2
CIA, "Threat of Impending al-Qaeda Attack to Continue Indefinitely," August 3

Warren Bass, a historian in his mid-thirties, was one of the 9/11 Commission staffers who reviewed National Security Council documents going to and from Rice during the commission's investigation. Bass found that Clarke repeatedly warned her and her deputy, Stephen Hadley, of the volume of alarming information about possible al-Qaeda plots during the summer of 2001.

On July 10, Tenet took the unusual step of calling Rice and asking her with some urgency for a meeting that same day to discuss the al-Qaeda threats. Barely fifteen minutes later, Tenet and two of his deputies were in Rice's White House office. One of Tenet's staff members got everyone's attention when he predicted, "There will be a significant terrorist attack in the next weeks or months. . . . Multiple and simultaneous attacks are possible and they will occur with little or no warning." Rice asked her counterterrorism adviser Richard Clarke if he shared this assessment and he gave an exasperated "Yes." Tenet and his staff thought he had finally gotten Rice's attention, but she did nothing following the meeting. This was especially surprising because Rice would later publicly testify before the 9/11 Commission that the Bush administration was at "battle stations" during this period. The historical record does not reflect this.

During August, Bush was at his vacation ranch in Crawford, Texas, clearing brush, doing some competitive bicycling, and attending to some of the business of government. On August 6 he was given an intelligence briefing titled "Bin Ladin Determined to Strike in U.S." The brief had been prepared in part by the veteran CIA analyst "Barbara S.," an Agency official who had tracked al-Qaeda for years. Bush later said the contents of the brief were only "historical" and told him nothing new about the danger from al-Qaeda.

Barbara S., now revealed to be Barbara Sude, says the president did not understand the intention of the briefing, which was to warn of a possible attack in America, not to rehash history: "Was the piece historical? No . . . So did the analysts think that something would happen in the United States? We did assess there was a major attack coming. We couldn't say definitively where. We had threats all year about various locations." Sude says that the CIA briefing was particularly influenced by the fact that just two month earlier, Ahmed Ressam, an Algerian on the fringes of al-Qaeda, had pleaded guilty to charges that he had planned to detonate a bomb at Los Angeles International Airport in the middle of the Christmas season of 1999. According to the briefing, there were seventy ongoing investigations by the FBI into supposed al-Qaeda cells inside the United States during the summer of 2001 and the Bureau had also come across information indicating "preparations for hijackings or other types of attacks." The number of FBI investigations was, in fact, exaggerated, but the briefing to Bush clearly made the point that there were several ongoing inquiries into possible al-Qaeda activities inside the United States.

Following the August 6 briefing, President Bush never publicly discussed the threat posed by al-Qaeda until after 9/11, and chose not to interrupt the longest presidential vacation in more than three decades, only returning to Washington from Texas as planned after Labor Day. The 9/11 Commission also found no evidence that he had any further discussion with his advisers about possible al-Qaeda attacks on the United States until after they had happened.

Despite Rice's testimony before the 9/11 Commission that the Bush administration was at battle stations during the summer of 2001, in a wide-ranging and emblematic interview with Fox News the night of August 6—the same day that President Bush had been briefed that there were dozens of investigations into possible al-Qaeda cells in the United States—Rice chose to discuss the troubled situation in Israel, the administration's missile defense plans, and its relations with Russia. The threat from al-Qaeda, bin Laden, and terrorism went unmentioned.

There is also no evidence that Rice did anything to "pulse" the national security system for additional information about the presence of jihadist militants in the United States. Might that have caused the information about Zacarias Moussaoui, a jihadist militant then in FBI custody in Minnesota who was keen on practicing flying a 747, to have been more widely distributed? Might that have caused the wider dissemination of the names of the al-Qaeda soon-to be-hijackers Nawaf al-Hazmi and Khalid al-Mihdhar, who were known to be in the United States? It is worth contrasting Rice's lackadaisical approach with that of Clinton's national security advisor, Sandy Berger, who held almost daily meetings of the National Security Council from mid-December 1999 as the new millennium approached and similar fears of a terrorist attack gripped the national security establishment.

For Donald Rumsfeld the most pressing threat in the summer of 2001 was not al-Qaeda but the Department of Defense itself, which he felt was blocking his efforts at "transformation" of the military into a lighter, more nimble force. During a speech on September 10, Rumsfeld described the Pentagon bureaucracy as "an adversary that poses a serious threat to the security of the United States." A day later Rumsfeld would be helping the victims of al-Qaeda's attack on the Pentagon.

The fact that al-Qaeda and its allies intended to attack the United States, and indeed had already done so before 9/11, was hardly a secret. The CIA briefing to President Bush headlined "Bin Ladin Determined to Strike in U.S." was simply stating the blindingly obvious. Al-Qaeda's leader had repeatedly said he was going to attack the United States, starting in 1997 in an interview with CNN, and he reiterated this threat over the next two years in interviews with ABC News and *Time*.

Rarely have the enemies of the United States publicly warned so often of their plans. Imagine for a moment that starting in 1937, Japanese government officials had repeatedly told American radio and newspaper correspondents that they were planning to strike the United States. Might not the events of Pearl Harbor have played out rather differently than they did on the morning of December 7, 1941?

The problem, then, was not a lack of information about al-Qaeda's intentions and capabilities, but the Bush administration's inability to comprehend that an attack by al-Qaeda on the United States was a real possibility, much more so than attacks by traditional state antagonists such as China or Iraq. Al-Qaeda's 9/11 assaults seemed especially surprising to senior Bush officials because the world's only superpower was bloodied by an organization, not a state. It should have been less surprising than it was; after all, bin Laden had declared war on the United States years earlier and he had followed through on that promise with the attacks on the two American embassies in Africa and the bombing of the *Cole*.

The 9/11 attacks were not the beginning of al-Qaeda's campaign against the United States. They were its climax.

Chapter 4

Kicking Ass

This crusade, this war on terrorism, is going to take a while. And the American people must be patient.

—President Bush to reporters on September 16, 2001

On the morning of September 11, Bush was visiting a kindergarten class in Sarasota, Florida, when he was informed that a plane had flown into the World Trade Center. A little later Andrew Card, his chief of staff, whispered in the president's right ear: "A second plane hit the second tower. America is under attack." An hour later, Bush, by now flying on Air Force One, spoke with Dick Cheney in the White House, telling the vice president, "We're going to find out who did this and we're going to kick their asses." Exactly whose asses to kick and how would consume much of the rest of Bush's presidency.

At eight-thirty that night Bush addressed tens of millions of Americans from the Oval Office in a speech that laid out a key doctrine of his administration's future foreign policy: "We will make no distinction between the terrorists who committed these acts and those who harbor them." While this was a reasonable rationale for the coming war against the Taliban, it also helped set the stage for the subsequent war with Saddam Hussein's Iraq, which the administration would repeatedly say was allied with al-Qaeda, although the evidence for that assertion was nonexistent.

Over the course of the coming weeks and months the Bush administration would set the course of policies that would have unforeseen consequences for many years into the future: a "light footprint" operation in Afghanistan, which would succeed brilliantly at toppling the Taliban but leave many of the top leaders of al-Qaeda at liberty following the failure to capture or kill them at the battle of Tora Bora in December 2001, and would also fail to secure Afghanistan for the long term. Bush also launched the nation on an ambiguous and open-ended conflict against a tactic, termed the "war on terror," which would warp U.S. foreign policy and distort key American ideals about the rule of law, while his administration's obsession with Iraq would lead the United States into fighting two wars in the Muslim world simultaneously, seeming to confirm one of bin Laden's key claims—that the West, led by America, was at war with Islam.

The idea that Iraq was behind 9/11 gripped senior members of the Bush administration within hours of the attacks. At 2:40 that afternoon Defense Secretary Donald Rumsfeld considered whether "to hit S. H. [Saddam Hussein] same time—not only UBL [bin Laden]," according to contemporaneous notes made by one of his top deputies. Douglas Feith, the number-three official at the Pentagon and a longtime neoconservative advocate of overthrowing the Iraqi dictator, was flying back from Europe the day of the attacks with a group of senior Pentagon officials. On the flight Feith broached the idea of overthrowing Saddam. General John Abizaid, the Arabic-speaking four-star general who two years later would assume responsibility for U.S. military operations in the Middle East, interrupted him, saying, "Not Iraq. There is not a connection with al-Qaeda."

A day later, Bush pulled Richard Clarke aside and asked him to look into the evidence to see if Saddam was involved. Clarke said, "But al-Qaeda did this," to which Bush replied, "I know, I know . . . but see if Saddam was involved." Clarke's deputy Roger Cressey remembers that this exchange with the president "struck us as odd, only because we knew there was no state sponsorship of al-Qaeda to do this type of thing. But it clearly reflected what their frontal lobe issue was. And they viewed Iraq as something that was an existential threat to the United States." In response, Clarke and Cressey's office worked up a memo that was sent to Condoleezza Rice a week after 9/11; titled "Survey of Intelligence Information of Any Iraqi Involvement in the September 11 Attacks," it concluded that there was "no compelling case" that Iraq was involved.

On September 14, Bush for the first time visited "Ground Zero," the smoking pile of what remained of the World Trade Center and the more than 2,700 people who had perished there. Three days earlier, when he had first spoken to the nation shortly after the attacks, Bush had appeared hesitant. On this day he was a man transformed. Standing on top of a wrecked fire truck, Bush grabbed a bullhorn to address the rescue crews working feverishly to find any survivors. When one of the workers said he couldn't hear what the president was saying, Bush made one of the most memorable remarks of his presidency, "I can hear you. The rest of the world hears you. And the people who knocked these buildings down will hear from all of us soon." Bush's robust response to the attacks drove his poll ratings from 55 percent favorable before 9/11 to 90 percent favorable in the days after, the highest ever recorded for a president.

The plan to bring some justice to those who had knocked down the Trade Center buildings was first laid out to Bush by Cofer Black, the head of the CIA's Counterterrorist Center. Black briefed the National Security Council on September 13 in the White House Situation Room, a subterranean, wood-paneled conference room that sits behind a well-insulated door next to the White House Mess. Black had something of a personal interest in al-Qaeda; while he was the CIA station chief in Sudan, during the mid-1990s, the terrorist group had tried to assassinate him. Black handled the episode with admirable sangfroid, deciding to consider the attempt an exercise to see how al-Qaeda was running its operations. Black, given to a certain bombastic brand of deadpan theatrics, assured the president that the CIA-led operation to destroy al-Qaeda and the Taliban would take only a matter of weeks and that they would shortly have "flies walking across their eyeballs."

During this meeting, Secretary of Defense Donald Rumsfeld claimed that Iraq was a threat, supported terrorists, and might give them weapons of mass destruction. Rumsfeld also pointed out that Iraq had far more military targets than the scant and rudimentary infrastructure in Afghanistan and that the United States could inflict on Iraq the kind of damage that would cause other terrorist-supporting regimes to take note. Bush replied that any U.S. military action in Iraq would have to go beyond simply making a statement and would have to bring about regime change. Only two days after 9/11, several of the key arguments for the Iraq War were discussed by Bush and his national security team. The discussions of military action against Iraq were more than merely academic. On September 13, Rumsfeld sent a directive to Third Army headquarters in Atlanta to draw up a plan within three days setting forth what it would take to seize Iraq's southern oilfields.

Early the following morning, in his office at CIA headquarters, a modernist glass and concrete box surrounded by woodlands in suburban Virginia, Cofer Black met with Gary Schroen, a fifty-nine-year-old CIA officer who had recently started the weeks-long process of retiring from the Agency. Schroen's three-decade career had taken him on many assignments around South Asia, including a clandestine trip into Afghanistan in 1996 to meet with Ahmad Shah Massoud to discuss efforts to capture bin Laden. Schroen had a good rapport with Massoud and his key aides and he also spoke Dari, the language of the Tajik ethnic group that dominated the Northern Alliance.

Black got straight to the point: "Gary, I want you to take a small team of CIA officers into Afghanistan. You will link up with the Northern Alliance and convince them to cooperate with the CIA and U.S. military as we go after al-Qaeda." Putting his retirement plans on hold, Schroen accepted the assignment and began packing the various necessities for his mission, which included millions of dollars in cash to sweeten the coming negotiations with the various commanders of the Northern Alliance.

The next day, on Saturday, September 15, Bush again met with his national security team, this time at Camp David, the presidential retreat in the Maryland hills. Seated around the retreat's large conference room table were the president, the vice president, Secretary of State Colin Powell, Donald Rumsfeld and his deputy Paul Wolfowitz, National Security Advisor Condoleezza Rice and her deputy Stephen Hadley, Attorney General John Ashcroft, FBI director Robert Mueller, CIA director George Tenet and his deputy John McLaughlin. Bush, as was his custom, offered a prayer to begin the meeting and then the members of what was now effectively his war cabinet, casually dressed in windbreakers, khakis, and jeans, began to discuss the future outlines of the American response to 9/11.

The mood at the meeting was somber. The president went around the room and asked for everyone's assessment about what had just happened, after which he said, "Let's have lunch, and then everyone take an hour, take a walk or something, get your thoughts together, and then we're going to come back and talk about what we're going to do about this," recalls John McLaughlin.

Bizarrely, the Department of Defense had almost nothing to offer in the way of a plan for attacking the Taliban. General Tommy Franks, the head of

U.S. Central Command (CENTCOM), whose area of operations covered the Middle East, Central Asia, and parts of South Asia, recalled that the Pentagon did not have an "off-the-shelf" plan for attacking the militants in Afghanistan. Douglas Feith, the number-three official in the Pentagon, also remembers that there was no military plan ready for attacking al-Qaeda or overthrowing the Taliban. Deputy National Security Advisor Stephen Hadley says that the plan the military did present at Camp David "was heavily weighted toward an airpower-based approach. And the president said, 'We're not going to do it that way. We need to send a whole new message, that we are serious about this.'"

But the CIA and its cigar-chomping, back-slapping director Tenet did have a plan, because from the time that the Taliban had first seized Kabul five years earlier, the Agency had remained in touch with the Northern Alliance. From February 1999 to March 2001, the CIA had inserted five teams successively into Massoud's Panjshir Valley stronghold to build up relations with the commanders of the Northern Alliance. Those relationships were supplemented by a CIA intelligence collection program inside Afghanistan that included tips and information flowing in from tribal leaders, criminals, low-level members of the Taliban, and al-Qaeda support staff such as drivers and cooks. On 9/11 the Agency had a total of some one hundred sources and subsources inside Afghanistan.

While the plan that Tenet presented to Bush's war cabinet was seemingly a somewhat risky one—inserting Agency officers into Afghanistan with the various warlords of the Northern Alliance armed with suitcases of cash to buy loyalty and fighters—it was the only plan on offer. Once on the ground in Afghanistan, CIA officers would coordinate the insertion of U.S. Special Forces teams who would then guide American bombing strikes on Taliban positions.

Rice remembers that when a map of Afghanistan was rolled out on the conference room table at Camp David, "the color drained from everybody's faces." Surrounding Afghanistan were potentially unstable Pakistan, hostile Iran, and autocratic states like Uzbekistan and Tajikistan. Rice says, "I think everybody thought: Of all the places to have a fight a war, Afghanistan would not be our choice."

At the Camp David meeting, Deputy Secretary of Defense Paul Wolfowitz, long an advocate of overthrowing Saddam Hussein, interjected that he estimated there was a 10 to 50 percent chance that the Iraqi dictator was involved in 9/11. There was no evidence at all for this assertion, but Wolfowitz seemed to have internalized his boss Donald Rumsfeld's well-known dictum that "the absence of evidence is not the evidence of absence." This phrase, which posed as deep thinking about the real world, will no doubt serve as an ironic epitaph for the Bush administration, which again and again after 9/11 took the position that the lack of hard evidence for its assertions in no way undercut their truthfulness.

Wolfowitz, whose bookish manner belied his ultrahawkish views, also made the case for striking Iraq in "this round" of the war on terror. John McLaughlin, the CIA deputy director, who spoke in the measured tones of the college professor he would later become, argued that this was "not the right conclusion to draw at this point. . . . We had been projecting a spectacular attack by al-Qaeda. Here it was. We had the names of some of the people involved that we recognized: They were al-Qaeda." The cabinet then voted to go to war against al-Qaeda and the Taliban in Afghanistan, although Rumsfeld abstained. At the end of the meeting Bush said, "I believe Iraq was involved, but I'm not going to strike them now."

Later that evening, Attorney General Ashcroft, a talented amateur musician, gathered the war cabinet around a piano for a sing-along of "Nobody Knows the Trouble I've Seen" and "America the Beautiful."

On Monday morning, September 17, in the Cabinet Room of the White House, Bush started barking instructions to his assembled national security team. "I want the CIA in there first," the president demanded. Bush also signed a top-secret directive about the war plan for Afghanistan, which also instructed the Pentagon to begin planning for an invasion of Iraq, one of many indicators that the march to war there began immediately after 9/11. That same day Wolfowitz wrote Rumsfeld a memo arguing that the odds were better than one in ten that Saddam was involved in 9/11, citing his praise for the attacks and (long-discredited) theories that Iraq was behind the first World Trade Center attack in 1993. Wolfowitz argued that eliminating Saddam needed to be a top priority. He met little resistance from Rumsfeld, who on September 29 instructed his incoming chairman of the Joint Chiefs, General Richard Myers, to begin preparing military options for Iraq, including plans for an invasion with a much smaller force than the army of five hundred thousand that had taken Kuwait back from Saddam following his 1990 invasion of the country.

Gary Schroen and his team of CIA officers left Washington on September 19 for the long trip to Uzbekistan, Afghanistan's neighbor to the north, where an Agency-owned helicopter was waiting to fly them over the border and insert them into the small patch of northeastern Afghanistan where the Northern Alliance continued to hold out against the Taliban. Before they left they met with Cofer Black at Agency headquarters for their final marching orders. They were unambiguous. Black told them, "I want bin Laden's head shipped back in a box filled with dry ice. I want to be able to show bin Laden's head to the president." This appears to have been the first time in decades that a CIA officer had been directly ordered to kill an enemy of the United States.

The next day President Bush gave the speech that would define his presidency. On September 20, nine days after 9/11, he addressed both houses of Congress and laid out the strategic doctrines of what for the first time he publicly referred to as the "war on terror." The doctrines laid out in the speech would set the course of the foreign policy of the United States for the next decade and would reshape the Middle East in then-unforeseen ways.

Before a packed congressional chamber and watched on TV live by eighty million Americans, Bush explained, "Our war on terror begins with al-Qaeda but it does not end there. It will not end until every terrorist group of global reach has been defeated." This war then would extend not only to the perpetrators of 9/11 but to other groups that might potentially threaten the United States, and the war could theoretically last for decades: "Americans should not expect one battle, but a lengthy campaign."

Then Bush turned to his analysis of why the United States was attacked on 9/11: "Why do they hate us? . . . They hate our freedoms—our freedom of religion, our freedom of speech, our freedom to vote and assemble and disagree with one another." Yet in all the tens of thousands of words that bin Laden had uttered, he was largely silent about American freedoms and values. He just didn't seem to care very much about the beliefs of the "Crusaders." Instead his focus was invariably on American foreign policies in the Middle East. If the first rule of war is "know your enemy," it would have been helpful if Bush had been more knowledgeable about the motives of al-Qaeda leaders, who cared far more about how U.S. foreign policy was conducted in the Middle East than about how Americans conducted themselves in their daily lives.

Bush then asserted that al-Qaeda followed in the footsteps "of the murderous ideologies of the 20th century . . . in the path of fascism, Nazism and totalitarianism." Certainly "bin Ladenism" seemed to share some commonalities with the Nazis and the Soviets: their anti-Semitism; their antiliberalism and general contempt for Enlightenment values; their cultlike embrace of charismatic leaders; their deft exploitation of modern propaganda methods;

and their bogus promises of utopia here on Earth if their programs were implemented. But the threat posed by al-Qaeda was orders of magnitude smaller than that posed by the Nazis, who instigated a global conflict that killed tens of millions and who perpetrated the Holocaust, and if the Cold War had ended with a bang instead of a whimper much of the human race would have vanished. Yet immediately after 9/11, President Bush raised al-Qaeda to the status of the strategic, existential threat that the group craved to be, rather than the serious-enough problem that it in fact presented.

Such a supposedly existential struggle merited that the coming war would have to be fought in black and white: "Either you are with us, or you are with the terrorists," said Bush. An alternative formulation could have been "If you are against the terrorists, then you are with us," and that formulation would have vastly increased the number of potential allies of the United States. Instead, much of the foreign policy of the first Bush term would be conducted in a high-handed and unilateral manner.

What went unsaid in Bush's speech was the idea that the United States, the consumer of a quarter of the world's energy, should launch a Manhattan Project–style energy policy to make Americans less dependent on the Middle Eastern countries that had helped to incubate al-Qaeda. This was a squandered opportunity, since at no other point in history would the American public have been more receptive to such a call. Bush would style himself as a "wartime president," but by way of sacrifice he stopped playing golf, cut taxes for the wealthiest Americans, and did not institute a draft. At the height of the Battle of Britain in 1940, Churchill could say with some truth, "Never in the field of human conflict was so much owed by so many to so few." After 9/11, never was so little asked from so many.

On 9/11 there was little question that al-Qaeda was at war with the United States; the critical question in the months that followed was, What kind of war was the United States going to fight against it? The dean of military strategists, Carl von Clausewitz, explained the importance of this decision making in his 1832 treatise *On War:* "The first, the supreme, the most far-reaching act of judgment that the statesman and commander have to make is to establish . . . the kind of war on which they are embarking; neither mistaking it for, nor trying to turn it into something that is alien to its nature."

Clausewitz's excellent advice about the absolute necessity of properly defining the war upon which one is about to embark was ignored by Bush administration officials, who instead declared an open-ended and ambiguous "war on terror." Sometimes known as the Global War on Terror, or by the clunky acronym "GWOT," it became the lens through which the Bush administration judged almost all of its foreign policy decisions. The GWOT framework propelled the Bush administration into its disastrous entanglement in Iraq, which had nothing to do with 9/11 but was launched under the rubric of the "war on terror" and the erroneous claims that Saddam Hussein had weapons of mass destruction that he might give to terrorists, including al-Qaeda, to whom he was supposedly allied, and that he therefore threatened American interests. None of this, of course, was true.

On September 14, 2001, Congress passed an "Authorization for Use of Military Force" against "those nations, organizations or persons [the president] determines planned, authorized, committed or aided the terrorist attacks." The coming American war against the Taliban was backed by the world; two days earlier the UN Security Council had passed an unusually forceful and unambiguous resolution "to combat by all means . . . terrorist acts." On the same day NATO invoked Article 5 for the first time in its history, which meant that the nineteen member states of the alliance considered the 9/11 attacks as an attack against all of them, to be responded to with force. (Interestingly, major Muslim clerics did not declare that the subsequent American war in Afghanistan necessitated a "defensive jihad," as had happened after the Soviets invaded the country in 1979.)

Bin Laden disastrously misjudged the possible American responses to the 9/11 attacks, which he believed would take one of two forms: an eventual retreat from the Middle East along the lines of the U.S. pullout from Somalia in 1993, or another ineffectual round of cruise missile attacks similar to those that followed al-Qaeda's bombings of the two American embassies in Africa in 1998. Of course, neither of these two scenarios happened. The U.S. campaign against the Taliban was conducted with massive American airpower, tens of thousands of Northern Alliance forces, allied with some three hundred U.S. Special Forces soldiers working with 110 CIA officers.

The first Americans into Afghanistan, Gary Schroen's seven-man CIA team, code-named JAWBREAKER, touched down on the afternoon of September 26. Two weeks later, on October 7, the American bombing campaign against the Taliban began. As it did, bin Laden made a surprise appearance in a videotape shown around the world. It was the first time he had been seen publicly since the 9/11 attacks. In an uncharacteristically brief statement, the al-Qaeda leader, dressed in a camouflage jacket with a submachine gun propped at his side, said that the attacks were revenge for the long-standing Western humiliation of the Muslim world, consistently his most important theme.

Nine days after bin Laden's videotaped appearance, the first U.S. Special Forces team arrived near the northern Afghan city of Mazar-e-Sharif and linked up with one of the leaders of the Northern Alliance, the Uzbek general Abdul Rashid Dostum. After spending their first night in a cattle stable, the Special Forces group teamed up with Dostum's heavily bearded, RPG-wielding Uzbek horsemen. Within twenty-four hours of their arrival the Americans started calling in airstrikes on the Taliban front lines, using their laser designators. Those strikes were so precise that Northern Alliance commanders came to believe that the U.S. forces possessed some kind of "death ray." The Americans did not disabuse them of this notion; once the Taliban got wind of the U.S. death ray, units would often surrender.

But the American press was already growing restive about the seeming lack of progress against the Taliban. On October 31, R.W. "Johnny" Apple wrote an indicative front-page story in the *New York Times* headlined "A Military Quagmire Remembered: Afghanistan as Vietnam." The fall of Kabul was less than two weeks away.

The CIA's top official on the ground in Afghanistan was Gary Berntsen. If some men can be described as laid-back, Berntsen is laid-forward, a bear-sized, gung-ho CIA officer with a pronounced Long Island accent who speaks Dari, one of the local Afghan languages. In early November Berntsen was liasing with the leaders of the Northern Alliance and helping to call in the airstrikes on the Taliban front lines on the Shomali Plains, north of Kabul. He remembers that at first the Taliban morale was very high: "They'd beaten the Soviets and figured they were going to beat us."

Berntsen recalls that there were several thousand Taliban soldiers on the front lines near Kabul who were being joined by many more Pakistani recruits. "The roads from Pakistan into Afghanistan were clogged with people all trying to get *in*." Berntsen's boss at the CIA, Hank Crumpton, said, "We're gonna let 'em all in so we kill 'em on the front lines. The more the merrier." AC-130 gunships and B-52 bombers made short work of the Taliban foot soldiers on the Kabul front lines.

In the weeks after the 9/11 attacks, bin Laden avoided all but his closest supporters. Only a handful of people outside al-Qaeda or the Taliban are known to have spent any time with him. A couple of weeks after the first American bombing raids had begun, the al-Qaeda leader met with Taysir Allouni of Al Jazeera, who interviewed the Saudi exile at length on October 21. During that interview bin Laden appeared relaxed and poised, explicitly linking himself to the 9/11 attacks for the first time publicly. The Al Jazeera correspondent asked him, "America claims that it has proof that you are behind what happened in New York and Washington. What's your answer?" Bin Laden came close to admitting his role, answering: "If inciting people to do that is terrorism, and if killing those who are killing our sons is terrorism, then let history be our judge that we are terrorists." At one point bin Laden made the interesting observation, "We practice the good terrorism."

Allouni followed up with the most important question that can be posed to al-Qaeda's leader: "How about the killing of innocent civilians?" Bin Laden replied, "The men that God helped [on September 11] did not intend to kill babies; they intended to destroy the strongest military power in the world, to attack the Pentagon," adding that "the [World Trade Center] Towers are an economic power and not a children's school."

Dr. Amer Aziz, a prominent Pakistani surgeon and Taliban sympathizer who had treated bin Laden two years earlier for a back injury, also met with him a few weeks after 9/11. Aziz was summoned to Kabul in the first week of November 2001 to treat Mohammed Atef, the military commander of al-Qaeda. While examining Atef, Aziz again encountered bin Laden. This meeting was significant because there had been widespread reports that the al-Qaeda leader suffered from potentially deadly kidney disease. Aziz said those reports were false: "When I saw him last he was in excellent health. He was walking. He was healthy. I didn't see any evidence of kidney disease. I didn't see any evidence of dialysis." (Similarly, Ahmed Zaidan of Al Jazeera television, who had interviewed bin Laden for two or three hours eight months before 9/11, says, "I didn't see anything abnormal." That was also the take of Bakr Atyani of the Middle East Broadcasting Corporation, who met him five months later. Atyani thought that bin Laden had put on weight and was in "good health.")

On November 9, Mazar-e-Sharif, the largely Uzbek city in the north of Afghanistan that had been the scene of some of the Taliban's nastiest massacres, fell to the Northern Alliance and the small team of U.S. Special Forces supporting the local warlord General Dostum. One of the American soldiers remembered the roads "were just lined with people cheering and clapping their hands and just celebrations everywhere. It was just unlike anything we'd ever seen, other than maybe on a movie screen." Three days later, Kabul also fell to the Northern Alliance. Peter Jouvenal, a British cameraman who had covered Afghanistan extensively since 1980, was the first Westerner to set foot in Kabul as it fell. He recalled, "The people were overjoyed to be relieved of such a suppressive regime."

The Taliban and members of al-Qaeda made a hasty retreat from Kabul following its liberation by the Northern Alliance. A few days later, Atef was killed in a U.S. Predator drone airstrike. Atef, a former Egyptian policeman, was one of the most hard-line members of al-Qaeda. To cement their relationship in January 2001, bin Laden had married his son Muhammad to Atef's daughter. The loss of al-Qaeda's military commander was a blow to the organization, since it was Atef who had performed as bin Laden's chief executive officer, and had worked around the clock to manage al-Qaeda's personnel, operations, and cash flow.

Hundreds of miles to the south of Kabul, the CIA was working to try to open up a rift between the Taliban and al-Qaeda. In late September, Robert Grenier, the dapper, smooth-talking CIA station chief in Islamabad, traveled to Baluchistan, a Pakistani province of vast, broiling deserts less than a hundred miles from the Taliban headquarters of Kandahar, for a clandestine meeting with Mullah Akhtar Mohammad Osmani, the number-two official in the Taliban. Meeting in the five-star Serena hotel in the Baluch capital of Quetta, Grenier offered Mullah Osmani a deal whereby the Taliban would let American forces covertly snatch bin Laden while they could plausibly maintain that they had no idea of the plan. Mullah Osmani took careful notes and said he would discuss the idea with the Taliban leader Mullah Omar. Grenier figured that even if Mullah Omar rejected this plan other Taliban leaders might embrace it, and so "we could at least sow some dissension within the ranks."

The proposal to snatch bin Laden came to nothing, but in their next meeting, on October 2, Grenier offered Mullah Osmani another deal: overthrow Mullah Omar, seize power, and then turn over al-Qaeda's leader. Grenier recalls telling Osmani, "You need to save your movement. So he said, 'How do I do that?' So I gave him a sort of textbook plan as to how you launch a coup d'état: Put Mullah Omar under house arrest. Don't let him communicate with anybody." Nothing came of this plan either.

More successful was the CIA effort to support the rise of an obscure Afghan dissident by the name of Hamid Karzai. Karzai, a Pashtun in his early forties then living in Pakistan, was from a distinguished tribe that had supplied a number of Afghanistan's monarchs. He had become a bitter enemy of the Taliban following his father's assassination in Quetta in 1999, a hit almost certainly ordered by Taliban leaders, who eliminated Pashtuns who threatened their monopoly on power.

Grenier explained the American thinking behind backing Karzai: "Those people who we encouraged to go inside Afghanistan essentially were going to be going on their own. They would need to demonstrate that they in fact had tribal support, and then we would attempt to reinforce them. That was the strategy."

On October 8, a day after the first American bombing raids in Afghanistan, Karzai and three comrades, wrapped under heavy turbans to disguise themselves, rode on motorbikes over the border into Kandahar province in southern Afghanistan, a sparsely populated region of deserts punctuated by rocky hills. Karzai had been plotting against the Taliban for years, and although he knew that riding into their home turf was quite risky, he was also confident he could recruit to his cause Pashtuns who were fed up with the incompetence and strictures of the religious warriors.

Once inside southern Afghanistan, Karzai led some fifty supporters on foot to an area where they could link up with an airdrop of American supplies, which he had requested in an earlier satellite phone call to the U.S. embassy in Islamabad. A CIA officer there told Karzai, "Tell your people to light fires; that's the only way we can find [you] out in the mountains." The supplies dropped into the mountains on October 30 included food and weapons, which Karzai used to sustain his growing band—now 150 men—who were already fighting off Taliban attacks. Under increasing pressure from the Taliban, Karzai urgently requested the Agency that he be airlifted to Pakistan. A CIA officer named "Greg" arranged for a helicopter to extract Karzai out of Afghanistan on November 5.

Eleven days later Karzai returned to Afghanistan, to Uruzgan province some eighty miles to the north of Kandahar. This time Karzai was also accompanied by a twelve-man Special Forces team and half a dozen CIA officers.

Tarin Kowt, the provincial capital of Uruzgan, is a dusty one-horse town around which would swirl one of the most crucial battles of the war against the Taliban. Captain Jason Amerine, the leader of the U.S. Special Forces team embedded with Karzai, explains the American mission in Tarin Kowt: "We were going to build a Pashtun guerrilla army effectively from scratch under Karzai's command, seize the town of Tarin Kowt in order to gain control of Uruzgan, and then we would build a larger Pashtun army and seize Kandahar as a final coup-de-grace against the Taliban. It all really hinged on Karzai's belief that the Pashtun were ready to rise up against the Taliban leadership."

On November 16, the people of Tarin Kowt did rise up against the Taliban and chased them out. A day later Karzai headed into the town in a twenty-vehicle convoy and set up shop in the governor's mansion, a modest two-story building surrounded by well-irrigated fields. Arriving around midnight, he met with local Pashtun tribal leaders, who welcomed him and told him with some trepidation that there was a column of some one hundred vehicles approaching from Kandahar containing up to five hundred Taliban, who would reach the town by the next day intent on taking it back.

Hearing this news, Captain Amerine excused himself from Karzai and his group of supporters, who were breaking their fast as Ramadan had just begun. Amerine started to plan how to repel the much larger Taliban force, while his combat controller sent out an urgent warning to Navy and Air Force aircraft in the area that they would be needed shortly. Amerine gathered as many of Karzai's guerrillas as he could. His plan was to stake out some higher ground with those guerrillas outside of Tarin Kowt and call in airstrikes from there onto the fast-approaching Taliban convoy.

The hundred-vehicle convoy sent to retake Tarin Kowt for the Taliban was Mullah Omar's last real shot at hanging on to power. Vahid Mojdeh, a Taliban foreign ministry official, recalled that Mullah Omar was now constantly on the move around Kandahar because of the American bombing campaign. "The intense bombardment made the situation very difficult for Mullah Omar. He was forced to spend his nights in open spaces or places where he had not been seen before."

Around two hours after Amerine was first alerted to the approaching Taliban column, Navy F-18 fighters spotted a group of around ten four-wheel drives and started bombing them. Three hours later, at 5 A.M., the larger convoy of dozens of Taliban vehicles came into view. Heavily outnumbered, Karzai's group of Afghan guerrillas took flight and sped back to Tarin Kowt, followed by Captain Amerine and his Special Forces team. Back in Tarin Kowt, Amerine told Karzai, "The Taliban are coming, there are a lot of them. These [Afghan] fighters we are with don't understand our capabilities; they kind of ran. I need to take these vehicles and get out there and keep doing what I'm doing." Amerine drove back outside the town at around 7 A.M. to direct deadly accurate bombing runs on the approaching Taliban convoy. Three hours later the battle was over and what remained of the convoy was in full retreat.

Hank Crumpton, who was running the CIA's operation in Afghanistan, recalls that this was a decisive battle because Karzai was the only man who could unify the country's fractious ethnic factions: "Karzai was the linchpin between north and south. The Uzbeks, the Tajiks, the Hazara, they all respected Karzai. They knew that he understood the concept of a nation-state." But the importance of the Tarin Kowt battle was not well understood at the time because the vast majority of the international media covering the war were concentrated in the north of the country and focusing on the fall of Kabul five days earlier.

Following the news of the debacle at Tarin Kowt, Mullah Omar finally abandoned Kandahar, the city he had controlled absolutely for the past seven years. Overtures to Karzai about surrendering started coming in from Taliban commanders. But taking no chances over the next two weeks, Karzai started gathering the large force necessary for what seemed likely to be a major battle for Kandahar.

Half a world away, in Washington, D.C., Ambassador James Dobbins, a veteran diplomat on the verge of retirement whose Waspy manner belied that he had successfully taken on some of America's most difficult peacekeeping missions in Bosnia, Haiti, and Kosovo, had recently been tapped by the Bush administration to be its new envoy to Afghanistan. Less than a week after Kabul fell, Dobbins flew into Afghanistan with Dr. Abdullah, a leader of the Northern Alliance, on a white cargo plane with no markings, chartered by the CIA.

As they were flying to Kabul, Dr. Abdullah told Dobbins that Karzai would be an acceptable choice to lead Afghanistan for the largely Tajik and Uzbek ethnic groups that made up the Northern Alliance. A few days earlier, Ehsan ul-Haq, the new head of Pakistan's intelligence service, which had played a critical role in the rise of the largely Pashtun Taliban, had also told Dobbins that Karzai would be acceptable to his government. If Pakistan and the Northern Alliance, long bitter enemies, could agree on Karzai as the next leader of Afghanistan, Dobbins knew that brokering a deal for him to run the new Afghan government would have a good chance of succeeding.

On November 27, in the former West German capital of Bonn, the various Afghan factions gathered for the opening of a United Nations conference to choose an interim government and its new leader. Dobbins headed the American delegation, which met frequently with Iranian officials, who were the first to push for democratic elections in Afghanistan. One day a senior Iranian diplomat was chatting with Dobbins over a breakfast of coffee and croissants and mentioned to him that there was a serious gap in the draft of the document that would later become the Bonn declaration: "It really doesn't make any mention of elections or democracy. Don't you think the Afghans should be pledging themselves to hold elections and build a democracy?" Dobbins recalls that "this was before the Bush administration had discovered democratization as its panacea for the region, so I didn't have any instructions on this subject, but it seemed a harmless suggestion, so I said, 'Yeah, that seems like a good idea.'"

Fasting for Ramadan and freezing in the bitter Afghan winter, Karzai addressed the delegates in Bonn by satellite phone from Tarin Kowt. Karzai remembers: "I was sitting with some of the poorest members of the Afghan community at that time when I was making the speech. I wasn't aware of the significance of it, nor were the people sitting around me." Karzai's dramatic call from the battlefields of southern Afghanistan to the delegates at the Bonn conference helped to seal his nomination to be the leader of the interim administration, which would run the country until nationwide elections could be held.

Early in the morning of November 28, Lieutenant Colonel David Fox, the highest-ranking American officer on the ground in southern Afghanistan, arrived in Tarin Kowt and met with Karzai to urge him to start moving on Kandahar to increase the pressure on the Taliban leadership to surrender. Two days later Karzai assembled a large convoy of vehicles and headed south toward Kandahar.

Karzai arrived just outside Kandahar on December 5 to begin the discussions of the terms of the Taliban surrender agreement. The following day, around 9 A.M., Karzai was talking with a local tribal chief when suddenly there was an enormous bang and the doors and windows of the building he was in blew out. "Greg," the CIA officer who had earlier arranged for Karzai to be pulled out to Pakistan, threw himself over the Afghan leader. It seemed likely the attack had been launched by the Taliban or al-Qaeda. A U.S. investigation later determined that the cause of the explosion was a two-thousand-pound American bomb that had fallen two kilometers short of its intended target, instead landing on Karzai and his security detail. Captain Amerine, who had grown close to Karzai in the weeks that he had protected him, was wounded in the leg and evacuated. Three other American Special Forces soldiers were killed.

Karzai was rushed away from the scene of the bombing and a nurse attended to minor wounds on his face. After having his wounds dressed, Karzai received an excited call from Lyse Doucet, a BBC correspondent and old friend, who told him that the delegates at the Bonn conference had chosen him to become the new leader of Afghanistan. Doucet told Karzai, "Hamid, we just got the news that you are being chosen as the chairman of the interim administration." Karzai recalls saying, "OK," but not being able to concentrate on much besides the evacuation of the dead and wounded lying around the site of the bomb's impact. A few minutes later he received another call, informing him that the Taliban ministers of defense and interior were on their way to see him to deliver their surrender.

In the space of three hours Karzai had survived a massive American bomb, had taken the surrender of the Taliban over the phone, and had received the news that he was the new leader of his country. It was a portent of the survivor skills that would serve him well over the next decade.

On December 7, after accepting the formal surrender of the Taliban, Karzai rolled into Kandahar at the head of a convoy of more than two hundred vehicles. Many of them sported the new black, red, and green flag of Afghanistan.

Chapter 5

The Great Escape

So let me be a martyr.
Dwelling in a high mountain pass
Among a band of knights who,
United in devotion to God,
Descend to face armies.

—poem by Osama bin Laden

As Kabul fell to the Northern Alliance, bin Laden and other al-Qaeda leaders quickly decamped to Jalalabad, in eastern Afghanistan. Fifty miles from the border with Pakistan, it is a compact city surrounded by lush fruit groves and gardens fragrant with jasmine and roses. Al-Qaeda's leader knew the city well, having first settled there in May 1996, after his expulsion from his previous base, in Sudan. During the late 1990s, bin Laden maintained a compound in a suburb of Jalalabad, which consisted of dozens of rooms spread out over more than an acre, a place that could house hundreds of people. Across the road was another large al-Qaeda compound. Neighbors knew to keep away and not ask too many questions.

It was quite predictable that bin Laden would eventually retreat to Jalalabad and from there to the neighboring mountainous redoubt of Tora Bora. In 1987 he had built a road to allow the movement of his Arab fighters from the

Pakistani border through the Tora Bora mountains down to Jalalabad, which was then occupied by the Soviets. It took the Saudi militant more than six months to build the road, which only four-wheel-drive vehicles could navigate. But the half year that bin Laden spent pushing the road through the Tora Bora passes would provide knowledge that he would put to good use almost a decade and a half later when he fled there, since he knew every ridge and track intimately.

Aside from its obvious advantage as a place from which to disappear, Tora Bora was a place that bin Laden loved. In the Tora Bora settlement of Milewa, a three-hour drive up a narrow mud-and-stone road from Jalalabad, the al-Qaeda leader maintained his own mini-jihadist kingdom for several years before 9/11. The buildings that made up the settlement were strung across a series of ridges that in winter lay far above the snow line, commanding lovely views of the verdant valleys below. They comprised a series of scattered lookout posts, a bakery, and bin Laden's two-bedroom house, all constructed of the baked mud and stone typical of Afghan villages. Next to bin Laden's house was a crude swimming pool and a broad field where al-Qaeda members cultivated their crops. From bin Laden's house all he could see was his own little feudal fiefdom; the nearest village was out of sight, thousands of feet below down a scree-covered slope.

In the winter of 1996 bin Laden took Abdel Bari Atwan, a Palestinian journalist based in London, on a walking tour of frigid Tora Bora. The al-Qaeda leader told Atwan, "I really feel secure in the mountains. I really enjoy my life when I'm here. I feel secure in this place." Bin Laden also well understood how the Tora Bora caves where he sat down with Atwan for an interview and a photographic session would have a certain resonance in the Muslim world, as it was in a cave in the mountains that the Prophet Mohammed had first received the revelations of the Koran.

Bin Laden would also routinely hike from Tora Bora into neighboring Pakistan, according to his son Omar. The treks could take anywhere between seven and fourteen hours. The Saudi exile instructed his sons on these walks, "We never know when war will strike. We must know our way out of the mountains." Bin Laden told his sons they had to memorize every rock on the escape routes to Pakistan. Omar bin Laden later recalled, "My brothers and I all loathed these grueling treks that seemed the most pleasant of outings to our father."

During the fall of 2001, Tora Bora was not yet a familiar name to many

Americans—but it would be soon enough. What unfolded there remains, many years later, the most consequential single battle of the war on terrorism. Presented with an opportunity to kill or capture al-Qaeda's top leadership just three months after September 11, the United States was instead outmaneuvered by bin Laden, who slipped into Pakistan, largely disappeared from American radar, and slowly began rebuilding his organization.

Abdallah Tabarak, bin Laden's chief bodyguard, says that during the month of Ramadan, which began on November 17, 2001, bin Laden and his top deputy, Ayman al-Zawahiri, made their way from Jalalabad thirty miles south to the mountains of Tora Bora, hard up on the border with Pakistan. Around the same time, Hazarat Ali, a local Afghan commander, told a *New York Times* reporter that the al-Qaeda leader had been recently spotted in Tora Bora.

Bin Laden's retreat from Kabul to Jalalabad and then on to the easily defended craggy ridges and cave complexes of Tora Bora was being closely monitored by the CIA. The Agency's top official on the ground was Gary Berntsen. Berntsen had arrived in Kabul on November 12, the same day that the Taliban had fled the capital, and within two days was receiving a stream of intelligence reports from the Northern Alliance that the al-Qaeda leader was in Jalalabad, giving pep talks to an ever-growing caravan of fighters.

Berntsen decided to push a four-man CIA team into Jalalabad. To provide them with local guides he made contact with the Afghan commander Hazarat Ali, a longtime opponent of the Taliban, who sent three teenage fighters to escort the American team into Jalalabad, an area that was now crawling with fleeing Taliban and al-Qaeda fighters. Berntsen's team arrived uneventfully in Jalalabad on November 21 and several days later they moved into a schoolhouse in the foothills of Tora Bora, which they used as a base. Berntsen says he was now receiving "multiple hits" from his sources on the ground that bin Laden was in Tora Bora.

Khalid al-Hubayshi, a Saudi bomb-making expert, was in the Tora Bora trenches as the al-Qaeda leader prepared for his showdown with the United States. Bin Laden, Hubayshi says, "was convinced" that U.S. soldiers would land in the mountains by helicopter. "We spent five weeks manning our positions in case the Americans landed," he recalls.

As bin Laden set about preparing for an American landing that never came, Gary Berntsen's team remained just one step behind him. At the end of November, the team, which had by now grown to eight, decided to split into two groups of four, one of which would head farther into the mountains with ten Afghan fighters as guides. The team's members included an air force combat controller who specialized in calling in airstrikes, and they took with them a laser capable of "painting" targets with a signal that American bombers could then lock on to. The expedition was delayed when a poorly packed set of grenades carried on a mule blew up, killing two of the Afghan guides. But as dusk was falling the group reached a mountaintop from which it could see several hundred of bin Laden's men arrayed below. For the following fifty-six hours straight, the team called in airstrikes from all the bombers available in theater.

Berntsen had not asked anyone for permission to begin the battle of Tora Bora. About twenty-four hours after the airstrikes had begun, Berntsen's boss, Hank Crumpton, the head of Afghan operations at the CIA, called him and asked, "Are you conducting a battle in Tora Bora?" Not quite knowing what his boss's reaction might be, Berntsen simply said, "Yes." Crumpton replied, "Congratulations! Good job!"

As the battle began to gear up, the *Times* of London ran an elaborate graphic purporting to show what bin Laden's hideaway in Tora Bora looked like, a report that was then picked up by media outlets around the world. The graphic showed a multifloored lair suitable for a James Bond villain, protected by iron doors, powered by hydroelectricity, built more than a thousand feet deep into the mountain, and replete with bedrooms and offices capable of sheltering up to a thousand al-Qaeda foot soldiers. The reality was more prosaic. The caves that dot the hills of Tora Bora are certainly well insulated from bombing raids, but even the larger ones are suitable only for holding several men standing up.

Shortly after 9/11, Adam Khan, an Afghan-American who had served in the Marines and who spoke Pashtu and Dari, the two main Afghan languages, received a call about deploying to Afghanistan. An American official asked him, "Do you want to read the news or do you want to make the news?" Khan (a pseudonym) arrived at Bagram Air Base north of Kabul at the end of November. There he was introduced to a team of half a dozen Delta Force operators and signals intelligence "collectors" led by Dalton Fury (also a pseudonym). Khan would be their eyes and ears on the ground in Jalalabad.

Fury, a thirty-seven-year-old major in the elite Delta Force commandos, would lead the small American and allied force at Tora Bora: forty Delta operators from "black" Special Forces, fourteen Green Berets from the less secretive "white" Special Forces, six CIA operatives, a few Air Force signals operators, and a dozen British commandos from the Special Boat Service. Their mission was to link up with the three Afghan warlords in the Tora Bora area, in particular Hazarat Ali, and provide them tactical advice and intelligence and above all accurately map out the al-Qaeda hideouts in the mountains and then call in American airstrikes. In the end, 1,110 precision-guided smart bombs were dropped on Tora Bora, many of them guided in by Fury's team.

Muhammad Musa, a laconic, massively built commander who led six hundred Afghan soldiers on the Tora Bora front lines, recalled the fanatical bravery with which some of al-Qaeda's fighters resisted to the end. "They fought very hard with us. When we captured them, they committed suicide with grenades. I saw three of them do that myself." But Musa said he was not impressed by the American forces on the ground. "They were not involved in the fighting," he said. "There were six American soldiers with us, U.S. Special Forces. They coordinated the airstrikes. My personal view is if they had blocked the way out to Pakistan, al-Qaeda would not have had a way to escape. The Americans were my guests here, but they didn't know about fighting."

In fact, the five dozen or so Americans on the ground at Tora Bora fought well; there were just far too few of them to cordon off a mountainous area of scores of square miles—something that their more numerous Afghan allies failed to do, as did the Pakistani military on the other side of the border.

At the end of November, Hank Crumpton, the veteran CIA officer who was overseeing the Agency's Afghan operation, briefed Bush and Cheney in the White House that bin Laden would likely flee Tora Bora since there were so many potential avenues of escape. Crumpton, a soft-spoken Georgian, recalled from his posting in Australia shortly after 9/11 to run the CIA's special operations, says, "I briefed the White House and said, 'You cannot expect the Pakistanis to seal that border.' That is impossible. You can't even expect the U.S. to be able to seal a border with Mexico. Borders just don't function that way. Moreover, we understood the limitations of the Pakistani military, both in terms of their resources and also in terms of their will." CIA director George Tenet remembers President Bush asking Crumpton directly if the Pakistanis would seal the border, to which the CIA veteran replied, "No, sir."

Meanwhile, the CIA commander on the ground, Gary Berntsen, realized that the Afghan militias the United States was relying on at Tora Bora were simply not up to the task of taking on al-Qaeda's hard core there. By the evening of December 3, one of his team, a former Delta Force operator who had gone deep into Tora Bora, was back in Kabul to brief Berntsen about the lay of the land there and what would be needed to deliver a knockout blow to bin Laden and his men. The task could be accomplished, he told Berntsen, but it would require hundreds of Rangers, elite soldiers who have gone through the Army's most rigorous physical training. That same night Bentsen sent out a lengthy message to CIA headquarters asking for a battalion of Rangers—up to eight hundred soldiers—to assault the complex of caves where bin Laden and his lieutenants were believed to be hiding and to block their escape routes. Berntsen's boss back at CIA headquarters, Crumpton, recalls, "I remember the message, I remember talking not only to Gary, every day, but to some of his men who were *at* Tora Bora. Directly. And their request could not have been more direct, more clear, more certain: that we needed U.S. troops there. More men on the ground."

By early December Crumpton was "one hundred percent" certain that bin Laden was bottled up in the Tora Bora mountains, so he called General Tommy Franks, who had overall control of the Tora Bora operation, to request additional soldiers. Crumpton recalls that Franks pushed back because of two issues: the small American "footprint" approach had already worked so well at overthrowing the Taliban, and the time it would take to get more U.S. soldiers on the ground into Tora Bora. Crumpton countered that taking on the al-Qaeda hard core hiding out in Tora Bora was not the same as defeating the Taliban: "This was different, this was a high mountain stronghold heavily defended. . . . And I maintained that we could not wait for weeks, even many days, because of my concern that al-Qaeda, bin Laden in particular, would escape to Pakistan."

General Franks explained by email his reasoning about why he did not send more U.S. soldiers to take on al-Qaeda's hard core: "My decision not to add American troops to the Tora Bora region was influenced, as Hank [Crumpton] reports, by several factors: The comparative light footprint of coalition troops in theater, and the fact that these troops were committed to operations ongoing across Afghanistan; the amount of time it would take to deploy additional troops would likely create a 'tactical pause' which would run the risk of losing the momentum our forces were enjoying across Afghanistan [and] uncertainty as to whether bin Laden was in fact in Tora Bora. Intelligence suggested that he was, but conflicting intelligence also reported that he was in Kashmir; at a recreational lake NW of Kandahar [and] at a stronghold on the Iranian border."

Franks also said that part of his calculation about not sending more American soldiers was his belief that the United States could rely on the Pakistanis to cut off fleeing members of al-Qaeda. This was wishful thinking. Like Crumpton, the Special Forces ground commander Dalton Fury had identified the central weakness in the plan at Tora Bora: there was no one to guard the back door into Pakistan. Fury recommended that his own team be dropped in from the mountainous Pakistani side of Tora Bora, an area where al-Qaeda would not expect an attack. For reasons that have never been satisfactorily clarified, that request was turned down somewhere in the Pentagon chain of command. Instead, as Fury later wrote, "For this most important mission to date in the global war on terror our nation was relying on a fractious bunch of AK-47-toting lawless bandits and tribal thugs, not bound by any recognized rules of warfare."

The ground forces at Tora Bora were overwhelmingly provided by a motley crew of Afghan commanders: Haji Zaman Gamsharik, an Afghan who had been living in exile in the comfortable environs of Dijon, France, before he returned to Afghanistan as the Taliban fell; Hazarat Ali, a nose-picking, semi-literate from a local tribe who spoke the obscure Pashai language; and Hajji Zahir, the twenty-seven-year-old son of a Jalalabad warlord. This team of rivals assembled some two thousand Afghans, who launched attacks on December 3 into Tora Bora. The Afghan commanders certainly disliked each other more than they did al-Qaeda, and their subcommanders were more than happy to take bribes from Arabs trying to break out of Tora Bora.

On December 7, the Delta team set up camp in the schoolhouse near Tora Bora from which they tried to press farther toward the al-Qaeda front lines and get "eyes on target." Then they would direct laser beams on the targets so that accurate airstrikes could be called in on them. According to the official U.S. Special Forces history of the battle, by now "the latest intelligence placed senior AQ [al-Qaeda] leaders and UBL [Usama bin Laden] squarely in Tora Bora."

But locals were reluctant to give the Delta team much in the way of useful information about al-Qaeda because civilians in the area had been killed in American bombing raids and bin Laden had been a generous guest over the several years that he had been their on-and-off neighbor. Many of the villagers also believed that the al-Qaeda men truly were holy warriors fighting infidels. Years after the battle, on one of Tora Bora's many rocky outcrops, several al-Qaeda graves became a well-maintained shrine marked by flying pennants of pink, green, blue, and orange.

As the fighting got under way, bin Laden sought to project an easy confidence to his men. Abu Bakr, a Kuwaiti who was at Tora Bora, said that early in the battle he saw bin Laden at the checkpoint he was manning. The al-Qaeda leader sat with some of his foot soldiers for half an hour, drinking a cup of tea and telling them, "Don't lose your morale. Don't worry. I'm here always asking about you guys." To the ultrafundamentalists of al-Qaeda, the fact that they were fighting the Americans during the holy month of Ramadan would have had additional resonance, since it was at the battle of Badr during Ramadan that the Prophet Mohammed had led a small group of Muslims to victory fourteen centuries earlier against a much larger army of infidels.

But by the first week of December, things were growing desperate. Rising up to fourteen thousand feet, Tora Bora's mountains are a tough environment at any time of year—and, in the middle of December, temperatures drop to well below zero at night. As the battle raged in the mountains, snow was falling steadily. Meanwhile, American bombs rained down on the snow-covered peaks ceaselessly, preventing sleep. In one four-day period alone, between December 4 and 7, U.S. bombers dropped seven hundred thousand pounds of ordnance on the mountains. The militant Abu Jaafar al-Kuwaiti recalled that, together with bin Laden and a larger group, he took up a position in trenches at nine thousand feet that they had built to protect them "from the insane American strikes."

Ayman Saeed Abdullah Batarfi, a Yemeni doctor who was treating the al-Qaeda wounded, paints a scene of desperation. "I was out of medicine and I had a lot of casualties," Batarfi later recalled. "I did a hand amputation by a knife, and I did a finger amputation with scissors." Batarfi said he personally told bin Laden that, if they did not leave Tora Bora soon, "no one would stay alive" under the American bombardment. But the al-Qaeda leader seemed mainly preoccupied with his own escape. "He did not prepare himself for Tora Bora," Batarfi said, "and to be frank he didn't care about anyone but himself."

Bin Laden recalled that "day and night, American forces were bombing us by smart bombs that weigh thousands of pounds and bombs that penetrate caves." On December 9, a U.S. bomber dropped an immense BLU-82 bomb on al-Qaeda's positions. Known as a daisy cutter, the fifteen-thousand-pound bomb was used in the Gulf War to clear minefields. Berntsen remembers that the daisy cutter was followed by a wave of additional American airstrikes. "We came right in behind it with B-52s," he says. "Each of them has twenty-five-hundred-pounders, so everything goes in there. Killed a lot of people."

That night, al-Qaeda member Abu Jaafar al-Kuwaiti and others "were awakened to the sound of massive and terrorizing explosions very near to us." The following day, Abu Jaafar "received the horrifying news" that the "trench of Sheikh Osama had been destroyed." But bin Laden was not dead. An al-Qaeda website offered the following description of what had happened: bin Laden had dreamed about a scorpion descending into one of the trenches that his men had dug, so he evacuated his trench, moving two hundred meters away.

On December 10, the U.S. National Security Agency, which sucks up signals intelligence around the world, picked up an important intercept from Tora Bora: "Father (bin Laden) is trying to break through the siege line." This was then communicated to the Delta operators on the ground. Around 4 P.M. the same day, Afghan soldiers said that they had spotted bin Laden and had him surrounded. Later that evening another intercept was picked up of bin Laden talking on the radio with some of his lieutenants, according to the Delta commander Dalton Fury. The information was so accurate that it appeared to pinpoint bin Laden's location down to within ten meters. Another intercept that same night placed him two kilometers further away, suggesting that the al-Qaeda leader was on the move.

For Fury this posed something of a quandary. This was the closest to bin Laden's position that any American forces had ever been, but at the same time three of Fury's men were now pinned down in a ferocious firefight with some al-Qaeda fighters. And as dusk fell, Fury's key Afghan ally, Hazarat Ali, had retreated from the battlefield back to Jalalabad for some dinner to break his Ramadan fast, as is the Afghan way. Fury was under explicit orders not to take the lead in the battle and only to act in a supporting role for the hundreds of Afghans in Hazarat Ali's ragtag army. Now he had no Afghan allies to guide him at night into the craggy moonscape of upper Tora Bora. Fury reluctantly made the decision to bail on that night's mission. "My decision to abort that effort to kill or capture bin Laden when we might have been within 2,000 meters of him, about 2,000 yards, still bothers me. It leaves me with a feeling of somehow letting down our nation at a critical time," Fury says.

On December 12, a defining moment came in the Tora Bora battle, and al-Qaeda would swiftly exploit it. Haji Zaman Gamsharik, one of the Afghan warlords leading the attack against al-Qaeda, had opened negotiations with members of the group for a surrender agreement. "They talked on the radio with Haji Zaman," an Afghan front-line commander explained, "saying they were ready to surrender at 4 P.M. Commander Zaman told the other commanders and the Americans about this. Then al-Qaeda said, 'We need to have a meeting with our guys. Will you wait until 8 A.M. tomorrow?' So we agreed to this. Those al-Qaeda who were not ready to be killed escaped that night. At 8 A.M. the following day no one surrendered, so we started attacking again."

News of the cease-fire with al-Qaeda did not sit well with the group of twenty Delta operators who by December 12 had made their way deeper into Tora Bora, into an area near bin Laden's now-destroyed two-room house. Strung out on a ridge above the Americans were about two hundred of Haji Zaman's men, who were looking down on what remained of bin Laden's bombed-out house. Haji Zaman's commanders told the Delta operators that al-Qaeda members would gather in the field in front of bin Laden's wrecked house to surrender the following morning. Instead, during that night, many of the militants who were supposed to surrender likely instead fled the Tora Bora mountains.

Back in Kabul, the CIA ground commander, Gary Berntsen, was screaming profanities into the phone when he was told about the surrender agreement. Berntsen remembers, "Essentially I used the f-word . . . I was *screaming* at them on the phone. And telling them, 'No cease-fire. No negotiation. We continue airstrikes.'" But there wasn't much the small number of Delta operators on the ground at Tora Bora could do once their Afghan allies had dug their heels in about the cease-fire. As Fury remembers it, U.S. forces only observed the cease-fire for about two hours on December 12—resuming bombing around 5 P.M. that day.

The next afternoon, American signals operators who had spent the past four days on the ground at Tora Bora intercepting radio transmissions heard that "Father" (bin Laden) was again on the move. Bin Laden himself then spoke to his followers: "The time is now. Arm your women and children against the infidel!" Following several hours of high-intensity bombing, the al-Qaeda leader broke radio silence again, saying, "I am sorry for getting you involved in this battle; if you can no longer resist, you may surrender with my blessing." One member of Berntsen's team, an Arabic-speaking CIA officer who had been listening to bin Laden's voice for several years, was in Tora Bora monitoring the al-Qaeda leader talking to his followers over an open radio channel: "Listening to bin Laden pray with these guys. Apologizing to them, for what's occurred. Asking them to fight on."

Khalid al-Hubayshi, one of the Saudis holed up in Tora Bora, says that bin Laden's aides instructed the hundreds of mostly Arab fighters who were still alive in the mountainous complex to retreat to Pakistan and surrender to their embassies there. Hubayshi remains bitter about the behavior of his leader: "We had been ready to lay down our lives for him, and he couldn't make the effort to speak to us personally."

On December 14, bin Laden's voice was again picked up by American signals operators, but, according to an interpreter translating for the Delta team, it sounded more like a prerecorded sermon than a live transmission, indicating that bin Laden had already left the battlefield area. He had likely used the cover of al-Qaeda's "surrender" to begin his retreat during the early morning of December 13, which is confirmed by the various American radio intercepts later that day in which bin Laden made his final good-byes to his troops.

December 13 was the twenty-seventh day of Ramadan, an especially sacred day in the Muslim calendar, when the Prophet Mohammed had received the first verses of the Koran. On the same holy day in 1987, not far from Tora Bora and surrounded by up to two hundred Soviet soldiers, bin Laden had witnessed a "miracle," which he later recounted to a journalist: "A Soviet airplane, a MiG I believe, passed by in front of us, when a group of our Afghan Mujahideen brothers grouped together [and attacked]. The plane then broke to pieces as it fell right in front of our eyes." Now bin Laden was once again delivered from the clutches of a superpower around the time of this most sacred day.

The top leaders of al-Qaeda separated as they made good their escape from Tora Bora; Ayman al-Zawahiri left the mountainous redoubt with Uthman, one of bin Laden's sons. Osama himself fled with another of his sons, seventeen-year-old Muhammad, accompanied by his guards. Meanwhile, Abdallah Tabarak, bin Laden's chief bodyguard, escaped Tora Bora with a group made up mainly of Yemenis and Saudis. He went in the direction of Pakistan, taking bin Laden's satellite phone with him on the assumption that U.S. intelligence agencies were monitoring satellite calls in the region. Tabarak continued to use the satphone as his boss made his own escape, to divert attention away from the leader of al-Qaeda.

Ghanim al-Harbi, a Saudi in his twenties, had gone to Afghanistan a year before 9/11 and trained at an al-Qaeda camp. As the Taliban fell, Harbi ended up with a group of around sixty-five Arabs in Tora Bora. Sometime around December 15, his group recruited two local guides for the arduous trek to the Pakistani border. As this large group passed through one of the local villages, a massive American airstrike killed forty of the Arabs and Harbi suffered serious injuries. He was subsequently captured with a group of others from Yemen, Kuwait, Egypt, and Tunisia.

By December 17, the battle of Tora Bora was over. Dalton Fury, the Delta commander on the ground, estimated that at battle's end there were some 220 dead militants and fifty-two captured fighters, who were mostly Arabs, with a dozen Afghans and a sprinkling of Chechens and Pakistanis. Around twenty of the captured prisoners were paraded for the cameras of the international press. They were a bedraggled, scrawny lot who did not look much like the fearsome warriors everyone presumed them to be.

Across the border from Tora Bora, in Pakistan, thousands of the paramilitary constabulary of the Pakistani Frontier Corps were posted in the general vicinity. But Pakistan's military leaders were distracted in the critical time period when al-Qaeda members started slipping out of Tora Bora, because of the attack by a group of Pakistani militants on the Indian Parliament on December 13. That attack led both countries to mobilize their soldiers on the India-Pakistan border and events in Afghanistan were quickly superseded by the possibility of war between the two nuclear-armed rival states. The Pakistani minister of the interior, Moinuddin Haider, recalled that India moved hundreds of thousands of soldiers to Pakistan's border: "We had to respond. All our armed forces went to combat that situation and we also moved to the borders. All of our second-line forces which guard our borders, especially with Afghanistan, they were deployed."

Despite the mobilization for a possible war with India, Pakistan's military dictator, General Pervez Musharraf, later claimed that Pakistani forces managed to arrest up to 240 militants retreating from Tora Bora, but clearly many others also escaped, including much of the leadership of al-Qaeda. And so was lost the last, best chance to capture bin Laden and his top deputies, at a time when they were confined to an area of several dozen square miles.

Al-Qaeda's leaders fled into the tribal areas of western Pakistan, where they began the long process of rebuilding their devastated organization.

Why did the United States military—the most powerful armed force in history—not seal off the Tora Bora region, instead relying only on a small contingent of American Special Forces on the ground? Part of the answer is that the U.S. military was a victim of its own earlier successes. In Afghanistan the Pentagon and CIA had just secured one of the most stunning unconventional military victories in modern history, overthrowing the Taliban in a matter of weeks with only some four hundred American soldiers and intelligence officers on the ground, working with the tens of thousands of men in the Northern Alliance and the targeted wrath of the U.S. Air Force.

However, substantial numbers of Americans on the ground were needed to throw up an effective cordon around al-Qaeda's hard core. Michael DeLong, a three-star Marine general and the deputy commander of U.S. Central Command (CENTCOM), which had overall responsibility for the Tora Bora battle, recalled that the Pentagon did not want to put many American soldiers on the ground because of a concern that they would be treated like antibodies by the locals. "The mountains of Tora Bora are situated deep in territory controlled by tribes hostile to the United States and any outsiders. The reality is if we put our troops in there we would inevitably end up fighting Afghan villagers—creating bad will at a sensitive time."

There may also have been reluctance at the Pentagon to send soldiers into harm's way. The Pentagon's risk aversion is now hard to recall, following the years of war in Afghanistan and Iraq and the thousands of American soldiers who have since died—but it was quite real at the time. Recall that in the most recent U.S. war—the 1999 conflict in Kosovo—not a single American had died in combat. And, at that point in the Afghan War, more journalists had died than U.S. soldiers. Fury says that the fourteen U.S. Green Beret soldiers from the "white" Special Forces who were on the ground at Tora Bora were told to "stay in the foothills" at least four kilometers from any action—"pretty much out of harm's way." The Green Berets did call in airstrikes but were not allowed to engage in firefights with al-Qaeda because of concerns that the battle would turn into a "meat grinder."

Finally, there was Iraq. In late November, as the battle of Tora Bora was gearing up in earnest, Defense Secretary Donald Rumsfeld told General Franks that President Bush "wants us to look for options in Iraq." Franks told

Rumsfeld that there was a planning document, known as OPLAN 1003, which was a detailed blueprint for an invasion of Iraq that ran to eight hundred pages, but whose assumptions were now "out of date." Rumsfeld instructed the general to "dust it off" and brief him in a week's time. The chairman of the Joint Chiefs, Richard Myers, recalls, "I realized that one week was not giving Tom and his staff much time to sharpen" the plan. Franks points out in his autobiography that his staff was already working seven days a week, sixteen-plus hours a day as the Tora Bora battle was reaching its climax. Although Franks doesn't say so, it is impossible not to wonder if the labor-intensive planning ordered by his boss for another major war was a distraction from the one he was already fighting.

The Pentagon's reluctance to send more soldiers to Tora Bora arose out of a combination of factors: fear of offending the Afghan warlords in eastern Afghanistan; worries about replicating the Soviet debacle in Afghanistan; concerns about the difficult terrain; and an unwillingness to take casualties. However, given that only three months earlier some three thousand Americans had died on 9/11 and that al-Qaeda's leaders and hundreds of the group's foot soldiers were now all concentrated at Tora Bora, the Pentagon's reluctance to commit more American boots on the ground is a decision that historians are not likely to judge kindly.

In the end, there were probably more journalists at Tora Bora than there were Western soldiers, who totaled around seventy or so Delta operators, Green Berets, and British Special Boat Service troops. CNN's veteran war correspondent Nic Robertson remembered that in the vicinity of Tora Bora there were "close to 100 journalists in tents, buses and mud houses." Since news organizations from around the world could arrange for their journalists and crews to cover Tora Bora, it is puzzling why the U.S. military could not have put more soldiers on the ground to entrap the hard core of al-Qaeda.

Could the Pentagon have deployed a substantial number of additional soldiers to Tora Bora during the battle? Yes: there were around two thousand American troops already in or around the Afghan theater. Stationed at the U.S. air base known as K2 in Uzbekistan, Afghanistan's neighbor to the north, were some one thousand soldiers of the 10th Mountain Division, which specializes in high-altitude warfare. Hundreds of those soldiers had already deployed forward to Bagram Air Base, an hour drive north of Kabul, as the Tora Bora battle heated up. In addition, 1,200 Marines from the highly mobile 15th and 26th Marine Expeditionary Units were stationed at Forward

Operating Base Rhino in the deserts near Kandahar in southern Afghanistan from November 25. Brigadier General James N. Mattis, the commander of the Marines in the Afghan theater, is reported to have asked to send his men into Tora Bora, but his request was turned down.

Dalton Fury, the on-scene Delta commander, estimates that three hundred U.S. soldiers could have secured the main passes out of Tora Bora. Was such an operation feasible? Perhaps. On the night of October 19, weeks before the Tora Bora battle, 199 Army Rangers had parachuted in total blackout conditions onto a Taliban-held desert landing strip near Kandahar, which they then secured. (To be fair, that operation was conducted without the expectation of Taliban resistance, and there was none.) And at the same time a further ninety-one U.S. Special Forces soldiers were dropped into Mullah Omar's own Kandahar compound, where they gathered intelligence and arrested members of the Taliban before pulling out after an hour. Those operations demonstrated that elite American units could be dropped anywhere into Afghanistan, a month and a half before the Tora Bora battle began in earnest.

Of course such a force would have had to deal with the treacherous weather conditions and high altitudes of Tora Bora as well as fierce resistance from al-Qaeda. An official U.S. military history of the Afghan War later stated that the mountainous terrain and lack of helicopter assets in the theater meant that it was "unrealistic" to think that more U.S. forces could have been inserted to "seal the passes into Pakistan." Maybe so, but what is not in doubt is that no effort was ever made by the Pentagon to test this proposition.

In the end there would be no American blocking forces securing the passes of Tora Bora, despite the fact that the *New York Times* story on November 25, quoting a local Afghan warlord, had explicitly made the point that bin Laden would likely "slip into Pakistan" when Tora Bora came under attack. And, as we have seen, Hank Crumpton, the CIA officer running the overall Afghan operation, had also briefed the White House and CENTCOM that this was a strong possibility.

What is most infuriating about all this is that bin Laden's presence at Tora Bora was well-known not just to those U.S. forces on the ground at the battle, but also to officials higher up the American chain of command, something that they *publicly acknowledged* at the time. According to a background briefing reported by CNN, Pentagon officials in mid-December 2001 told reporters that there was "reasonable certainty" that bin Laden was at Tora Bora, a judgment that they based on intercepted radio transmissions. Similarly, the

New York Times reported on December 12, 2001, that a "senior military officer" in Washington placed bin Laden at Tora Bora, based on "intercepted radio communications." And in late November, as the battle raged on in Tora Bora, when asked on ABC News if bin Laden was there, Vice President Dick Cheney said, "I think he's probably in that general area." Two weeks later, Cheney was on NBC's *Meet the Press* also explaining that "the preponderance of reporting at this point" was that bin Laden was in Tora Bora. The next day, Paul Wolfowitz, the number-two official at the Pentagon, when asked if bin Laden was in Tora Bora, told reporters, "We don't have any credible evidence of him being in other parts of Afghanistan or outside of Afghanistan." Even General Franks himself recounted in his autobiography that in December 2001 he briefed President Bush, saying, "Unconfirmed reports that Osama has been seen in the White Mountains, Sir. The Tora Bora area." And shortly after the battle, on January 7, 2002, Franks told thc Associated Press that bin Laden had indeed been at Tora Bora, "at one point or another."

The official U.S. military history of the Afghan War later concluded that bin Laden was indeed at Tora Bora during the battle: "All source reporting corroborated his presence on several days from 9–14 December." And Lieutenant General Michael Delong, Franks's deputy at CENTCOM, also wrote in his memoir that his superiors and he were well aware at the time that bin Laden was at Tora Bora: "We were hot on Osama bin Laden's trail. He was definitely there when we hit [the Tora Bora] caves. Every day during the bombing, Rumsfeld asked me, 'Did we get him? Did we get him?'"

None of this was sufficient for anyone in the Bush administration or at the higher echelons of the Pentagon to order more U.S. soldiers into the battle zone. Later, top Bush administration officials and General Franks himself would simply deny that the al-Qaeda leader had ever been at Tora Bora.

The question of whether the United States had missed an opportunity to kill bin Laden during the battle of Tora Bora became a particular issue during the razor-close 2004 U.S. presidential campaign. During the September 30 presidential debate, Democratic contender Senator John Kerry said, "When we had Osama bin Laden cornered in the mountains of Tora Bora, 1,000 of his cohorts with him in those mountains. With the American military forces nearby and in the field, we didn't use the best-trained troops in the world to go kill the world's number one criminal and terrorist."

This charge produced a furious response from the Bush campaign, since it went to the heart of the president's claim that he was the "strong on terrorism" contender. Writing in the *New York Times*, General Franks, a Bush supporter and the overall commander of the Tora Bora operation, stated, "We don't know to this day whether Mr. bin Laden was at Tora Bora." At a town hall meeting in Ohio, the same day that Franks's piece appeared in the *Times*, Vice President Dick Cheney charged that Kerry's critique of the Tora Bora campaign was "absolute garbage."

On October 27, President Bush himself weighed in at a campaign rally a week before voters went to the polls, accusing Kerry "of saying anything it takes to get elected. Like when he charged that our military failed to get Osama bin Laden at Tora Bora, even though our top military commander, General Tommy Franks, said, 'The senator's understanding of events does not square with reality,' and intelligence reports place bin Laden in any of several different countries at the time."

Two days later, bin Laden himself suddenly appeared on a videotape on Al Jazeera, his first appearance on video in more than a year. The tape was then replayed on TV stations across the United States. In the video, bin Laden spoke directly to the American people from behind a desk, dressed formally in gold robes and a white turban, his long beard streaked with gray. Bin Laden was well lit, suggesting a careful production, and he was without a gun at his side, a rare sight. That nonbelligerent visual message mirrored what bin Laden said: "Your security is not in the hands of Kerry, or Bush, or al-Qaeda. It is in your own hands and any state that does not violate our security has automatically guaranteed its own," implying that al-Qaeda would suspend its attacks if there were a change in U.S. foreign policy in the Muslim world. On the videotape bin Laden for the first time made an unequivocal public admission of his own involvement in the 9/11 plot, saying that he had agreed with the lead hijacker Mohammed Atta, "that his mission be accomplished in twenty minutes before Bush and his administration had time to notice."

The most obvious message of the election-eve videotape was that bin Laden was not only alive but doing quite well, a potent reminder that the Bush administration had not brought the al-Qaeda leader to justice. By now Bush and Kerry were running neck and neck and Kerry was quick to point out that "when George Bush had the opportunity in Afghanistan and Tora Bora he didn't choose to use American forces to hunt down and kill Osama bin Laden." President Bush immediately responded to Kerry's charge, saying, "My opponent tonight continued to say things he knows are not true . . . it is especially shameful in the light of a new tape from America's enemy."

Kerry was correct about what had taken place at Tora Bora, most importantly the fact that hundreds of al-Qaeda's hard core, including bin Laden, escaped from the grasp of the United States to live to fight another day, while Bush, Cheney, and General Franks either misled the American public about what had happened at Tora Bora or were simply ignorant of what had really taken place during the most important battle of the "war on terror."

Just how close bin Laden came to death at Tora Bora was illustrated by a videotape that aired on December 27, 2001, a couple of weeks after the battle had ended. As we have seen, bin Laden said, "I am just a poor slave of God. If I live or die, the war will continue," his choice of words seeming to confirm his recent brush with death at Tora Bora. A visibly aged bin Laden did not move his entire left side during the thirty-four-minute videotape, suggesting he had sustained a serious injury. Abdel Bari Atwan, who had spent two days interviewing bin Laden in Tora Bora in 1996, says that in late December 2001, "I was in the Gulf region and I met somebody from al-Qaeda and he told me that Osama bin Laden was injured during the Tora Bora bombing, and he was operated on his left shoulder."

On December 14, around the time bin Laden fled Tora Bora, he wrote a final testament that included a bleak message to his offspring: "As to my children, forgive me because I have given you only a little of my time since I answered the jihad call. I have chosen a road fraught with dangers and for this sake suffered from hardships, embitterment, betrayal, and treachery. I advise you not to work with al-Qaeda."

Bin Laden retreated from the Tora Bora battlefield demoralized, wounded, and contemplating his own death, while the organization he had so carefully nurtured for more than a decade was now on life support. He was forty-four.

Chapter 6

The Destruction of the Base

The tactics took over the strategy.

—Noman Benotman, one of bin Laden's companions-in-arms during the jihad against the communists in Afghanistan, when asked to explain the 9/11 attacks

Tactics without strategy is the noise before defeat.

—Sun Tzu

Omar bin Laden, the fourth son of the al-Qaeda leader, cuts quite a figure. In one photo, he stares out from beneath an Adidas baseball cap, his beard closely trimmed—an entirely different look from his father's seventh-century aesthetic. He wears jeans and sits next to his wife, a striking British woman more than two decades his senior and with five other marriages under her belt, who once was known as Jane Felix-Browne but preferred the name Zaina al-Sabah following her marriage into the bin Laden family. While his father would hardly have approved of his lifestyle choices, few men knew the terrorist mastermind so well. After the Sudanese government had exiled bin Laden in 1996, Omar spent four years living in and around the notorious training camps that his father had then assembled in Afghanistan.

But between his departure from Sudan and his marriage, something happened to Omar: he turned against his father. During a Hajj pilgrimage to Mecca in 2003, where Omar spent four days performing religious observances and talking about life in Afghanistan, he heaped abuse on his father for attacking the United States. "Those guys are dummies," he told Hutaifa Azzam, the son of the Palestinian cleric Abdullah Azzam, who had been Osama bin Laden's most important mentor. "They have destroyed everything, and for nothing. What did we get from September 11?" In fact, these attacks drove a permanent wedge between father and son. Omar left Afghanistan in disgust in 2000 as the 9/11 plans were advancing.

After 9/11, Omar bin Laden was not the only al-Qaeda insider critical of his father. A letter written by an al-Qaeda member—and addressed to Khalid Sheikh Mohammed, the operational commander of the September 11 attacks—gives a sense of just how demoralized the group was: "Consider all the fatal and successive disasters that have afflicted us during a period of no more than six months. . . . Today we are experiencing one setback after another and have gone from misfortune to disaster."

These feelings of despair extended even to the al-Qaeda leader himself. In June 2002, bin Laden and one of his younger sons, Hamzah, posted comments to an al-Qaeda website that underlined how precarious life on the run had become. Hamzah wrote, "Oh father! Why have they showered us with bombs like rain, having no mercy for a child? Oh father! What has happened for us to be chased by danger?" The al-Qaeda leader replied, "Pardon me my son, but I can only see a very steep path ahead. A decade has gone by in vagrancy and travel, and here we are in our tragedy. Security has gone, but danger remains."

Al-Qaeda's leaders and foot soldiers were right to be dispirited following 9/11. The United States appeared to have smashed the terrorist organization. But what exactly had been smashed? Successful militant organizations tend to be defined by two characteristics: inspirational leadership and effective management practices. Before 9/11, al-Qaeda had both. Not only did al-Qaeda have a charismatic leader who attracted recruits from around the Muslim world, but the organization also oversaw training camps in Afghanistan that had churned out an estimated ten thousand to twenty thousand recruits in the five years before 9/11. Some of those camps were operated by al-Qaeda itself and others by affiliated groups such as the Islamic Movement of Uzbekistan and the Pakistani Harakat-ul-Mujahideen. Most recruits learned just the basics of insurgent warfare. Others graduated to more specialized terrorist training, and an elite group of recruits were inducted into al-Qaeda itself by swearing a personal religious oath of allegiance known as *bayat* to bin Laden. Only around two hundred in number at the time of the 9/11 attacks, al-Qaeda inductees were required to sign an oath of allegiance that read, "I pledge by God's creed to become a Muslim soldier to support God's religion."

The training camps were tough. Omar Nasiri (a pseudonym) attended the Khaldan training facility in 1996. Despite the poor diet and harsh conditions, Nasiri loved his time in the camps and proved an adept student of insurgent and terrorist tactics. To his surprise, training patrols at night sometimes involved being shot at with live ammunition. He learned to fire every conceivable weapon, from German pistols to Russian artillery pieces, and he worked with explosives ranging from Semtex to blast mines. He also learned how to arrange kidnappings and assassinations. Nasiri went on to bomb school, where he was taught how to make high explosives from common household products. He even learned how to make a bomb from his own urine.

Nasiri's account tracks closely with what Moroccan L'Houssaine Kherchtou experienced when he attended al-Qaeda's Farouq training camp near Kandahar in the early 1990s. Kherchtou trained on a variety of automatic rifles, including the AK-47, M-16, and Uzi. He also learned how to handle explosives such as C3, C4, and dynamite. Kherchtou, who had once attended a catering school in France, lost a lot of weight during the rigorous training, more than forty pounds.

In addition to al-Qaeda's training camps in Afghanistan, the *Encyclopedia of Jihad* was the organization's most important contribution for instructing jihadists about guerrilla warfare and terrorist tactics. The *Encyclopedia* is a massive work of several thousand pages that was posted to the Internet in Arabic. It contains advice for every imaginable hostile situation, from how to booby-trap a napkin, to how to conduct a drive-by shooting, to how to recognize a rattlesnake or treat a scorpion sting.

Internal memos from the time it was based in Afghanistan demonstrate that al-Qaeda, like many of the murderous organizations that had preceded it, was highly bureaucratic. Al-Qaeda's bylaws covered annual budgets; who controlled which money accounts; salary levels (including a discussion of extra pay for those members with multiple wives); the frequency of airline tickets for members of the group to visit families back home; the proper distribution of medical benefits; the scale of furniture allowances; the special provisions that were made for those with disabilities; and the grounds for dismissal from the group. Al-Qaeda even had a generous vacation policy with a week off for its married recruits for every three weeks served. Requests for vacation had to be submitted two and a half months in advance.

Abu Jandal, bin Laden's chief bodyguard, told FBI interrogators that al-Qaeda's pre-9/11 management structure consisted of a military committee, public relations committee, finance committee, an administrative section for its training camps, and even a farming committee, which took care of the group's agricultural pursuits. Abu Jandal explained that each section filed regular reports to the group's leadership on a computer and that the al-Qaeda leader met regularly with the head of each committee "to discuss their issues."

Rather than an ad hoc collection of like-minded jihadists who had gathered in Afghanistan in the late 1990s, as some had portrayed it, al-Qaeda was, in fact, one of the most bureaucratic terrorist organizations in history. A detailed application form that potential recruits had to fill out before they were accepted at one of al-Qaeda's training camps asked them about their education level, religious background, how they had arrived in Afghanistan, military skills, involvement in other jihads, marital status, language skills, and political affiliations. The application form also outlined al-Qaeda's requirements for those entering its camps, including that they agree not to leave before their basic two-month training course was finished and that they not bring any "forbidden items" such as tape recorders, radios, and cameras. They were reminded to pack appropriate running shoes and clothes suitable for paramilitary training.

The picture that emerges of the pre-9/11 al-Qaeda from the myriad accounts of trainees in bin Laden's camps, from its own internal documents, and from accounts by its leaders to journalists and to Western interrogators, is of a paramilitary organization with a strict chain of command, at the top of which stood the absolute leader, bin Laden. It was bin Laden who set the group's strategy, and key members of the group had sworn a binding religious oath of obedience to the man they referred to as their "emir," or prince. Below bin Laden were his deputies, who enforced strict discipline and handled the operational details of terrorist plots and promotions within the hierarchy, all of which they managed with a heavy flow of paperwork more reminiscent of an insurance company than a group dedicated to revolutionary jihad.

Instead of being a terrorist organization sponsored by a state, al-Qaeda was an organization that ran something of a parallel state alongside that of the Taliban regime in Afghanistan. (This was the exact opposite of the state-sponsored terrorist groups that so many Bush administration officials believed to be the real threat posed by terrorism.) Al-Qaeda conducted its own foreign policy independent from the Taliban beginning in 1998 in the form of multiple strikes on American government, military, and civilian targets. And the 9/11 plot demonstrated that al-Qaeda was an organization of global reach. The plot played out across the globe with planning meetings in Malaysia, operatives taking flight lessons in the United States, coordination by plot leaders based in Hamburg, money transfers from Dubai, and the recruitment of suicide operatives from countries around the Middle East—all activities that were ultimately overseen by al-Qaeda's leaders in Afghanistan.

Despite the fact that following 9/11 al-Qaeda—whose name in Arabic means "the base"—lost the best base it ever had in Afghanistan, Saif al-Adel, one of the group's military commanders, explained in an interview four years later that the strikes on New York and Washington had, in fact, been a brilliant success and were part of a far-reaching and visionary plan to provoke the United States into some ill-advised actions: "Such strikes will force the person to carry out random acts and provoke him to make serious and sometimes fatal mistakes. . . . The first reaction was the invasion of Afghanistan."

But there is not a shred of evidence that in the weeks before 9/11, al-Qaeda's leaders made any plans for an American invasion of Afghanistan. They prepared instead only for possible U.S. cruise missile attacks or airstrikes by evacuating their training camps. Also, al-Qaeda insiders well understood that the overthrow of the Taliban hardly constituted an American "mistake," as the loss of the first and only regime in the modern Muslim world that ruled according to al-Qaeda's rigid precepts was hardly a victory, nor was the loss of an entire country that they had once enjoyed as a safe haven. And in the wake of the fall of the Taliban, al-Qaeda would never again recover anything like the status it once had as a terrorist organization with considerable sway over Afghanistan.

In 2004, Abu Musab al-Suri, a precise, intellectual Syrian jihadist who had known bin Laden since the late 1980s, released on the Internet a history of the jihadist movement titled "The Call for Global Islamic Resistance." In his history Suri was at pains to praise bin Laden, but he also painted a grim picture of the scale of the strategic disaster that had engulfed the Taliban and al-Qaeda following bin Laden's foolhardy decision to attack the United States: "America destroyed the Islamic Emirate [of the Taliban] in Afghanistan, which had become the refuge for the mujahideen. . . . The jihad movement rose to glory in the 1960's, and continued through the 70's and 80's, and resulted in the rise of the Islamic Emirate of Afghanistan [the Taliban], but it was destroyed after 9/11."

Suri's bleak assessment was seconded by Hank Crumpton, the CIA supervisor of operations in Afghanistan in the months after 9/11, who says that by the winter of 2001 twenty training camps had been secured, yielding a treasure trove of hundreds of documents, videotapes, and phones, all of which led to many new leads, while at least five thousand militants had been killed, mostly in the massive American bombing raids on Taliban positions.

While the loss of its sanctuary in Afghanistan was a major blow for al-Qaeda's leaders, they could take solace in some of the other outcomes of 9/11, which above all demonstrated that the world's only superpower was indeed vulnerable. If terrorism had previously been a form of murderous theater in which "terrorists want a lot of people watching, not a lot of people dead," as the terrorism expert Brian Jenkins had once observed, then on 9/11 al-Qaeda amped up that formula by orders of magnitude into a made-for-TV horror movie. Untold millions of people watched thousands of civilians die on *live* television.

The 9/11 attacks were an enormous tactical success for al-Qaeda. They involved well-coordinated strikes on multiple targets in the heart of the enemy, magnified through their global broadcast. The 9/11 "propaganda of the deed" took place in the media capital of the world, which ensured the widest possible coverage of the event. Not since television viewers had watched the abduction and murder of Israeli athletes during the Munich Olympics in 1972 had a massive global audience witnessed a terrorist attack unfold in real time. If al-Qaeda had been a largely unknown organization before 9/11, in the days after it became a household name.

An unexpected bonus of the 9/11 attacks for the al-Qaeda leadership was their financial impacts. Bin Laden later gloated that every dollar al-Qaeda invested in the operation cost the U.S. economy $1 million: a leveraged investment of $500,000 by al-Qaeda in its "Holy Tuesday" operation ultimately cost the American economy $500 billion. Sounding more like an economist than a terrorist leader, bin Laden ticked off a number of the economic consequences of the attacks: Wall Street stocks lost 16 percent of their value, airlines and air freight companies laid off 170,000 employees, and the hotel chain Intercontinental fired twenty thousand workers. As a result of the lessons he learned from 9/11, around the first anniversary of the attacks bin Laden released an audiotape announcing a new al-Qaeda policy aimed at disrupting the global economy.

While 9/11 may have brought bin Laden and al-Qaeda a great deal of notoriety and some personal satisfaction that they had bloodied the nose of the superpower, it did not achieve any of the group's larger goals. It was certainly bin Laden's intention to set off a Clash of Civilizations of the kind first predicted by the Harvard political scientist Samuel Huntington. In his post-9/11 interview with Al Jazeera, the Saudi exile was asked: "[Do] you support the 'Clash of Civilizations'?" Bin Laden replied: "No doubt about that. . . . The Jews and the Americans made up this call for peace in the world. The peace they're calling for is a big fairy tale. They're just drugging the Muslims as they lead them to slaughter." Militant Islamists like bin Laden are fans of Huntington's concept, which they see as an accurate description of the inevitable battle between the West and Islam—a battle that Islam will win in the long term.

But the Clash of Civilizations that bin Laden had hoped to spark never happened. Tens of millions, perhaps hundreds of millions of people around the world watched bin Laden's call for holy war in his improbable global broadcast on October 7, 2001, as the United States launched its first aerial assaults against Taliban and al-Qaeda forces in Afghanistan. But bin Laden's call did not resonate with the planet's more than one billion Muslims. Instead of mass outpourings of support for bin Laden, in the vast cities of Karachi and Jakarta there were demonstrations against the United States that numbered only in the low tens of thousands. And governments of Muslim countries lined up to help the fight against al-Qaeda, from the military regime of Pakistan, which had formerly been supportive of the Taliban, to countries like Yemen and Jordan, which during the Gulf War had sided with Saddam Hussein.

So why did bin Laden's call for a global jihad against the "unbelievers" fall on so many deaf ears? First, and most obviously, it is simply *un-Islamic* to murder thousands of civilians. There is scant justification for such an attack in the Koran or other key Islamic texts, and indeed, when bin Laden was asked how such attacks could possibly be justified, he generally fell back on the political argument that American taxpayers are complicit in the policies of the U.S. government. Second, Middle Eastern governments well understood that bin Laden's ultimate aim was regime change across the region to create a swath of Islamist theocracies and therefore that bin Laden's followers posed as much of a threat to their own governments as they did to the United States.

And so bin Laden's grand project—to transform the Muslim world into a militant Islamist caliphate—has been, by any measure, a resounding failure. In large part, that's because bin Laden's strategy for arriving at this Promised Land is a fantasy. Al-Qaeda's leader prided himself on being a big-think strategist, but for all his brains, leadership skills, and charisma, he fastened on to an overall strategy that was self-defeating. Bin Laden's main goal was to bring about regime change in the Middle East and to replace the Arab governments with Taliban-style rule. He believed that the way to accomplish this was to attack the "far enemy" (the United States), then watch as the supposedly impious, U.S.-backed Muslim regimes he called the "near enemy" collapse.

This might have worked if the United States really had been a paper tiger that could sustain only a few blows from al-Qaeda. While the costs to the American economy of the 9/11 attacks were indeed high, at an estimated $500 billion, that could be absorbed in an economy with an annual output of $10 trillion, costing America around 5 percent of her 2001 gross domestic product.

Not only did bin Laden not achieve his war aims, but the attacks on Washington and New York resulted in the direct opposite of his stated goal of forcing a U.S. withdrawal from Muslim lands. After 9/11, American soldiers occupied both Afghanistan and Iraq and relations between the United States and the authoritarian Middle Eastern regimes became stronger than ever, based on their shared goal of defeating violent Islamists out for American blood and the regimes' power.

For most leaders, such a complete strategic failure would require a rethinking. Not for bin Laden. He could have formulated a new policy after U.S. forces toppled the Taliban in the winter of 2001, and have al-Qaeda and its allies directly attack the sclerotic "near enemy" regimes; he could have told his followers that, in strictly practical terms, provoking the world's only superpower would clearly interfere with al-Qaeda's goal of establishing Taliban-style regimes from Indonesia to Morocco. Instead, bin Laden continued to conceive of the United States as his main foe, as he explained in the many audio- and videotapes that he released after 9/11.

9/11 demonstrated that from a *tactical* standpoint, bin Laden was an effective leader. He intervened to make two key decisions that ensured the success of the attacks. The first was to appoint Mohammed Atta to be the lead hijacker; Atta would carry out his responsibilities with grim efficiency. The second was to curb the 9/11 operational commander Khalid Sheikh Mohammed's early plans for ten hijacked planes to crash into targets in both Asia and the East Coast of America simultaneously. Such a large number of attacks would have been hard to synchronize and might not have succeeded.

But as the *strategic* leader of al-Qaeda, bin Laden was an abject failure. His total dominance of al-Qaeda meant it was hostage to his strategic vision, and that became a problem for the organization because bin Laden's cultlike control over his group was not matched by any depth of strategic insight. Because he was so blinded by his intense hatred for America, bin Laden's strongly held belief that the United States was a paper tiger capable of only withstanding a few strikes before it would fall, taking down with it its client regimes in the Middle East, would turn out to be a disastrously naive view of the American response to 9/11. He showed no understanding of the intensity of outrage that would follow the first serious attack on the continental United States since the British burned the White House in 1814.

Chapter 7

The Gloves Came Off

All you need to know is that there was "before" 9/11 and "after" 9/11. After 9/11 the gloves come off.

—Cofer Black, the head of CIA's Counterterrorist Center, to the Senate and House Intelligence Committees on September 26, 2002

A state of war is not a blank check for the president.

—Supreme Court Justice Sandra Day O'Connor, on June 28, 2004

While al-Qaeda was reeling from its near-destruction in Afghanistan, the Bush administration was gripped by fears that the group might launch another devastating attack. National Security Advisor Condoleezza Rice remembers that the daily briefing, which now started the White House day at 7 A.M. with an update of the detailed, raw intelligence of terrorist threats from around the globe, only served to stoke those fears. "We went from basically no information to floods. It just started flooding with everything. So now you were getting un-assessed intelligence. You know, just about anything anybody said might be a threat."

Roger Cressey, a White House counterterrorism official, similarly recalls, "You're being flooded with some of the most dogshit, inaccurate threat reporting possible. And the obligation was to put it out there. When Ground Zero is still on fire, and we're kicking the shit out of the Taliban in Afghanistan, it was a price of doing business in that environment. . . . So, threat reporting that I would laugh out of my working group on threats was now making it directly into the White House. And making it directly into the Oval Office because God forbid the FBI or the CIA didn't tell the president or the White House of a threat and it became true."

Adding to the intense concerns in the White House about the possibility of another wave of attacks was the news that on October 5, 2001, a photo editor at the *National Enquirer* in Florida had died after inhaling anthrax. In the next weeks an assistant to the NBC News anchor Tom Brokaw tested positive for the biological agent, and letters containing anthrax were found at the offices of Senators Tom Daschle and Patrick Leahy. The anthrax letters closed down the Capitol Hill mail delivery system as well as a major postal sorting station in Washington and eventually killed five people. The anthrax-laced letters all contained the message: "DEATH TO AMERICA. DEATH TO ISRAEL. ALLAH IS GREAT."

Scott McClellan, the deputy White House press secretary, recalled that the anthrax attacks had "an enormous impact on President Bush's mind-set." The attacks seemed to be part of a second wave of terrorist assaults and added to the sense of imminent peril posed by terrorists this time armed perhaps with weapons of mass destruction. (The FBI would eventually identify the man behind the anthrax attacks as an American government scientist.)

Shortly before 9/11, an exercise positing a biological weapons attack on the United States conducted by the Johns Hopkins Center for Civilian Biodefense Studies and the Center for Strategic and International Studies, a heavyweight Washington think tank, had received considerable attention from Vice President Cheney. Conducted in late June 2001, the exercise named "Dark Winter" gamed out the effects of a major smallpox attack on the United States, concluding that three million would be infected and a million would die. In the exercise the role of the president was played by former Senator Sam Nunn, who more than almost any other political figure had sounded the alarm on the parlous security of Russia's nuclear weapons. Nunn's participation in the simulated attack, and that of other establishment Washington insiders, ensured that the exercise received plenty of attention, as did the fact that Iraq was (incorrectly) believed by the participants in the exercise to possess smallpox.

In the months following 9/11, Cheney became convinced that the United States might be the subject of a smallpox attack, perhaps from Iraq, and pushed for the immunization of the entire American population. It was estimated that those smallpox inoculations would probably kill three hundred Americans. Cheney believed the immunization program was still worth it, given that a smallpox attack might kill so many more. Bush nixed the idea.

The crisis atmosphere in the White House linking terrorism and WMD became more pronounced on October 29, 2001, when Tenet briefed the president and his senior advisers about a supposedly credible threat that terrorists might blow up a radiological bomb in Washington or New York. Following Tenet's briefing, Cheney, who had spent decades involved in "Continuity of Government" exercises designed to ensure that elements of the American government could survive a nuclear attack, announced he was decamping for an "undisclosed location," which was typically Camp David.

Bush administration officials were not alone in their fears of another serious attack. In the years after the attacks on New York and Washington, *Foreign Policy* magazine regularly surveyed some one hundred of the country's top foreign policy experts; around a quarter of them consistently believed that a 9/11-style attack was likely within six months, while two-thirds or more believed that such a large-scale assault was likely within five years.

Before 9/11 senior Bush administration officials were narrowly focused on the threats posed by traditional state antagonists and were therefore utterly surprised by the attacks by al-Qaeda, and so overreacted. Compounding their real fears of another wave of assaults by bin Laden's men, none of the key officials and lawyers who set the course of Bush administration policies on the detention and interrogation of suspected terrorists had any meaningful knowledge about al-Qaeda nor had any of them served as federal prosecutors or in law enforcement, the professions that best understand the value and efficacy of standard, noncoercive interrogation techniques. And none of the senior Bush national security team had fought in the U.S. military and so they had little understanding that upholding the Geneva Conventions is a core value of American soldiers on the battlefield. (The one cabinet official who had fought in a war, Secretary of State Colin Powell, vigorously objected to the overturning of Geneva protections for prisoners captured in Afghanistan.)

All of these factors help explain the Bush team's subsequent decisions to jettison the country's core principle: that it is a nation of laws. Bush administration officials outsourced more than fifty suspected terrorists to countries that practice torture, set up a prison camp at Guantánamo for around 800 prisoners where the Geneva Convention supposedly did not apply, and authorized the coercive interrogations of some two dozen prisoners, which in some cases amounted to torture.

For hours, the words come pouring out of Abu Omar as he describes his years of torture at the hands of Egypt's security services. Spreading his arms in a crucifixion position, he demonstrates how he was tied to a metal door as shocks were administered to his nipples and genitals. His legs tremble as he describes how he was twice raped. He mentions the hearing loss in his left ear from the beatings, and how he still wakes up at night screaming, takes tranquilizers, finds it hard to concentrate, and has unspecified "problems with my wife at home." He is, in short, a broken man.

There is nothing particularly unusual about Abu Omar's story. Torture is a standard investigative technique of Egypt's intelligence services and police, as the State Department and human rights organizations have documented myriad times over the years. What is somewhat unusual is that Abu Omar ended up inside Egypt's torture chambers courtesy of the United States, via an "extraordinary rendition"—in this case, a spectacular daylight kidnapping by the CIA on the streets of Milan, Italy.

First employed while Clinton was in office, extraordinary renditions—in which suspected terrorists are turned over to countries known to use torture—were used to a much larger degree following 9/11 as Bush officials took every measure they could to head off the next attack and to disrupt militant networks overseas. But Abu Omar's case was unique: unlike any other extraordinary rendition case, it prompted a massive criminal investigation—though not in the United States. An Italian prosecutor launched a probe of the kidnapping in 2003, resulting in the indictment of twenty-six Americans, almost all of them suspected CIA officials, and the case generated thousands of documents about the secretive rendition program that detailed how it actually worked.

A little before noon on February 17, 2003, Abu Omar, one of a circle of Egyptian Islamist militants living in exile in Italy, was headed to his mosque in a gritty section of Milan. He strolled down Via Guerzoni, a quiet street mostly empty of businesses and lined with high, view-blocking walls. A red Fiat pulled up beside him and a man jumped out, shouting "Polizia! Polizia!" Abu Omar (whose full name is Osama Hassan Mustafa Nasr) produced his ID. "Suddenly I was lifted in the air," he recalled. He was dragged into a white van and beaten by wordless men wearing balaclavas. After trussing him with restraints and blindfolding him, they sped away.

Hours later, when the van stopped, Abu Omar heard airplane noise. His clothes were cut off and something was stuffed in his anus, likely a tranquilizing suppository. His head was entirely covered in tape with only small holes for his mouth and nose, and he was placed on a plane. Hours later he was hustled off the jet. He heard someone speaking Arabic in a familiar cadence; in the distance, a muezzin was calling the dawn prayer. After more than a decade in exile, Abu Omar was back in his native Egypt.

And so began Abu Omar's descent into one of the twenty-first century's nastier circles of hell. His cell had no lights or windows, and the temperature alternated between freezing and baking. He was kept blindfolded and handcuffed for seven months. Interrogations could come at any time of the day or night. He was beaten with fists, electric cables, and chairs, stripped naked, and given electric shocks. His tormentors' questions largely revolved around his circle of fellow Egyptian militants in Italy, though every now and then the interrogators would indicate that they knew he wasn't a big-time terrorist. They were detaining him only because "the Americans imposed you on us."

In the fall of 2003, Abu Omar was taken to another prison; it was here that he was trussed in the crucifixion position and raped by the guards. After seven more months of torture, a Cairo court found there was no evidence that Abu Omar was involved in terrorism and ordered him freed. He was told not to contact anyone in Italy—including his wife—and not to speak to the press or human rights groups. Above all, he was not to tell anyone what had happened.

After agreeing to the conditions, Abu Omar was deposited at his mother's home in Alexandria, Egypt. He promptly called his wife in Italy. It was the first time she'd heard from him in fourteen months. Italian investigators, who'd been monitoring Abu Omar's phone in Milan for years, recorded the call. His wife asked him how he had been treated. He told her sarcastically, "They brought me food from the fanciest restaurant," though nearly three weeks later, he admitted to her, "I was very close to dying." He also spoke with a friend in Milan whose phone was also being tapped by Italian investigators. "I was freed on health grounds," he told the friend in one of the recorded calls. "I was almost paralyzed; still today I cannot walk more than 200 yards."

And then, just as suddenly as Abu Omar had reappeared, he vanished again. Egyptian authorities had gotten wind of his calls to Italy. This time he was imprisoned for three years. He smuggled out a letter describing his ordeal, which found its way to the Arab and Italian press and international human rights organizations. Inevitably, that led to more torture.

Was it illegal for American officials to transport Abu Omar to Egypt? Yes, according to the United Nations Convention Against Torture, which prohibits delivering someone to a country where there are "substantial grounds" to assume that he might be tortured. Were there substantial grounds to believe that transferring Abu Omar to Egypt would result in his being tortured? Plenty, according to a State Department report that detailed the methods used by Egypt's security services during the year that Abu Omar was abducted and confined. Those methods included the stripping and blindfolding of prisoners; beatings with fists, whips, and metal rods; administering electric shocks; and sexual assault.

The Bush White House routinely claimed that when the United States rendered individuals to other countries it received assurances that, as President Bush asserted at a press conference in March 2005, "They won't be tortured. . . . This country does not believe in torture." Several months later, Secretary of State Condoleezza Rice reiterated, "The United States has not transported anyone, and will not transport anyone, to a country when we believe he will be tortured."

But in the case of Abu Omar, Rice's assertions were demonstrably false. Fourteen documented extraordinary renditions of suspected jihadist militants took place under the Clinton administration. Almost all of those prisoners were rendered to Egypt, where at least three were executed. Generally those prisoners faced some kind of trial. After 9/11 the pace of extraordinary renditions sped up dramatically. Prisoners were now also transferred to Jordan, Yemen, Morocco, Algeria, and even Libya, Sudan, and Syria. These prisoners were rarely put on trial and the transfers were motivated largely by a desire to extract information from the detainees by any means necessary. Fifty-three documented cases of extraordinary rendition took place between September 2001 and February 2008; only one prisoner specifically said he had not been tortured. Of the sixteen men who were released, eight claimed they were tortured and/or mistreated while in foreign custody; one died within weeks of being released. Nineteen of the rendered men have not been heard from since they disappeared.

Philip Bobbitt, a leading American constitutional scholar, pointed out that the policy of extraordinary renditions "outsources our crimes, which puts us at the mercy of anyone who can expose us, makes us dependent on some of the world's most unsavory actors and abandons accountability. It is an approach we associate with crime families, not with great nations."

Brad Garrett is a former FBI special agent who obtained uncoerced confessions from two of the most high-profile Islamist terrorists in American history: Ramzi Yousef, who bombed the World Trade Center in 1993, and Mir Aimal Kasi, who shot and killed two CIA employees outside the Agency's headquarters the same year. Garrett dismisses the idea that useful intelligence can be garnered by depositing suspects in countries where they are tortured. "The whole idea that you would send anyone to some other country to obtain the intel you want is ludicrous," he said. "If we want the intel there are approaches that will render the information without torture. The problem is that someone in the U.S. government became convinced that torture is the way to go, and so if we are not allowed to do it, then send them to someplace where torture is sanctioned."

Robert Dannenberg, who ran operations for the CIA's Counterterrorist Center (CTC) from the summer of 2003 until late 2004, says that the critics of the rendition program should consider the effects that the fear of rendition has had on members of al-Qaeda and allied groups: "Are they looking over their shoulder because they don't know whether they're going to get a hood thrown over their head at any given moment of the day and get carried off to vanish? And the answer we got back for that question was, yes, that this is having a real chilling effect in the jihadists." Dannenberg points out that the climate of the times was also important. "If you really want to understand the mentality of the Agency and its CTC particularly at the time, it was all about making sure 9/11 never happens again. We had absolutely clear instruction from the president of the United States, and from the Congress, frankly, do whatever it takes to make sure it never happens again, and that was the mindset. And we felt that the rendition program was an important element in the make-sure-it-never-happens-again category."

Dannenberg says that the Justice Department produced legal guidance that the renditions were lawful, something that was important to him and his peers: "A lot of us had been around the block a few times performing that type of a mission for the executive and the legislative branch of our government, and then had later been hung out to dry. So to the extent that we could get assurance from the lawful authorities that what we were doing was legal and in line with the mission we'd been given, then we wanted to seek that reassurance." CIA officials even bought professional liability insurance to pay for their legal bills if they were indicted or had to have a lawyer represent them before Congress, in case their participation in operations such as the rendition program came back to haunt them, as the Abu Omar case in Milan was to do for some two dozen CIA employees.

Milan's slate-gray skies glower over the city in both summer and winter, and charmless skyscrapers dominate the skyline of the financial, media, and fashion capital of Italy. It's an unlikely setting for the operatic tale of Abu Omar's CIA kidnappers and their nemesis, Deputy Chief Prosecutor Armando Spataro. Spataro launched the first-ever criminal case against American officials over an extraordinary rendition, but he was hardly a bleeding-heart Euro-liberal. A prosecutor for more than three decades, he had put droves of drug traffickers, mafia dons, and terrorists behind bars. Spataro had been building a potential terrorism case against Abu Omar for months before his kidnapping; as a result of his investigation, a number of Abu Omar's acquaintances were convicted of terrorism offenses and in 2005 Abu Omar himself was indicted in absentia on charges that he had been recruiting fighters to go to Iraq. But his sudden disappearance into the bowels of Egypt's prisons had set back Spataro's probe dramatically.

The prosecutor also didn't appreciate being lied to—American officials had let it be known around Milan that Abu Omar had likely fled to the Balkans. It didn't take Spataro long to get past this smoke screen and even track down an eyewitness to the abduction. But the bulk of his case would revolve around a rookie mistake made by the kidnappers: using cell phones, and unencrypted ones at that. Spataro's investigators reviewed the records from three Italian cell phone companies with relay towers in the vicinity of where the Egyptian militant had disappeared and ran them through a commercial data-crunching program. Of the more than ten thousand cell phones in use during a three-hour window around the time of the kidnapping, seventeen were in constant communication with each other. The investigators also determined that soon after the abduction, some of those cell phones' users traveled to Aviano Air Base, a major American installation several hours east of Milan.

The suspicious cell phones had been used to make calls to the American consulate in Milan and to numbers in Virginia (where the CIA is headquartered). The phones, most registered under bogus names, had also been used to make many calls to prominent hotels in Milan—hotels where, the Italian investigators found, a dozen Americans had stayed in the weeks before the kidnapping. They had registered under addresses in the Washington, D.C., area. And their movements matched those of the suspicious cell phones. Over the course of several weeks the Americans had blown more than one hundred thousand dollars on easily traceable credit cards at hotels such as the ultra-fancy Principe di Savoia, which offers a special room-service menu for dogs. Others took side trips to Venice, where they stayed at the five-star Danieli and Sofitel hotels.

Next, Spataro's investigators began reviewing records from Italian air-traffic control, NATO, and the main European air-traffic facility in Brussels. They discovered that a ten-seat jet had departed from the Aviano base a few hours after Abu Omar was abducted and flew to Ramstein Air Base in Germany. An hour after it landed, an Executive Gulfstream with the tail number N85VM departed Ramstein for Cairo, a jet that was owned by Phillip Morse, a partner in the Boston Red Sox and one of a number of individuals whose planes were occasionally rented by the CIA.

One of the suspicious cell phones had been used to make hundreds of calls in the vicinity of both the Milan residence and the country house of the CIA's station chief in Milan, Robert Lady. Armed with a warrant, Spataro's investigators searched Lady's country house in June 2005 and found that he'd gone on a ten-day trip to Cairo a week after Abu Omar's abduction. The investigators also found surveillance photos of Abu Omar taken on the street where he was abducted.

In February 2007, Abu Omar was finally released from his Egyptian jail. "Without the human rights and media campaign, I would still be in prison," he said. When the Abu Omar kidnapping case went to trial in Milan, as expected none of the indicted CIA officials showed up. All of the officials were found guilty in absentia in 2009 and were sentenced to prison terms of up to eight years.

The torture of Abu Omar was just one of many cases in the U.S. conduct of the "war on terror" that was at odds with America's own legal traditions and international law and was part of a larger pattern in which the United States ceded the moral high ground in an often futile, counterproductive, and extralegal effort to protect itself. The president's lawyers wrote briefs that allowed the government to abuse and coerce prisoners in ways that amounted to torture. Bush's lawyers also ruled that prisoners in American detention were not to be accorded the protections of the Geneva Convention, international standards of conduct that the Eisenhower administration had first signed on to.

Many key decisions about the conduct of the war on terror were made in secret by Cheney and Defense Secretary Donald Rumsfeld. The pair's close working relationship went back decades to 1969, when Rumsfeld had hired the future vice president to be his assistant in the Nixon White House. On November 10, 2001, Cheney chaired a small group at the White House that authorized the president to detain anyone who had "engaged in, aided or abetted, or conspired to commit acts of international terrorism." Those detainees were not presumed to be innocent nor were they entitled to a public trial.

In a portent of the dominance that Cheney would wield over policy making in the Bush administration, Secretary of State Colin Powell and National Security Advisor Condoleezza Rice only found out about this decision after Bush and Cheney had met for their weekly private lunch on November 13, during which Cheney had given the president the four-page text of the detention directive to sign. Powell, who would be the official who would have to deal most directly with the leaders of the four dozen nations whose citizens would end up at Guantánamo, learned about this decision from CNN. "What the hell just happened?" Powell exclaimed to a colleague when he watched the report. The military order titled "Detention, Treatment, and Trial of Certain Non-Citizens in the War Against Terrorism" was news even to the Joint Chiefs of the military.

In December 2001, faced with the problem of where to house prisoners as the Taliban fell, the administration alighted on the idea of holding them at Guantánamo Bay, a naval base the U.S. had leased from Cuba since 1903. As Rumsfeld put it on December 27, 2001, "I would characterize Guantánamo Bay, Cuba, as the least worst place we could have selected." Guantánamo was attractive to administration officials because they believed it placed the detainees outside the reach of American laws, such as the right to appeal their imprisonment, yet it was only ninety miles off the coast of Florida, so it was accessible to the various three-letter agencies that would need to travel there to extract information from what was believed to be a population of hundreds of dangerous terrorists. But as the constitutional scholar Philip Bobbitt points out, the notion that Guantánamo was not subject to American laws simply because the territory was a long-term lease from Cuba was a flimsy and Jesuitical interpretation of the law: "The whole theory of the U.S. Constitution is that it applies laws to the acts of the State."

On January 9, 2002, two days before prisoners arrived for the first time at Guantánamo from Afghanistan, John Yoo, a thirty-four-year-old lawyer in the White House Office of Legal Counsel, circulated a draft memorandum to Bush officials that would provide much of the legal reasoning for the administration's future actions concerning the detention and interrogation of prisoners. Yoo, a former law professor and clerk to Supreme Court Justice Clarence Thomas, concluded that neither the Taliban nor al-Qaeda were entitled to prisoner-of-war status, or the protections of the Geneva Convention. Yoo reasoned that al-Qaeda was a stateless entity not protected by Geneva and that the Taliban ran a "failed state," which meant that their treaty rights could be ignored. Much of Yoo's reasoning made little sense. The concept of a "failed state" wasn't recognized by international law. Also, Afghanistan was a signatory to the Geneva Convention, and while the United States had not officially recognized the Taliban government, U.S. officials had met with Taliban officials on many occasions before 9/11 and had treated them as the de facto government of Afghanistan. In addition, there were no clauses in the Geneva Convention allowing states to unilaterally opt out of any of its provisions. And Article 3 of the Convention banned "humiliating and degrading treatment" of prisoners even in the cases of conflicts that were not between two states. The Geneva Convention plainly stated that all prisoners in *any* type of conflict were given certain rights.

William Taft IV, a patrician lawyer who was a great-grandson of President Taft and had served in Republican administrations going back to Nixon, submitted the State Department's response to Yoo's memorandum. Taft described Yoo's reasoning as "seriously flawed," "procedurally impossible," and "unsound." Taft pointed out, "In previous conflicts, the United States has dealt with tens of thousands of detainees without repudiating its obligations under the [Geneva] Convention." (Four years later the Supreme Court would endorse this elementary point when it granted Geneva protections to all prisoners held in American custody.)

But it was Yoo's arguments that would win the day. On February 7, 2002, Bush signed an executive order endorsing Yoo's opinion that the Geneva Convention did not apply to al-Qaeda and asserting that the Taliban were "unlawful combatants." Bobbitt, who had served in Democratic and Republican administrations going back to President Carter, made an acute observation about the contorted policy implications that flowed from the Bush administration's decision to treat prisoners as "unlawful combatants" who could also be prosecuted for crimes. "Like prisoners of war, these persons may be held indefinitely without formal charge. Like criminals, they can be tried and sentenced for planning or carrying out acts of violence for which soldiers are not prosecuted."

Given the fog of propaganda surrounding the Guantánamo prisoners—whom Rumsfeld described on a well-publicized visit to the base on January 27, 2002, as "among the most dangerous, best-trained, vicious killers on the face of the earth"—it may be surprising to learn that only some 5 percent of all the detainees held at Guantánamo were ever apprehended by U.S. forces to begin with. Why is that? Almost all of the prisoners there were turned over to American forces by foreigners, some with an ax to grind, or more often for a hefty bounty or reward. After U.S. forces invaded Afghanistan in late 2001, a reward of five thousand dollars or more was given to Pakistanis and Afghans for each detainee turned over. While rewards can be a valuable law enforcement tool, they have never in the past absolved law enforcement authorities of the necessity of corroborating the information that motivated the reward. But the U.S. military accepted the uncorroborated allegations of the award claimants with little independent investigation.

As a result of the fact that many in Guantánamo were either foot soldiers for the Taliban or innocents swept up in the fog of war, FBI Special Agent Daniel Coleman, who was arguably the most knowledgeable person in the U.S. government about al-Qaeda, says as a source of information the Guantánamo camp was a bust: "I never saw anything useful." Coleman wasn't the only FBI veteran who felt this way. Michael Rolince, a top FBI counterterrorism official, says, "I don't recall any information that was relevant [to my office] coming out of Guantánamo."

Guantánamo was also a bust as a place to bring terrorists to justice. By the time the Obama administration came into office seven years after the prison had opened, of the some eight hundred detainees sent to Guantánamo, the government had convicted only three prisoners. One was David Hicks, an Australian who plea-bargained his way out. Another was Salim Hamdan, bin Laden's driver, whom the prosecution had portrayed as some sort of big deal within al-Qaeda, but when it came to his sentencing he was given time served plus five months. The Hamdan case was ridiculous on its face; at the end of World War II, Hitler's driver was not tried as if he were a senior Waffen SS officer. Self-confessed al-Qaeda operative Ali Hamza al-Bahlul was convicted of conspiracy, solicitation to commit murder, and providing material support for terrorism in November 2008 and was sentenced to life. But these three cases represented a successful prosecution rate of less than 0.5 percent at the prison camp.

And Guantánamo was a place where American interrogators in at least one case tortured an al-Qaeda member to the point he was no longer prosecutable in any U.S. court. This was not the conclusion of a liberal advocacy organization but of a senior Pentagon official, Susan Crawford. Crawford was a retired judge who had served as general counsel for the U.S. Army under President Reagan and was appointed to oversee the military commission process at Guantánamo by the Bush administration. In January 2009, Crawford said that the cumulative effects of sustained isolation, sleep deprivation, nudity, and prolonged exposure to cold on the Saudi prisoner Mohammed al-Qahtani met the legal definition of torture. Crawford also said that this treatment had threatened to kill Qahtani and as a result of this abuse she could not refer his case for prosecution.

Qahtani had tried to enter the United States at the airport in Orlando, Florida, in the summer of 2001. Given the fact that lead hijacker Mohammed Atta was probably waiting for him outside the airport, Qahtani was likely to be the twentieth hijacker. But he was turned back by a savvy immigration official who was suspicious of the fact that Qahtani spoke no English, had very little money, and was traveling on a one-way ticket.

Qahtani was later detained in Afghanistan and sent to Guantánamo. At one point there he was interrogated for forty-eight days, more or less continuously, between November 23, 2002, and January 11, 2003. Loud music and white noise were played to prevent him from sleeping. Qahtani was forced to perform dog tricks and often exposed to low temperatures. At a certain point his body started closing down and he was given drugs and enemas so that the interrogations could continue. An FBI official noted in a letter to the Pentagon in June 2004 that Qahtani began "evidencing behavior consistent with extreme psychological trauma (talking to non-existent people, reporting hearing voices, crouching in a cell covered with a sheet for hours on end)."

It should have been obvious that using coercive interrogation techniques on Qahtani was not going to yield much. Anyone with the most superficial understanding of al-Qaeda would have understood that Qahtani, as one of the "muscle" hijackers, might have known a great deal about the training regime at al-Qaeda's camps in Afghanistan, but that would be the extent of his knowledge. Until the last moments of the operation, the muscle hijackers didn't even know what the targets were on 9/11, let alone the outlines of other al-Qaeda plots, nor did they have much contact with the leaders of the terrorist organization. The abuse of Qahtani produced little valuable intelligence and, in the end, meant that he would not stand trial for his peripheral role in the 9/11 attacks.

Critics of Guantánamo compared it to a gulag. This, of course, was nonsensical. The Soviet gulags killed millions through starvation, executions, and forced labor. The issue at Guantánamo was not, generally speaking, the problem of the prisoners' treatment. The real issue was that many of the prisoners at Guantánamo were innocent; were held for years without explanation, some in solitary confinement and were unable to see lawyers during the first three years that the prison operated. Their very presence at the facility was kept a secret for years because the military would not release the names of detainees until April 2006. Such forced disappearances were human rights violations that the United States had in the past condemned, whether committed by right- or left-wing dictatorships.

Prisoners at Guantánamo faced trial before "military commissions," a legal concept that many Americans probably assumed was similar to the court-martial system for U.S. servicemen or foreign soldiers captured on the battlefield accused of all manner of crimes, including war crimes. In fact, a military commission is a very different proceeding than a court-martial, which gives defendants many of the same kind of rights that an American civilian trial entitles them to. In the military commission system the accused was not able to see all of the evidence against him, and "evidence" obtained by coercion and hearsay was admissible in the proceedings.

In June 2006 the Supreme Court ruled in *Hamdan v. Rumsfeld* that the prisoners in Guantánamo were covered by the Article 3 protections of the Geneva Convention, which prohibit abusive or humiliating treatment of prisoners, something that the Bush administration had denied was the case for four years. It was a landmark decision of the court because it determined that even in a war no president was above the law. There was an irony here: Cheney and others on his staff had pushed hard to turn the presidency into a quasi-monarchical office and in so doing had ended up creating case law and precedent that would serve as an important brake on presidential powers for the foreseeable future.

On August 1, 2002, the White House lawyer John Yoo wrote a classified memo narrowly defining the crime of torture. According to Yoo, American interrogators could legally inflict pain short of that "accompanying serious physical injury such as organ failure, impairment of bodily function, or even death." Interrogators could also inflict mental pain, but only short of the point where it resulted "in significant psychological harm of significant duration, e.g., lasting for months or even years." The memo also concluded that inflicting "cruel, inhuman, or degrading" treatment on a prisoner wasn't necessarily something that American interrogators risked being prosecuted for. This seemed more the reasoning of a mob enforcer than an official in the Office of Legal Counsel, the White House's elite group of in-house lawyers, whose opinions guide the actions of the executive branch. (And if these were the opinions of a Harvard-educated, Supreme Court clerk turned law professor, as Yoo was, it is not entirely surprising that, as these ideas filtered down to soldiers in the rank and file, you ended up with the human pyramids of naked Iraqi prisoners at Abu Ghraib.)

Zein al-Abideen Mohamed Hussein, generally known as Abu Zubaydah, a Palestinian al-Qaeda logistician in his early thirties, was believed to be the highest-ranking member of the terror group to be taken alive in the first months after 9/11. That made him the subject of intense interest from American officials, since, by early 2002, there was no one as yet in custody who they believed could tell them about what form the next terror attack might take. As a result, many of the Bush administration's coercive interrogation techniques would first be applied to Abu Zubaydah.

In February 2002, the CIA station in Islamabad had learned that Abu Zubaydah was either in Lahore or Faisalabad, Pakistani cities with large populations in the east of the country. Intelligence officials also discovered Abu Zubaydah's cell phone number, but he used it only briefly and infrequently. Agency officials narrowed down to fourteen the possible locations where Abu Zubaydah might be living. At 2 A.M. on March 28, 2002, Pakistani army units hit all of them.

Abu Zubaydah was captured in a shoot-out in Faisalabad in which he was shot three times and critically wounded, losing a testicle in the firefight. So grave was Abu Zubaydah's condition that the CIA arranged for a leading surgeon from the Johns Hopkins Medical Center in Baltimore to fly to Pakistan to save his life and revive him to the point that he could be interrogated.

The interrogation of Abu Zubaydah set the stage for a carefully concealed battle between the FBI and elements of the CIA, backed by senior Bush administration officials, about how best to obtain information from suspected terrorists in American custody. The Bureau favored traditional rapport-building techniques, while some Agency and White House officials successfully pushed for coercive interrogations that verged on torture.

Abu Zubaydah was the first detainee to be placed in a secret overseas CIA prison, this one located in Thailand. There he was interrogated by Ali Soufan, one of the few Arabic-speaking FBI agents. Soufan softened up Abu Zubaydah by calling him "Hani," the childhood nickname his mother had used for him, a fact that the FBI agent had gathered from intelligence files. The approach started yielding quick results.

When Abu Zubaydah was shown a series of photos of al-Qaeda members by Soufan, he identified Khalid Sheikh Mohammed as "Mukhtar," meaning "the chosen" in Arabic. This was a key to unraveling one of the great mysteries of the attacks on New York and Washington, because in an al-Qaeda videotape recovered by American forces in Afghanistan a few months after 9/11, bin Laden had referred to a "Mukhtar" as someone who had some sort of a plan for a "tall building in America."

Soufan remembers puzzling over the bin Laden videotape. "It was annoying the shit out of me: Who is Mukhtar?" Abu Zubaydah had now identified Mukhtar to be Khalid Sheikh Mohammed. KSM had been known as a jihadist to U.S. authorities since 1993, when his name surfaced in the FBI's investigation of the World Trade Center bombing; but his central role in 9/11 came as a complete surprise to investigators.

Abu Zubaydah's confirmation of KSM's role in 9/11 was the single most important piece of information uncovered about al-Qaeda after the attacks on the Trade Center and Pentagon, and it was discovered during the course of a standard interrogation, without recourse to any form of coercion. Soufan recalled that Abu Zubaydah gave up the information about a week or so into his interrogation.

In the top-secret memoranda prepared by the White House's Office of Legal Counsel that authorized coercive interrogation techniques on Abu Zubaydah, he was variously described as "one of the highest ranking members of al-Qaeda," either the number three or four in the terror group, and as one of the planners of 9/11. In fact, within weeks of Abu Zubaydah's capture it became clear to at least some U.S. officials that he was not "al-Qaeda's chief of operations," as he had been publicly described by President Bush on June 6, 2002, but rather someone who was a logistician for militants in Pakistan on their way to training camps in Afghanistan. Daniel Coleman, the al-Qaeda expert at the FBI, says that Abu Zubaydah was simply a "travel agent; he wasn't a member of the inner circle" who would know about future operations, although he did know many members of al-Qaeda by virtue of his role as a "safe house keeper."

But believing that Abu Zubaydah was, in fact, a very big al-Qaeda fish, the White House lawyers authorized continuous sleep deprivation of up to 180 hours (one week), face slapping, extended nudity (including in front of females), dietary manipulation, confinement in cramped boxes, being slammed into a flexible wall and, of course, "the waterboard." The Office of Legal Counsel noted that these techniques were supposed to induce "a state of learned helplessness" in the detainee, who would then supposedly be putty in his interrogator's hands.

This piece of pseudoscience was the brainchild of James E. Mitchell, a retired psychologist who had worked with the military's SERE program (Survival, Evasion, Resistance and Escape), which is used to train American soldiers how to resist coercive interrogations, in the event that they are captured. In late 2001, Mitchell had coauthored a classified paper, "Recognizing and Developing Countermeasures to Al-Qaida Resistance to Interrogation Techniques." Mitchell had never conducted a real interrogation and so had no sense of what worked in the real world to elicit information from prisoners, but that did not stop him from helping to develop aggressive "Enhanced Interrogation Techniques" to be used on al-Qaeda detainees. Those techniques included confinement in a small box, stress positions, sleep deprivation for days, and waterboarding; one or more of these were later used on a total of twenty-eight detainees in American custody.

In mid-April, around ten days after Soufan had first started interrogating Abu Zubaydah, and over the FBI agent's vociferous objections, a CIA contractor stepped in to take over the interrogation. The FBI's standard, noncoercive techniques were jettisoned and Abu Zubaydah was stripped naked, deprived of sleep, subjected to loud noise and wide variations in temperature, and isolated from Soufan and other professional interrogators. The CIA contractor would now appoint a colleague to be Abu Zubaydah's "God," who would exercise total control over him. Soufan recalls: "Only one person and one person only from now on would have access to Abu Zubaydah. . . . The interrogation style was to go in and tell him, 'Tell me what I need to know.'"

The CIA contractor, a psychologist, had not interrogated anyone before, nor did he know anything about Islamist extremists or the Middle East. Soufan and the other professional interrogators with him watched the new approach unfold with astonishment. Soufan says that at one point Abu Zubaydah was sitting naked on the floor, and the CIA contractor insisted that his new experimental interrogation techniques were working on the prisoner:

"He's like, 'See! See! He tilted his head to the right: That means it's working. He's contemplating, he's thinking, because he tilted his head to the right—he's in agreement, he's going with the program.' . . . The contractor gets so excited he had a fucking boner.'" Abu Zubaydah then promptly fell asleep, snoring loudly.

Soufan objected to the CIA that Zubaydah was being subjected to "borderline torture," and "other people who were on the ground were going on the computers and shooting cables back to Washington" to complain about the new interrogation regime. By now Abu Zubaydah was no longer giving up any significant information.

Eventually, Soufan and the other professional interrogators were allowed to resume their questioning of Zubaydah. It was then that he described an Hispanic al-Qaeda wannabe whose physical description jibed with that of Jose Padilla, an American small-time hood who would later be arrested at Chicago's O'Hare Airport in May 2002, supposedly planning to detonate a radiological "dirty bomb" in the United States.

Scott Shumate, a psychologist working with the CIA who was present during Abu Zubaydah's interrogations, was so disgusted by the interrogation regime instituted by the Agency contractor that he flew home. On May 25, almost two months after he had first started interrogating Abu Zubaydah, so too did Ali Soufan, pulled out on the orders of his FBI superiors, who did not want the Bureau's agents to be involved in coercive interrogations.

Abu Zubaydah was later "waterboarded" eighty-three times by the CIA. This form of simulated drowning is generally considered torture, but none of it produced much in the way of useful information. General Michael Hayden, who served as CIA director in the last two years of the Bush administration, claimed that waterboarding Abu Zubaydah did yield key information that led to the capture of Ramzi Binalshibh, who had helped to oversee the 9/11 plot. But there may be a problem with Hayden's chronology because waterboarding wasn't authorized until August 1, 2002, four months *after* Zubaydah was arrested, and Binalshibh's name was by then already well-known to the U.S. government and indeed to the world, as he was the subject of a front-page story in the *New York Times* ten weeks *before* he was captured, on September 11, 2002.

In the end the multiple waterboardings of Abu Zubaydah provided no specific leads on any plots, although clearly his role as an al-Qaeda logistician did give him insights into the organization and its personnel. Dozens of videotapes of the CIA interrogations of Abu Zubaydah were destroyed in 2005 by a senior CIA official, Jose Rodriguez, who seems to have calculated that if the tapes ever entered the public domain they would have caused the same kind of outrage that greeted the Abu Ghraib prison abuse photographs from Iraq. It is one thing to read about abuses; it is quite another to watch them unfold in front of your eyes.

Following the Supreme Court *Hamdan* decision requiring the administration to respect the Geneva Convention's ban on "humiliating and degrading treatment" of prisoners, the CIA prohibited its operatives from waterboarding, a practice that the Agency had ended, in any event, in 2003. And on September 6, 2006, President Bush announced he was transferring 14 "high-value" prisoners—including al-Qaeda leaders like Khalid Sheikh Mohammed (KSM)—held in secret, overseas CIA prisons into Guantánamo. Some of the CIA's high-value prisoners had been held in jails in Poland and Romania; KSM was imprisoned at a Polish facility north of Warsaw at Stare Kiejkuty.

Officials of the International Committee of the Red Cross wrote a memo describing the treatment of detainees at these CIA prisons in Eastern Europe, which included continuous solitary confinement and incommunicado detention, waterboarding, prolonged stress standing, lengthy nudity, sleep deprivation, exposure to cold temperatures, and the prolonged use of handcuffs and shackles. The Red Cross concluded that, "The ill-treatment to which they were subjected while held in the CIA program, either singly or in combination, constituted torture."

A reader might be thinking that while the Bush administration's approaches to incarceration and interrogation were perhaps unsavory and even unlawful—still, weren't they necessary because of the large threat posed by al-Qaeda? To help answer that question, consider the case of Abu Jandal, who provided a vast amount of intelligence about al-Qaeda's inner workings immediately after the attacks on New York and Washington under no duress whatsoever.

A week after 9/11, FBI Special Agent Ali Soufan and Robert McFadden, an investigator from the Naval Criminal Investigative Service, interrogated Abu Jandal, who had served as bin Laden's chief bodyguard for years and was privy to many of his secrets. Abu Jandal, whose real name is Nasser Ahmad Nasser al-Bahri, had been jailed in a Yemeni prison since 2000. The two American investigators, who both spoke Arabic and had significant experience investigating al-Qaeda, used the "Informed Interrogator" approach on him while plying the diabetic bin Laden confidant with sugar-free cookies. Soufan recalls the cookies were a gesture that "kind of broke the ice." As a result Abu Jandal disgorged a great deal of information about the terror network. Soufan recalls that he "named dozens and dozens of people" in the organization.

The rich intelligence haul from Abu Jandal is confirmed by the official FBI summaries of his interrogations, covering the gamut from al-Qaeda's structure, leadership, membership, and training camps to its communication methods. The al-Qaeda insider also picked out eight of the 9/11 hijackers from photos and he identified ten members of bin Laden's security detail and described how they were armed with SAM-7 missiles, Russian PK machine guns, and rocket-propelled grenades. He also explained that the al-Qaeda leader usually traveled in a group of around a dozen bodyguards in a motorcade of three vehicles each containing a maximum of five armed guards. And the bin Laden confidant provided a richly detailed seven-page account of the various machine guns, mortars, mines, sniper rifles, and surface-to-air missiles possessed by al-Qaeda and the Taliban. None of this bonanza of timely intelligence was acquired using coercive measures, but all of it was especially valuable as Abu Jandal was the first al-Qaeda insider to explain the inner workings of the group during the period after bin Laden had moved his men to Afghanistan in 1996.

Contrast Abu Jandal's treatment and the wealth of information he quickly gave up with that of Khalid Sheikh Mohammed, the operational commander of the 9/11 attacks. When KSM finally goes on trial, the most potent challenge his lawyers will surely raise is that their client was waterboarded 183 times. In the mid-1980s, President Reagan's Justice Department prosecuted a group of police officers who had waterboarded prisoners; they were convicted and served long sentences.

The mistreatment of KSM was entirely unnecessary insofar as the 9/11 case was concerned. Before he was captured, KSM and his colleague Ramzi Binalshibh had laid out in great detail the entire 9/11 operation in a 2002 interview with Yosri Fouda, an Al Jazeera correspondent. Fouda's interviews resolved key questions that investigators still had about the plot—for instance, that United Flight 93, before it crashed into a field in Pennsylvania, was on its way to destroy the U.S. Capitol, rather than the White House. KSM and Binalshibh also explained how they had kept bin Laden informed about the timing of the attacks, and they discussed the coded correspondence they had conducted with Mohammed Atta, the lead 9/11 pilot, when he was living in the States.

The CIA provided detailed summaries of the interrogations of KSM and Binalshibh to the 9/11 Commission. There was little or no difference between the account that KSM and Binalshibh had freely volunteered to Fouda in the spring of 2002 and the version the commission published in its 2004 report. Nor was Fouda's reporting difficult to find: he hosted a documentary on Al Jazeera about KSM and Binalshibh and wrote a long piece in London's *Sunday Times* about the terror duo. By the time CIA officials started interrogating the pair, a full account of their 9/11 plotting was only a Google search away.

Following his arrest in Pakistan in 2003, KSM was taken to the secret CIA prison in northern Poland, where he initially proved resistant to interrogation, saying he would talk only when he was provided a lawyer. Following his defiance, KSM was subjected to a number of coercive interrogation techniques besides being waterboarded the 183 times: he was kept up for seven and a half days straight while diapered and shackled, and he was told that his kids, who were now being held in American custody, would be killed. KSM then provided a wealth of information about al-Qaeda's inner workings as well as details about past and future plots. In the words of the CIA's inspector general, "Khalid Shaykh Muhammad, an accomplished resistor, provided only a few intelligence reports prior to the use of the waterboard, and analysis of that information revealed that much of it was outdated, inaccurate or incomplete."

Over time, KSM would become so compliant that he would treat his interrogators to seminars on a wide variety of topics. A senior Agency official recalled that KSM "used to take great pride in holding lectures for us on the jihad . . . He'd come in; he'd say, 'Can we talk on Sunday? You know, I've got another idea I want to put in front of you guys.' Some of it was bullshit and a lot of it was sort of not operationally useful, but it reinforced the condition of him talking and sharing with us, which was really useful." In short, the waterboarding of KSM *worked*, but what did it really *reveal*?

Bush administration officials often asserted that coercive interrogation techniques, especially those used on KSM, had saved many American lives. After he left office, former vice president Dick Cheney vehemently defended the practices of the Bush administration, saying in February 2009, "If it hadn't been for what we did—with respect to the terrorist surveillance program, or enhanced interrogation techniques for high-value detainees, the Patriot Act, and so forth—then we would have been attacked again."

In a speech he gave three months later at the right-wing American Enterprise Institute (AEI) in Washington, D.C., Cheney said, "In top-secret meetings about enhanced interrogations, I made my own beliefs clear. I was and remain a strong proponent of our enhanced interrogation program." Cheney gave this speech the same day that President Obama was giving his own major speech on his administration's revamped detention and interrogation policies just a couple of miles away at the National Archives. Giving such a dueling policy speech was something of a first for a just-stepped-down vice president, a role that is generally supposed to entail a comfortably obscure retirement spent fly-fishing and attending rubber-chicken fund-raisers. But Cheney did not go gently into that vice presidential night. At AEI, he amped up his usual sky-is-falling rhetoric, claiming that the coercive interrogations of al-Qaeda detainees had "prevented the violent death of thousands, if not hundreds of thousands, of innocent people."

This speech was essentially a remix of the arguments that Cheney had made in the run-up to the Iraq War: that if only ordinary American citizens had seen the top-secret information he had access to, they would be even more alarmed than he was. And the Bush administration had only prudently taken every measure necessary to keep Americans safe.

Hiding behind a wall of classification had been a quintessential Cheney trope. But that wall crumbled in August 2009 when the CIA released two secret documents that assessed the information derived from its "high value detainees," which showed that while al-Qaeda leaders like KSM had indeed provided information under duress to their American interrogators, the content of that information was less than earth-shattering. One of the CIA reports stated that "reporting from KSM has greatly advanced our understanding of al-Qa'ida's anthrax program," in particular about the role of a Malaysian scientist named Yazid Sufaat, who was recruited by al-Qaeda to research biological weapons. But what the CIA report did not say is that Sufaat was never able to buy or produce the right strain of anthrax suitable for a weapon. And so while KSM may have helped the CIA to understand something of al-Qaeda's anthrax program, either he had little understanding of the science of biological weapons or the Agency officials who wrote the report were also similarly handicapped. In fact, al-Qaeda's anthrax program was a dud that never produced anything remotely threatening, a point that the CIA report was silent on.

A piece of useful information that KSM did offer up to his CIA interrogators after he had been waterboarded concerned a man named Hambali who was the interface between al-Qaeda and its Southeast Asian affiliate, Jemaah Islamiyah. Hambali was the mastermind of the October 12, 2002, bombing of two nightclubs in Bali, which killed around two hundred people, many of them Western tourists. Former CIA director George Tenet says that KSM's information about Hambali led to the latter's capture in Thailand. In his memoir, Tenet writes that the coercive interrogation techniques used on KSM were necessary because "none of these successes would have happened if we had treated KSM like a white collar criminal—read him his Miranda rights and got him a lawyer who surely would have insisted his client simply shut up." Hambali's capture then also led to the arrest of more than a dozen Southeast Asian operatives slated for attacks against the U.S. homeland.

A 2005 top-secret memo by the White House Office of Legal Counsel released by the Obama administration pointed out that KSM had only given up his plans for the "Second Wave" of attacks on the United States after he had been subjected to "enhanced techniques," that is, waterboarding and the like. But did KSM's coerced interrogations really lead to any substantive plots against the American homeland being averted?

A fact sheet that the government released around the time that KSM was transferred out of his secret CIA prison to Guantánamo in 2006 offered details on the plots he had hatched against the United States:

> KSM launched several plots targeting the U.S. Homeland, including a plot in late 2001 to have . . . suicide operatives hijack a plane over the Pacific and crash it into a skyscraper on the U.S. West Coast; a plan in early 2002 to send al-Qa'ida operatives to conduct attacks in the U.S.; and a plot in early 2003 to employ a network of Pakistanis . . . to smuggle explosives into New York and to target gas stations, railroad tracks, and a bridge in New York.

While this "Second Wave" of attacks all sounded very frightening, there is no indication that these plots were ever more than just talk. The chances of success, for instance, of al-Qaeda's plan to attack the skyscraper on the West Coast—since identified as the 73-story Library Tower in Los Angeles—were described by KSM in one court document to be "dismal." KSM also explained in the same document that the "Second Wave" of al-Qaeda attacks on the United States was put on the "back burner" after 9/11.

A CIA inspector general's report on al-Qaeda detainees stated that KSM "provided information that helped lead to the arrests of terrorists including Sayfullah Paracha and his son Uzair Paracha, businessmen who Khalid Shaykh Muhammad planned to use to smuggle explosives into the United States; Saleh Almari, a sleeper operative in New York; and Majid Khan, an operative who could enter the United States easily and was tasked to research attacks [redacted]. Khalid Shaykh Muhammad's information also led to the investigation and prosecution of Iyman Faris, the truck driver arrested in early 2003 in Ohio." However, based on a review of KSM's plots aimed at the United States, the CIA inspector general "did not uncover any evidence that these plots were imminent."

The man identified by the CIA as "Saleh Almari, a sleeper operative in New York" whom KSM gave up to his interrogators was in fact Ali Saleh Kahlah al-Marri, who had been arrested on December 12, 2001, in Peoria, Illinois, a year and a half before KSM was captured, and was by then already imprisoned in a New York jail awaiting trial on credit card fraud charges. He was someone that the feds had already identified as being in contact with members of al-Qaeda. The Parachas are a father-and-son team; the former was arrested in Thailand in the summer of 2003 and was transferred to Guantánamo and has yet to face trial, while his son was convicted of providing "material support" to al-Qaeda in 2006. Majid Khan was arrested in Pakistan only four days after KSM was captured, suggesting that this lead came not from interrogations but from KSM's many computers and cell phones that were picked up when he was captured.

Of the terrorists, alleged and otherwise, cited by the CIA that KSM fingered during or after his coercive interrogations, only the Ohio truck driver Iyman Faris was an actual al-Qaeda foot soldier living freely in the United States with the serious intention to wreak havoc in America. However, he was not much of a competent terrorist: in 2003 he researched the feasibility of bringing down the Brooklyn Bridge by using a blowtorch to cut through its cables, an enterprise akin to demolishing the Empire State Building with a firecracker.

If this was the most threatening plot the United States could discover by waterboarding the most senior al-Qaeda member in American custody, it was thin stuff. And when the FBI director Robert Mueller was asked in 2008 if he was aware of any attacks on America that had been disrupted thanks to intelligence obtained through "enhanced techniques," Mueller replied: "I don't believe that has been the case." The CIA's inspector general arrived at a similar conclusion when he judged that: "it is difficult to determine conclusively whether enhanced interrogations have provided information critical to interdicting specific imminent attacks," which was the supposed standard necessary for the imposition of coercive measures on the al-Qaeda prisoners in the first place.

The putative intelligence gains made by the abusive interrogation techniques were easily outweighed by the damage they caused to the United States' moral standing, according to Admiral Dennis Blair, then the director of national intelligence, who wrote in April 2009, "These techniques have hurt our image around the world, the damage they have done to our interests far outweighed whatever benefits they gave us and they are not essential to our national security."

The U.S. government belatedly realized in 2006 that the CIA's treatment of KSM could seriously jeopardize the trial of the man who had planned the largest mass murder in American history. FBI and military interrogators known as the "Clean Team" started independently collecting the same information from KSM and other al-Qaeda members that they had previously given to the CIA, this time using standard rapport-building techniques. Still, legal experts have questioned whether the new interrogations can entirely remove the taint of the CIA's coerced confessions, as the al-Qaeda defendants may be able to draw on the legal doctrine known as the "fruit of the poisonous tree," that evidence found through unconstitutional means may not be introduced at trial. (In KSM's case this may be moot, as he has voluntarily admitted his role in 9/11 on a number of occasions.)

Might another approach have worked with KSM, which did not involve coercion? It's worth recalling not only that KSM had given Al Jazeera two days of interviews a year before his capture in which he laid out every detail of the 9/11 plot, but also that his nephew Ramzi Yousef had given a fulsome uncoerced confession to the FBI agent who arrested him about his role directing the 1993 Trade Center bombing. And the most well-informed American official about KSM's case was Frank Pellegrino, the FBI agent who had been tracking him since 1993, when he had wired several hundred dollars to his nephew in the run-up to the first Trade Center attack. Pellegrino did not get the chance to interrogate KSM, since by the time of his capture in 2003 such "high-value" detainees were in CIA custody, and the Bureau did not want anything to do with the Agency's coercive interrogations.

President Bush's extralegal approach to the war on terrorism was not only unnecessary and counterproductive, but it also helped to torpedo America's good reputation around the world. In a BBC survey in 2007, of the more than 26,000 people polled in twenty-five different countries, seven out of ten disapproved of the treatment of Guantánamo inmates, while half thought the United States played a mostly negative role in the world. The numbers were far worse in Muslim countries—including democratic ones that should have been natural American allies. According to another poll the same year, America's favorability rating stood at 9 percent in Turkey (down from 52 percent before September 11, 2001) and 29 percent in Indonesia (down from 75 percent before September 11). These low numbers were, in part, because of the widely held view in the Muslim world that the Bush administration kept preaching the virtues of democracy and human rights, but hypocritically reserved the right to ignore such principles when it suited its own purposes.

Chapter 8

Home Front: The First Bush Term

One by one we're hunting the killers down.

—President Bush on September 14, 2002, following the arrest of a group of Yemeni-Americans accused of being members of an al-Qaeda sleeper cell

On December 21, 2001, in Paris, Richard Reid attempted to board American Airlines Flight 63 to Miami. Reid, a six-foot-four British-Jamaican with an unkempt semi-Afro and a straggly beard, attracted considerable attention from security officers, particularly when they found a magazine he was carrying that showed a picture of Osama bin Laden. A small-time criminal and convert to Islam (a type that would become increasingly common among jihadist terrorists after 9/11), Reid was flagged as a potential troublemaker and he was extensively searched. That search did not turn up the bomb hidden in his ankle-high hiking boots and the next day Reid successfully boarded the same flight for Miami.

Reid, an al-Qaeda recruit, had instructed a friend to send an email to his mother after what he believed would be his certain death in which he told her, "What I am doing is part of the ongoing war between Islam and disbelief . . .

Forgive me for all the problems I have caused you both in life and death and don't be angry for what I have done."

Three hours into the flight, which was almost full with 184 passengers and fourteen crew members, Reid attempted to light his shoe bomb with matches. Passengers complained of a smoky smell and a flight attendant found Reid with one shoe in his lap, a fuse leading into the shoe, and a lit match. She tried grabbing Reid twice, but he pushed her to the floor each time, and she screamed for help. A second flight attendant tried to grab Reid and he bit one of her hands. Reid was disabled by passengers who tied him down with seat belts. It was later determined that Reid's shoe bomb was made with a high explosive that likely would have ripped a hole in the outside skin of the plane, bringing it down in the middle of the Atlantic and making any investigation into the resulting crash close to impossible. Reid told investigators that bombing a U.S. passenger jet during the Christmas season would have caused substantial damage to the American economy.

There was enough evidence of a possible second series of al-Qaeda attacks after 9/11 to merit the serious concern of the Bush administration. One of the possible perpetrators of that second wave was Zacarias Moussaoui, the French citizen who had attracted attention to himself in the summer of 2001 at a flight school in Minnesota and was already in jail during the attacks on Washington and New York. While Moussaoui was often portrayed as the "twentieth hijacker," in fact he had nothing to do with that operation but had instead been tasked by al-Qaeda to go to the States to participate in some way in the next round of attacks.

Another al-Qaeda plant was Ali Saleh Kahlah al-Marri, the citizen of Qatar who had arrived in the United States on September 10, 2001, on a student visa, ostensibly to study computer programming at Bradley University in Peoria, Illinois. Following 9/11, at least 1,200 mostly Muslim men were detained in a post–9/11 dragnet that caught almost no really threatening person except Marri, who was questioned a month after the attacks and again in December 2001. After Marri was questioned for the second time, the FBI searched his laptop and found that he had conducted extensive research on chemical weapons, including the manufacture of hydrogen cyanide. Investigators concluded that the highly technical information found on his computer "far exceeds the interest of a merely curious individual." Marri had also stored on his computer the usual panoply of bin Laden lectures typical of an al-Qaeda acolyte. At the time of his arrest Marri had set up multiple fake credit card accounts. He was charged with credit card fraud and lying to federal investigators and was jailed.

Two years later, Marri was named an enemy combatant by the Bush administration and was incarcerated in a Navy brig in Charleston, South Carolina, where he was then held in solitary confinement for almost six years. Khalid Sheikh Mohammed (KSM), who was captured in March 2003, appears to have been the source of some of the information that led the Bush administration to treat Marri as an enemy combatant. Marri had trained at al-Qaeda camps in Afghanistan beginning in 1998, and during the summer of 2001 he met with KSM and volunteered for some kind of operation in the States. Marri then traveled to Dubai, where he met Mustafa al-Hawsawi, the paymaster for much of the 9/11 operation, who gave him ten thousand dollars. Marri arrived in the States the day before the attacks on New York and Washington along with his wife and five kids, good cover that pegged him as a family man.

In the following months Marri placed calls from payphones in the Peoria area to members of al-Qaeda, sometimes traveling as far as 150 miles from his home to elude detection. Ali Soufan, the Arabic-speaking FBI agent, remembers that Marri was placing calls to Hawsawi, the 9/11 paymaster: "He was using a payphone outside the motel where he was staying with his family to call Hawsawi. There is one person that called Hawsawi before; it was Mohammed Atta." Having denied the charges against him for years, Marri finally entered a plea agreement in April 2009 in which he admitted his deep ties to al-Qaeda.

Marri was not the only al-Qaeda foot soldier planning attacks on Americans in the wake of 9/11. The Ohio trucker Iyman Faris was born in Pakistani Kashmir in 1969. As a young man Faris had fought against the Soviets in Afghanistan and after a spell fighting in Bosnia he slipped into the States in 1994 where he promptly married an American, Geneva Bowling. Five years later, by now an American citizen, Faris divorced his wife. Around this time, on a trip to Pakistan he met with KSM, who recruited him to work for al-Qaeda.

Always dreaming up the next terror spectacular, KSM tasked Faris with severing the cables on the Brooklyn Bridge, an idea he got from watching the movie *Godzilla*. Faris explored the idea of bringing down the bridge by cutting its suspension cables with an acetylene torch. In February 2003, Faris concluded that this harebrained scheme was not going to work and via a Baltimore contact told KSM "the weather is too hot," unsubtle code for nixing the operation. He was detained on March 20, 2003, and for six weeks Faris's arrest was kept secret, during which time he gave investigators a considerable amount of information about al-Qaeda (without any coercive measures being applied).

While Reid, Marri, and Faris were genuine al-Qaeda recruits, many of the terrorism cases during the first Bush term did not amount to very much. A critical element of the Bush administration's approach to the threat after 9/11 was that there were large numbers of al-Qaeda "sleeper cells" in the United States. The week after the attacks on New York and Washington, three North African Muslim men living in Detroit were arrested on suspicion of being such a cell. Attorney General John Ashcroft said the Detroit cell members were "suspected of having knowledge of the Sept. 11 attacks." Much of the evidence against the men, however, had been supplied by a known con man facing a prison sentence who was hoping to cut a deal for himself.

U.S. officials found a videotape of a trip the "Detroit cell" had made to Disneyland and became convinced that it was a "casing tape" for a future terrorist attack. Prosecutors said that the Arabic narration on the tape described Disneyland as "a rising cemetery," but the translator for the defense said the correct translation was, "What a lovely view!" Ron Hansen, a reporter for the *Detroit News* who covered the case, explained that the Disneyland video didn't look like a terrorist casing tape: "I could never get past the fact that the tape looked just like a tourist tape. The Disneyland ride, for example, was a lengthy queue, people just making their way to the ride. The camera occasionally pans to look at the rocks on the wall, made to look like an Indiana Jones movie, and after several minutes the camera, it pans across and shows a trash can momentarily, and then continues off to look into the crowd. The [government] expert basically said that, by flashing on that trash can for a moment, the people who are part of this conspiracy to conduct these kinds of terrorist operations—they would understand what this is all about: how to locate a bomb in Disneyland in California."

The case became even more bizarre when officials also charged that the members of the Detroit sleeper cell were planning to attack a U.S. Air Force base in Turkey. Drawings of the base, discovered in a diary, were later determined to be the demented doodles of a Yemeni who variously believed he was Yemen's minister of defense and Saudi Arabia's president and who had committed suicide a year before any of the accused had arrived in Detroit. Eventually, the terrorism convictions of the three North African men were overturned.

The Detroit case was emblematic of a number of the "terrorism" cases during the first Bush term, which often followed the trajectory of a tremendous initial trumpeting by the government only to collapse, or to be revealed as something less than earth-shattering, when the details emerged months later. Take Chaplain James Yee, the supposed al-Qaeda spy at Guantánamo who turned out to be cheating not on his country but on his wife. Or Brandon Mayfield, the unfortunate Oregon lawyer busted for his alleged role in the 2004 Madrid bombings. Mysterious Spanish documents found in Mayfield's possession later turned out to be his son's homework.

An iconic image of the war against the Taliban was the interview of "American Taliban" John Walker Lindh by CNN after Lindh was captured in northern Afghanistan in December 2001. Lying on a stretcher, heavily bearded and caked in dirt, Lindh explained in a vaguely Middle Eastern accent, "I was in [Pakistan's] North-West Frontier Province. The people there in general have a great love for the Taliban. So I started to read some of the literature of the scholars and my heart became attached." That an American citizen would admit just months after the 9/11 attacks that his "heart had became attached" to the Taliban made him, needless to say, the object of a great deal of hostility in the United States; many Americans wanted Lindh to be tried for treason.

Despite initial claims by Attorney General John Ashcroft that Lindh would be charged with conspiracy to kill Americans, the eventual plea agreement that the government reached with him was only that he had provided "services" to the Taliban contravening the 1999 Clinton executive order that had slapped sanctions on them. What services had Lindh provided to the Taliban? Himself, it turned out. Lindh had refused offers by al-Qaeda leaders to take part in operations against Americans and there was no proof that he was involved in any militant activity other than training at a Taliban camp, but that was enough to convict him of providing "services" to the Taliban.

Lindh's conviction on the charge that he had provided his own services to the Taliban set an important precedent for a number of cases in the "war on terror." The same charge of providing their own services to a terrorist group would also be the undoing of a group of Yemeni-Americans living in upstate New York who traveled to Afghanistan on something of a jihad vacation in 2001. A year later the group would be portrayed by the Bush administration with great fanfare as the first genuine al-Qaeda sleeper cell discovered in the United States since 9/11.

The group of six Yemeni-Americans making up the supposed cell lived in the small, decaying Rust Belt town of Lackawanna, New York, where they had grown up as American as Big Macs. One dated and married a high school cheerleader, and many of them played soccer on the high school team. But in 2000 they fell under the spell of Kamal Derwish, a charismatic, deeply religious, fellow Yemeni-American, who told them stirring tales of derring-do about his role in the early-1990s war between the Bosnian Muslims and Serbs. Over late-night bull sessions fueled by pizza, Derwish led the group of very ordinary men—telemarketers, delivery men, and car salesmen—in discussions about the plight of Muslims around the world; gradually they came to embrace a militant form of Islam.

Derwish eventually persuaded the six men that they should go to Afghanistan to see the Taliban in action and deepen their commitment to jihad by attending training camps there. Under the cover that they were traveling to Pakistan as part of Tablighi Jamaat, a generally apolitical missionary organization with a large following in the Muslim world, Derwish and his buddies traveled to Afghanistan in two groups during the spring and summer of 2001.

At one of al-Qaeda's Afghan training camps, the men trained on M-16 rifles, RPGs, and AK-47s. During their training bin Laden and Zawahiri appeared at the camp to announce the merger of their organizations. One of the Lackawanna group, Sahim Alwan, a twenty-nine-year-old father of three, was asked by bin Laden how Americans felt about suicide operations. Alwan did not give the al-Qaeda leader the answer he was looking for: "We don't even think about it." Realizing that he was in well over his head, Alwan faked an ankle injury and finagled his way out of the camp. Eventually almost all of the Yemeni-Americans returned home to Lackawanna. They kept their training in Afghanistan a secret, pushing it to the back of their minds, and if they recalled it at all they remembered the bad food, the uncomfortable rigors of life at the camp—four of them had washed out of their training early—and the depth of hatred for the United States among al-Qaeda's recruits.

It was their bad luck that in the spring of 2002 a handwritten, anonymous letter arrived at the FBI office in Buffalo, New York, charging that terrorists had come to Lackawanna "for recruiting the Yemenite youth." When Sahim Alwan was asked by an FBI agent what he had done on his trip to Pakistan a year earlier, he lied and said he had gone only for religious instruction.

The FBI's investigation went into high gear during the summer of 2002 as the first anniversary of al-Qaeda's assaults on Washington and New York fast approached. One of the Lackawanna group, Mukhtar al-Bakri, was then traveling in the Middle East. On July 18 Bakri sent a mystifying email message home to a buddy in Lackawanna, subject "Big Meal," which was intercepted by the feds. The email said, "The next meal will be very huge. No one will be able to stand it." Bakri's friend wrote back, "Are you talking about a hamburger meal, or what?" The cryptic message about the "huge" meal was compounded by chatter picked up from Bakri that his "wedding" was fast approaching. As the word *wedding* was believed to be code for an impending al-Qaeda attack, this raised the Lackawanna investigation to a matter that President Bush was now being regularly briefed on.

The decision was made to arrest Bakri, who was now in Bahrain. But the wedding was not a code; on the first anniversary of the 9/11 attacks Bakri was arrested in his marital chamber, pulled from the tender caresses of his just-married teen bride. He soon admitted attending the Afghan training camp and his five friends were swiftly detained in the United States.

The Justice Department held a press conference to announce the disruption of an "al-Qaeda terrorist cell" and President Bush told journalists, "One by one, we're hunting the killers down." And in his January 2003 State of the Union address, Bush claimed that an al-Qaeda cell had been recently broken up in Buffalo, referring to the Lackawanna case. This was a reach. None of the Lackawanna Six was ever accused of planning an act of terrorism nor had they ever joined al-Qaeda. A New York Police Department report concluded, "There was never any evidence of any operational targeting or planning in the United States." But the Lackawanna Six had certainly exercised very poor judgment to travel to an al-Qaeda training camp after the organization had already bombed the American embassies in Africa and the USS *Cole*.

In the charged atmosphere of the first years after 9/11, it was obvious to the lawyers for the Lackawanna Six that the "material support" they had offered to al-Qaeda in the form of their own "services" was a charge that would stick, and there was always a possibility that the government could play the "enemy combatant" card against them, which would mean their clients could be held indefinitely without charge. Eventually all six took plea bargains and received prison terms of between seven and ten years.

The ringleader of the group, Kamal Derwish, had fled to Yemen, although his escape would prove short-lived. On November 3, 2002, Derwish was incinerated in a CIA drone strike on the car he was riding in across the Yemeni desert, along with one of the USS *Cole* conspirators. He was the first American citizen to be killed in a U.S. drone strike.

Many jihadist terrorism cases during the first Bush term had no real connection to al-Qaeda at all but simply involved Americans inspired by bin Laden's ideas. Some involved feckless wannabes, such as the Portland Six, a group of mostly African-American converts to Islam from Oregon who tried to join the Taliban or al-Qaeda immediately after 9/11. They were not subtle. Only two weeks after the attacks on New York and Washington, members of the group—several sporting Taliban-style turbans and long robes—were spotted shooting off automatic weapons at a gravel pit in the Portland area. It's hard to imagine a performance more likely to garner the attention of the feds. The group then traveled to China in 2002 in a vain bid to cross from there into Afghanistan, but were detained by Chinese officials and arrested after their return to the States. None of them had gotten within a thousand miles of Afghanistan.

During the summer of 2004, as Bush campaigned for a second term, the outlines of what seemed to be another wave of serious al-Qaeda attacks on the East Coast appeared, this one linked to an al-Qaeda operative, Dhiren Barot. Barot, a British convert from Hinduism to Islam, was, like many converts, more zealous than most of his coreligionists and had volunteered at age twenty to fight against the Indian army in Kashmir and later worked in Taliban-controlled Afghanistan in the late 1990s as an instructor at a military training camp.

U.S. investigators believe that bin Laden tasked Barot to conduct surveillance of financial and Jewish targets in New York and Washington. Barot then applied to a college in New York, which gave him some plausible cover for casing financial targets on the East Coast between August of 2000 and April of 2001. Those targets included the New York Stock Exchange, the Citigroup building, and the International Monetary Fund and World Bank in Washington. Barot's casing notes were quite detailed, running to eighteen dense pages about the structure of the buildings; the locations of toilets where bombs might be assembled; and the likely sources of shrapnel that could amplify the effects of a bomb blast. Barot then sent his casing documents on to al-Qaeda Central in Pakistan.

Those casing notes were discovered in an al-Qaeda safe house in Pakistan during the summer of 2004. The discovery of the documents caused something close to panic in Washington. Frances Fragos Townsend, Bush's top counterterrorism adviser, recalls being briefed by the acting CIA director, John McLaughlin, someone not given to hyperbole: "I'll never forget McLaughlin saying to me, he had looked at these casing reports, and said to me, they were as good if not better than anything he had ever seen done, including from the most senior CIA case officers. We realized that they had clearly been in these buildings, and they clearly had the intention to do it, and the buildings were vulnerable, and so there was a scramble then, before any of this became public, to talk to the folks in the financial sector, particularly the folks in the buildings that had been cased. We had enough to know to be very concerned about it, and not enough to know if the plot was still active."

But a careful reading of the casing notes showed that they were "little more than a graduate school report on some famous buildings," in the words of Michael Sheehan, who was then in charge of counterterrorism for the New York Police Department (NYPD). And, most importantly, the reconnaissance of the financial landmarks had all taken place *before* 9/11. Sheehan remembers that he and David Cohen, the head of intelligence at NYPD and a three-decade veteran of the CIA, examined the casing documents carefully. "We're like, 'Holy shit, this is the real deal.' Then we went back and reread it, and the more I looked at it, the more I looked at Cohen and said, 'Wait a second. This *sounds* really ominous. But this could be done by any jackass having a cup of coffee at a Starbucks across from the Citigroup building, and on the Internet.' . . . Within an hour after reading it, I knew this was one guy, educated, who did a pre-9/11 reconnaissance of these buildings, and the information was five years old."

That did not stop Secretary of Homeland Security Tom Ridge from going public with specific warnings about the four landmark buildings in Washington, New York, and New Jersey. Sheehan was "flabbergasted," as not only were the warnings completely unnecessary but Barot wasn't yet in custody and surely would flee the United Kingdom where he was then living. But Barot did not flee and was arrested by British police two days later.

Barot's arrest resulted in the Department of Homeland Security elevating the threat level to the orange "high" risk category for the financial services sectors in New York City, northern New Jersey, and Washington, D.C., on August 1, 2004, despite the fact that there was absolutely no indication that the plot was anything other than historical. The raising of the unnecessary alert to orange in the final months of the tight presidential campaign between Bush and John Kerry obviously did not hurt the "strong on terrorism" president.

Bush's homeland security adviser Fran Townsend says that she "knew to be concerned that our motives would be questioned, and I worked incredibly hard to get hold of the Kerry campaign and brief them before it went public. I insisted that we reach out to them, that they not get blindsided, because I knew Kerry was going to be out in public and was going to get asked about it. I did not want him to say, 'I don't know what you're talking about.'"

The alert was lowered only on November 10, a week after the election campaign was over.

Chapter 9

Building the Case for War with Iraq

How are nations ruled and led into war? Politicians lie to journalists and then believe those lies when they see them in print.

—Austrian journalist Karl Kraus,
explaining the causes of World War I

You are entitled to your own opinion, but you are not entitled to your own facts.

—Senator Patrick Moynihan

In the spring of 1997, I traveled to eastern Afghanistan for CNN to produce Osama bin Laden's first television interview, during the course of which the Saudi militant told a Western audience for the first time that he was launching a holy war against the United States. After the formal interview was over, the correspondent Peter Arnett asked bin Laden what he thought about Saddam Hussein, a subject that wasn't then freighted with any of the significance it would later come to have. Bin Laden replied that Saddam was not sufficiently Islamic and had invaded Kuwait in 1990 for his own aggrandizement, statements with which few could disagree.

What bin Laden told us in 1997 represented his unvarnished opinion of

Saddam, a view from which he did not later waver. And there is no subsequent evidence that al-Qaeda and Saddam had anything but the most distant and frigid of relationships. However, following the 9/11 attacks the American public became convinced that Saddam and al-Qaeda were in league. By September 2003, six months into the war with Iraq, nearly 70 percent of Americans believed that Saddam was implicated in the attacks on New York and Washington, despite the fact that there was not a shred of evidence that this was the case. Even five years later, more than a quarter of Americans continued to believe that Saddam had had a *personal* role in 9/11, showing how effective Bush administration efforts to link the Iraqi dictator to the attacks had continued to be.

Why were Americans persuaded that there was an alliance between Saddam and bin Laden? Just as faulty intelligence and exaggerated claims by Bush officials made the case for a dangerous and threatening Iraqi weapons of mass destruction (WMD) program, a case that went largely unchallenged by a pliant media, the same set of factors also allowed the Bush administration to create a useful myth: that there was a substantial connection between al-Qaeda and Iraq. The widespread belief that there was an al-Qaeda–Iraq alliance was a necessary precondition to create the public consensus to go to war in Iraq because Saddam's supposed WMD programs were, of themselves, not enough to threaten American security. Even if the most exaggerated claims about Saddam's WMD capabilities were in fact true, those weapons posed no threat to the United States because Saddam did not possess the ballistic missile systems to deliver them to American targets. For Saddam to present a threat to the United States you had to make the case that Saddam was in league with terrorists including bin Laden and that he might give WMD to a group like al-Qaeda, which would then deploy them against the United States.

Myriad variations of that argument were presented by Bush officials as a pressing reason to go to war against Iraq. A year after 9/11, Secretary of Defense Donald Rumsfeld said that there was "bulletproof" evidence of an Iraq–al-Qaeda connection. In his January 2003 State of the Union address, President Bush said, "Saddam Hussein aids and protects terrorists, including members of al-Qaeda."

Despite the many statements of Bush officials positing an al-Qaeda–Iraq axis, and a raft of stories in the media that seemed to confirm such an alliance, an examination of the historical record demonstrates that while al-Qaeda members and Iraqi officials had some limited contacts during the mid-1990s, there were never any *outcomes* from those discussions. There is also no evidence that Saddam and al-Qaeda ever cooperated in any specific act of terrorism, nor that Iraq funded al-Qaeda. The evidence that Saddam passed WMD material or know-how to bin Laden's men is also nonexistent.

Of course, the fact that Saddam, a secular dictator, and bin Laden, an Islamist zealot, were ideologically opposed does not mean they might not have cooperated with each other. The question is, did bin Laden's ideological antipathy for Saddam ever diminish to the point that al-Qaeda entered into anything resembling a marriage of convenience with the Iraqi dictator? Among the reasons that suggest such an accommodation was implausible was the fact that bin Laden had been an antagonist of Saddam for many years. "A year before Hussein entered Kuwait," bin Laden recalled in the 1997 CNN interview, "I said many times in my speeches at the mosques, warning that Saddam will enter the Gulf. No one believed me. I distributed many tapes in Saudi Arabia." Khaled Batarfi remembers his childhood friend delivering those same warnings about Saddam to a salon of intellectuals in Mecca six months before his armies invaded Kuwait on August 1, 1990. Bin Laden told the group, "We should train our people, our young, and increase our army and prepare for the day when eventually we are attacked. This guy [Saddam] can never be trusted."

As we have seen, after Saddam's forces invaded Kuwait, bin Laden immediately volunteered the services of his "holy warriors," who had recently returned from fighting the Soviets in Afghanistan, to defend Saudi Arabia. The fact that bin Laden was willing to lead his own troops into battle against Saddam hardly suggested a desire to ally himself with the Iraqi dictator—rather, it underlined the contempt that bin Laden had long felt for him.

Bin Laden's visceral dislike of the Baathist secular socialism of Saddam's regime did not abate over the years. Hamid Mir, the Pakistani journalist who has interviewed the Saudi terrorist a number of times, says that when he interviewed bin Laden in the late 1990s the al-Qaeda leader passionately condemned Saddam, saying, "The land of the Arab world, the land is like a mother and Saddam Hussein is fucking his mother."

Iraqi officials and al-Qaeda members were certainly in contact while the terrorist group was headquartered in Sudan between 1991 and 1996. Cofer Black, the CIA's station chief in Sudan during the mid-1990s, says, "I'm personally aware of contacts between Iraq and members of al-Qaeda. The real question is the comprehensiveness of this. Was there holding of hands? You betcha." This is hardly surprising. The then de facto ruler of Sudan, Hassan

Turabi, was closely allied to Saddam, while he was also playing host to terrorist groups from around the Middle East. But al-Qaeda's desultory contacts with Iraqi officials stopped after bin Laden's departure from Sudan for Afghanistan in May 1996. Roger Cressey, a counterterrorism official who served at the National Security Council under President Clinton, says, "I don't recall any intelligence reporting of Iraqis going to Afghanistan or vice versa, and if there was such reporting it was never deemed credible." However, in October 2002, CIA director George Tenet wrote a letter to Senator Bob Graham, the head of the Senate Intelligence Committee, saying that the CIA had "solid reporting of senior-level contacts between Iraq and al-Qaeda going back a decade." This was a seriously misleading construction. The contacts between al-Qaeda and Iraq did date back a decade, but they did not continue past the mid-1990s.

The investigation into the U.S. embassy bombings in Africa in 1998, at the time the largest overseas investigation ever mounted, found no Iraqi connection. The investigation into the USS *Cole* attack found no evidence of Iraqi complicity. And the most wide-ranging criminal inquiry in history, involving chasing down half a million leads and interviewing 167,000 people, uncovered no Iraq link to 9/11. The congressional intelligence committees and the bipartisan 9/11 inquiry that exhaustively investigated the attacks on the Trade Center and Pentagon also found no Iraqi connection. In September 2003, more than two years after the attacks, even President Bush himself tersely conceded for the first time that there was "no evidence" that Saddam played any role in the 9/11 atrocities.

Yet the belief that Saddam posed an imminent threat to the United States was an article of faith within the Bush administration, a conviction that was successfully sold to the American public and then embroiled the United States in a costly war in Iraq, so it's fair to ask: Where did this faith come from?

An important element of that faith originated with the research of an obscure academic named Laurie Mylroie. Mylroie possessed an array of credentials that appeared to certify her as an expert on the Middle East and Iraq. She had held faculty positions at Harvard and the U.S. Naval War College and had served as some kind of adviser on Iraq to the 1992 Clinton presidential campaign. Until this point there was little controversial about Mylroie's career. That would change with the 1993 bombing of the World Trade Center, the first time that a group of jihadist terrorists had struck inside the United States. The Trade Center attack would launch Mylroie on a quixotic quest to prove that Saddam's regime was the most important source of terrorism directed against the United States. Mylroie laid out her case for Iraqi involvement in the 1993 attack in *Study of Revenge: Saddam Hussein's Unfinished War Against America*, a book published a year before 9/11 by the American Enterprise Institute (AEI), the right-wing think tank.

It was not an accident that the AEI published Mylroie's book, since it was at the AEI in particular that the idea took shape that overthrowing Saddam should be a fundamental goal of U.S. foreign policy. Neoconservative hawks such as Richard Perle, a key architect of President Bush's get-tough-on Iraq policy, had a long association with AEI. Still, not one of the thinker/operatives at AEI, or indeed any of the other Iraq hawks such as Deputy Defense Secretary Paul Wolfowitz, was in any real way an expert on the country or had served in the region. Moreover, the majority of those in and out of government who were Middle East experts had grave concerns about the wisdom of invading Iraq and serious doubts about claims that Saddam's regime posed an urgent threat to American security. What, then, gave neoconservatives like Wolfowitz and Perle such abiding faith in their own positions?

A good deal of their certainty came from Mylroie's findings that Saddam was the central source of anti-American terrorism going back a decade. *Study of Revenge* makes it clear that Mylroie and the neoconservatives worked hand in glove to push her theory that Iraq was behind the 1993 Trade Center bombing. Richard Perle glowingly blurbed the book as "splendid and wholly convincing." I. Lewis "Scooter" Libby, later Vice President Cheney's chief of staff, was thanked in the acknowledgments for his "generous and timely assistance." Wolfowitz was also instrumental in the genesis of *Study of Revenge:* "At critical times, he provided crucial support for a project that is inherently difficult," Mylroie wrote.

None of this was out of the ordinary, except for the fact that Mylroie became enamored of her theory that Saddam was the mastermind of a vast terrorist conspiracy against the United States against virtually all evidence and expert opinion. In what amounted to the discovery of a unified-field theory of terrorism, Mylroie wrote that Saddam was not only behind the 1993 Trade Center attack, but also every anti-American terrorist incident of the past decade, from the bombings of the embassies in Kenya and Tanzania in 1998 to the attack on the USS *Cole* two years later.

Mylroie's influence could be seen in the Bush cabinet's reaction to 9/11. As we have seen, Rumsfeld, Wolfowitz, Bush, and Cheney immediately jumped to the conclusion that Saddam was implicated. This was far from an obvious conclusion to arrive at, as every significant anti-American terror attack of the past decade had been the work of the al-Qaeda network, while the U.S. State Department's counterterrorism office had concluded in its comprehensive, yearly report for 2000 that "[Iraq] has not attempted an anti-Western attack since its failed attempt to assassinate former President Bush in 1993 in Kuwait." In other words, it was the *official conclusion* of the U.S. government by the time of the 9/11 attacks that Iraq had not been involved in any anti-American terrorism for almost a decade.

Why was it then that key members of the Bush administration believed that Iraq had been deeply involved in anti-American terrorism for many years? For that we must turn in more detail to Laurie Mylroie, who claimed to have discovered something that everyone else had missed: that the mastermind of the 1993 Trade Center plot, a man generally known by one of his many aliases, "Ramzi Yousef," was an Iraqi intelligence agent. Mylroie wrote that sometime after Iraq's invasion of Kuwait in 1990, Yousef assumed the identity of a Pakistani whose family lived in Kuwait, named Abdul Basit, in order to disguise his real identity as an Iraqi agent. Mylroie came to that deduction following an examination of Abdul Basit's passport records and her discovery that Yousef and Abdul Basit were apparently four inches different in height. On such wafer-thin pieces of "evidence" Mylroie built her case that Yousef must have therefore been an Iraqi agent and that therefore Iraq had masterminded the 1993 Trade Center attack. However, U.S. investigators had long ago found that the man Mylroie described as an Iraqi agent was in fact a Pakistani born in Kuwait who had ties to al-Qaeda. The FBI, the U.S. attorney's office in the Southern District of New York, the CIA, and the State Department had all found no evidence implicating the Iraqi government in the first Trade Center attack.

It is possible, of course, that the neoconservatives did not find Mylroie's research to be genuinely persuasive, but rather that her findings simply fit conveniently with their own desire to overthrow Saddam. But there are reasons to think that they actually were persuaded by her research. Given that she was the one member of the neoconservative team with any real credentials on Iraq, Mylroie's opinions would naturally have carried special weight. That she was a genuine authority, whose "research" confirmed their worst fears about Saddam, could only have strengthened their convictions.

After 9/11, Wolfowitz pressed top Justice Department officials to declare Ramzi Yousef, the mastermind of the first Trade Center attack, who was jailed in Colorado, an "enemy combatant." This would have allowed Yousef to be transferred from federal prison into U.S. military custody. Wolfowitz apparently believed such a move might get Yousef to finally confess that he was indeed an Iraqi intelligence agent. Wolfowitz's request was turned down by Justice officials. A veteran CIA official specializing in al-Qaeda said that throughout late 2002 and early 2003 he and his colleagues were constantly being asked to provide briefings to Bush administration officials about Mylroie's theory that both the 9/11 operational commander Khalid Sheih Mohammed and Ramzi Yousef were Iraqi agents.

On July 8, 2003, Mylroie appeared as an "expert witness" before the 9/11 Commission. She testified: "There is substantial reason to believe that these masterminds [of both the 1993 and 2001 Trade Center attacks] are Iraqi intelligence agents." Mylroie explained that this had not been discovered by the U.S. government because "a senior administration official told me in specific that the question of the identities of the terrorist masterminds could not be pursued because of bureaucratic obstructionism." We were expected to believe that the Bush administration officials whom Mylroie knew so well could not find anyone in intelligence or law enforcement to investigate the supposed Iraqi intelligence background of the mastermind of 9/11, at the same time that 150,000 American soldiers had just been sent to fight a war in Iraq under the banner of the war on terrorism.

Saddam was guilty of many crimes, not least the genocidal policies he unleashed on the Marsh Arabs, Shia, and Kurds of Iraq, but there is no evidence linking him to acts of anti-American terrorism since the failed 1993 attempt to assassinate former president George H. W. Bush in Kuwait. Unfortunately, Mylroie's research proved to be more than merely academic, as her theories swayed key opinion makers in the Bush administration, who then managed to persuade seven out of ten Americans that the Iraqi dictator had a role in the attacks on Washington and New York. So Mylroie's specious theories of Iraq's involvement in anti-American terrorism became part of the zeitgeist in the United States and were an important factor in leading America into the costly war in Iraq.

Meanwhile, in November 2003, Mylroie observed: "I take satisfaction in the fact that we went to war with Iraq and got rid of Saddam Hussein. The rest is details." Now she tells us.

A few weeks after 9/11, Mike Maloof, a Defense Department official who specialized in high-tech export controls, was asked by Douglas Feith, the number-three official at the Pentagon, to investigate the exact nature of the supposed Iraq–al-Qaeda connection. Maloof, who had worked for Richard Perle in Reagan's Defense Department together with David Wurmser, a neoconservative scholar known for his close ties to the Israeli right, set up a two-man office at the Pentagon known as the Policy Counter Terrorism Evaluation Group (PCEG), which reported to Feith.

Both Feith and Wurmser were longtime advocates of overthrowing Saddam. Together with Richard Perle, in 1996 they even wrote a position paper for Israeli Prime Minister Benjamin Netanyahu that made the bizarre suggestion that Israel should encourage the Hashemite monarchy of Jordan "to control Iraq." In 1999, Wurmser, then at the American Enterprise Institute, had written a book, *Tyranny's Ally: America's Failure to Defeat Saddam Hussein*, which argued that Saddam's fortunes had revived since the mid-1990s after the U.S. government had withdrawn its backing from the neoconservatives' favorite Iraqi, Ahmad Chalabi, and his Iraqi National Congress. Wurmser, who subsequently became Dick Cheney's Middle East expert, was hardly a disinterested observer when it came to reviewing the case for the connections between al-Qaeda and Saddam.

Between October and December 2001, Maloof and Wurmser, who called themselves "Team B," combed through a decade of CIA and Defense Intelligence Agency (DIA) files looking to find hitherto-overlooked connections, particularly between Saddam's regime and al-Qaeda. Maloof said, "We did not leave any dot unconnected. We took the information from CIA and DIA, material that was overlooked. They were missing a lot because they had a preconceived idea that secular and religious groups would not work together. Anything that didn't fit that theory was just disregarded."

In an unusual arrangement, some of Team B's information came directly from Ahmad Chalabi's Iraqi National Congress (INC), rather than from U.S. intelligence. Maloof says, "I found that information was useful and I never found it inaccurate" (in fact much of the INC-supplied information turned out to be false). Once they had completed their analysis, Maloof and Wurmser presented their findings to Feith. Maloof says Feith "expressed amazement at what we found." Team B concluded that there was "consultation, training, financing and collaboration" between al-Qaeda and Iraq. The fruits of Team B's labors were eventually distilled into a 150-page slide presentation that was made available to senior Bush officials.

While Team B came to the conclusion that there were substantive connections between Saddam and al-Qaeda, veteran U.S. counterterrorism analysts would come to a different conclusion. In the fall of 2002, Michael Scheuer, the former head of the CIA's bin Laden unit, led a review of nineteen thousand Agency documents, consisting of around eighty thousand pages of material going back more than a decade, looking for al-Qaeda–Iraq links. Scheuer says, "We worked very hard on it, coming to a solidly reached conclusion that there was no formal or ongoing relationship" between al-Qaeda and the Iraqi dictator, a finding that was communicated to the top levels of the CIA. And, strikingly, following the fall of the Taliban, no documents were found in Afghanistan that substantiated an Iraqi link, despite the fact that al-Qaeda was a highly bureaucratic organization.

Daniel Coleman, the FBI special agent whose knowledge of al-Qaeda was unrivaled, says that in August 2002 someone called him from Cheney's office, something both memorable and quite unprecedented, and asked him "to review everything" on Iraq and the al-Qaeda connection. Coleman recalls: "We had already reviewed the material twice. Again we came up empty." Coleman, whose son was then serving in Afghanistan as an Army Ranger, subsequently told the staffer from Cheney's office, "If you came to me for a casus belli you are not going to get it."

On August 15, 2002, Feith presented Team B's conclusions at CIA headquarters. By then two new researchers were at work for him: DIA analysts Tina Shelton and Chris Carney. Shelton gave the presentation, arguing that Iraq's alliance with al-Qaeda was an "open and shut case" and that they had a "mature, symbiotic relationship." CIA director Tenet remembers that he listened politely to this briefing for a few minutes, thinking this is "complete crap," and quickly found a way to excuse himself. At the CIA, the Team B approach came to be known as "Feith-based analysis."

Two months earlier, on June 21, 2002, the CIA had issued its own classified assessment, "Iraq and al-Qa'ida: Interpreting a Murky Relationship." The assessment noted that it was "purposefully aggressive in seeking to draw connections, on the assumption that any indication of a relationship between these hostile elements would carry great dangers for the United States." The paper concluded that there was no evidence of cooperation on terrorist operations but there was enough intelligence on supposed contacts and training, including on chemical and biological weapons, that the relationship between al-Qaeda and Saddam was worrying. Three days earlier the CIA had issued another report concluding that the interaction between Saddam and bin Laden appeared to be "more akin to activity between rival intelligence services, each trying to use the relationship to its own advantage."

In January 2003, the CIA produced a paper that was the Agency's definitive take on the matter, concluding that there was no Iraqi "authority, direction and control" over al-Qaeda. Deputy Director of the CIA John McLaughlin recalls that this did not go down well with the Bush administration: "It took the form of phone calls from people on the vice president's staff, saying, 'Here are another dozen questions we'd like you to look at,' at which point I'd have to say, 'No, we've turned over every rock we can on this, and, frankly, there will be a rebellion in this building if we go any further, because we've taken our stand on this.' Now, intelligence people always have to be alert to new information. So you're arrogant if you say, 'Nothing will ever change my view!' But at that point, we could see nothing that would change our view."

Within the intelligence community there were serious doubts about Saddam's supposed relationship with al-Qaeda, but several prominent media stories appeared in the run-up to the Iraq War that seemed to provide independent corroboration of some of the more sensational claims that the Bush administration was then making. Take Jeffrey Goldberg's March 2002 story in *The New Yorker*, in which he wrote that "Iraqi intelligence agents smuggled conventional weapons, and possibly even chemical and biological weapons into Afghanistan." Aside from the obvious implausibility of smuggling weapons into Afghanistan, a nation already awash in every kind of weaponry after two decades of war, a further problem with Goldberg's story was identified by the British al-Qaeda expert Jason Burke. Goldberg's source on the arms smuggling story was Mohammed Mansour Shahab, an Iranian arms dealer imprisoned by the Kurds, who claimed to have smuggled the Iraqi weapons to Kandahar, the Taliban stronghold. Burke, who had reported from Kandahar repeatedly over the years, interviewed Shahab after Goldberg's story had appeared and concluded that the arms smuggler was lying about his Kandahar trip since he could not describe the city accurately. And, of course, no evidence has subsequently emerged that Iraqi intelligence agents ever smuggled any weapons into Afghanistan.

A further exhibit that was advanced by proponents of the supposed links between al-Qaeda and Saddam was the Salman Pak training camp, some twenty miles from Baghdad, where Islamist terrorists were supposedly taught how to hijack aircraft. Several defectors associated with the anti-Saddam opposition group, the Iraqi National Congress (INC), made this claim to a variety of major media outlets in the run-up to the Iraq war. One of the defectors, a former Iraqi general, Jamal Abu Zeinab al-Qurairy, told *Vanity Fair* in January 2003 that he helped to train "non-Iraqi Islamic fundamentalists at the Salman Pak camp . . . to hijack aircraft with knives." Sound familiar?

Over the course of two days in November 2001, another INC-supplied defector, former Iraqi "army colonel" Sabah Khalifa Khodada al-Lami, gave a series of media interviews about Salman Pak, telling the Agence France-Presse wire service that he had worked at the training camp and had observed Arabs from a number of countries learning how to hijack planes. The *New York Times* similarly quoted Khodada—although in this incarnation he had been mysteriously demoted to captain—saying that Islamist radicals from countries such as Saudi Arabia, Yemen, Algeria, and Egypt had passed through the camp. Khodada was described in the *Vancouver Sun* as an "intelligence officer," while the London *Times* quoted him as a "former Iraqi army officer." During his various interviews Khodada had changed in rank from colonel to captain, and had also morphed from an army officer to an intelligence officer.

Khodada's bogus claims also made their way into a White House "white paper" drafted by Bush aide Jim Wilkinson, which charged that Salman Pak was a training camp for anti-American terrorists. The paper, dated September 12, 2002, recycled the nonsense about Salman Pak being used to train "non-Iraqi-Arabs" in "hijackings," showing that the INC fabrications were making their way into official White House documents. After the invasion of Iraq, the Defense Intelligence Agency's investigation of Salman Pak found no "credible reports that non-Iraqis were trained to conduct or support transnational terrorist operations at Salman Pak."

The Salman Pak story was emblematic of a wider problem: information that seemed to prove the Iraq–al-Qaeda connection often came from the INC. Vincent Cannistraro, the head of the CIA's Counterterrorist Center in the early 1990s, says, "Ahmad Chalabi is a fraud and provided us with a stream of coached alleged defectors with information to get us into Iraq. Chalabi flooded the system with so much of this crap."

A road map of where that crap ended up in the media and the U.S. government is provided in a 2002 letter that the Washington office of the INC wrote to the Senate Appropriations Committee to justify the tens of millions of dollars of American taxpayer money then being lavished on the INC. The letter said that "defectors, reports and raw intelligence are cultivated and analyzed by the INC and are reported through the . . . western media." Attached to the memo was a list of more than a hundred stories that the INC had successfully planted in venues ranging from NPR to the *Washington Post*, many of which were later demonstrated to be false. The memo went on to note that recipients of INC information included senior officials at the Department of Defense and the Office of the Vice President. This was significant because it shows that INC's nonsensical information was bypassing American intelligence agencies and instead going directly to those in the Pentagon and the vice president's office who were most gung-ho about the coming Iraq War.

Exhibit A for the "connection" theory between Iraq and al-Qaeda was the supposed April 9, 2001, meeting in Prague between the lead 9/11 hijacker, Mohammed Atta, and Ahmed Khalil Ibrahim Samir al-Ani, an Iraqi agent. This story was first put into play by Czech government officials who shortly after 9/11 said that Atta met the Iraqi intelligence official in Prague before flying to the United States. In congressional testimony on June 18, 2002, CIA director George Tenet said, "Atta allegedly traveled outside the US in early April 2001 to meet with an Iraqi intelligence officer in Prague. We are still working to confirm or deny this allegation." Despite Tenet's uncertainty about the Atta-Ani meeting, in January 2003 Cheney's chief of staff, Scooter Libby, briefed senior Bush officials that Atta had in fact met with the Iraqi intelligence agent as many as four times. Libby's presentation was deemed "a strong case" by Wolfowitz.

The centerpiece of the Bush administration's case for going to war in Iraq was Secretary of State Colin Powell's presentation to the UN Security Council on February 5, 2003, six weeks before the invasion. Cheney's office pressed for the most expansive case for the connection between Saddam and al-Qaeda in the speech, which was supposed to replicate the presentation that Adlai Stevenson, the U.S. ambassador to the United Nations, had given in 1962 at the height of the Cuban Missile Crisis. In that speech Stevenson had used aerial photographs to convince the world that the Soviets had installed nuclear missiles in Cuba.

Powell's deputy, Richard Armitage, remembers that the vice president's office wrote up a submission for his boss to deliver to the UN that included "every kitchen sink that you could imagine," including the increasingly dubious idea that Atta had met in Prague with the Iraqi intelligence agent before 9/11. A month earlier a CIA report titled "Iraq Support for Terrorism" had already concluded that "we are increasingly skeptical that Atta traveled to

Prague in 2001 or met with the [Iraqi official]." Deputy CIA director John McLaughlin recalls that the White House material about the putative al-Qaeda–Iraq connections had not been cleared by the Agency. McLaughlin told Powell and his staff, "This is not our draft. There's all sorts of garbage in here." Despite the good-faith efforts to exclude questionable material about Saddam's connections to al-Qaeda in Powell's speech, much that remained in the final text would later be discounted following the occupation of Iraq.

Powell's presentation was a bravura performance that seemed to establish beyond a doubt that Saddam was actively concealing an ongoing WMD program and was in league with al-Qaeda. At one point the secretary of state dramatically brandished a small vial of a white powder of supposed anthrax, saying "about this amount . . . shut down the US Senate in the fall of 2001." As Powell gave his speech, sitting directly behind him was CIA director Tenet, giving a visual imprimatur to what Powell was saying. Tenet later wrote, seemingly without irony, that "it was a great presentation, but unfortunately the substance didn't hold up."

One section of Powell's UN speech tried to make the case for an emerging alliance between Saddam and al-Qaeda. Powell was careful not to use any material that was obviously suspect, such as the supposed meeting between Atta and the Iraqi intelligence agent in Prague. Instead he said:

> Iraq today harbors a deadly terrorist network headed by Abu Musab al-Zarqawi, an associate and collaborator of Osama bin Laden and his al-Qaeda lieutenants. . . . When our coalition ousted the Taliban, the Zarqawi network helped establish another poison and explosive training center camp, and this camp is located in northeastern Iraq. . . . Baghdad has an agent in the most senior levels of the radical organization Ansar al-Islam that controls this corner of Iraq. In 2000, this agent offered al-Qaeda safe haven in the region. . . . After we swept al-Qaeda from Afghanistan, some of those members accepted this safe haven. They remain there today. Zarqawi's activities are not confined to this small corner of northeast Iraq. He traveled to Baghdad in May of 2002 for medical treatment, staying in the capital of Iraq for two months while he recuperated to fight another day. During his stay, nearly two-dozen extremists converged on Baghdad and established a base of operations there.

Powell's speech made a gossamer-thin case for the Iraq–al-Qaeda nexus, even with the faulty intelligence that was then available. The relationship between Zarqawi and al-Qaeda was already known to be far from clear-cut. Until 2004, Zarqawi ran an organization separate from al-Qaeda, known as *Tawhid,* whose name corresponds to the idea of monotheism in Arabic. Indeed, Shadi Abdalla, a member of Tawhid who was apprehended in Germany in 2002, told investigators that the group saw itself to be in competition with al-Qaeda. An indication of his independence from bin Laden is that when Zarqawi founded a training camp in Afghanistan in 1999, he established it near the western city of Herat, near the border with Iran, several hundred miles away from al-Qaeda's training camps, which were in southern and eastern Afghanistan.

Even after the Iraq War began in March 2003, Zarqawi was still running his own outfit independent of al-Qaeda. Unlikely support for that fact came from Secretary of Defense Donald Rumsfeld, who said of Zarqawi at a Pentagon briefing in June 2004, "Someone could legitimately say he's not al-Qaeda." Not only did Zarqawi run a terrorist organization that was separate from and even competitive with al-Qaeda, but he also was independent of Saddam Hussein. On June 23, 2004, Zarqawi released an audiotape on a jihadist website that delivered a blistering critique of Saddam, whom he described as a "devil" who "terrified the people." That audiotape came a week after President Bush had described Zarqawi as "the best evidence" of Saddam's connection to al-Qaeda. On October 25, 2005, the CIA released a report that finally disposed of the myth that Saddam and Zarqawi had ever been in league, assessing that prior to the war, "the regime did not have a relationship, harbor, or turn a blind eye towards Zarqawi."

An additional exhibit in Powell's UN speech that was intended to prove an al-Qaeda–Saddam–WMD nexus was the Kurdish Islamist group Ansar al-Islam, which was experimenting with crude chemical weapons in its training camp in northeastern Iraq, a facility that was described as a "poison factory" in the aerial photograph of the camp that Powell displayed in his UN presentation. However, the only reason that Ansar al-Islam could exist in that part of Kurdish Iraq was because the U.S. Air Force had been enforcing a no-fly zone in the region for more than a decade, which meant that the Pentagon had more control over that part of Kurdistan than Saddam did. Obviously well aware of the fact that Saddam did not control Kurdish Iraq, Powell said that the Iraqi dictator had a high-level spy in Ansar al-Islam. However, while Saddam may have had a spy in Ansar al-Islam, this hardly meant that he had control over the group.

Charles Faddis, the senior CIA officer on the ground in Kurdistan during the summer of 2002, spent many weeks investigating the poison factory as well as Ansar al-Islam and its al-Qaeda allies: "What we did night and day, seven days a week, eighteen to twenty hours a day for two months was suck every piece of data we could get on that place because what we had were reports of al-Qaeda on the ground and chem-bio work." Faddis discovered that at their poison factory the Ansar militants were ordering large quantities of cyanide and experimenting with chemical weapons on donkeys. But he found that none of this activity was in any way linked to Saddam. Faddis told his team, "If we find intelligence that's credible, that says that Saddam Hussein is in bed with al-Qaeda and Ansar al-Islam, I will be more than happy to be the guy who gets to press the buttons and send the report back. . . . The only Iraqi intelligence we ever found in that area were doing the exact same thing we were doing, which is keeping an eye on Ansar."

When a group of reporters visited the Ansar al-Islam "poison factory" in Kurdistan a week after Powell's UN presentation, in the words of the *New York Times* they found a "wholly unimpressive place." The poison factory turned out to be a collection of some dozen mud houses without plumbing and whose electricity was provided by a generator. If this was the poison factory linking Saddam and al-Qaeda, it just didn't seem very threatening, and if it really was that threatening, then why not just bomb it? After all, the United States controlled the airspace in the Kurdish no-fly zone. Faddis repeatedly requested to his bosses at CIA headquarters in August 2002 to mount an operation to take out the poison factory as well as the hundred or so al-Qaeda foot soldiers and the larger group of allied Ansar al-Islam fighters concentrated in the immediate vicinity of the facility, all of whose positions had been painstakingly mapped out by Faddis's team. Faddis recalls: "We submitted a series of proposals to Washington to go get rid of these guys. . . . None of those proposals were accepted largely because it was concluded that it might somehow or another derail the plans for the invasion of Iraq and that had already taken priority."

Two days after Powell's speech to the United Nations, on February 7, 2003, the administration raised the national terrorism alert from yellow or "elevated" risk to the orange "high" risk category. Health-care officials were told to be on the lookout for symptoms of biochemical contamination. Secretary of Homeland Security Tom Ridge urged that "families in the days ahead take some time to prepare for emergency," while officials said the attacks could come in the form of biological, chemical, or radiological weapons. The Bush administration issued detailed advice about how the public should prepare for a WMD attack, including stocking up with food and water, and recommended that families keep a supply of duct tape and plastic sheeting handy to seal windows in the event of a chemical or biological weapons attack. Those warnings generated a surge in sales of plastic sheeting and duct tape in the Washington, D.C., area and generated a number of panicky media stories. This scare about an imminent WMD terrorist attack on the United States was politically quite useful for the Bush administration, which was only six weeks away from ordering the invasion of Iraq under the flag of disarming the supposedly WMD-armed regime of the terrorist-supporting Saddam Hussein.

Five weeks before the invasion of Iraq, Tenet testified before the Senate Armed Services Committee that Iraq had "provided training in poisons and gases to two al-Qaeda associates," a point that Powell had also made in his UN presentation. Such claims were, of course, not checkable by the media or the American public, as they relied on highly classified intelligence, and, in any event, they could only be refuted or confirmed by invading Iraq.

What the American public did not know about Tenet's and Powell's crucial claim that Iraq was training al-Qaeda associates on poison gases was that it didn't show a nexus between bin Laden, Saddam, and some of the world's nastiest weapons but was in fact the tainted fruit of an "extraordinary rendition," in which militants, as we have seen, were transported by American officials to countries that routinely used torture, where they would finally divulge whatever secrets they had supposedly been keeping from their American interrogators.

In December 2001, Ibn al-Shaykh al-Libi, a Libyan militant who had run the al-Qaeda–affiliated Khaldan training camp, was captured in Pakistan. The two FBI agents at Bagram Air Base in Afghanistan who were assigned to interrogate Libi sought advice from Jack Cloonan, a veteran FBI investigator who was deeply immersed in al-Qaeda because of his extensive interrogations of three members of the group who were already in American custody. Cloonan told his two FBI colleagues, "I don't care what anyone else says, I would like you to do the following, which is advise al-Libi of his rights." Cloonan briefed the two agents that Libi was an important person because of his position as "amir," or commander, of the Khaldan camp, and someone they should be looking to get as much cooperation from as possible, as they would from any other suspect in any other case.

Under no duress, Libi spoke to the agents about Richard Reid, the so-called shoe bomber, who had recently been arrested in Boston after trying to blow up an American Airlines flight over the Atlantic. Reid had trained in the Khaldan camp under Libi, as had the supposed twentieth hijacker, Zacarias Moussaoui, so naturally what the Libyan had to say about these two men was of great interest to investigators. Libi also said there were no ties between Saddam Hussein and al-Qaeda.

Several days into Libi's interrogation, an Arabic-speaking CIA official named Albert burst into Libi's cell and in front of one of the FBI interrogators yelled at the prisoner, "You know where you are going. And while you're there I'm going to find your mother and fuck her." The CIA then rendered Libi to Egypt.

To improve his chances of better treatment once in Egypt's notorious prisons, Libi fed his interrogators a number of fairy tales, including the nonsensical idea that al-Qaeda had cooperated with Russian organized crime to smuggle "canisters containing nuclear materials into New York." But most importantly he told them that bin Laden had sent two operatives to Iraq to learn about biological and chemical weapons.

Because Libi's story encapsulated the key arguments for the Iraq War, his tale was picked up by President Bush in a keynote speech in Cincinnati on October 7, 2002, in which Bush laid out his rationale for the coming conflict with Iraq, saying, "We've learned that Iraq has trained al-Qaeda members in bomb-making and poisons and deadly gases." But once he was back in American custody, on February 14, 2004, Libi recanted what he had falsely told his Egyptian jailors. Libi told his U.S. interrogators that he had "fabricated" his tale of the Saddam–al-Qaeda–poison connection to the Egyptians following "physical abuse and threats of torture."

Several months before any of the false claims of that connection based on Libi's coerced statements were first made by Bush officials, the Defense Intelligence Agency (DIA) had concluded that Libi was likely making everything up. On February 22, 2002, DIA noted that Libi "lacks specific details on Iraq's involvement. . . . It is possible he does not know any further details: it is more likely that he is intentionally misleading the debriefers." The CIA followed that report up with its own six months later, finding that "questions persist about [Libi's] forthrightness and truthfulness . . . he seems to have fabricated information." Two key American intelligence agencies had raised serious doubts about Libi's reliability yet those concerns were either not briefed to senior Bush officials or were simply ignored, despite the fact that this was the *only* evidence offered to the American public that made the key argument for the war—that Saddam had WMDs and that his regime had instructed members of al-Qaeda about their use.

Despite the absence of evidence that Saddam and bin Laden were allied, senior Bush officials maintained an almost theological certainty that they were joined at the hip. Vice President Dick Cheney told NBC's Tim Russert in September 2003 that "[Iraq] was the geographic base of the terrorists that have had us under assault for many years, most especially on 9/11." Cheney never corrected this egregious misstatement of the facts. During the same interview, Russert asked Cheney if Saddam had any role in 9/11, to which Cheney replied, "We don't know," which was a curious thing to say, since the most wide-ranging criminal investigation in American history had long before determined that Saddam had had no role in the attacks.

On June 16, 2004, the bipartisan 9/11 inquiry staff report was released, and it concluded that there was no operational relationship between Saddam and al-Qaeda. The report also established that the lead hijacker Mohammed Atta's cell phone records showed that he was in Florida at the time of his supposed meeting with the Iraqi spy in Prague on April 9, 2001. Calls from Atta's cell were made multiple times on April 6, 9, 10, and 11 using cell phone transmitting sites in Florida.

The day after the 9/11 staff report came out—the conclusions had been trumpeted in a front-page story in the *New York Times*—an unusually animated Cheney was interviewed by Gloria Borger of CNBC about the supposed Iraq–al-Qaeda connection and, in particular, the supposed meeting in Prague between Atta and the Iraqi intelligence agent.

CHENEY: We have never been able to confirm that nor have we been able to knock it down. We just don't know.

BORGER: Well, this report says it didn't happen.

CHENEY: No, this report says they haven't found any evidence.

BORGER: That it happened.

CHENEY: Right.

BORGER: But you haven't found the evidence that it happened either, have you?

CHENEY: No. All we have is that one report from the Czechs. We just don't know.

BORGER: So does this put it to rest for you or not on Atta?

CHENEY: It doesn't—it doesn't add anything from my perspective. I mean, I still am a skeptic. I can't refute the Czech claim; I can't prove the Czech claim. I just don't know. It's the nature of the intelligence business lots of times.

The claim that Atta had met in Prague with the Iraqi intelligence agent had just been definitively refuted by the 9/11 Commission (an inquiry that the Bush administration had fought to prevent from ever happening). And by the time that Cheney spoke on CNBC, the evidence that Atta could not have been in Prague to meet with the Iraqi agent was already well-known to the U.S. government. According to the 2003 FBI's "Hijackers Timeline," Atta had cashed a check for eight hundred dollars at a SunTrust bank in Virginia Beach, Virginia, on April 4, 2001, and a week later had rented an apartment in Coral Springs, Florida. The three-hundred-page FBI timeline painstakingly retraced the hijackers' steps in the United States and found no evidence that Atta was out of the country at the time of his supposed meeting in Prague with the Iraqi agent. By October 2003, Ahmed Khalil Ibrahim Samir al-Ani, the very same Iraqi intelligence agent who was supposed to have met with Atta, was in American custody, and he denied ever meeting him.

When Bush was asked by reporters about the 9/11 Commission's findings in June 2004 that there was no "collaborative relationship" between al-Qaeda and Saddam, he resorted to tautology: "The reason I keep insisting that there was a relationship between Iraq and Saddam and al-Qaeda; because there was a relationship between Iraq and al-Qaeda."

Not according to Saddam Hussein, who had been captured six months earlier. Appointed to be his interrogator was George Piro, a Lebanese-American who, unusually for an FBI agent, spoke excellent Arabic. Piro, a thirty-six-year-old avid student of Middle Eastern history who had already served tours in Iraq and Afghanistan, would spend the next seven months with the former Iraqi dictator, speaking with him every day for anywhere between five and seven hours. Using standard (noncoercive) interrogation techniques, Piro built up a strong rapport with Saddam, even giving him some of his mom's home-baked cookies when the Iraqi celebrated his sixty-eighth birthday.

Several months into his interrogations, Piro elicited the real story behind Iraq's supposed WMD. Saddam told him that they had all been destroyed in the mid-1990s by UN inspectors, or by the Iraqis themselves, but this was kept secret to protect the regime's aura of power among both its internal and external enemies. During the course of one of their discussions on June 28, 2004, Piro probed Saddam about his putative connections to al-Qaeda. The former Iraqi dictator dismissed the idea, explaining that bin Laden was a zealot with whom his regime did not cooperate. Just as Bush was assuring the world that al-Qaeda and Saddam had a relationship, the FBI, and through it the entire U.S. intelligence community, was confirming for the umpteenth time that there was no such thing.

Why did the Bush administration cling so tenaciously to the fiction of the Saddam–al-Qaeda alliance, given the fact that the bipartisan 9/11 Commission had concluded by June 2004 that there was no operational relationship between them? Part of the answer could be found in the fact that six months earlier, David Kay, the head of Iraq Survey Group, had admitted publicly to the world what was already painfully obvious: There were no weapons of mass destruction in Iraq. (Three months earlier, Bush had already obliquely acknowledged this at the annual Radio & TV Correspondents black-tie dinner in Washington, where he joked about how no weapons of mass destruction had been found in Iraq. At one point Bush showed a photo of himself searching under the furniture in the Oval Office, saying "Nope. No weapons over there.")

On January 28, 2004, Kay testified before the Senate Armed Services Committee, saying, "We were all wrong" about Saddam's WMD. Needless to say this was something of a surprise to the American public, which, following all of the Bush administration's rhetoric about smoking guns and mushroom clouds, had been expecting there would be truckloads of WMD uncovered by American inspectors. Instead there was nothing, and instead of being greeted with flowers, as promised in the run-up to the invasion of Iraq, by now American soldiers were being greeted with IEDs, and hundreds of U.S. servicemen had already died.

In an interview around the time that Kay was telling the world there was no WMDs in Iraq, Vice President Cheney asserted, "We haven't really had the time to pore through all those records in Baghdad. We'll find ample evidence confirming the link; that is, the connection if you will between al-Qaeda and Iraqi intelligence." But no documents were ever unearthed in Iraq proving the Saddam–al-Qaeda axis despite the fact that, like other totalitarian regimes, Saddam's government kept meticulous records. The U.S. military had by 2006 translated 34 million pages of documents from Saddam's Iraq and found there was nothing to substantiate a "partnership" between Saddam and al-Qaeda. And two years later the Pentagon's own internal think tank, the Institute for Defense Analyses (IDA), concluded after examining 600,000 Saddam-era documents and several thousand hours of his regime's audio- and videotapes that there was no "smoking gun (in other words, evidence of a direct connection between Saddam's Iraq and al-Qaeda)."

IDA did find a document from 1993 in which Iraqi intelligence agents wrote that they had agreed to renew relations with Egypt's Jihad Group, then led by Ayman al-Zawahiri, and also to continue to support financially Gulbuddin Hekmatyar, an Afghan warlord long allied to al-Qaeda. By the time of the Iraq invasion a decade later, nothing had come of those relationships and they were long defunct. And the IDA found nothing that substantiated any of the prewar claims about al-Qaeda's relations with Saddam.

After the invasion of Iraq, the U.S. military did, however, discover a memo from the office of Saddam Hussein to his Mukhabarat intelligence organization, dated August 17, 2002. The letter asked the director of the Mukhabarat to be on the lookout for al-Qaeda associates who might have entered the country and to give the matter "extreme importance" and search "hotels, residential apartments and rented houses." Attached to the letter was a photo of a man named "Ahmed Fadel al-Khalaylah," Abu Musab al-Zarqawi's real name. This letter showed that rather than having any kind of relationship with Zarqawi, Saddam's regime was *trying to find him* before the war and had instructed its intelligence agency to conduct a thorough search of all the accommodations that he might have been conceivably staying in.

In June 2008, the Senate Select Committee on Intelligence concluded, as every other investigation had before, that there was no "cooperative relationship" between Saddam and al-Qaeda. The committee also found that "most of the contacts cited between Iraq and al-Qa'ida before the war by the intelligence community and policy makers have been determined not to have occurred." The only meeting that had actually taken place was eight years before the invasion of Iraq, between Farouq Hijazi, a senior Iraqi intelligence official, and bin Laden in Sudan in early 1995. Once he was in U.S. custody, Hijazi told his American interrogators that he had been admonished by Saddam before the meeting not to negotiate or promise anything to the al-Qaeda leader but "only to listen." Bin Laden asked to open an office in Baghdad and for military training for his men. Those requests were turned down flat by Saddam.

The only matter that Saddam's agents and bin Laden did agree upon was for Iraq to broadcast the speeches of Salman al-Awdah, a cleric revered by bin Laden because he was sharply critical of the Saudi royal family. It is not clear if those speeches were ever broadcast. The sum total of the much-vaunted Saddam–al-Qaeda "relationship" that had been relentlessly touted by the Bush administration turned out to be an eight-year-old agreement to broadcast the speeches of a fiery Saudi cleric, something that, in any event, may have never happened.

Obviously, the American public would hardly have supported a war to interrupt a supposedly growing relationship between Saddam and al-Qaeda that boiled down to a decade-old discussion about some nonexistent radio broadcasts.

Chapter 10

The War of Error

There is always an easy solution to every human problem—neat, plausible, and wrong.

—H. L. Mencken

In his State of the Union speech of January 29, 2002, President Bush laid out a new doctrine of preemptive war, which went well beyond the long-established principle that the United States would go to war to prevent an adversary launching an attack that imminently threatened the country. The new doctrine, by contrast, meant that Bush could launch a war whenever the United States might be threatened by another country at any point in the future, a determination the president reserved to himself. "I will not wait on events while dangers gather. I will not stand by as peril draws closer and closer. The United States of America will not permit the world's most dangerous regimes to threaten us with the world's most destructive weapons," Bush declared.

Bush identified those dangerous regimes as an "axis of evil" that comprised Iran, Iraq, and North Korea, echoing the United States' wars against the Axis states of Nazi Germany, Fascist Italy, and Imperial Japan. Quite how this axis functioned was never explained, since in reality, Iran and Iraq had fought a bitter war throughout much of the 1980s, while Iranian involvement in the conference held in Bonn a month before Bush's speech had helped to install the new American-backed interim government in Afghanistan.

At the graduation ceremony for West Point cadets on June 1, 2002, Bush elaborated on his preemptive war doctrine, saying, "If we wait for threats to fully materialize we have waited too long." By then Bush had already decided on war with Saddam. A few weeks later, when Richard Haass, director of policy planning at the State Department, was attending one of his regular meetings with Condoleezza Rice, he started to raise concerns about the possible war. Rice cut him off, saying, "Save your breath. The president has already made up his mind."

In the fall of 2002, Rand Beers was working at the White House as one of Bush's top counterterrorism advisors. Beers, who had fought in Vietnam as a Marine officer and had served in administrations going back to Nixon, found the Bush administration's unilateral rush to war in Iraq quite alarming, as he believed it was both distracting from the unfinished conflict in Afghanistan and would simply confirm bin Laden's master narrative about America's negative role in the Muslim world. He had noticed during the winter of 2002 that the number of White House meetings held on Afghanistan had dropped to around one a week, while those held about Iraq were now averaging around five a week.

In December 2002, Beers attended a meeting at the White House that crystallized his gathering concern about the looming Iraq War. At a cabinet meeting that included the president, the issue was tabled about how best to delegitimize bin Laden. Beers remembered that CIA director George Tenet raised the issue first. Then the Deputy Defense Secretary, Paul Wolfowitz, generally seen as a hawk, said, "We need to think really hard about this." Beers remembers that then "the president says, 'Stop! Victory will take care of that issue! Victory in Iraq will take care of that issue!'" Beers was taken aback, thinking, "He doesn't get it. He somehow thinks that the use of power in so effective a fashion will . . . show how powerful we are and then we didn't have to think about that issue—of delegitimizing bin Laden—because our power would be so clearly visible and dominant."

While it is difficult to decipher precisely why Bush was so convinced that Iraq needed to be attacked—by any rational standard, the country did not pose a real threat to the United States—what Bush said at this cabinet meeting shows that he believed that there would be a "demonstration effect" in destroying Saddam's regime that would deter groups like al-Qaeda or indeed anyone else who might be inclined to attack America. Undersecretary of Defense Douglas Feith confirmed this when he explained the thinking of senior Bush administration officials: "What we did after 9/11 was look broadly at the international terrorist network from which the next attack on the United States might come. And we did not focus narrowly only on the people who were specifically responsible for 9/11. Our main goal was preventing the next attack."

Five days before the invasion of Iraq, Beers quietly tendered his resignation, something almost unheard-of for a senior member of the National Security Council staff in a time of war. Beers recalls his thinking at the time: "We were taking our eye off bin Laden and we were going to pay for it, both with respect to the capture, kill, dismantle, neutralize effort against al-Qaeda and equally, or more important, our longer-term effort to delegitimize him and his movement."

Just as bin Laden made a large strategic error in attacking the United States on 9/11, so too President Bush—having presided over the campaign in Afghanistan that came close to destroying al-Qaeda—would make his own deeply flawed decision to attack Iraq, which breathed new life into bin Laden's holy war.

On March 19, 2003, on the eve of the invasion of Iraq, President Bush issued the order for war: "For the peace of the world and the benefit and freedom of the Iraqi people, I hereby give the order to execute Operation Iraqi Freedom. May God bless the troops." The next day the American-led invasion of Iraq began. Within three weeks U.S. forces controlled Baghdad and the famous images of the massive statue of Saddam Hussein being toppled from its plinth were broadcast around the world. After a stunning military victory the United States quickly lost the ensuing peace. First, the American military stood by as the country's government buildings were looted, which implied—rightly, as it turned out—that chaos would replace Saddam's iron fist. Second, instead of handing the baton of control to an Iraqi interim administration, as had happened in Afghanistan after the fall of the Taliban, the country was subjected to a full-blown American occupation under the Coalition Provisional Authority (CPA).

The CPA would prove to be one of the more inept imperial administrations in modern history, preoccupied by fantasies such as turning Iraq's sclerotic socialist economy into a free-market paradise by privatizing state industries, ending fuel and food subsidies, and introducing a flat tax.

CPA order number 1, on May 16, 2003, mandated the removal of some thirty thousand members of Saddam's Baath party from whatever positions they had once held. In one stroke the CPA had swept the board of Iraq's most experienced administrators in government ministries, universities, hospitals, and state-run industries, many of whom had joined the Baath party for personal gain or simple survival, a common story in totalitarian states. But a much more serious error was CPA order number 2, which dissolved all of the Iraqi military, including the army, intelligence service, Republican Guard units, and their respective ministries. At least four hundred thousand men lost their jobs, many of them Sunnis.

Colonel Derek J. Harvey, a cerebral, Arabic-speaking intelligence officer serving as the head of the U.S. military cell examining the resulting insurgency, concluded after talking with a number of insurgent leaders that those decisions were pivotal to fueling the insurgency. The Iraqi military and Baath party were dominated by Sunni Iraqis who largely ran the country under Saddam, and the CPA dismissal of them had "flipped the social, economic and political order on its head," creating a large group of disenfranchised men willing to take up arms against the new rulers of Iraq.

Simultaneously, the U.S. military did not secure the massive weapons caches that the Iraqi army had stashed around the country, estimated to amount to *one million tons*. Lieutenant General Ricardo S. Sanchez, the commanding general in Iraq, remembers that there were hundreds of weapons stashes in Baghdad alone and thousands of other ammunition dumps around the country, some of which "covered areas that were measured in kilometers." There were not enough American soldiers on the ground to secure and destroy the weapons and ammunition sites, a task estimated by the U.S. military to take three to five years to complete. Sanchez recalls that by May 2003 "the Iraqis began holding open-air bazaars that sold everything from small handguns to rocket-propelled grenades."

And because the overwhelming priority was to find Saddam's supposed stockpiles of WMD, as the insurgency gathered steam in the summer of 2003 American policy makers had little understanding of who exactly the insurgents were. CPA official Clayton McManaway remembers that "the imbalance was staggering between the intelligence analysts working on weapons of mass destruction and those working on the insurgency."

So the insurgency was born in a perfect storm of American errors—not establishing order; not providing the semblance of any government; confirming to the Sunnis who had once lorded it over Iraq's Shia majority that they were officially the underdogs, and throwing hundreds of thousands of soldiers onto the streets in an economy where the jobless rate was around 50 percent, while simultaneously ensuring that there was an unlimited supply of weaponry at hand for those angry young men.

Ali Allawi, the minister of defense in the Iraqi government that replaced the CPA, explains that "the searching of homes without the presence of a male head of household, body searches of women, the use of sniffer dogs, degrading treatment of prisoners, public humiliation of the elderly and notables, all contributed to the view that the Americans had only disdain and contempt for Iraq's traditions." When the pictures of naked prisoners at Abu Ghraib, tethered on dog leashes and stacked like cordwood in human pyramids, were broadcast around the world, they served as further confirmation of the supposed contempt Americans had for Arabs.

Instead of working with Iraq's powerful Sunni tribes to reel in the insurgency, the CPA rejected such efforts, according to General Sanchez, who remembers that he met repeatedly with Paul Bremer, the head of the CPA, urging him "to work with us in the process of tribal engagement and reconciliation. But he adamantly refused to do so. The reason I believe was more philosophical than practical. The Bush administration's—and therefore CPA's—grand vision for Iraq was to create a democratic state where tribes had minimum to no influence in running the government." And CIA director George Tenet also remembered the CPA's hostility to engaging with the tribes. (Three years later, of course, American engagement with the Sunni tribes would help to dramatically tamp down the violence in Iraq.)

By November 2003, as U.S. military fatalities in the conflict drifted over the four hundred mark, the CIA station chief in Baghdad was seriously worried and wrote a long formal assessment back to Washington that, for reasons which are obscure, is known at the Agency as an AARDWOLF. The AARDWOLF, titled "the Expanding Insurgency in Iraq," concluded that the insurgents were largely Sunnis who saw themselves as being excluded from Iraq's emerging new political order but "believe they will ultimately succeed in returning to power as they have in the past." As a result of the intensifying insurgency, the CIA station chief predicted that U.S. military deaths would rise to two thousand. His prediction would of course turn out to be optimistic.

On November 11, 2003, Tenet and a number of the Agency's top Iraq analysts gathered in the White House Situation Room to brief the president,

Cheney, Rumsfeld, Rice, Wolfowitz, and Bremer about the gathering insurgency. One of the analysts explained that Iraq was just one of a long series of jihads that al-Qaeda had exploited in the past, such as the Afghan war against the Soviets, and this one had come along "at exactly the right time for al-Qaeda," allowing it to tap into a whole new generation of supporters, including Iraqis.

Robert Grenier, the CIA's Iraq mission manager, remembers the several-hour meeting: "We were trying to convey that this was a full-blown insurgency. I kept saying that it was sort of the functional equivalent of civil war." Grenier says the mood of the meeting was "heavily colored by the presence of Secretary of Defense Donald Rumsfeld, who interrupted one of the analysts who had first used the term *insurgency* to ask him why he had used that word, explaining, 'This is not a term that we should use publicly because it conveys legitimacy on them that we obviously don't want to convey.'" The analyst countered that what was happening in Iraq conformed to the Pentagon's own definition of an insurgency. Grenier recalls that Bush then said, "We're not calling it an insurgency. So fine, within the room, we can call it what we want. But just so you all understand, we are not going to go out of here and call it an insurgency."

As the violence accelerated, those in charge of the war compounded the problem by acting as if nothing untoward was happening. Bush administration officials seemed to have internalized the Orwellian idea that if you could successfully frame the language that was used to describe the rising violence, then you could snow the public about its underlying reality. As the insurgency picked up steam, Rumsfeld referred to it as "pockets of dead enders" during a Pentagon briefing, while President Bush explained at a White House press conference that "the more progress we make on the ground . . . the more desperate these killers become." Ascribing the rising violence to the supposed increasing desperation of the insurgents would become a standard rhetorical device of the administration.

On June 23, 2004, Deputy Secretary of Defense Paul Wolfowitz went on MSNBC to assure viewers that "it's not an insurgency." Almost exactly a year later, Cheney didn't quibble about the term *insurgency* when he was speaking with Larry King on CNN but instead told viewers that it was in its "last throes." And three years into the war, Cheney told CBS that the insurgents were in a state of "desperation" and denied that Iraq was in the middle of a civil war.

All of those blithe assessments were quite at odds with the bloodbath that Iraq had become following the invasion. Taking the most conservative figures of Iraqi civilian dead from Iraq Body Count, which relied on morgue data and media accounts, and therefore almost certainly undercounted the total numbers of victims, at least ninety thousand Iraqis had died in the war by the time Bush left office. Another measure of how intense the Iraq civil war became was the numbers of Iraqis who fled their homes or left the country; 4.7 million Iraqis, around a sixth of the population, fled the conflict, about half to other countries and half displaced internally. This was the largest single movement of refugees in the history of the Middle East, and the majority were displaced after 2006, as the war intensified.

As Iraq spiraled out of control, the Bush administration and its supporters resorted to blaming the media, which was supposedly ignoring the "good news" in Iraq. Curiously, this charge did not accompany the glowing coverage of the rapid overthrow of Saddam, but only came into play after Iraq's descent into chaos. In 2004 Defense Secretary Donald Rumsfeld lamented that positive news stories "apparently aren't as newsworthy, and they seem not to make the press," bizarrely citing Iraq's fielding of an Olympic team as evidence of progress at a time when Iraq was already one of the most dangerous places on the planet.

Dexter Filkins, a correspondent for the *New York Times,* recounted what it was actually like to be in Baghdad as the war accelerated: "There was no law anymore, no courts, nothing—there was nothing at all. They kidnapped children now; they killed them and dumped them in the street. The kidnapping gangs bought and sold people; it was like its own terrible ecosystem." And Filkins recalled that the good news, what little of it existed, was almost impossible to cover: "One of the favorite targets of the suicide bombers were American ribbon-cuttings—a pump station, for instance, or a new school, because of the crowds they brought. It got so bad that the Americans sometimes kept the unveilings of new projects a secret."

What was especially cynical about the charge that the media was ignoring the "good news" was that the Iraq War was the most dangerous war the press had covered since World War II. Some 130 journalists were killed in the Iraqi conflict, more than double the number that had died in Vietnam. Indicative of how dangerous it became were the physical changes that took place over the course of the war at the Baghdad bureau of the *New York Times,* which gradually morphed into a fortress festooned with searchlights and machine gun emplacements on its roof, surrounded by concrete blast walls, a foot thick and twenty feet high, protected by forty armed guards.

Demands that the U.S. media cover more of the good news in Iraq were strange given that over the course of the war seven American journalists were kidnapped and two were killed, and simply surviving the mayhem of what was one of the world's most lethal wars became a daily chore for the press. Just to cover the story in Baghdad journalists had first to survive the five-mile trip between Baghdad International Airport and the capital, a road known as "Route Irish," which was a gantlet of suicide bombers and rocket attacks during the first two years of the war. In one three-month period alone between September and November 2004, Route Irish was the scene of eighteen suicide bombings.

At the height of the Iraqi conflict, which like many civil wars combined aspects of an insurgency with those of a sectarian conflict, one hundred civilians were dying every day, some in the most unspeakable manner, killed by having their skulls drilled in. By October 2006, more than three thousand civilians were dying a month.

No one person was more responsible for all this chaos than a Jordanian gangster turned religious zealot known as Abu Musab al-Zarqawi. Zarqawi would rise to become the pathologically brutal leader of the group known as Al-Qaeda in Iraq by a circuitous route that would take him from a Jordanian prison cell to Taliban-controlled Afghanistan and finally to Iraq. Zarqawi embraced a particularly virulent form of militant Islam while in prison in Jordan during the 1990s, an experience that would sharpen his zeal, as it had for al-Qaeda's number two, Ayman al-Zawahiri. But there the resemblance ended, for while Zawahiri is the scion of a family of ambassadors, lawyers, and clerics and is himself a surgeon, Zarqawi, one of a family of ten born into an impoverished Bedouin family, came up from the mean streets of the city of Zarqa, a charmless conglomeration of concrete block houses and trash-strewn streets just north of Amman, the Jordanian capital. Zarqawi whiled away his youth in Zarqa (hence his *nom de jihad*), dropping out of high school, running with gangs, and boozing, a vice discouraged by Islam. Zarqawi opened a video rental store, which failed. Even his mother conceded to a journalist, "He wasn't that smart."

Zarqawi acquired his first taste for warfare during the jihad against the communists in Afghanistan. Fellow Jordanian Hutaifa Azzam met Zarqawi on Afghanistan's eastern border with Pakistan in 1990 while the mujahideen were besieging the town of Khost. Azzam remembers that Zarqawi, then in his mid twenties, was a "street guy" with a long rap sheet, a brawler quick with a knife and a propensity for drink, who had come to fight in the holy war because he had "finally decided to return to Allah." Azzam also remembers that the blood ran cold in Zarqawi's veins. "He doesn't know what is the meaning of frightened or to be afraid. He can fight an army alone."

After the fall of the communist regime in Afghanistan, Zarqawi returned to Jordan in 1993, by now a militant with some serious jihad cred. Zarqawi began conspiring to overthrow the Jordanian government and a year later he was jailed. In prison Zarqawi worked out manically, learned the Koran by heart, and gradually rose to become a jailhouse capo whom other inmates learned to fear and to obey without question. Zarqawi had now completed his transformation from a hoodlum to a steely Islamist warrior, so devoid of the normal range of human emotions that even those close to him referred to him as Al Ghraib, "the Stranger," the name he would use to sign his letters to family members.

In March 1999, the newly crowned king of Jordan, Abdullah II, gave an amnesty to thousands of political prisoners, among them Zarqawi, who quickly made his way back to Afghanistan. Letting Zarqawi go free was a decision that the Jordanians would have good reason to regret in the coming years. Around the time of the new millennium, Zarqawi's group in Jordan plotted to blow up a Radisson hotel in Amman and other sites frequented by Western tourists. This plot was broken up by Jordanian intelligence but the group did succeed in killing Laurence Foley, an American diplomat, who was assassinated at his home in the Jordanian capital on October 28, 2002.

In Afghanistan, Zarqawi set up a training camp in the western part of the country near the city of Herat, by the Iranian border, a small affair for a group of his mostly Jordanian followers. Saif al-Adel, one of al-Qaeda's Egyptian military commanders, remembers that when the al-Qaeda leadership first met with Zarqawi in Kandahar in 1999 he did not seem sophisticated: "A sturdy man who was not really very good at words. He expressed himself spontaneously and briefly." Adel says that the al-Qaeda leadership did not seek Zarqawi's allegiance and, for his own part, Zarqawi maintained his independence from al-Qaeda.

When the war against the Taliban began in the winter of 2001, Zarqawi rushed to defend Kandahar, where he narrowly escaped being killed in an American bombing raid, ending up with some broken ribs when a ceiling collapsed in on him. After the fall of the Taliban, Zarqawi fled to Iran, where the Afghan warlord Gulbuddin Hekmatyar—then living in exile there—provided fleeing al-Qaeda militants with apartments. Zarqawi and his fellow Jordanians then opted to move to Iraq, where their complexions and accents would enable them to integrate into Iraqi society easily and where they anticipated that there would be some kind of American invasion. Unlike the Arab volunteers who were drawn to the 1980s jihad against the Soviets in Afghanistan only years after the conflict had begun, foreign fighters such as Zarqawi started to arrive in Kurdish Iraq in 2002, months before the American invasion.

Zarqawi traveled to northern Iraq with around two dozen fighters and met with Mullah Krekar, the leader of the Kurdish militant group Ansar al-Islam, sometime in mid-2002. They agreed to conduct operations against American targets. Zarqawi's initial Iraq operation was limited to Kurdistan, part of the no-fly zone established by the United States in northern Iraq that was outside Saddam Hussein's control.

After the American invasion, Zarqawi's group quickly moved to make Iraq a no-go area for the international community, sabotaging efforts to put the country back on its feet. On August 19, 2003, Zarqawi's men bombed the United Nations headquarters in Baghdad, killing twenty-two, including Sergio de Mello, the head of the UN mission in Iraq. A month later the UN pulled out, which precipitated the withdrawal of the International Monetary Fund, the World Bank, and Oxfam, a leading British relief organization. Also in August, Zarqawi's group bombed the Jordanian embassy, killing at least seventeen. On November 12, it attacked an Italian police barracks in southern Iraq, a bombing in which twenty-five died. These attacks all helped to scare off countries and companies considering getting involved in the reconstruction of Iraq.

Zarqawi also made a quite original if sickening contribution to the conduct of the insurgency and to warfare in general. The Jordanian terrorist seemed to have intuitively understood that Iraq was the first open-source war. Based on this intuitive understanding, Zarqawi's group routinely videotaped its operations, including kidnappings, executions, IED attacks, and suicide bombings for immediate posting to the Web. Zarqawi's revolution was not only televised but also promptly uploaded to the Internet for almost real-time global distribution. His rise to become the most feared leader of the Iraqi insurgency benefited considerably from the fact that around the same time broadband Internet access was becoming more available, ensuring that these bandwidth-consuming videos had a wide distribution. If Vietnam had been the first television war, and the 1991 war to liberate Kuwait from Saddam Hussein's armies had been the first cable news war, Iraq was the first Web war.

It was in part his skill as a Web propagandist that turned Zarqawi from a division B commander in Iraq to the most feared leader of the insurgency. Zarqawi's videotape of the beheading of twenty-six-year-old American businessman Nicholas Berg was posted on the Web on May 11, 2004. The videotape of the murder, titled "Sheikh Abu Musab Al Zarqawi Slays an American Infidel," was viewed millions of times.

On the tape Berg is shown sitting in front of five armed, hooded men and is dressed in an orange jumpsuit to mimic the clothes worn by the detainees at the American prison camp at Guantánamo. Berg made a final statement: "My name is Nicholas Berg. My father is Michael. My mother's name is Susan. I have a brother and a sister, David and Sarah. I live in West Chester near Philadelphia." It was almost certainly Zarqawi who then wielded the machete-like knife that cut off his American captive's head. Given the extreme anti-Semitism of al-Qaeda, it does not seem a coincidence that the group's Iraqi affiliate's first beheading victim was a Jewish-American, reenacting almost to the letter al-Qaeda's videotaped execution of the Jewish-American journalist Daniel Pearl two years earlier.

The beheading specifically videotaped for Web distribution became something of a Zarqawi signature. He made it a commonplace event of his kidnappings in Iraq, which included two other Americans, Eugene Armstrong and Jack Hensley, the Englishman Kenneth Bigley, and other victims from South Korea, Bulgaria, and Turkey. Those kidnapping-murders recorded for video distribution on the Internet of course further dissuaded the international community from getting involved in Iraq.

But Zarqawi's special demonic genius was to launch Iraq down the road to civil war. In early 2004, the U.S. military intercepted a letter from Zarqawi to bin Laden in which he proposed provoking a civil war between Sunnis and Shia. This was something in which bin Laden had shown little interest in the past, partly because since 2002, senior al-Qaeda leaders had been living under some form of arrest in largely Shia Iran, including one of his own sons, Saad bin Laden. (It is also not impossible that bin Laden's beloved Syrian mother is herself an Alawite, as that Shia sect is concentrated in Latakia, Syria, the region she hails from.)

In the letter Zarqawi argued that the Shia, whom he described variously as snakes and scorpions, were "the key to change. . . . If we succeed in dragging them into the arena of sectarian war, it will become possible to awaken the inattentive Sunnis as they feel imminent danger." Zarqawi explained that without a civil war, Iraqi Sunnis sympathetic to al-Qaeda would continue to prefer "the arms of their wives" to engaging in jihad.

Zarqawi's strategy was to hit the Shia so that they would in turn strike the Sunnis, so precipitating a vicious circle of violence in which al-Qaeda would be cast as the protector of the Sunnis against the wrath of the Shia. It was a strategy that worked all too well, provoking first sectarian conflict in Iraq and later civil war. On August 29, 2003, Zarqawi's father-in law drove a massive truck bomb outside a Shia mosque in Najaf, killing around a hundred, including Ayatollah Baqir al-Hakim, one of the most important spiritual leaders of the Shia. Al-Qaeda in Iraq also regularly attacked Shia religious processions, shrines, and clerics. The tipping point in the slide toward full-blown civil war was al-Qaeda's February 2006 attack on the Golden Mosque in Samarra, which is arguably the most important Shia shrine in the world.

One of the seeming triumphs of the post-invasion period was the election of the new Iraqi government on January 30, 2005. That election received extensive coverage from networks around the world, which broadcast pictures of excited Iraqis showing off their ink-stained purple fingers, indicating that they had voted in Iraq's first election in decades. But the election turned out to be effectively a census of the adult Shia population of Iraq because Iraqis voted almost entirely on sectarian lines and Sunnis boycotted the voting; in Anbar province, the heartland of the Sunni insurgency, only two thousand people voted.

The election was, in fact, a disaster, serving to further deepen the sectarian divide in the country. The new Iraqi government was, in all but name, a Shia government, and key departments, such as the Ministry of the Interior, which controls the country's internal security, quickly became populated by Shia death squads.

The center of the Sunni insurgency was Fallujah, a small city in Anbar province forty miles west of Baghdad. On April 28, 2003, soldiers of the 82nd Airborne had shot into a crowd of demonstrators in the city, killing seventeen. Resistance to the American occupation gathered strength and Fallujah increasingly attracted Sunni insurgent groups, including al-Qaeda. On March 31, 2004, Fallujah became a household name in the States when SUVs carrying four American security contractors from Blackwater USA ran into an ambush. They were killed, their bodies set on fire, and two were strung up from a bridge over the Euphrates River.

In retaliation, U.S. Marines were ordered to launch a major operation to retake Fallujah, which they did, killing hundreds of insurgents and Iraqi civilians, an operation halted by Bremer on April 9 as the widespread coverage of the assault brought considerable pressure from Iraqi leaders to stop the bloodshed. The resulting cease-fire seemed to be a victory for the insurgents, who had generally avoided set-piece battles with the better-trained and equipped U.S. military.

Lieutenant General Ricardo Sanchez, the commanding general in Iraq, remembers that Fallujah was a turning point. "To say that the Fallujah offensive angered the Sunni Muslims of Iraq would be a gross understatement. Up to that point many had been still on the fence and were working with us to create a more stable government." After the first battle for Fallujah, Sunnis, who make up around a fifth of the Iraqi population, concluded—if they hadn't done so already—that they were going to be marginalized in the new Iraq. Sanchez recalls that the "Sunni triangle exploded in violence" with attacks in Baghdad, around Mosul in the north, in central Iraq along the Euphrates River, and around Karbala in the south.

The Marines went back into Fallujah on November 7, 2004. By now it was controlled by thousands of jihadist insurgents. In the heaviest urban combat the Marines had seen since the battle of Hue in Vietnam, they fought block to block, largely pacifying the city within a couple of weeks. But retaking Fallujah came at a tremendous cost; thousands of the city's buildings were destroyed and hundreds of thousands of its inhabitants fled, including Abu Musab al-Zarqawi and other members of al-Qaeda. Thirty-five U.S. troops had died. But Sunni insurgents would never again challenge the U.S. military to a battle on the scale of Fallujah.

Early in the war, Bush spoke to reporters at the White House and remarked of the insurgents in Iraq, "Bring 'em on." Unfortunately, thousands of militants from around the Muslim world took him up on that offer. As other rationales for the Iraq War evaporated—WMD, peace between Israel and the Palestinians, a democratic domino effect around the Middle East—the administration and some in the U.S. military started trying to make a virtue of the fact that foreign jihadists were flocking to the Iraq conflict, leaning on the so-called "flypaper" theory that terrorists would be drawn to Iraq like bugs to a strip, only to be killed or captured there. General Sanchez told CNN that Iraq "is what I would call a terrorist magnet . . . and that will prevent the American people from having to go through attacks back in the United States." Similarly, Bush asserted at a campaign event in Colorado in 2004, "We are fighting these terrorists with our military in Afghanistan and Iraq and beyond so we do not have to face them in the streets of our own cities."

Art Keller, a CIA officer stationed in the tribal areas of Pakistan in 2006, points out that the Iraqi "flypaper" didn't prove to be particularly sticky: "People were going from the Afghan/Pakistan border to Iraq to learn the tactics and then came back. Seems like the reverse of the way the War on Terror was supposed to work."

Of course, before the war the administration could not have sold the American public on the idea that American men and women in uniform were deploying to Iraq to act as bait for the al-Qaeda terrorists who would flood into the country. And the flypaper theory was based on the comforting, but false, premise that there was a finite group of terrorists that could be attracted to one place and killed. In fact, as the administration's own 2006 National Intelligence Estimate explained, "The Iraq War has become the cause célèbre for jihadists . . . and is shaping a new generation of terrorist leaders and operatives."

The most prominent of that new generation was, of course, the Jordanian Abu Musab al-Zarqawi. Although the Bush administration tended to gloss over the fact, al-Qaeda only formally established itself in Iraq a year and a half after the U.S. invasion. On October 17, 2004, Zarqawi issued an online statement pledging allegiance to bin Laden. Zarqawi's pledge was fulsome: "By God, O sheikh of the mujahideen, if you bid us plunge into the ocean, we would follow you. If you ordered it so, we would obey." And so, nearly two years after Bush administration officials had first argued that Zarqawi was part of al-Qaeda, the Jordanian terrorist finally got around to swearing allegiance to bin Laden. Three months later the al-Qaeda leader responded warmly to Zarqawi in an audiotape that aired on Al Jazeera: "It should be known that the *Mujahid* brother Abu Musab al-Zarqawi is the *Amir* [prince] of the al-Qaeda organisation in the Land of the Two Rivers [Iraq]."

Despite his oath of allegiance, Zarqawi did not act as if he were under al-Qaeda's control. Ayman al-Zawahiri sent a letter to an associate of Zarqawi's, which was intercepted by U.S. forces in Iraq in July 2005, urging him to exercise more restraint in his campaign against the Shia: "Many of your Muslim admirers amongst the common folk are wondering about your attacks on the Shia." Zawahiri also gently advocated an end to Zarqawi's televised executions: "Among the things which the feelings of the Muslim population who love and support you will never find palatable are the scenes of slaughtering the hostages." This was all excellent advice that Zarqawi largely ignored, continuing to attack the Shia without restraint and brutalizing Sunnis who did not conform to al-Qaeda's Talibanesque social policies.

In 2006 the CIA estimated that there were thirteen hundred foreign fighters on the battlefield in Iraq, almost all of whom were attached to al-Qaeda. Made up largely of foreigners at its inception in 2004, the Agency estimated that three years later Al-Qaeda in Iraq (AQI) was largely Iraqi. Those estimates suggest that at the height of its power, AQI fielded no more than several thousand fighters. But AQI punched well above its relatively small weight because of its predilection for extreme violence and the fact that it was the group that supplied most of the suicide attackers in Iraq.

By April 2008 suicide attacks had killed more than ten thousand Iraqis. And more suicide attacks were conducted in Iraq between 2003 and 2007 than had taken place in every other country of the world combined since 1981. While Iraqis made up the great bulk of the insurgents, a number of studies showed that the suicide attackers in Iraq were generally foreigners. The U.S. military assessed that AQI's foreign recruits were responsible for up to 90 percent of the suicide attacks in Iraq. Similarly, Mohammed Hafez, the author of the authoritative study *Suicide Bombers in Iraq*, found that of the 139 "known" suicide bombers in Iraq, fifty-three were from Saudi Arabia and only eighteen were Iraqi, while the rest came from other Arab countries and even Europe. And the Israeli academic Reuven Paz found that of the 154 fighters identified as "martyrs" in Iraq on jihadist forums, 61 percent were Saudi, and the rest were from a variety of other Middle Eastern countries. The most extensive suicide campaign in modern history was conducted in Iraq largely by foreigners animated by the deeply held religious belief that they had to liberate a Muslim land from the "infidel" occupiers.

Those findings were broadly confirmed in October 2007 by the discovery of a trove of al-Qaeda documents by the U.S. military in Sinjar, close to the Syrian border. They documented foreign fighters who had traveled to Iraq since August 2006. Of the 606 foreign fighters whose biographies were detailed in the documents, 41 percent of them were Saudi, 19 percent were Libyan, and smaller percentages from other Middle Eastern countries made up the rest of the total. Of the 389 fighters who designated their "work," more than half wrote that they intended to be suicide bombers. Those bombers saw themselves as acting on behalf of the *umma*, the global community of Muslim believers, a supranational concept that doesn't recognize national boundaries. The suicide attackers who often attacked Shia shrines and religious processions in Iraq were motivated by vicious anti-Shiism that was also obviously religious in character.

In short, the suicide attackers in Iraq were as far from being nationalists as it's possible to imagine, paying their own way to travel to Iraq, a country that most of them had never previously visited, to commit suicide. The only explanation for their suicidal missions was the rationale that the foreign volunteers themselves offered—that they were doing this for Islam and a one-way ticket to Paradise. In the Sinjar documents, for instance, a "martyr's will" made no mention of Iraq at all and simply said instead, "Make my burial gathering as my wedding party."

Not content with whipping up mayhem only in Iraq, al-Qaeda's Iraqi affiliate also exported its terror campaign. On November 9, 2005, the group launched simultaneous suicide bombings at three American hotels in the Jordanian capital of Amman—the Radisson, Hyatt, and Days Inn—killing sixty. Most of the victims were Jordanians attending a wedding party and the attack provoked a wave of revulsion against Zarqawi in his birthplace. His hometown of Zarqa issued a formal condemnation of its most infamous son and tens of thousands of Jordanians took to the streets in protest, an early indication of how counterproductive Zarqawi's tactics were becoming. Even Zarqawi felt it necessary to defend the bombings, releasing an audiotape two days after the attacks claiming that the hotels were targeted because they were frequented by Israeli spies.

At the height of its power, Al-Qaeda in Iraq, like its parent organization, was a highly bureaucratized group. AQI asked its non-Iraqi recruits to fill out application forms that asked for their countries and cities of origin; real names; aliases; date of birth; who their jihadist "coordinator" was; how they were referred to al-Qaeda in the first place; their occupation; how they had entered the country from Syria (the usual transit point for foreign fighters arriving in Iraq); who in Syria had facilitated their travel; an assessment of how they had been treated there; what cash and ID cards they had with them when they arrived in Iraq; any relevant knowledge—such as computer skills—they might have; and whether they were volunteering to be fighters or suicide attackers.

AQI also recorded detailed battle plans for attacks that would take place over the course of three months; the organization maintained pay sheets for brigade-size units of hundreds of men; it recorded the detailed minutes of meetings, kept prisoner rosters, maintained death lists of enemies, and kept the records of vehicles in its motor pool. Most chillingly, AQI's Anbar branch videotaped eighty executions, which were not used for propaganda purposes but simply as a record of having done the job. The tapes showed prisoners thrown from bridges with ropes tied around their necks.

AQI was well financed, as was demonstrated by a 2005 letter from al-Qaeda's number two, Ayman al-Zawahiri, in which he requested a $100,000 transfer from al-Qaeda's Iraqi affiliate to al-Qaeda headquarters in the tribal areas of Pakistan. Al-Qaeda's "border emirate," on Iraq's Syrian border, recorded income of $386,060 and spending of $173,200 in a six-month period during 2007.

AQI also brought many tactical innovations to its terror campaign, for instance deploying two vehicles for double suicide attacks, as it did for the November 18, 2005, bombing of the Hamra hotel in Baghdad, which housed a number of Western journalists and security contractors. One suicide truck bomb breached the concrete blast wall protecting the hotel, followed quickly by a flatbed truck loaded with explosives that plowed though the breached area and then detonated, killing at least six.

AQI's suicide campaign increasingly used female suicide bombers, something that other Salafi jihadist groups had largely avoided. In one Iraqi province alone, Diyala, there were twenty-seven suicide bombings by women between 2007 and 2009. And the campaign also saw the innovation of husband-wife suicide teams. In November 2005, Muriel Degauque, a Belgian woman who worked as a baker's assistant, and her husband were recruited by AQI from Belgium to carry out suicide attacks on American convoys in Iraq. Degauque became the first female European jihadist to launch a suicide operation anywhere. And only hours after Degauque's attack, Sajida al-Rishawi, a thirty-five-year-old Iraqi woman also recruited by AQI, walked into a wedding reception at the Radisson hotel in Amman, dressed festively, as was the man accompanying her, Hussein Ali al-Samara, whom she had married just days earlier. Under their clothes they were both wearing explosive belts. According to the televised confession she later gave, when her belt failed to explode her husband pushed her out of the hotel and exploded his device.

Al-Qaeda also deployed children as suicide bombers. In late August 2008, a fifteen-year-old girl wearing a suicide vest turned herself in to police in Baquba, in the region near Baghdad where Degauque had killed herself. And AQI exploited the mentally unstable, strapping bombs, for instance, to two women, one of whom had undergone psychiatric treatment for depression or schizophrenia, who together killed around one hundred in Baghdad's central market on February 1, 2008.

It was above all in the manufacture of homemade bombs, known as improvised explosive devices (IEDs), that the insurgents made warp-speed innovations. The first IEDs were simple "passive" victim-operated trip devices. They then progressed to cell-phone-triggered devices; IED "daisy chains" of multiple charges rigged together; and bombs relying on infrared triggers. Another innovation was the use of chlorine in bombs, although the insurgents stopped this tactic in 2007, in part because the gas was not especially effective.

The insurgents would often set off multiple IED explosions close together, the first one to cause casualties and the second to maim or kill first responders tending to the injured and dying, or those investigating the scene of the attack. Sergeant Brian Doyne, an Army bomb tech who had served in Afghanistan and was in Iraq on his first tour, responded to an IED targeting an American tank south of Tikrit on February 24, 2005. Doyne recalled: "At first look you really don't know there's anything else to this incident." But as Doyne was gathering evidence at the scene of the bombing, a second and then a third bomb detonated, and at the age of twenty-six he lost both his left arm and left eye.

In many ways it was a car- and truck-bomb war, since this was the delivery method for many of the most effective attacks of the insurgency. Typically the insurgents would use 155 mm Chinese shells left over from Saddam's arsenals as the basic bomb, an explosive charge that came already wrapped in a steel case, which was guaranteed to produce plenty of high-velocity fragments. When the bomb went off those fragments would travel faster than the speed of sound, and if one hit a person's head, it would likely burst it open.

During World War II, 3 percent of American combat deaths were caused by mines or booby traps. By 1967, during the Vietnam War, the figure rose to 9 percent. In Iraq during the latter half of 2005, IEDs were the leading cause of American combat deaths; by October 2007 some one thousand American soldiers had been killed by homemade bombs. Some of those deaths might have been avoidable, but only one in ten of the some nine thousand military transport trucks in Iraq in 2004 were armored.

Three years into the Iraq War, AQI seemed all but unstoppable. A classified Marine intelligence assessment dated August 17, 2006, found that AQI had become the de facto government of the western Iraqi province of Anbar, which is strategically important as it borders Jordan, Syria, and Saudi Arabia and makes up about a third of the landmass of Iraq. The Marine report's downbeat conclusion: AQI had become "an integral part of the social structure in western Iraq" and was so deeply entrenched in Anbar that it could not be defeated there with a "decapitating strike that would cripple the organization." In addition, AQI controlled a good chunk of the exurban belts around Baghdad, the "Triangle of Death" to the south of the capital, and many of the towns north of it, up the Tigris River to the Syrian border. Thus AQI controlled territory larger than New England and maintained an iron grip on much of the Sunni population. And in a country with a stratospheric unemployment rate, AQI was paying its foot soldiers salaries and raking in millions of dollars from various oil smuggling scams, kidnapping rings, extortion schemes, and overseas donations. In other words, the Bush administration had presided over the rise of precisely what it had said was one of the key goals of the Iraq War to destroy: a safe haven for al-Qaeda in the heart of the Arab world.

It was not only militants who were radicalized by the Iraq War. When the United States went to war against the Taliban in the wake of 9/11, it was understood by many around the world as a just war. The war in Iraq drained that reservoir of goodwill and dragged the United States into what many saw as a conflict with Muslims in general. The Iraq War was widely viewed by Muslims as a classic "defensive" jihad. This was not an arcane matter of Islamic jurisprudence, but in fact a key reason why thousands of Americans died in Iraq, and also the reason that the al-Qaeda movement was reinvigorated by the conflict. The Koran has two sets of justifications for holy war. One concerns a "defensive" jihad, when a Muslim land is under attack by non-Muslims, while another set of justifications concerns grounds for an "offensive" jihad, which countenances unprovoked attacks on infidels. Muslims consider the defensive justifications for jihad to be the most legitimate.

The Bush-appointed Director of National Intelligence, John Negroponte, contradicted the findings of his own intelligence agencies when he testified to Congress in January 2007 that he was "not certain" that the Iraq War had been a recruiting tool for al-Qaeda and stated, "I wouldn't say there has been a widespread growth of Islamic extremism beyond Iraq. I really wouldn't."

In fact, a study by New York University's Center on Law and Security comparing the period after September 11 through the invasion of Iraq in March 2003 with the period from March 2003 through September 2006, found that the rate of deadly attacks by jihadists had actually increased *sevenfold* after the invasion. Even excluding terrorism in Iraq and Afghanistan, fatal attacks by jihadists in the rest of the world increased by more than one-third in the three years following the invasion of Iraq. The Iraq War, of course, did not cause all of this terrorism, but it certainly increased the tempo of jihadist attacks from London to Kabul to Amman.

The administration's focus on war in Iraq also undermined America's place in the world in other ways. A poll taken a few months after the 2003 invasion found that Indonesians, Jordanians, Turks, and Moroccans all expressed more "confidence" that bin Laden would "do the right thing" than that President Bush would.

On May 1, 2003, aboard the USS *Abraham Lincoln*, President Bush announced that "major combat operations" in Iraq had ended. The defeat of Saddam Hussein, he told the American people, was "a crucial advance in the campaign against terror." For the umpteenth time Bush once again bracketed Saddam and 9/11: "The battle of Iraq is one victory in a war on terror that began on September 11th, 2001 and still goes on." The president went on to describe the 9/11 attacks, "the last phone calls, the cold murder of children, the searches in the rubble," as if this had any bearing on the Iraq War. The president also made the definitive statement that Saddam was "an ally of al-Qaeda," something that his own intelligence agencies had determined was not the case before the war.

There is no question that the United States liberated Iraqis from Saddam's demonic tyranny, but that argument was not what persuaded Americans that a preemptive war against the Iraqi dictator was in their best interests. They were hustled to war by the invocation of putative Iraqi mushroom clouds and the argument that there was a genuine and threatening Saddam–al-Qaeda–WMD nexus. The war against Saddam wasn't conducted under the banner of the liberation of the Iraqi people, but rather under the banner of winning the war on terrorism. And by that standard it was a failure, giving the jihadist movement around the world a new battlefront and a new lease on life.

What the Bush administration did in Iraq is what bin Laden could not have hoped for in his wildest dreams: America invaded an oil-rich Muslim nation in the Middle East, the very type of imperial adventure that bin Laden had long predicted was the United States' long-term goal in the region; the United States deposed the secular socialist Saddam, whom bin Laden had long despised; the war ignited Sunni and Shia fundamentalist fervor in Iraq; and it provoked a "defensive" jihad that galvanized jihadi-minded Muslims around the world.

Chapter 11

Almost Losing the War the United States Thought It Had Won

It is very important to keep our focus on this war in Afghanistan. It's a classic military mistake to leave a partially defeated enemy on the battlefield in one form or another.

—Paul Wolfowitz, deputy secretary of defense, at a Pentagon news conference on December 10, 2001, just days before Osama bin Laden disappeared from Tora Bora

You have all the watches and we have all the time.

—saying commonly attributed to the Taliban

Kabul under the Taliban was simultaneously quiet, grim, and boring. Black-turbaned vigilantes roamed its streets like wraiths dispensing their ferocious brand of "Islamic" justice. Curfew started at 9 P.M. and by 8 P.M. the streets were deserted except for the young Taliban soldiers in turbans who stood at every traffic circle, carefully checking passing vehicles. Some wore kohl, a black eyeliner that gave them a look both feline and foreboding. The Taliban had banned pretty much any form of diversion and entertainment and had presided over the total collapse of the economy. A doctor earned only six dollars a month. Government ministries worked without computers, their offices unheated in the brutal Kabul winter. There were no banks and the treasury of the country consisted of a box from which the Taliban leader Mullah Omar distributed wads of cash; the Taliban had pulled Afghanistan back into the Middle Ages.

In the years after the fall of the Taliban the capital slowly sprang to life. Kabuli men shaved off their beards while others celebrated by listening to music, flying kites, and watching television, pleasures that had long been denied them. The money-changers down by the Kabul River started doing a roaring trade and packed movie houses played Bollywood flicks. On Chicken Street, the decrepit Madison Avenue of the capital, a bookshop sold American and British newspapers. Other shops offered rich coats of fox fur and tiger skin. There were even traffic jams, the first time that the city had seen them since Afghanistan had been plunged into a series of wars more than two decades earlier. Refugees don't return to places they don't see having a real future and in 2002 alone almost two million Afghans came home from neighboring Pakistan and Iran. And there were millions of Afghan kids in school, including, of course, many girls.

Kandahar, the former Taliban stronghold in the south of the country, was now firmly in the grip of the United States. Kandahar airport, where once Taliban soldiers had shown off their anti-aircraft missiles to members of the international media, was now a vast U.S. base housing thousands of soldiers, as well as a twenty-four-hour coffee shop, a North Face clothing store, a day spa, and a PX the size of a Walmart. Next door, what had once been a base for bin Laden was now an American shooting range, while in downtown Kandahar, Mullah Omar's gaudy compound was home to American Special Forces units.

The relative absence of the Taliban and al-Qaeda throughout Afghanistan during 2003 meant fewer U.S. casualties. Forty-eight U.S. servicemen were killed there that year, the lowest number of American deaths for any year in the decade after the fall of the Taliban. And by mid-2005 the Afghan government had succeeded in disarming almost all of the private warlord-led militias that had plagued Afghanistan since the early 1990s. More than sixty thousand men were disarmed and tens of thousands of light and heavy weapons were handed in to the government, all part of a larger pattern of seeming progress in Afghanistan.

During his first years in power, the new Afghan leader, Hamid Karzai, seemed like a shrewd player of the kind of hardball politics that would have warmed the heart of Lyndon Johnson. Karzai forced Ismail Khan, the powerful governor of the western province of Herat, to resign, giving him instead the consolation prize of the ministry of energy. Uzbek strongman Abdul Rashid Dostum was given a job in 2003 with a fancy title but no real power at the ministry of defense. The next year Karzai dropped Mohammad Fahim from his post as minister of defense; the power-hungry general had awarded himself the title of Field Marshal after the fall of the Taliban. With these moves Karzai not only skillfully neutralized his most powerful rivals, men who could field their own private armies, but he also increased the authority of the central government.

The presidential election held on October 9, 2004, was a success by any standard. Ten million Afghans registered to vote, far more than was initially projected, and almost half of those who signed up were women. The day of the election Afghans streamed to the polls. In conservative Pashtun areas such as Gardez—where weeks earlier insurgents had fired rockets at Karzai's helicopter, and where even fully covered women are rarely seen on the streets—turnout was heavy. Groups of women clad in blue burqas besieged polling stations in Gardez, eager to vote.

In the end, Karzai won 55 percent of the vote against more than a dozen other candidates in a reasonably fair election. Eight million Afghans voted, a more than 70 percent voter turnout, a rate not seen in any American presidential election since 1900. The election was the high water mark of Afghanistan's recovery. An ABC/BBC poll taken in 2005 captured this well. Eighty-three percent of Afghans approved of President Karzai's work and the same number expressed a favorable opinion of the United States, unheard-of in a Muslim nation. Eight in ten Afghans supported the presence of U.S. and other international forces on their soil, while only 8 percent supported the Taliban. Three out of four Afghans said their living conditions were better than they had been under the Taliban and roughly the same number felt that the country was heading in the right direction. Contrast that with Iraq, where ABC/BBC also polled in 2005 and found that less than one in five Iraqis supported international forces in their country and were evenly split on the question of whether their lives were better or worse following the American-led invasion.

The generally positive feelings Afghans had about their future and the role that the international community was playing in their country—attitudes that lasted for several years after the fall of the Taliban—were not entirely surprising when you considered what the country had suffered through during the previous grim two decades of its history: the occupation by the Soviets, the civil war that followed, and the rule of the Taliban, which brought a certain measure of security to the country but at the cost of forcing Afghans to live under an authoritarian, theocratic state incapable of delivering the most basic of services.

Almost every Afghan had a member of their immediate family who had been killed or maimed in the wars of the previous decades, and the whole country seemed to be in the grip of post-traumatic stress disorder. No country in history had been subjected to a communist occupation, followed by warlordism, followed by rigid Islamist fundamentalist rule—approaches to politics and economics that individually could have crippled any country, but in combination were devastating to ordinary Afghans.

There were many grim statistics one could enumerate about how damaged the country was after decades of war, but suffice to say that even several years after the United States had toppled the Taliban, the countries of Afghanistan and Burkino Faso, in central Africa, were running neck and neck on their abysmal quality-of-life indicators. Life expectancy for an Afghan was forty-two, while in neighboring Iran it was seventy. And despite the tens of billions of dollars in aid supposedly spent on Afghan reconstruction, the Kabul River, which snakes through the center of the city, was still clogged with garbage and raw sewage many years after the departure of the Taliban.

One of the homes of Kabul's ubiquitous street kids underlined the grinding poverty that was the lot of the vast majority of Afghans. Muzhgan, a slight, shy eleven-year-old girl, begged on the street and collected scraps of paper and cardboard for cooking fuel, while her fourteen-year-old sister Hamida worked in a textile factory. Their father, Abdullah, a day laborer, was unemployed throughout the long winter months when building construction stopped. Luckily, Muzhgan attended the Aschiana School, which provided her a hot lunch and some schooling, as it did for some six thousand other street kids in the Kabul area who would otherwise have gone hungry and uneducated. Together with her sister, Muzhgan brought in ten dollars a week, which was barely enough to cover the rent on the well-kept one-room home they shared with six other members of their family in one of Kabul's burgeoning slums. Theirs was the lot of millions of the residents of Kabul.

On the other end of town, on a dimly lit road in Wazir Akbar Khan, the Upper East Side of Kabul, it was a whole other story. A couple of street kids gestured toward an unmarked iron gate, behind which, they assured passersby, you can find what you are looking for. An Afghan guard gave prospective patrons a wary once-over and opened the gate onto a dark garden, at the end of which a door was slightly ajar and through which you stepped into a world far removed from the dust-blown avenues of Kabul and its street kids like Muzhgan.

At one end of a long room was a well-stocked bar tended by a Chinese madam who assessed prospective customers with a practiced calculus. In front of her were more than a dozen scantily clad, smiling young Chinese women sprawled over a series of bar stools and couches. Adorning the walls were red lanterns and large posters of Bruce Lee and Jackie Chan. Nestling next to the ladies of the night were several mustached, glazed-eyed Afghan men who occasionally took unsteady steps onto a makeshift dance floor to bust some surprisingly graceful traditional moves. A couple of the women tittered as they gamely joined in.

Several of the women tried to make conversation, most of which consisted of "Me no speak English." Conversation was not really the point here. One of the prostitutes whispered, "You guys worry about the attacks?" She was referring to the massive car bomb that had blown up a day earlier a couple of hundred yards from the U.S. embassy, killing two American soldiers, one of them a fifty-two-year-old female reservist, and more than a dozen Afghan bystanders. Shortly after the attack, body parts that looked like fried pieces of meat and bone were found scattered a couple of blocks away from where the bomb had exploded.

Years after the fall of the Taliban, Kabul had a distinctly *fin-de-siècle* air. An economy steeped in corruption and driven by the heroin/opium trade and foreign aid enriched an elite who partied into the night, taking advantage of new freedoms that under the Taliban might have earned them a reprimand from the religious police (listening to music); landed them in prison (drinking alcohol); or had them stoned to death (sex outside marriage). Hotels played loungey house music at night and discreetly served beer and wine. Private parties featured vodka Jello shots and sound systems blasting techno. One restaurant even boasted a pool where comely French female aid workers could display their charms. But, as the years went by, the establishments catering to foreigners and rich Afghans increasingly took on the look of fortresses. Hotels invested in bomb shelters and restaurants deployed armed guards. These were sensible precautions; in May 2006 an angry anti-American mob shot out the ground-floor windows of Kabul's five-star Serena hotel, and a year later Taliban fighters shot the guards outside the same hotel and went room to room hunting and shooting Westerners.

The Taliban played on the fears of a generally conservative population who worried about the corrupting foreign influences exemplified by the thriving bar scene and the bustling Chinese brothels of Kabul. Graeme Smith, a reporter based in Kandahar for Canada's *Globe and Mail*, interviewed forty-two Taliban foot soldiers through an intermediary and was able to make some observations about the insurgents in the Kandahar region: that the Taliban at its core was an uprising by rural Afghans who often had a distaste for the "corruption" foreigners had brought into their cities; that it was a rebellion largely driven by tribes excluded from government; and that the majority of Taliban fighters were engaged in poppy farming.

The Taliban also benefited from American missteps in the early years of the war, which were the result of a number of the Bush administration's ideological positions. The first was an intense dislike of "nation building" being performed by the U.S. military, something that was regarded as the preserve of Clintonian liberals. During the 2000 election campaign, Condoleezza Rice said that "we don't need the 82nd Airborne escorting kids to kindergarten." And, as a candidate, Bush explained in a debate with his Democratic rival, Al Gore, "The vice president and I have a disagreement about the use of troops. He believes in nation building. I would be very careful about using our troops as nation builders." The results of this attitude could be seen in a memo written to Secretary of Defense Donald Rumsfeld by one of his top deputies, Douglas J. Feith. Four days after the American campaign against the Taliban had begun on October 7, 2001, Feith wrote his boss that "nation building is *not* our key strategic goal" (emphasis in original).

The trio who ran the Pentagon—Rumsfeld, Feith, and Wolfowitz—prided themselves on their big-picture strategic thinking, yet the most cursory knowledge of Afghan history suggested that the absence of a strong supportive relationship between the United States and the government in Kabul would be a prelude to the Taliban returning to power. By 9/11 the story of the American neglect of Afghanistan was well-known. Following the expulsion of the Soviets, the George H. W. Bush administration had closed the American embassy in Kabul in 1989 and for more than a decade U.S. policy makers paid virtually no attention to Afghans. As the country was battered by multiple civil wars, the Taliban and later al-Qaeda took good advantage of the resulting vacuum. On 9/11 the United States learned a deadly and expensive lesson about how mistaken it was to stand on the sidelines as Afghanistan sank into chaos.

Following the 2001 attacks on New York and Washington, the Defense Department's attitude and that of the George W. Bush administration in general was: Overthrow the Taliban. Go home. General Tommy Franks recalled that he and Rumsfeld agreed that they would keep the number of American troops in Afghanistan to a minimum. "'We don't want to repeat the Soviets' mistakes,' I told the secretary." But this was a mistaken analogy. The Soviets employed a scorched-earth policy in Afghanistan, killing more than a million Afghans and forcing some five million more to flee the country, creating what was then the world's largest refugee population.

On April 17, 2002, President Bush gave a speech at the Virginia Military Institute, where General George C. Marshall had studied a century earlier, and seemed to promise some kind of Marshall Plan to Afghanistan. Bush said, "Marshall knew that our military victory against enemies in World War II had to be followed by a moral victory that resulted in better lives for individual human beings." But no such plan was forthcoming in Afghanistan. Aid per capita to Bosnians following the end of the Balkan civil war in the mid-1990s was around thirty times that given to Afghans in the first two years after the fall of the Taliban. U.S. monies for reconstruction and humanitarian purposes hovered around an average of $1.75 billion a year between 2002 and 2009, which worked out at about $60 per year per Afghan. Ambassador James Dobbins, the Bush administration's first American envoy to the new Afghan government, observed that "the American administration's early aversion to nation building" meant there was "low input" and therefore "low output," which resulted in "low levels of security and economic growth."

As a result of the Bush administration's early disdain for nation building and its desire to keep the U.S. military presence to a minimum, Admiral Michael Mullen, the chairman of the Joint Chiefs of Staff under both Bush and Obama, observed in a nice piece of understatement in 2008 that Afghanistan had been an "economy of force" operation since the fall of the Taliban. And you get what you pay for. According to a study by RAND, "Afghanistan has received the least amount of resources out of any major American-led, nation-building operation over the last 60 years." Specifically, the initial deployment of American soldiers to Afghanistan following the fall of the Taliban was the smallest per capita peacekeeping force of any U.S. post-conflict deployment since World War II—some six thousand soldiers, about the size of the police force in a city like Houston; hardly sufficient for a country the size of Texas.

Both Karzai and Kofi Annan, then the head of the United Nations, wanted to post international peacekeepers around Afghanistan in early 2002. But the Bush administration blocked any non-U.S. troops from deploying outside Kabul for the first two years of the occupation. Dobbins recalls a meeting in the White House Situation Room in February 2002 in which Rumsfeld killed any idea of expanding the role of the largely European International Security Assistance Force (ISAF) then securing Kabul. Not only was the United States unwilling to police Afghanistan; it wasn't going to let anyone else do it, either.

The six thousand U.S. soldiers in Afghanistan in 2002 had one mission: to hunt the Taliban and al-Qaeda—not to secure the population or help in reconstruction, the classical tasks of a successful counterinsurgency campaign—while the four thousand soldiers in ISAF remained only in Kabul. In the words of the official U.S. military history of the Afghan War, "The strong antipathy towards large-scale reconstruction and governance efforts at high levels in the US government persisted through 2002 and into 2003." Of course, during this period Rumsfeld and other senior officials knew that war in Iraq was looming as a virtual certainty, which also entered into their calculus about maintaining only the lightest of footprints in Afghanistan. Lieutenant General John Vines, the U.S. commanding general in Afghanistan at the time, told Army historians that his bosses were "under enormous pressure not to over commit resources to Afghanistan to make sure everything possible was available for Iraq."

As a result, security was often entrusted to local warlords—which, in turn, slowed the formation of a real Afghan national army. Afghanistan is a country ideally suited to guerrilla warfare, with its high mountain ranges and a landmass that is a third larger than Iraq's, while its population is some four million or so greater. Yet, by the end of the second Bush term there were four times more soldiers and policemen in Iraq than there were in Afghanistan.

The relatively low number of soldiers meant that American and NATO forces could clear the Taliban out of areas but couldn't hold many of those cleared areas and then rebuild them, the critical sequence in any successful counterinsurgency. One Western diplomat in Kabul described military operations in the south of the country as much like "mowing the lawn" every year. NATO forces went in and cleared out Taliban sanctuaries and then had to go back and do it all over again in the same place the following year.

Robert Grenier, the CIA station chief in Islamabad who had helped Hamid Karzai in his battle against the Taliban, was back in Washington in the summer of 2002 in the newly created job of Iraq mission manager. In October, Grenier traveled to Kuwait City to meet with Lieutenant General David McKiernan, who was in the advanced stages of planning the Iraq invasion. Grenier asked McKiernan what he would need for the coming conflict. "As much as you can give me," said the general. Throughout late 2002 and early 2003, the best Agency paramilitary officers, counterterrorism specialists, case officers, and targeting personnel were shifted from dealing with Afghanistan and Pakistan to dealing with Iraq. Grenier described the movement of resources focused on Iraq as a "big surge."

"Operation Iraqi Freedom" consistently received around five times more U.S. funding than "Operation Enduring Freedom" in Afghanistan. And Iraq consumed the bulk of President Bush's focus and effort. Senior U.S. intelligence official David Gordon recalls: "The president was just way too committed to Iraq to think about changing the weight of the commitments."

As NATO expanded its role in Afghanistan in late 2005, on December 19 Rumsfeld ordered that three thousand U.S. soldiers, a sixth of the force, be pulled out of the country. Though this was little noticed in the United States—and in the end didn't happen because of the worsening security situation—Lieutenant General David Barno, who was then commanding U.S. forces in Afghanistan, later explained that this announcement sent exactly the wrong signal to other countries in the region: "Tragically, I believe that this misunderstood message caused both friends and enemies to recalculate their options—with a view toward the U.S. no longer being a lead actor in Afghanistan. . . . Many of the shifts in enemy activity and even the behavior of Afghanistan's neighbors, I believe, can be traced to this period."

The U.S. commanding officer in Afghanistan in 2006 was Lieutenant General Karl Eikenberry, an intense, intellectual soldier who speaks Mandarin and was on his second tour in the country. Eikenberry conceded that "the strength and coherence of the Taliban movement is greater than it was a year ago." In addition to citing tribal and land disputes and narcotrafficking as reasons for the Taliban resurgence, Eikenberry made the following interesting observation about the relationship between reconstruction and violence: "Where the road ends, the Taliban begins."

Certainly, Afghanistan needed much more reconstruction (which in itself was a misnomer—there was little to "reconstruct"; everything needed to be built from scratch). The key road from Kabul to Kandahar, which under the Taliban had been a nightmarish seventeen-hour slalom course with giant potholes that could swallow cars whole, was rebuilt as a black-topped freeway with much hoopla in 2004. By then it was the only large-scale reconstruction project completed in the country since the U.S. invasion, and only two years after the new road was finished the security situation had deteriorated so much that the highway was a suicidal journey for anyone who was foolhardy enough to drive it without substantial security.

Afghans hadn't seen much for the billions of dollars of reconstruction aid that had supposedly been lavished on the country; a decade after the fall of the Taliban, Afghanistan remained one of the poorest countries in the world, on par with such basket cases as Somalia. Much of the aid was consumed by the various international organizations whose four-wheel drives clogged the streets of Kabul. In 2008 the leading British charity Oxfam released a report finding that some 40 percent of aid to Afghanistan was funneled back to donor countries to maintain offices in the West and pay for Western-style salaries, benefits, and vacations. And another study found that less than 20 percent of the international aid ended up being spent on local Afghan projects. Too often Western donor countries had, in effect, generously paid themselves in the guise of helping poor Afghans.

The Bush administration's single-minded focus on Iraq and the relatively small number of American boots on the ground in Afghanistan and the desultory reconstruction efforts there all helped to create a vacuum of security and governance in the country, which the Taliban would deftly exploit.

In January 2007, somewhere in Logar province, forty miles south of Kabul, a twenty-year-old goat herder named Imdadullah strapped on a bulky black waistcoat lined with packages of TNT. The packages were wrapped with newspaper printed in Urdu, the lingua franca of Pakistan, and tied together with a cord that led to a switch attached to a battery capable of detonating the explosives. Glued to the newspapers were nails and ball bearings.

Imdadullah was in Afghanistan at the time, but he was originally from the Pakistani town of Bannu in the North-West Frontier Province, where he had trained for his mission. In that sense he was typical of suicide bombers in Afghanistan, many of whom were Pashtuns from Pakistan. He had been given his explosives-laden vest by a Pakistani Taliban commander named Akthar

Mohammed, but, unlike some suicide bombers, he was not given tranquilizers before setting off on his assignment: to blow up a convoy of Western soldiers and so earn his ticket to Paradise.

But as Imdadullah approached the convoy, fiddling with his detonator switch, he was spotted by an eagle-eyed Afghan policeman. Whether because of faulty wiring or because he simply lost his nerve, Imdadullah's bomb never went off, and, instead of Paradise, he ended up in jail. Three months later, he sat in an interrogation room at a dingy Kabul prison, wrapped in a dark cloak to ward off the building's chill. A cataract had occluded one of his eyes, turning it from brown to a milky color. He said he was not being mistreated by Afghanistan's National Directorate of Security—which had arranged the interview—and was speaking of his own free will.

It's not often that you get to chat with a failed suicide bomber, which is perhaps as good a definition of failure as any other, and it was interesting to hear what Imdadullah had hoped to achieve. "I regret that Almighty Allah did not allow me to sacrifice myself. I wanted to attack the British and foreigners and Americans," he said, expressing confidence that as a martyr he would have been granted the promised seventy-two virgins.

Had Imdadullah's bomb gone off, he almost certainly would have killed a number of Muslims. Eight of every ten victims of suicide attacks in Afghanistan in the previous year were civilians. Suicide bombers like Imdadullah seemed oblivious or unaware of the high civilian toll of their operations (which, however, never matched the carnage inflicted in Iraq by suicide attackers).

Imdadullah explained that he wanted to kill Americans and other foreigners because "it's written in the Holy Koran to do jihad against the infidels." It was pointed out to Imdadullah that it is also written in the Koran that to kill one person is as if to kill the whole of humanity, and that the holy book also admonishes warriors not to kill civilians, which he would undoubtedly have done as his explosive vest—heavy with ball bearings and nails—was designed to be a devastating antipersonnel device. Imdadullah parried: "It's not fair to kill Muslims. It is fair to kill the British and the Americans. Allah has promised us Paradise if we do this." When asked if he still hoped to be a martyr once he got out of jail, Imdadullah replied "Of course," in a tone that suggested he had just been asked a stupid question.

By 2006 in the south and east of Afghanistan, the Taliban were back with a vengeance, propelled in part by suicide attackers like Imdadullah. Suicide attacks went up more than fivefold, from seventeen in 2005 to 123 a year later, while IED attacks doubled; attacks on international forces tripled; Afghan civilian deaths at the hands of the insurgents reached a record seven hundred; and American and NATO military deaths were at their highest levels since the Taliban were ousted.

On September 11, 2006, as the fifth anniversary of the 9/11 attacks was commemorated with the mournful dirge of a bagpiper on the small U.S. base of Bermel, a few miles from the Pakistani border, incoming rockets forced the 150 soldiers of the 10th Mountain Division's Bravo Company gathered together to observe a minute of silence to run for cover. Bravo Company fired back long-barreled 105 mm howitzers, which rocketed off with an earsplitting report. Captain Jason Dye, who commanded Bravo Company, explained that "we used to get a rocket attack once a week. Now it's every other day."

This was an interesting observation because just a week before, the Pakistani government had signed a peace deal with the militants in North Waziristan, a tribal area of Pakistan just across the border from the Bermel base. While the peace agreement might have lowered the tempo of militant attacks inside Pakistan, the deal brought more attacks into Afghanistan. Up in the steep hills high above the Bermel base, Dye's men found cross marks and horizontal slashes cut deep into the trees, reference points the Taliban used for calibrating and bracketing the rocket attacks on the American base below them.

The movement of religious warriors had regrouped substantially since their seeming defeat five years earlier. A key to the resurgence of the Taliban could be summarized in one word: Pakistan. After 9/11 the Pakistani government was either unwilling or incapable of clamping down on the Taliban. According to a U.S. military official, between 2001 and 2006 not a single senior Taliban leader was arrested or killed in Pakistan. This was despite the fact that the leaders of the Taliban mostly lived in Pakistan. Amir Haqqani, the leader of the Taliban in Zabul province in 2006, for instance, never came across the border into Afghanistan.

General James Jones, then the Supreme Allied Commander of NATO (and later President Obama's national security advisor), testified in 2006 before the Senate Foreign Relations Committee that it was "generally accepted" that the Taliban maintained their headquarters in Quetta, a city of one million that is the capital of Baluchistan province, in southwestern Pakistan. A senior U.S. military intelligence official said of the Taliban leader Mullah Omar's location: "At one point we had it down to a particular section of Quetta." The official explained that Mullah Omar continued to supply "high level guidance" to his movement of religious warriors, although he was not involved in day-to-day military operations.

In 2007 Abdul Haq Hanif, a lanky, bearded, twenty-six-year-old former spokesman for the Taliban, serving a six-year prison sentence in a jail in Kabul, confirmed that the Taliban leadership had settled across the border in Pakistan. "I was dealing with provincial Taliban leaders," he explained. "They were calling from Pakistan."

Despite its general acquiescence in allowing its old Taliban allies to operate from its territory, the Pakistani army would sometimes act against them. A U.S. military official characterized Pakistani cooperation on the Taliban as "schizophrenic." The official pointed to the case of Mullah Osmani, a leading Taliban commander killed by a U.S. airstrike inside Afghanistan on December 19, 2006, as an example of what Pakistan's government could do when it wanted to: "We would not have got him without Pakistani information."

In the years after 9/11 the Pakistani government routinely denied that it provided a haven for the Taliban leadership. An explanation for the seeming dichotomy between the fact that U.S. military and intelligence officials universally held the view that the Taliban were headquartered in Pakistan and the government denial of this, is that the Pakistani government has never completely controlled its own territory. And ISI, the Pakistani military intelligence agency, at some levels continued to tolerate and/or maintain links with certain Taliban leaders throughout the "war on terror."

The Taliban also had deep roots in Pakistan. Many members of the movement of religious warriors had grown up in refugee camps there. Not only that, but the Taliban, an almost entirely Pashtun organization, drew strength from the fact that, at some 40 million, the Pashtuns are one of the largest ethnic groupings in the world without their own state. They straddle both sides of the Afghan-Pakistan border, a line that was drawn by the British in 1893 and that many Pashtuns don't recognize; there are almost twice as many Pashtuns in Pakistan as there are in Afghanistan. And after the U.S. invasion of Afghanistan, the Taliban were increasingly seen by some Pashtuns as the defender of their rights. That's why when pollsters asked Afghans of all ethnic groups their view of the Taliban, in any given year after 9/11 no more than 10 percent viewed them favorably, but in Kandahar and Helmand provinces, in the Pashtun-dominated south of Afghanistan, one survey found favorable numbers as high as 27 percent by 2007.

One of the key leaders of the Taliban as it surged in strength was Mullah Dadullah, a thuggish but effective commander who, like his counterpart in Iraq, Abu Musab al-Zarqawi, thrived on killing Shia, beheading his hostages, and media celebrity. In interviews in 2006, Mullah Dadullah said that Taliban forces numbered some 12,000 fighters. That was larger than a U.S. military official's estimate the same year of between 7,000 and 10,000, but a number that likely had some validity given the numerous part-time Taliban farmer/fighters. Dadullah also conceded what was obvious as the violence dramatically expanded in Afghanistan between 2005 and 2006: that the Taliban had increasingly morphed together tactically and ideologically with al-Qaeda. "Osama bin Laden, thank God, is alive and in good health. We are in contact with his top aides and sharing plans and operations with each other."

A U.S. military official estimated that in 2006 there were several hundred foreign militants tied to al-Qaeda in Afghanistan, mostly Uzbeks, but also some North Africans, Saudis, and Egyptians. "They won't be taken, though we have captured some," said the official. Those foreign militants helped the Taliban become a more effective military force. A Taliban member explained: "The Arabs taught us how to make an IED by mixing nitrate fertilizer and diesel fuel and how to pack plastic explosives and to connect them to detonators and remote-control devices like mobile phones. We learned how to do this blindfolded so we could safely plant IEDs in the dark." Another recounted that "Arab and Iraqi mujahideen began visiting us, transferring the latest IED technology and suicide-bomber tactics they had learned in the Iraqi resistance." Small numbers of al-Qaeda instructors embedded with much larger Taliban units functioned something like U.S. Special Forces do—as trainers and force multipliers.

The Taliban commander Mullah Dadullah explained that bin Laden himself had supervised the suicide operation targeting Vice President Cheney at Bagram Air Base during his visit to Afghanistan on February 27, 2007, an attack that killed nearly two dozen, including an American soldier. The U.S. military dismissed that claim but said that another al-Qaeda leader, Abu Laith al-Libi, was behind the operation, which seemed more of a confirmation than a denial of al-Qaeda's role in the attack.

Militants based on the Afghan-Pakistan border also traveled to Iraq for on-the-job training. Evidence for the migration of al-Qaeda members to Iraq from Afghanistan can be found in the stories of Hassan Gul, an al-Qaeda courier from Pakistan who was arrested while entering northern Iraq in January

2004, and in the case of Omar al-Farouq, a high-ranking al-Qaeda official who escaped from American custody at Bagram Air Base outside of Kabul in 2005 and was killed in Iraq a year later. Similarly, in late 2006 the Pentagon announced that Abdul Hadi al-Iraqi, an al-Qaeda leader based on the Afghan-Pakistan border, had been captured as he was making his way to Iraq. Hamid Mir, the Pakistani journalist, said that militants he had interviewed had traveled from Afghanistan to Iraq. "I met a Taliban commander, Mullah Mannan, in Zabul in 2004 who told me that he was trained in Iraq and subsequently he set up his own training camp in Zabul."

In 2009, Mustafa Abu al-Yazid, one of al-Qaeda's founders, described his group's rapport with the Taliban during an interview with Al Jazeera in Afghanistan. "We are on a good and strong relationship with them," he explained, "and we frequently meet them." He also said that his organization continued to regard Mullah Omar as the "Commander of the Faithful"—in effect acknowledging that the Taliban leader is al-Qaeda's religious guide, a position he had enjoyed for more than a decade.

When the Taliban had ruled Afghanistan they were a provincial bunch. Mullah Omar rarely visited Kabul in the five years that he ran the country and made a point of avoiding meeting with most non-Muslims and journalists. Omar, whose education was not more than that of a village mullah, was far from worldly; when the Taliban leader was given a toy camel by visiting Chinese diplomats, he recoiled in horror as if they had handed him a piece of red-hot coal because he believed all representations of living beings to be against Islam.

But in the decade after their fall from power, this was no longer your father's Taliban. They began courting the press and Taliban spokesmen were available at any time of the day or night to discuss the latest developments, even publishing their cell phone numbers on jihadist web sites. The Taliban's public statements were now filled with references to Iraq and Palestine in a manner that mirrored bin Laden's. They had also adopted the playbook of the Iraqi insurgency wholesale, embracing suicide bombers and IED attacks on U.S. and NATO convoys. The Taliban only began deploying suicide attackers in large numbers after the success of such operations in Iraq had become obvious to all. Where once the Taliban had banned television, now they boasted an active video propaganda operation named Umar, which posted regular updates to the Web. Hundreds of dollars were paid to the cameramen who successfully recorded the Taliban's suicide operations. Those videos were then distributed on DVDs for purchase for the equivalent of fifty cents in city markets or were posted to jihadist websites.

A typical sequence in one of those videotapes shows a smiling young man getting into one of Afghanistan's ubiquitous white and yellow Toyota taxis. He sits down in the driver's seat and the camera pans to the ignition switch next to him, which is in turn connected to a series of homemade bombs. The driver may wave at the camera, or he may not. It's his call; after all, this is going to be the suicide bomber's first and only fifteen minutes of fame. Jihadi chants swell in the background (but not actual music because that is *haram*, forbidden). The camera follows the taxi as it drives out of frame. And then the video cuts to an intersection filmed on a long zoom lens several hundred yards from the cameraman's position. The taxi speeds toward the intersection, gathering speed as it hits a NATO convoy. A plume of smoke goes up first; then, a few moments later, you hear the sound of the explosion because sound travels slower than light. The cameraman shouts "Allah Akbar! Allah Akbar!" and the sequence ends. By 2007 there were literally scores of videos like this in circulation in Afghanistan.

The Taliban also offered something concrete to ordinary Afghans, which was rough and ready justice. The Afghan judicial system remained a joke long after the Taliban had fled Kabul, and so farmers and their families—the vast majority of the population—looking to settle disputes about land, water, and grazing rights could find a swift resolution of these problems in a Taliban court. In some areas the Taliban even set up their own parallel government, appointing shadow governors as well as judges. By late 2008 the Taliban were running two dozen law courts in southern Afghanistan. They were regarded as fairer than the central government's courts.

By 2006, NATO, at least on paper, had taken over military operations in much of Afghanistan. But in practice, of the twenty-six countries that made up the alliance, few would do any real fighting. A senior NATO commander in Kabul in December 2005 explained that he had fourteen pages of "national caveats" to contend with. German forces, for instance, would only operate in the relative safety of northern Afghanistan. Three years later, a U.S. military official griped that "only a handful of countries are doing the real work," such as the British and Canadians then fighting in the south.

The military chain of command in Afghanistan passed through a spaghetti bowl of acronyms—ISAF, CENTCOM, and the many countries that made up NATO—that was so bewildering that only five people in the world could have possibly explained how it was all supposed to work together, and they would have had to do it in French because they all lived in Brussels at NATO headquarters. "Unity of command," in which authority is vested in one commander, is a basic principle of counterinsurgency, indeed of warfare in general, yet once NATO took over it was never really clear who was in charge of military operations in the country. That problem lingered on for three years, until finally, in the summer of 2008, General McKiernan, who had led the ground invasion of Iraq, was made the commander of all U.S. and NATO forces in the country. (American Special Forces retained their own chain of command.)

The Taliban had banned poppy growing in 2000, but half a decade later they started killing government forces eradicating poppy fields, and were profiting handsomely from the opium trade. It is no coincidence that opium and heroin production, which by 2007 was equivalent to one-third of Afghanistan's licit economy, spiked at the same time that the Taliban staged a comeback. Afghanistan was the source of more than 90 percent of the world's heroin. Individual donations from the Middle East were also boosting the Taliban's coffers. These twin revenue streams—drug money and Mideast contributions—allowed the Taliban to pay some of their fighters $100 or more a month, which compared favorably to the $70 salary of an Afghan policeman. Kidnappings also fueled the Taliban, who could make millions of dollars abducting a foreigner, as they did with Daniele Mastrogiacomo, an Italian journalist kidnapped in 2007.

In his jail cell in Kabul, the Taliban spokesman Abdul Haq Hanif acknowledged the linkage between the Taliban and the drug trade, conceding what pretty much every Afghan and U.S. official in Afghanistan has been saying for years, that the Taliban was, in part, a drug cartel. Hanif explained: "The Taliban said to people to cultivate poppies in your lands and we will protect you."

"First, do no harm" is a sensible injunction in combating any insurgency, but the United States adopted a counterproductive poppy eradication strategy in Afghanistan. That policy was championed by William B. Wood, the American ambassador in Afghanistan from April 2007 to January 2009, who was known locally as "Chemical Bill" because of his preference for the eradication of poppy fields by chemicals dispersed from the air. This idea did not sit well with Afghans who still retained unpleasant memories of the Soviets spraying napalm and other defoliants from the air. Wood told Karzai that the chemicals that would be used to eradicate the poppy fields were so safe that he was willing to go to Massoud Circle, a major traffic intersection in Kabul, and jump into a fifty-five-gallon drum of the chemicals in his Speedos to prove just how safe they were. This argument proved unpersuasive and the Afghan government rejected aerial spraying.

Poppy eradication was a particularly hard sell in the south of Afghanistan. In April 2007, General Mohammed Daud, who headed his government's eradication efforts, traveled down to Uruzgan, an isolated, poverty-stricken province that retained a strong Taliban presence. Tarin Kowt, the dusty, flyblown provincial capital, was devoid of any women, its central market peopled by fierce Pashtun tribesmen wearing the black turbans favored by the Taliban. General Daud met with Uruzgan's deputy governor to discuss how and where eradication efforts might proceed. During a break in the meeting, one of Daud's aides stepped out onto a balcony in the governor's mansion and was greeted by the sight of a sea of lush poppy fields stretching from the walls of the governor's mansion to a range of mountains several miles away. Already the distinctive red flowers of the mature poppy plants could be seen in some of the fields. The Afghan counternarcotics official said, "Uruzgan is a very beautiful place." Smiling, he added, "And a very dangerous place."

According to the UN, Uruzgan in 2007 had the fifth-largest poppy harvest of any of the thirty-four provinces in Afghanistan, making eradication efforts distinctly unpopular locally. No wonder the governor of the province had some pressing business elsewhere and was out of town for General Daud's visit with his eradication force, the first high-level delegation from Kabul to spend any time in Tarin Kowt in years.

One morning Daud and his aides drove out to a scrubby, desert flatland area several miles out of Tarin Kowt, where they met up with what looked like a large traveling circus, albeit a heavily armed one. Two hundred policemen trucked in from Kabul had set up large green tents to live in during the two-week eradication program that was planned for the province. The policemen were members of the Afghan Eradication Force, which traveled around the country destroying poppy fields if the locals didn't have the will or ability to do it for themselves, as was obviously the case in Uruzgan.

Large trucks disgorged some twenty all-terrain vehicles, powerful, four-wheel-drive mini-tractors with large tires. The ATVs were brought in because Afghan peasants would sometimes flood their fields to prevent ordinary tractors from doing the eradication. On the back of the vehicles workmen affixed long metal bars that would be dragged over the poppy stalks to break them down. The entire operation, nominally an Afghan one, was directed by employees of DynCorp, a large American contractor. The DynCorp guys were easy to spot, as they were wearing the uniform of the American contractor in Afghanistan—Oakley shades, goatees and beards, baseball caps, T-shirts, tan pants, and work boots.

Three days into the eradication effort, Taliban fighters, some disguised in burqas, sprang a series of ambushes on the eradication force, pinning them down in an intense several-hour firefight that seriously injured four policemen.

The Uruzgan attack demonstrated, for those who hadn't yet figured it out, just how the Taliban was seeking to exploit popular resentment against eradication efforts. All across the country, Afghan support for poppy cultivation was then on the upswing; almost 40 percent of Afghans considered it acceptable if there was no other way to earn a living, and in the southwest, where much of the poppy crop was grown, two out of three people said it was acceptable.

Instead of taking such findings to heart, the Bush administration's counternarcotics policy placed eradication at its center, even though it was met with growing Afghan skepticism and, in some cases, violence. Why was the policy so unpopular? Afghanistan is one of the poorest countries in the world and many rural Afghans have few options to make money other than by poppy growing. Abruptly ending the poppy/opium trade was not an option, as that would have put up to three million people out of work, or around a tenth of the population, and impoverished millions more; the only really functional part of the economy was poppy and opium production. Farmers could earn as much as twelve dollars a day growing poppy, while a tailor might make that in a month. You simply could not eviscerate the livelihoods of the millions of Afghans who grew poppies and not expect a backlash.

Manual eradication by Afghan policemen working together with DynCorp's contractors failed to wipe out the drug trade. Quite the reverse: trade boomed and the eradication approach only created more enemies, since the farmers who had their crops destroyed were generally the poorer ones who couldn't pay the bribes to have their fields left alone. Those farmers proved easy recruits to the Taliban cause. The U.S. government, in short, was deeply committed to an unsuccessful drug policy that helped its enemies. (The measure of a successful counternarcotics policy should not have been hectares of poppy destroyed every year, but hectares of other crops that were planted.)

The drug trade not only helped fund the Taliban; it also fueled Afghanistan's pervasive corruption. By 2008, according to the watchdog group Transparency International, Afghanistan was rated one of the most corrupt countries on the planet, alongside such completely failed states as Somalia, in part because government officials were reaping the benefits of the drug trade, and not just the Taliban. In June 2005, U.S. Drug Enforcement Administration officials and Afghan police raided the office of the governor of Helmand, Sher Mohammed Akhundzada, and found nine tons of opium in his office. Wali Karzai, President Karzai's brother and an important politician in Kandahar, was repeatedly identified in news reports as profiting from the drug business. Yet a culture of impunity existed for those at the top of the heroin trade, exemplified by the vast, gaudy mansions that the drug barons built for themselves in the center of Kabul.

By 2006, Karzai, now often derided as the "mayor of Kabul," seemed to be losing his grip. Not only would he not move against the drug lords, but some of the most competent officials, such as foreign minister Dr. Abdullah and the finance minister Ashraf Ghani, had left the government. There was also little true representation of Pashtun political interests in parliament because Karzai appeared to distrust political parties.

In the latter half of the second Bush term, Afghanistan's drift into chaos became a matter of concern at the White House. Meghan O'Sullivan, Bush's adviser on Iraq and Afghanistan, had instituted a review of Afghan policy while Iraq was still on fire in 2006 but no substantive changes of policy emerged out of that review. O'Sullivan recalls: "The recommendations were made, and they were accepted, and then people were told to go and ferret out the resources, and we didn't have them. And so, they weren't executed." Another official at the White House working on Afghanistan recalls that during this period, "There were many discussions about expanding the small Afghan national army," but nothing of substance happened.

In 2007, the U.S. ambassador in Kabul, William Wood, and the commanding general in Afghanistan, Dan McNeill, were telling White House officials in videoconferences that everything was fine. One official recalled, "They believed it from their bubble."

But a group of senior Bush administration officials who dubbed themselves "the shura"—the Arabic word means council—had begun traveling to the country regularly and did not share this rosy view. Key members of the shura were Lieutenant General Douglas E. Lute, who had been appointed "war czar" at the White House for Iraq and Afghanistan in May 2007, and Eliot Cohen, one of Condoleezza Rice's top deputies at the State Department. Cohen recalls that during the summer of 2007 he and his staff started examining color-coded maps of Afghanistan going back five years that the United Nations had drawn up to show where in the country it was safe for aid organizations to work: "And you can just see the green shrinking, the yellow growing, and the red really growing." By the summer of 2008, after one of the trips of the shura to Afghanistan, it was obvious to the group that the country's downward trajectory was now a real problem. General Lute recalled: "There was a point where we basically just concluded, this was really going bad on us: There's no sort of seminal event but we were not winning. And in a counterinsurgency, that's not good enough."

The growing alarm about Afghanistan precipitated a soup-to-nuts review during the fall of 2008. David Kilcullen, who had recently served in Iraq as General David Petraeus's counterinsurgency adviser, was then advising Secretary of State Condoleezza Rice. Kilcullen says, "By September there was critical mass in the Bush administration for a new review. Part of it was that this pressure had been building, to look at Afghanistan again; part of it was Iraq started to turn in the middle of '07, and finally they got enough bandwidth back that they could think about something other than Iraq. It was very, very hard to get their attention on Afghanistan until Iraq started to turn around. They were just all Iraq, all the time."

In mid-September 2008, as the formal review began, President Bush's instructions to his team were: "I don't want a written report out of this thing any time before the twentieth of January '09, and I want you to look at two issues. One, things I have to do now, as president, which are urgent. And secondly, what are we handing off to the next administration, and how do we help them understand the issue?" There was no disagreement among the couple of dozen officials who worked on the review that Afghanistan was on a downward slope. Participants were told that violence had gone up more than 500 percent in the past five years and Afghan support for international forces had plummeted by 33 percent in the past few months, according to private polling commissioned by the U.S. government.

Two weeks before Americans went to the polls to vote for John McCain or Barack Obama in the 2008 presidential election, Bush administration officials briefed advisers to both campaigns about the deteriorating situation in Afghanistan. The meeting was held at the Army and Navy Club in downtown

Washington, D.C., and was organized, in part, by Barnett Rubin, a professor at New York University and the country's leading Afghan expert. Kilcullen remembers, "We gave them a briefing on the Afghanistan review. Sort of swore them to silence, and we told them everything we'd done. That was the point at which I realized Obama was going to win the election, because the McCain people were defeated and slumping and not even taking notes. And the Obama people were sitting up straight and they were taking notes. They were clearly people who expected to take office and assume responsibility for the problem."

After Obama won the election, and under instructions from Bush, National Security Advisor Stephen Hadley briefed his incoming replacement, General James Jones, about the content of the Afghan review. Hadley recalls, "The president said, basically, 'Why don't you talk to Jones about it, ask him what he wants to do. My guess is they'll opt to have us give them the strategy review and not announce it.' I did talk to Jones, and they were briefed on the strategy review, and Jones said, 'Leave it for us.' So we did." The unpublicized Bush review outlined some of the policies that the Obama administration would later adopt, including treating Afghanistan as a regional problem that included Pakistan and building up the Afghan state at the provincial level, something that hitherto had been largely ignored, and it advocated an expanded counterinsurgency mission.

General David McKiernan had recently consolidated control over U.S. and NATO forces in Afghanistan and started adjusting their tactics. McKiernan issued an order on September 2, 2008, that U.S./NATO forces should change their rules of engagement by emphasizing the need for proportional force in reacting to Taliban attacks so as to lower civilian casualties, the issue that was most damaging to the standing of the coalition among the Afghan population. A key part of McKiernan's new strategy involved reaching out to Afghanistan's many tribes. It was an approach that the U.S. military had successfully adopted in Iraq, where tens of thousands of Sunni tribe members involved in the "Sunni Awakening" were put on the American payroll. To attempt to replicate elements of that approach, the U.S. military and NATO started mapping the approximately four hundred tribes and their many subtribes across Afghanistan. And in the winter of 2008 a pilot program in the central Afghan province of Wardak, thirty miles from Kabul, was put in place to arm local militias to fight the resurgent local Taliban. In late 2008, McKiernan also requested more than 20,000 new troops to supplement the relatively small force of 32,000 then on the ground; around 10,000 of them were authorized by President Bush in the waning months of his final term.

But these incremental measures could not hide the fact that by the time Bush left office, the Taliban were stronger than at any point since they had lost Kabul seven years earlier. By one estimate the Taliban had a permanent presence in 72 percent of the country. The Taliban, which in 2002 had barely been more than a nuisance, now controlled large sections of Afghanistan's most important road, the three-hundred-mile Kabul to Kandahar highway, and by 2008 more American soldiers were dying in Afghanistan than in Iraq.

Afghanistan should have been a demonstration project of American resolve and American compassion: a signal to her enemies that, once evicted from their sanctuaries, they would never be allowed back; and a signal to her friends that a peaceful, stable state could flourish in a land where militant Islamists had once reigned. But as Lieutenant General David Barno, the commanding general in Afghanistan between 2003 and 2005, later dryly noted of the U.S. effort in Afghanistan, "'Nation-building' was explicitly *not* part of the formula."

America's neglect of Afghanistan after 2001 was an enormous missed opportunity and something that Bush officials only really began to grapple with seriously during their last year in office.

Chapter 12

Al-Qaeda 2.0

God has bestowed on our beloved emir Sheikh Osama bin Laden and his brothers the mujahideen what they wished for—and that is the globalization of the concept of jihad.

—Mustafa Abu al-Yazid, al-Qaeda's commander in Afghanistan, in a video released to Al Jazeera in 2007

We are at war and I am a soldier.

—Mohammed Siddique Khan, a British primary school teacher, who blew himself up on the London Underground, speaking on his al-Qaeda "martyrdom" videotape in 2005

The plague bacillus never dies or vanishes entirely . . . it can remain dormant for years and years in furniture and linen chests . . . it waits patiently in bedrooms, cellars, trunks, and bookshelves and . . . perhaps the day will come when, for the instruction of mankind, the plague will rouse its rats again and send them forth to die in a well-contented city.

—Albert Camus

On the morning of July 7, 2005, at around eight-thirty, four men hugged each other at Kings Cross railway station in London, a moment that was caught on one of the capital's ubiquitous surveillance cameras. The men appeared to be happy, even euphoric before they separated to board three trains on the Underground and a double-decker bus. Within the next hour and a half the men detonated bombs that killed themselves and fifty-two commuters and maimed hundreds more. It was the deadliest terrorist attack in British history and the first time that British citizens had conducted suicide operations in their own country. The attacks took place as Prime Minister Tony Blair was hosting the G-8 meeting of world leaders in Scotland and appeared to be timed for maximum embarrassment to the government.

A few days after the bombings, police identified all four of the suicide attackers from surveillance camera footage. The bombers were relatively easy to spot because three were of Pakistani descent and all of them were carrying large backpacks inside which were packed their bombs. They were an unremarkable bunch of blokes. Ringleader Mohammed Siddique Khan, known widely as "Sid," was a beloved teacher at a primary school in the northern city of Leeds, teaching handicapped children, and the happily married thirty-year-old father of a baby daughter, with another kid on the way. Shehzad Tanweer, a keen cricketer, was the twenty-two-year-old son of a relatively prosperous businessman who owned a slaughterhouse and fish-and-chips shop in Leeds. Tanweer, a fastidious dresser, tooled around town in a red Mercedes that his father had given him. Eighteen-year-old Hasib Hussain was faring poorly at school and drifting in life, while Germaine Lindsay was an unemployed, nineteen-year-old Jamaican-British convert to Islam.

While all the London bombers were known for their strict religious observance, none was regarded by their friends and families as a militant. They seemed utterly ordinary, their leisure time made up of cricket and soccer practice, working out together and going on paintballing trips. But there was another hidden dimension to their lives that centered on an Islamic bookshop in the bleak Leeds suburb of Beeston where they would go to buy jihadi videos. The Beeston cell bonded around watching videos of atrocities against Muslims in Iraq, Palestine, and Chechnya.

Once radicalized in Britain, the two ringleaders, Khan and Tanweer, traveled to Pakistan to link up there with militant groups. Before making what would be his final trip to Pakistan in the winter of 2004, Khan made a farewell video of himself in his Leeds home. On the tape Khan addressed his baby daughter cradled in his arms and said, "Not too long to go now and I'm going to really miss you." Khan, it seems, expected to die on his last trip to Pakistan, but something changed for him there, and instead he returned to his native land with plans to wreak mayhem in London.

Once they got over the shock of the fact that the London attacks were conducted by their own citizens, the British press and government initially portrayed the bombings as an entirely "homegrown" plot with no links to an overseas group, carried out by "self-starting" militants who had radicalized themselves in their hometown of Leeds. Typical of this view was a report in the well-sourced *Sunday Times* newspaper, which said that British authorities had found no evidence linking the bombers to al-Qaeda and they were instead a new breed of "unaffiliated" militants. But while the London bombings were certainly implemented by homegrown terrorists, what had in fact turned them from a group of angry young men into an effective terrorist cell was the training and direction that the leader of the group had received from al-Qaeda in Pakistan.

Two months after the London bombings, a videotape of Khan, the lead suicide attacker, appeared on Al Jazeera branded with the distinctive, golden Arabic logo of al-Qaeda's Pakistan-based media arm, *Al-Sahab* ("the Clouds"). On his "martyrdom" videotape—a standard accoutrement of al-Qaeda attackers since 9/11—Khan addressed his audience in the broad accent of his native Yorkshire, saying softly, "I'm going to talk to you in a language that you understand. Our words are dead until we give them life with our blood." Khan, wearing a Palestinian-style red and white checkered head scarf, went on to describe bin Laden and his deputy Ayman al-Zawahiri as "today's heroes."

On the same videotape Zawahiri himself made an appearance, explaining that the London bombings were revenge for Britain's participation in the war in Iraq, and came as a result of ignoring bin Laden's earlier offer of a "truce" with those European nations participating in the coalition in Iraq that were willing to pull out of the country. That truce offer expired on July 15, 2004, almost exactly a year before the London attacks took place. (In 2006 a martyrdom video of bomber Shehzad Tanweer appeared; this one was also made by Al-Sahab, further evidence of al-Qaeda's role in the bombings.)

Khan returned to England in February 2005 and made his first purchase of hydrogen peroxide chemicals with which to build bombs. In an apartment in Leeds that Khan and his fellow plotters rented to serve as their bomb factory, they mixed the chemicals, which were so noxious that neighbors noticed that their plants were wilting. As they brewed up the batches of chemicals, the bombers wore disposable masks because of the high toxicity of the materials, which bleached their dark hair a noticeably lighter color. They also installed a commercial-grade refrigerator in the apartment to keep the highly unstable bomb ingredients cold. The four bombs that detonated in London on July 7, 2005, were all hydrogen-peroxide-based devices, a signature of plots that have had a connection to al-Qaeda's Pakistani training camps since 9/11.

The bombings were largely financed by Khan using credit cards and a personal loan from a bank. (Much of the hysterical analysis about "Saudi funding" for terrorism, which was pervasive after 9/11, fell apart when you looked at particular terrorism cases in any detail; the plots were often self-financed and, in any event, generally didn't cost much money.) Underlining the fact that terrorism is a cheap form of warfare, the British government found that the entire London operation cost around £8,000 ($14,000), including airfares to Pakistan and the chemicals to make the bombs.

Two weeks after the 7/7 attacks, on July 21, 2005, a second wave of hydrogen-peroxide-based bombs was set off in London, this one organized by a cell of Somali and Eritrean men who were first-generation immigrants. Like the 7/7 bombers, the 7/21 cell members would gather in each other's flats to watch videos of the Iraq War and the beheadings of "infidels." Fortunately, while four bombs were set to detonate on 7/21—three on the London Underground and one on a bus, mimicking the attacks two weeks earlier—their faulty construction rendered them harmless. One of the conspirators fled London wearing an all-enveloping black burqa, accessorized with a handbag, and was recorded by surveillance cameras in Birmingham a day after the failed bombings. With the July 21 bombing attempts, Londoners, who had taken the 7/7 attacks somewhat in their stride, were now facing the unnerving possibility that there would be a sustained campaign of suicide attacks in the capital.

At the trial of the would-be bombers, a scientist testified that the explosive devices they had used were similar to the bombs used on 7/7. Prosecutors said Mukhtar Ibrahim, the leader of the July 21 group, had traveled to Pakistan in 2005 around the time that the 7/7 cell leader, Mohammed Siddique Khan, was there. Ibrahim denied this, but a year before the attacks, he had been searched by British authorities on his way to Pakistan and was found to be carrying camping equipment, cold weather gear, three thousand pounds in cash, and pages from a first-aid manual about how to treat ballistic injuries, suggesting that he was not embarking on a conventional vacation. Ibrahim had also previously traveled to Sudan "to do jihad." Jurors convicted Ibrahim and three of his sidekicks of conspiracy to murder despite their claims that they had designed their bombs only to make a symbolic noise and had no intention to harm anyone.

The grim lesson of the London 7/7 attacks was that al-Qaeda was still able to inspire and direct simultaneous bombings in a major European capital, thousands of miles from its base on the Afghan-Pakistan border. By the summer of 2005, al-Qaeda had recovered sufficient strength that it could now undertake multiple, successful bombings aimed at targets in the West. And the London bombings underlined the fact that no Western country was more affected by Pakistan's jihadist culture than the United Kingdom, because many British terrorists are either second-generation Pakistanis or have trained with militant groups in Pakistan.

Despite the success of the London bombings, as the 9/11 attacks faded into history, some believed that al-Qaeda's leader and the organization he headed had largely faded into irrelevance, not able to carry out an attack on the United States and seemingly able only to threaten Americans with video- and audiotapes that occasionally popped up on the Internet. At a press conference in 2006, President Bush asserted, "Absolutely, we're winning. Al-Qaeda is on the run." American officials weren't the only ones who believed this. On the fifth anniversary of 9/11, the *Atlantic* ran a cover story headlined simply "We Won."

The most prominent exponent of the view that al-Qaeda was largely out of business was Dr. Marc Sageman, a sociologist and former CIA case officer who in 2004 had published an influential study of jihadist terrorists titled *Understanding Terror Networks*. A year later he told PBS that "Al-Qaeda is operationally dead." And in early 2008 Sageman published another book, *Leaderless Jihad*, which claimed that "the present threat has evolved from a structured group of al-Qaeda masterminds controlling vast resources and issuing commands, to a multitude of informal groups trying to emulate their predecessors by conceiving and executing plans from the bottom up. These 'homegrown' wannabes form a scattered global network, a leaderless jihad." In the *Washington Post* Sageman further argued that these homegrown militants "must now be seen as the main terrorist threat to the West."

In the spring of 2008, Bruce Hoffman, a Georgetown University professor who had worked at the CIA after the 9/11 attacks and was the author of the standard text *Inside Terrorism*, launched a blistering critique of Sageman's claim that "leaderless" jihadis unconnected to a formal terror group were now the main threat to the West. Hoffman wrote in *Foreign Affairs* that this was "a fundamental misreading of the al-Qaeda threat," pointing out that the terrorist group had reorganized and reinvigorated itself in the years following the fall of the Taliban. Sageman, a frequent consultant to government agencies, and the New York Police Department's freshly minted first scholar-in-residence, fired back at Hoffman in the *New York Times*, saying "maybe he's mad that I'm the go-to guy now."

Henry Kissinger is supposed to have quipped that "the reason why academic quarrels are so nasty is that the stakes are so small." But in the case of the Sageman-Hoffman spat the stakes were enormously high; if indeed Sageman was correct that the West was threatened largely by "self-starting" homegrown militants, then why spend hundreds of billions of dollars in a "Global War on Terror" in places like Afghanistan, Pakistan, Iraq, and Yemen, where al-Qaeda and its affiliated groups were headquartered? If Hoffman was correct, then the course that the Bush administration had followed, of taking the war to wherever al-Qaeda and its allies had found sanctuary, made a great deal of sense.

The idea of a "leaderless jihad" was not a new one. In a different context, Louis Beam, a prominent American racist, advocated the idea of "leaderless resistance" during the 1980s as a technique for his fellow racists to struggle successfully against the American government without fear of being penetrated by law enforcement agencies. Beam explained: "Utilizing the Leaderless Resistance concept, all individuals and groups operate independently of each other, and never report to a central headquarters or single leader for direction or instruction, as would those who belong to a typical pyramid organization." Timothy McVeigh, who bombed the Murrah Federal Building in Oklahoma City in 1995, killing 168, the deadliest terrorist attack on the American homeland hitherto, carried out this attack largely as an independent operator functioning with no support from any formal organization, which demonstrated that the "leaderless resistance" model really worked.

The "leaderless jihad" concept had also percolated within al-Qaeda itself in the years before 9/11. Abu Musab al-Suri, the intense Syrian intellectual who was at once an ally and internal critic of bin Laden's, in 2000 set up his own training camp in eastern Afghanistan, where he laid out the principles of such an approach, which was quite contrary to al-Qaeda's existing heavily bureaucratized, top-down structure.

Videotapes recovered in Afghanistan after the fall of the Taliban showed Suri in front of a whiteboard addressing one of his classes, explaining that he wanted to demonstrate how to keep jihadist cells secure. Suri then launched into a critique of the hierarchical structures prevalent in al-Qaeda, drawing a diagram indicating how easy it is to round up a cell structure in which many cells can be traced back to the leader of the organization. Suri urged that the best approach for jihadists in the future was to organize themselves in small cells with a flatter structure. "In the new stage," Suri told his class, "I advise that your brigade doesn't exceed ten members." And Suri outlined the importance of self-starting militants taking the jihad into their own hands: "If a man living in Sweden spots a Jewish security target, he should attack it."

In his magnum opus, the fifteen-hundred-page *Call for Global Islamic Resistance*, which Suri released to the Internet in 2004, he formalized his concept into the slogan "nizam la tanzim"—"a system, not an organization"—meaning that there should be no organizational bonds between the "Resistance fighters" who are bound together only by their common ideology: defeating the supposed enemies of Islam.

After the fall of the Taliban, al-Qaeda of necessity had to adopt a flatter structure because the group had been flattened by the American assault on Afghanistan and it would subsequently never resurrect its network of Afghan-era, large-scale training camps that had churned out thousands of graduates every year. But al-Qaeda and its affiliated groups continued to try to build organizational structures from Iraq to Pakistan, as it was those structures that gave them the ability to carry out large-scale operations.

The "leaderless" approach to jihad could be seen in its purest form three years after 9/11 during the assassination of Theo van Gogh, a Dutch filmmaker known more in Holland for his role as a professional provocateur than for any merit as an auteur. Van Gogh had collaborated with the Somali-Dutch politician Ayaan Hirsi Ali to make a film about the subjugation of women under Islam, *Submission*, in which verses of the Koran were projected onto the naked bodies of several young women. The film was designed to provoke, and it did.

Mohammed Bouyeri, a twenty-six-year-old Moroccan Dutchman who had recently embraced a militant form of Islam, calmly shot van Gogh on November 2, 2004, as the filmmaker was bicycling through the streets of

Amsterdam, after which he slashed the filmmaker's throat with a machete. The assassin then pinned a letter to the dead man's chest addressed to Ali, in which he accused her of betraying her childhood faith. Bouyeri had no links to any existing terror organizations and his murder of Van Gogh was purely the work of a "lone wolf."

The most deadly act of "leaderless jihad" had taken place a few months earlier, on March 11, 2004, when a group of mostly Moroccan Spaniards had launched multiple bombings on Madrid's transportation system, killing 191 and wounding hundreds more, attacks designed to protest Spanish support for the war in Iraq. There had been some discussion on an al-Qaeda website three months earlier that attacking Spain might result in its troops being pulled out of Iraq, and bin Laden had in October 2003 for the first time mentioned Spain as a potential target. However, the Madrid attacks were largely the work of leaderless jihadis who financed the bombings with the proceeds of substantial drug deals, and only some of whom were affiliated with a known jihadist organization, the Moroccan Islamic Combatant Group. The Madrid attacks worked; a new Spanish government quickly announced that it would be pulling its troops out of Iraq.

Sageman's view of the evolving, homegrown nature of the jihadist threat was largely shared by key counterterrorism officials in Europe, who said that several years after 9/11, although bin Laden was an important inspirational figure, they didn't find any evidence of al-Qaeda operations in their countries. Armando Spataro, one of Italy's leading terrorism prosecutors, said that in his investigations he found "there is no longer a hierarchical organization, now there are many groups without links to al-Qaeda." And Baltasar Garzon, a judge who had investigated terrorist groups in Spain since the mid-1990s, said that while bin Laden was "a fundamental reference point for the al-Qaeda movement," he didn't see any of the terror organization's fingerprints in his inquiries.

This view of al-Qaeda's increasing irrelevance, and by extension bin Laden's, was emphatically not shared by top counterterrorism officials in the United Kingdom and the United States. The sixteen American intelligence agencies that collectively make up the U.S. intelligence community all signed off on a 2007 National Intelligence Estimate that concluded that al-Qaeda was resurging, particularly in the wake of its 7/7 bombings in London. Jonathan Evans, the head of Britain's domestic intelligence service MI5, said a year later that there were some two thousand citizens and residents of the United Kingdom whom the British government considered a serious threat to security, a good number of them with connections to al-Qaeda.

Why was there such a starkly differing view of the al-Qaeda threat in much of Europe compared to the way the governments of the United Kingdom and the United States saw it? The difference in the perception of the threat was because of the deadly nexus that had developed from 2003 onward between militant British Muslims and al-Qaeda headquartered in Pakistan's tribal areas. The lesson of a number of the terrorist plots uncovered in the United Kingdom was that the "bottom-up" radicalization described by Sageman only became really lethal when the "'homegrown' wannabes"—often radicalized by jihadi videos on the Internet—managed to make contact with "Al-Qaeda Central" in the tribal areas of Pakistan along its border with Afghanistan. For just as the U.S. military doesn't conduct its training over the Internet but at boot camps, it turns out that effective jihadist terrorists are generally the graduates of training camps or war zones, rather than the passive consumers of jihadist propaganda on the Web.

Michael Sheehan, the deputy police commissioner in New York City responsible for counterterrorism until 2006, explained that "hotheads in a coffeehouse are a dime a dozen. Al-Qaeda Central is a critical element in turning the hotheads into an actual capable cell," providing them with the skills in bomb making and maintenance of operational security that turns them from angry young men into effective killers. Philip Mudd, the number two in the CIA's Counterterrorist Center who later worked at the FBI to help improve its intelligence capabilities, agreed: "There is a very clear almost mathematical increase in lethality as soon as plotters touch the FATA," the Federally Administered Tribal Areas in Pakistan, where al-Qaeda is headquartered. What was worrying for the Bush administration was the trend highlighted by the Director of National Intelligence, Michael McConnell, in congressional testimony in 2008. He noted that "We have seen an influx of new Western recruits into the tribal areas since mid-2006."

After 9/11, jihadist terrorist attacks were carried out by a mixture of true "leaderless" cells and a resurgent al-Qaeda regrouped in Pakistan, but the deadliest or most threatening attacks on commercial aviation, oil interests, and Western and Jewish targets were not generally carried out by leaderless jihadis but rather by leader-led, organized groups. There was a certain logic to this. The more complex and deadly the attack, the more likely it was to be organized not by a group of ad hoc "self-starting" jihadists but by an organization with cadre trained in bomb making and other pertinent skills such as countersurveillance. After all, 9/11 itself, the most lethal terror attack ever, was carried out by arguably the most organized terrorist group in history.

The 7/7 London bombings were carried out by an al-Qaeda–directed cell; the bombings of two nightclubs on the Indonesian island of Bali in 2002, which killed some two hundred mostly Western tourists, were the work of Jemaah Islamiyah, al-Qaeda's Southeast Asian affiliate, and were the most deadly terrorist attack in the history of the world's most populous Muslim country; the bombings in Istanbul a year later that killed sixty-two were directed by al-Qaeda; the most protracted suicide bombing campaign in history, in which thousands of Iraqis were murdered, was largely conducted by al-Qaeda's affiliate in Iraq; and the wave of suicide attacks in Pakistan that killed many hundreds after 2006 was carried out by groups allied to or inspired by al-Qaeda.

Attacking commercial aviation—the central nervous system of the global economy—continued to preoccupy al-Qaeda after 9/11. Hydrogen-peroxide-based bombs would again be the signature of a cell of British Pakistanis trained by al-Qaeda who plotted to bring down seven passenger jets flying to the United States and Canada from Britain during the summer of 2006. The plotters were intent on committing suicide when they detonated their bombs on the passenger jets. Six of them made "martyrdom" videotapes recovered by British investigators. The ringleader, twenty-five-year-old Abdullah Ahmed Ali, recorded a video wearing a Palestinian-style black-and-white checkered head scarf in which he lectured into the camera in a heavy Cockney accent, "Sheikh Osama warned you many times to leave our lands or you will be destroyed. Now the time has come for you to be destroyed." Like a number of aspiring British suicide bombers, Ali was married and had a young son, and in the years before his arrest he had made frequent trips to Pakistan, including a six-month sojourn there in 2005. And, like many other jihadist militants before him, he had a technical background, with a degree in computer science.

British authorities were tracking Ali and his crew intensively during the summer of 2006. On July 4 Ali sent an email to his al-Qaeda handler in Pakistan saying, "my black mate said he is cool with a trial run." A month later he followed up with another email: "all I have to do now is sort out opening time table and bookings." British police wired Ali's bomb factory for sound and video and on August 10, the day he was arrested, Ali was heard saying that in "a couple of weeks" the plan would be ready to go. One of the bomb makers was also heard to say triumphantly, "We've got our virgins," likely a reference to the fragrant black-eyed *houris* of Paradise supposedly awaiting the suicide bombers in their next life.

Juan Zarate was the point person at the U.S. National Security Council on counterterrorism during the summer of 2006. "My job, in some ways, was to serve as a kind of tripwire for the White House," he says. Intelligence about the planning of the plot to bring down the airliners began crossing Zarate's desk in early July. By the second half of that month, Zarate recalls, senior officials at the White House viewed the plot as quite alarming, with the 9/11 fifth anniversary looming and attacks on American passenger jets a real possibility. Frances Fragos Townsend, Bush's top homeland security adviser, began to chair meetings that eventually included President Bush in the Roosevelt Room of the White House.

Townsend, a former federal prosecutor in New York, recalls the "planes plot" as the greatest crisis of her tenure: "They had a bomb-making factory, they were trying to put the thing together, there were communications and links back to Pakistan." A thirteen-year veteran of the Justice Department, she remembers that the plot posed a dilemma, "because you want to see how far you can trace the conspiracy back into the tribal areas and up the command chain of al-Qaeda, yet at the same time as we understood the contours of the plot—liquid explosives, multiple simultaneous explosions, American airlines targeted—our feeling was, 'How long can we let this thing go and have planes flying?' Because every time a plane took off, it was a risk." The sense of urgency picked up in early August as the plotters seemed to be preparing some kind of trial run. Townsend recalls, "How would we know that it was only a trial run? You've got some intelligence officers arguing, 'Well, if it's a trial run and you don't have anything on them, let them go. Let's watch it.' I was like, 'I don't think so!'"

When Ali was arrested in East London on August 10, he was carrying a Memory Stick storing flight plans for United Airlines, American Airlines, and Air Canada jets flying from the United Kingdom to destinations such as Chicago, Washington, Los Angeles, San Francisco, Montreal, and Toronto. Ali had also downloaded security advice from Heathrow Airport's website about items that were restricted as hand luggage. Also recovered was his diary, in which were found diagrams of bombs and notations about "time taken to dilute in HP [hydrogen peroxide]."

Investigators later found several large bottles containing hydrogen peroxide concentrated to between 20 and 40 percent—concentrations suitable for turning the liquids into effective bombs—that one of the conspirators had dumped in a London park. The plotters were planning to bring the liquid explosives onto the flights they had targeted disguised as soft drinks, together with other innocuous-looking items such as disposable cameras—the flashes of which could act as triggers—and assemble their bombs on the planes. At the East London apartment that served as the plotters' bomb factory, police found traces of HMTD, a high explosive made from concentrated hydrogen peroxide.

During the trial of the men accused in the planes plot, the prosecution argued that some fifteen hundred passengers would have died if all seven of the targeted planes had been brought down. The plot seemed designed to "celebrate" the upcoming fifth anniversary of 9/11 by once again targeting commercial aviation, a particular obsession of al-Qaeda, and most of the victims of the attacks would have been Americans, Britons, and Canadians. Three years after the aborted attack, Ali and two of his co-conspirators were found guilty of planning to blow up the transatlantic airliners. Some of the key evidence against them was emails they had exchanged with their handler in Pakistan, Rashid Rauf. A British citizen who has worked closely with al-Qaeda, Rauf ordered them "to get a move on" with their operation in an email he had sent them on July 25, 2006. Those emails were intercepted by spy agencies, and Rauf's arrest in Pakistan at the behest of American officials on August 9 quickly triggered the arrest of his jihadist buddies in London. When Rauf was arrested in Pakistan he was found to be in possession of twenty-nine bottles of hydrogen peroxide.

The planes plot case resulted in the immediate ban of all carry-on liquids and gels, and rules were later put in place to limit the quantities of these items that travelers could bring on planes to prevent liquid-based bombs from being carried onto future flights. The plot also revealed a new generation of al-Qaeda leaders hitherto little understood by Western intelligence agencies, says Bruce Riedel, a three-decade veteran of the CIA: "When the August 2006 plot was uncovered, and the threads led back to Pakistan, we'd never heard of any of these people. This was a whole group of people, clearly important, clearly tied to bin Laden. . . . And then we started learning about Rashid Rauf, and it was like, 'Huh? Who are these people?'"

The U.K.-based planes plot did not stand alone: four years earlier an al-Qaeda affiliate in Kenya almost succeeded in bringing down an Israeli passenger jet with a surface-to-air missile, while in 2003 a plane belonging to the DHL courier service was struck by a missile as it took off from Baghdad airport. The same year militants cased Riyadh airport and were planning to attack British Airways flights into Saudi Arabia. And if the Nigerian Umar Farouk Abdulmutallab had brought down the Northwest Airlines flight over Detroit on Christmas Day of 2009, it would have been al-Qaeda's most successful attack on an American target since it destroyed the World Trade Center towers and a wing of the Pentagon.

After the 9/11 attacks, al-Qaeda and its affiliated groups increasingly attacked economic and business targets. The shift in tactics was in part a response to the fact that the traditional pre-9/11 targets, such as American embassies, warships, and military bases, were now better defended, while so-called soft economic targets were both ubiquitous and easier to hit. The suicide attacks in Istanbul in November 2003—directed at a British consulate, two synagogues, and the local headquarters of the HSBC bank—were indicative of this trend. The plotters initially planned to attack Incirlik Air Base, a facility in western Turkey used by American troops, but concluded that the tight security at the base made the assault too difficult. The plotters transferred their efforts to the bank, consulate, and synagogues because they were relatively undefended targets. Al-Qaeda provided tens of thousands of dollars to the conspirators, and the leaders of the Turkish cell met with bin Laden in Kandahar around a week after the 9/11 attacks.

Al-Qaeda had also learned an important lesson from its attacks on New York and Washington: disrupting Western economies and, by extension, the global economy was useful for its wider jihad. In a videotape released in October 2004, bin Laden pointed out that for al-Qaeda's $500,000 investment in the 9/11 attacks, the United States economy sustained a $500 billion loss. Bin Laden crowed over al-Qaeda's investment: "Every dollar al-Qaeda invested defeated a million dollars."

Thus al-Qaeda's leaders now believed (naively) they could bleed the West dry, prompting the group to launch multiple attacks on the oil business. Al-Qaeda's affiliate in Yemen launched an attack on the French oil tanker the *Limburg* on October 6, 2002, as it steamed off the Yemeni coast. An explosives-laden dinghy rammed the tanker and detonated. The vessel caught on fire and one crewman was killed. In Yanbu, Saudi Arabia, al-Qaeda's Saudi Arabian affiliate attacked the offices of a contractor for ExxonMobil on May 1, 2004, killing six Westerners. Four weeks later, in Al Khobar, Saudi Arabia, al-Qaeda attacked the office buildings and residential compounds of Western oil firms. Twenty-two were killed. On December 16, 2004, bin Laden drew attention to al-Qaeda's operations in Saudi Arabia and the need to target oil interests, saying in an audio recording, "One of the most important reasons that led our enemies to control our land is the theft of our oil. . . . Be active and prevent them from reaching the oil, and mount your operations accordingly." In February 2006, al-Qaeda in Saudi Arabia unsuccessfully attacked the Abqaiq facility, perhaps the most important oil production facility in the world, through which approximately 10 percent of the world's oil supply flows.

Al-Qaeda and affiliated terrorist groups also targeted companies with distinctive Western brand names. In 2003, suicide attackers bombed the J. W. Marriott hotel in Jakarta and attacked it again six years later, simultaneously also attacking the Ritz Carlton hotel in the Indonesian capital. Similarly, a Marriott was bombed in Islamabad in 2008. In 2002 a group of eleven French defense contractors were killed as they left a Sheraton hotel in Karachi, which was heavily damaged. In October 2004, in Taba, Egyptian jihadists attacked a Hilton hotel. In Amman, Jordan, in November 2005, Al-Qaeda in Iraq attacked three hotels with well-known American names—the Grand Hyatt, Radisson, and Days Inn. And five-star hotels that catered to Westerners in the Muslim world were a perennial target for jihadists: the Taj and Oberoi in Mumbai in 2008, the Serena in Kabul the same year, and the Pearl Continental in Peshawar in 2009.

Attacking Jewish and Israeli targets was an al-Qaeda strategy that only emerged strongly after 9/11. Despite bin Laden's declaration in February 1998 that he was creating the "World Islamic Front against the Crusaders and the Jews," al-Qaeda only started attacking Israeli or Jewish targets in early 2002. Al-Qaeda and affiliated and like-minded groups then directed a campaign against such targets, killing journalist Daniel Pearl in Karachi, bombing synagogues and Jewish centers in Tunisia, Morocco, Turkey, and India, and attacking an Israeli-owned hotel in Mombasa, Kenya.

Seven years after 9/11, influenced by al-Qaeda, the Taliban began planning seriously to attack targets in the West. According to Spanish prosecutors, the leader of the Pakistani Taliban, Baitullah Mehsud, dispatched suicide bombers to Barcelona in January 2008. A Pakistani Taliban spokesman confirmed this eight months later in a videotaped interview in which he said that those suicide bombers "were under pledge to Baitullah Mehsud" and were sent because of the Spanish military presence in Afghanistan.

Two years later, Faisal Shahzad, a Pakistani-American who had once worked as a financial analyst at the Elizabeth Arden cosmetics company in

Stamford, Connecticut, traveled to Pakistan where he received bomb-making training from the Taliban. Armed with that training, Shahzad returned to Connecticut, where he purchased an SUV, placed a bomb in it and detonated it in Times Square on May 1, 2010 when the sidewalks were thick with tourists and theatergoers. The bomb, which was designed to act as a fuel-air explosive, luckily was a dud and Shahzad was arrested two days later as he tried to leave JFK Airport for Dubai.

The extent of the cooperation between the Pakistani Taliban and al-Qaeda could be seen in the suicide bombing that killed seven CIA officers and contractors in the American base at Khost in eastern Afghanistan on December 30, 2009. The suicide bomber, Humam Khalil Abu-Mulal al-Balawi, a Jordanian doctor, was a double agent: information he had earlier provided to the CIA was used to target militants in Pakistan. Two months after Balawi's suicide attack, al-Qaeda's video production arm released a lengthy interview with him in which he laid out how he planned to attack the group of Agency officials using a bomb made from C-4. Mustafa Abu al-Yazid, the number three in al-Qaeda, praised the suicide attack targeting the CIA officers, saying it was "to avenge our good martyrs" and listing several militant leaders felled by U.S. drone strikes, while the chief of the Pakistani Taliban, Hakimullah Mehsud, appeared alongside Balawi in a prerecorded video saying the attack was revenge for the drone strike that had killed Hakimullah's ruthless predecessor, Baitullah Mehsud, six months earlier.

And in the same period al-Qaeda's influence was extending well beyond the Afghanistan-Pakistan theater as the terrorist organization added new "franchises" around the Muslim world. In September 2006, the Algerian Salafist Group for Preaching and Combat's leader, Abu Musab Abdul Wadud, explained that al-Qaeda "is the only organization qualified to gather together the mujahideen." Subsequently taking the name "Al-Qaeda in the Islamic Maghreb," the group conducted a range of operations: bombing the United Nations building in Algiers, attacking the Israeli embassy in Mauritania, and murdering French and British hostages.

Al-Qaeda in the Islamic Maghreb joined the already well-established franchises of Al-Qaeda in Iraq and Al-Qaeda in the Arabian Peninsula, which comprised many hundreds of militants in Saudi Arabia and Yemen. In 2009 al-Qaeda extended its influence in the Horn of Africa when the Somali militant group Al Shabab announced that it was joining bin Laden's group. Indicative of bin Laden's continuing importance to militant jihadists around the world is that when these groups announced they were joining al-Qaeda they pledged an oath of allegiance not to al-Qaeda but to bin Laden himself.

Al-Qaeda Central also retained some control over its affiliate in Saudi Arabia, according to a senior Saudi law enforcement official: "There is evidence that al-Qaeda in Afghanistan/Pakistan is communicating with al-Qaeda in the Kingdom." Al-Qaeda in Saudi Arabia took a beating after the group made the strategic error of killing scores of Saudi civilians in a campaign of violence that began with multiple bombings in the kingdom in May 2003. According to the Saudi official, the green light for that campaign came from Saif al-Adel, al-Qaeda's military commander, who was then living under some form of house arrest in Iran. Saudi forces subsequently killed more than 150 militants and imprisoned thousands more, but "Al-Qaeda in the Arabian Peninsula" continued to retain some capabilities years later, as was demonstrated on August 28, 2009, by its assassination attempt against the top Saudi counterterrorism official, Prince Mohammed bin Nayef, who was lucky to survive.

The Mumbai attacks of 2008 showed that al-Qaeda's ideas about attacking Western and Jewish targets had also spread to Pakistani militant groups like Lashkar-e-Taiba (LeT), which had previously focused only on Indian targets. Over a three-day period in late November 2008, LeT carried out multiple attacks in Mumbai on five-star hotels housing Westerners and a Jewish-American community center.

Undoubtedly, one of al-Qaeda's key successes after 9/11 was spreading its ideas widely. Bin Laden has observed that 90 percent of his battle is conducted in the media and al-Qaeda understands that what the Pentagon terms IO (information operations) are vital to its continued viability. Al-Qaeda's media production arm Al Sahab's first major production debuted on the Internet in the summer of 2001, signaling a major anti-American attack was in the works. Subsequently it significantly increased its output; in 2007, Al Sahab released more audio- and videotapes than in any other year of its six-year history, nearly one hundred.

These tapes were increasingly complex productions with subtitles in languages such as English, animation effects, and studio settings. As Sahab's growingly sophisticated and regular output was evidence that al-Qaeda had recovered to a degree that it was capable of managing a relatively advanced propaganda operation. Al-Qaeda the organization also evolved after 9/11 into an ideology of "bin Ladenism," which reached a vast global audience as a result of the wide dissemination of bin Laden's multiple statements. The Internet created a multiplier effect for his ideas. After 9/11, on constantly moving websites with names such as Alneda.com and mujahidoon.net, al-Qaeda disseminated its propaganda. Now it was no longer necessary to go to Afghanistan to sit at the feet of al-Qaeda's leaders. Signing up for the jihad was just a click of a mouse away.

While it is certainly the case that al-Qaeda and other jihadist groups have used the Web quite adeptly for propaganda and recruitment, there is no evidence that any terrorist attack anywhere has been successfully operationalized or coordinated mainly through the Internet. It is also worth recalling that the most lethal terrorist attack in history was directed from Afghanistan under the Taliban, a country with—forget the Internet—almost no phone system and little electricity. Watching jihadist videos on the Internet may help to radicalize young men, but screening a beheading video in your pj's doesn't turn you into a successful terrorist or insurgent. Nor do bomb-making recipes on the Internet teach people how to kill or how to build effective bombs. That is achieved by learning on the job in a war zone or at a jihadi training camp. Indeed, the countries with the highest levels of jihadist terrorist activity in the world, such as Afghanistan and Iraq, all have tiny percentages of Internet users; no more than 3 percent of their populations use the Web.

If terrorism conducted through the Internet is an overblown fear, there are two tactics that al-Qaeda could easily employ in the next few years that would have significant detrimental effects on Western interests. Neither has been successfully used by the group before, but both are well within the organization's capability; unlike the threat of al-Qaeda detonating a nuclear device, they do not represent Chicken Little scenarios. The first such tactic is the use of a surface-to-air missile or bomb to bring down a commercial jetliner. Al-Qaeda has already tried such an attack, against the Israeli passenger jet in Kenya in 2002. That attempt almost succeeded, as did the abortive plot to bring down the Northwest flight over Detroit with a bomb seven years later.

The second scenario is the detonation of a radiological bomb, most likely in a European or Asian city, which would cause widespread panic, leading many to believe that terrorists had "gone nuclear," even though a radiological "dirty bomb" is nothing like a nuclear device, only dispersing radioactive material rather than setting off an atomic explosion. A dirty-bomb attack in a Western or Asian city would kill relatively few people but it would engender panic and likely damage global investor confidence. The quest for such a device and other exotic weapons has preoccupied al-Qaeda for two decades.

Chapter 13

Al-Qaeda's Quixotic Quest for Weapons of Mass Destruction

Acquiring nuclear and chemical weapons is a religious duty.

—Osama bin Laden in 1999

The single biggest threat to U.S. security, both short-term, medium-term, and long-term, would be the possibility of a terrorist organization obtaining a nuclear weapon.

—President Barack Obama, April 2010

Two months after 9/11, Osama bin Laden for the first time claimed publicly to possess some kind of nuclear capability. On the morning of November 8, 2001, the Saudi militant was eating a hearty meal of meat and olives as Hamid Mir, the Pakistani journalist, interviewed him in a house in Kabul. Mir remembers that bin Laden was in a jocular frame of mind, although what he had to say was anything but a laughing matter. Mir asked bin Laden to comment on reports that he had tried to acquire nuclear and chemical weapons, to which the al-Qaeda leader replied: "I wish to declare that if America used chemical or nuclear weapons against us, then we may retort with chemical and nuclear weapons. We have the weapons as deterrent." Mir asked, "Where did you get these weapons from?" Bin Laden responded coyly: "Go to the next question."

After the interview was finished, Mir followed up this exchange over tea with bin Laden's deputy, Dr. Ayman al-Zawahiri. "I asked this question to Dr. al-Zawahiri: that it is difficult to believe that you have nuclear weapons. So he said, 'Mr. Hamid Mir, it is not difficult. If you have thirty million dollars, you can have these kind of nuclear suitcase bombs from the black market of Central Asia (in the former Soviet Union).'"

These claims by al-Qaeda's leaders about the group's nuclear weapons capabilities had come after a long quest by the terror organization to learn about atomic weapons and acquire nuclear materials. Sensing the inadequacy of his own knowledge about nuclear weapons, Abu Khabab al-Masri, the terror group's in-house weapons of mass destruction researcher, in a pre-9/11 memo to his al-Qaeda bosses asked if it was possible to get more information about atomic weaponry "from our Pakistani friends who have great experience in this sphere."

For that information al-Qaeda's leaders turned to Dr. Sultan Bashiruddin Mahmood, a recently retired senior Pakistani nuclear scientist in his early sixties whose bushy beard advertised his deep attachment to the Taliban. After studying nuclear engineering in Britain in the 1960s, Mahmood had spent nearly four decades working in the heart of Pakistan's nuclear program and helped to develop the Kahuta facility near Islamabad that produced enriched uranium for nuclear devices, although he was never directly involved in the production of nuclear weaponry.

Despite his years working in Pakistan's nuclear establishment, Mahmood was also something of a kook, entertaining decidedly eccentric ideas about the role that Islamic spirits known as *djinns* supposedly might have in helping to solve the energy crisis. Pervez Hoodbhoy, a leading Pakistani nuclear scientist with a Ph.D. from MIT, recalls Mahmood as "a rather strange man" who also wrote a book about the supposed role that sunspots had played in influencing significant historical events such as the French Revolution. Hoodbhoy says that when Mahmood's book on sunspots was published, "We had a rather unpleasant exchange of letters since he claimed that it was based on physics."

Tiring of his religiosity and eccentricity, in 1999 Pakistani authorities quietly relieved Mahmood of his job as the head of a facility that produced weapons-grade plutonium. Mahmood then spent part of his retirement in Afghanistan helping the Taliban with his charity Ummah Tameer-e-Nau

(UTN, "Islamic Reconstruction"). But UTN's charitable cover masked more ambitious plans. The charity aimed to establish uranium-mining facilities in Afghanistan, part of a larger plan to establish some type of nuclear program in the country. And at UTN's offices in Kabul after the fall of the Taliban, reporters found a drawing of a balloon designed to deliver weaponized anthrax and documents about anthrax disease, items suggesting that UTN was not a conventional charity.

Dr. Mahmood failed polygraph tests about his meetings with al-Qaeda's leaders once those encounters became known to U.S. and Pakistani investigators. The nuclear scientist had met with bin Laden over the course of two meetings just weeks before the 9/11 attacks, during which Mahmood had provided information to the al-Qaeda leader about the infrastructure needed for an atomic weapons program.

Veteran CIA officer Charles "Sam" Faddis was dispatched to Islamabad to get to the bottom of what exactly had taken place between bin Laden and Mahmood. Faddis says there was a great deal of urgency surrounding the investigation of Mahmood in the weeks immediately following 9/11: "People were legitimately thinking in the context of that time—they already have an atomic bomb. What if they already have one? What if it's already moving? What if that's the next thing that's happening?"

Faddis spent many hours debriefing Mahmood over the course of the three months that he spent in Pakistan investigating the case. Faddis says the nuclear scientist "tried to paint this as almost as if this is a very normal thing to be sitting around just having a conversation with Osama bin Laden and he asks you about a nuclear weapon," adding, with a tinge of sarcasm, "I mean, wouldn't you tell him about nuclear weapons if you were having tea with Osama bin Laden?"

Bin Laden had claimed to Mahmood that he possessed fissile material suitable for an atomic device that a Central Asian jihadist group, the Islamic Movement of Uzbekistan, had provided al-Qaeda and he asked Mahmood if he could recruit other scientists who knew how to build a nuclear weapon. Bin Laden showed the Pakistani nuclear scientist some of the "fissile material," which Mahmood quickly recognized to be only some formerly radioactive materials from a medical facility that were now "dead." Faddis says, "It was a real medical source, but like with so many of those radiological materials, their half life is such that they don't last very long."

After a painstaking investigation of Mahmood, Faddis concluded: "There was no atomic bomb under construction; that we were nowhere close to anything remotely resembling that, but the real danger here was that we had this guy, with his influence and his connections and his cachet, sitting down talking about atomic bombs with Osama bin Laden, and if this thing hadn't been squashed and had been allowed to just trundle along, and a few years had gone by, what we would have found was that in the interim, he would have brought in other people who knew very well how to build weapons."

Following 9/11, additional worrisome evidence of al-Qaeda's interest in mass casualty weaponry emerged. "American Taliban" John Walker Lindh told his interrogators that the second wave of al-Qaeda attacks on the United States would involve weapons of mass destruction (WMD), while several months later the operational manager of the 9/11 attacks, Khalid Sheikh Mohammed, told Al Jazeera television that al-Qaeda had contemplated attacking American nuclear facilities. And the 9/11 hijackers had looked into purchasing crop-dusting planes in the States that they believed might be suitable for dispersing chemical or biological agents.

After the attacks on New York and Washington, al-Qaeda's leaders also stepped up their rhetoric about their plans to use WMD. Suleiman Abu Ghaith, a Kuwaiti who served as al-Qaeda's official spokesman, wrote an essay on the organization's website Al Neda ("The Call") in June 2002 in which he laid out the case for al-Qaeda having the "right" to kill and maim millions of Americans using weapons of mass destruction. "The Americans have still not tasted from our hands what we have tasted from theirs. Those killed in the World Trade Center and the Pentagon are but a tiny part of the exchange for those killed in Palestine, Somalia, Sudan, the Philippines, Bosnia, Kashmir, Chechnya, and Afghanistan. We have not reached parity with them. We have the right to kill four million Americans—two million of them children."

This statement was followed a year later by the fatwa of a Saudi cleric, Nasir bin Hamad al-Fahd, who gave religious sanction for the use of WMD to kill American civilians. In his May 2003 "Treatise on the Legal Status of Using Weapons of Mass Destruction Against Infidels," the cleric explained that large-scale slaughter of civilians was permissible because in the Prophet Mohammed's time his commanders would employ "catapults and similar weapons that cause general destruction" when they were laying siege to cities. Never mind that seventh-century siege engines such as catapults generally killed a relatively small number of civilians while nuclear weapons can kill hundreds of thousands; al-Qaeda had now been given the religious sanction to use nukes against American civilians.

Leonid Smirnov is the world's first known atomic thief. For decades during the Cold War, the unassuming lab worker labored at the Luch nuclear laboratories near Moscow. In 1992, as the Russian economy went into free fall following the collapse of the Soviet Union, Smirnov cooked up a scheme to stage a spectacular act of nuclear theft. By then Smirnov was a foreman at the lab so it was relatively easy for him to get his hands on highly enriched uranium, the same material that was used in the bomb dropped on Hiroshima. The risk was small as there were few security checks at the facility and Smirnov only stole tiny amounts of uranium that would not attract notice. He recalled, "I was the shift leader, so it wasn't hard for me. The main thing was not to take too much."

At the end of each working day Smirnov would save the pieces of uranium he had stolen and store them in vials that he would then smuggle out of the facility. Eventually Smirnov stole around three pounds of the uranium, about one-fortieth of the amount needed for a simple atomic weapon. (The "gun-type" atomic bomb, the simplest nuclear device, dropped on Hiroshima used around 130 pounds of highly enriched uranium.)

Smirnov lived in a dingy block of apartments in the shadow of the nuclear facility where he worked. Like much of the former Soviet Union, it is a grim place whose inhabitants wear an air of defeat, not least Smirnov himself, who lived there in a cramped one-bedroom apartment with his wife and two well-fed cats. Years after his theft was discovered Smirnov explained that his motives for carrying out his nuclear heist were quite pedestrian: "Mainly because I just wanted a little bit of money, to get a few material things; a refrigerator; a gas stove; fix up the apartment."

While the Smirnov case seemed more pathetic than a real threat to global security, it underlined the fact that the desperate circumstances of many Russians after the fall of the communist regime might unleash a nightmarish supply of materials for nuclear weapons that could fall into the hands of terrorists. But who might be interested in this material? Terrorist groups have generally avoided acquiring or deploying any kind of WMD because the use of such weapons would likely eliminate whatever popular support or legitimacy they might enjoy. And the few terrorist groups that have had an interest in developing such weapons have had scant success in their plans for mass murder. Still, al-Qaeda members dreamed of superweapons that would eliminate the United States and their other enemies at one stroke. That dream launched the organization on an ultimately ill-fated quest for not only nuclear weapons, but also chemical and biological devices.

What distinguished al-Qaeda from other terrorist groups was that its leaders made it clear publicly that they would deploy such weapons without hesitation, despite the fact that privately some al-Qaeda leaders were aware that their WMD program was strictly an amateur affair. This was the mirror image of the Cold War, where the Soviets had enough nuclear devices to end civilization, yet their intentions about what they might do with those weapons were so opaque that the art of Kremlinology sprang up to divine what their plans might be. The Soviets had the capability to wipe out the United States, but never really had the intention to do so, while al-Qaeda's leaders have often said they intend to kill millions of Americans, but their ability to do so has been nonexistent.

Bin Laden's first public pronouncement about WMDs was his reaction to the news of an Indian nuclear test on May 11, 1998, at a remote desert test site less than one hundred miles from the Pakistani border. Three days later bin Laden issued a statement calling for an "Islamic" bomb: "We call upon the Muslim nation in general, and Pakistan and its army in particular; to prepare for the Jihad imposed by Allah. . . . This should include a nuclear force."

The Indian nuclear test helped to provoke a lively debate within al-Qaeda about whether the group should acquire and deploy such weapons. Abu Walid al-Masri, the Egyptian editor of the Arabic-language magazine of the Taliban, recalled that al-Qaeda hard-liners, like the military commander Mohammed Atef, pushed for acquiring nuclear, biological, and chemical weapons capabilities. Another wing of al-Qaeda assessed, correctly as it turned out, that these types of weapons would only bring small tactical benefits because the group was likely only to acquire or build weapons that were quite primitive.

But even al-Qaeda's "doves" understood that they should call those primitive devices "weapons of mass destruction" to create fear, knowing the psychological warfare advantage that seeming to possess WMD had against the West. In fact, ironically it was Western preoccupations with the danger posed by biological and chemical weapons that piqued al-Qaeda's interest in them in the first place. On an al-Qaeda computer, recovered after the fall of the Taliban, Ayman al-Zawahiri wrote to Mohammed Atef on April 15, 1999, saying, "Despite their extreme danger, we only became aware of [chemical and biological weapons] when the enemy drew our attention to them by repeatedly expressing concerns that they can be produced simply with easily available materials."

In the late 1990s al-Qaeda set up a secret WMD program innocuously code-named the "Yoghurt project" and earmarked a piddling $2,000–$4,000 as the budget for it. Bin Laden remained convinced that more conventional types of assaults on the United States would likely be more effective than crude WMD attacks, but he kept those doubts largely to himself. The Egyptian, Abu Walid al-Masri, recalled that bin Laden "refused to voice publicly his rejection of the idea, probably because of his extreme politeness with those around him."

Despite the private doubts of its leader, al-Qaeda had long been in the market for nuclear or radioactive materials, as was revealed by the New York trial of the four men implicated in the attacks on the U.S. embassies in Africa in 1998. At the trial, Jamal al-Fadl, an al-Qaeda member who had lived in Sudan in the mid-1990s and who later defected from the group, explained that he had witnessed al-Qaeda's attempts to acquire uranium. Fadl said that members of al-Qaeda based in Khartoum were prepared to pay up to $1.5 million for a consignment of uranium and that he once saw a cylinder purporting to contain uranium that al-Qaeda members were contemplating buying. However, the deal seemed to have never gone through and, in any event, even if it did the sale of the "uranium" was one of the many times that al-Qaeda was scammed in its search for nuclear materials.

Bin Laden's skepticism about WMD was not unfounded. Before 9/11 Taliban authorities had stockpiled a considerable quantity of radioactive materials seized or purchased from smugglers traveling from the Central Asian countries of the former Soviet Union. Mullah Khaksar, the Taliban deputy interior minister, recalled that some of his colleagues in Kandahar were even trafficking in capsules of "uranium" that they would sometimes stuff in a sock. Mullah Khaksar advised the Taliban leader Mullah Omar that the uranium trade was likely a scam, telling him, "Don't spend money on this stuff. I don't think it's real."

After the fall of the Taliban, American officials discovered an underground facility near Kandahar airport where uranium 238 was stored; it is used in nuclear processing but cannot be used in nuclear weapons (which require highly enriched uranium 235). Uranium 238 might, however, have been considered by the militants to be useful to make a radiological weapon.

Based on an analysis of the fatalities caused by an accident involving radioactive materials in Brazil in 1987, analysts writing for the U.S. National Defense University concluded that "some forms of radiological attack could kill tens or hundreds of people and sicken hundreds or thousands." And the risk of a dirty bomb attack has grown rapidly in past years. In 1996 there were only some thirty incidents involving nuclear or radioactive smuggling, but in 2006 there were over 140.

Emblematic of the dangerous trade in radioactive materials suitable for a dirty bomb that were shipped out of the former Soviet Union was the truck loaded with some twenty tons of scrap metal that approached the busy Gisht-Kuprik border crossing on Uzbekistan's border with Kazakhstan on March 30, 2000. When Uzbek border guards stopped the truck, their radiation detectors—issued to them two years earlier courtesy of U.S. Customs—went off, showing levels of radiation one hundred times above normal levels. When they checked the truck, under a pile of scrap metal the guards found ten lead-lined containers, the source of the radiation.

According to U.S. Customs officials who followed the case, inside the containers were likely spent fuel rods from a nuclear reactor. Even more worrisome, the truck driver gave the Uzbek border guards paperwork for his cargo showing that the final destination for the shipment was Quetta in Pakistan, a city that is just across the Afghan border from Kandahar, which was then the headquarters of both al-Qaeda and the Taliban. According to the truck driver's shipping manifest, the firm that was supposed to receive the shipment in Quetta was listed as Ahmadjan Haji Mohamed, roughly the local equivalent of John Smith and quite likely a fictitious entity.

The Uzbek border guards did not have the authority to impound the truck but only to send it back across the border to Kazakhstan, where it promptly disappeared. It is quite likely that this shipment of highly radioactive material was destined for militants in Afghanistan, as Pakistan already had its own nuclear program and so would have had little need of spent fuel rods or other similar radioactive materials.

Bin Laden and Zawahiri's portrayal of al-Qaeda's nuclear capabilities in their post-9/11 statements to the Pakistani journalist Hamid Mir was psychological warfare against the West and not based in any reality; there is not a shred of evidence that their quest for nukes ever got beyond the talking stage. And the whole notion of "missing" Russian nuclear suitcase bombs floating around for sale on the black market that Zawahiri mentioned to Hamid Mir is a Hollywood construct greeted with great skepticism by nuclear proliferation experts.

In 2002 the former UN weapons inspector David Albright examined all the available evidence about al-Qaeda's nuclear research program and concluded it was virtually impossible for al-Qaeda to have acquired any type of nuclear weapon, while U.S. government analysts also came to the same conclusion. There is, however, evidence that the group was experimenting with crude chemical weapons, was exploring the use of biological weapons such as botulinum, salmonella, and anthrax, and also made multiple attempts to acquire radioactive materials suitable for a dirty bomb.

After the group moved from Sudan to Afghanistan in 1996, al-Qaeda members ramped up their WMD program, experimenting on dogs with some kind of chemical, possibly cyanide gas. An al-Qaeda videotape from this period shows a small white dog tied up inside a glass cage. A milky gas slowly filters into the cage. An Arabic-speaking man with an Egyptian accent says: "Start counting the time." Nervous, the dog starts barking and then moaning. After flailing about for some minutes, it succumbs to the poisonous gas and stops moving. This experiment almost certainly occurred at the Darunta training camp near the eastern Afghan city of Jalalabad, conducted by the Egyptian WMD experimenter Abu Khabab. The dogs that were used in these experiments were puppies from the litters of dogs kept by one of the al-Qaeda leader's sons, Omar bin Laden, an animal lover. He pleaded with his father to stop the puppies from being killed for the chemical weapons tests, but his pleas were ignored.

In the late 1990s, Abu Khabab set up the terrorist group's WMD research program. One of the fruits of this program was al-Qaeda's seven-thousand-page *Encyclopedia of Jihad*, which was made available on CD in 1999 and devoted a chapter to how to develop chemical and biological weapons. This work has had wide distribution in jihadist circles.

Abu Khabab, by training a chemical engineer, taught hundreds of militants how to deploy poisons such as ricin and cyanide gas, and he singled out Uzbekistan, a country on Afghanistan's northern border that was formerly part of the Soviet Union, as a possible source of chemical weapons. In an order he wrote on April 2, 2001, Abu Khabab directed, "Obtain the liquid and non-liquid chemicals as soon as possible from Uzbekistan because we need them. Take all necessary precautions to ensure the correct delivery of the materials and the lives of our men. Try and recruit Uzbek army individuals who are experienced in this field. Procure necessary face-masks, protective clothing and protective footwear."

Disturbingly, al-Qaeda has been able to recruit American-educated scientists such as Aafia Siddiqui, who has a degree in biology from MIT and a Ph.D. in neuroscience from Brandeis. When the slight Pakistani-American mother of three in her mid-thirties was arrested in eastern Afghanistan in 2008, authorities maintain she was carrying documents about the manufacture of chemical, biological, and radiological weapons and descriptions of various New York City landmarks. Another al-Qaeda recruit with an American science degree is Yazid Sufaat, a graduate in biochemistry of California Polytechnic State University who set up Green Laboratory Medicine Company in Kandahar in 2001 to acquire anthrax and other biological weapons. But Sufaat was never able to buy the right strain of anthrax suitable for a weapon and was arrested in Malaysia three months after 9/11. Similarly, Abdur Rauf, a biologist working for the Pakistani government, traveled around Europe on behalf of Ayman al-Zawahiri in the late 1990s looking for anthrax suitable for weaponization. In a letter recovered in Afghanistan in December 2001, Rauf explained to Zawahiri that he was unable to acquire "pathogenic" anthrax, that is, the lethal strain of the agent.

Al-Qaeda's inability to acquire lethal strains of anthrax or to "weaponize" anthrax should not be surprising. The anthrax attacks in the United States in the fall of 2001 targeting several politicians and journalists caused considerable panic but only killed five people. The author of that attack, Bruce E. Ivins, was one of the leading biological weapons researchers in the United States. Even this brilliant scientist could only weaponize anthrax to the point that it killed a handful of people. Imagine then how difficult it would be for the average terrorist, or even the above-average terrorist, to replicate Ivins's efforts. (Gary Ackerman, an American scholar of the use of WMD by terrorists, points out, however, that Ivins, who mailed out a number of anthrax-laced letters, could have infected far more people if he had put the anthrax spores in a salt shaker, gone to the top of a building and sprinkled the spores on passersby. Of course, this also would have quickly led to Ivins's arrest.)

If al-Qaeda's research into WMD was strictly an amateur affair, its plots to use these types of weapons have wavered between the ineffectual and the plain nutty. Take the 2003 "ricin" case in the United Kingdom, which was widely advertised as a serious WMD plot and ended up amounting to nothing. In the months before the invasion of Iraq, media in the United States and Great Britain were awash in stories about a group of men arrested in London who possessed highly toxic ricin to be used in future terrorist attacks. Not only that, but those arrested were reported to be "associates" of Abu Musab al-Zarqawi, whom the Bush administration was then presenting as the key link between al-Qaeda and Saddam Hussein. This supposed confluence of WMD, al-Qaeda, and Saddam was, of course, a useful building block of the case for war against the Iraqi dictator. On January 16, 2003, two months before the U.S.-led invasion of Iraq, CNN reported this story under the headline "Ricin Suspects Linked to al-Qaeda." And three weeks later, when Secretary of State Colin Powell gave his speech at the United Nations laying out the American case for war against Iraq, he put up a slide that linked the "UK poison cell" to Zarqawi.

But two years later, at the trial of the men accused of the ricin plot, a government scientist testified that the men never had ricin in their possession, a charge that had been triggered by a false positive on a test. The men were cleared of the poison conspiracy except for an Algerian named Kamal Bourgass, who was convicted of conspiring to commit a public nuisance by using poisons or explosives.

A similar nonevent was the widely trumpeted plan by the al-Qaeda recruit Dhiren Barot to build a dirty bomb to be detonated either in the United Kingdom or the United States after 9/11. Barot wrote a letter to the leaders of al-Qaeda proposing that he would mine the small amount of radioactive material known as americium that can be found in ordinary smoke detectors and use it to build a radiological device. In his presentation document to al-Qaeda, Barot said that the americium from around ten thousand smoke detectors would be needed to make the bomb effective and that once the device was detonated the subsequent radioactive cloud "has the potential to affect around 500 people." Barot estimated that buying the ten thousand smoke detectors necessary to make the bomb would cost more than one hundred thousand dollars. Neither Barot nor anyone in al-Qaeda ever implemented any part of this harebrained scheme, which Michael Sheehan, who was in charge of counterrorism for the New York Police Department at the time of Barot's 2004 arrest, describes as "comical." Indeed, of the 177 cases of individuals charged or convicted of a jihadist terrorist crime in the United States between 9/11 and the spring of 2011, none involved chemical, biological, radiological, or nuclear weapons.

The only post-9/11 cases where al-Qaeda or any of its affiliates actually *used* any kind of WMD was in Iraq, where al-Qaeda's Iraqi affiliate laced more than a dozen of its bombs with the chemical chlorine in 2007. Those attacks sickened hundreds of Iraqis but the victims who died in these assaults did so largely from the blast of the bombs, not because of inhaling chlorine. Al-Qaeda stopped using chlorine in its bombs in Iraq in mid-2007 in part because the insurgents never figured out how to make the chlorine attacks especially deadly, and the bombmakers were captured or killed.

Charles Faddis, who headed up the CIA's operations against the Iraqis who were building the chlorine bombs, recalls "there was a lot of effort to secure the chlorine, to get a hold of the tanks, to track these guys down, to kill them or capture them. Meanwhile the attacks are not being particularly successful. . . . The people are dying in the blast, but fortunately nobody is dying from chlorine."

Despite the difficulties associated with terrorist groups acquiring or deploying weapons of mass destruction and al-Qaeda's sorry record in the matter, there was a great deal of hysterical discussion about this issue after 9/11. Clouding everything was the semantic problem of the ominous term "weapons of mass destruction," which is really a misnomer as it suggests that chemical, biological, and nuclear devices are all equally lethal. In fact, there is only one true weapon of mass destruction that can kill tens or hundreds of thousands of people and that is a nuclear device.

The Bush administration in particular tended to conflate chemical, biological, and nuclear weapons under the rubric of WMD as if they were all equally dangerous. The false claims advanced by the Bush administration that Saddam was building up a serious WMD program and that his regime had given training in "poisons and deadly gases" to al-Qaeda associates in Iraq were the apogee of this hysteria, as they helped to embroil the United States in the disastrous Iraq War.

But there were many other examples of such hysteria. In his 2004 book, *Osama's Revenge: The Next 9/11*, Paul L. Williams, a sometime consultant to the FBI, trotted out the dubious tales about the missing Soviet suitcase nukes and quoted Yossef Bodansky, the head of the Congressional Task Force on Terrorism, who had told a congressional committee in 1998 that "there is no longer much doubt that bin Laden has succeeded in his quest for nuclear suicide bombs," whatever that means.

A widely publicized piece of hyperbolic reporting by the Pulitzer Prize–winning journalist Ron Suskind in his 2006 book, *The One Percent Doctrine*, told the story of a group of jihadists who had been arrested in Bahrain three years earlier. One of them had an illustration of a device called a "*mubtakar*" stored on his computer. The *mubtakar* could supposedly be used to mix sodium cyanide with hydrogen to create lethal hydrogen cyanide, similar to the Zyklon B gas that was used by the Nazis in their concentration camps.

Suskind described the device as "a fearful thing, and quite real" and that "in the world of terrorist weaponry, it was the equivalent of splitting the atom." Milton Leitenberg of the University of Maryland, who had worked on chemical and biological weapons issues for four decades, said that Suskind's "splitting the atom" claim was "the stupidest statement I have heard in many years," and pointed out that the much-vaunted *mubtakar* likely wouldn't work at all. And there is no evidence that al-Qaeda terrorists actually built a *mubtakar* (an Arabic word, ironically, for "invention"), or that al-Qaeda ever developed hydrogen cyanide gas.

In *The One Percent Doctrine*, Suskind also reported that sometime in early 2003 al-Qaeda set in motion a hydrogen cyanide attack on the New York City subway but Ayman al-Zawahiri called off the attack for some unknown reason. In an excerpt of the book that ran prominently in *Time* magazine, Suskind was credited with discovering that "al-Qaeda terrorists came within 45 days of attacking the New York subway system with a lethal gas similar to that used in Nazi death camps."

This story was entirely false, according to Michael Sheehan, who ran counterterrorism operations for the New York Police Department (NYPD) at the time of the supposed hydrogen cyanide plot. Sheehan recalls that when he and his colleagues at NYPD "drilled down" on the supposed cyanide gas threat, they found "there was some reports of sketchy reliability that said there was a couple of guys in New York City that were going to use this improvised chemical thing in the subway, and we never identified that those two guys existed or came to the U.S. or that the source really knew what he was talking about." Sheehan also dismisses the notion that Zawahiri had ever canceled what was, after all, a nonexistent operation. "That's ridiculous. There was no evidence that he had ever called it off." John McLaughlin, the deputy director of the CIA at the time, also says the *mubtakar* story "has been blown out of proportion. We did take the device seriously, but this was one of a dozen or a hundred things we were looking at, and we had no indication that there was a specific plot about to unfold." As a matter of "due diligence" the Agency did alert local authorities to what a *mubtakar* might look like if it were ever constructed. McLaughlin recalls, "We built a model of it, and we took it around so people could see what it was, but we were not saying this is the main thing you have to worry about."

Even the sober political scientist Graham Allison, a founding dean of the Kennedy School at Harvard, wrote a 2004 book titled *Nuclear Terrorism* predicting that "on the current path, a nuclear terrorist attack on America in the decade ahead is more likely than not." Coming from Allison, who had served in the Pentagon as a senior official under President Clinton, this dramatic warning received considerable attention. Yet, many years after Allison first made his grim prediction, not a shred of evidence has emerged to substantiate this doomsday claim.

Similarly, the congressionally authorized Commission on the Prevention of Weapons of Mass Destruction Proliferation and Terrorism issued a report in December 2008 that concluded: "It is more likely than not that a weapon of mass destruction will be used in a terrorist attack somewhere in the world by the end of 2013." The findings of this report received considerable ink in the *New York Times* and *Washington Post* and plenty of airtime on networks around the world. And the day the report was released, incoming vice president Joe Biden was briefed on its contents.

The report's overall conclusion that WMD terrorism is likely to happen "somewhere in the world" in the next five years was simultaneously stating the obvious—because terrorists had already engaged in crude chemical and biological weapons attacks—but also highly unlikely because the prospects of al-Qaeda or indeed any other terrorist group having access to a true WMD—a nuclear device—is near zero for the foreseeable future.

To understand how complex it is to develop an atomic weapon, it is worth recalling that Saddam Hussein put hundreds of millions of dollars into his nuclear program with no success. Iran, which has had an aggressive nuclear program for two decades, is still years away from developing a nuclear bomb. Terrorist groups simply don't have the resources of states and so the notion that they could develop their own, even crude, nuclear weapons is fanciful.

Even if they did have access to such resources, acquiring sufficient highly enriched uranium (HEU) to make a bomb is next to impossible for terrorists. The total of all the known thefts of HEU around the world tracked by the International Atomic Energy Agency between 1993 and 2006 was just less than eight kilos, far short of the twenty-five kilos needed for the crudest bomb. (And none of the uranium thieves were linked to al-Qaeda.) So, even building the simple gun-type nuclear device of the kind that was dropped on Hiroshima would be extraordinarily difficult for a terrorist group because of the problem of accumulating sufficient quantities of HEU.

What about terrorists who might be given a nuke by a state? This was one of the underlying rationales of the push to topple Saddam in 2003. But governments are not about to hand over their crown jewels to organizations that they don't control, and giving a terror group a nuclear weapon exposes the state sponsor to large-scale retaliation. The United States destroyed Saddam's regime on the mere *suspicion* that he might have a nuclear weapons program and that he might give some kind of WMD capacity to terrorists; imagine what would happen to a country that actually *did* what Saddam was accused of doing. Also, nuclear states are well aware that their atomic weapons give off distinctive signatures after they are detonated, which means that even in the unlikely event that they wanted to get away with giving a nuke to terrorists, they couldn't.

For the same reason that states won't give nukes to terrorists, they also won't sell them, either. This leaves the option of stealing a nuclear weapon, but nuclear-armed governments, including Pakistan, are quite careful about the security measures they place around their most valued weapons. After 9/11 the United States gave Pakistan some $100 million in aid to help secure its nukes. And the Department of Defense has assessed that "Islamabad's nuclear weapons are probably stored in component form," meaning that the weapons are stored unassembled, with the fissile core separated from the nonnuclear explosive. Such disassembling is one layer of protection against potential theft by jihadists. A further layer is Permissive Action Links (PAL), essentially electronic locks and keys designed to prevent unauthorized access to nuclear weapons, and Pakistan asserts that it has the "functional equivalent" of these. As a result of these measures, Michael Maples, the head of the Defense Intelligence Agency, told the Senate Armed Services Committee in March 2009 that "Pakistan has taken important steps to safeguard its nuclear weapons."

Though a true WMD attack by terrorists in the United States that would kill hundreds of thousands is extraordinarily unlikely, former vice president Cheney—in the course of defending the Bush administration's use of waterboarding and other such measures—claimed in February 2009 that such an attack was "a high probability," adding that "whether or not they can pull it off depends on whether or not we keep in place policies that have allowed us to defeat all further attempts, since 9/11, to launch mass-casualty attacks against the United States." In other words, if there were an attack on the United States that killed many tens of thousands, it would be the Obama administration's fault, since, in Cheney's telling, it was the Bush administration's extralegal policies that kept America safe after 9/11, including safe from terrorists wielding weapons of mass destruction.

Luckily, the chances of such an attack are quite remote, but the story of A. Q. Khan, the founder of Pakistan's nuclear weapons program, does provide some pointers about how a group like al-Qaeda might be able to recruit scientists with the know-how to build an atomic weapon. After obtaining his Ph.D. in Belgium in 1972, Khan, a metallurgist by training, traveled to Holland, where he secured a job in a company that made centrifuges suitable to enrich uranium for a nuclear device. Khan was able to steal the blueprints for the centrifuges and send them to officials in Pakistan, who eventually built devices based on those designs to enrich enough uranium to make a number of atomic weapons.

For his role in building Pakistan's bomb, Khan became a national hero, but motivated by greed, Khan also proliferated nuclear technology to rogue states like Libya. That made him a rich man with four houses in Islamabad, a collection of vintage cars, and a villa on the Caspian Sea, but eventually Khan's career of nuclear proliferation was discovered by the United States and he was placed under house arrest by the Pakistani government in 2003, where he remains.

One of the worrisome features of Khan's story is that while he was not an Islamist ideologue himself, one of the younger scientists working with Khan in the mid-1970s on Pakistan's program to build a nuclear weapon with stolen technology was Sultan Bashiruddin Mahmood, the same pro-Taliban nuclear scientist who more than two decades later would be discussing atomic weaponry with Osama bin Laden in Afghanistan.

Governments must, of course, be cognizant that scientists motivated either by greed or ideology might give WMD know-how to terrorist groups. But even a group armed with such scientific knowledge would still have to overcome enormous technical challenges to build a workable nuclear device or to weaponize agents such as anthrax. And so groups like al-Qaeda will for the foreseeable future continue to use the tried-and-true tactics of hijackings, truck bombs, and suicide attacks, rather than being able to successfully pull off the deeply uncertain, complex, and prohibitively expensive task of developing true weapons of mass destruction. This, of course, does not preclude al-Qaeda or its affiliates from deploying crude biological, chemical, or radiological weapons over the coming years, but these will not be weapons of mass destruction. Rather, they will be weapons of mass disruption, whose principal effect will be panic and few deaths.

Part II

Nemesis?

Wars begin when you will, but they do not end when you please.

—Niccolò Machiavelli

Chapter 14

The United States of Jihad

Although we have discovered only a handful of individuals in the United States with ties to al-Qa'ida senior leadership since 9/11, we judge that al-Qa'ida will intensify efforts to put operatives here.

—National Intelligence Estimate of July 2007, representing the collective judgment of the United States' sixteen intelligence agencies

Najibullah Zazi, a lanky Afghan-American man in his mid-twenties, walked into the Beauty Supply Warehouse in Aurora, Colorado, a suburb of Denver, on July 25, 2009, in a visit that was captured on a store video camera. Wearing a baseball cap and pushing a shopping cart down the aisles of the store, Zazi appeared to be just another suburban guy, although not too many suburban guys buy six bottles of Clairoxide hair bleach, as Zazi did on this shopping trip. He returned to the same store a month later and purchased another dozen bottles of "Ms. K Liquid," which is also a peroxide-based hair bleach. Aware that these were hardly the typical purchases of a heavily bearded, dark-haired young man, Zazi—who had lived in the States since the age of fourteen—kibitzed easily with the counter staff, joking that he had to buy such large quantities of hair products because he "had a lot of girl friends."

Zazi, a sometime coffee cart operator on Wall Street, was in fact planning to launch what could have been the deadliest terrorist attack in the United States since 9/11 using the seemingly innocuous hair bleach to assemble homemade bombs, a signature of al-Qaeda plots in recent years. During early September 2009, at the Homewood Studio Suites motel in Aurora, Zazi mixed and cooked batches of the noxious chemicals in the kitchenette of his room. On the night of September 6, as Zazi labored over the stove, he made a number of frantic calls to someone whom he asked for advice on how to perfect the bombs. Two days later Zazi was on his way to New York in a rented car. By now President Obama was receiving daily briefings about Zazi, sometimes as many as three or four a day.

Zazi was spotted in downtown Manhattan on Wall Street on the eighth anniversary of the 9/11 attacks just a few blocks from the gaping hole where the World Trade Center had once stood. By then he was under heavy FBI surveillance and eight days later Zazi was arrested. He later admitted that "the plan was to conduct martyrdom operations on subway lines in Manhattan."

Zazi was the first genuine al-Qaeda recruit to be discovered living in the United States in six years. On his laptop the FBI discovered he had stored pages of handwritten notes about the manufacture and initiation of explosives and the components of various detonators and fusing systems, technical know-how he had picked up at one of al-Qaeda's training facilities in Pakistan's tribal regions sometime between the late summer of 2008 and January 2009, when he finally returned to the United States. The notations included references to TATP, an explosive used in Richard Reid's shoe bomb and the London 7/7 suicide bombings.

A constellation of serious domestic terrorism cases surfaced during the last years of the second Bush term and during Obama's first years in office, which showed that a small minority of American Muslims were not immune to the al-Qaeda ideological virus. And quite a number of those terrorism cases were more *operational* than *aspirational*, unlike many of the domestic terror cases that had preceded them following 9/11. The jihadists in these cases were not just talking about violent acts to a government informant but had actually traveled to an al-Qaeda training camp; had fought in an overseas jihad; had purchased guns or explosives; were building bombs and casing targets; and in a couple of cases, had actually killed Americans.

The Zazi case was a reminder of al-Qaeda's ability to attract recruits living in America who were "clean skins" without previous criminal records or known terrorist associations and who were intimately familiar with the West. Similarly, Bryant Neal Vinas, a twenty-something Hispanic-American convert to Islam from Queens, New York, traveled to Pakistan's tribal areas in the summer of 2008. There he attended al-Qaeda training courses on explosives and handling weapons such as rocket-propelled grenades, lessons that he put to good use when he participated in a rocket attack on an American base in Afghanistan in September 2008. Vinas was captured in Pakistan the same month and was turned over to the FBI. He told his interrogators that he had provided al-Qaeda members details about the Long Island Rail Road, which the terror group had some kind of notional plan to attack. (The fact that seven years after 9/11 a kid from Long Island managed to waltz into an al-Qaeda training camp, a feat that no American spy had done, despite the some $75 billion a year that the United States was spending on its intelligence agencies, says a great deal about how the U.S. intelligence community actually works.)

An American who rose to prominence in al-Qaeda several years after 9/11 was Adam Gadahn, a Californian convert to militant Islam. Gadahn, a heavily bearded man in his twenties wearing a white robe and turban, became a regular on-camera presence in al-Qaeda videos using his jihad handle of "Azzam al-Amriki" and delivering finger-wagging lectures about the perfidious United States. Typical of those appearances was a video in which Gadahn said "fighting and defeating America is our first priority. . . . The streets of America shall run red with blood." In 2006 Gadahn became the first American charged with treason in more than five decades.

Surprisingly, even almost a decade after 9/11 a number of Americans bent on jihad also managed to travel to al-Qaeda's headquarters in the tribal regions of Pakistan. In addition to Zazi and Vinas, David Headley, an American of Pakistani descent living in Chicago—he had legally changed his name from Daood Gilani in 2006 to avoid suspicion when he traveled abroad—also had significant dealings with militants based in Pakistan's tribal areas.

Sometime in 2008, Headley hatched a plan to attack the Danish newspaper *Jyllands-Posten*, which three years earlier had published cartoons of the Prophet Mohammed that were deemed to be offensive by many Muslims. In a message to a Pakistan-based Yahoo group on October 29, 2008, Headley wrote, "Call me old fashioned but I feel disposed towards violence for the offending parties."

The cartoons of the Prophet had become a particular obsession of al-Qaeda. In March 2008, bin Laden publicly denounced the publication of the cartoons as a "catastrophe" for which punishment would soon be meted out. Three months later, an al-Qaeda suicide attacker bombed the Danish embassy in Islamabad, killing six. For al-Qaeda and allied groups, the Danish cartoon controversy had assumed some of the same importance that Salman Rushdie's fictional writings about the Prophet had for Khomeini's Iran two decades earlier.

In January 2009, Headley traveled to Copenhagen, where he reconnoitered the *Jyllands-Posten* newspaper on the pretext that he ran an immigration business that was looking to place some advertising in the paper. In coded correspondence with militants in Pakistan, Headley referred to his plot to take revenge for the offensive cartoons as the "Mickey Mouse project." On one of his email accounts Headley listed a set of procedures for the project that included "Route Design," "Counter Surveillance," and "Security."

Following his trip to Denmark, Headley met with Ilyas Kashmiri in the Pakistani tribal regions to brief him on his findings. Kashmiri headed a terrorist organization, Harakat-ul-Jihad Islami, closely tied to al-Qaeda. Headley returned to Chicago in mid-June 2009 and was arrested there three months later as he was preparing to leave for Pakistan again. He told investigators that he was planning to kill the *Jyllands-Posten*'s cultural editor, Flemming Rose, who had first commissioned the cartoons, as well as Kurt Westergaard, who had drawn the cartoon he found most offensive: the Prophet Mohammed with a bomb concealed in his turban.

Headley said that he also cased a synagogue near the *Jyllands-Posten* headquarters at the direction of a member of Lashkar-e-Taiba (LeT) in Pakistan, the same group that had carried out the Mumbai attacks that killed some 170 people in 2008. The Lashkar-e-Taiba militant whom Headley was in contact with mistakenly believed that the newspaper's cultural editor was Jewish. When he was arrested, Headley had a book titled "How to Pray Like a Jew" in his luggage and a Memory Stick containing a video of a close-up shot of the entrance to the *Jyllands-Posten* offices in Copenhagen.

Headley also played a key role in LeT's massacre in Mumbai in late November 2008, traveling to the Indian financial capital on five extended trips in the two years before the attacks. There Headley made videotapes of the key locations attacked by the ten LeT gunmen, including the five-star Taj Mahal and Oberoi hotels and the Nariman House, a Jewish community center, which was a particular target of LeT's gunmen and would help further explain why Headley had the book about Jewish prayer rituals in his luggage at the time of his arrest. Headley also scouted out possible locations on Mumbai's seafront where the attackers, who originated in the Pakistani seaport of Karachi, could land their boat before they launched their attacks.

For many years after 9/11, the United States government had largely worried about terrorists coming into the country. David Headley was an American *exporting* the jihad overseas. But he was far from the only one. By the summer of 2010 some three dozen American citizens or residents had been charged with traveling to an overseas training camp or war zone for jihad since 9/11: three who trained with the Taliban; ten who trained with al-Qaeda; eight who trained with the Pakistani terrorist group Lashkar-e-Taiba; three who had trained with some other unspecified jihadist outfit in Pakistan; and more than a dozen who had fought with the Somali al-Qaeda affiliate, Al Shabab. (The actual number of Americans who had traveled overseas for jihad since 9/11 was likely larger, as not everyone who did so ended up being charged or convicted of a crime.)

In September 2009, the Somali Islamist insurgent group Al Shabab formally pledged allegiance to Osama bin Laden following a two-year period in which it had recruited Somali-Americans and other U.S. Muslims to fight in the war in Somalia. Six months earlier bin Laden had given his own imprimatur to the Somali jihad in an audiotape he released titled "Fight On, Champions of Somalia."

In 2006, with American encouragement and support, Ethiopia, a predominantly Christian country, invaded Somalia, an overwhelmingly Muslim nation, to overthrow the Islamist government there known as the Islamic Courts Union (ICU). While far from ideal, the ICU was the first government in two decades to have brought some measure of stability to the failed Somali state, but its rumored links to al-Qaeda–like groups had put it in the Bush administration's crosshairs.

Some two dozen Somali-Americans, motivated by a combination of nationalist pride and religious zeal, traveled to Somalia in 2007 and 2008 to fight the Ethiopian occupation. Most of them associated themselves with *Al Shabab*—"the youth" in Arabic—the insurgent group that would later proclaim itself to be an al-Qaeda affiliate. Many of Al Shabab's recruits hailed from Minnesota, where the largest number of Somali-Americans are concentrated.

Al Shabab managed to plant al-Qaeda–like ideas into the heads of even its American recruits. Shirwa Ahmed, an ethnic Somali, graduated from high school in Minneapolis in 2003, then worked pushing passengers in wheelchairs at the Minneapolis airport. During this period Ahmed was radicalized; the exact mechanisms of that radicalization are still murky but in late 2007 he traveled to Somalia. A year later, on October 29, 2008, Ahmed drove a truck loaded with explosives toward a government compound in Puntland, northern Somalia, blowing himself up and killing about twenty people. The FBI matched Ahmed's finger, recovered at the scene of the bombing, to fingerprints already on file for him. Ahmed was the first American suicide attacker anywhere. It's possible that eighteen-year-old Omar Mohamud of Seattle was the second. On September 17, 2009, two stolen United Nations vehicles loaded with bombs blew up at Mogadishu airport, killing more than a dozen peacekeepers of the African Union. The FBI suspected that Mohamud was one of the bombers.

Al Shabab prominently featured its American recruits in its propaganda operations, releasing two videos in 2009 starring Abu Mansoor al-Amriki ("the father of Mansoor, the American"), who was in fact Omar Hammami, a twenty-five-year-old from Alabama who was raised as a Baptist before converting to Islam while he was in high school. In the video Amriki delivered an eloquent rejoinder to President Obama's speech in Cairo, in which the president had extended an olive branch to the Muslim world. Mansoor addressed himself to Obama in a flat American accent: "How dare you send greetings to the Muslim world while you are bombing our brothers and sisters in Afghanistan. And how dare you send greetings to Muslims while you are supporting Israel, the most vicious and evil nation of the modern era." Another Al Shabab video from 2009 shows Amriki preparing an ambush against Ethiopian forces and featured English rap lyrics extolling jihad intercut with scenes of his ragtag band traipsing through the African bush.

The chances of getting killed in Somalia were quite high for the couple of dozen or so Americans who volunteered to fight there; in addition to the two men who conducted suicide operations, six other Somali-Americans between eighteen and thirty years old were killed in Somalia between 2007 and 2009, as was Ruben Shumpert, an African-American convert to Islam from Seattle. Given the high death rate of the Americans fighting in Somalia, as well as the considerable attention this group received from the FBI, it was unlikely that American veterans of the Somali war posed much of a threat to the United States itself. It was, however, plausible, now that Al Shabab had declared itself to be an al-Qaeda affiliate, that U.S. citizens in the group might be recruited to engage in anti-American operations overseas.

The shuttered U.S. embassy in Kabul, Afghanistan in 1993—an all too apt metaphor for the United States' neglect of Afghanistan before the 9/11 attacks. *Photo by Peter Bergen.*

During the mid-1990s civil war that tore Afghanistan apart, child soldiers like these were a common sight. It was out of this chaos that the Taliban would arise. *Photo by Peter Bergen.*

Osama bin Laden and Ayman al-Zawahiri, al-Qaeda's top leaders, in Afghanistan in early November 2001. During this interview, they improbably claimed al-Qaeda possessed some kind of nuclear weapon. *Visual News/ Getty Images.*

An exceptionally rare photograph of the reclusive Taliban leader Mullah Omar, taken in Kandahar sometime before the 9/11 attacks. Face partially concealed, third from left. *Photo courtesy of CNN.*

Noman Benotman, seen here in Afghanistan, a onetime companion-in-arms of Osama bin Laden, who met with him a year before 9/11 and warned him of the folly of attacking the United States. *Photo courtesy of Noman Benotman.*

CIA al-Qaeda expert Barbara Sude in Yemen. The 9/11 Commission Report identified her as one of the principal authors of the August 6, 2001 briefing to President Bush entitled "Bin Ladin Determined to Strike in U.S." *Photo courtesy of Barbara Sude.*

Gary Berntsen headed CIA operations on the ground in Afghanistan in the winter of 2001. *Photo courtesy of Gary Berntsen.*

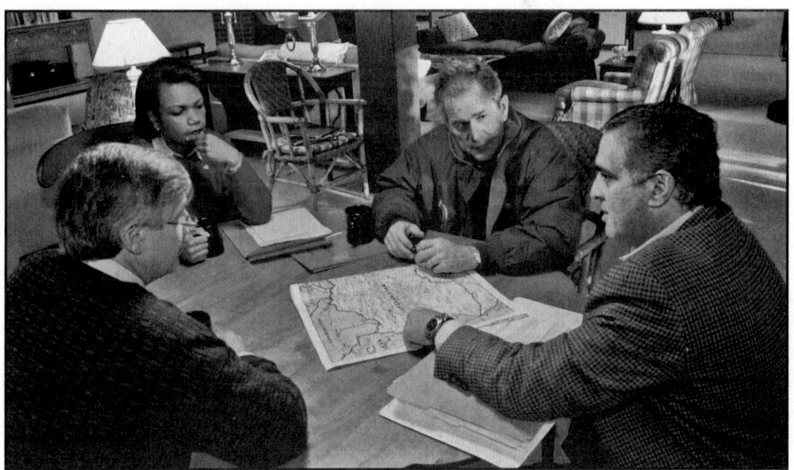

CIA Director George Tenet briefs President Bush and National Security Advisor Condoleezza Rice about the Agency's plans to attack the Taliban and al-Qaeda in Afghanistan, at Camp David in Maryland on September 29, 2001. *White House photo by Eric Draper. Courtesy of the George W. Bush Presidential Library.*

Inside a cave in Tora Bora in eastern Afghanistan; this was the last confirmed location of Osama bin Laden before he was killed in Pakistan in 2011. The caves there are rudimentary affairs, but can withstand heavy bombing. *Photo by Peter Bergen.*

Future Afghan president Hamid Karzai surrounded by the team of U.S. Special Forces who helped him in the fight against the Taliban, outside Kandahar on December 3, 2001. *Photo courtesy of Major Jason Amerine.*

Ali Soufan, left, one of the few Arabic-speaking agents at the FBI before 9/11, was able to solicit a great deal of uncoerced information from al-Qaeda insiders. *Photo courtesy of Ali Soufan.*

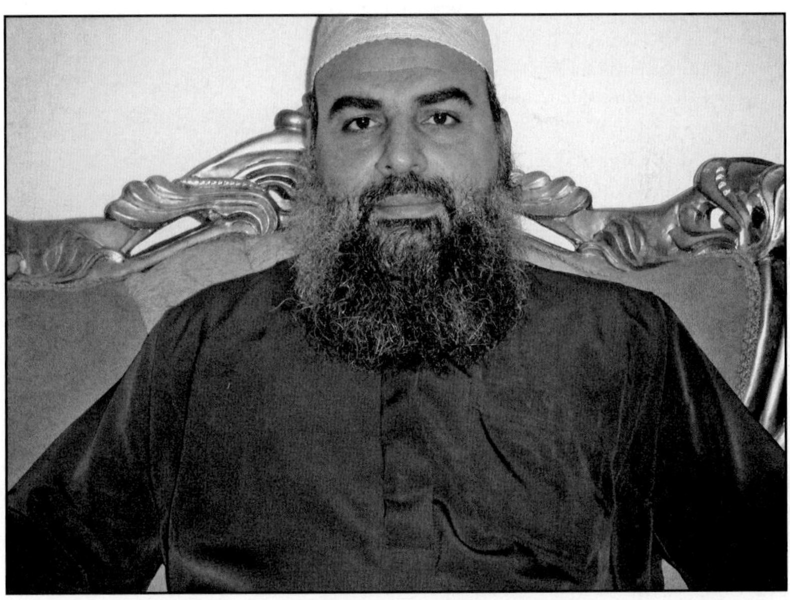

Egyptian militant Abu Omar was abducted from the streets of Milan by CIA officers in 2003. He spent four years in Egypt's hellish prisons. *Photo by Peter Bergen.*

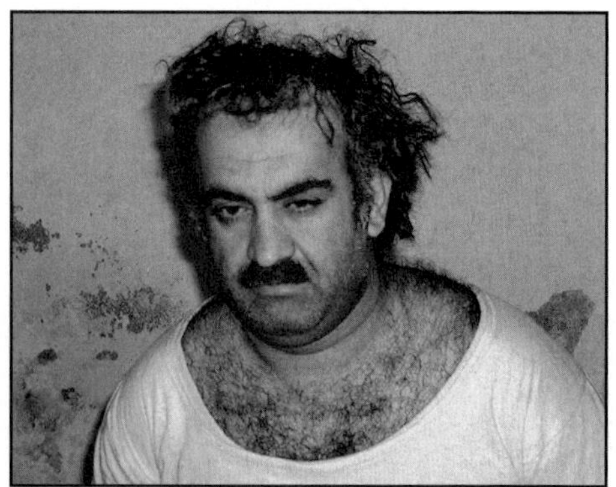

Khalid Sheikh Mohammed, the operational commander of the 9/11 attacks, was roused from his bed in the middle of the night and arrested in Pakistan on March 1, 2003. *U.S. government photo via Associated Press.*

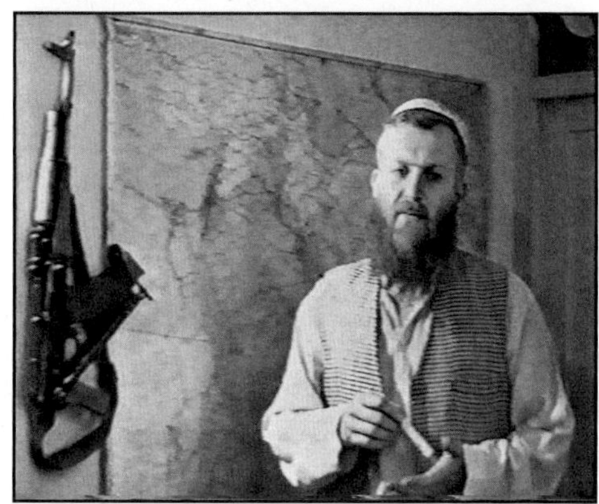

Abu Musab al-Suri, seen here in an instructional videotape made before 9/11 in which he criticized the existing hierarchical and bureaucratic nature of al-Qaeda and instead advocated for a less centralized jihadist movement. *Photo courtesy of Peter Bergen.*

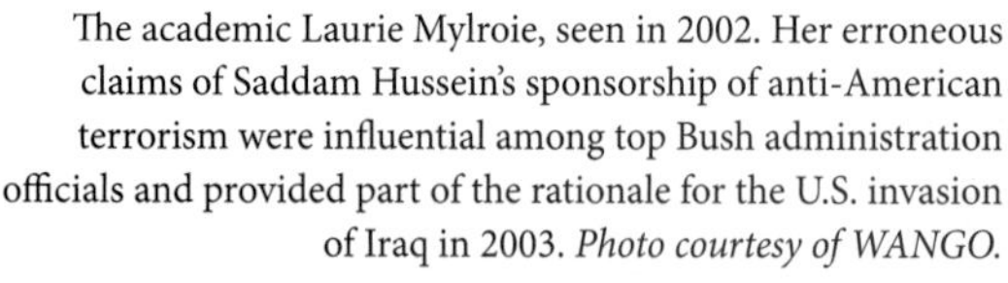

The academic Laurie Mylroie, seen in 2002. Her erroneous claims of Saddam Hussein's sponsorship of anti-American terrorism were influential among top Bush administration officials and provided part of the rationale for the U.S. invasion of Iraq in 2003. *Photo courtesy of WANGO.*

Abu Musab al-Zarqawi, the thuggish leader of al-Qaeda in Iraq, shows his face publicly for the first time in this video in March 2006. A few weeks later he would be killed in an American airstrike. *Department of Defense.*

Vice President Dick Cheney, left, National Security Advisor Stephen Hadley, center, and Iraq adviser Meghan O'Sullivan, second right, listen to President Bush discuss the death of Abu Musab al-Zarqawi, on June 8, 2006. Hadley and O'Sullivan played a critical role in developing the "surge" strategy in Iraq. *Brendan Smialowski/AFP/Getty Images.*

On the sixth anniversary of September 11, General David Petraeus, the top U.S. commander in Iraq, testified before the Senate Foreign Relations Committee about conditions there. Then-Senator Hillary Clinton told the general his report required a "willing suspension of disbelief." *Carol T. Powers/Bloomberg via Getty Images.*

Former Pakistani Prime Minister Benazir Bhutto returns home to Pakistan triumphantly from eight years of exile on October 18, 2007. Two months later she would be assassinated by the Pakistani Taliban. *Daniel Berehulak/Getty.*

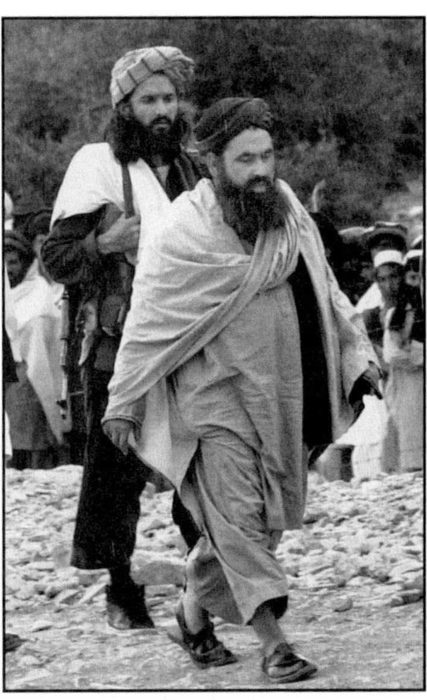

Baitullah Mehsud, the leader of the Pakistani Taliban who ordered Bhutto's assassination. In August 2009 he would die in a U.S. drone strike in South Waziristan. *A Majeed/AFP/Getty.*

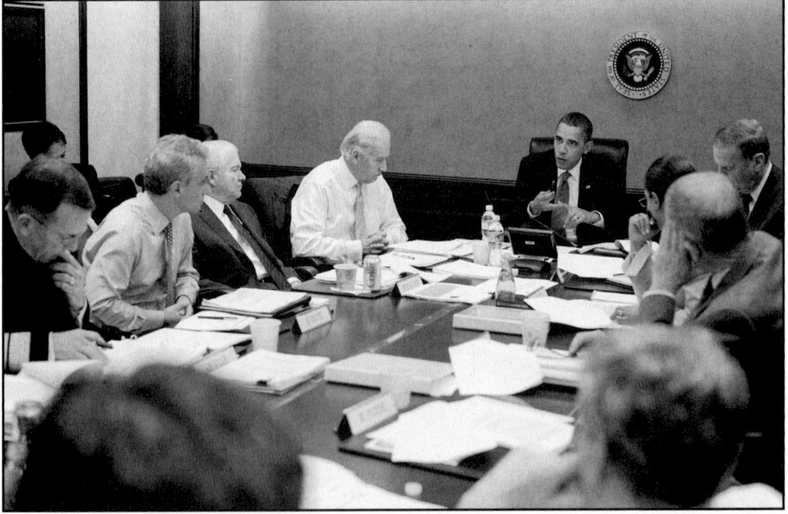

President Barack Obama meets with his national security team to discuss Afghanistan and Pakistan in the Situation Room of the White House on Nov. 11, 2009. During this meeting, Obama instructed the U.S. military to come up with a timetable to surge troops into Afghanistan more quickly than the Pentagon had planned. *White House photo by Pete Souza.*

The fact that American citizens had engaged in suicide operations in Somalia raised the possibility that suicide operations could start taking place in the United States itself; to discount this possibility would be to ignore the lessons of the British experience. On April 30, 2003, two Britons of Pakistani descent launched a suicide attack in Tel Aviv; the first British suicide bomber, Birmingham-born Mohammed Bilal, blew himself up outside an army barracks in Indian-held Kashmir in December 2000. Despite those attacks, the British security services had concluded after 9/11 that suicide bombings would not be much of a concern in the United Kingdom itself. Then came the four suicide attackers in London on July 7, 2005, which ended that complacent attitude.

Major Nidal Malik Hasan, a Palestinian-American medical officer and a rigidly observant Muslim who made no secret to his fellow officers of his opposition to America's wars in Iraq and Afghanistan, went on a shooting spree at the giant Army base at Fort Hood, Texas, on November 5, 2009, killing thirteen and wounding many more. This attack seems to have been an attempted suicide operation in which Hasan planned a jihadist "death-by-cop." In the year before his killing spree, Hasan had made Web postings about suicide operations and the theological justification for the deaths of innocents, and had sent more than a dozen emails to Anwar al-Awlaki, an American-born cleric living in Yemen who is a well-known al-Qaeda apologist. Awlaki said he first received an email from Major Hasan on December 17, 2008, and in that initial communication he "was asking for an edict regarding the [possibility] of a Muslim soldier [killing] colleagues who serve with him in the American army."

Hasan was a social misfit who never married, largely avoided women (except, apparently, strippers), and had few friends, while the psychiatric counseling he gave to wounded veterans when he worked at Walter Reed Army Medical Center in Washington, D.C., might have contributed to a sense of impending doom about his own deployment to Afghanistan. But while Hasan was undoubtedly something of an oddball, in what he assumed to be his final days he seems to have conceived of himself as a holy warrior intent on martyrdom.

Early on the morning of the massacre, the deadliest ever on a military base in the United States, Hasan was filmed at a convenience store buying his regular snack, dressed in white, flowing robes. The color white is often associated with martyrdom in Islam, as the dead are wrapped in white winding sheets. In the previous days Hasan had given away many of his possessions to his neighbors in the decrepit apartment block they shared. Neighbor Lenna Brown recalled, "I asked him where are you going, and he said Afghanistan." Asked how he felt about that, Hasan paused before answering: "I am going to do God's work." He gave Brown a Koran before he left for what he believed to be his last day on earth.

As he opened fire in a room full of fellow soldiers who were filling out paperwork for their deployments to Afghanistan and Iraq, Hasan shouted at the top of his lungs, "Allah Akbar!" God is Great! It has been the battle cry of Muslim warriors down the centuries. Hasan survived being shot by a police officer and was put in intensive care in a hospital in San Antonio, Texas. After he woke up he found himself not in Paradise but being interrogated by investigators and paralyzed from the waist down.

For Americans fired up by jihadist ideology, American soldiers fighting two wars in Muslim countries were particularly inviting targets. A few months before Hasan's murderous spree, Abdulhakim Mujahid Muhammad, an African-American convert to Islam, had shot up a U.S. military recruiting station in Little Rock, Arkansas, killing a soldier and wounding another. Despite the fact that the FBI had had him under surveillance following a mysterious trip that he had recently taken to Yemen, Muhammad was still able to acquire guns and attack the recruiting station in broad daylight. When Muhammad was arrested in his vehicle, police found a rifle with a laser sight, a revolver, ammunition, and the makings of Molotov cocktails. (The middle name that Muhammad had assumed after his conversion to Islam, Mujahid, or "holy warrior," should have been a red flag, as this is far from a common name among Muslims.)

A group of some half-dozen American citizens and residents of the small town of Willow Creek, North Carolina, led by Daniel Boyd, a charismatic convert to Islam who had fought in the jihad in Afghanistan against the Soviets, was also alleged to have had some kind of plan to attack American soldiers. Starting in 2008, Boyd purchased eight rifles and a revolver and members of his group did paramilitary training on two occasions in the summer of 2009. According to federal prosecutors, members of Boyd's cell conceived of themselves as potential participants in overseas jihads from Israel to Pakistan. And Boyd obtained maps of Quantico Marine Base in Virginia, which he cased for a possible attack on June 12, 2009. He also possessed armor-piercing ammunition, saying it was "to attack Americans," and said that one of his weapons would be used "for the base," an apparent reference to the Quantico facility.

Similarly, in 2007 a group of observant Muslims—a mix of Albanians, a Turk, and a Palestinian—living in southern New Jersey and angered by the Iraq War told a government informant they had a plan to kill soldiers stationed at the Fort Dix Army base. One of the group made an amateur mistake when he went to a Circuit City store and asked for a videotape to be transferred to DVD. On the tape a number of young men were shown shooting assault weapons and shouting "Allah Akbar!" during a January 2006 training session. An alarmed clerk at the store alerted his superiors; quickly the FBI became involved in the case and an informant was inserted inside the group.

One of the plotters, Serdar Tatar, knew the Fort Dix base well because he made deliveries there from his family's pizza parlor. The Fort Dix plotters assembled a small armory of rifles and pistols and regularly conducted firearms training in the Pocono Mountains of Pennsylvania. They also went on paintball trips together, a not uncommon form of bonding for jihadist militants living in the West. The plotters also looked into purchasing an array of automatic weapons. And on August 11, 2006, the ringleader, Mohamad Shnewer, surveilled the base and told the government informant, "This is exactly what we are looking for. You hit four, five, six Humvees and light the whole place [up] and retreat completely without any losses."

Another group that planned to attack U.S. military installations was led by Kevin Lamar James, an African-American convert to Islam who formed a group dedicated to holy war while he was jailed in California's Folsom Prison during the late 1990s. James, who viewed his outfit as "Al-Qaeda in California," cooked up a plan to recruit five people, in particular those without criminal records, to help him with his plans. One of his recruits had a job at Los Angeles International Airport (LAX), which James thought could be useful. In notations he made of potential targets, James listed LAX, the Israeli consulate in Los Angeles, a U.S. Army base in Manhattan Beach, California, and "Army recruiting centers throughout the country."

James's crew planned to attack a U.S. military recruiting station in L.A. on the fourth anniversary of 9/11, as well as a synagogue a month later during Yom Kippur, the most solemn of Jewish holidays. Members of the group financed their activities by sticking up gas stations; their plans only came to light during the course of a routine investigation of a gas station robbery when police in Torrance, California, found documents that laid out the group's plans for jihadist mayhem.

Between 9/11 and the summer of 2010 the government had charged or convicted at least twenty Americans and U.S. residents who had direct connections to al-Qaeda and were conspiring with the group to carry out some type of attack; another nine had attended one of al-Qaeda's training camps but did not have an operational terrorist plan; and two dozen other militants aspired to help al-Qaeda in some other way but had failed to connect with the group because of their own incompetence or because they had been ensnared by a government informant.

Typical of the latter group was the posse of mostly Haitian-Americans who imagined they had sworn allegiance to al-Qaeda in 2006 in Liberty City, Miami, one of the city's poorest neighborhoods. After their arrests Attorney General Alberto Gonzales commented, "Homegrown terrorists may prove to be as dangerous as groups like al-Qaeda." As far as the Liberty City group was concerned this was nonsense; the group of men, who were arrested for plotting to blow up the Sears Tower in Chicago, smoked a great deal of marijuana and subscribed to the obscure beliefs of an outfit called the Moorish Science Temple; so nascent were their terrorist plans that they never even bothered to travel to Chicago. A government informant from Yemen who portrayed himself as an emissary from al-Qaeda had provided them with military-style boots, money, and weapons. It took putting the Liberty City crew on trial three times to get a jury to convict them.

The domestic terrorism cases during the latter years of Bush's second term and Obama's first years in office were a mix of purely "homegrown" militants of limited or no competence, like the Liberty City crew; jihadist lone wolves like Major Hasan and Abdulhakim Mujahid Muhammad, who nonetheless both were able to pull off deadly attacks against U.S. military targets; "self-starting" radicals with no connections to al-Qaeda but inspired by its ideas, like the Torrance, California, cell who posed a serious threat to Jewish and military targets and whose plans for mass mayhem were, crucially, not driven forward by an informant; homegrown militants opting to fight in an overseas jihad with an al-Qaeda affiliate, such as the Somali-American recruits to Al Shabab; militants like David Headley, who played an important operational role for the Pakistani terrorist group Lashkar-e-Taiba, which is acting today with an increasingly al-Qaeda–like agenda; and finally those American citizens like Najibullah Zazi, who had managed to plug directly into al-Qaeda Central in Pakistan's tribal regions.

Some of the men drawn to jihad in America in the decade since 9/11 looked like their largely disadvantaged and poorly integrated European Muslim counterparts. The Afghan-American al-Qaeda recruit, Najibullah Zazi, a high school dropout, earned his living as an airport shuttle bus driver; the Somali-American community in the Cedar-Riverside neighborhood of Minneapolis where some of the young men who volunteered to fight in Somalia had grown up is largely ghettoized. Family incomes there average less than fifteen thousand dollars a year and the unemployment rate is 17 percent. Bryant Neal Vinas, the kid from Long Island who volunteered for a suicide mission with al-Qaeda, skipped college, washed out of the U.S. Army, and later became a truck driver, a job he quit for good in 2007. Three of the five men in the Fort Dix cell were illegal immigrants who supported themselves with construction or delivery jobs.

Decades ago the anger and disappointments or thirst for adventure of some of these men might have been funneled into revolutionary anti-American movements like the Weather Underground or Black Panthers. Today, militant jihadism provides a similar outlet for the rage of disaffected young men, with its false promises of a total explication of the world, which is grafted onto a profound hatred for the West, in particular the United States.

This raises the question of what kind of exact threat to the homeland was posed by this cohort of militants, who ran the gamut from incompetent "homegrowns" to American citizens trained by al-Qaeda. If Zazi had managed to detonate his bombs on Manhattan's subway lines he could have killed scores of Americans, as his plan looks similar to that of the al-Qaeda–directed bombers in London who killed fifty-two commuters in 2005 with the same kind of hydrogen-peroxide-based bombs that Zazi was assembling in his Denver motel room. But the Zazi case also represented the outer limit of al-Qaeda's capabilities inside the United States in the decade after 9/11, indicating that al-Qaeda no longer posed a national security threat to the American homeland of the type that could launch a mass-casualty attack sufficiently large to reorient completely the country's foreign policy as the 9/11 attacks had done, and instead represented a second-order threat similar to that posed by American domestic terrorists such as Timothy McVeigh, who killed 168 when he bombed the Oklahoma City federal building in 1995.

Some claimed the reason that al-Qaeda had not successfully attacked the United States again after 9/11 was that the group was waiting to match or top the attacks on Washington and New York. In 2006, Michael Scheuer, the former head of CIA's bin Laden unit, asserted that "they are not interested in an attack that is the same size as the last one." This proposition could not be readily tested, as the absence of a 9/11-scale attack on the United States was, in this view, supposedly just more evidence for the assertion that al-Qaeda was waiting to hit the States with a massive attack. Of course, al-Qaeda wanted to mount an attack on the States on the scale of 9/11 or larger but intent is not the same thing as capability. And the Zazi case forcefully demonstrated that al-Qaeda was not waiting to launch "the big one," but was in fact content to get any kind of terrorist operation going in the United States, even a relatively small-bore attack.

A frequent question after the attacks on the World Trade Center and Pentagon was why didn't al-Qaeda mount an attack on a mall in some midwestern town, thus showing the American public its ability to attack in Anywheresville, USA? For the Muslims around the globe whom al-Qaeda is trying to influence, an attack on an obscure, unknown town in the Midwest would have little impact, which explains al-Qaeda's continuing fixation on attacks on cities and targets well-known in the Islamic world. That explains Zazi's travel to Manhattan from Colorado and al-Qaeda's many attempts to bring down American passenger jets in the past decade. That is not, of course, to say that someone influenced by bin Laden's ideas—but not part of al-Qaeda or one of its affiliates—might not attempt an attack in the future in some obscure American town, but the terrorist organization itself remains fixated on symbolic targets.

After 9/11, al-Qaeda did continue to pose a substantial threat to U.S. interests overseas and it demonstrated that it could still organize an attack that would kill hundreds of Americans, as was the plan during the "planes plot" of 2006 and the attempt to bring down Northwest Flight 253 three years later as it flew between Amsterdam and Detroit on Christmas Day, 2009.

No Western country was more threatened by al-Qaeda than the United Kingdom. Despite the relatively serious terror cases emerging in the United States as the Bush administration transitioned to that of Obama, America did not have a jihadist terrorism problem anywhere on the scale of Britain, where in 2009 British intelligence identified as many as two thousand citizens or residents who posed a "serious" threat to security, many of them linked to al-Qaeda, in a country with only a fifth of the population of the United States.

Why was the post-9/11 threat from al-Qaeda lower in the United States than it was in the United Kingdom? For all of President Bush's obvious missteps, as he left office after his second term his defenders pointed out that he had "kept America safe" from attack (although that was obviously not the case on 9/11). Bush was not shy about taking credit for this. Al-Qaeda, he explained in 2006, had failed to strike the United States a second time "because our government has changed its policies—and given our military, intelligence, and law enforcement personnel the tools they need to fight this enemy and protect our people." And a fair-minded observer might ask: Was it possible that, despite all he got wrong in Iraq and Afghanistan, Bush somehow managed to get this right?

There is little doubt that some of the measures the Bush administration and Congress took after 9/11 made Americans safer. First, the Patriot Act accomplished something quite important, which was to break down the legal wall that had been blocking the flow of information between the CIA and the FBI. Second, the creation of the National Counterterrorism Center led to various government agencies sharing data and analyzing it under one roof (although the center was the brainchild of the 9/11 Commission, whose establishment the Bush administration had fought against for more than a year). Third, the FBI moved from being largely a crime-solving organization to one more driven by intelligence-gathering, assigning two thousand agents to national security cases and hiring an additional two thousand intelligence analysts. This was supplemented by the creation of some one hundred Joint Terrorism Task Forces around the country integrating the FBI with local law enforcement. Fourth, it became much harder for terrorists to get into the country thanks to no-fly lists. Before 9/11 the total number of suspected terrorists banned from air travel totaled just sixteen names; nine years later there were around four thousand.

One of the most dramatic instances of how heightened security measures prevented potential terrorists from arriving in the United States was the case of Raed al-Banna, a thirty-two-year-old Jordanian English-speaking lawyer who was denied entry at Chicago's O'Hare Airport on June 14, 2003, because border officials detected "multiple terrorist risk factors." A year and a half later, on February 28, 2005, Banna conducted a suicide bombing in Hilla, Iraq, that killed 132 people; his fingerprints were found on the severed hand chained to the steering wheel of his bomb-filled truck.

Finally, cooperation between U.S. and foreign intelligence agencies was generally strong after September 11. For instance, al-Qaeda's 2006 plot to bring down the seven American and Canadian airliners leaving Heathrow was disrupted by the joint work of U.S., British, and Pakistani intelligence services.

That said, a key reason the United States escaped a serious domestic terrorist attack had little to do with either the Bush or Obama administrations. In sharp contrast to sections of the Muslim populations in European countries such as Britain, the American Muslim community—generally a higher-skilled group of immigrants than their European counterparts—has overwhelmingly rejected the ideological virus of militant Islam. The "American Dream" has generally worked well for Muslims in the United States, who are both better educated and wealthier than the average American. More than a third of Muslim-Americans have a graduate degree or better, compared to less than one in ten of the population as a whole.

For European Muslims there is no analogous "British Dream," "French Dream," or, needless to say, "EU Dream." None of this is to say that the limited job opportunities and segregation that are the lot of many European Muslims are the *causes* of terrorism in Europe—only that such conditions may create favorable circumstances in which al-Qaeda can recruit and feed into bin Laden's master narrative that the infidel West is at war with Muslims in some shape or form all around the world. And in the absence of those conditions, militant Islam has never gained much of an American foothold—largely sparing the United States from the scourge of homegrown terrorism. This is fundamentally a testament to American pluralism, not any action of the American government.

Between 9/11 and the spring of 2011 only seventeen Americans were killed in jihadist terrorist attacks in the United States, something that would hardly have been predicable in the immediate aftermath of al-Qaeda's assaults on the World Trade Center and Pentagon. However, in 2009 there were a record 43 jihadist terrorism cases against U.S. citizens and residents, indicating that while the American melting pot had successfully absorbed the vast majority of American Muslims, a tiny—but growing minority—were now embracing the ideology of violent jihad.

Chapter 15

Pakistan: The New Base

Only jihad can bring peace to the world.

—Baitullah Mehsud, leader of the Pakistani Taliban in 2007

Carry out a thought experiment in which al-Qaeda was founded in Iran in the late 1980s and remains headquartered there today, while the Taliban, which was substantially aided by the Iranian government during the 1990s, is now headquartered in Iran. And then add to this toxic brew the notion that Iranian nuclear scientists met with Osama bin Laden before 9/11, and that still other senior officials in Iran's nuclear program proliferated nuclear technology to rogue states such as Libya.

Needless to say, if all of this were the case then the United States would almost certainly have gone to war against Iran following 9/11. But, of course, none of this is true, and instead it was in Pakistan—nominally an ally of the United States—that al-Qaeda and Taliban leaders rebased themselves following their expulsion from Afghanistan in the winter of 2001. And it was veterans of Pakistan's nuclear program who met with bin Laden in Kandahar in the months before 9/11 to discuss his pressing interest in atomic weapons, and it was A. Q. Khan, the dean of Pakistan's nuclear program, who sold nuclear weapons technology to a rogues' gallery that included Libya's bizarre dictator Muammar Ghaddafi.

To understand why the Taliban and al-Qaeda rebased themselves in Pakistan following the fall of the Taliban regime it is helpful to recall a little of the country's history. Pakistan's on-and-off conflict with India, in particular over the disputed Kashmir region, was critical to the rise of the Pakistani military-jihadi complex. One-third of Kashmir is on the Pakistani side of the border and the rest is on the Indian side, but the majority of Kashmiris are Muslims and they wish to secede from predominantly Hindu India. India and Pakistan have fought two full-blown wars, in 1947 and 1965, over the region whose high mountains and lakes suggestive of Switzerland belie its violent history.

Unable to best the much larger Indian army in battle, Pakistan's government supported the rise of Kashmiri militant groups that could infiltrate Indian-held Kashmir and tie down tens of thousands of Indian soldiers. In doing so they fused the political dispute over Kashmir with Pakistan's increasing religiosity and created a state-sanctioned jihad movement. Pakistan's generals supplemented their policy of supporting Kashmir jihadi groups with a doctrine they termed "strategic depth," which meant they wanted to ensure that they had a pliant, pro-Pakistani Afghan state on their western border in the event that India attacked over their eastern border. In practice, the doctrine of strategic depth led Pakistan to support militant Pashtun Islamists in Afghanistan like the Taliban, who the Pakistani government believed were most closely aligned with their own anti-Indian policies.

After their near-death experience in Afghanistan during the winter of 2001, members of al-Qaeda and their Taliban allies didn't disintegrate: they simply moved across the border, a few hundred miles into Pakistan, comfortably out of range of the U.S. military. In a sense, al-Qaeda was just going home, since it was in the Pakistani city of Peshawar in 1988 that bin Laden had founded the group. The Taliban also felt at home in Pakistan. Indeed, several of their leaders had attended the Haqqania madrassa just outside of Peshawar, known as the Harvard of the Taliban.

In their first years on the run, many of al-Qaeda's leaders avoided Pakistan's remote tribal areas along the border with Afghanistan, choosing instead to live in the anonymity of its teeming cities. In particular, Karachi, a barely governable megacity of fifteen million people on Pakistan's southern coast, emerged after 9/11 as a hub of jihadist violence perpetrated by a toxic alliance between al-Qaeda, Kashmiri militant groups, and Sunni sectarian fanatics who had long been at war with Pakistan's Shia minority. After 9/11, militants in Karachi bombed the Sheraton hotel, killing a group of French defense contractors; mounted three attacks on the U.S. consulate, one of which killed a dozen Pakistanis; and killed the American journalist Daniel Pearl.

Karachi's slums are violent no-go areas for the police, making the city an attractive place to hide for Khalid Sheikh Mohammed (KSM), the 9/11 operational commander, as it was for Omar Sheikh, a British-Pakistani militant released from an Indian jail following the hijacking of an Indian Airlines jet to Kandahar in 1999. Omar Sheikh and KSM would fatefully cross paths during the murder of Daniel Pearl, which perhaps better than any one single event demonstrates the nexus between Pakistan's powerful military intelligence agency, ISI, and Kashmiri militant groups tied to al-Qaeda such as Jaish-e-Mohammed ("Army of Mohammed").

One of the *Wall Street Journal*'s star reporters, Pearl had made a name for himself writing deeply reported, often quirky stories from around Asia and the Middle East. As a journalist working in the Muslim world, Pearl had made no secret of his Jewish ancestry. This would make Pearl an inviting target for Omar Sheikh and later too for KSM, once al-Qaeda itself became involved in his abduction.

As the 9/11 attacks unfolded, Pearl had recently married Mariane, a French radio journalist, and she was pregnant with their first child. The Pearls, who were then based in New Delhi, traveled together to Pakistan. There Danny, as he was universally known, began reporting on the various Pakistani militant groups. One in particular aroused his interest, an obscure sect named Jamaat-ul-Fuqra ("Party of the Poor"), which recruited African-Americans from its base in the Pakistani city of Lahore and maintained a number of communes in the United States. Of particular interest to Pearl in mid-January 2002 was Richard Reid, the British-Jamaican "shoe bomber," who had recently tried to blow up an American Airlines flight with explosives hidden in his sneakers. Reid had visited the Fuqra headquarters in Lahore before 9/11.

Pearl set out to interview Fuqra's founder, Sheikh Mubarak Ali Gilani, who, unlike many Pakistani militant clerics, shunned the spotlight. The contacts he reached out to in Pakistan's militant community did not lead Pearl to the shadowy cleric but instead to Omar Sheikh, posing as someone who could arrange a meeting with Gilani. Omar Sheikh was quite adroit at conning Pearl; in his breezy email exchanges with the reporter, Sheikh played hard to get, apologizing for delays in setting up the supposed meeting with

Gilani because he had given Pearl some incorrect contact information, or because his wife was supposedly gravely ill in the hospital.

The last person to see Pearl before his abduction on the night of January 23, 2002, was Karachi businessman Jameel Yusuf, the chief of the Citizen Police Liaison Committee, a group that he had founded in the mid-1990s to help the police solve the epidemic of kidnappings then gripping the city. Yusuf recalled that Pearl "dropped in to talk to me about the reforms after September 11th—How much is the international community doing to strengthen the law enforcement agencies?" Yusuf was struck, as were many others, by Pearl's engaging and open manner: "Very humble down to earth person."

Yusuf remembered that during their meeting Pearl received two calls on his cellphone. Pearl told the caller that he was close by and would be able to meet at 7 P.M. Pearl then met with Omar Sheikh in a fast-food restaurant, where he made the fatal mistake of agreeing to be driven to another location. Pearl did not show up later that night at the house he was living in, which prompted a search in which Yusuf was quickly involved since his organization was the leading investigator of kidnappings in Karachi. Yusuf remembers their worst fears being confirmed when they examined the phone number of Pearl's last caller. "It was a prepaid telephone card, not traceable."

The Pearl case was the first successful act of anti-American terrorism conducted by the al-Qaeda network after 9/11. And it would be the first time that members of the network, rabid anti-Semites to a man, would specifically target a Jew. Until Pearl's kidnapping, international journalists had had little reason to fear doing their jobs in Pakistan. Now the rules had changed.

On January 24, an email was sent to a number of reporters in Pakistan from the account kidnapperguy@hotmail.com. The message demanded the release of all Pakistani prisoners in American custody, including those held at the just-opened Guantánamo Bay prison camp. The email said "CIA officer" Daniel Pearl was now in the custody of "The National Movement for the Restoration of Pakistani Sovereignty." Attached to the message was a photo of a handcuffed Pearl wearing a pink and blue jogging suit. A man was holding a gun to Pearl's head.

Using a specialized computer program, Pakistani and FBI investigators analyzed phone calls made by Pearl before he was kidnapped, and subsequent calls made by those Pearl had contacted, thus building up a phone tree of anyone who might have had a role in the kidnapping. The FBI also dispatched experts in computer forensics to Karachi who worked on tracing where the emails from kidnapperguy@hotmail.com might have originated. Both of these approaches successfully pinpointed several of the conspirators in the kidnapping, but none of this investigative work was enough to prevent Pearl from being murdered by three Arab men on February 1 in the cruelest manner: his head was cut off with a knife, a scene that was recorded on video and posted to the Internet in late February 2002. Another new low for al-Qaeda.

One of the great mysteries of the Pearl case is that kidnapper Omar Sheikh had surrendered to Brigadier Ejaz Shah, a former ISI official, on February 5, 2002, more than a week before the Pakistani government announced to the world that he had been captured. His surrender to the former ISI official strongly suggests that Sheikh had ties to the Pakistani military intelligence agency, and the official silence about his capture, at a time when the Pearl kidnapping was a leading story around the world, also suggests that ISI was debriefing one of its own before he entered into the public Pakistani court system.

Much remains murky about Pearl's kidnapping and murder but what is clear is that Omar Sheikh—who had shown no propensity for murder in the past—kidnapped Pearl on behalf of the Kashmiri militant group Jaish-e-Mohammed in order to spring fellow jihadists from jail. But as the kidnapping evolved, a number of Arabs entered the scene, including KSM, and matters then took a darker turn and the kidnapping became instead a murder; KSM has claimed that he was the man who beheaded Pearl. While some have cast doubt on this assertion, there is little debate today that it was Arab members of al-Qaeda who killed Pearl.

Two months after Pearl's murder, Yosri Fouda, Al Jazeera's chief investigative reporter, scored a journalistic coup: an interview with both KSM and Ramzi Binalshibh, who had together overseen al-Qaeda's attacks on Washington and New York. Buttressing KSM's assertions of his role in the slaying of Pearl is the fact that he gave Fouda an unedited videotape of Pearl's murder.

Fouda, an urbane Egyptian based in London not averse to a pint or two in his local pub, remembers his phone ringing in early 2002 and the man on the other end of the line making him an unusual offer: "He asked me if I was thinking of preparing something special with my program, *Top Secret*, for the first anniversary of September 11th. If so, he would be able to give me some exclusive stuff for the program." Fouda, a secular journalist ideologically far removed from the militant Islamists of al-Qaeda, would then accomplish what it would take *another year* for the CIA to do: track down the man who more than any other was the operational commander of 9/11.

Fouda made his way to Karachi and was met there on April 20, 2002, by an intermediary and driven around the city at night, blindfolded, until they arrived at an apartment block. Fouda recalls, "I counted four floors as I was walking upstairs. I hear a doorbell ringing, and then someone snatches my hand, pulls my hand inside. And then he started taking my blindfolds off." Fouda remembered, "Khalid Sheikh Mohammed asked me, have you recognized us yet? I said, 'You look familiar.'"

One of Fouda's first observations to KSM was, "They say you are terrorists." KSM quickly replied, "They are right. That is what we do for a living." Ever the terrorist technocrat, KSM explained that his main concern about the attacks on Washington and New York was their mechanics: finding the pilots like Mohammed Atta, "people who would know first of all how to fly, people who would mix nicely in a Western atmosphere; people who would speak English well." KSM said that finding the "muscle hijackers" willing to die in the operation was "the least of his worries . . . they had at the time a department for martyrs and that his problem was the office had too many volunteers."

By contrast, Ramzi Binalshibh was more concerned about making the case that the 9/11 attacks were religiously justified, explaining, "Targeting civilians in particular was, in Islam, permitted because America is considered to be a country at war. And that's a very old concept from the early age of Islam."

Much of what KSM and Binalshibh freely volunteered to Fouda was later confirmed by the 9/11 Commission. Fouda remembers that KSM said he had originally contemplated targeting American nuclear power plants with the hijacked planes, "and he said that later they decided to take it off the list because they were not sure if they could control the operation."

The al-Qaeda leaders also explained that the hijacked United Flight 93, which Ziad Jarrah crashed into a field in Pennsylvania, was routed to fly into the U.S. Capitol building in Washington, D.C. "The White House was initially on the list, but they decided that it be taken off the list for navigation reasons. Apparently it was difficult to hit it from the air, according to them. And it was later replaced by another spectacular target, Capitol Hill." The two al-Qaeda operatives told Fouda every detail of how they managed the operation; what codes they had used when communicating with the hijackers in the United States; how they had kept bin Laden in Afghanistan apprised of developments; and the kind of training they had given the hijackers about how to operate in the West.

KSM's and Binalshibh's interview with Al Jazeera would turn out to be a monumental act of hubris. On September 11, 2002, within hours of the first airing of Fouda's documentary featuring the 9/11 masterminds, Binalshibh was arrested in Karachi following a four-hour gun battle and was transferred to American custody. KSM had already slipped away to Quetta, the capital of Baluchistan, the western desert region of Pakistan, where his family had hailed from.

Between 2001 and 2004, none of the key captured al-Qaeda operatives were captured in Pakistan's remote tribal areas along the border with Afghanistan; instead they were all run to ground in its teeming cities, not only in Karachi, but also in Peshawar, Quetta, Faisalabad, Gujrat, and Rawalpindi. Those arrested included Abu Zubaydah, who provided logistical support to al-Qaeda recruits; Walid bin Attash, who played a role in the attack on the USS *Cole* in Yemen; Ahmed Khalfan Ghailani, who was one of the conspirators in the 1998 bombing of the U.S. embassies in Kenya and Tanzania; and Mustafa Ahmed al-Hawsawi, who bankrolled the 9/11 hijackers.

The most important al-Qaeda member to be captured was KSM, who was arrested in Rawalpindi on March 1, 2003, in a 3 A.M. raid in the city that happens to be home to the headquarters of Pakistan's army. A Western diplomat in Pakistan remarked, "What the fuck was this guy doing just down the road from GHQ [army headquarters]?" KSM was run to ground with the help of an informant in Pakistan who would later pick up a substantial cash reward. The informant text-messaged his American controllers, "I am with KSM," when he had slipped into the bathroom of a house in Rawalpindi where the al-Qaeda leader was staying. Later that night KSM was arrested. After KSM was captured, the CIA gave the Associated Press a photo of what the mastermind of 9/11 looked like freshly rousted from his bed in the middle of the night. It was not a pretty sight. KSM, dressed in a rumpled T-shirt, looks dopey, disheveled, and paunchy, the exact opposite of his own heroic self-conception as the James Bond of Jihad.

After KSM's capture there was a brief flurry of anticipation that bin Laden himself would soon be arrested, but according to a U.S. intelligence official interviewed some months after KSM's arrest, bin Laden's "personal signature trail has gone cold." However, computer hard drives seized at the time of KSM's capture did contain a trove of information about al-Qaeda, including spreadsheets listing families who had received financial assistance from the terror group, three letters from bin Laden, a list of wounded and killed al-Qaeda "martyrs," a summary of operational procedures and training requirements for the organization, and passport photos of al-Qaeda operatives.

In the five years after 9/11, Pakistan handed over 369 suspected militants to the United States, for which its government earned bounties of millions of dollars. The high rate of capture of al-Qaeda operatives meant that two or three years after the fall of the Taliban, many militants made the collective decision that the anonymity of Pakistan's teeming cities was not quite as protective as they had once assumed. In fact, typical urban activities like making cell phone calls or dialing up Internet connections had provided many important clues to the whereabouts of al-Qaeda's operatives. Robert Dannenberg, the head of CIA counterterrorism operations at the time, says that the Agency developed new technologies and techniques to target al-Qaeda members in Pakistan, exploiting signals from cell phones and electronic traces from Internet usage: "There's some very creative young engineers and technology people in the Agency who got right on geolocation technologies and used them to grind in on these guys. It's as impressive a technological and operational performance as I've ever seen." The result was that "it absolutely demolished al-Qaeda's operational capability" in Pakistan's urban areas, recalls Dannenberg.

And so al-Qaeda migrated to the remote Pakistani tribal regions on the Afghan border known as the Federally Administered Tribal Areas (FATA). Dannenberg says that al-Qaeda members "retreated to the tribal areas because they felt safer there and they were willing to sacrifice the ability to communicate efficiently with their networks for their own safety." Indicative of this trend was Ahmed Khalfan Ghailani, the Tanzanian member of al-Qaeda involved in the 1998 bombings of the U.S. embassies in Africa, who decided to leave Karachi for the tribal agency of South Waziristan in April 2003.

The term "Federally Administered Tribal Areas" is really a misnomer, since the region has never really been administered nor under the federal government's control. The British fought the Pashtun tribes there in the nineteenth and twentieth centuries. A young Winston Churchill wrote his first book, *The Story of the Malakand Field Force*, about his experiences fighting those tribes, whom he described as possessed of a "wild and merciless fanaticism." The British concluded that the tribal regions were more trouble than they were worth and allowed the tribes de facto independence and the right to enforce their own system of laws. After World War II, Pakistan inherited this arrangement and did little to change it.

The general backwardness of the tribal regions can be gauged by the female literacy rate, which is only 3 percent. And an indicator of the ferocity of the Pashtun tribes is the kind of compounds in which they live, generally mud or concrete fortresses studded with gun ports ideal for fighting off raiding parties. Larger compounds are defended by artillery. In Pashtu the words for "cousin" and "enemy" are roughly the same, which is indicative of the endemic low-level warfare that is the way of life in the FATA, where all males are armed and the blood feud is a multigenerational pursuit that the tribesmen seem to genuinely enjoy.

It was in this remote, ungovernable region that al-Qaeda started rebuilding its operations. A former American intelligence official stationed in Pakistan said that by 2008 there were more than two thousand foreign fighters in the region, while a U.S. intelligence official who tracked al-Qaeda put the number somewhat lower, saying the foreign militants in the FATA consisted of around 100 to 150 members of the core of al-Qaeda who had sworn *bayat,* a religiously binding oath of personal allegiance to bin Laden; a couple of hundred more "free agent" foreigners, mostly Arabs and Uzbeks, living there who were "all but in name al-Qaeda personnel"; and thousands of militant Pashtun tribal members, into whose families some of the foreigners had intermarried.

To root out those militants, the Pakistanis first tried the hammer approach in the FATA in 2004 with a number of military operations. They were essentially defeats for the Pakistani army, which was geared for land wars with India, rather than effective counterinsurgency campaigns. Those military operations were sometimes designed to coincide with the arrival in Pakistan of top Bush administration officials, as was the case in Waziristan in March 2004, when the campaign there kicked off at the same time that Secretary of State Colin Powell was visiting Islamabad. At the time of Powell's visit, President Pervez Musharraf went on CNN to explain that a "high value target," likely Ayman al-Zawahiri, was now surrounded in Waziristan by Pakistani troops. That proved to be wishful thinking, and the failed military operations were followed by appeasement in the form of "peace" agreements with the Taliban in 2005 and 2006, which were really admissions of military failure and allowed the militants to establish even greater sway in the FATA.

By 2009 the Taliban wholly controlled all seven of the tribal agencies in the

FATA and their writ extended into the "settled" areas of the North-West Frontier Province, almost up to the gates of Peshawar, the provincial capital. They also controlled the northern region of Swat, whose verdant valleys and towering mountains had once been one of Pakistan's leading tourist destinations. In areas they controlled, the Taliban conducted their own kangaroo courts, publicly hanging men for infractions such as drinking, and shooting burqa-clad women for supposed promiscuity. The Taliban, who had once banned television, filmed their executions for distribution on DVDs and posting to the Internet. And militants in Waziristan set up a parallel judicial system, lynching and torturing civilians for infringements of their code. Much of what was going on in the tribal areas was opaque because the Pakistani government prevented international journalists from traveling anywhere near these areas, and journalists were sometimes detained or even killed when they reported on the tribal regions.

Pakistan's ruler in the years after 9/11 was General Pervez Musharraf. He had come to power following a bloodless military coup in 1999 that ended a decade of civilian rule, which had been characterized by the incompetence and corruption of Pakistan's elected rulers. For the first years of his tenure as Pakistan's leader Musharraf was wildly popular, but gradually he managed to alienate much of his country's population. His first blunder was to rig a 2002 election so that pro-Taliban religious parties, in an alliance known as the MMA, did better at the polls than they had ever done in Pakistani history, taking over the North-West Frontier Province. The MMA also did well at the polls in the province of Baluchistan, which is where Mullah Omar, the leader of the Taliban, had fled following the fall of his regime. Under Musharraf's rule, two out of Pakistan's four provinces were now largely controlled by the Islamists of the MMA, who were broadly sympathetic to the Taliban and al-Qaeda. The same year Musharraf also held a rigged referendum, boycotted by all the political parties, that extended his power as president for five years, which did much to damage his earlier reputation as a disinterested patriot rather than a power-hungry officer in the mold of other Pakistani military dictators who had preceded him.

On January 12, 2002, Musharraf made an important televised speech to the nation in which he said that Pakistan would no longer tolerate organizations that practiced terrorism in the name of religion. Musharraf banned the militant Kashmiri groups Lashkar-e-Taiba and Jaish-e-Mohammed, both of which had played a role in a gun battle outside the Indian Parliament building in New Delhi a month earlier in which seven guards died. That attack almost brought Pakistan and India to the brink of war again, this time with each side possessing nuclear weapons.

Musharraf's ratcheting up of the pressure on the militant groups made him the target of their wrath. He survived two serious assassination attempts in December 2003 in the garrison city of Rawalpindi. In the first plot, a cell of Pakistani air force personnel bombed Musharraf's convoy. In the second attempt, members of Pakistan's elite commando Special Services Group conspired to kill Musharraf using suicide bombers. While military personnel were integrated into the plots, both assassination attempts were masterminded by al-Qaeda or its close affiliate, Jaish-e-Mohammed. And both attacks came three months after al-Qaeda's number two, Ayman al-Zawahiri, had for the first time issued a tape specifically calling for attacks on Musharraf because of his cooperation with the United States in the "war on terror."

A symptom of the increasingly visible and vocal role of the militant Islamists in Pakistan that characterized the latter years of Musharraf's rule was the standoff between his government and radicals based at the Red Mosque in Islamabad. In the early months of 2007, the militant imam of the Red Mosque, Abdul Rashid Ghazi, was suddenly a force to be reckoned with in Pakistani politics, as his students were staging a series of violent protests. The proximate cause of their anger was the demolition of several mosques in Islamabad that authorities said had been built without the required authorizations, but their agenda had broader elements, including a demand that Musharraf implement sharia law. Masked students armed with batons visited video store owners in Islamabad and told them to close their businesses, while others destroyed music CDs.

In the early summer of 2007, around the mosque grounds heavily bearded men and younger boys milled about, some armed with AK-47s. Inside the mosque, Ghazi, his face framed by professional gold-rimmed glasses, a bushy salt-and-pepper beard, and a reddish knit cap, explained his views on women. "Females should be educated," he said, explaining why the two madrassas he managed included, somewhat unusually, a large number of female students. At the time Ghazi's female charges were staging regular protests against the government, their pictures splashed across newspapers around the world, an army of women clad in black burqas wielding long wooden staves. The extent to which the al-Qaeda ideological virus that justifies suicide operations had infected even relatively cosmopolitan parts of Pakistan could be seen in Ghazi's claim that "a lot of people come to us and ask us if it is permitted to do suicide operations." Asked for clarification on the exact numbers of would-be suicide bombers seeking his counsel, he replied, "Hundreds."

When asked what would happen if the government tried to use force to take the mosque back from his armed militants, Ghazi said with a smile, "We will resist." And they did. Ghazi was killed on July 10, 2007—along with dozens of his supporters—when Pakistani troops stormed his mosque after a weeklong siege.

The soldiers attacked the Red Mosque, which is just a few minutes' drive from Pakistan's parliament, after Ghazi's followers had committed their most brazen act yet: kidnapping six Chinese women in Islamabad from what they said was a brothel. The women were released only after the Chinese ambassador intervened with the government, which in turn pressured Ghazi to free the abducted citizens of one of Pakistan's closest allies.

The bloody siege of the Red Mosque increasingly spread the scourge of militancy from the FATA into the "settled" areas of the North-West Frontier Province and beyond into Pakistan's Punjabi heartland. And the Red Mosque showdown became both a rallying cry for the militants and a pivot point that caused many of the different jihadist groups in Pakistan to turn against their government.

All this mayhem was quite out of character for Islamabad, which has a well-deserved reputation as one of the most boring cities in South Asia. Its regimented neighborhoods—with anodyne names like F6 and E11—are filled with comfortable villas, home to diplomats and senior government officials who are attended by fleets of servants. Their gardens are shaded by jasmine trees and generously scented with the wild marijuana that grows throughout the city.

Around the same time that Musharraf was clamping down on the Red Mosque militants, he also faced another mushrooming political crisis in the usually sedate capital. In March 2007, Musharraf made what would turn out to be a spectacular mistake, suspending the Supreme Court chief justice Iftikhar Chaudhry, ostensibly because he was abusing his office but more likely because he had shown refreshing independence from the government—for instance, by looking into the fates of some of the hundreds of "disappeared" Pakistanis who were widely believed to have been sucked into the maw of the ISI, the powerful military intelligence agency.

Almost overnight, the fired chief justice became a hero to all sorts of disparate groups fed up with Musharraf's despotic ways. The first wave of protests was undertaken by the most unlikely of demonstrators: lawyers wearing black suits, pressed white shirts, and black ties. When they stormed the entrance to the Supreme Court building, it made for great television. In the days when Pakistan had only government-controlled TV, such footage never would have seen the light of day. But one of Musharraf's positive legacies was that he presided over the rise of a genuinely independent media, and a number of private channels had sprung up under his rule, most prominently GEO Television.

And that's where the government made another mistake. A week into the crisis, on March 16, GEO was carrying live pictures of demonstrations around the Supreme Court. Hamid Mir, GEO's Islamabad bureau chief, had set up cameras on the roof of his office: "We were showing police firing rubber bullets on the protesters and tear gas—the first time that the Pakistani people were seeing these scenes live." About an hour later, policemen armed with guns and lathi sticks started gathering outside the GEO office, then entered the building's reception area and beat the receptionist. Mir says, "We retreated into our newsroom area"—rows of computer screens and televisions—"and made a human chain, including with our female colleagues." Pakistani police are reluctant to attack women, so they stood down, but not before they had trashed an adjoining news organization's office. GEO naturally videotaped much of this and carried it live. Within hours, Musharraf appeared on GEO to apologize for the government's actions.

Meanwhile, Chaudhry, the fired chief justice, traveled to rallies around the country, where he was routinely greeted by boisterous crowds of tens of thousands of Pakistanis from all walks of life. Their demands were simple: that the government should uphold the independence of the judiciary and that Musharraf make good on his repeated promises to doff his uniform and surrender his dual role as president and chief of the military. This emergence of a grassroots, democratic movement suggested that wide swaths of the public wanted Pakistan to emulate neighboring India—a democratic state that had not constantly reverted to military rule, as Pakistan had done four times since the countries had both gained independence from the British in 1947.

Unfortunately for those who wanted a return to genuine civilian rule, Musharraf appeared to have something of a messiah complex, making him loath to relinquish any of his power. During the 2007 crisis, Secretary of State

Condoleezza Rice kept up a constant barrage of calls to Musharraf, urging him not to declare martial law as he repeatedly seemed poised to do. But in November, Musharraf declared emergency rule, making it clear that he would never willingly give up his position as both head of the military and president.

Perhaps it was not surprising that a dictator would convince himself that only he could save his country. What was surprising is that Musharraf managed to convince others as well. No one fell for this hoax harder than President Bush. It was a central plank of the administration's foreign policy that democratization was the best way to counter militant Islamists. Yet Bush, so keen to promote democracy in the rest of the Muslim world, was strikingly silent on the need for Musharraf to loosen his dictatorial grip on Pakistan, which had been a democracy on and off over the past six decades of its history and also is the world's second-most-populous Muslim country.

In September 2006, Musharraf had made one of his periodic visits to the United States. At a joint Washington press conference, after telling Musharraf, "I admire your courage and leadership," Bush went on to address a deal that the Pakistani government had recently signed with the Taliban in the tribal area of North Waziristan on the Afghan border. It was very similar to a cease-fire that the Pakistanis had done a year earlier in South Waziristan that had failed. Bush assured the assembled reporters that his Pakistani counterpart had a plan: "When the president looks me in the eye and says, the tribal deal is intended to reject the Talibanization of the people, and that there won't be a Taliban and won't be al-Qaeda, I believe him." Privately, Bush was delivering a different message about the second "peace" deal to Musharraf. National Security Advisor Stephen Hadley recalls that during a dinner at the White House, Bush told the Pakistani general, "We got real concerns about this, whether it's going to work." And Musharraf said, "I want to try it. If it doesn't work, I'm prepared to end it."

Frances Fragos Townsend, Bush's top counterterrorism adviser, was worried by these "peace" agreements. "I think that over time we were getting diddled. It took us a while before we figured that out. By the second one, I had had it. Obviously I didn't win that debate inside the administration, but after what I saw about the first peace agreement, I had no patience for the second one. Complete waste of time."

As part of that second "peace" deal, the Pakistani government even gave local militant leaders $540,000 so they could repay the loans they had taken out from members of al-Qaeda. Several months after the cease-fire agreement was signed, on September 5, 2006, Lieutenant General Karl Eikenberry, the top American commander in Afghanistan, disclosed that cross-border attacks from that area of Pakistan were 200 percent higher than the year before. Hadley says that by the spring of 2007 it was obvious to the Bush team that the peace deal wasn't working and that letting the militants regroup unmolested in the tribal areas as a result of the cease-fire was having disastrous consequences for both Afghanistan and Pakistan.

The Bush administration handed some $11 billion to the Pakistani military after September 11, 2001, for its help in the "war on terror." Yet the Taliban and al-Qaeda remained headquartered in Pakistan throughout the Bush administration's two terms. By July 2007, the sixteen American intelligence agencies that collectively make up the U.S. intelligence community had all signed off on a National Intelligence Estimate that concluded that al-Qaeda "has protected or regenerated key elements of Homeland attack capability, including a safe haven in Pakistan's Federally Administered Tribal Areas (FATA), operational lieutenants, and its top leadership."

Not only that, but the Pakistanis had proven either unwilling or incapable (or both) of effectively taking on the militants. In the spring of 2007, a U.S. military official in Afghanistan with access to intelligence information said that Taliban leader Mullah Omar "is still in Quetta," a Pakistani city. And a U.S. military official based in Pakistan said that detailed "target folders" about the specific locations of high-value Taliban and al-Qaeda targets were provided by the U.S. government to Pakistan in late 2006, but were never acted upon. Moreover, on at least one occasion the Bush administration refused to do what Pakistan would not: In 2005 Donald Rumsfeld nixed a proposed attack on a meeting of al-Qaeda leaders in the tribal region—a group thought to include Ayman al-Zawahiri—in part because the operation, which would have involved more than a hundred Special Forces and CIA personnel, could have destabilized Musharraf.

Musharraf seemed to have convinced the Bush administration that he was the only person who could prevent radical Islamists from taking over his country and getting their hands on Pakistan's nuclear weapons. But this was a self-serving fiction. Contrary to the myth that democracy would merely empower Pakistan's Islamists, pro-Taliban political parties won only 11 percent of the countrywide vote in the 2002 elections, which Musharraf had fixed to disadvantage the two main secular parties. And when Musharraf was finally forced to hold a free and fair election in February 2008 under pressure from both the United States and ordinary Pakistanis, the pro-Taliban parties won only a piffling 2 percent of the vote.

By the summer of 2007 the Bush administration had wearied of Musharraf's dictatorial ways and inability to roll back the militants, and put its weight behind the return of former prime minister Benazir Bhutto from a decade of exile. Bhutto's Pakistan People's Party (PPP) was one of the two leading political parties in the country and Bhutto was its most popular politician. In the months before the election that was scheduled for early 2008, Musharraf and Bhutto cut a deal that allowed her to return to Pakistan to campaign for the PPP, while Musharraf dropped the corruption charges that he had used to chase her out of the country in the first place.

Bhutto's life was the stuff of Shakespeare: her father, a former prime minister, had been executed; one of her brothers was poisoned in France, while another brother was killed in a shoot-out with police outside her Karachi home; her husband was jailed for eight years without charge under Musharraf; and she had endured decades of house arrest and exile. She was also a rather complex political character despite the widespread impression in the West that she was a liberal, based on her years of study at Oxford and Harvard. She was the first female prime minister of a Muslim country, yet her government was instrumental in the rise of the Taliban. And both Bhutto and her husband, Asif Ali Zardari, were widely believed to have looted the country while in office.

In fairness to Bhutto, the handsome, self-assured, and charming woman who returned to Pakistan at age fifty-four was very different from the woman who had first become prime minister at the age of thirty-five. Callow and inexperienced no longer, but rather a politician who had matured dramatically in her years in exile, Bhutto had put the Taliban and al-Qaeda on notice many times before her return to her beloved Pakistan that she would crack down on them hard once she was in a position of power again.

The threats Bhutto had made against the Taliban and al-Qaeda certainly got the attention of the militants, and on October 19 two suicide bombers targeted the former prime minister in Karachi as she made her triumphant return from exile mobbed by hundreds of thousands of supporters. The bombings, the most deadly in Pakistani history, killed some 140 bystanders and almost succeeded in killing her.

On December 27, Bhutto's enemies struck again, this time deploying a gunman to finish the job. In the minutes before Bhutto was killed in Rawalpindi, she was standing up through the sunroof of her armored vehicle—a sunroof that she had installed despite the pleas of many others. A videotape of the attack shows a clean-shaven young man, wearing a dark jacket, tie, and rimless black shades, stepping toward the vehicle. Using only one hand, the gunman shoots three times in Bhutto's direction. Bhutto's back is toward the camera. Her head scarf billows slightly, and she starts to drop inside the vehicle; the assassin detonated a bomb and the screen goes black.

The government quickly fingered Baitullah Mehsud as the mastermind, an all-too-plausible candidate since he was the head of the Pakistani Taliban. Shortly after the Bhutto hit, the Pakistani government released a transcript of a phone call in which Mehsud yukked it up with a mullah crony, crowing: "Congratulations to you. Were they our men?" To which the mullah replied, "Yes, they were ours." Through a spokesman, Mehsud later disavowed any role in the attack. (U.S. officials, using voice match technology, authenticated that it was Mehsud's voice on the tape.)

Several months after Bhutto's assassination, in late May 2008, some forty Pakistani journalists received a summons to an unusual press conference given by the man who had ordered her death. Reporters were given twenty-four hours' notice about the event, which was held in a high school in South Waziristan on Pakistan's western border with Afghanistan. Surrounded by a posse of heavily armed Taliban guards, Mehsud boasted that he had hundreds of trained suicide bombers ready for martyrdom and that he would continue to wage his jihad against American and coalition forces in Afghanistan. Over the course of the three-hour meeting, which climaxed with a lavish lunch of lamb and goat meat, reporters called in news about the press conference on their satellite phones. For a man who was supposedly on the run it was an extraordinarily public performance and it was emblematic of Pakistan's inability to clamp down on leading militants on its territory.

On February 18, 2008, Pakistanis went to the polls and overwhelmingly rejected Musharraf's political party, installing a civilian government led by Bhutto's widower, Asif Ali Zardari, who then maneuvered Musharraf into retirement and himself assumed the presidency. To signal their contempt for Pakistan's new civilian government, militants detonated a truck bomb outside Islamabad's Marriott hotel, long a gathering place for the capital's elite, killing about fifty-five on September 20, 2008, just hours after Zardari had made his first speech as president in the Parliament. The attack was likely masterminded by an al-Qaeda leader in Pakistan, Osama al-Kini. It was the deadliest terrorist atrocity in the capital's history, turning the Marriott into a giant fireball, and may have been planned to take out the entire Pakistani cabinet, which reportedly had been scheduled to eat dinner there following Zardari's speech. The venue for the dinner was changed at the last minute.

There were some promising signs that the Pakistani establishment began to wake up to its domestic militant threat in the waning days of the second Bush administration. In July 2008, Pakistani Prime Minister Yousuf Raza Gilani told reporters in Lahore, "Pakistan is not fighting the war of any other country. The war on terror is in our own interests." When Gilani made this comment, the government had just launched an operation against Mangal Bagh, a former bus driver, who had turned himself into an Islamist capo in the Khyber tribal agency.

Despite years of hysterical analysis by the commentariat in the United States, as the Obama administration came into office Pakistan was not poised for an Islamist takeover similar to what had happened in the Shah's Iran. There was no major religious figure around whom opposition to the Pakistani government could form, and the alliance of pro-Taliban parties known as the MMA, which had come to power in two of Pakistan's four provinces in 2002 and had implemented some window-dressing measures such as banning the sale of alcohol to non-Muslims, did nothing to govern effectively. In the election in 2008 it was annihilated at the polls. Ordinary Pakistanis were also increasingly fed up with the tactics used by the militants. Between 2005 and 2008, Pakistani support for suicide attacks dropped from 33 percent to 5 percent.

Despite American criticisms that the Pakistanis could do more to fight the Taliban and al-Qaeda, Pakistan's officer class felt strongly that their country was doing as much as it could to combat the militants, citing as evidence the nearly 3,000 Pakistani soldiers and police who had died fighting the militants between 2001 and the start of 2010, a number that outweighed the some 1,500 NATO and U.S. forces who had died during the same time period fighting the Taliban across the border in Afghanistan.

While there was no doubt that elements of the Pakistani army had done much to combat the militants, suspicions lingered about the military intelligence agency ISI, which had been instrumental both in the rise of the Taliban and in a number of the Kashmiri militant groups. The most dramatic evidence of the continued links that some in ISI maintained with terrorists was the suicide bombing of the Indian embassy in Kabul on July 7, 2008, which killed more than fifty, the worst attack in the capital since the fall of the Taliban seven years earlier. Both the U.S. and Afghan governments said the bombing was aided by elements of the ISI, an assertion they based on intercepted phone calls between the plotters and phone numbers in Pakistan.

The Mumbai attacks in late November 2008 also underlined how little things had really changed inside Pakistan's jihadi culture since 9/11. The Pakistani group that carried out the attacks, Lashkar-e-Taiba (LeT), had, as we have seen, been officially banned in January 2002, but that did not prevent it from organizing the sixty-hour attack on Mumbai, much of it carried live by news channels around the world. The series of assaults was often described as "India's 9/11." LeT dispatched ten militants armed with assault rifles and grenades from Karachi on a boat out to sea, where they hijacked an Indian trawler for the five-hundred-mile trip to the oceanfront city of Mumbai. Once in Mumbai the terrorists sprayed gunfire at passengers at the central train station, took hostages, and executed guests at two five-star hotels, the Taj and the Oberoi, and attacked residents of the Nariman House Jewish center, leaving some 170 dead in their wake.

The Mumbai attacks also demonstrated the fact that Pakistan had lost control of its jihadists, who sought to undermine the creeping rapprochement between India and Pakistan over the Kashmir issue, something that Musharraf had, to his credit, pushed forward in the years after LeT's attack on the Indian Parliament in 2001. The steps toward peace between the two countries were small but symbolic—restored bus and flight services between them and joint cricket matches—but these "confidence building measures" were exactly the kinds of steps toward a deal over Kashmir that LeT and the Mumbai attackers sought to sabotage.

What was worrying as Pakistan headed into the second decade of the twenty-first century was the fact that its economy was in free fall, a plunge that had preceded the global financial crisis. And the high Pakistani fertility rate put the country on track to become the fifth-largest country in the world by 2015 with a population of almost 200 million. The combination of a sharply rising population with not enough jobs will likely play into the hands of the militants, who often recruit young men with time on their hands. Unless Pakistan can change that equation the plague of the militant groups will only continue.

Chapter 16

The Fall of Al-Qaeda in Iraq and the Rise of an Iraqi State

Just because you invade a country stupidly doesn't mean you have to leave it stupidly.

—Lieutenant Colonel David Kilcullen, counterinsurgency adviser to General David Petraeus

Security may be ten percent of the problem, or it may be ninety percent, but whichever it is, it's the first ten percent or the first ninety percent. Without security, nothing else we do will last.

—John Paul Vann, one of the leading proponents of counterinsurgency warfare during the Vietnam War

In the summer of 2006, Sterling Jensen, a lanky, intense twenty-eight-year-old Mormon with a talent for languages, wasn't in Utah anymore; he was living in Ramadi, perhaps the most dangerous city in what was then perhaps the most dangerous country on the planet. Jensen had volunteered to go to Iraq to work as an interpreter with the U.S. military and was assigned to the 1st Brigade of the 1st Armored Division, which took over responsibility for Ramadi in June 2006.

But there wasn't much of anything to take over. Al-Qaeda had made Ramadi the capital of its soon-to-be-named "Islamic State of Iraq," presiding over Mogadishu levels of violence while banning smoking, music, and television. The group's enforcers killed anyone who didn't follow their dictates to the letter and local tribal sheikhs who did not bend to their will. In the city of some three hundred thousand there were no public services and only one hundred cops would dare to show up for work. Ramadi and much of the surrounding Anbar province had become a nightmarish mash-up of the Taliban and al-Qaeda's appallingly violent leader, Abu Musab al-Zarqawi, whose signature execution method was the televised beheading.

Even Saddam Hussein had left the staunchly independent Sunni tribes of Anbar pretty much to their own devices—mostly small-bore smuggling rackets—and the tribes did not appreciate al-Qaeda muscling into their turf, nor did they subscribe to its vision of a Taliban-style utopia. In the summer of 2006, masked Anbar tribesmen began a covert campaign of killing al-Qaeda members. Jensen remembers: "We were finding dead people with signs on them saying, 'This was what you get when you work with al-Qaeda.'" American commanders were pleasantly surprised by the dead al-Qaeda foot soldiers who were showing up in the streets of Ramadi but were puzzled as to who might be engineering the killings.

On September 9, 2006, a number of Anbar tribal sheikhs went public with their plan to destroy al-Qaeda. They named their movement *Sahwa,* meaning "Awakening." Colonel Sean MacFarland, the U.S. brigade commander in Ramadi, met with the Awakening leader, Sheikh Abdul Sattar Abu Risha, and his tribal allies at the charismatic sheikh's house. Abdul Sattar had good reason to loathe al-Qaeda, members of which had killed his father and three of his brothers, acts that demanded revenge in the tribal code. And Abdul Sattar was also quietly making good money working as a contractor for the Americans.

Abdul Sattar announced to the crowd of some fifty sheikhs, "The coalition forces are friendly forces, not occupying forces!" Some of the tribal leaders seemed nervous about this idea but within six months many of them were also allied with the United States. This was quite a surprising development, as the insurgency then gripping Iraq was largely led by Sunni groups, and all the more so because the U.S. Marines, which had bases around Anbar, had assessed in a secret intelligence report just three weeks earlier that al-Qaeda effectively ruled the province.

But the Anbar Awakening sheikhs would soon change that. Jensen, who had learned Arabic in Syria and Morocco and was interpreting the exchanges between Colonel MacFarland and the Awakening tribal leaders, collared the American commander during a break in their first meeting with the sheikhs, saying, "I think this is awesome." MacFarland enthused, "I love it." Abdul Sattar Abu Risha, the leader of the Awakening, would later be rewarded with a meeting with President Bush during one of his surprise visits to Iraq, but al-Qaeda still managed to kill him on September 13, 2007. However, killing the leader of the Anbar Awakening did not do anything to halt the spread of the tribal rebellion against Al-Qaeda in Iraq (AQI).

The American-Sunni tribal alliance would help to bring a measure of stability to Iraq. AQI, which more than any other group had brought the country to the brink of complete collapse, was by 2008 on life support. It was something of an assisted suicide because AQI had forced on the Sunni population Taliban-style strictures, which had alienated its natural allies. And American commanders in Iraq followed Napoleon's excellent advice, "Never interrupt your enemy when he is making a mistake." General George W. Casey, the ground commander in Iraq, had ordered Colonel MacFarland in 2006 not to take Ramadi in an aggressive assault, as the United States had done in neighboring Fallujah two years earlier.

At the same time that he was allying with the Anbar sheikhs, MacFarland started putting small American combat outposts into hot spots in Ramadi to live side by side with the population to protect them, a tactic that had worked the previous year in the anarchic city of Tal Afar in northern Iraq for Colonel H. R. McMaster, who is credited, among others, with developing the "clear, hold, and build" strategy that was to become a commonplace of American counterinsurgency operations. In Tal Afar, McMaster had established twenty-nine small outposts in the city to separate the Sunnis and Shia then waging a ghastly war in which headless corpses would be left to rot on the streets.

This was the exact opposite of the U.S. strategy of the time, which was to hand over ever more control to the Iraqi army and police and withdraw the bulk of American soldiers to massive (misnamed) "Forward Operating Bases," known as FOBs. Camp Victory, the main U.S. base in Baghdad, housed an astonishing fifty thousand soldiers. This strategy gave birth to the wonderful neologism *fobbits* to describe the FOB dwellers, who enjoyed Starbucks-style coffee, giant flat-screen TVs, PXs that channeled Walmart and Target, and football-field-sized DFACs (dining facilities) groaning with enough food to feed the populations of small African countries. From the FOBs out would sally armored Humvee patrols, which had little or no understanding of the country they were supposedly pacifying.

By contrast, the on-the-ground intelligence provided by Sunni tribesmen to American forces living "among the population" in Ramadi during the winter of 2006 meant that more and more IED caches were being found, as well as the hiding places of al-Qaeda cells in Anbar's western deserts. The tribes also began providing recruits for the police, who now showed up for work in the thousands. As neighborhoods became safer, MacFarland poured Commander's Emergency Response Program (CERP) funds into projects such as building schools, and a virtuous circle of rising security brought more jobs and reconstruction to Ramadi. By the summer of 2008 the city looked just like any other scrappy town in the Middle East with small shops open for business along its main roads. By then the surrounding Anbar province was also one of the safest regions in the country.

At the height of its power, on February 22, 2006, AQI bombed the Golden Mosque at Samarra, one of the most important pilgrimage sites for the Shia, turning the already nasty Iraqi sectarian conflict into a full-blown civil war. In addition, AQI controlled a good chunk of the exurban belts around Baghdad, the "Triangle of Death" to the south of the capital, and many of the towns north of it, up the Tigris River to the Syrian border. And in a country with an unemployment rate of something like 50 percent, AQI was paying its foot soldiers salaries and raking in money from various oil-smuggling scams, kidnapping rings, extortion schemes, and overseas donations.

In late April 2006, as AQI appeared to be unstoppable, the group's shadowy leader, Abu Musab al-Zarqawi, showed the world his face for the first time in a video posted to jihadist websites. Zarqawi was taped pontificating to a group of hooded acolytes and shooting off a machine gun in the desert, but within a couple of months he was dead.

The breakthrough that nailed Zarqawi was the patient (noncoercive) interrogation of a Sunni insurgent who eventually told his American interrogators that the best way to find the al-Qaeda leader was by tracking his "spiritual advisor," a man who would change cars several times before meeting with Zarqawi and who would invariably use a blue car just before the meeting took place. That information was enough to track Zarqawi to a remote desert compound, where he was killed with two five-hundred-pound bombs dropped from an F-16 on June 7, 2006.

In much of Shia Iraq there was celebratory gunfire, feasting, and cheers at the news of Zarqawi's death. And privately Osama bin Laden might not have mourned Zarqawi's death as excessively as he would publicly profess when he said on an audiotape released two weeks later, "The Muslim nation was shocked by the death of its courageous knight, the lion of jihad." The thuggish Jordanian had proved difficult to control and had even managed the neat trick of tarnishing the al-Qaeda brand with his excessive violence.

Despite Zarqawi's death, the violence in Iraq continued to spiral upward throughout the remainder of 2006, reaching a peak around the New Year of 2007. The civil war that Zarqawi had helped to precipitate was so much larger than any one man. Air Force interrogator Matthew Alexander (a pseudonym), who had played a critical role in eliciting the information from the detainee that had led to locating Zarqawi, recalls, "It was obvious that just because Zarqawi was killed that Sunnis weren't going to drop their arms and go, 'OK, you beat us.' And we could have killed every foreigner in Iraq and it wouldn't have solved the insurgency."

As its stock fell precipitously with Iraq's Sunni population, al-Qaeda recognized belatedly that it needed to put a more Iraqi face on the group. Zarqawi was himself, of course, a Jordanian, and four months after his death AQI changed its name to the Islamic State of Iraq and appointed an Iraqi, Abdullah Rashid al-Baghdadi, to be its nominal boss. But with the death of Zarqawi, AQI no longer had a charismatic leader.

A cache of al-Qaeda documents discovered in the fall of 2007 by U.S. forces in the northern Iraqi town of Sinjar provided the best account of what was then going on inside al-Qaeda's operation. One of the Sinjar documents was an unsigned oath of allegiance to the group that was meant to be signed by tribal leaders in Diyala province; it well illustrated AQI's tone-deaf approach to local politics. The leaders had to swear to reject tribal rules, not something that any self-respecting Sunni tribal leader could possibly agree to.

By early 2008 the foreign-fighter flow into Iraq had declined from around 120 a month to around forty-five a month, which was a key to peace, since roughly half of these foreign fighters were volunteers for suicide missions. And a year later the foreign-fighter flow had slowed to a dribble of only five or six a month. As a result AQI defaulted to increasingly using women as suicide attackers. Needless to say, this did little for its poor image in Iraq.

AQI was also demoralized; in November 2007 American soldiers raided a house in northern Iraq and found the diary of an al-Qaeda leader in the area, a man who called himself Abu Tariq, "the emir of al-Layin and al Mashadah sectors." The diary lamented that his force, which had once been six hundred strong, was down to twenty men. Abu Tariq blamed local Sunni tribes for "changing course" and bringing about his group's present travails. Similarly, a letter found by the U.S. military around the same time and written by an unnamed emir of AQI referred to the situation in Anbar province in western Iraq as being "an exceptional crisis." The letter also cited the difficulties foreign fighters eager to participate in suicide operations were having, forced to wait for months in the western desert regions of Iraq with nothing to do because the organization was under such pressure.

By early 2008, Al-Qaeda in Iraq was a wounded organization. U.S. military officials said that by then they had killed 2,400 suspected members of AQI and captured 8,800, whittling the group's strength down to 3,500. The situation became so grave for AQI that in October 2007, bin Laden accused his Iraqi affiliate of fanaticism and exhorted the Sunni insurgent groups to unite. "Beware of division. . . . The Muslim world is waiting for you to gather under one banner," he said.

Al-Qaeda's untrammeled violence and imposition of Taliban ideology on the Sunni population provoked a countrywide Sunni backlash against AQI that took the form of the "Awakening" militias. Many of those militias were put on Uncle Sam's payroll in a program known as the "Sons of Iraq." The combination of the Sunni militias' on-the-ground intelligence about their onetime AQI allies and American firepower proved devastating to al-Qaeda's Iraqi franchise. And so, between 2006 and 2008, AQI shrank from an insurgent organization that controlled territory larger than the size of New England to a rump terrorist group that would still remain a spoiler of Iraq's fragile peace, but it was never likely to regain its iron grip on much of Sunni Iraq.

The tribal revolt that spread from Anbar to many other provinces in Iraq was the most important development in the country since the 2003 invasion. In the summer of 2007, Lieutenant Colonel David Kilcullen, the fast-talking, erudite Australian anthropologist and infantry officer who was the senior counterinsurgency adviser to General David Petraeus, noted in a lengthy post on *Small Wars Journal*, the website that served as the internal bulletin board for the counterinsurgency community, that 85 percent of Iraqis claim some tribal affiliation. In his post, Kilcullen concluded that "the tribal revolt is not some remote riot on a reservation: it's a major social movement that could significantly influence most Iraqis where they live."

Al-Qaeda not only drove the Sunni tribes into a quite unexpected alliance with the Americans; around the same time the terrorist organization made another error that was to anger its allies in other Sunni insurgent groups, such as the 1920s Brigade and Islamic Army of Iraq, by killing some of their leaders. This was a serious mistake because members of those groups also ended up on the American payroll in the Sons of Iraq program, which by the spring of 2009 had grown to around 100,000 men. Many of those men used to be shooting at Americans; now they were shooting at al-Qaeda. This was in itself a surge of spectacular proportions—when 100,000 men who used to be shooting at you start shooting at your enemies it effectively adds 200,000 to your overall numbers.

In the spring of 2006, following al-Qaeda's bombing of the Golden Mosque shrine at Samarra, it was obvious to senior Bush administration officials that Iraq was falling apart. National Security Advisor Stephen Hadley recalls that he kept a chart that showed incidents of violence per week, and this chart "since 2003, just goes up. And I say to my people, every time when they say, 'Well, we're making progress,' in '04, '05, '06, and I would always say, 'When I see this violence chart start to head down, I'll believe we're making progress.'"

The Samarra bombing was the final straw for the Shia, who had generally not engaged in sectarian conflict despite repeated provocations by al-Qaeda and other Sunni terrorist groups. This policy was largely the result of the Grand Ayatollah Ali al-Sistani, their most important spiritual leader, urging restraint on his flock. Hadley recalls: "The patience of the Shia finally gave out. Sistani had been holding them back from retaliating. But after the Samarra bombing, they lose confidence in the Iraqi forces. And Shia death squads start getting active."

By the early summer of 2006, Meghan O'Sullivan, a deputy national security advisor who had spent two years living in Iraq and who had the respect of the president, was able to communicate to him her mounting concern about the rising level of violence. Hadley recalls the conversation: "The president says, 'How are your friends in Baghdad?' She says, 'They're terrified, Mr. President. They're more terrified than they've ever been. It's impossible to live in that city.' Well, this is from somebody the president knows, who knows Iraq, as much as any American can, has personal friends in Baghdad, and is committed to success. And she's telling him, 'Mr. President, this is a whole new game. And everybody's terrified.' That gets your attention."

In the face of the accelerating civil war, O'Sullivan and her deputy, Brett McGurk, concluded that lowering the American profile in Iraq was going to lose the war and so they started secretly exploring a "surge" strategy that would instead send more troops to Iraq. They were both so convinced that this was the right approach that they privately dubbed themselves the "surgios."

Throughout late 2006 an intense debate about not only a possible surge but also the overall U.S. military strategy in Iraq raged inside the halls of the Pentagon and the White House and in the conference rooms of Washington think tanks, a debate that was largely obscure to the American press and public. The debate pitted on one side the U.S. commander on the ground in Iraq, General George Casey, and his boss, CENTCOM commander General John Abizaid, as well as their overall boss Donald Rumsfeld, against an unlikely alliance that included the "surgios" at the National Security Council; Jack Keane, a retired four-star general who continued to wield considerable influence inside the Beltway; Fred Kagan, an historian based at the neoconservative American Enterprise Institute; Stephen Biddle, a military strategist at the centrist Council on Foreign Relations; Eliot Cohen, an influential professor at the School of Advanced International Studies at Johns Hopkins; and even General Casey's own deputy, Lieutenant General Raymond Odierno, who was quietly lobbying for more troops behind the back of his boss.

Casey, Abizaid, and Rumsfeld were also supported by almost all of the senior leaders of the U.S. military who advocated lowering the profile of U.S. forces to put more of an Iraqi "face" on the occupation, on the theory that American soldiers were antibodies in the Arab world and that, in any event, Iraqis had to "take the training wheels off" and learn to drive their own bike themselves. This approach could be best summarized as standing down the American presence in the country, while simultaneously the United States helped to "stand up" the Iraqi security services that would increasingly take control of the country.

In the early summer of 2006, O'Sullivan, who had served in Baghdad as an official in the Coalition Provisional Authority, found out that General Casey was recommending the withdrawal of two brigades from Iraq, as many as ten thousand soldiers. O'Sullivan, whose doctorate from Oxford was about the Sri Lankan civil war, found this strange: "Violence was going up, the situation was deteriorating, and we were going to pull two brigades out of Iraq. And I remember thinking, 'What possible justification is there for this?' There's *no* strategic reason for this, unless you really believe that we are the cause of the violence." O'Sullivan's deputy, McGurk, who had lived in Baghdad in 2004 and returned there in May 2006, was shocked by the chaos in the city. There didn't seem to be any real plan to stem the violence. "When you'd sit with Casey and the military at that time, there was zero new thinking. It was like, 'We're going to have a new Baghdad Security Plan.' OK, well, what is the plan? And it was just the same old thing, over and over again," recalls McGurk.

During the summer of 2006, as the violence in Baghdad reached stratospheric levels, the Iraqi security services and the U.S. military jointly conducted two major offensives in the capital, Operation Together Forward I and II, to reclaim the city from the feuding Sunni and Shia militias. Both operations failed because the Iraqi army and police were incapable of holding neighborhoods once they had been cleared of insurgents.

By now O'Sullivan was convinced that handing off responsibility to Iraq's security services in the short term in much of the country was a pipe dream. "We would transfer responsibility to Iraqi police or the Iraqi army, and violence would go way up. And we would see this pattern, over and over again." Not only were the Iraqi security services incapable of halting the sectarian strife, but they had also become infiltrated by Shia militias. General David Petraeus recalls that "the National Police, which in the beginning was a fairly tough outfit, had been hijacked by the militias."

McGurk recalls this being an especially bleak time for those who worked on Iraq. "I told friends at the White House at that time, 'If we do not rapidly change our strategy to do something radically different, I can't keep working on this issue.' . . . So late August, we were building the case, or trying to be able to build the case for more force. But it couldn't be discussed in polite company. Steve [Hadley] would say to us, 'I don't want to hear about a surge,' and you still had Rumsfeld in place." Whatever his initial misgivings about a surge, in late September Hadley instructed O'Sullivan and McGurk to start discreetly exploring all options in Iraq, telling them, "Do a top-to-bottom strategic review in a more formalized way, but quietly: close-hold."

That the United States could play a helpful role in the burgeoning Iraqi civil war if it employed a different strategy was first argued publicly and comprehensively by Stephen Biddle in a lucid essay early in 2006 in *Foreign Affairs*, the bible of the foreign policy establishment. Biddle, a Waspy, cerebral military strategist who taught at the Army War College in Carlisle, Pennsylvania, explained that the main problem in Iraq was not an anti-American insurgency but a "communal civil war." Biddle pointed out that this called into question the main American strategy of the time, which was the "standing up" of the Iraqi security services, because "Iraq's Sunnis perceive the 'national' army and police force as a Shiite-Kurdish militia on steroids"; in short, the main American strategy of the time was actually *helping to fuel the civil war.* In order to reverse that process Biddle advocated "a wider amnesty for former Baathists and insurgents" so as to reassure the Sunnis that the United States was an honest broker in the sectarian war. Biddle made this suggestion six months before the first of such deals was cut in Anbar province by the U.S. military.

The recently retired four-star general Jack Keane, who had risen from commanding a platoon in Vietnam to Army vice chief of staff, was watching events unfold in Iraq with growing unease in 2006: "The strategy on the ground largely belonged to the U.S. military in Vietnam as it did in Iraq. And in both cases we had it wrong." In September he went to see Rumsfeld at the Pentagon and told him that to reverse the downward spiral in Iraq he needed to deploy an additional five to eight brigades—up to forty thousand soldiers—or risk losing the war. Rumsfeld listened intently but Keane was not certain he had made any headway with him.

In late October 2006, O'Sullivan and Hadley traveled to Iraq to assess the situation for themselves. O'Sullivan recalls a large gulf between the strategy being pursued by the Army leadership and what those further down the chain of command were finding on the ground: "We had a meeting with battalion and brigade commanders in Baghdad. We didn't have any other senior people in the room. I asked every single one of them, 'How do the Iraqis react to you when you and your guys come into their neighborhoods?' And *without exception* they responded along the lines: 'They welcome us and they are desperate for us to stay when it comes time for us to hand over to Iraqi Security Forces.'"

This flew in the face of the prevailing American strategy in Iraq, while it simultaneously confirmed a classic counterinsurgency doctrine, which is that to win required putting *more* of an American face on the occupation by getting U.S. soldiers out of their vast bases and into Iraqi neighborhood outposts to "protect the population." A good deal of the intellectual heavy lifting that had helped to inform this view had gone into the unglamorously named *Counterinsurgency Field Manual 3-24*, the Army and Marines' new handbook on counterinsurgency, the work for which was directed by General David Petraeus in 2006 at the Army's training center at Fort Leavenworth, Kansas.

John Nagl is a Rhodes Scholar with a doctorate from Oxford. In 2002 he published *Learning to Eat Soup with a Knife: Counterinsurgency Lessons from Malaya and Vietnam*. The title was taken from T. E. Lawrence, better known as Lawrence of Arabia, who had helped organize the insurgency known as the Arab Revolt against the Ottoman Empire during World War I. Lawrence wrote of fighting insurgents that "making war on a rebellion is messy and slow, like eating soup with a knife." A year after publishing his book, Nagl was in Iraq serving as a battalion commander in the troubled province of Anbar. Following his tour there, Nagl worked in the Pentagon as a military assistant to Rumsfeld's top deputy, Paul Wolfowitz, where he became known as one of the most persistent proponents that the Army needed a new counterinsurgency doctrine. In November 2005, Petraeus gave a lunchtime speech at a counterinsurgency conference in Washington, D.C. Nagl recalls that Petraeus, his former history professor at West Point, "announced that he was going to write a counterinsurgency manual, and he announced that I was going to be the lead pen, which was the first time I'd heard of it!"

After the conference Nagl and a couple of other officers who would also be recruited to help write the new manual repaired to the Front Page bar in downtown Washington and sketched out on a cocktail napkin the outlines of a new doctrine. Nagl assumed the role of managing editor of the manual and Petraeus recruited Conrad Crane, a military historian and a former West Point classmate, to be the lead writer. But there was no doubt who was in charge. Nagl recalls that Petraeus "was the driver, he was the vision, he was the copy editor, he read the whole thing twice, he turned around chapters in twenty-four hours with extensive edits and comments."

The writings of the French soldier-intellectual David Galula were quite influential on the group working on the manual. Galula had fought in Indochina and Algeria in the 1950s as an officer in the French army as it was attempting to stamp out nationalist insurgencies in France's colonial possessions. Around a decade later Galula published *Counterinsurgency Warfare: Theory and Practice*, which distilled the lessons of fighting and observing insurgencies in the Middle East and Southeast Asia. Galula laid down a general principle that is recognized as the core of a successful counterinsurgency strategy: "The population becomes the objective for the counter-insurgent as it was for his enemy." This meant that seizing territory became far less important than it was in a conventional war; ensuring that people felt secure enough so they were not forced to side with the insurgents and, eventually, even felt secure enough to provide intelligence about them, became the prize.

Once a first draft of the counterinsurgency manual was completed, Petraeus and the lead writer, Crane, decided to convene a group of outside experts to critique it. Crane recalls, "We had a vetting conference to go over the doctrine, and I agreed with the general that we would do it, and I said, 'Yeah, let's bring in thirty smart people to talk about it'; he brought in a hundred and fifty. It was quite a three-ring circus out at Fort Leavenworth." Over the course of two days officials from the CIA and State Department, and leading academics and journalists such as Eliot Cohen, James Fallows, and George Packer were instructed to give their critiques, which generated hundreds of pages of new ideas. Cochairing the conference was Sarah Sewall, the director of Harvard's Carr Center on Human Rights Policy; that sent a significant signal about the content of the manual. Nagl says, "Sarah's influence was incredibly important in encouraging the military to accept more risk in order to put the population at lesser risk," as well as in helping to establish the importance of a legal regime that respected the rights of detainees.

The Army and Marines published the final version of the *Counterinsurgency Field Manual* in December 2006. The Web version of the manual was downloaded 1.5 million times and the *New York Times* gave it a serious review, something of a first for a dense military tome that weighed in at some four hundred pages.

The doctrines in the new manual permeated the subsequent actions of the U.S. military both in Iraq and Afghanistan. The following points from the manual summarize its central message: Unsuccessful practices: overemphasize killing and capturing the enemy rather than securing and engaging the populace; conduct large-scale operations as the norm and concentrate military forces in large bases for protection. Successful practices: focus on the population, its needs, and its security and provide amnesty and rehabilitation for those willing to support the new government. In a section titled "Paradoxes," the manual made a number of recommendations that were hardly typical of prevailing U.S. military doctrine: "Sometimes doing nothing is the best reaction" and (drawing on T. E. Lawrence) "the host nation doing something tolerably is normally better than us doing it well."

These commonsense prescriptions would, in time, help to change the course of the Iraq War.

By the fall of 2006 the American public had long tired of the war, and on November 4 it dealt the Republican Party what President Bush accurately termed a "thumping" in the congressional midterm elections, which brought Democratic majorities to both the House and the Senate. A day after that thumping Bush dumped his secretary of defense, Donald Rumsfeld, who had become a lightning rod for all the dissatisfactions surrounding the Iraq War, and installed in his place the consummate Washington insider, former CIA director Robert Gates.

A week later National Security Advisor Stephen Hadley convened a meeting on Iraq at the White House that included Secretary of State Condoleezza Rice. Rice and her counselor Philip Zelikow argued that the time to do much more in Iraq had come and gone and that the United States had other important strategic interests to attend to in the world in places like Iran, Afghanistan, and Pakistan. Bush's point person on Iraq, Meghan O'Sullivan, and her deputy, Brett McGurk, argued for an alternative approach: "We need to try something radically different, because the consequences of not doing so are really catastrophic."

Hadley says Bush was becoming increasingly alarmed as he saw the reports of the rising American casualties in Iraq. "The president sees, every morning, the blue sheets, a Situation Room report indicating who was killed overnight. That gets his attention, and that helped convince him we needed a review." In mid-November the president launched a formal review of the war.

There were four approaches on the table: first, the "stay the course" option of continuing the strategy that was clearly failing; second, the State Department's "targeted" approach, which was to focus on al-Qaeda in Iraq but not expand the American role further; third, the "double down" option, which was the surge; and fourth, "bet on Maliki," the Iraqi prime minister who was telling Bush administration officials that he wanted to clamp down on the sectarian violence that elements of his own government were fueling, but that he did not have the forces to do it.

These options were considered at four formal meetings of the National Security Council with the president during the first week of December. The CIA had an important input in this process because when it forecast what would happen to the Iraqi military in the event of a reduced American role, the Agency found a very high level of risk that the Iraqi army would fracture along sectarian lines. Bush said, "I'm not taking that risk." McGurk recalls, "That's when the debate started to shift towards 'we're going to have to do something here.'" Over the course of the rest of December that "something" became a mix of the surge and betting on Maliki.

Meanwhile, at the American Enterprise Institute (AEI) think tank in Washington, D.C., a home to Laurie Mylroie and many of the other leading advocates of the war in Iraq, the historian Fred Kagan, whose academic specialty is the Napoleonic wars, was becoming increasingly frustrated at the tenor of the debate in Washington, which seemed more about managing an exit from Iraq than actually winning the war. In the fall of 2006, Kagan and some of his think tank colleagues decided to set up their own planning exercise to work out what number of additional troops in Iraq might put what Kagan termed a "tourniquet" on the bloody civil war.

At AEI's office near the White House, Kagan convened a number of Iraq experts and, crucially, American officers who were veterans of Iraq to work through the planning exercise. Kagan's research team used open-source reporting and Google maps of Iraq to construct "heat maps" of where the violence was most intense to determine where additional American boots on the ground could make the most difference. To make the exercise even more realistic they used the Army's own "force generation" model, the briefing slide for which someone had helpfully posted on Wikipedia, so that their recommendations could be matched by the Army's actual capability to generate new forces. Kagan recalls, "The slide was on Wikipedia, it was unbelievable. We did a little bit of diligent calling to make sure it was accurate, but it was."

Using the Army's force-generation model, the AEI exercise came to the conclusion that five Army combat brigades and two Marine regiments were available to reverse Iraq's descent into chaos, almost exactly the troop increase that President Bush would announce a month later. Kagan says, "I don't know that I ever gave this more than a thirty or forty percent chance of succeeding. The only argument that I made was that the consequences of all of the alternative strategies that were being proposed were so unacceptable that it was worth trying."

Kagan and his team turned the conclusions of the planning exercise into a PowerPoint presentation, and on December 11 he and Jack Keane, the retired four-star general, went to brief Vice President Cheney about its findings. Cheney did not show his hand during the meeting. Kagan says, "He is a Sphinx. He was asking good questions, but we didn't have a particular takeaway from that meeting; one never does."

Before the meeting Keane had had a long discussion with Lieutenant General Raymond Odierno, the newly arrived number-two military commander in Iraq, an officer whom he had mentored over the course of many years. Odierno and his boss, General Casey, fundamentally disagreed about how many more American boots on the ground were needed in Iraq. Casey would only accept two brigades while Odierno wanted five and, in addition, two Marine battalions. This was almost exactly what the AEI exercise had independently determined to be a plausible number to help reverse the momentum of the civil war.

On December 11, Bush also met privately with a number of outside experts, including General Keane, Stephen Biddle, and Eliot Cohen, who were advocating major changes in the way that the war was being fought. Collectively they made the case that the Iraq strategy needed to be changed; new leadership had to be installed to implement that strategy, specifically to replace General Casey, and more troops were needed.

Biddle recalls that the White House meeting was "unbelievably somber; the president looked depressed to me. The setting around the room was maybe not quite funereal, but the impression I got was that whatever you thought of this administration before, they looked like a bunch of people who were staring into the abyss, and had made the decision that they were looking at a failed war with potentially grave, cataclysmic consequences, and had come up full-stop against the reality that there weren't any really appealing options at the moment, and that the consequences of failure were very high."

Cohen had published *Supreme Command: Soldiers, Statesmen, and Leadership in Wartime* in 2002. The book argued that to win a war civilian leaders sometimes had to get really involved in the nitty-gritty details of how to conduct it. Now Cohen urged the president to do just that, something he had tried to articulate at a previous meeting with Bush at Camp David some months earlier: "When I left that first meeting in June, I felt as if I'd pulled my punches a little bit, which is hard not to do when you're meeting with the president of the United States." This time was going to be different. Cohen's son was deploying to Iraq, "and that gave me the steel that I needed. And so I was really quite direct. . . . Although I like Casey as a human being, I thought you had to get rid of him, and I said you have to put in Petraeus. And I was very blunt about it."

Keane says, "We got around to talking about a potential successor to Casey; we all agreed that Petraeus was the guy." Bush's reaction to this, according to Biddle, was "'How am I supposed to know that this guy is a great general and that guy's a poor general?' He didn't feel like he had the knowledge space required to make decisions about which general to back in a war like this. At the time he was clearly very uncomfortable with this, and yet that's ultimately exactly what he did. For all intents and purposes, he fired Casey. He kicked him upstairs, but his tour ended early."

Keane addressed the president directly, saying, "We don't have a military strategy to defeat the insurgency." Keane recalls that the president "didn't say anything, but his nonverbal reaction, I could tell that he was quizzical about it. He asked very few questions of any of us, but I sensed something. And then I went on to lay out what we needed to do, which was a counterinsurgency strategy designed to protect the people. I said the center of gravity is Baghdad; the enemy has chosen that as its center of gravity, and that has to be where we start. We don't have to do all of Baghdad, and some of what I presented I took from the AEI analysis. I said, 'We're dealing with a city of five to six million people. And we've got to demonstrate that we're gonna protect the Shias and the Sunnis, and we're gonna be equitable about it. So we should start with the mixed Sunni-Shia neighborhoods.'" Keane explained that this approach would be costly: "'This is a military counteroffensive, and as a result of that casualties are going to rise, because the level of violence is going to go up. But if we are right, and I believe we are, then the casualties will eventually not only go down; they'll drop dramatically.' And I told them this was twelve to eighteen months duration, closer to eighteen, not to twelve."

As the White House was secretly considering the surge, on December 6 the congressionally mandated bipartisan Iraq Study Group released its keenly awaited report. Headed by former secretary of state James Baker, the Bush family's most faithful ally in the Republican Party, and Lee Hamilton, the longtime former Democratic chair of the House Foreign Relations Committee, the Iraq Study Group's report arrived with a considerable splash in Washington. The report made the observation that the situation in Iraq was "grave and deteriorating," which few could quibble with, but it was nonetheless strong language coming from Baker, given his decades-long close friendship with the president's father. And the report urged that the "Iraqi government should accelerate assuming responsibility for Iraqi security by increasing the number and quality of Iraqi Army brigades. While this process is under way, and to facilitate it, the United States should significantly increase the number of U.S. military personnel, including combat troops, imbedded in and supporting Iraqi Army units." The report argued that with this approach most combat brigades could be out of Iraq by early 2008.

The Iraq Study Group endorsed a key element of what the Bush administration had already been doing for the past three years—"standing up" the Iraqi security forces—while giving a sop to those who wanted more troops sent to Iraq, but only in the form of trainers for the Iraqi army, and simultaneously giving a lukewarm endorsement to a drawdown over the course of the next eighteen months. While these were, of course, all desirable *goals*, as a strategy for success in Iraq, as the violence peaked there during the winter of 2006, this advice was a muddle. It was a predictable muddle because a successful strategy to prosecute a complex war was unlikely to be generated by a committee of Democratic and Republican elder statesmen, no matter how wise. O'Sullivan recalls her reaction to these recommendations: "If we do this, on the timeline they're suggesting, we're going to lose. And really badly. The Baker-Hamilton approach looked very much like where we wanted to be in Iraq, but it wasn't where we were." National Security Advisor Steve Hadley privately referred to the Baker-Hamilton report as a "dog's breakfast," while President Bush "hated it. . . . He saw it as calling for a withdrawal," according to Brett McGurk, the NSC staffer.

For the surge to work Bush had to enlist the support of the Joint Chiefs of Staff, the six senior officers who head the military services, who were generally opposed to sending five more brigades to Iraq. On December 13, Bush made a rare visit to the secure Joint Chiefs conference room at the Pentagon known as "the tank." He came armed with some "sweeteners," including larger budgets and an expansion of the Army and Marine Corps, and he brushed aside concerns advanced by some of the chiefs about the Iraq War's strain on the ground forces and the depletion of America's strategic reserve.

Hadley recalls that the meeting with the Joint Chiefs was critical to moving the surge forward: "If the president had just decided, without going through this process, and bringing the military on board, you would have had a split between the president and his military in wartime. Not good. That's a constitutional crisis. But more to the point, Congress—who did not like the surge and was appalled that the president would do this—would have brought forward all those military officers who'd had any reservation about the surge in order to defeat it. And the president would have announced his surge, but he'd have never gotten it funded."

The new defense secretary, Robert Gates, who had been a member of the Iraq Study Group before his appointment to run the Pentagon, met Lieutenant General Odierno in Baghdad on December 19 and for the first time a senior American military commander in Iraq directly told him "we need more troops." Around the same time, Gates told Casey he was being replaced and offered him the top job of Army chief of staff.

After it was announced that he would be replacing Casey, Petraeus called Odierno to ask him what his recommendation was on troop levels. Odierno told him that he should bring in all five brigades as soon as possible. "A blind man on a dark night could see that there was no alternative," recalled Petraeus, who had been watching the failure of Iraqi security services to hold cleared neighborhoods for years.

Iraqi Prime Minister Nouri al-Maliki, however, was concerned about the political implications of having five new American brigades arrive in Iraq and was pushing for two, the same number that Casey was in favor of. McGurk recalls, "The president said something to the effect of 'Goddammit, does this guy want to win or not? If he wants to win, I'm with him. But if he doesn't wanna win, what's the point?'" Bush spoke to Maliki in one of his many one-on-one videoconferences with the Iraqi prime minister, who eventually agreed to the five additional brigades.

Never an accomplished orator, President Bush announced the new surge of twenty thousand soldiers in an especially wooden speech to the American public from the White House library on January 10, 2007. Almost four years after the invasion of Iraq and with some three thousand American soldiers now in their graves, he publicly acknowledged for the first time that all had not gone according to plan and that he had played a role in the decisions that had wrecked Iraq: "Where mistakes have been made, the responsibility lies with me."

Immediately after the speech, the junior senator from Illinois, Barack Obama, went on MSNBC to say, "I am not persuaded that the 20,000 additional troops in Iraq is going to solve the sectarian violence there. In fact, it will do the reverse. I think it takes the pressure off the Iraqis to make the sort of political accommodations that every observer believes is the ultimate solution to the problems we face there. So I'm going to actively oppose the president's proposal." Obama was joined in his opposition to the surge by more or less the entire Democratic Party, including then-Senator Joe Biden and much of the foreign policy establishment on both sides of the aisle who felt that Bush was doubling down on a bad bet. Republican Senator Chuck Hagel described the escalation as "the most dangerous foreign policy blunder in this country since Vietnam." A survey of "100 of America's most respected foreign policy experts" by *Foreign Policy* magazine eight months after the surge was announced found that more than half thought the surge was having a "negative impact" on the war. Most Americans were also against the surge: a poll the day after Bush made his surge announcement found that 61 percent opposed sending more troops to Iraq.

But to those who were most closely following the Iraq War—such as the "surgios" at the NSC, commanders like Odierno and Petraeus with extensive experience on the ground in Iraq, and those outside the government, like General Keane and AEI's Fred Kagan—the fact that Iraq needed both more American boots on the ground and a better strategy to stanch the civil war there was quite obvious. It was so obvious to them that they all arrived at quite similar conclusions at more or less the same time during the fall of 2006, sometimes working independently of each other and at other times feeding off each other.

Petraeus, for instance, had a back channel to O'Sullivan, to whom he could not have been more clear about his need for a significantly larger force just before he was about to assume command in Iraq. Petraeus remembers saying to O'Sullivan, "Give me everything—find everything you can and get it all." Similarly, Odierno had a back channel to both Keane and Petraeus, and Keane had a back channel to Vice President Cheney. And coordinating all this was Stephen Hadley, an unassuming, thoughtful workaholic, who deftly managed the policy-making process around the surge so that the senior Pentagon and State Department officials who had once opposed it eventually and, in some cases, begrudgingly, endorsed the surge.

Emma Sky is a lively British graduate of Oxford who studied Arabic there and then went on to work in Palestine doing development work. With that background it was hardly predictable that she would end up working as a key aide to the top U.S. military commanders in Iraq. After the American and British invasion of Iraq in 2003, Sky became the Coalition Provisional Authority representative in the key northern city of Kirkuk, and as a result met regularly with both Petraeus and Odierno.

As the surge started four years later, Odierno, now the number-two commander in Iraq, asked Sky to work as his political adviser. Contemporary coverage of the surge tended to fixate on the numbers of new troops going to Iraq, which would eventually amount to an additional thirty thousand soldiers. Sky suggests that the most important, and often undervalued aspect, of the surge was "the huge psychological impact it had on us—and on Iraqis. We proved to ourselves—and to our critics—that we were not defeated."

Sky became part of a small team of a half dozen or so known as the Initiatives Group advising Odierno, which included Derek Harvey, an Arabic-speaking intelligence officer who had first laid out for President Bush at the White House the real scale and nature of the Sunni insurgency in the winter of 2004, and Colonel Mike Meese, an instructor at West Point's Social Sciences Department. (Former and present faculty at West Point provided a good deal of the intellectual firepower that reshaped the American strategy in Iraq, including Meese, John Nagl, H. R. McMaster, Fred Kagan, and Petraeus himself.)

During January 2007, the Initiatives Group worked through the strategy that the surge of new troops would help implement. Sky recalls that the National Security Council "gave permission for there to be a surge: great. They gave no details about what that meant." The Initiatives Group started to sort out the key question of who the reconcilables and irreconcilables were, a pragmatic approach to success that recognized that the United States had to make deals with even those insurgent groups that had American blood on their hands. Sky recalls that an important first symbolic step was to stop labeling all the insurgents with the Orwellian and obscuring name of "Anti-Iraqi Forces," as the U.S. military was then calling them. Sky explains, "The biggest mind-set change was for us to look at Iraqis as not the enemy, but to look at the Iraqis as people who needed protecting."

Just as the surge began in February 2007, General Petraeus arrived as the new U.S. commander in Iraq. He had not been back in Iraq for sixteen months. Shortly after his arrival he took a tour of Baghdad neighborhoods he knew from his past deployments. "I just couldn't believe it . . . here's literally tumbleweed rolling down the street of what I remembered as a very prosperous, upper-middle-class, former military officers' neighborhood in northwest Baghdad. It was just . . . Wow!" There were now well over two hundred car bombings and suicide attacks every month in Iraq. Six months earlier there were around a quarter of that number. "Security incidents" that ran the gamut from attacks on Iraqi government forces to rocket attacks were averaging more than 1,600 every week, up from 600 or so a year earlier. Iraq was simultaneously exploding and imploding.

Petraeus, an intensely competitive officer with a Ph.D. from Princeton, assembled a brilliant staff to reassess and redirect the war. Laughing, he recalls, "I didn't get all these superstars in Iraq because people wanted to send me their best people. I got them because I said I've just been picked for mission impossible; the president supports it; and, with respect I'd like to get H. R. McMaster over here and I'm going to take this guy and I want that guy."

Petraeus brought with him to Iraq a sense that there was a *plan*. And he also had the full support of Bush, with whom he held a weekly private videoconference, which was unprecedented since the president was circumventing several levels in the chain of command to speak to his field commander. Watching Petraeus's BUA, or Battlefield Update Assessment, held every morning at "Camp Victory" in Baghdad, was to see a master at work, cajoling and cheerleading his commanders across the country via video link as they reported on every variable of the Iraqi body politic from the grandest of political issues to the minutest of water projects.

The new team and new approach got American soldiers out of their bases and into the neighborhoods and was amplified by the arrival of what would eventually become the thirty thousand soldiers of the surge. Petraeus outlined that "population-centric" strategy in a three-page letter he distributed to all of the soldiers under his command. "You can't commute to this fight. . . . Living among the people is essential to securing them and defeating the insurgents . . . patrol on foot and engage the population. Situational awareness can only be guaranteed by interacting with people face-to-face, not separated by ballistic glass."

Sky says that Petraeus played another key role, which was buying time in Washington for the new strategy to work. "In showing that there was somebody in charge, somebody credible, that there was a policy. He owned the policy and he owned the implementation. Now without his strategic communications, without people's belief in Petraeus we would never have got the time."

O'Sullivan says the concern at the White House during the summer of 2007 was that the political will to do what was necessary to roll back the violence in Iraq was beginning to evaporate: "Where everyone was very worried was with Congress. I think we were very nervous that we would lose the opportunity to fully execute." A telling defection in Congress was that of Senator Richard Lugar of Indiana, the foreign policy eminence grise of the Republican Party. On June 25 Lugar took to the Senate floor to withdraw his support from the surge, saying, "Persisting indefinitely with the surge strategy will delay policy adjustments that have a better chance of protecting our vital interests over the long term."

The greatest test of whether the political will existed to continue with the ramped-up Iraq effort was the congressional hearings held on the sixth anniversary of 9/11. On September 11, 2007, Petraeus and Ryan Crocker, the veteran diplomat who was U.S. ambassador to Iraq, were grilled by both the Senate Foreign Relations and Armed Services committees, on which happened to sit five senators all seriously vying for the presidency—Joe Biden, Christopher Dodd, Barack Obama, John McCain, and Hillary Clinton—one of whom would become president of the United States in just over a year. Petraeus recalls that the hearing "was just charged beyond belief. I mean, you could just feel the spotlight of the world on you. It was carried live in Baghdad."

Petraeus and Crocker gamely tried to present a picture of progress in Iraq but the Democrats were having none of it. Clinton interjected at one point: "You have been made the de facto spokesmen for what many of us believe to be a failed policy. Despite what I view as your rather extraordinary efforts in your testimony . . . I think that the reports that you provide to us really require the willing suspension of disbelief." This is Washington-speak for "you are either wrong or lying."

The day before, the duo had also testified before a joint hearing of the House Armed Services and Foreign Affairs committees. Petraeus knew it was going to be a rough day when he received a heads-up that the *New York Times* was running a full-page ad about him, paid for by the left-wing advocacy group MoveOn.org. Under a banner headline GENERAL PETRAEUS OR GENERAL BETRAY US? the general was accused of "Cooking the Books for the White House." The ad copy went on to assert, "Every independent report on the ground situation in Iraq shows that the surge strategy has failed. . . . Most importantly, General Petraeus will not admit what everyone knows: Iraq is mired in an unwinnable religious civil war." Around six o'clock on the morning of his testimony, Petraeus, an avid runner, went for a lonely run as a new day dawned gray in Washington, D.C. "Talk about feeling like an 'Army of One.' . . . Man, I've just been called a traitor, in a newspaper I used to read every morning," recalls Petraeus, a native of New York state.

The two days of contentious congressional hearings each lasted a grueling eight or nine hours. Petraeus remembers sitting outside the PBS studio in northern Virginia where he and Ryan Crocker were scheduled to give interviews following one of the hearings, saying to his colleague, "'You know, Ryan, I am never going to do this again.' And he said, 'Neither am I.' It's a little bit like the sentiment after you run a particularly grueling marathon, not just any marathon, but one in which you sort of ran into the wall at the nineteenth-mile mark, instead of the twenty-three- or twenty-five-mile mark."

General Ray Odierno, Petraeus's massively built deputy, known as "Big O," put two brigades of the newly arrived soldiers of the surge into Baghdad's toughest neighborhoods and three more brigades into the "belts" surrounding the capital where AQI had established bases. This operational approach emerged following the December 2006 capture by U.S. Special Forces of documents that outlined al-Qaeda's plan to control the belts around Baghdad so as to slowly strangle the city. It was in those belts that al-Qaeda hid its car-bomb factories and rest houses for its fighters. Odierno set out to destroy those havens.

The surge of American soldiers brought a surge of American combat deaths as their deployments into neighborhood outposts exposed them to greater risk. In May 2007, 120 American soldiers died, the deadliest month in two years. For those who worked on the surge it was agonizing. "It was awful. We had a hundred a month we were losing. Everywhere we went, a little note would come to Odierno, 'another guy dead, another guy dead,'" remembers his political adviser, Emma Sky. Odierno recalls, "The worst was May and June; the most difficult times. I was obviously concerned, but the reason I was still fairly confident it would work is because the majority of the deaths and the casualties were coming from us breaching these defensive belts that had been put in these safe havens."

Stephen Biddle of the Council on Foreign Relations, a critic of how the Iraq War was going, was recruited by Petraeus to be one of two outside civilians to sit on his Joint Strategic Assessment Team (JSAT) to help him work up the new campaign plan for the war. The JSAT, which was chaired by Colonel H. R. McMaster, who had restored order to Tal Afar two years earlier, recommended that the Anbar Awakening model be expanded to the rest of Iraq. Biddle described this approach as "Tony Soprano does Iraq: we had to manipulate the incentive structures of all three of the major actors—the Kurds, the Shiites, and the Sunnis. We could not simply permanently align with any one of them. There are no good guys and bad guys; there are just ethnosectarian groups that are at war with each other in a security dilemma. Our job is to resolve the dilemma by compelling them against their will to come to compromises."

Odierno also enthusiastically endorsed embracing America's former enemies. Soon after assuming his new job as deputy commander, Odierno traveled in January 2007 to Ramadi, the city where the Awakening movement had first started, to meet with its leader, Sheikh Abdul Sattar Abu Risha. Odierno says Abdul Sattar "was somebody who was convinced that, together with the U.S. forces, they could beat al-Qaeda. And he was all in. . . . There were thirteen different tribes out there, and at that time there were only eight who were working with us. There were still five more that we were trying to bring over, and he was helping us to do that."

Odierno says that by then other Sunni tribes in other provinces were clamoring to ally with the Americans against al-Qaeda: "We started getting feedback from other Iraqis saying, 'Why can't we have an Awakening movement?' . . . So we had a large internal discussion, how do you reach out to someone who's been trying to kill you, and fighting against you?" Odierno issued guidance to his commanders in February and March about how to move forward to set up Awakening movements around Iraq so that the Anbar model could be extended to the rest of the country.

Odierno recalls that this was a hard sell to some of his commanders. "Initially, people were nervous about it, and rightfully so. . . . Once they got out there, and they started seeing the results and how willing people were to do this, they really bought into it." The new approach precipitated literally hundreds of local cease-fires with insurgents and tribal leaders, deals that were often sweetened by substantial cash payments. Odierno points out that the new soldiers of the surge also helped this process: "As we were able to establish ourselves in areas we'd never been able to establish ourselves in, it gave them confidence to become part of the Awakening." Odierno explains how this process worked: "We would go set up a patrol base. When we first got there nobody would talk to us, but when they saw the walls go up, and the permanent base, they'd come out of the woodwork. They'd go, 'OK, they're going to stay. So they will be here to help us; they're not just going to leave and we'll be left here and be slaughtered by al-Qaeda.' When they knew we were going to stay and be there for a while, they gave us help and information."

There were also shifting dynamics on the ground in Iraq that would make the additional combat brigades of the surge a force multiplier rather than simply more cannon fodder for Iraq's insurgents. Those changes included not only al-Qaeda's weakening grip and the rise of the Awakening movements but previous sectarian cleansing that had forced more than four million Iraqis to flee their homes, and which made it harder for the death squads to find their victims. In Baghdad by the end of 2006, half the Sunni population had fled the city. Around the same time efforts to register all military-age Iraqi males using biometrics created a useful database of that population. And walls built around vulnerable neighborhoods kept insurgents out. Petraeus recalls that "we literally created gated communities all over Baghdad. And in some cases, we created gated cities like Fallujah. There was a period where we didn't allow vehicles into Fallujah. There were massive parking lots outside the city of several hundred thousand people."

The better integration of human intelligence from the former insurgents on the American payroll and information from the vastly increased number of hours flown by unmanned aerial vehicles over Iraq—hours flown by UAVs in Iraq jumped from nearly 165,000 flight hours in 2006 to more than 258,000 in 2007—supplemented by signals intelligence and cell phone chain analysis, combined with the efforts of U.S. and Iraqi special forces, all integrated together, put the insurgents on the run in provinces across Iraq. Senior U.S. intelligence official David Gordon recalls, "By 2008, Special Forces were going on two rounds a night! They were going on an attack, getting new information; they were *destroying* the enemy . . . and that's part of what happens when all of this works, is that you get this huge flow of intelligence that enables us."

Better bomb detection devices, such as drones equipped to spot subtle anomalies in roads indicating the presence of bombs; the increasing deployment of hulking armored vehicles with V-shaped hulls known as MRAPs, which are largely immune from roadside bombs; and an aggressive effort to map and target the networks of Iraq's bomb makers all led to a decline in the number of deaths caused by the leading killer of U.S. soldiers—the improvised explosive device. The number of IED attacks in Iraq dropped from almost 5,000 in 2006 to around 3,000 two years later. Petraeus recalls that all of these factors were mutually reinforcing. "So you reverse a death spiral, basically. It wasn't just a downward spiral. . . . And one aspect reinforces another, which makes something else possible, which reinforces another and then promotes better security which means, you just keep going up."

By 2008 the Sunni insurgent organizations in Iraq were largely defeated, but that was only one, albeit critically important, aspect of the problem that faced American commanders, because al-Qaeda had something of a Shia analogue, the Jaish al-Mahdi (the "Army of the Savior"), known by its initials as JAM. Operating at the behest of the sullen young cleric Moqtada al-Sadr, JAM fought pitched battles in 2004 with American forces in the southern Iraqi city of Najaf. Two years later JAM had grown to a force of some sixty thousand men, far larger than any of the Sunni insurgent groups.

But as AQI gradually faded in importance, so too did JAM's role as the protector of the Shia against the Sunni terrorists, and increasingly JAM began to be seen by the Shia population as just another predatory militia. The best predictor of future ethnic strife is acts of revenge for previous ethnic violence, and so as AQI and JAM declined in strength a reinforcing positive feedback loop began to take hold, and the numbers of Iraqi civilians dying in sectarian violence began a sharp decline from a high of around ninety *every day* in December 2006 to single digits two years later.

The PowerPoint briefing slides so beloved of the U.S. military showed the violence in Iraq peaking in almost every category in the first months of 2007 and steadily dropping after that. That decline was true across the board, including attacks by insurgents, civilian deaths, U.S. soldiers killed, Iraq security forces killed, car-bomb attacks, and IED explosions. In December 2006, the U.S. military map of "ethno-sectarian" violence in Baghdad was colored mostly yellow, orange, and red, indicating medium to intense violence. The same map two years later was mostly colored green, indicating that the sectarian violence in Baghdad had largely subsided.

JAM compounded its problems when in late August 2007 it started fighting another Shia militia, the Badr Corps, around the shrine of the holy city of Karbala, in southern Iraq, during pilgrimage season, clashes that killed scores. It was as if two mafia families had waged pitched gun battles in the vicinity of the Vatican in the middle of Easter, and it horrified most Shia. As a result Moqtada al-Sadr ordered JAM to stand down in a six-month truce that he later renewed.

In the spring of 2008, JAM overreached yet again when it unleashed barrages of mortar and rocket attacks on the hitherto largely safe Green Zone in

Baghdad, attacks that had landed close to the prime minister's own house. By the last week of March, Maliki decided to launch an assault on the city of Basra, the key to the southern province that is the source of some 70 percent of Iraq's oil wealth, which had been largely taken over by JAM.

Maliki's attack plan reflected his mounting frustration about the Shia gangs running rampant in Basra. He barely gave American commanders any warning about what he was doing. Petraeus recalls that this was a make-or-break moment for Maliki: "We saw it as a game-changer if he didn't win. I remember the president saying, 'This is a decisive moment,' and I was telling Ryan [Crocker, the U.S. ambassador to Iraq], 'Boy, I hope it's decisive in the way I think he means,' because it was such a rapid, such a sudden, frankly, arguably impulsive decision."

Senior U.S. intelligence official David Gordon recalls, "There were all of these questions being raised about Maliki, and President Bush said, 'You know, we don't have the luxury of choosing who our partners are.' And I give President Bush . . . really, very high grades for his personal management of the relationship with Maliki." National Security Advisor Stephen Hadley was in the Oval Office as Bush heard the news about Maliki's impulsive move into Basra and recalls the president saying, "If he succeeds on this, it will transform him as a leader. He will become the leader of this country, and he will become a nonsectarian leader of his country. That's what I've been looking for ever since we toppled Saddam Hussein. So, not only are we gonna support Maliki in this, but the Pentagon and the military better get some people down there and help get control of this operation, and make it a success." American advisers and air support soon arrived in Basra and the Shia militias were decimated.

Maliki followed up the Basra operation with a similar American-supported drive by the Iraqi military into the vast Shia slums of Sadr City in Baghdad, from which many of the rocket and mortar attacks into the Green Zone were being launched. Maliki's operations against JAM, however, were not just simple acts of single-minded patriotism, since they had the side benefit for the prime minister of neutralizing a major competing power center in the world of Shia politics.

The Basra and Sadr City operations sent an important signal to the Sunni population that the Shia-dominated government would act against Shiite militias. It is hard to imagine a more anti-Shia and anti-Iranian group than the Sunni sheikhs of the Anbar Awakening, but after the Basra operation a group of four of them all took turns to say variations of "We are pleased with Maliki. The rest of the government other than the prime minister is Shia." Before the Basra operation, their praise for Maliki, who had spent decades living in Iran and came to power because of his onetime alliance with Sadr, would have been inconceivable.

And the operations in Sadr City and other parts of the country underlined the importance of another "surge," the significance of which was largely missed in the United States: the Iraqi security services were now quite substantial and somewhat effective. By 2009 there were some six hundred thousand Iraqi soldiers and policemen, four times more than was then the case in Afghanistan, which is a much larger country with a larger population and is harder to control because of its mountainous topography.

For years the Iraqi police had been seen by Sunnis, with ample justification, as just another ethnic-cleansing Shia militia. But in 2008 the new head of the police force, Major General Hussein al-Awadi, fired eighteen of the more sectarian of his twenty-seven battalion commanders and the force became much better balanced ethnically. Similarly, the Iraqi army was increasingly able to operate as a genuinely national force. For instance, the 1st Brigade of the 1st Division had no problem operating in the 2008 Basra operation despite the fact that it was a mixed force of 60 percent Sunni and 40 percent Shia.

Another positive development was the emergence of Iraqi politics conducted by parliamentary maneuver rather than with rockets. A legitimate criticism of the security gains in Iraq was that they weren't matched by concomitant political progress. But a provincial election law was finally passed in September 2008 and provincial elections followed on January 31, 2009. The election went largely peacefully and Iraqis voted for more nationalist, secular-leaning parties over the religious parties that had won in the elections of 2005.

The long-contentious Status of Forces Agreement that was finally hammered out between the Bush administration and the Iraqi government and passed by the Iraqi parliament in late November 2008 was another sign of deepening political maturity. This agreement provided a framework for the incoming Obama administration to plan the withdrawal of all American soldiers by the end of 2011. The Bush administration did not get caveats inserted into the agreement that would have prolonged the occupation potentially indefinitely; Iraqi politicians who voted for the agreement had a date certain for a complete American withdrawal, and the Iranians who were, in effect, another partner in the negotiations, because of the influence they wielded over Iraq's Shia parties, secured a guarantee that Iraq would not be used by American forces for offensive operations against other countries.

Emma Sky, the political adviser to the U.S. military in Iraq, points out that the agreement had a key clause that U.S. forces had to be out of the cities by June 2009: "Now making us do that was huge, because without that clause we would have always found a reason that we couldn't leave the cities. Violence would never be down to a good enough level to justify it." On June 30 the last American units pulled out of Iraq's cities. Sky remembers the "Sovereignty Day" celebrations and watching the Iraqi Security Forces march by, and thinking, "I just never believed we would get to this day. It was really, really huge. For them, to actually see that we had no long-term interest in occupying their country; that this was genuine."

More than half a decade after Casey, Abizaid, and Rumsfeld had first decided that their most important goal in Iraq was to put a more Iraqi face on the American occupation, it was now finally realized with the withdrawal of U.S. forces from Iraq's cities. But to get there had required a wholesale change in U.S. strategy; putting at first an even more American face on the occupation by putting more GI boots on the ground in some of Iraq's toughest neighborhoods, which helped to stanch the bloodbath that had engulfed the country.

None of these positive developments was to suggest that the Iraq War was somehow *post facto* worth the blood and treasure consumed—more than 4,500 American soldiers dead and thirty thousand wounded; at least one hundred thousand Iraqis killed; costs to U.S. taxpayers that will rise above a trillion dollars; and jihadist terrorist attacks that had increased around the world sevenfold in the three years following the 2003 invasion.

It bears recalling that almost none of the goals of the war as described by proponents of overthrowing Saddam were achieved. An alliance between Saddam and al-Qaeda wasn't interrupted because there wasn't one, according to any number of studies, including one by the Institute for Defense Analyses, the Pentagon's own internal think tank. There was no democratic domino effect around the Middle East; quite the opposite: the authoritarian regimes became more firmly entrenched. Peace did not come to Israel, despite the prediction of the well-known academic Fouad Ajami, writing before the war in *Foreign Affairs* that the road to Jerusalem went through Baghdad. Nor did the war pay for itself, as posited by Paul Wolfowitz, who told Congress in 2003 that oil revenues "could bring between 50 and 100 billion dollars over the course of the next two or three years. We're dealing with a country that could really finance its own reconstruction, and relatively soon." Quite the reverse: Iraq was a giant money sink for the American economy. The supposed threat to the United States from Saddam wasn't ended because there wasn't one to begin with. And in his place arose a Shia-dominated Arab state, the first in modern history. Meanwhile, American prestige overseas evaporated, while the U.S. military was stretched to the breaking point.

And Al-Qaeda in Iraq might still regain a role despite its much weakened state today. In 2008 there was a sense that al-Qaeda's Iraqi affiliate was on the verge of defeat. The American ambassador to Iraq, Ryan Crocker, said, "You are not going to hear me say that al-Qaeda is defeated, but they've never been closer to defeat than they are now." Al-Qaeda had by then certainly lost the ability to control large swaths of the country and a good chunk of the Sunni population as it had two years earlier, but the group proved surprisingly resilient, as demonstrated by the fact that it pulled off a number of bombings in Baghdad in 2010 that killed hundreds.

The jury is, in short, still out on whether the Iraq War was the United States' most spectacular foreign policy blunder of the past several decades, or whether, out of the wreckage, something resembling a coherent Iraq will eventually arise. Petraeus famously asked Rick Atkinson, the *Washington Post* reporter who was embedded with him during the 2003 invasion of Iraq, "Tell me how this ends?" That question remains a good one today. Petraeus's successor as the top commander in Iraq, General Raymond Odierno, says that the Iraqi government elected in 2010 will be the key to answer that question. "They will really be the government that decides whether Iraq continues to move towards a more open economy, and move towards a more democratic process, or do they decide to move back towards a more closed economy, back to an Islamic state or a dictatorship. . . . From what I'm seeing, they're going to go towards a democratic process and an open economy, but we'll see."

For President Bush, the surge was the single most consequential decision of his second term, a decision that he made against the advice of almost the entire leadership of the military and in the face of opposition from much of the foreign policy establishment, and at a time when his favorability ratings with the American people were in the tank, hovering around 30 percent in most polls. The military historian Eliot Cohen says, "There's only one guy who deserves the credit. And that's George W. Bush. He deserves all the blame for the other stuff, too. He deserves the blame, but he deserves the credit . . . for supporting the surge decision, but also the Petraeus decision, and both are very important."

In part because of the surge, as well as the other factors considered in this chapter, al-Qaeda suffered a strategic defeat in Iraq. For the Arab leaders of al-Qaeda, the large role their Iraqi affiliate played during the Iraq War was a source of considerable pride, as was reflected in the several tapes issued by bin Laden in which he crowed about the successes of Iraq's insurgents against American forces. But after Al-Qaeda in Iraq was put on the run in 2007, bin Laden was largely silent on the issue of Iraq. And the declining fortunes of Al-Qaeda in Iraq were, in fact, a harbinger of the decline of the larger al-Qaeda organization and movement.

Chapter 17

The Jihad Within

Striking the World Trade Center, I consider that to be a criminal act.

—Abdullah Anas to Al Arabiya television in 2005; Anas had once been bin Laden's companion-in-arms during the jihad against the Soviets in Afghanistan

Will al-Qaeda eventually be condemned to what President Bush once eloquently termed "history's unmarked grave of discarded lies"? To a large degree that depends not on the West but on the Islamic world, for it is Muslims who are making the choices that are leading to the marginalization of both al-Qaeda and the ideology of "bin Ladenism" that it has spawned. Indeed, it is mainstream Islam itself that poses the largest ideological threat to al-Qaeda.

Despite a widespread view in the West that Muslim religious leaders had not done enough to condemn the 9/11 attacks, within days of the assaults Mohamed Tantawi, the grand mufti of Al-Azhar University in Cairo, the foremost center of Sunni learning, denounced them saying "attacking innocent people is not courageous, it is stupid and will be punished on the day of judgment." Around the same time, another leading Sunni cleric, Yusuf al-Qaradawi, said "Islam, the religion of tolerance, holds the human soul in high esteem, and considers the attacks against innocent human beings a grave sin." And the most senior cleric in Saudi Arabia, Abdul Aziz Abdullah al-Sheikh, similarly issued a fatwa stating, "These matters that have taken place in the United States . . . are expressly forbidden and are amongst the greatest of sins."

Around half a decade after 9/11, a surprising wave of criticism about the legitimacy of al-Qaeda's actions also emerged from some of Osama bin Laden's onetime religious mentors and former companions-in-arms. The repercussions for al-Qaeda could not be underestimated, because, unlike most mainstream Muslim leaders, al-Qaeda's new critics had the jihadist credentials to make their criticisms bite. One of the most prominent was Abdullah Anas, who had fought side by side with the Afghan commander Ahmad Shah Massoud in Afghanistan for years during the 1980s. At that time Anas and bin Laden were close friends. Anas's jihadist credentials were further burnished by the fact that he is the son-in-law of Abdullah Azzam, the godfather of the global jihad movement. In a wide-ranging 2006 interview in *Al-Sharq al-Awsat*, one of the leading newspapers in the Arab world, Anas said that al-Qaeda's suicide bombings in London a year earlier were "criminal" acts and that "blowing up a train here and a restaurant that leads to the death of innocent victims—as happened in London and elsewhere—will not force the United States to change its policy." Al-Qaeda's leaders did not respond to Anas's well-publicized condemnations as he is difficult to impugn, as both a jihadi war hero and the son-in-law of the founder of the modern jihadist movement.

Around the sixth anniversary of September 11, al-Qaeda received another blow from one of bin Laden's erstwhile heroes, Sheikh Salman al-Awdah. Awdah, a leading Saudi religious scholar, addressed al-Qaeda's leader on MBC, a widely watched Middle East TV network: "My brother Osama, how much blood has been spilt? How many innocent people, children, elderly, and women have been killed . . . in the name of al-Qaeda?" What was noteworthy about Awdah's statement was that it was not a boilerplate condemnation of terrorism, or even of 9/11, but a *personal* rebuke of bin Laden, something clerics in the Muslim world had generally shied away from.

Dressed in the long, flowing black robe fringed with gold that is worn by those accorded respect in Saudi society, Awdah recalled first meeting with bin Laden in the northern Saudi region of Qassim in 1990, and finding him to be a "simple man without scholarly religious credentials, an attractive personality who spoke well." Awdah explained that he had publicly criticized al-Qaeda for years but was now directing his criticism at bin Laden himself: "I don't expect a positive effect on bin Laden personally as a result of my statement. It's really a message to his followers."

Awdah's rebuke was also significant because he is considered one of the fathers of the *Sahwa*, the fundamentalist awakening movement that had swept through Saudi Arabia in the 1980s. His sermons against the U.S. military presence in Saudi Arabia following Saddam Hussein's 1990 invasion of Kuwait helped turn bin Laden against the United States. And bin Laden told CNN in 1997 that Awdah's imprisonment three years earlier by the Saudi regime was one of the reasons he was calling for attacks on American targets. Awdah was also one of twenty-six Saudi clerics who in 2004 handed down a religious ruling urging Iraqis to fight the U.S. occupation. He was, in short, not someone al-Qaeda could paint as either an American sympathizer or a tool of the Saudi government.

More doubt about al-Qaeda was planted in the Muslim world when Sayyid Imam al-Sharif, an important ideological influence on al-Qaeda, withdrew his support for the terrorist organization in a 2007 book written from his prison cell in Cairo. Sharif, generally known as "Dr. Fadl," is the author of the 1993 tract *The Basic Principles in Making Preparations for Jihad* and an architect of the doctrine of *takfir*, arguing that Muslims who did not support armed jihad or who participated in elections were *kuffar*, unbelievers.

So it was an unwelcome surprise for al-Qaeda's leaders when Dr. Fadl's new book, *Rationalization of Jihad*, was serialized in an independent Egyptian newspaper in November 2007. Dr. Fadl ruled that al-Qaeda's bombings in Muslim nations were illegitimate and that terrorism against civilians in Western countries was wrong. He also took on al-Qaeda's leaders directly in an interview with *Al Hayat* newspaper. "Zawahiri and his Emir Bin Laden [are] extremely immoral," he said. "I have spoken about this in order to warn the youth against them." And a year later, leaders of the Libyan Islamic Fighting Group, which had once loosely aligned themselves with bin Laden, turned against al-Qaeda, issuing statements against the terrorist group's ideology from their prison cells in Libya and their offices in London.

Why did militants and clerics once considered allies by al-Qaeda's leaders turn against them? To a large extent it is because al-Qaeda and affiliated groups had increasingly adopted the doctrine of *takfir*, by which they claimed the right to decide who was a "true" Muslim, something that in mainstream Islamic theology is something only Allah can truly know. Al-Qaeda's Muslim critics knew what resulted from this *takfiri* view: first the radicals deemed some Muslims apostates; after that, the radicals started killing them. From 2003 this could be seen most dramatically in Iraq, where al-Qaeda's suicide bombers killed thousands of Iraqis, many of them targeted simply because they were Shia.

Additionally, al-Qaeda and its affiliates had killed thousands of Muslim civilians elsewhere since 9/11, including the hundreds of ordinary Afghans killed every year by the Taliban, and the scores of Jordanians massacred at a wedding at a hotel in Amman in November 2005. For groups that claimed to be defending Muslims this was not impressive. All this created a dawning recognition among Muslims that the ideological virus that had unleashed 9/11 and the terror attacks in London and Madrid was the same virus that was now also wreaking havoc in the Islamic world.

Conscious that al-Qaeda was getting seriously damaged by all this criticism, in December 2007 Ayman al-Zawahiri and his handlers took the unprecedented step of soliciting questions from anyone over the Internet, which the deputy al-Qaeda leader then answered four months later in a Q&A format online. The Q&A did not go well. When Zawahiri was asked how he could justify al-Qaeda's killings of Muslim civilians, he answered defensively in dense, recondite passages that referred readers to other dense, recondite things he had already said about the matter. Someone identifying himself as "Madaris Jughrafiya" (a geography teacher) asked, "Excuse me, Mr. Zawahiri, but who is killing with your Excellency's blessing the innocents in Baghdad, Morocco and Algeria. Do you consider that to be Jihad?" Bin Laden himself released a tape trying to tamp down this line of attack, in which he said that "the Muslim victims who fall during the operations against the infidel Crusaders are not the intended targets."

Is al-Qaeda going to dissipate as a result of the rising tide of criticism it faces in the Muslim world? Not in the short term. Though losing the favor of Muslim populations certainly doesn't help al-Qaeda, history shows that small violent groups from the anarchists of the early twentieth century to the leftist terrorists of the 1970s can sustain their bloody work for years with virtually no public support.

However, encoded in the DNA of militant jihadist groups like al-Qaeda are the seeds of their own long-term destruction because they have four crippling strategic weaknesses. First, their victims are often Muslim civilians. This is a real problem for al-Qaeda as the Koran forbids both killing civilians and fellow Muslims. Al-Qaeda in Saudi Arabia, for instance, lost a great deal of support after its campaign of attacks in 2003 that killed mostly Saudis. By

2007, Saudi society, which had once been cheerleaders for bin Laden, had turned against al-Qaeda; only 10 percent of Saudis had a favorable view of the terrorist network.

Second, al-Qaeda and its allies don't offer a positive vision of the future. We know what bin Laden is *against*, but what's he really *for*? If you asked him he would say the restoration of the caliphate. By that he does not mean the restoration of something like the last caliphate, the Ottoman Empire, a relatively rational polity, but rather the imposition of Taliban-style theocracies stretching from Indonesia to Morocco. A silent majority of Muslims don't want that. Many Muslims admire bin Laden because he "stood up" to the West, but that doesn't mean they want to live in his grim Islamist utopia. Afghanistan under the Taliban is not an attractive model of the future for most Muslims.

Third, the jihadist militants are incapable of turning themselves into genuine mass political movements because their ideology prevents them from making the kind of real-world compromises that would allow them to engage in normal politics. Bin Laden's principal political grievance, the large-scale U.S. military presence in Saudi Arabia, ended in 2003, yet bin Laden never acknowledged this change. And to satisfy his political demands fully would have involved stamping out all American influence in the Muslim world; destroying the state of Israel; the overthrow of every Middle Eastern regime; the rollback of India from Kashmir; the installation of Taliban regimes in Afghanistan and Pakistan; the ending of any democratic elections anywhere in the Islamic world—the list went on and on.

While bin Laden has enjoyed a certain amount of personal popularity in much of the Muslim world, that has not translated into mass support for al-Qaeda in the manner that Hezbollah enjoys such support in Lebanon. That is not surprising—there are no al-Qaeda social welfare services or schools. An al-Qaeda hospital is a grim oxymoron. Even al-Qaeda's leaders are aware of the problem of their lack of mass support. In the 2005 letter sent by Zawahiri to Abu Musab al-Zarqawi, al-Qaeda's number two urged the terrorist leader in Iraq to prepare for the U.S. withdrawal from the country by not making the same mistakes as the Taliban, who had alienated the masses in Afghanistan.

Fourth, the militants keep adding to their list of enemies, including any Muslim who doesn't exactly share their ultrafundamentalist worldview. Al-Qaeda has said it is opposed to all Middle Eastern regimes; the Shia; most Western countries; Jews and Christians; the governments of India, Pakistan, Afghanistan, and Russia; most news organizations; the United Nations; and international nongovernmental organizations. It's very hard to think of a category of person, institution, or government that al-Qaeda does not oppose. Making a world of enemies is never a winning strategy.

Given the religio-ideological basis of al-Qaeda's jihad, the condemnation being offered by religious scholars and fighters once close to the group was arguably the most important development in stopping the spread of the group's ideology since 9/11. These new critics, in concert with mainstream Muslim leaders, created a powerful coalition countering al-Qaeda's ideas. Simultaneously al-Qaeda began losing significant traction with ordinary Muslims. The numbers of people having a favorable view of bin Laden or supporting suicide bombings, for instance, in the two most populous Muslim countries, Indonesia and Pakistan, dropped by at least half between 2002 and 2009.

By the end of the second Bush term it was clear that al-Qaeda and allied groups were losing the "war of ideas" in the Islamic world, not because America was winning that war—quite the contrary: most Muslims had a quite negative attitude toward the United States—but because Muslims themselves had largely turned against the ideology of bin Ladenism.

It is human nature to be concerned mostly with threats that directly affect one's own interests, and so as jihadi terrorists started to target the governments of Muslim countries and their civilians, this led to a hardening of attitudes against them. Until the terrorist attacks of May 2003 in Riyadh, for instance, the Saudi government was largely in denial about its large-scale al-Qaeda problem. The Saudi government subsequently arrested thousands of suspected terrorists, killed more than a hundred, and arrested preachers deemed to be encouraging militancy. A similar process also happened in Indonesia, where Jemaah Islamiyah, the al-Qaeda affiliate there, was more or less out of business within half a decade of 9/11, its leaders in jail or dead, and its popular legitimacy close to zero.

Zawahiri acknowledged in his autobiography that the most important strategic goal of al-Qaeda is to seize control of a state, or part of a state, somewhere in the Muslim world, explaining that "without achieving this goal our actions will mean nothing." But after 9/11, al-Qaeda had lost control of Afghanistan, where it had once had a large role, and its attempt in Iraq to set up a state that dominated the Sunnis dramatically backfired.

A decade after 9/11, by Zawahiri's own standard, the group had achieved "nothing."

Chapter 18

The End of the "War on Terror"?

Americans can always be counted on to do the right thing; after they have exhausted all other possibilities.

—Winston Churchill

A couple of weeks after assuming office, President Barack Obama was interviewed in the White House by CNN anchor Anderson Cooper. Cooper asked Obama: "I've noticed you don't use the term 'war on terror.' . . . Is there something about that term you find objectionable or not useful?" Obama replied: "I think it is very important for us to recognize that we have a battle or a war against some terrorist organizations." Cooper followed up: "So that's not a term you're going to be using much in the future?" Obama said: "What I want to do is make sure that I'm constantly talking about al-Qaeda and other affiliated organizations because we, I believe, can win over moderate Muslims to recognize that that kind of destruction and nihilism ultimately leads to a dead end."

Obama may have abandoned the Global War on Terror (GWOT) framing of the Bush administration but he did not embrace the view that was common on the left of his Democratic Party and among many Europeans, who have lived through the bombing campaigns of various nationalist and leftist terror groups for decades: that al-Qaeda was just another criminal/terrorist group that could be dealt with by law enforcement alone. After all, a terrorist organization like the Irish Republican Army would call in warnings before its attacks and its largest massacre only killed twenty-nine people. By contrast, al-Qaeda had declared war on the United States repeatedly during the late 1990s and then had made good on that declaration with attacks on American embassies, a U.S. warship, the Pentagon, and the financial heart of the United States, killing thousands of civilians without warning—acts of war by any standard. Al-Qaeda was obviously at war with the United States and so Obama understood that to respond by simply recasting the GWOT as the GPAT, the Global Police Action against Terrorists, would be both foolish and dangerous.

For Obama, America was still at war but the conflict was now bounded, as he put it, to "al-Qaeda and its allies." Within a year of Obama assuming office, one of those allies demonstrated that this war was far from over. On Christmas Day of 2009, Umar Farouk Abdulmutallab, a twenty-three-year-old from a prominent Nigerian family who had graduated a year earlier from the top-flight University College London with a degree in engineering, boarded Northwest Airlines Flight 253 in Amsterdam, which was bound for Detroit with some three hundred passengers and crew on board. Secreted in his underwear was a bomb made with eighty grams of PETN, a plastic explosive that was not detected at airport security in Amsterdam or the Nigerian city of Lagos, from where he had originally flown. He also carried a syringe with a chemical initiator that would set off the bomb.

As the plane neared Detroit the young man, who was only fifteen at the time of the 9/11 attacks, tried to initiate his bomb with the chemical, setting himself on fire and suffering severe burns. Some combination of his own ineptitude, faulty bomb construction, and the quick actions of the passengers and crew who subdued him and extinguished the fire prevented an explosion that might have brought down the plane near Detroit killing all on board and also likely killing additional Americans on the ground. Immediately after he was arrested Abdulmutallab told investigators that the explosive device "was acquired in Yemen along with instructions as to when it should be used."

The Northwest Airlines plot had been presaged in almost every detail a few months earlier, several thousand miles to the east of Detroit. On August 28, the Saudi deputy minister of interior, Prince Mohammed bin Nayef, survived a bombing attack launched by an al-Qaeda cell based in Yemen, Saudi Arabia's southern neighbor. Because he leads Saudi Arabia's counterterrorism efforts against al-Qaeda, the prince is a key target for the terrorist group.

Prince Nayef was responsible for overseeing the kingdom's terrorist rehabilitation program, and some two dozen important members of al-Qaeda had previously surrendered to him in person. Abdullah Hassan al-Asiri, the would-be assassin, a Saudi who had fled to Yemen, posed as a militant willing to surrender personally to Prince Nayef. During the month of Ramadan, traditionally a time of repentance in the Muslim world, Asiri gained an audience with the prince at his private residence in Jeddah, presenting himself as someone who could also persuade other militants to surrender. Pretending that he was reaching out to those militants, Asiri briefly called some members of al-Qaeda to tell them that he was standing by Prince Nayef. After he finished the call, the bomb blew up, killing Asiri but only slightly injuring the prince, who was a few feet away from his would-be assassin. A Saudi government official characterized the prince's narrow escape as a "miracle."

According to the official Saudi investigation, Asiri concealed the bomb in his underwear; it was made of PETN, the same plastic explosive that would be used in the Detroit plot, and he exploded the hundred-gram device using a detonator with a chemical fuse, as Abdulmutallab would attempt to do on the Northwest flight. Prince Nayef's assassin also had to pass through metal detectors before he was able to secure an audience with the prince. (It was also PETN that Richard Reid, the al-Qaeda recruit who tried to bring down the American Airlines flight from Paris to Miami, had used in his shoe bomb almost exactly eight years before the attempt to bring down the Northwest flight. According to a senior U.S. counterterrorism official, it is "rare" for PETN to be used in terrorist attacks.)

Shortly after the failed attacks on both Prince Nayef and the Northwest passenger jet, al-Qaeda's affiliate in Yemen took responsibility for the operations and released photographs of the two bombers taken while they were in Yemen. A Saudi counterterrorism official said that "after the attack on the prince, the fear of using similar techniques against airplanes, which was discussed openly in the media, has encouraged al-Qaeda cells to try it." The official also explained that American government agencies had participated in the forensic investigation of the Prince Nayef plot, which meant that they should have been aware that a PETN bomb concealed in underwear would evade metal detectors.

The plot to bring down the Northwest flight demonstrated that al-Qaeda was still targeting commercial aviation, which after 9/11 had become one of the hardest targets in the world. And it also demonstrated that the group retained some ability to mount large-scale plots against American targets despite all the damage that had been inflicted on the group. If Umar Farouk Abdulmutallab had succeeded in bringing down Northwest Airlines Flight 253, the bombing would not only have killed hundreds but would also have had a large effect on the U.S. economy, already reeling from the effect of the worst recession since the Great Depression, and would have devastated the critical aviation and tourism businesses.

If the attack had succeeded it would also have dealt a crippling blow to Obama's presidency. According to the White House's own review of the Christmas Day plot, there was sufficient information known to the U.S. government to determine that Abdulmutallab was likely working for al-Qaeda's affiliate in Yemen and that the group was looking to expand its terrorist attacks beyond the Arabian Peninsula. Yet the intelligence community "did not increase analytic resources working" on that threat. Also information about the possible use of a PETN bomb by the Yemeni group was well-known within the national security establishment, including to John Brennan, Obama's top counterterrorism adviser, who was personally briefed by Prince Nayef about the assassination attempt against him. As Obama admitted in a meeting of his national security team a couple of weeks after the Christmas Day plot, "We dodged a bullet."

On January 21, 2009, on his second day in the Oval Office, surrounded by a photo-op-ready bevy of sixteen retired generals and admirals, President Obama signed executive orders that made good on the best line in his inaugural address: "As for our common defense, we reject as false the choice between our safety and our ideals." As he appeared to be drawing down a curtain on the "war on terror," Obama ordered the Guantánamo prison to be closed within a year, officially ended the use of secret prisons by the CIA, and required all interrogations to follow the noncoercive methods of the Army field manual. And he ordered a six-month review of all the cases of the 245 prisoners then held at Guantánamo, which effectively ended any of the trials going on at the base. These moves seemed to presage a wholesale rollback of Bush's "war on terror."

The issue of what the Obama administration would do with the remaining prisoners at Guantánamo boiled down to how dangerous these prisoners actually were. Sixty had already been cleared for release by the Bush administration but some would likely face persecution if they returned to their home countries, in particular, a hapless group of seventeen Chinese Muslims known as Uighurs. In 2009 some of those Uighurs were flown to the island nation of Bermuda, where they were released.

There were also some one hundred Yemenis in the prison camp who could not, for the foreseeable future, be returned to Yemen because of the Yemeni government's weak prison system. There had been not one but two jailbreaks in Yemen in recent years by men involved in the USS *Cole* attack.

Complicating the issue, some of the detainees who had already been released from the prison camp then engaged in terrorism, such as Said Ali al-Shihri, a Saudi who was released in November 2007 and who, like all other Guantánamo detainees released to Saudi custody, entered a comprehensive reeducation program. After passing through the program, Shihri left Saudi Arabia for Yemen and became the deputy leader of al-Qaeda's Yemeni affiliate, the group that planned the botched Christmas Day 2009 attack.

Other released detainees appear to have been so radicalized by their time at Guantánamo that they turned to violence. Abdullah Salih al-Ajmi, a Kuwaiti held in Guantánamo until November 2005, conducted a suicide attack in the Iraqi city of Mosul on April 26, 2008, killing thirteen Iraqi soldiers. Ajmi had changed while incarcerated at Guantánamo. Letters to his Washington lawyer, Thomas Wilner, chart his changing character. His first letter is upbeat and friendly: "How are you and how is your nice team doing? I hope you are doing well. Tell me how you are doing, Mr. Tom, and what is going on in the outside world." Ajmi's final letter to Wilner was a different matter: "To the vile, depraved Thomas, descendant of rotten apes and swine." Wilner said that Ajmi became more radicalized while he was jailed: "Guantánamo took a kid—a kid who wasn't all that bad—and it turned him into a hostile, hardened individual."

In May 2009 a Pentagon fact sheet about Guantánamo detainees who had been released but had since taken up arms was made public. What dominated news stories about the report was the claim that seventy-four of those released from Guantánamo, or one in seven, had "returned to the battlefield." On May 21 the *New York Times* ran a story on its front page about the report under the headline "1 in 7 Detainees Rejoined Jihad." The paper subsequently issued a correction, noting it had conflated those "suspected" by the Pentagon and those "confirmed" of engaging in violence, but the media splash surrounding the report overwhelmed the later correction. The *Times* story ran on the same day that President Obama and former vice president Cheney gave their dueling keynote speeches in Washington about Guantánamo. Unsurprisingly, Cheney seized on the findings of the new report, saying of the released detainees, "One in seven cut a straight path back to their prior line of work and have conducted murderous attacks in the Middle East." However, when threats to the United States were considered, the true rate for those released from Guantánamo who were either confirmed or suspected of taking up arms was 6 percent, according to a review of the public record by the New America Foundation.

Despite Obama's declarations that the "war on terror" was a construct of the past and the implication that his administration would dramatically move away from Bush's policies, the shift was more one of tone than of substance. Guantánamo did not close a year after Obama was inaugurated, as he had promised; indeed in 2011 around 175 prisoners remained incarcerated there, some fifty of whom were likely to be detained indefinitely as they were deemed too dangerous to release, yet at the same time there wasn't enough evidence to put them on trial; the some one hundred Yemenis in the jail similarly could not be released because of the lax Yemeni prison system, while the rest of the inmates would eventually face either a civilian trial or a military commission. Under pressure from New York politicians, Obama backed away from a promised trial in a federal court in Manhattan for Guantánamo's most infamous inmate: 9/11 operational commander Khalid Sheikh Mohammed. Instead, Mohammed would be tried by a military commission at Guantánamo.

There were other continuities with the Bush administration: While Obama did ban the use of the euphemistically named "Enhanced Interrogation Techniques," the practice of waterboarding had already ended in 2003 and the other coercive interrogation techniques were suspended three years later because of a ruling by the Supreme Court. And Obama dramatically increased the Bush administration policy of the targeted killing of militant leaders in Pakistan by drone strikes, while greatly expanding the war against "al-Qaeda and its allies" in neighboring Afghanistan.

Chapter 19

Obama's War

The Taliban regime is out of business, permanently.

—Vice President Dick Cheney in March 2002

[The Taliban] have a dominant influence in 11 of Afghanistan's 34 provinces.

—Admiral Mike Mullen, Chairman of the U.S. Joint Chiefs of Staff, in December 2009

On January 22, 2009, two days after his inauguration, President Obama gave a speech at the State Department declaring that Afghanistan and Pakistan were the "central front in our enduring struggle against terrorism and extremism." Of course, this was true, but few commented at the time how strange an outcome this was. After all, hadn't the Taliban been defeated in the winter of 2001? And wasn't Pakistan a close American ally in the "war on terror"?

At the State Department, Obama announced he was creating a new diplomatic post, appointing a U.S. special representative to Afghanistan and Pakistan. The special representative would be Richard C. Holbrooke, the veteran diplomat who had cajoled, charmed, and bullied the warring parties in the Balkans to make peace, at Dayton, Ohio, in 1995. His appointment was a recognition by the Obama administration that stability could not come to Afghanistan without a stable Pakistan, and vice versa, and also of how much work needed to be done in the region to end its status as the "central front" for al-Qaeda and its allies.

Just as Holbrooke was making his first official visit to the region, eight Taliban fighters carrying AK-47s and wearing explosive vests mounted simultaneous attacks on several government buildings in Kabul, including the Ministry of Justice and the Prisons Department, spraying gunfire indiscriminately and killing at least twenty. It was a particularly brazen daytime assault designed to demonstrate that the Taliban could penetrate even the most sensitive Afghan government ministries. And the attacks, which took place on February 11, 2009, just hours before Holbrooke landed in Kabul, were designed to send a message from the Taliban to the United States: We own Afghanistan. The Taliban seemed to understand instinctively that what the Pentagon termed "information operations"—that is, sending political messages—should always play a key role in their military planning.

Between the rising Taliban insurgency, the epidemic of attacks by suicide bombers, and spiraling criminal activity fueled by the drug trade, by the time Obama took office Afghanistan looked something like Iraq in the summer of 2003, when the descent into violent conflict had begun. According to a threat assessment map provided by the Afghan National Security Forces to the United Nations in April 2009, 40 percent of Afghanistan was now either under direct Taliban control or a high-risk area for insurgent attacks. These high-risk and Taliban-controlled areas were located primarily in the troubled south and east of the country, along the fifteen-hundred-mile border with Pakistan. As a former senior Afghan cabinet member explained, "If international forces leave, the Taliban will take over in one hour." A U.S. military slide of "security incidents" in Afghanistan, running the gamut from small-arms attacks to ambushes, showed that while there had been some 30 a week in 2004, that number had risen to 300 a week during the summer of 2008.

By then the Taliban had largely re-created the command structure they had before the U.S. invasion of Afghanistan in fall 2001. The new structure was headed by the "inner shura" (inner council), an eighteen-member group led by Taliban leader Mullah Omar that arrived at decisions based on consensus, but "within Omar's guidance." Those decisions were then communicated to regional shuras of up to twenty members, then to provincial shuras and the Taliban's shadow provincial governors. The Taliban had effectively created a parallel government, in competition with the Kabul government. Eleven of the thirty-four Afghan provinces had a Taliban shadow governor in 2005. By 2009 there were thirty-three.

A couple of weeks before he was inaugurated, Obama had sent his running mate, Joe Biden, to Afghanistan to get a feel for the deteriorating situation. Biden was already quite skeptical about what could be achieved there. A year earlier, in late February 2008, then-Senator Biden sat down to a formal dinner with Afghan President Hamid Karzai at the presidential place in Kabul. The subject of corruption in Afghanistan, among the worst in the world, was discussed. According to one of the dinner guests, the discussion "was just going around and around in circles and Karzai not really acknowledging the corruption issue and just sort of saying, you know, we're working on things." Biden said, "Look, I think we've come to the point where we're not getting much more out of this discussion," threw down his napkin and declared, "This dinner is over." And he and his delegation walked out of the dinner early.

A year later, in early January 2009, Biden and his top aide, Antony J. "Tony" Blinken, visited Karzai again, this time as emissaries of Obama. On their return to the States, Biden briefed Obama at their transition headquarters in Washington. Blinken recalls, "The vice president said if there's one thing I bring back to you, in terms of Afghanistan—and it's obviously intimately related to Pakistan—it's that if you ask ten of our people in Afghanistan what we're trying to accomplish, what the mission is, you'll get ten different answers. And we need strategic clarity on what we're trying to accomplish. And the president said, 'That's exactly the first thing I want to come out of this review that I'll order when we get in.'"

Tapped to do that review was Bruce Riedel, a three-decade veteran of the CIA who had played a critical role in helping to formulate South Asia policy in the Clinton administration. In 1999, Clinton, advised by Riedel, had helped to pull Pakistan and India back from the brink of what could have turned into a nuclear war over the disputed territory of Kashmir. Riedel was now retired and had no desire to go back into government: "And they asked me if I wanted to be considered for various things, and I said, 'No, I really *don't* want to go back in.' So I'm minding my own business on the thirtieth of January, and the phone rings. 'Please hold for the president.' And ten seconds later, 'Hi, Bruce, it's Barack.'"

The president asked Riedel if he would chair the Afghan review, which, given Obama's election campaign rhetoric about the importance of the war in Afghanistan, was the most predictable foreign policy challenge of his young presidency. Riedel remembers asking, "Can I talk to my wife?" The president replied, "Smart move." "And I immediately knew I was cornered," Riedel recalls. "But he came up with this idea of a sixty-day review. And there was logic to the sixty days; it wasn't arbitrary. He had to be in Strasbourg on the third of April for the NATO Sixtieth Anniversary Summit, and he had to have an Afghanistan/Pakistan strategy by then." Also driving the pace of the review was the upcoming Afghan presidential election scheduled for the summer of 2009, which necessitated the deployment of more troops to protect polling stations. At the same time the Taliban were also gaining momentum, which needed to be blunted if that election were to be held safely.

Key members of Riedel's team on the review included Holbrooke; General David Petraeus; Michèle Flournoy, the number-three official at the Pentagon and the highest ranking female ever at the Defense Department; Lieutenant General Douglas Lute, the Afghan "war czar" in the Bush administration who had been held over in that job; and Tony Blinken. Riedel recalls there was largely a consensus in the group: "People agreed on the threat: al-Qaeda; that al-Qaeda and the Taliban are closely linked; not a monolith, but closely linked, and unlikely to delink when they think they're winning; delinkable if they think they're losing, maybe, but not when they think they're winning; that the war in Afghanistan is going very, very poorly."

But most of the participants in the review also believed that Afghanistan could be turned around because the marked deterioration in security was largely confined to the south and east of the country, home to most of the country's Pashtun ethnic group, which makes up about half of the Afghan population. Riedel said that provided an important basis for hope: "Because not all Pashtuns are Taliban, either. So the population the Taliban can work with is probably less than a quarter, maybe less than a fifth of the population. Now, they can intimidate and terrorize more, but they're not going to recruit from a broader audience."

This calculation had an important impact on the discussion of overall troop numbers in Afghanistan. Classic counterinsurgency doctrine indicated that to stabilize Afghanistan you needed a ratio of one member of the security forces to every twenty of the population, and that would dictate you needed some 600,000 soldiers and policemen given the Afghan population of 30 million. But an insurgency largely confined to the south and east of the country suggested a lower number of security forces could work. Petraeus, the leading American practitioner and theorist of counterinsurgency, made the point that the number of forces needed to stabilize Afghanistan was in fact closer to 300,000, a figure that seemed relatively doable given that at the time the Afghan army and police numbered some 150,000 men and the U.S./NATO contingent was already around 50,000 strong, supplemented by a force of around 12,000 additional American soldiers that Bush had ordered deployed there in the last months of his second term.

Vice President Biden was a strong outlier from this consensus. Riedel recalls, "He had real doubts that Afghanistan can be stabilized; much gloomier appraisal of the prospects to stabilize Afghanistan. But second and I think much more important to the vice president, very gloomy about the prospects for sustaining domestic political support for the war, and especially Democrats' political support for the war. And in that case, I think he read the tea leaves better than almost anyone else."

Biden favored an approach that emphasized the use of American drones and U.S. Special Forces to take on al-Qaeda and its Taliban allies and eschewed any large-scale ramp-up of U.S. troops and counterinsurgency efforts. Riedel recalls, "The killer argument against his approach, in political terms, is—Well, that's what Bush and Cheney did. [The vice president was] much more a naysayer on this than someone who had a viable alternative. And that's why, at the end of the day, the president was not swayed by that argument."

For Obama's key political advisers—David Axelrod; his chief of staff, Rahm Emanuel; and Biden—the ghost hovering over the discussion of any ramping-up of the Afghan war effort was that of Lyndon Johnson, who had destroyed his presidency as he expanded the American involvement in Vietnam. Riedel recalls, "They are just very, very mindful that a Democratic president with big ideas for domestic change can see all of that destroyed in a war in Asia that destroys the party in the process. . . . Biden does not want to be the Hubert Humphrey. He doesn't want to be the guy who went along with something which he profoundly disagreed with, but he went along with it because he was a loyal supporter of the president."

But was Afghanistan really likely to be a rerun of Vietnam? Hardly. The similarities between the Taliban and the Viet Cong ended with their mutual hostility toward the U.S. military. Although the Taliban had roughly quadrupled in size between 2006 and 2009, still the some twenty-five thousand Taliban full-time fighters were too few to hold even small Afghan towns, let alone mount a Tet-style offensive on Kabul. As a military force, they were armed lightly enough to constitute a significant tactical problem, not a strategic threat. By contrast, the Viet Cong and North Vietnamese army at the height of the Vietnam War numbered more than half a million men, were equipped with artillery and tanks, and were well supplied by both the Soviet Union and Mao's China. And the scale of casualties in Afghanistan was orders of magnitude smaller than in Vietnam. One hundred and fifty-four American soldiers died in 2008 in Afghanistan, the largest number since the fall of the Taliban. In 1968, the deadliest year of the Vietnam conflict, the same number of U.S. servicemen were dying *every four days.*

One participant in the Riedel review recalls that early on in the process, "the military came in and said look, we really need to get more troops in now, kind of in a holding pattern because we're losing ground and we need to make sure that we stop losing ground while we think about the longer-term strategy. And we need to secure the elections better than we can secure them with the forces we have in place now." So Obama agreed to send in 21,000 more soldiers in addition to the some 12,000 that President Bush had already ordered in at the end of his administration but hadn't yet arrived in-country. The net result was that there would be around 33,000 additional American forces going into Afghanistan in 2009 from January to the summer, so doubling the U.S. military presence there.

While agreeing to the significant troop increases, Obama told his national security team, "I want to see the impact of that; I want to constantly assess where we are, and the critical assessment point will be the Afghan elections, because we're doing some of this to secure the elections. Let's see where we are then and let's make sure that the strategy is appropriately on target."

On March 19, five weeks into the review, Riedel sat down with Obama on Air Force One on the long flight to California, where the president would later appear as a guest of Jay Leno's on *The Tonight Show*. During the trip Obama asked Riedel, "Is it sustainable to really send more American troops. What assurance is there that that's going to turn things around?" Riedel's reply was blunt: "There's no guarantee. This has a chance of success; the alternatives are worse. And I am firmly of the view that you should have a pretty good idea if it's working in eighteen to twenty-four months. . . . It's either going to work, or all those statistical indicators that are going bad, will just keep going bad. And if that happens, then the patient arrived on Mr. Obama's doorstep, dead on arrival. And a brave attempt to resuscitate it hasn't produced. But I think you're better off having tried to see if you can revive the patient, than to just give up right now.'"

On March 27, as the Riedel review debuted publicly, Obama announced that the goal of his campaign in South Asia was "to disrupt, dismantle, and defeat al-Qaeda in Pakistan and Afghanistan, and to prevent their return to either country in the future." Few could quibble with that goal, but the Riedel review would set the stage for another eight months of wrangling about how best to achieve it. Recommendation number one of the Riedel review was a fully resourced counterinsurgency campaign in south and eastern Afghanistan, but the likely costs to implement such a campaign, in particular the sizable number of American boots on the ground needed to execute it, were poorly understood by key players in the administration, which was by now only two months old.

As a result of the Riedel review, Obama announced he would aim to modestly improve the size and professionalism of Afghanistan's police force, and nearly double the ranks of the Afghan army over the next two years. To help train those Afghan security services, Obama ordered to Afghanistan some four thousand trainers from the 82nd Airborne.

President Obama had now made Afghanistan a defining element of his foreign policy, and just as Iraq became "Bush's war," so the conflict that now embroiled both Afghanistan and Pakistan was "Obama's war." This caused consternation among some in the Democratic Party. On May 14, 2009, fifty-one House Democrats voted against continued funding for the Afghan War. Around the same time, David Obey, the chairman of the powerful House Appropriations Committee, which helps determine federal spending, said the White House had to show concrete results in Afghanistan within a year, implying that if it didn't do so he would move to turn off the money spigot. It wasn't just politicians who were souring on the Afghan War. A March 2009 *USA Today* poll found that 41 percent of Americans believed the war was a mistake, up from only 6 percent in 2002. American opposition to the Afghan War rose to 57 percent five months later. The media only added to the gloom and doom. *Newsweek* ran a cover story speculating that Afghanistan could be Obama's Vietnam. And the *New York Times* ran prominent opinion pieces with headlines like "The 'Good War' Isn't Worth Fighting" and "Fearing Another Quagmire in Afghanistan."

But the growing skepticism about Obama's chances for success in Afghanistan were largely based on some deep misreadings of both the country's history and the views of its people, which were often compounded by facile comparisons to the United States' misadventures of past decades in Southeast Asia and the Middle East. Afghanistan would not be Obama's Vietnam, nor would it be his Iraq, although it could be his Afghanistan.

Objections to Obama's ramp-up in Afghanistan began with the observation that Afghanistan has long been the "graveyard of empires": as went the disastrous British expedition there in 1842 and the Soviet invasion in 1979, so too the current American occupation was doomed to follow. In fact, any number of empire builders, from Alexander the Great to the Mogul emperor Babur in the sixteenth century to the British in the successful Second Afghan War three decades after their infamous defeat there, have won military victories in Afghanistan. The graveyard-of-empires metaphor belonged in the graveyard of clichés.

More importantly, Afghans had generally embraced international forces after the fall of the Taliban. In a 2005 poll by BBC/ABC, eight out of ten Afghans expressed a favorable opinion of the United States and the same number supported foreign soldiers in their country. Contrast that with Iraq, where BBC/ABC also polled the same year and found that less than one in five Iraqis supported international forces in their country. While the same poll taken in Afghanistan in 2009 found, for the first time, that just under half of Afghans had a favorable view of the United States, that was still a higher approval rating than the United States received in any other Muslim-majority country save Lebanon. And a solid majority of Afghans continued to approve of the international forces in their country. What Afghans wanted was not for American and other foreign soldiers to leave, but rather to deliver on their promises of helping to midwife a more secure and prosperous country.

A corollary to the argument that Afghanistan was unconquerable was the argument that it was ungovernable: that the country has never been a functioning nation-state, that its people, mired in a culture of violence not amenable to Western fixes, had no interest in helping to build a more open, peaceful society. Certainly endemic low-level warfare is embedded in Pashtun society, but the level of violence in Afghanistan was actually far lower than most Americans believed. In 2008 more than two thousand Afghan civilians had died at the hands of the Taliban or coalition forces out of a population of 30 million—that was too many, but it was also less than a fourth as many as had died the year before in Iraq, which is both more sparsely populated and often assumed to be easier to govern. At the height of the violence in Iraq, some three thousand civilians were dying *every month*, making the country around twenty times more violent than Afghanistan was as Obama assumed control of the war.

An assertion that deserved a similarly hard look was that nation building in Afghanistan was doomed because the country wasn't a nation-state, but rather a jerry-rigged patchwork of competing tribal groupings. In fact, Afghanistan is a much older nation-state than, say, Italy or Germany, both of which were only unified in the late nineteenth century. Modern Afghanistan is considered to have emerged with the first Afghan empire under Ahmad Shah Durrani in 1747—it has been a nation for decades longer than the United States, and Afghans have an accordingly strong sense of nationhood. What they have had just as long, however, is a weak central state. The last king of Afghanistan, for instance, Zahir Shah, who reigned from 1933 to 1973, presided lightly over a country that Afghans recall with great nostalgia as a time of relative peace and prosperity.

Skeptics of Obama's Afghanistan policy said that the right approach to the country was either to reduce American commitments there or just get out entirely. The short explanation of why this wouldn't work is that the United States had tried this already. Twice. In 1989, after the most successful covert program in the history of the CIA helped to defeat the Soviets in Afghanistan, the George H. W. Bush administration closed the U.S. embassy in Kabul. The Clinton administration then effectively zeroed out aid to one of the poorest countries in the world. Out of the chaos of the Afghan civil war in the early 1990s emerged the Taliban, who then gave sanctuary to al-Qaeda. In 2001, the next Bush administration returned to topple the Taliban, but its ideological aversion to nation building ensured that Afghanistan was the least resourced per-capita reconstruction effort the U.S. has engaged in since World War II. An indication of how desultory those efforts were was the puny size of the Afghan army, which two years after the fall of the Taliban numbered only six thousand men.

America got what it paid for with this Afghanistan-on-the-cheap approach: as we have seen, after 2001 the Taliban reemerged, this time fused ideologically and tactically with al-Qaeda, and the new Taliban adopted wholesale al-Qaeda's Iraq playbook of suicide attacks, IED operations, hostage beheadings, and an aggressive video-based information campaign.

At the end of March 2009 the Pentagon was tasked to develop an operational plan to implement the fully resourced counterinsurgency campaign envisioned by the Riedel review, a task that fell to General David McKiernan. The commander of the land war in Iraq that had toppled Saddam Hussein's regime in only three weeks in the spring of 2003, McKiernan was now the commander in Afghanistan. But his immediate bosses, Secretary of Defense Robert Gates, Chairman of the Joint Chiefs Admiral Mike Mullen, and CENTCOM commander General David Petraeus, had grown increasingly concerned that he was not up to the complex job of managing a successful counterinsurgency campaign. They decided to replace him with General Stanley McChrystal, a commander who had distinguished himself running Special Operations in Iraq and had presided over the hunt for Abu Musab al-Zarqawi, al-Qaeda's leader there. Petraeus remembers, "It was a very close-hold decision; it was basically three people." Just as Gates had told General George Casey in Iraq two years earlier that he was being replaced early in his tour by Petraeus, so now the secretary of defense went to Kabul to tell McKiernan that his tour was over. Gates announced that McKiernan was retiring on May 11. This was widely portrayed as the first time that an American theater commander had been fired since President Truman had sacked General Douglas MacArthur during the Korean War, but in truth Casey had also been relieved of his job, albeit in a far more graceful fashion than was the case with McKiernan.

Removing McKiernan had important consequences because instead of an operational plan for the new counterinsurgency strategy going to the White House in June, the campaign plan would now be given to McChrystal to write, thus delaying its arrival until late August. "During those three months, the bottom fell out of the Democratic Party's support for the war," recalls Riedel.

To write the assessment of the situation on the ground that would provide the basis for his campaign plan, McChrystal assembled a dozen outside civilian academics and think tank staffers to help him. Stephen Biddle, of the Council on Foreign Relations, who had worked with Petraeus in Iraq, was one of those summoned to Kabul on short notice in early June 2009 to work on the assessment, which had to be finished in two months. Biddle recalls McChrystal as being surprisingly open to dissent for a senior general: "It's very unusual to have an officer who's already been assigned this mission asking a dozen outsiders to tell him if his mission could be achieved or not. What would have happened if we'd said no?"

Another of the civilian advisers recruited by McChrystal was former army captain Andrew Exum, a veteran of the Afghan War, who now worked at the

Washington think tank Center for a New American Security, which served as something of a farm team for key members of Obama's national security apparatus. Exum recalls that American intelligence about what was really going on in Afghanistan was quite poor. "I think what shocked me is that I first went there in 2002, and I don't think we really knew that much more about Afghanistan in June of 2009 than we did back then."

The neoconservative military historian Fred Kagan, who had helped shape the debate in Washington about the "surge" in Iraq, was also tapped for the McChrystal assessment, as was his wife, Kimberly Kagan, similarly a military historian. They saw their mission as taking a hard look at the available intelligence on the Taliban's capabilities and strategy. Kagan says, "The take in the theater was 'They don't have a plan—no terrain is more important than any other piece of terrain.' And this is what drove us crazy. Because you're describing a group such as has never existed. I've taught many, many cases of counterinsurgency, from the Boers to the American Revolutionaries. . . . I've never heard of a group that had no plan. So we spent a lot of time trying to figure out, what's their plan? And one of the things that emerged from that was the importance, the centrality of Kandahar." The Kagans also concluded that the Taliban were effectively the government in Kandahar province: "They've got provincial shadow governors, district shadow subgovernors for every district, they've got sharia courts. . . . We were going to wake up one day and discover that the Taliban controlled Kandahar."

That Kandahar was the key to the Taliban's strategy was not surprising. The Taliban movement had first emerged in Kandahar in 1994, it was the traditional capital of the Pashtuns, and it was also the largest city in southern Afghanistan. Yet the main American effort in the summer of 2009 was in the neighboring province of Helmand, where ten thousand Marines had begun to be deployed in July. This was akin to trying to end World War II by attacking Austria but not Germany. In counterinsurgency doctrine "protecting the population" is the key to success, yet in Helmand there wasn't much of a population to protect. In the southern half of Helmand lived less than 1 percent of the Afghan population. One senior U.S. official recalls, "So you've got car bombs going off in Kandahar, but Nawa and Garmsir districts of Southern Helmand have ten thousand fucking Marines in them. . . . We sent [them] to the place which was only very marginally important—very minimally important. So that was a huge fucking mistake." That mistake had been grandfathered into the system because the two commanding generals in Afghanistan in 2008, Dan McNeill and later David McKiernan, had already signed off on the deployment of the Marines to Helmand.

There was, however, some logic to that decision because while Helmand might not have been the strategic prize that Kandahar was for the Taliban, it certainly was their bank. If Helmand were a country, by 2009 it would have been the world's leading producer of opium and its derivative, heroin. More than half the world's heroin originated there—much of it destined for the veins of junkies living in Europe. And money from that drug trade helped support the Taliban, who used it to help fund their operations. According to a threat assessment by the Afghan army in April 2009, Helmand had the highest percentage of territory controlled by the Taliban of any of the country's thirty-four provinces. Nearly 60 percent of Helmand in April was fully Taliban-controlled, and the remainder was classified as "high risk" for Taliban attacks.

In early July 2009, some 4,500 U.S. Marines and hundreds of Afghan soldiers launched offensives against the Taliban in Helmand and, according to a senior U.S. Marine officer, three months later the Taliban were "on their ass, literally." The officer claimed that of the thirteen districts in Helmand, only one was now fully controlled by the Taliban.

During the summer of 2009, in Nawa district, in central Helmand, Marines living at Camp Jaker, a dusty, spartan base with no electricity or running water, ventured out on several-hour foot patrols. They moved through canal-fed cornfields armed with metal detectors and a bomb-sniffing dog looking to discover and disable IEDs. The IEDs ranged from simple victim-operated bombs, typically pressure-plate devices made from wood and springs, to more complex devices that were remotely detonated using a command wire. The corn rows standing ten feet high provided ideal cover in which the IED triggermen could hide. An astonishing 80 percent of the U.S. casualties in Helmand were caused by IEDs. Improvised explosives did for the Taliban what surface-to-air missiles once did for the Afghan mujahideen fighting the Soviets—somewhat equalizing the fight against a superpower.

At the end of August, a few weeks after the Marines had deployed in force into Helmand, the McChrystal assessment arrived on Secretary of Defense Robert Gates's desk. The assessment made a number of key points—that the situation in Afghanistan was "serious," that the Taliban, as the Kagans had described, were running a de facto government in southern Afghanistan with shadow governors, sharia courts, tax collectors, and even Taliban ombudsmen to handle the complaints of the population, and that their key objectives were the control of Kandahar and Khost provinces in southeastern Afghanistan. To reverse this McChrystal recommended a "comprehensive counterinsurgency campaign" to be achieved by protecting key population centers and main roads and doubling the size of the Afghan army and police. McChrystal also pointed out that "resources will not win the war, but under-resourcing could lose it." Translation: *We need significantly more troops or we will lose this war.*

Three weeks later, as is the Washington way, the closely held assessment landed on the front page of the *Washington Post* under the byline of Bob Woodward and the unambiguous headline "McChrystal: More Forces or 'Mission Failure.'" The public airing of McChrystal's dire assessment did not come at a propitious moment for the Obama administration. A month earlier, on August 20, Afghans had gone to the polls for the first time in five years to elect their new president. The election was marred not so much by predictable Taliban violence, but rather by low turnout and by multiple and credible allegations of serious election day fraud, in particular by supporters of the incumbent president, Hamid Karzai.

The flawed election of Karzai and the pervasive corruption of his government raised serious questions connected to a key aspect of counterinsurgency doctrine: Was there a legitimate Afghan government for the United States to support? The day after the election, Richard Holbrooke met with Karzai and over a meal the American envoy asked, "Mr. President, supposing no one gets fifty percent in the first round?" Karzai became quite agitated, saying, "That's not possible. I know how the people voted. I know that I got fifty-three, fifty-four percent." Holbrooke replied, "OK, congratulations—but supposing you didn't? You need a fair election according to your own procedures. If no one gets fifty percent, it calls for a runoff."

Karzai was not happy about this exchange and over the next weeks he continued to insist he had won the election, and denied the charges of fraud, but a panel of experts appointed by the United Nations issued findings in October showing that fraud was in fact so widespread that almost a quarter of all the votes had to be thrown out and as a result Karzai had not won the 50 percent of the vote he needed to be declared the winner.

On September 13, 2009, President Obama convened the first meeting of his war cabinet to develop a strategy to stabilize Afghanistan and reverse the gains that the Taliban had made during the past several years. The meetings took place in the White House Situation Room, a basement conference room whose walls are lined with digital clocks showing the time in Baghdad and Kabul, one end of which is dominated by large flat-screen TVs connected to secure video links. It was in this same room eight years ago to the day that President Bush had first been briefed about the CIA plans to overthrow the Taliban.

Obama's Afghanistan review process is reconstructed here based on interviews with several of the participants. Unlike the earlier Riedel review, which was largely conducted at the subcabinet level, this review involved Obama's top national security officials and his key political advisers in all of its phases. The first couple of sessions of the ten-week review focused on three foundational questions: the exact nature of the relationship between al-Qaeda and the Taliban, the relationship between events in Afghanistan and those in Pakistan, and what was actually achievable in Afghanistan. One senior administration official attending recalls, "A lot of the assumptions and premises that everyone brought to the table were kind of exploded like a piñata with a baseball bat. . . . A number of us thought that it was not at all a given that if the Taliban were to reemerge in a more significant way in Afghanistan, that al-Qaeda would necessarily follow."

In short, wouldn't the Taliban change their tune if they returned to power in some form? Wouldn't Mullah Omar and his allies become deterrable in the same way that leaders of most other states are deterrable—and realize it was in their interest to drop al-Qaeda? It was impossible to know for sure, but the last time the Taliban had controlled a state, they were not so interested in realpolitik; after September 11, the group made clear that it was prepared to lose everything (and it did) rather than betray bin Laden. And since then, the Taliban's leadership had grown more closely aligned with al-Qaeda's ideology and tactics—not less.

Another key discussion at the White House centered on Pakistan. Vice President Biden often made the point, "We have al-Qaeda Central in Pakistan, nuclear weapons in Pakistan, the Afghan Taliban leadership's in Pakistan, and yet our resourcing is thirty to one in favor of Afghanistan over Pakistan. Does that make strategic sense? Obviously, there are good reasons why it's thirty to one. We have sixty-eight thousand troops there; they cost a lot of money. That's fine, but do we need to think more over time whether sustaining that ratio makes sense." (Biden, along with Republican Senator Richard Lugar, had long pushed for legislation that funneled American aid more directly to Pakistani civilian institutions rather than to the military, the recipient of the lion's share of U.S. aid during the Bush administration.)

But there were real limits about what the United States could do in Pakistan. Obviously the United States could not go to war with a country which hadn't attacked America, possessed nuclear weapons and a half-million-man army, and was deeply opposed to any American boots on the ground. But just because the United States couldn't send ground forces into Pakistan was not an argument for scaling back in Afghanistan. It was into the vacuum caused by Afghanistan's civil war in the mid-1990s that militants with deep roots in Pakistan such as the leaders of the Taliban, many of whom were educated in Pakistani madrassas, and al-Qaeda itself, had expanded.

On October 1, the day after the second Afghan review meeting, McChrystal gave a speech in London at the International Institute for Strategic Studies, a leading think tank. During his speech and in the course of the Q&A with the audience, McChrystal made it clear that he believed that a policy in Afghanistan that focused largely on counterterrorism, the vice president's preferred option, would lead to failure there, instead it required a full-blown counterinsurgency campaign. While this was in line with the conclusion of the Riedel review, McChrystal had by then already participated in two meetings with Obama's war cabinet in which considerable skepticism had been voiced about the need for a large-scale counterinsurgency campaign. The uniformed military now seemed to be staking out a hard position publicly ahead of the conclusion of the formal Afghanistan review by Obama. (Nine months later, following the publication of an article in *Rolling Stone* in which McChrystal and his aides made disparaging remarks about Biden and other civilian leaders, he was forced to retire.)

On October 7, during the third Afghan review meeting, McChrystal explained over his video link to the Situation Room that his counterinsurgency strategy depended on securing key infrastructure such as the Ring Road around Afghanistan and important cities such as Kandahar. A participant recalled that the reaction to this in the room was "Well, that all sounds kind of reasonable."

There was another White House meeting on October 9, in which the mood dramatically shifted after McChrystal presented what this counterinsurgency campaign would cost to execute. McChrystal explained the thinking that had gone into his "force options paper," which presented three options for additional troop deployments to Afghanistan; on the low end he requested 11,000 soldiers who would act only as trainers for the Afghan army and police, in the midrange he asked for 40,000 additional soldiers, and at the high end an additional 80,000 troops. According to a senior military officer the low-end and high-end options were both seen by the Pentagon as "throwaways," since not much could be done in Afghanistan with just a cadre of new trainers, while the 80,000 number was recognized to be a political impossibility.

During the Situation Room meeting McChrystal advocated the middle 40,000 option and elaborated that "I'm actually looking for American troops here; I'm not really interested in allied troops. And in my estimate, we'll know if this is working in 2013. And in the course of doing this, we need to build an Afghan national security force of 400,000. And the building of that ANSF will be about $10–12 billion a year for five years."

Since the beginning of 2009, 33,000 additional American troops had already poured into Afghanistan and now the military was asking for 40,000 *more*. This provoked a case of severe sticker shock in the Situation Room. One of the participants recalls: "In the course of '09, we doubled the number of American troops on the ground in Afghanistan. And at the very tail end of that, we got McChrystal, who said, 'Oh, that was a down payment, OK' . . . One comeback was—'Wait a second, what happened to the 33,000 we sent you this year? Where are those fuckers?' "

Another problem with McChrystal's troop request was that he envisaged those additional 40,000 U.S. soldiers to be on the ground through 2013. A quick back-of-the-envelope calculation showed that was going to cost $160 billion in addition to the $55 billion a year the Afghan operation was already consuming. The reaction around the Situation Room to this was quite negative, with a number of officials saying versions of "Given the other priorities of the administration, we're not going to go to 100,000 Americans in Afghanistan all through this term and into the next term—all through the 2012 election season, no end in sight."

A White House official said a further problem with the McChrystal plan was the cost of doubling the size of the Afghan army and police—at a cost of up to $60 billion—something that America could ill afford at a time of economic crisis and that also conflicted with other Obama priorities such as extending health-care coverage. And, in any event, it was well known at the White House that the Afghan security services were quite weak. A 2008 report from the U.S. Government Accountability Office had found that $10 billion had *already* been spent to develop the Afghan army, yet only two of its

105 units were fully capable of operating, and a further $6 billion had been spent on the Afghan police and none of its units were fully capable of operating. A White House official recalls, "There was a whole debate about whether it was necessary or even possible to double the size of the Afghan security forces. . . . The conclusion of our review was that no, that wasn't necessary and it might not be possible."

The sum result of the McChrystal presentation about how much a full-blown counterinsurgency campaign would cost was a reevaluation of whether such a strategy was really necessary anyway, something the Riedel review had not considered in any detail. "There was a general assessment that Riedel had done a bit of a rush job and, gosh, you know, we should have done this in the spring," recalls one national security official advising Obama. Another political appointee says, "The idea of a nationwide nation-building effort seemed to be beyond our capacity, both in terms of the drain on military resources, economic resources, and then third—less important, but nonetheless real—political capital was included. Would we be able to sustain that?"

Simultaneously, senior military officers came to realize that the Obama administration would not simply rubber-stamp their requests for large-scale ramp-ups in troops and resources that would then go on for more than four years. One national security official says, "There was a point where the Defense Department realized that there had been an election in November of '08. This is not the [era of] 'Just tell us what you need; you're going to get it.' And there was a real 'ah-ha' moment that this was going to be a two-way street between what was requested and what was provided. And once that soaked in—and it wasn't immediate, because remember who you've got around the table: you've got McChrystal, who got everything he ever wanted as the JSOC [Joint Special Operations Command] commander; you've got Petraeus, who got everything he ever asked for—and they're sort of saying, 'Hey look, we don't understand what the problem is: We're the military. We're all together on this. We're telling you what this is going to take. We kind of expect you to deliver it.'"

One official says Obama's national security advisor, James Jones, a former U.S. Marine four-star general, was "the most effective intermediary because of his links back into the Pentagon. So he was able to go back to [Chairman of the Joint Chiefs] Mullen, for example, and Gates and Petraeus, and say 'Look, you know, I've got all this, but it's not in the cards, guys.'"

The real costs of a full-scale counterinsurgency campaign in terms of blood and treasure prompted a narrowing of the focus of the American effort in Afghanistan. The key question became: Was it really necessary to "defeat" the Taliban? "Several folks argued, including Biden, that it was neither possible nor necessary to defeat the Taliban . . . They were going to be part of the fabric of Afghan society, whether we liked it or not," recalls one White House official.

Another official says, "The president led us to the conclusion that even the Riedel objective, which was intended to be circumscribed, and constrained and focused on al-Qaeda, was not. And there was this sort of 'ah-ha' moment that we had really bitten off more than we needed to chew and probably could chew, with regard to defeating the Taliban, and that was central. Now, once you got past that, all sorts of things open up. So now, reintegration, reconciliation, a political settlement of some sort, a counterinsurgency that's limited in scale, and scope and duration—all those things start kicking in, because you no longer have to defeat them; you just have to degrade them to a point where they can't take over Kandahar, and Kabul."

During these discussions, Obama, the former law professor, did not show his hand but rather asked focused questions throughout, synthesizing the debates at the end of each meeting by saying, "OK, here's what I've taken out of this."

Outside the White House, the deliberative pace of the Afghan review was drawing fire. On October 22, former vice president Cheney charged in a speech that "the White House must stop dithering while America's armed forces are in danger." This was, of course, quite rich coming from the number-two official of the administration that had shortchanged Afghanistan for most of the eight years that it was in office.

October was also the deadliest month of the war so far for American troops; fifty-nine had died. On October 29, Obama visited Dover Air Force Base in Delaware late at night with a small group of journalists to salute eighteen American servicemen and Drug Enforcement Administration officials who had recently been killed and whose bodies were coming home for burial. Obama's visit to Dover signaled that the rising death toll in Afghanistan was going to play an important part in his calculations about what he planned to do there. On the forty-five-minute helicopter ride home to the White House, the normally affable president was silent.

If one ghost hovering over the discussion of Afghanistan was that of Vietnam, another ghost was that of the Iraq "surge," which had been opposed by many of the officials presiding over the Afghan review, including the president himself, the vice president, and Secretary of State Hillary Clinton. Of course, the surge in Iraq had succeeded for a number of reasons, including the Sunni Awakening, but Obama, who had never publicly conceded that he had been wrong about the Iraq surge, ironically now used its success as an important way of informing his way forward in Afghanistan. A national security official recalls, "He admitted inside the Situation Room that 'look, basically [the Iraq surge] worked. Now, we're not going to settle, today, why it worked.' . . . And there was the laughter around the table [and someone said] 'OK, Mr. President, we're just going to leave that where it is.'"

On November 11, Obama examined what the military had named "Option 2A" for the deployment of new troops to Afghanistan. The 2A schedule would take a year and a half to get all the additional troops into place. Obama was annoyed when he saw the chart describing this option, saying, "I don't know how we can describe this as a surge."

Obama jokingly quizzed General McChrystal about the leisurely pace of this new deployment, saying, "Wait a second, Stan. You know, I read your assessment in the *Washington Post*. I had my own version but I could have read it in the *Post*. And you paint a very urgent picture here. So OK, how does that urgent picture get addressed by deploying troops deliberately over eighteen months?" Obama turned to General Petraeus, telling him he was "looking for a surge" and peppering him with questions about how he had implemented the surge in Iraq: "How fast did we get them in? How many were there? How long? How long did they stay before we started thinning them out?"

Obama was looking not only for a surge into Afghanistan but also for a deployment that pulled the soldiers of the surge out far faster than the 2013 pullout envisaged by his senior military officers. Secretary of Defense Robert Gates came up with a compromise, saying, "We propose to surge troops for eighteen to twenty-four months and then we can begin to come down," which translated into a withdrawal date for at least some of the surge troops in July 2011.

While a target withdrawal date could send a message of lack of resolve to the Taliban, it also provided an important signal to both the American domestic audience and to the Afghan government that the large U.S. troop commitment would not run on for many years into the future. "Obama, at the end of the day, thought it was more important to light a fire for the Afghans as well as to demonstrate to our own people this was not an open-ended thing. That weighed more heavily than any risk in sending a message to the Taliban, that it could wait us out," says a national security official.

The July 2011 withdrawal date also papered over the real policy differences that continued to exist between senior officers in the Pentagon and top White House officials about what the ideal length of the Afghan deployment should be. Both sides could take from the July 2011 date that they had won the battle: for the Pentagon the important point about the timing of the withdrawal was that it would be "conditions based," which meant that the drawdown could be relatively token if, as seemed likely, conditions in Afghanistan continued to be largely insecure, while White House officials could point to a date certain for a real withdrawal.

During the course of the review an important signal of growing American impatience with his government had been sent to Karzai: that he had to abide by the electoral laws of his own country. When the votes in the August presidential election were finally tallied Karzai had only 49 percent, just under the 50 percent he needed to be declared the outright winner, which meant that under the Afghan constitution he had to go to a runoff election with his main challenger, the former foreign minister Dr. Abdullah. Karzai refused to do this, which added to the aura of illegitimacy that now surrounded his government. As Holbrooke recalls, the stakes were quite high if Karzai refused to accept a constitutionally mandated runoff: "It would turn him from a legitimately elected leader to a man whose tenure in office was so tainted by the refusal to follow procedures he had sworn to uphold, that we would have had a constitutional political crisis which could have ended or destroyed our venture in Kabul."

Over several days in late October, Senator John Kerry, the head of the powerful Senate Foreign Relations Committee, met with Karzai in Kabul for twenty bruising hours of talks. Kerry recalls, "I think we were able to work through things in constructive ways so that he felt comfortable that I was helping to guarantee a structure for a second round [of elections] that wouldn't be artificial; that wouldn't be a trumped-up, 'Remove Karzai' initiative." Finally Karzai acceded to the American pressure and agreed to the runoff, which in any event his challenger Dr. Abdullah had never had the votes to win. Recognizing that fact, Dr. Abdullah announced he was standing down on November 1, leaving Karzai the legitimate winner of the presidential election.

Five days later, U.S. ambassador Karl Eikenberry filed the first of two stinging cables to his boss, Hillary Clinton, and the rest of the participants in the review. The first described Karzai as "not an adequate strategic partner" and raised serious questions about the abilities of the Afghan army and police to grow in size and efficacy. In his next cable, Eikenberry poured considerable cold water on McChrystal's counterinsurgency plan, which he pointed out was not matched by a similar effort on the civilian side, and would cost a great deal, while it had scant chance of success if the Taliban continued to have a safe haven in Pakistan. Eikenberry's cable came as a surprise to the military, especially to McChrystal and his staff, who typically met with Eikenberry three times a week. The broad outlines of Eikenberry's dissents, of course, quickly leaked.

Meetings of the Obama national security team continued through November, yet the participants remained unsure where the president would finally come down. In the penultimate meeting, on November 23, Hillary Clinton, a vocal opponent of the surge in Iraq, sided with the military and was the most forceful advocate in the room for a substantial troop increase. The final meeting took place on Sunday, November 29. Obama appears to have made his decision the day before. As dusk fell Obama gathered Gates, Mullen, Petraeus, Jones, and Rahm Emanuel in the Oval Office to tell them that his mind was made up: he would be sending 30,000 more troops, asking NATO for at least 5,000 more; a review of the strategy would take place in December 2010; and at least some of the troops would be coming home in July 2011. From there Obama went to the Situation Room, where he had a videoconference with General McChrystal and Ambassador Eikenberry, who would be responsible for implementing the new strategy.

Why did the alternative offered by the Obama administration, committing large numbers of boots on the ground and significant sums of money to Afghanistan, have a better chance of success than the policies of Bush there? In part, because the Afghan people—the center of gravity in a counterinsurgency—were rooting for the Taliban to lose. BBC/ABC countrywide polling found that in 2009, 58 percent of Afghans named the Taliban—whom only 7 percent of Afghans viewed favorably—as the greatest threat to their nation. There was nothing quite like living under Taliban rule to convince one that their promises of creating a seventh-century utopia here on earth were fantasies. And the same poll found that an astonishing 63 percent of Afghans continued to have a favorable view of the U.S. military even eight years after the fall of the Taliban. (To those who say you just can't trust polls in Afghanistan, it's worth noting that the same organizations that commissioned polls in Afghanistan also did so in neighboring Pakistan, which was consistently found to be one of the most anti-American countries in the world.)

By early 2010, 70 percent of Afghans said their country was going in the right direction. Considering Afghanistan's rampant drug trade, pervasive corruption, and rising violence, this seemed counterintuitive—until you recalled that no country in the world had ever suffered Afghanistan's combination of an invasion and occupation by a totalitarian regime followed by a civil war, with subsequent "government" by warlords and then the neo-medieval misrule of the Taliban. In other words, the bar was pretty low. No Afghan was expecting that the country would turn into, say, Belgium, but there was an expectation that Afghanistan could be returned to the somewhat secure condition it had enjoyed in the 1970s before the Soviet invasion, and that the country would be able to grow its way out of being simply a subsistence agricultural economy.

There was one potential skunk at this garden party, and it was a rather large one: Afghanistan's nuclear-armed, al-Qaeda- and Taliban-headquartering neighbor to the east. The Pakistani dimension of Obama's "Af-Pak" strategy was his critics' most reasonable objection to his plans for the region. It was difficult for the United States to have an effective strategy for Pakistan if *Pakistan* didn't have an effective strategy for Pakistan.

Pakistan had also long stirred the pot in Afghanistan by supporting elements of the Taliban, in particular the Haqqani Network, which was paid by the Pakistanis to conduct operations against Indian targets in Afghanistan, including the bombings of the Indian embassy in Kabul in 2008 and 2009. That was compounded by the fact that the so-called Afghan Taliban continued to be headquartered in Pakistan, particularly in and around the western city of Quetta.

The most worrisome development in Pakistan as Obama assumed office was the gradual Talibanization of Swat, a northern region of lakes and mountains that had been one of the country's premier tourist attractions. In February 2009 the provincial government did a deal with the Taliban leader in Swat, Maulana Fazlullah (in his previous life a ski-lift operator), which allowed his self-styled religious warriors to impose their version of sharia law on the region's inhabitants. As they had with other "peace" deals, the Taliban took the agreement as an opportunity to expand into new territory, pushing this time into the neighboring Buner district just sixty miles from Islamabad.

By 2009 there were some hopeful signs that the militants had shot themselves in the feet in Pakistan. Jihadist violence had grown exponentially, insurgent attacks had increased nearly 800 percent since 2005, and suicide attacks had increased *twentyfold.* Suicide bombers managed, for instance, to strike in three different places in Pakistan in just one twenty-four-hour period on April 4, 2009. There was no single "9/11 moment," but the cumulative weight of the Taliban's assassination of Benazir Bhutto; al-Qaeda's bombing of the Marriott hotel in Islamabad in 2008; the widely circulated video images of the Taliban flogging a seventeen-year-old girl; and on October 10, 2009, the twenty-hour Taliban attack on Pakistan's equivalent of the Pentagon, provoked revulsion and fear among the Pakistani public. Where once the Taliban had enjoyed something of a religious Robin Hood image among ordinary Pakistanis, they were now increasingly seen as just thugs.

The Taliban's decision to take up positions only sixty miles from Islamabad was the tipping point that finally galvanized the sclerotic Pakistani state to confront the fact that the jihadist monster it had helped to spawn was now trying to swallow its creator. When the Taliban had been largely confined to Pakistan's tribal regions (which are known in Urdu as "foreign area"), the Pakistani government and military could more or less live with them, but as they marched on the capital, bombing police stations and military posts along the way, the Pakistani establishment began to see the Taliban as a real threat.

After ordering more than a million residents out of the Swat Valley during the spring of 2009, the Pakistani military launched operations against the Taliban, which largely ended the reign of terror of the militants there. Then, after having suffered three defeats in the tribal region of South Waziristan over the course of the previous five years, the Pakistani army went in there again in October 2009, this time with a force of at least thirty thousand troops, following several months of bombing of Taliban positions. These operations were done with the support of at least half of the Pakistani public, which did not view them as solely for the benefit of the United States, as previous military operations against the Taliban had generally been seen.

Simultaneously, President Obama, far from curtailing the drone program he had inherited from President George W. Bush, dramatically increased the number of U.S. drone strikes into Pakistan's tribal regions, targeting not only al-Qaeda but also the Taliban. There were fifty-one American drone strikes in Pakistan in 2009 alone under Obama, compared to forty-five in the entire eight years of the Bush administration. The leader of the Pakistani Taliban, Baitullah Mehsud, the mastermind of Benazir Bhutto's December 2007 assassination and many of the suicide bombings in Afghanistan, was a frequent target of these drone attacks. But he still didn't see it coming. On August 5, 2009, Mehsud, a diabetic former gym instructor, was receiving a leg massage on the roof of a house in South Waziristan when a drone slammed into his hideout, killing one of his wives and the terrorist chief himself.

The Pakistani press was jubilant. "Good Riddance, Killer Baitullah" was the lead headline in the quality *Dawn* newspaper. Much of the previous coverage in Pakistan of U.S. drone strikes in the tribal region had ranged from critical to downright hostile. But in the case of Mehsud, U.S. strategic interests and Pakistani interests were closely aligned because the Pakistani Taliban's victims had included not only Bhutto, the country's most popular politician, but also hundreds of Pakistani policemen, soldiers, and civilians. Now the Pakistani military and government—cognizant that American drones were often targeting militants who were attacking the Pakistani state—offered less pushback on this issue than they had in the past.

As a result of the unprecedented number of drone strikes authorized by the Obama administration aimed at Taliban and al-Qaeda networks, in 2009 about a half-dozen leaders of militant organizations were killed, including the head of an Uzbek terrorist group allied with al-Qaeda, as were hundreds of lower-level militants and civilians.

Despite the exponential rise in U.S. drone strikes, Afghanistan and Pakistan still faced high levels of violence, much of it traceable to militants based in the tribal regions. In 2009, there were a record eighty-seven suicide attacks in Pakistan, which killed around 1,300 people, while in Afghanistan nearly 6,000 Afghan civilians were killed or injured, the highest number of casualties recorded since the fall of the Taliban. While the drones were killing significant numbers of militant leaders and foot soldiers, these losses were clearly being absorbed. Nor had the expanded drone program stopped al-Qaeda and its allies from continuing to train Western recruits. Around 100 to 150 Westerners in total were believed to have traveled to the Federally Administered Tribal Areas in 2009 alone, including Faisal Shahzad, the failed Times Square bomber.

Of course, the drones program did create some real problems for the Taliban and its allies in the tribal regions. David Rohde, the *New York Times* reporter who was held by the Haqqani Taliban network for months in 2009, called the drones a "terrifying presence" in South Waziristan. And the Taliban regularly executed suspected "spies" in Waziristan accused of providing information to the United States, suggesting they feared betrayal from within. But the U.S. drone strikes didn't seem to have had any great effect on the Taliban's ability to mount operations in Pakistan or Afghanistan or deter potential Western recruits, and they no longer had the element of surprise. By early 2010, after around eighteen months of sustained drone strikes, many of Pakistan's militants had likely moved out of their once-safe haven in the tribal regions and into other parts of the country.

A December 2009 briefing prepared by the top U.S. intelligence official in Afghanistan mapped out the strategy and strength of the Taliban, concluding that the insurgency was increasingly effective. The briefing warned that the Taliban's "organizational capabilities and operational reach are qualitatively and geographically expanding" and predicted that "security incidents [are] projected to be higher in 2010."

It was in this context that President Obama announced his new Afghan strategy. On December 1, 2009, Obama traveled to the U.S. Military Academy in West Point, New York, to deliver the key speech of his presidency about the war. Obama recalled, "That was probably the most emotional speech that I've made in terms of how I felt about it, because I was looking out over a group of cadets, some of whom were gonna be deployed to Afghanistan. And potentially some might not come back."

Obama explained the reasoning behind the new strategy: "I make this decision because our security is at stake in Afghanistan and Pakistan. This is the epicenter of the violent extremism practiced by al-Qaeda. It is from here where we were attacked on 9/11, and it is from here that new attacks are being plotted as I speak." Obama announced the thirty thousand new troops of the Afghan surge, but most news accounts of the speech seized on the fact that the president also said that some of those troops would be coming home in July 2011 as they transferred responsibility for a number of Afghanistan's provinces to Afghan security forces. However, there was a large and little-noticed caveat inserted in the speech: that this drawdown would be based on conditions on the ground. And at the time only *one* of Afghanistan's thirty-four provinces was under the control of the Afghan army and police, and that was Kabul itself.

In late June 2010, after accepting General McChrystal's resignation in the wake of the controversial *Rolling Stone* article, Obama appointed General David Petraeus as commander of the Afghan war; the second American president to pick the cerebral strategist to turn around a war that the United States wasn't winning.

At a meeting of NATO member states in Lisbon in November 2010, Obama promised that the American commitment in Afghanistan would now stretch to the end of 2014. Rather than substantially winding down the American military presence in Afghanistan a year before the 2012 presidential election, as Obama had seemed to promise he would do a year earlier, he had now committed the United States to another four years in Afghanistan with a troop presence of some 100,000. (Imagine the moaning and gnashing of teeth this would have precipitated on the left if a Republican president had embraced such a policy.)

Why was the announcement of the 2014 withdrawal date a potential game changer in Afghanistan? For many reasons: Taliban leaders now had the difficult task of having to explain to their foot soldiers that they would have to hang on for yet another four years against a much larger and better resourced American military presence. It would give the rapidly growing Afghan army time to get to the point where it could fight back against the Taliban. It reassured Afghan elites that they could plan for a more secure and prosperous future without moving their funds or themselves out of the country. It allowed for some kind of genuine (uncorrupt) political force to challenge the Karzai mafia that dominated the country. It signaled to regional players, above all Pakistan, that the United States had a long-term commitment to a stable Afghan state and that it was going to be a waste of time for Pakistani intelligence services to continue playing footsy with elements of the Taliban in the hopes of a quick American exit from the region. All those developments would not eliminate the Taliban, but they could make the Taliban irrelevant, which was about as good a definition of victory as one could hope for.

What you don't often see in the news from Afghanistan is how lovely a place it can be. The city of Kabul sits six thousand feet above sea level and is rimmed by snow-tipped mountains. In spring the warming sun sends soft winds during the day and at night a pleasant chill begins to descend with dusk and the muezzin's call to prayer. And as night falls it's possible to remember that in the 1970s, before the series of wars that wrecked Afghanistan, Kabul was a major pit stop on the hippie trail to India and something of a tourist destination.

One day the tourists may come back, but for the moment, that all seems a long, long way off.

Chapter 20

The Long Hunt

So my Lord, if my demise has come, then let it not be
Upon a bier draped with green mantles.
But let my grave be an eagle's belly, its resting place
In the sky's atmosphere amongst perched eagles.

—poem by Osama bin Laden released in the weeks before the U.S.-led invasion of Iraq in March 2003

I have an excellent idea of where [bin Laden] is.

—CIA director Porter J. Goss on June 22, 2005

Flying over the valleys and peaks of the Hindu Kush, which march in serried ranks toward the Himalayas, dividing Central Asia from the Indian subcontinent, you got a sense of the scale of the problem: Osama bin Laden was hiding somewhere out there. And despite the most extensive manhunt in history, he eluded capture for about a decade.

The conventional wisdom after the fall of the Taliban was that tracking bin Laden down wouldn't make much of a difference to the larger war on terrorism. At a March 2002 press conference, President Bush referred to bin Laden as "a person who's now been marginalized." Three years later the CIA even closed "Alec Station," its dedicated bin Laden unit, which had been tasked with the mission of hunting al-Qaeda's top leaders, and reassigned its analysts and officers. Senior CIA officials decided to close Alec Station because they believed that al-Qaeda was no longer the hierarchical organization it once was. However, although it was certainly the case that the global jihadist movement would carry on, whatever bin Laden's fate, it was quite wrong to have assumed that it didn't really matter whether he was apprehended.

Finding bin Laden remained of utmost importance for three reasons. First, there was the matter of justice for the roughly three thousand people who died on 9/11, and for the thousands of other victims of al-Qaeda's attacks around the world. Second, every day that bin Laden remained at liberty was a propaganda victory for al-Qaeda. Third, although bin Laden and his deputy Ayman al-Zawahiri didn't exert day-to-day control over al-Qaeda, statements from bin Laden and, to some degree, Zawahiri were always the most reliable guide to the future actions of jihadist movements around the world and this remained the case even while both men were on the run.

After 9/11, bin Laden issued more than thirty video and audio tapes. Those messages reached untold millions worldwide via television, the Internet, and newspapers. The tapes not only instructed al-Qaeda's followers to continue to kill Westerners and Jews; some carried specific instructions that militant cells then acted on. In 2003, bin Laden called for attacks against members of the coalition in Iraq; subsequently terrorists bombed a British consulate in Turkey, and commuters on their way to work in Madrid. In December 2004, bin Laden called for attacks on Saudi oil facilities, and in February 2006, al-Qaeda's affiliate in Saudi Arabia attacked the Abqaiq facility, arguably the most important oil production facility in the world. Luckily that attack was a failure. Bin Laden also called for attacks on the Pakistani state in 2007, which is one of the reasons that Pakistan had more than fifty suicide attacks that year.

Bin Laden also continued to be the key inspiration for many jihadist terrorists. The Saudi government commissioned a private study of the mind-set of some of the militants in its custody, interviewing one group of 639 extremists arrested before 2004 and another sample of fifty-three arrested between 2004 and 2006. In both studies participants cited bin Laden as their most important role model.

Bin Laden's continued influence on militant foot soldiers could be seen in their public statements. In the United Kingdom, for instance, some of the key terrorist plotters made emblematic remarks about al-Qaeda's leader on videos or in suicide notes, believing that these would be their final statements on earth before going on to Paradise. Mohammed Siddique Khan, the leader of the July 7, 2005, suicide attacks in London, described bin Laden and Zawahiri as "heroes" on his "martyrdom" video. Similarly, Abdullah Ahmed Ali, the ringleader of the plot to bring down seven passenger jets over the Atlantic in the summer of 2006, made a suicide video in which he declared, "Sheikh Osama warned you many times to leave our lands or you will be destroyed. Now the time has come for you to be destroyed." And on May 22, 2008, Nicky Reilly, an autistic twenty-two-year-old British convert to Islam who would set off a homemade bomb in a restaurant in the southwestern city of Exeter, wrote in a suicide note, "Sheikh Usama has told you how to end this war between us and many others but you ignore us. Our words are dead until we give them life with our blood. Leave our lands and stop your support for Israel." This was an efficient summary of bin Laden's basic religio-political message, demonstrating that even someone like Reilly could grasp the essentials of bin Laden's description of the supposed war between "true" Islam and the West.

Given bin Laden's continued importance to jihadists around the world, what was the American-led hunt for bin Laden turning up during the Bush administration? The short answer was nothing. The U.S. government hadn't had a solid lead on al-Qaeda's leader since the battle of Tora Bora in the winter of 2001. While there were informed hypotheses that he was in Pakistan's North-West Frontier Province on the Afghan border, perhaps in one of the more northerly areas such as Bajaur, Dir, or Chitral, these were simply hypotheses, not actionable intelligence. A longtime American counterterrorism analyst explained: "There is very limited collection on him personally." That's intelligence community shorthand for the fact that the usual avenues of "collection" on a target such as bin Laden were yielding little or no information about him. Those avenues typically include signals intercepts of phone calls and emails, as well as human intelligence from spies. Given the hundreds of billions of dollars that the "war on terror" had consumed, the inability of the intelligence and military communities to capture or kill al-Qaeda's leader for almost a decade was one of the war's signal failures.

The incompetence that sometimes characterized the hunt for bin Laden was well illustrated sometime after 9/11 when American planes dropped thousands of matchboxes across southern Afghanistan offering cash rewards for information about al-Qaeda's leader. The reward offer was made in

Dari, not Pashtu, the quite different language of southern Afghanistan, and it suggested that those with relevant information should call a number in the United States or email in pertinent information. Ninety-eight percent of Afghans don't have access to the Internet and very few of them can afford to call America.

What was the proof that the al-Qaeda leader was still alive in the years after 9/11? Plenty. After the attacks on New York and Washington, bin Laden released a slew of video and audiotapes, many of which discussed current events. On one such tape he said the suffering of the Palestinians was amplified when Arab leaders supported an Israeli-Palestinian peace conference that the U.S. government had hosted in Annapolis, Maryland, in 2007. After a nine-month silence bin Laden released an audiotape on March 14, 2009, sharply condemning the recent Israeli invasion of Gaza. In late January 2010, bin Laden released a tape praising the Nigerian who had recently tried to blow up the Detroit-bound airliner on Christmas Day, saying, "The message delivered to you through the plane of the heroic warrior Umar Farouk Abdulmutallab was a confirmation of the previous messages sent by the heroes of September 11."

Could these tapes have been fakes? Not one of the dozens of tapes released by bin Laden after 9/11 was a fake; the U.S. government authenticated many of them using bin Laden's distinctive voiceprint. And what about the reports he was ill? In 2002, Pakistani President Pervez Musharraf said bin Laden had kidney disease, for which he required a dialysis machine, and was therefore likely dead. But the persistent stories of bin Laden's life-threatening kidney problems were false, judging by his appearance in videotapes that he released in 2004 and again in 2007, where he showed no signs of illness. His son Omar has said his father did suffer from painful kidney stones, which is perhaps where the idea that he had kidney disease got started. On the 2007 tape the al-Qaeda leader had even dyed his white-flecked beard black, suggesting that as the Saudi militant entered his fifth decade he was not immune to a measure of vanity about his personal appearance. In fact, bin Laden looked much better in those videos than in the tape he released in December 2001 following the battle of Tora Bora, where he had narrowly escaped being killed in the massive American bombing raids.

Why was it so hard to find bin Laden? First, there was his obsession with security, which began in earnest long ago. In 1994, while bin Laden was living in Sudan, he was the target of a serious assassination attempt, when gunmen raked his Khartoum residence with machine-gun fire. After that attack bin Laden took much greater care of his security, an effort that was coordinated by Ali Mohamed, an Egyptian-American former U.S. Army sergeant who had once worked as an instructor at Special Forces headquarters, at Fort Bragg, North Carolina. And bin Laden and Zawahiri had spent their entire adult lives in organizations that prize discipline and secrecy. Zawahiri joined a jihadist cell in Egypt when he was only fifteen; bin Laden became involved in clandestine efforts against the Soviets in Afghanistan when he was in his early twenties.

In 1997, when I was a producer for CNN, I met with bin Laden in eastern Afghanistan to film his first television interview and witnessed the extraordinary lengths to which members of al-Qaeda went to protect their leader. My colleagues and I were taken to bin Laden's hideout in the middle of the night; we were made to change vehicles while blindfolded; and we had to pass through three successive groups of guards armed with submachine guns and rocket-propelled grenades.

The hunt for al-Qaeda's leaders was further complicated because shortly after the fall of the Taliban, bin Laden and Zawahiri were almost certainly hiding out in or around the tribal areas of Pakistan on the Afghan border. The Pakistan-Afghan border stretches some fifteen hundred miles—roughly the distance from Washington, D.C., to Denver. It is lightly guarded and undefined; clandestine travel in the region is therefore relatively easy. The two Pakistani provinces that abut Afghanistan are Baluchistan, a vast, inhospitable expanse of broiling deserts, and the North West Frontier Province, a flinty, mountainous region punctuated by the fortresses of tribal chiefs. Pashtun tribes, who constitute one of the largest tribal groups in the world without a state, are a major presence in both provinces. They subscribe to Pashtunwali, the law of the Pashtuns, which places an enormous premium on hospitality and on the giving of refuge to anybody who seeks it, an obvious boon to fugitive members of al-Qaeda.

Arthur Keller, a CIA officer who ran a spy network in Pakistan's tribal areas in 2006, explained the problems of working in the region: "It's an incredibly remote area. They're hiding in a sea of people that are very xenophobic to outsiders, so it's a very, very tough nut to crack." That assessment was shared by Admiral William J. Fallon who, until he retired in March 2008, ran Central Command, which is responsible for all U.S. military activities in the Middle East and Central Asia. Fallon explained that "even Pakistani forces are treated as antibodies in the tribal areas."

This situation was compounded by the fact that for years after 9/11, few American spies were operating in Pakistan's tribal areas. Keller said that when he was posted there in early 2006 he was one of only a "handful" of CIA officers working in the seven tribal regions where al-Qaeda and Taliban militants were concentrated. "A great deal of the resources has gone to Iraq," he explained. "I don't think it's appreciated that the CIA is not really a very large organization in terms of field personnel." Keller said that in the summer of 2006 the Agency did start putting more resources into the tribal region.

Bin Laden had long been something of a hero in Pakistan, a standing that helped him while he was in hiding. In 2004 a Pew poll found al-Qaeda's leader had a 65 percent favorability rating among Pakistanis, the highest rating in any of the four Muslim countries that Pew had polled that year. And while bin Laden's popularity had eroded over the years it still stood at 18 percent in Pakistan in 2010.

Bin Laden also had been preparing for life on the run for decades, adopting a lifestyle of monklike detachment from material comforts. Bin Laden would regularly take his sons out on desert trips designed to toughen them up. His son Omar recalled his father telling him and his brothers, "We must be prepared to face desert warfare when the infidel West attacks the Muslim world." Bin Laden's first wife, his Syrian cousin Najwa, also remembered desert expeditions in the mid-1990s when they were based in Sudan in which her husband made all of his wives and kids sleep at night in trenches dug in the desert while limiting their intake of liquids and food and telling them, "There will come a day when you will not have a shelter over your head."

Bin Laden pushed his survivalist ideas to absurd lengths, forbidding his family to use refrigerators and air-conditioning even when they lived in the scorching Sudanese capital of Khartoum. And when he moved to Kandahar from Jalalabad sometime in 1997, bin Laden chose to base himself and his men at the Kandahar airport housing complex, a place with no running water or electricity. In the words of his chief bodyguard Abu Jandal, "He wanted his followers to live an austere and modest life in this world."

Those outside his immediate circle also witnessed the al-Qaeda leader's determination to live a life of austerity. Abdel Bari Atwan, the Palestinian journalist who interviewed him in Afghanistan in 1996, recalls that dinner for bin Laden and several of his inner circle consisted of salty cheese, a potato, five or six fried eggs, and bread caked with sand. Zaynab Khadr, whose family lived with the al-Qaeda leader in Afghanistan during the late 1990s, remembers that "he didn't allow [his children] to drink cold water . . . because he wanted them to be prepared that one day there's no cold water." Noman Benotman, the Libyan who once fought alongside al-Qaeda, says that when bin Laden lived in Afghanistan he instructed his followers, "You should learn to sacrifice everything from modern life like electricity, air conditioning, refrigerators, gasoline. If you are living the luxury life, it's very hard to evacuate and go to the mountains to fight."

Cofer Black, who ran the CIA's Counterterrorist Center at the time of the 9/11 attacks and who told President Bush that his operatives would bring him bin Laden's head "in a box," explained that bin Laden had a dilemma after the fall of the Taliban: to avoid being captured he had to adopt a "hermit on the hilltop" approach. On the other hand, if he remained "in business," he opened himself to the possibility that his communications would be detected. Al-Qaeda's leaders were surely cognizant of this fact, which might explain why bin Laden sometimes sharply reduced the number of tapes he released, going eleven months without releasing one in 2002.

Ahmed Zaidan, Al Jazeera's bureau chief in Pakistan, an intense Syrian intellectual who speaks English faster than most native speakers, described what it was like to receive one of those audiotapes: "It was November 2002, just after the Bali incident. Somebody called me saying 'I want you urgently now.' I met a man with a half-covered face who handed me a cassette. I said to him 'What is this?' He said 'No questions.'" Once the mysterious man had disappeared Zaidan played the cassette and realized that it was bin Laden's voice on the tape.

On the audiotape, which aired first on Al Jazeera on November 12, 2002, and then was picked up by media outlets around the globe, bin Laden referenced a string of recent terrorist attacks perpetrated by al-Qaeda or one its affiliates, from the bombing of a synagogue in Tunisia on April 11, 2002, which killed twenty, to the attack on a French oil tanker, the *Limburg*, off the coast of Yemen on October 6, to the October 12 suicide bombings of two nightclubs on the holiday island of Bali in Indonesia, which killed two hundred mostly young Western tourists.

At eight o'clock on the evening that the bin Laden audiotape was released, National Security Advisor Condoleezza Rice called President Bush with the unwelcome news that there was a proof of life from al-Qaeda's leader. The next day Bush walked into his morning staff meeting very intense. The man he had promised to capture Dead or Alive was very much Alive.

Tracing back the chain of custody of audiotapes such as the one received by Al Jazeera's Ahmed Zaidan would conceivably eventually lead to al-Qaeda's leaders, but such an investigation was complicated by the fact that the group used cutouts and varied the media outlets that received its messages. In the nine years after 9/11, al-Qaeda's two top leaders had released more than one hundred audio and videotapes, on average about one tape a month. However, despite the fact that many of these tapes were released first to Al Jazeera, U.S. intelligence services (which were funded to the tune of around $75 billion a year) were seemingly incapable of tracing the chain of custody of the tapes.

The release of a bin Laden videotape just before the 2004 U.S. presidential election was no exception to this pattern. Five days before the election, on October 29, Zaidan again received a mysterious videotape at his Islamabad office. CNN reported that Pentagon officials were not surprised that bin Laden would issue such a statement around the time of the American election, yet there was nothing to indicate that U.S. intelligence agencies were staking out the most obvious recipient of such a tape: Al Jazeera's bureau in Pakistan.

The new bin Laden videotape played on Al Jazeera and on television networks around the world; on the tape al-Qaeda's leader responded directly to President Bush's frequent claim that his group was attacking the United States because of its freedoms rather than its foreign policy. The terrorist leader said sardonically, "Contrary to what Bush says and claims that we hate your freedom. If that were true, then let him explain why did we not attack Sweden?"

The unexpected reappearance of bin Laden did remind Americans that the Bush administration still had not caught the terrorist mastermind, but it also reminded them of the threat from terrorism, an issue on which Bush was seen as stronger than his rival, Senator John Kerry. Kerry later said that the bin Laden tape's appearance in the final days of the close election race was a critical factor in his loss to Bush. "It froze our polls that night, and over the weekend, we went down one point by Monday," Kerry recalls, adding, "There was no other issue, other than 48 hours of talk about the War on Terror and Osama bin Laden. It had a profound impact."

It was clear from the videotapes of bin Laden and Zawahiri that aired in the years after 9/11 that they were not living in caves. On those tapes both men's clothes were clean and well pressed. Caves generally don't have laundry facilities. And the videotapes that they released were well-lit and well-shot productions, suggesting access either to electrical outlets or generators to run lights. Zawahiri was often filmed in a library setting and on one of his videotapes from March 2006 there were curtains clearly visible behind him, suggesting that the tape was shot in a house.

And the statements made by al-Qaeda's leaders while they were on the run were surprisingly well informed about what was going on around the world. In a 2004 videotape, bin Laden made a reference to the scene in Michael Moore's film *Fahrenheit 9/11* where President Bush continued to read a story about a goat to a kindergarten class after he had been informed that passenger jets had crashed into the World Trade Center. In 2003, bin Laden issued an audiotape that inserted himself into an arcane debate then going on in Saudi clerical circles over the meaning of jihad. Similarly, a year later, Zawahiri issued tapes criticizing France's push to ban Muslim head scarves in schools. And in a 2007 tape bin Laden favorably mentioned the work of the leftist American author Noam Chomsky.

The content of these tapes implied that while they were on the lam both of al-Qaeda's leaders had access to a variety of Arab and English sources—not the sort of materials readily available in a cave. This also suggested that bin Laden and Zawahiri were either in or near an urbanized area.

In 2006, a top U.S. military intelligence official familiar with the hunt for bin Laden said that he might be living in the remote northern Pakistani region of Chitral, on the Afghan border, an analysis that was based in part on trees that are peculiar to that region and can be seen in a 2003 video of bin Laden walking in a mountainous area. In addition, the official said, that analysis was based on the length of time it took for bin Laden's audiotapes to make their way from this presumed location in the remote mountains on the Afghan-Pakistan border to outlets such as Al Jazeera when he commented on important news events, such as the death of al-Qaeda's leader in Iraq, Abu Musab al-Zarqawi. It took three weeks, for instance, for bin Laden's reaction to Zarqawi's death to appear on the world's television screens.

Given that al-Qaeda is highly secretive, compartmentalized, and security conscious, what strategies could have worked to flush out bin Laden? Could the $25 million bounty on his head have worked? In the past, cash rewards have been useful in bringing terrorists to justice. Mir Aimal Kasi, a Pakistani who killed two CIA employees outside the Agency's headquarters in Virginia in 1993, was apprehended in part because of the $2 million reward offered. A $25 million reward played a role in the apprehension of Khalid Sheikh

Mohammed. However, these men did not inspire the spiritual awe that bin Laden did. That bin Laden's inner circle would turn him over for money was unthinkable. Bin Laden had a multimillion-dollar bounty on his head as far back as 1999, but there were no takers.

FBI Special Agent Brad Garrett is a former Marine, habitually dressed entirely in black, who ran Kasi to ground in Pakistan after a four-year hunt. He explained what methods had worked to find Kasi, and how they might be applicable in the hunt for bin Laden. "The key is developing sources," Garrett said. "You have to sort out what is BS from what is the truth, and develop multiple sources to see what is real. You hope to get an associate to give up real-time information about the fugitive. The intelligence is very perishable, so another factor is one's ability to react to it in a timely fashion."

Garrett encountered many dry holes in his four-year hunt for Kasi, finally tracking him down in the dusty backwater of Dera Ghazi Khan, in central Pakistan, which "felt like it was out of *The Good, the Bad, and the Ugly*." Garrett explained that although Kasi was helped by a loose network of people who "respected" him for his attack outside CIA headquarters, he did not have an organization he could rely on, as bin Laden did. In short, Kasi was more vulnerable to detection than the terrorist mastermind, because he was essentially a lone wolf.

Robert Grenier, the CIA station chief in Pakistan during the fall of the Taliban, said that a local-informant-based approach was likely to yield the best results. Those informants would be looking for "anomalies" such as unusual amounts or types of food being provided to a particular location in areas where the al-Qaeda leader was believed to be hiding. Also, bin Laden had certain lifelong habits he was unlikely to break that could provide what CIA analysts call a "signature" of his presence. Bin Laden was a family man who over time accumulated five wives and some twenty kids. While two of his wives had left him, as had many of his children, some of his kids remained in the region.

U.S. intelligence services failed to insert agents in al-Qaeda's inner circle, the only surefire way to get real-time intelligence about bin Laden's whereabouts. Colonel Patrick Lang, a fluent Arabic-speaker who ran Middle Eastern "HUMINT" (human intelligence) for the Defense Intelligence Agency in the early 1990s, said that the lack of HUMINT remained a problem after 9/11. "Everybody talks about effective HUMINT," he said, "but nothing is happening. The people who do this kind of work are gifted eccentrics, who the bureaucrats don't like, or they are the criminal types, who the lawyers don't like. If only we were the ruthless bastards everyone thinks we are."

Signals intelligence, known as "SIGINT," could have been bin Laden's undoing. SIGINT was critical in the case of the Colombian drug kingpin Pablo Escobar, the subject of a massive manhunt by the Colombian police in his native city of Medellin in 1993. The operation used CIA eavesdropping and direction-finding technology. When Escobar made a cell phone call to his son that lasted longer than a few minutes, Colombian forces swarmed his neighborhood and shot him dead. But bin Laden was savvier than Escobar; a U.S. official said that he had "quit any kind of device that can be listened to." That included satellite phones, cell phones, and handheld radios. When communication was absolutely necessary he relied on couriers. There had been some success in intercepting these messengers in the past. "We have hit couriers from time to time," a U.S. military official said.

The same official said, "My sense is that he has been hunkered down in one place for a long time," making it harder to track him. The official said that Zawahiri, by contrast, is "more operational and is moving more." That may account for why the United States believed it had sufficiently good intelligence to launch a strike from a pilotless drone aimed at killing Zawahiri on January 13, 2006, in the village of Damadola, on Pakistan's border with Afghanistan. The strike missed Zawahiri by a couple of hours but resulted in the death of five militants, including one of the al-Qaeda leader's relatives. But a little over two weeks after the strike, Zawahiri released a videotape thumbing his nose at President Bush and celebrating the fact that he had survived the attack.

In the face of the intense Pakistani opposition to American boots on the ground, the Bush administration chose to rely on drones to target suspected al-Qaeda and Taliban leaders. Bush ordered the CIA to expand its attacks with Predator and Reaper drones during the summer of 2008, and the U.S. government stopped notifying Pakistani officials when strikes were imminent or obtaining their "concurrence" for the attacks. As a result, the time that it took for a target to be identified and engaged dropped from many hours to forty-five minutes.

The Predator and Reaper drones were operated by a squadron of pilots stationed in Nevada and were equipped to drop Hellfire missiles and JDAM bombs, respectively. More than two-dozen feet in length, the drones lingered over the tribal areas looking for targets. Between July 2008 and the time he had left office, President Bush had authorized thirty Predator and Reaper strikes on Pakistani territory, a fivefold increase compared to the six strikes that the CIA had launched during the first half of 2008.

Those drone strikes killed dozens of lower-ranking militants and at least ten mid- and upper-level leaders within al-Qaeda or the Taliban. One of them was Abu Laith al-Libi, who had orchestrated a 2007 suicide attack targeting Vice President Dick Cheney while the latter was visiting Bagram Air Base in Afghanistan. Libi was then described as the number-three man in the al-Qaeda hierarchy, perhaps the most dangerous job in the world, given that the half-dozen or so men who had occupied that position since 9/11 have ended up in prison or dead. Other militants killed in the stepped-up drone strikes included Abu Khabab al-Masri, al-Qaeda's WMD researcher, and Abu Jihad al-Masri, the group's propaganda chief. None of these strikes targeted bin Laden, who seemed to have vanished like a wraith.

The pace of drone attacks ramped up further during the waning days of the Bush administration—likely a legacy-building effort to dismantle the entire al-Qaeda top leadership. Cheney seemed to acknowledge this in an interview with CNN eleven days before Obama took office, saying optimistically of efforts to kill bin Laden, "We've got a few days left yet." A week earlier, the Bush administration had received the welcome news that Osama al-Kini and his lieutenant, Sheikh Ahmed Salim Swedan, had been killed by a Hellfire missile launched from a drone over Waziristan. Kini and Swedan had played a central role in planning the 1998 bombings of the two American embassies in East Africa. Bush told CNN's Larry King with a slight smirk that bin Laden would eventually be found "just like the people who allegedly were involved in the East African bombings. Couple of them were brought to justice recently."

As the drone program was in full swing, the CIA director, General Michael Hayden, explained in November 2008 that "by making a safe haven feel less safe, we keep al-Qaeda guessing. We make them doubt their allies; question their methods, their plans, even their priorities." Hayden went on to say that the key outcome of the drone attacks was that "we force them to spend more time and resources on self-preservation, and that distracts them, at least partially and at least for a time, from laying the groundwork for the next attack."

Privately, American officials raved about the drone program. One Bush administration official said that the drones had so crimped the militants' activities in Pakistan's tribal regions that they had begun discussing a move to Yemen or Somalia. The number of "spies" al-Qaeda and the Taliban killed rose dramatically after the summer of 2008, suggesting that the militants were turning on themselves in an effort to root out the sources of the often pinpoint intelligence that had led to what officials described as the deaths of half of the top militant leaders in the tribal regions by early 2009.

One way of measuring the pain that the drone program had inflicted on al-Qaeda was the number of audio- and videotapes that the terrorist group had released through its propaganda arm, Al Sahab. Al-Qaeda takes its propaganda operations seriously and in 2007 Al Sahab had a banner year, releasing almost one hundred tapes. But the number of releases dropped by half in 2008, indicating that the group's leaders were more concerned with survival than public relations.

Pakistan was not the only country where al-Qaeda's top leaders fled following the fall of the Taliban in the winter of 2001. A number of important al-Qaeda operatives fled to Iran, where they were taken into Iranian custody. Saif al-Adel, number three in the al-Qaeda hierarchy; Suleiman Abu Ghaith, the group's spokesman; and Abu al-Khayr, a deputy of Zawahiri's, were all apprehended by Iranian authorities a year or so after 9/11. What the Iranians planned to do with their al-Qaeda guests was something of a mystery: "We wish we could predict how this is going to turn out," said one U.S. intelligence official. They appeared to be bargaining chips that the Iranians could use in the event of some normalization of relations with the United States.

Even with the capture or death of key al-Qaeda leaders in both Iran and Pakistan, al-Qaeda can continue to sustain blows because the members of the group firmly believe that they are doing God's work. In their own narrative of their struggle, setbacks here on earth simply recall the Prophet Mohammed's many years of exile in the wilderness fighting the enemies of Islam. For al-Qaeda's leaders and foot soldiers, setbacks are, in fact, simply more evidence of their part in God's plan to prevail over the infidels.

Despite the difficulty it remained a vital interest of the United States to catch or kill bin Laden. While bin Laden remained on the lam al-Qaeda was far from defeated. Ahmed Zaidan, the Al Jazeera reporter, who has written an Arabic biography of bin Laden, explained "As long as Osama bin Laden is alive he has defeated America." "How do we close the 9/11 chapter with him still being out there?" said Roger Cressey, who was responsible for the coordination of counterterrorism policy at the time of the September 11 attacks.

Bin Laden had long made it clear that he would never be taken alive. His former bodyguard Abu Jandal explained that al-Qaeda's leader gave him a pistol that "had only two bullets, for me to kill Sheikh Osama with in case we were surrounded or he was about to fall into the enemy's hands so that he would not be caught alive." In a tape posted to Islamist websites in 2006, bin Laden confirmed his willingness to be martyred: "I have sworn to only live free. Even if I find bitter the taste of death, I don't want to die humiliated or deceived."

In the early morning of May 2, 2011, bin Laden finally got his wish, dying with a bullet to his head in a raid carried out by a team of US Navy SEALs in the small city of Abbottabad in northern Pakistan, where al-Qaeda's leader had been hiding out for several years.

Bin Laden's death left a large void for his organization. Between the founding of al-Qaeda in 1988 and the death of bin Laden more than two decades later those who had joined al-Qaeda had all sworn a religious oath of allegiance not to the organization, but to bin Laden himself, in much the same way that Nazi Party members had sworn an oath of personal fealty to Hitler rather than to Nazism.

This made bin Laden a difficult person to replace. While Ayman al-Zawahiri was the deputy leader of the terror group and therefore technically bin Laden's successor, he was not regarded as a natural leader. Zawahiri did not command the respect bordering on love that was accorded to bin Laden by members of al-Qaeda. Indeed, even among his fellow Egyptian militants Zawahiri was seen as a divisive force and so he was unlikely to be able to step into the role of the unquestioned leader of al-Qaeda and of the global jihadist movement that was once occupied by bin Laden. (A wild card is that one of bin Laden's dozen or so sons—endowed with an iconic family name—could eventually rise to take over the terrorist group. Already, Saad bin Laden, one of the oldest sons, had played a middle management role in al-Qaeda.)

In the longer term bin Laden's "martyrdom" will likely give something of a boost to the power of his ideas. Sayyid Qutb, generally regarded as the Lenin of the jihadist movement, was a relatively obscure writer before his execution by the Egyptian government in 1966. After his death, Qutb's writings, which called for offensive holy wars against the enemies of Islam, became influential. The same process will likely happen with the death of bin Laden, but to a larger degree as bin Laden's prestige and fame far eclipses Qutb's. And so, in death, bin Laden's ideas will likely attain some lasting currency. As bin Laden himself put it to his bodyguard, Abu Jandal, in death "his blood would become a beacon that arouses the zeal and determination of his followers."

"Bin Ladenism" will, however, never enjoy the mass appeal of other destructive ideologies of the modern era, such as communism, but it certainly enjoys some measure of support today. And this is important, because many thousands of underemployed, disaffected men in the Muslim world will continue to embrace bin Laden's doctrine of violent anti-Westernism. In a telling 2008 survey of opinion in the Muslim world in countries as diverse as Morocco, Indonesia, Jordan, and Turkey, people expressed more "confidence" in bin Laden than in President Bush by significant margins. Thus while eliminating the top leadership of al-Qaeda is useful in terms of seeking justice for the victims of 9/11 and heading off other spectacular attacks by the group, make no mistake: this will not end the war of the terrorists. Bin Laden's ideas have circulated widely and will continue to attract adherents for years to come. Killing people is one thing; killing ideas is another matter.

That said, beginning in December 2010 a series of protests and revolts spread across the Middle East, from Tunisia to Egypt and then on to Bahrain, Yemen, and Libya, events in which al-Qaeda's leaders, foot soldiers, and ideology were all notably absent. Bin Laden must have watched this "Arab Spring" unfold with a mixture of glee and despair. Glee, because overthrowing the dictatorships and monarchies of the Middle East had for so long been his central goal. Despair, because none of the Arab revolutions had anything to do with him.

There were no revolutionaries in the streets of Cairo carrying placards with pictures of bin Laden's face, nor were the protesters in Bahrain spouting al-Qaeda's venomous critiques of the West. Those calling for the overthrow of the Libyan dictator Moammar Gadhafi were not graduates of bin Laden's training camps, while the Facebook revolutionaries who launched the revolution in Egypt represented everything that al-Qaeda hates: Secular, liberal and anti-authoritarian, they also included women. Even the Muslim Brotherhood, the Islamist mass movement in Egypt, which joined the Egyptian revolution as it was already in motion, is opposed by al-Qaeda. The Brotherhood participates in conventional politics and elections, which bin Laden and his followers believe are against Islam; Zawahiri, bin Laden's top deputy, has even written an entire book condemning the Muslim Brotherhood.

Predictably, Zawahiri released an audiotape in February 2011 opportunistically seeking to position al-Qaeda as having some sort of role in the momentous events unfolding in the Arab world. In the tape Zawahiri called for his native Egypt to be governed as an Islamic state. Of course, Egypt is already a country where Islam plays a key role, as about nine out of 10 Egyptians are Muslim, and Al-Azhar University in central Cairo is the nearest that Sunni Islam comes to having a Vatican. What Zawahiri meant by his call for an Islamic state is that Egypt should be run as a Taliban-style theocracy with no rights for women or minorities.

Whatever the outcome of the Arab revolts they will not be to al-Qaeda's satisfaction, because few in the streets of Cairo, or Benghazi, Libya, or San'a, Yemen, are clamoring for the imposition of a Taliban-style theocracy, al-Qaeda's desired end state in the Middle East. Rather, the protesters want accountable governments that don't abuse their population, elections and the rule of law—just like pretty much everyone else except members of al-Qaeda, who regard the Taliban as the closest thing to an ideal government that has existed in the modern era.

Media stories that al-Qaeda was playing no role in the revolts in the Middle East provoked a furious response from the Yemeni-American cleric Anwar al-Awlaki, a leader of "Al-Qaeda in the Arabian Peninsula." In his group's *Inspire* magazine, a slick Web-based publication, heavy on photographs and graphics that, unusually for a jihadist organ, was written in colloquial English, Awlaki penned an essay titled "The Tsunami of Change." In the article, Awlaki made the uncontroversial point that the regimes based on fear were ending in the Arab world because of the revolutions and protests from Egypt to Bahrain. But he went on to assert that, contrary to commentators who had written that the Arab revolts represented a total repudiation of al-Qaeda's founding ideology, the world should "know very well that the opposite is the case." Awlaki also turned to this author, writing, "for a so-called 'terrorism expert' such as Peter Bergen, it is interesting to see how even he doesn't get it right this time. For him to think that because a Taliban-style regime is not going to take over following the revolutions is a too short-term way of viewing the unfolding events." In other words: Just you wait—Taliban-type theocracies will be coming to the Middle East as the revolutions there unfold further. Awlaki also wrote that it was wrong to say that al-Qaeda viewed the revolutions in the Middle East with "despair." Instead, he claimed that "the Mujahedeen (holy warriors) around the world are going through a moment of elation and I wonder whether the West is aware of the upsurge in Mujahedeen activity in Egypt, Tunisia, Libya, Yemen, Arabia, Algeria, and Morocco?"

We do not, of course, know the final outcome of the Arab revolutions, but there is little chance that al-Qaeda or other extremist groups will be able to grab the reins of power as the authoritarian regimes of the Middle East crumble. But while al-Qaeda and its allies cannot take power anywhere in the Muslim world, these groups do thrive on chaos and civil war. And the whole point of revolutions is that they are inherently unpredictable even to the people who are leading them, so anything could happen in the coming years in Libya and Yemen, and much is unpredictable in Egypt, and even in Saudi Arabia.

Still, it is hard to imagine two more final endings to the "war on terror" than the popular revolts against the authoritarian regimes in the Middle East and the death of bin Laden. If the Arab Spring was a large nail in the coffin of al-Qaeda's ideology, the death of bin Laden was an equally large nail in the coffin of al-Qaeda the organization.

In 2011 the Longest War, finally, began to wind down.

Note on Sources

I was able to interview many of the sources in the book on more than one occasion and the dates and places of all those interviews are noted in the footnotes. A partial list of the several hundred interviews I conducted for this history can be found in the next section. (A number of the people I interviewed were subsequently jailed, killed by security services, assassinated, or have gone into hiding, and I have noted those in the list of interviewees.) Of course, many interviewees chose to remain anonymous.

I have also drawn on documents filed in criminal cases involving jihadist militants in the United States, Italy, Belgium, Spain, Germany, and the United Kingdom. And I have mined books written by al-Qaeda's leaders and former Taliban officials; thousands of pages of transcripts of U.S. military tribunal proceedings of prisoners held at Guantánamo Bay; first-hand accounts about al-Qaeda from newspapers from around the Muslim world; and a trove of al-Qaeda-related documents and publications going back to the late 1980s that I have collected over the years.

I also used material derived from several hundred books that touch on aspects of the story and thousands of articles and government documents and other reports that I have collected on this subject, the most useful of which are referenced in the endnotes and bibliography. Also useful were the many publications and statements by al-Qaeda's leaders or other militant strategists.

When it comes to transliterating Arabic names or terms, I have used conventional English spellings, for instance, Osama bin Laden, al-Qaeda, and Omar Abdel Rahman.

Interviewees

Hassan Abbas
Dr. Abdullah
Zachary Abuza
David Albright
"Matthew Alexander"
Sydney Alford
Hazarat Ali
Imtiaz Ali
Jason Amerine
Abdullah Anas (Boudjema Bounoua)
Peter Arnett
Abdel Bari Atwan
Hussein al-Awadi
Salman al-Awdah
Hutaifa Azzam
Mahfouz Azzam
Robert Baer
Omar Bakri Mohamed
Kenneth Ballen
Arianna Barbazza
David Barno
Khaled Batarfi
Milt Bearden
Noman Benotman
James Bernazzani
Gary Berntsen
Benazir Bhutto (Assassinated in Pakistan in 2007)
Stephen Biddle
Cofer Black
Antony Blinken
Jason Burke
Daniel Byman
Vincent Cannistraro
Yigal Carmon
Frank Cilluffo
Peter Clarke
Richard A. Clarke
Jack Cloonan
Eliot Cohen
David Cohen
Daniel J. Coleman
Aukai Collins
Elizabeth Colton
Conrad Crane
Roger Cressey

Henry "Hank" Crumpton
Robert Dannenberg
Mohammed Daud
Essam Deraz
James Dobbins
Brian Doyne
Joshua Dratel
Assad Durrani
Jason Dye
Paul Eedle
Karl Eikenberry
Charles "Sam" Faddis
Saad al-Fagih
Christine Fair
William J. Fallon
Mahmoun Fandy
Khaled al-Fauwaz (Jailed in the UK in 1998)
Yosri Fouda
Tommy Franks
Joe Frost
"Dalton Fury"
Brad Garrett
Baltasar Garzon
Fawaz Gerges
Abdul Rashid Ghazi (Killed by Pakistani security forces in 2007)
Susan Glasser
David Gordon
Karen Greenberg
Robert Grenier
Stephen Grey
Alain Grignard
Abdul Rahman al-Hadlag
Stephen Hadley
Mohammed Hafez
Moinuddin Haider
Hamid al-Haiys
Kemal Halbawy
Abu Hamza (Mustafa Kamel Mustafa, jailed in the UK in 2004)
Abdul Haq Hanif (Jailed in Afghanistan)
Sami ul-Haq
Husain Haqqani
Ali Hatem
Neil Herman
Thomas Hegghammer
Gulbuddin Hekmatyar (In hiding)
Andrew Higgins
Bruce Hoffman
Richard Holbrooke
Pervez Hoodbhoy
Ed Husain
Zahid Hussain
Mansoor Ijaz
Faraj Ismail
Jamal Ismail
Imdadullah (Jailed in Afghanistan)
Abd al-Jabbar
Saad al-Jabri
Wael Jalaidan
Sadritdin Jalilov
Said Jawad
Sterling Jensen
Seth Jones
Sydney Jones
Peter Jouvenal
Fred Kagan
Hekmat Karzai
Rita Katz
Art Keller
Jack Keane
John Kerry
Mullah Abdul Samad Khaksar (Assassinated in Kandahar in 2006)

Jamal Khalifa (Murdered in Madagascar in 2007)
Rhamad Khan
Ismail Khan
Jamal Khashoggi
Khalid Khawaja (Assassinated by Taliban in 2010)
David Kilcullen
Daniel Kimmage
Osama bin Laden (In hiding)
Arif Lalani
William Lambert
Robert Lambert
Patrick Lang
Carie Lemack
Clare Lockhart
Douglas Lute
Norine MacDonald
Jean MacKenzie
Michael Maloof
Michele Malvesti
Omar Khan Masoudi
Ahmad Shah Massoud (Assassinated in Afghanistan in 2001)
Brett McGurk
John McLaughlin
Richard Melton
Joseph Melrose
John Miller
Khary Miller
Hamid Mir
Assaf Moghadam
Haji Deen Mohammed
Saad Mohseni
Vahid Mojdeh
Rolf Mowatt-Larssen
Philip Mudd
Ursula Mueller
Abdul Hakim Mujahid
Mohammed Musa
Wakil Ahmed Muttawakil
Muzhgan
John Nagl
Syed Mohsin Naqvi
Octavia Nasr
Vali Nasr
Maajid Nawaz
Shuja Nawaz
Raymond Odierno
Michael O'Hanlon
Abu Omar (Osama Hassan Mustafa Nasr)
Meghan O'Sullivan
Ralph Paredes
David Petraeus
William Pierce
George Piro
Kenneth Pollack
Mohammed Asif Qazizanda
Amir Rana
Ahmed Rashid
Joel Rayburn
Bruce Riedel
Nic Robertson
Michael A. Rolince
Eric Rosenbach
Barnett Rubin
Osama Rushdi
Thomas Ruttig
Marc Sageman
Omar Samad
Habiba Sarabi
Michael Scheuer
Michael Semple
Mohammed al-Shafey

Michael Sheehan
Mitch Silber
Steven Simon
Yasser al-Sirri
Julie Sirrs
Emma Sky
Leonid Smirnov
Ali Soufan
Armando Spataro
Frank Sturek
Barbara Sude
Abu Musab al-Suri (Mustafa Setmariam Nasar—captured in 2005, now jailed, location not known, perhaps Syria)
Jassim Suwaydawi
Camille Tawil
Frances Fragos Townsend
Tom Tullius
Ben Venzke
John Vines
Hussein al-Wadi
Doug Wankel
Dale Watson
Matthew Waxman
Gabriel Weimann
Mary Jo White
Andy Worthington
Daoud Yacub
Judith Yaphe
Jameel Yusuf
Rahimullah Yusufzai
Asif Zadari
Mohammed Zahir
Mohammed Haji Zahir
Ahmed Zaidan
Juan Zarate
Montasser al-Zayyat

Notes

Part I

1 "As a general rule": Christopher Andrew, *For the President's Eyes Only* (New York: Harper Collins, 1996), p. 538.

1 "No one loves": Maximilien Robespierre, "On the War," Speech to the Jacobin Club, Paris, January 11, 1792.

Chapter 1

3 a riddle: Yosri Fouda and Nick Fielding, *Masterminds of Terror: The Truth Behind the Most Devastating Attack The World Has Ever Seen* (New York: Arcade, 2003), p. 140.

3 turned down: National Commission on Terrorist Attacks Upon the United States Final Report (Washington, D.C.: 2004) ("9/11 Commission Report,"), p. 168.

3 "Jenny": Fouda and Fielding, *Masterminds of Terror*, pp. 158, 139.

4 dispatched a messenger: ibid. pp. 140–141.

4 trainers at the facility said: Musad Omar is a Yemeni being held at Guantánamo Bay. Omar claims to have gone to Afghanistan "to observe the situation" under the Taliban after being recruited to do so by an acquaintance in Yemen. In extracts from his testimony before a U.S. military tribunal at Guantánamo he recalls what it was like to be in al-Qaeda's camps around the time of the 9/11 attacks. He says he saw bin Laden in Khost in mid-October 2001 a month before the fall of Kabul on November 12, 2001. Guantánamo Bay tribunal transcripts. Author's collection.

4 In Kandahar: According to Abu Musab al-Suri, the Syrian jihadist who had sometimes had clashed with bin Laden, in September 2001, the al-Qaeda leader told some of his followers that it was time to leave Kandahar and go back to Yemen. Abu Musab al Suri, *The Call for Global Islamic Resistance*, published on jihadist websites, 2004.

4 Feroz Ali Abbasi: Feroz Ali Abbasi, Guantánamo Bay Prison Memoirs, 2002–2004.

4 Lindh heard an instructor: FBI report, "Interview of John Philip Walker Lindh," December 9–10, 2001. Author's collection.

4 Atyani asked bin Laden: Bakr Atyani, phone interview, Islamabad, Pakistan, August 22, 2005.
4 an open secret: Vernon Loeb, "U.S. forces in Gulf on highest alert; threats also prompt travel warning," *Washington Post*, June 23, 2001.
4 tightly held: 9/11 Commission Report, p. 532 fn 180. According to KSM, only bin Laden, Mohamed Atef, Abu Turab al-Jordani, Ramzi Binalshibh, and a few of the senior hijackers knew the specific targets, timing, operatives, and methods of attack. Intelligence reports, interrogations of KSM, Oct. 27, 2003.
4 formally contracted its alliance: 9/11 Commission Report, op. cit., p. 470, fn. 82: Intelligence report, interrogation of KSM, Jan. 9, 2004.
5 learned about the attacks: Osama bin Laden, December 13, 2001, op. cit.
5 for a suicide mission: Osama bin Laden, December 13, 2001, op. cit.
5 suicide "wills": Fouda and Fielding op. cit., p. 141; Such tapes were released in April 2002, September 2002, September 2003, and September 2006. Joel Roberts, "Video shows bin Laden, 9/11 hijackers," CBS News, September 7, 2006, http://www.cbsnews.com/stories/2006/09/07/terror/main1982773.shtml.
5 Despite his increasing militancy: Terry McDermott, *Perfect Soldiers: The 9/11 Hijackers: Who They Were, Why They Did It* (New York: HarperCollins, 2005), pp. 50–53; "personality clashes": 9/11 Commission Report op. cit., p. 246; "the Ayatollah": McDermott, *Perfect Soldiers*, p. 37.
5 "How do you feel?": Yosri Fouda interview with Ramzi Binalshibh, Karachi, Pakistan, April 20–21, 2002. Aired in Al Jazeera documentary, September 11, 2002. http://www.guardian.co.uk/world/2002/sep/09/september11.afghanistan.
5 "Holy Tuesday": Yosri Fouda, "We left out nuclear targets, for now," *The Guardian*, March 4, 2003, http://www.guardian.co.uk/world/2003/mar/04/alqaida.terrorism.
5 three or four floors: Tape transcript available from CNN.com, December 13, 2001. http://archives.cnn.com/2001/U.S./12/13/tape.transcript/. The tape was translated by George Michael, a translator at Diplomatic Language Services and Dr. Kassem M. Wahba, of Johns Hopkins University for the Department of Defense.
6 gathered around radios: *United States of America* v. *Ali Hamza Ahmad Sulayman al Bahlul*. Obtained through www.findlaw.com.
6 "Be patient": Osama bin Laden, mid-November 2001, Kandahar, Afghanistan. http://www.foxnews.com/story/0,2933,40750,00.html.
6 "Our brother Marwan": Fouda, Yosri. "Top Secret: The Road to September 11." Al-Jazeera (Qatar). First aired: September 11, 2002. Author collection.
6 Binalshibh remembers: Fouda and Fielding op. cit., p. 159.
6 understood that the game was up: Interview by author with Vahid Mojdeh, Kabul, Afghanistan, April 2006.
6 "As evidence he": Abu Walid al-Masri, *The History of the Arab Afghans from the Time of their Arrival in Afghanistan until their Departure with the Taliban*. Serialized in *Al Sharq al Awsat*, December 8–14, 2004.
6 "was not convinced": ibid.
7 There were others: 9/11 Commission Report, op. cit., pp. 251–252.
7 would be counterproductive: Peter Bergen and Paul Cruickshank, "The Unraveling," *The New Republic*, June 11, 2008. Noman Benotman, interview by author, London, UK, August 30, 2005.
7 known bin Laden: Benotman interview op. cit.
7 wanted to rein him in: Vahid Mojdeh, *Afghanistan under Five Years of Taliban Sovereignty*, translated by Sepideh Khalili and Saeed Gangi (Kabul, 2001).
7 put bin Laden on notice: 9/11 Commission Report, p. 251–252.
8 "Sheikh, if you give in": Omar bin Laden, Najwa bin Laden, Jean Sasson, *Growing Up Bin Laden* (New York: St. Martin's Press, 2009), p. 247.

8 the head of Ahmed Shah Massoud: 9/11 Commission Report, p. 252.
8 wiry warrior: Description of Massoud from author interview August 1993 northern Afghanistan.
8 one working helicopter: Interview by author, Dr. Abdullah, Washington, D.C., September 2000.
9 the Massoud hit: Description of Massoud's assassination from Gary Schroen, *First In: An Insider's Account of How the CIA Spearheaded the War on Terror in Afghanistan* (New York; Presidio Press, 2005), pp. 1–6.
9 about the Massoud assassination on the radio: Feroz Ali Abbasi, op. cit.
9 worried that the Northern Alliance was finished: Craig Pyes, and William C. Rempel, "Slowly stalking an Afghan lion,'" *Los Angeles Times*, June 12, 2002. http://articles.latimes.com/2002/jun/12/world/fg-masoud12.
9 the most cosmic of terms: Voice of America interview, "Mullah Omar," September 21, 2001.
10 "A U.S. campaign against Afghanistan": Array of al-Qaeda Memos and Forgotten Computer Reveals Thinking Behind Four Years of al-Qaeda Doings," *Wall Street Journal,* December 1, 2001. See also Alan Cullison, "Inside al-Qaeda's Hard Drive," *The Atlantic Monthly*, September 2004.
10 at least he was both pious and courageous: Vahid Mojdeh, *Afghanistan Under Five Years of Taliban Sovereignty,* translated by Sepideh Khalili and Saeed Gangi (Kabul, 2001).
10 "I'm sure he didn't do it": Faraj Ismail, interview by author, Cairo, Egypt, June 2005. The interview with Mullah Omar ran in *Al Majallah* on October 14, 2001.
10 longer than any conflict: There is some debate about the exact length of the U.S.'s involvement in the Vietnam War, which can vary anywhere between eight years and one and a half decades depending on which start and end dates for America's involvement are selected. According to Stanley Karnow's authoritative history *Vietnam*, in February 1962, an American military assistance command was formed in South Vietnam, and by the end of 1963 15,000 American military advisers were there. A cease-fire agreement was formally signed in Paris in January 1973, and the last American troops left Vietnam two months later. Karnow's account indicates that America's role in the war lasted at least a decade.
10 could last for generations: Ayman al-Zawahiri pointed out in his autobiography that it took two centuries to eject the Crusaders from the Middle East in the Middle Ages and it took almost as long to expel the French from Algeria in the 19th and 20th centuries. *Knights Under the Banner of the Prophet,* excerpts published by *Al Sharq al Awsat*, December 2001.

Chapter 2

11 "When people see": Osama bin Laden, December 13, 2001, translation by the Department of Defense. http://www.foxnews.com/story/0,2933,40750,00.html.
11 closest buddy: Khaled Batarfi, interviews by author, Jeddah, Saudi Arabia, September 5 and 9, 2005.
11 The Musharifa district: author visits to Jeddah, Saudi Arabia September 5–9, 2006.
11 fasted twice a week: Batarfi interview.
12 "He was frustrated": Khaled Batarfi, "First ever interview with the woman who brought up the world's most wanted man," *The Mail on Sunday*, December 23, 2001.
12 in the 1950s: Bergen 2006, p. 72.
12 charismatic Syrian physical education teacher: Steve Coll, *The Bin Ladens* (New York: Penguin, 2008), pp. 144–146.
12 was religiously conservative already: Jamal Khalifa, interviews by author, Jeddah, Saudi Arabia, September 6 and 9, 2005.

12 more than just observing: ibid.
13 married with a couple of toddlers: bin Laden and Sasson op. cit., pp. 292–293.
13 found his religiosity a bit much: Yeslam bin Laden, interview by Al Arabiya television, May 28, 2005.
13 died in a plane crash: Osama bin Laden, Al Jazeera interview, 1999 op. cit.
13 fifty-four children: Jamal Khalifa, interview by author, Jeddah, Saudi Arabia, September 6 and 9, 2005.
13 "I am the one son": Hamid Mir, interview by author, Islamabad, Pakistan, September 1998.
14 twenty-five sons: Khalifa op. cit.
14 founded the Services Office: The section about Abdullah Azzam draws on my 2001 book, *Holy War Inc.*, pp. 56–59.
14 an influential fatwa: Abdullah Azzam, *Defense of Muslim Lands: The Most Important Personal Duty*, published in booklet form by Modern Mission Library, Amman, 1984.
14 "The relationship between": Faraj Ismail, interview by author, Cairo, Egypt, June 2005.
14 "I feel so guilty": Basil Muhammed, *Al Ansar Al Arab fi Afghanistan* ("The Arab Volunteers in Afghanistan").
14 most of his time: Jamal Ismail, interview by author, Islamabad, Pakistan, March 2005.
15 Abdullah Anas: Abdullah Anas, interview by author, London, UK, June 15, 17, and 20, 2005.
15 "He became more assertive, less shy": Khaled Batarfi, interviews by author, Jeddah, Saudi Arabia, September 5 and 9, 2005.
15 no longer tolerate disagreement: Jamal Khalifa, interviews by author, Jeddah, Saudi Arabia, September 6 and 9, 2005.
15 ambitious plan: This section draws on chapter 3 of *The Osama bin Laden I Know* (Bergen 2006).
15 the first thing: Basil Muhammed, *Al Ansar Al Arab fi Afghanistan* ("The Arab Volunteers in Afghanistan").
15 "Every drop of blood": Khalifa op. cit.
16 the making of bin Laden: Essam Deraz, interviews by author, Cairo, Egypt, January 2000 and May 2005.
16 "sound of the explosions": Jamal Khashoggi, "Arab youths fight shoulder to shoulder with Mujahedeen," *Al Majallah* (Issue #430), May 4, 1988.
16 ranged up to 175,000: Mark Urban, *War In Afghanistan* (London: Macmillan, 1988), p. 244. According to Urban the total number of guerrillas that would be operating on any given day would not be below 35,000 and not above 175,000. Milt Bearden, who ran the CIA's Afghan operation, says the maximum number of mujahideen at any given time was 250,000, but that figure includes mujahideen fighters who cycled through Pakistani refugee camps to see their families, or had to return to their native villages for harvesting, etc. Milt Bearden, interview by author, Washington, D.C., September 2000.
16 several hundred: Abdullah Anas, interview by author, London, UK, June 15, 17, and 20, 2005.
16 no impact: Bergen 2006 op. cit., p. 50.
17 "For God's sake": Jamal Ismail, interview by author, Islamabad, Pakistan, March 2005.
17 "gentle, enthusiastic young man": Jamal Khashoggi, "Interview with Prince Turki al Faisal," *Arab News* and MBC Television, November 4–9, 2001.
17 Azzam did not approve: Anas op. cit.
17 "regime change": Ismail op. cit.

17 Osama Rushdi: Osama Rushdi, interview by author, London, UK, August 9, 2005.

18 He was assassinated: Bergen 2006 op. cit., p. 92.

18 "a volcanic temper": Bergen 2006 op. cit., p. 73.

18 The minutes of al-Qaeda's founding meetings: The documents are taken from the Government's Evidentiary Proffer Supporting the Admissibility of Co-Conspirator Statements, *United States v. Enaam Arnaout*, No. 02-CR-892 (North District of Illinois, filed January 6, 2003). Some of this material can be found in the proffer. The information is also retained by Motley Rice, the lead law firm for the 9/11 victims' families.

18 about a quarter: Coll op. cit., p. 189.

18 "My husband and I": Sasson and bin Laden op cit, pp. 26–27.

18 urging Muslims to boycott American products: Osama bin Laden interview by Taysir Allouni, Al Jazeera, south of Kabul, Afghanistan, October 20, 2001.

19 Pepsi and Coca-Cola: Jamal Ismail, interview by author, Islamabad, Pakistan, March 2005.

19 Omar recalls: Sasson and bin Laden op cit, p. 60.

19 "He changed": Turki op. cit.

19 "Women! Defending Saudi men!": Sasson and bin Laden op cit., p. 84.

19 an important impact: Osama bin Laden, interview by Peter Arnett and CNN, late March 1997, eastern Afghanistan.

19 raising his own jihadist army: Abu Musab al-Suri, a Syrian militant close to bin Laden recalled that during this period, "Osama's main passion was the jihad in South Yemen." Abu Musab al-Suri, *The Call for Global Islamic Resistance*, posted on the Internet in December 2004.

19 was given a passport: Khaled al-Hammadi, "Bin Laden's former bodyguard interviewed on al-Qaeda strategies," *Al-Quds al-Arabi*, in Arabic, August 3, 2004 and March 20–April 4, 2005.

20 sold their properties: Rushdi op. cit.

20 "head of the snake": United States v. Usama bin Laden, et al. S(7) 98 Cr. 1023 (LBS). United States District Court, Southern District of New York. Trial Transcript, February 6, 2001, pp. 280–285.

20 the first attack against an American target: Bergen 2001 op. cit., chapter 9.

20 traveled to Somalia: Daniel Benjamin and Steven Simon, *Age of Sacred Terror* (New York: Random House, 2002), p. 121.

20 eighteen American soldiers: Mark Bowden, "Team members try to free pilot's body," *Philadelphia Inquirer*, January 28, 1998.

20 the most effective way: Mark Bowden, *Black Hawk Down* (New York: Penguin, 2000), p. 110.

21 Within a week: Mark Huband, *Warriors of the Prophet: The Struggle for Islam* (Boulder, Colorado: Westview Press, 1998), p. 41.

21 "reviewed by Osama bin Laden": "Excerpts from guilty plea in terrorism case," *New York Times*, October 21, 2000. http://www.nytimes.com/2000/10/21/nyregion/excerpts-from-guilty-plea-in-terrorism-case.html.

21 "It was an unacceptable activity": Jamal Khashoggi, "Former Saudi intel chief interview on Saudi-Afghan ties, bin Laden—Part 5," *Arab News*, November 8, 2001.

21 Medina of the new age: Al-Qaeda recruitment videotape, summer 2001, accessed on August 14, 2001 at www.moonwarriors.com.

21 "hugely embittered": Sasson and bin Laden op cit, p. 207.

22 "Declaration of war": Osama bin Laden, "Declaration of war against the Americans occupying the land of the two holy places," August 1996. Available from PBS: http://www.pbs.org/newshour/terrorism/international/fatwa_1996.html.

22 in 1949: Lawrence Wright, *The Looming Tower: Al-Qaeda and the Road to 9/11* (New York: Vintage, 2007). "Baby, it's cold outside": Wright op. cit., p. 26.

22 jail-cell manifesto: Syed Qutb, *Milestones* (Mumbai: Bilal Books, 1998 edition), p. 62; repeatedly cited Qutb: Zawahiri op. cit.; "bin Laden would attend": Jamal Khalifa, interviews by author, Jeddah, Saudi Arabia, September 6 and 9, 2005.

23 The conventional view: This was largely the thrust of "The Man Behind bin Laden," Lawrence Wright's 2002 *New Yorker* piece, which remains the best account of Zawahiri's life. It's also an analysis that I had made in the 2001 book *Holy War, Inc.* Montasser al-Zayyat, an Egyptian lawyer who had been imprisoned with Zawahiri in the early 1980s, described him to me in December 2000 as "bin Laden's mind." But based on subsequent interviews with militants who know both men and an analysis of bin Laden's own actions it is clear that sometime in the mid-90s the al-Qaeda leader reversed the roles that had previously existed between himself and Zawahiri, who had once been one of his mentors and who he gradually eased instead into the role of one of his followers; albeit an important one. Zayyat himself has reversed himself writing in his 2002 book *The Road to Al-Qaeda: The Story of Bin Laden's Right-Hand Man*, "Osama bin Laden had an appreciable impact on Zawahiri though the conventional wisdom holds the opposite to be the case. Bin Laden advised Zawahiri to stop armed operations in Egypt and to ally with him against their common enemies: the United States and Israel. His advice to Zawahiri came upon their return to Afghanistan [in 1996], when bin Laden ensured the safety of Zawahiri and the [Egyptian] Islamic Jihad members under the banner of the Taliban."

24 "near enemy" regimes could not survive: Abu Musab al-Suri, *The Call for Global Islamic Resistance*, posted on the internet in December 2004.

24 "the main enemy is the Americans": Noman Benotman, interview by author, London, August 30, 2005.

24 came to this strategic analysis: Al-Suri op. cit.

24 in a Russian jail: Andrew Higgins and Alan Cullison, "Saga of Dr. Zawahiri Illuminates Roots of al-Qaeda Terror," *Wall Street Journal*, July 2, 2002.

24 Zawahiri was the penniless leader: Lawrence Wright, "The man behind bin Laden," *New Yorker*, September 16, 2002.

24 not especially well-liked: Jamal Ismail interview by author, Islamabad, Pakistan, 2004.

24 formally merged with al-Qaeda: The merger was de facto complete by February 1998, although the formal "contract" would not be signed until June 2001. See Intelligence report, Incorporation of Zawahiri's organization into bin Ladin's Al-Qa'ida, and recent [1998] activities of Egyptian Associates of Al-Qa'ida, Sept. 22, 1998; see also Intelligence report, interrogation of detainee, Feb. 8, 2002. 9/11 Commission Report op. cit., p. 470, fn 82.

24 "more like the assimilation": Feroz Ali Abbasi, Guantánamo Bay Prison Memoirs, 2002–2004, author's collection.

25 outlined the dictatorial powers: Substitution for the testimony of KSM, trial of Zacarias Moussaoui, http://en.wikisource.org/wiki/Substitution_for_the_Testimony_of_KSM.

25 requesting permission: Sasson and bin Laden op cit, p. 161 and 213.

25 modeled his life of jihad on the life of the Prophet: Batarfi op. cit.

25 "as a father": Al Hammadi op. cit.

25 "'seduced' many young men": Excerpts of Shadi Abdalla's interviews with German authorities that occurred between April 2002 and May 2003: "Summary Interrogation S. Abdalla: UK and European Connections plus Background Al Tawid/Zarqawi," author's collection.

25 "was so impressed": Trabelsi was subsequently arrested in Brussels on September 13, 2001, where he was planning a possible attack on a NATO base. Trabelsi was questioned in French and the text of his interrogation was later provided in Italian to prosecutors in Milan investigating one of Trabelsi's associates. Documents translated by investigative journalist Leo Sisti of *L'Espresso*. Author's collection.
25 "very inspirational": "Affidavit in support of pre-trial detention," filed by Special Agent Kiann Vandenover, U.S. District Court of Minnesota, Crim. 04-29 (JRT/FLN), February 6, 2004. Author's collection.
26 "godlike reverence": John Miller, interview by author, Washington, D.C., September 2005.
27 "What America is tasting now": transcript of the tape can be found from the Associated Press, October 7, 2001. http://www.guardian.co.uk/Archive/Article/0,4273,4272288,00.html.
27 "the Bush-Blair axis": Lawrence op. cit., p. 187.
27 ordinary American citizens: bin Laden quoted in Raymond Ibrahim, *The al-Qaeda Reader* (Broadway Books: New York, 2007), p. 281.
28 "Allah legislated": Lawrence op. cit., p. 165. (The verse in the Koran, 2, 194 is "And one who attacks you, attack him in the like manner as he attacked you.")
28 "completely justified": John Esposito and Dalia Mogahed, *Who Speaks for Islam? What a Billion Muslims Really Think* (New York: Gallup Press, 2007).
28 1.2 billion Muslims: PBS, "Islam Today," http://www.pbs.org/empires/islam/faith-today.html.
28 "organized Islamic faction": The founding minutes of al-Qaeda can be found in Bergen 2006, p. 81.
28 "This war is fundamentally religious": Al Jazeera op. cit. October 20, 2001.
29 quoted approvingly: Lawrence op. cit., p. 187.
29 an additional pillar: Fawaz Gerges, *The Far Enemy: Why Jihad Went Global* (Cambridge University Press: New York, 2005), p. 10.
29 religiously sanctioned warfare: David Cook, *Understanding Jihad* (University of California Press: Los Angeles, 2005), p. 2.
29 an able military commander: ibid., p. 6. This point is also buttressed by W. Montgomery Watt, *Muhammad: Prophet and Statesman* (New York: Oxford University Press, 1974), p. 124; Malise Ruthven, *Islam in the World* (New York: Oxford University Press, 2000), p. 48.
29 *Beit al-Ansar:* Bergen 2001 op. cit., p. 51.
29 also present were the sons: Hamid Mir, interview by author, Islamabad, Pakistan, July 9, 2003; Nic Robertson, "Previously unseen tape shows bin Laden's declaration of war," CNN, August 20, 2002; Ismail Khan, interview by author, Islamabad, Pakistan, September 1998.
29 a life sentence: Federal Bureau of Prisons, U.S. Department of Justice, Inmate Locator: http://www.bop.gov.
29 "Extract the most violent revenge": The card was translated into English for the first time in *The Osama bin Laden I Know*, pp. 204–5. This section on Sheikh Rahman draws on pp. 200–210.
30 *Dar al-Ansar:* Yosri Fouda and Nick Fielding, *Masterminds of Terror: The Truth Behind the Most Devastating Attack The World Has Ever Seen* (New York: Arcade Publishing, 2003), p. 108.
30 Abu Abdul Rahman: Fouda and Fielding, op. cit., p. 10.
30 declaration of war: Lawrence op. cit., p. 29.
31 "Manual for a Raid": Hans G. Kippenberg and Tilman Seidensticker, *The 9/11 Handbook* (London: Equinox Publishing, 2007), p. 21.
31 initial scheme: 9/11 Commission Report, p. 154.

32 70 percent of the recruits were Saudi: 9/11 Commission Report op. cit., p. 232.
32 the issue of Israel and Palestine: Samuel R. Berger and Mona Sutphen, "Commandeering the Palestinian Cause: Bin Laden's Belated Concern," in James F. Hoge Jr. and Gideon Rose, eds., *How Did This Happen? Terrorism and the New War* (New York: Public Affairs, 2001), p. 123.
32 "like a burning fire": Osama bin Laden, "Declaration of war against the Americans occupying the land of the two holy places," published in *Al Quds al Arabi*, August 1996. http://www.pbs.org/newshour/terrorism/international/fatwa_1996.html.
32 responsible for its restoration: Coll op. cit., p. 89.
32 "a routine of his father": Hamid Mir, interview by author, Islamabad, Pakistan, March 2005. Bin Laden also told the same story to Al Jazeera reporter Jamal Ismail.
33 "the green light": Kepel op. cit., p. 72.
33 first and only press conference: Nic Robertson, "Previously unseen tape shows bin Laden's declaration of war," CNN.com, August 20, 2002, http://archives.cnn.com/2002/U.S./08/19/terror.tape.main/.
33 al-Qaeda's first videotape production: The video was found on a jihadist website, www.moonwarriors.com, that is no longer operational. Author's collection.
33 "gave her name of Safia": Mir interview.
33 two letters: Intelligence reports, interrogations of KSM, June 3, 2003; February 20, 2004; April 3, 2004. 9/11 Commission Report op. cit., p. 532 fn 178.
33 a humble man: Noman Benotman, interview by author, London, UK, August 30, 2005.
34 "a poor slave of God": Osama bin Laden, December 27, 2001, Al Jazeera.
34 "afraid that if he does not": Jamal Khalifa, interview by author, Jeddah, Saudi Arabia, September 6 and 9, 2005.
34 "Jihad is in my mind": Abdul Sattar, "Osama urges Ummah to continue jihad," The News, May 7, 2001. Accessed via World News Connection, Dialog® File Number 985 Accession Number 134150902.
34 "My sons": bin Laden and Sasson op. cit., pp. 262–263.
35 "only way to get immunity": Noman Benotman, interview by author, London, June 13, 2009.
35 the Koranic injunction: The Holy Koran: Translation, N. J. Dawood (London: Penguin, 1997). Surah 5:51: "The Table."
35 "Every Muslim": Quoted in Bruce Lawrence, *Messages to the World: The Statements of Osama bin Laden* (New York: Verso, 2005), p. 87.

Chapter 3

36 CIA analyst Gina Bennett: Gina Bennett, *National Security Mom: Why "Going Soft" Will Make America Strong* (Deadwood, Oregon: Wyatt-MacKenzie Publishing, 2009), pp. 18–19.
37 "morning sickness": Bennett op. cit., p. 24.
37 developed a plan: Philip Shenon, "FBI knew for years about terror pilot training," *New York Times*, May 18, 2002.
37 memo that Sude had coauthored: 9/11 Commission op. cit., p. 260–262.
37 "I told my boss": author interview with Barbara Sude, Washington, D.C., December 16, 2009.
38 "I'm the kind of guy": Author interview with Daniel Coleman, Princeton, New Jersey, December 19, 2009.
38 debriefing the first defectors: FBI Affidavit on Ali Mohamed, submitted by Special Agent Daniel Coleman, September 1998. Author's collection.
38 In December 1995: Coleman interview op. cit.
38 smelled strongly of kerosene: Author interview with Daniel Coleman, op. cit.

39 "came up right away": Author interview with Barbara Sude, Washington, D.C., December 16, 2009.

39 "And I failed you": Rebecca Leung, "Your government failed you," CBS News, March 24, 2004. http://www.cbsnews.com/stories/2004/03/24/terror/main608526.shtml

39 immediately relieved: Department of the Navy, "Rear Admiral Husband Edward Kimmel," http://www.history.navy.mil/photos/pers-U.S./uspers-k/h-kimml.htm.

39 first congressional report: Richard Ben-Veniste, *The Emperor's New Clothes: Exposing the Truth from Watergate to 9/11* (New York, Thomas Dunne, 2009), pp. 205–207 describes the Roberts Commission in more detail.

39 *nine* official inquiries: Office of the Under Secretary of Defense for Personnel and Readiness, Advancement of Rear Admiral Kimmel and Major General Short on the Retired List, December 1, 1995, "The Pearl Harbor Investigations," http://www.ibiblio.org/pha/pha/dorn/dorn_3.html.

39 acceded to an investigative commission: Margaret Warner, PBS NewsHour, November 27, 2002. http://www.pbs.org/newshour/bb/terrorism/july–dec02/investigation_11-27.html

39 "circus atmosphere": Dick Cheney, *NBC Meet the Press with Tim Russert*, May 19, 2002.

40 public version of his report: Richard Shultz, "Showstoppers," *The Weekly Standard*, January 26, 2004. http://www.weeklystandard.com/Content/Public/Articles/000/000/003/613twavk.asp.

40 "Clinton wanted a rapier": Author interview with Michael Scheuer, Washington, D.C. December 23, 2009.

40 "brand-new Ferrari": Richard Shultz Jr., "How Clinton let al-Qaeda go," *Weekly Standard*, January 19, 2004.

41 sanctions on the Taliban: "Case Studies in sanctions and terrorism: Afghanistan," Peterson Institute, Case 99–1. http://www.petersoninstitute.org/research/topics/sanctions/afgh anistan.cfm.

41 "imposed an arms embargo: "UN passes arms embargo against Taliban," *Arms Control Association*, January/February 2001. http://www.armscontrol.org/node/2891.

41 followed that up: Neil King Jr. and David Cloud, "On High Alert: Casting a global net, U.S. security forces survive terrorist test." *Wall Street Journal*, March 8, 2000; Gutman op. cit., p. 197. Sheehan's own account can be found in his book, *Crush the Cell: How to Defeat Terrorism without Terrorizing Ourselves* (New York: Random House, 2006), p. 136.

41 "responsible for any attacks": Author interview with Michael Sheehan, November 21, 2009, New York.

41 "nucleus of opposition": Abu Walid al-Masri, "*The History of the Arab Afghans from the time of their arrival in Afghanistan until their departure with the Taliban*," serialized in *Al Sharq al Awsat*, December 8–14, 2004; was also told: interview with Abdul Hakim Mujahid by author in February 1999.

41 reopened after the fall off the Taliban: Office of the Inspector General, Department of State, "Inspection of Embassy Kabul, Afghanistan." http://oig.state.gov/lbry/reporthighlights/60040.htm.

42 only $2 million a year: Roy Gutman, *How We Missed the Story: Osama Bin Laden, the Taliban and the Hijacking of Afghanistan* (Washington, D.C., USIP, 2008), p. 56.

42 a political challenge: Gutman op. cit., p. 3.

42 "urgently": Richard Clarke, "Memorandum for Condoleezza Rice," January 25, 2001. George Washington University National Security Archive. http://www.gwu.edu/~nsarchiv/NSAEBB/NSAEBB147/clarke%20memo.pdf

42 "Strategy for Eliminating": Richard Clarke, "Strategy for Eliminating the Threat

from the Jihadist Networks of al Qada: Status and Prospects," George Washington University Security Archive. http://www.gwu.edu/~nsarchiv/NSAEBB/NSAEBB147/clarke%20attachment.pdf.

42 In the memo: Richard Clarke, "Memorandum for Condoleezza Rice," January 25, 2001. George Washington University National Security Archive. http://www.gwu.edu/~nsarchiv/NSAEBB/NSAEBB147/clarke%20memo.pdf.

42 businesslike but not urgent pace: Author correspondence with former 9/11 Commission staffer, Warren Bass February 1, 2010; 9/11 Commission Report op. cit., p. 205.

42 the same one: On March 22, 2004, Rice would write in the *Washington Post* that "No al-Qaeda plan was turned over to the new administration," which was simply not the case, as the December 2000 strategy paper did just that. Condoleezza Rice, "9/11: For the Record," *Washington Post*, March 22, 2004.

42 during a 2000 interview: Condoleezza Rice, interview with WJR Radio, Detroit, MI, October 2000.

42 "had succeeded": Condoleezza Rice, Testimony before the 9/11 Commission. Washington, D.C., May 19, 2004. http://www.cnn.com/2004/ALLPOLITICS/04/08/rice.transcript/.

43 "her facial expression": Richard Clarke, *Against All Enemies*, (New York: Free Press, 2004). p. 229.

43 "suspect connections": Paul Wolfowitz before the House of Representatives National Security Committee, Washington, D.C., September 16, 1998.

43 "trying to study": 9/11 Commission Report op. cit., p. 259.

43 thirty-three "principals" meetings: 9/11 Commission Report op. cit., p. 509 n. 174.

43 February 5: Elizabeth Bumiller, *Condoleezza Rice: An American Life* (New York: Random House, 2007), p. 141.

43 first cabinet-level meeting: 9/11 Commission Report op. cit., p. 212.

43 regularly briefed: "more than forty briefing items on al-Qaeda" before 9/11 according to Rice's testimony before the 9/11 Commission, April 8, 2004.

44 "Team B": Intelligence Community Experiment in Competitive Analysis: Soviet Strategic Objective—An Alternative View. Report of Team "B." December 1976. http://www.gwu.edu/~nsarchiv/NSAEBB/NSAEBB139/nitze10.pdf.

44 wrongly: Anne Cahn, *Killing Détente: The Right Attacks the CIA* (Philadelphia: University of Pennsylvania Press, 1998).

44 "the Vulcans": The phrase Vulcan came from the large statue of the Roman god Vulcan that looms over Rice's hometown of Birmingham, Alabama. See James Mann, *The Rise of the Vulcans: The History of Bush's War Cabinet* (New York: Penguin, 2004), p. x.

44 stood down: Richard Clarke, *Against All Enemies* (New York: Free Press, 2004), pp. 220–221; and Barton Gellman, "A strategy's cautious evolution," *Washington Post*, January 20, 2002.

44 turned down: James Risen and David Johnston, "FBI was warned it could not meet counterterrorism threat," *New York Times*, June 1, 2002. http://www.nytimes.com/2002/06/01/national/01INQU.html. Adam Clymer. "How September 11 changed goals of Justice Dept.," Florida State University, February 28, 2002.

44 top ten priorities: Philip Shenon, *The Commission: the Uncensored History of the 9/11 Investigation*. (New York: Hachette Book Group, 2008), p. 246.

45 had filmed bin Laden: Lisa Myers, "Osama bin Laden: missed opportunities," NBC News, March 17, 2004. http://www.msnbc.msn.com/id/4549030/

45 $3 million each: 9/11 Commission Report, op. cit., p. 211.

45 "was pounding on the [CIA]": Michael Sheehan interview New York, November 21, 2009; "had built a replica": Roger Cressey interview, Washington, D.C., November 24, 2009; and Gellman 2002 op. cit.

45 "I was at the meeting at the Agency": Cressey interview.
45 "We knew one hundred percent": Author interview with Ali Soufan, Manhattan, New York, December 17, 2009.
45 "preliminary judgment": 9/11 Commission Report, op. cit., p. 195.
46 simple exhaustion: My own analysis based on discussions with U.S. national security officials familiar with the handling of the *Cole* incident.
46 "possibility of a missile attack": The Combating Terrorism Center at West Point has released a series of documents and analyses relating to al-Qaeda; this document comes from that series. Document AFGP-2002-801138 from West Point's release of "Harmony" documents. http://ctc.usma.edu/harmony/harmony_menu.asp; http://ctc.usma.edu/aq/pdf/AFGP-2002-801138-Trans.pdf.
46 split up: 9/11 Commission Report, op. cit., p. 191.
46 Cheney was briefed: Gellman 2002 op. cit.
46 "We know all we need to": 9/11 Commission Report op. cit., p. 509, fn 180. Around this time, Clarke wrote Rice and Hadley that the Yemeni prime minister told a State Department official that while Yemen was not saying so publicly the Yemeni government was 99 percent certain that bin Laden was responsible for the *Cole* operation.
46 "no enthusiasm, no interest": Roger Cressey interview, Washington, D.C. November 24, 2009.
46 strongly implying its responsibility: 9/11 Commission Report, op. cit., p. 509, fn 180.
47 "inadequate, ineffective responses": Stephen Hadley, interview by author, Washington, D.C., December 15, 2009.
47 "we are untouchables": Ali Soufan interview by author, Manhattan, New York, December 17, 2009.
47 had renewed in June 2001: "Bush decides to keep Afghan sanctions," *Reuters*, July 3, 2001. http://www.nytimes.com/2001/07/03/world/bush-decides-to-keep-afghan-sanctions.html.
47 "blinking red": 9/11 Commission Report, op. cit., p. 259; "unprecedented": 9/11 Commission Report, op. cit., p. 262.
47 a representative sampling: 9/11 Commission Report, op. cit., pp. 533–535.
48 repeatedly warned: 9/11 Commission, op. cit., p. 199, and interview by author with Warren Bass, February 1, 2010.
48 "Multiple and simultaneous attacks": George Tenet, *At the Center of the Storm* (New York: Harper Collins, 2007), pp. 150–153.
48 "battle stations": Rice 9/11 Commission testimony, op. cit.
48 On August 6: 9/11 Commission Report op. cit. p 260 and p. 534 fn 35.
48 only "historical": 9/11 Commission Report op. cit., p. 260.
48 "Was the piece historical": Barbara Sude, interview by author, December 16, 2009, Washington, D.C.
48 seventy ongoing investigations: 9/11 Commission Report, op. cit., p. 262.
49 never publicly discussed: Michael Allen and Dana Milbank, "Bush gave no sign of worry in August 2001," *Washington Post*, April 11, 2004.
49 longest presidential vacation: Jim VandeHei, Peter Baker, "Vacationing Bush poised to set a record," *Washington Post*, August 3, 2005. http://www.washingtonpost.com/wp-dyn/content/article/2005/08/02/AR2005080201703.html.
49 no evidence: 9/11 Commission Report op. cit., p. 262.
49 wide-ranging and emblematic interview: Fox Special Report with Brit Hume, August 6, 2001. Interview with Jim Angle.
49 daily meetings: Clarke op. cit., p. 213, Michael Sheehan interview, New York City, November 21, 2009, and Roger Cressey interview and Bruce Riedel, *The Search for al-Qaeda* (Brookings: Washington, D.C., 2008), p. 96.

49 "an adversary that poses a serious threat": Andrew Cockburn, *Rumsfeld: His Rise, Fall, and Catastrophic Legacy* (New York: Simon & Schuster, 2007), p. 118.

Chapter 4

51 "A second plane": Bob Woodward, *Bush At War* (New York: Simon & Schuster, 2003), p. 15.

51 "kick their asses": Woodward, *Bush At War*, op. cit., p. 18.

52 "not only UBL": Bob Woodward, *Plan of Attack* (New York: Simon & Schuster, 2004), p. 25, and 9/11 Commission Report op. cit., p. 559, fn. 63.

52 "Not Iraq": David Cloud and Greg Jaffe, *The Fourth Star* (New York: Crown Publishing, 2009). p. 125.

52 "see if Saddam was involved": Richard Clarke, *Against All Enemies* (New York: Free Press, 2004), p. 32.

52 "their frontal lobe issue": Roger Cressey interview Washington, D.C., November 24, 2009.

52 worked up a memo: 9/11 Commission Report op. cit., p. 334.

53 "I can hear you": George W. Bush, New York, NY, September 14, 2001, http://georgewbush-whitehouse.archives.gov/news/releases/2001/09/20010914-9.html.

53 "poll ratings": ABC News/Washington Post Poll, "Backing for War on Terrorism," September 20, 2001. http://abcnews.go.com/images/PollingUnit/865a1%20Bush%20Address.pdf

53 personal interest: Interview by author with Amb. Cofer Black, Washington, D.C., February 6, 2003.

53 a matter of weeks: Tenet op. cit., pp. 175–176.

53 "flies walking across their eyeballs": Woodward op. cit., 2004, p. 52.

53 several of the key arguments: Douglas J. Feith, *War and Decision: Inside the Pentagon at the Dawn of the War on Terrorism* (New York: HarperCollins, 2008), pp. 13–16.

53 Rumsfeld sent a directive: Michael R. Gordon and Bernard E. Trainor, *COBRA II* (New York: Vintage, 2006), p. 22.

54 many assignments around South Asia: Schroen op. cit., pp. 57–60.

54 "take a small team": Schroen op. cit., pp. 15–16.

54 at Camp David: Tenet op. cit., p. 177.

54 the future outlines: Karen DeYoung, *Soldier: the Life of Colin Powell* (New York: Vintage, 2007), p. 350.

54 meeting was somber: John McLaughlin, interview by author, December 7, 2009, Washington, D.C.

54 off-the-shelf-plan: 9/11 Commission Report op. cit., p. 332.

55 no military plan ready: Feith op. cit., p. 88.

55 "airpower-based approach": Stephen Hadley, interview by author, Washington, D.C., December 15, 2009.

55 one hundred sources and sub sources: Hank Crumpton, "Intelligence and War: Afghanistan, 2001–2002," in Jennifer Sims and Burton Gerber, *Transforming U.S. Intelligence* (Washington, D.C.: Georgetown University Press, 2005). p. 163, and Hank Crumpton interview Washington, D.C. November 6, 2009.

55 the plan Tenet presented to Bush: Woodward op. cit., 2004, p. 51.

55 "the color drained": Condoleezza Rice, PBS Frontline, "Campaign Against Terror," July 12, 2002. http://www.pbs.org/wgbh/pages/frontline/shows/campaign/interviews/rice.html

55 "10 to 50 percent": Woodward op. cit. 2004, p. 83.

56 the lack of hard evidence: See chapters 9 and 10 in this book for more on this point.

56 "this round": 9/11 Commission Report op. cit., p. 335.

56 "projecting a spectacular attack": John McLaughlin, PBS Frontline, "The Dark Side," January 11, 2006. http://www.pbs.org/wgbh/pages/frontline/darkside/interviews/mclaughlin.html.

56 voted to go to war: Rumsfeld abstained and Cabinet voted; Tenet op. cit., p. 306.

56 Iraq was involved: Woodward op. cit., 2004, p. 99, and Bob Woodward and Dan Balz, "Combating terrorism: it starts today," Washington Post, February 1, 2002. http://www.washingtonpost.com/wp-dyn/content/article/2006/07; sh18/AR2006071800703_pf.html (which says the president made this comment the following morning of September 17).

56 a sing-along: Bumiller op. cit., p. 166.

56 "the CIA in there first": John McLaughlin, interview by author, December 7, 2009, Washington, D.C.

56 Bush also signed: Glenn Kessler, "U.S. decision on Iraq has puzzling past; opponents of war wonder when, how policy was set," *Washington Post*, January 12, 2003.

56 better than one in ten: 9/11 Commission Report, op. cit., p. 336.

56 military options for Iraq: Feith op. cit., p. 218. Also on September 17, Bush sent a 12 page memorandum to the CIA Director authorizing him to detain terrorists and set up a secret detention program for them outside the United States. United Nations Human Rights Council, "Joint study on global practices in relation to secret detention in the context of countering terrorism of the Special Rapporteur on the promotion and protection of human rights and fundamental freedoms while countering terrorism." January 26, 2010, p. 51. http://www2.ohchr.org/english/bodies/hrcouncil/docs/13session/A-HRC-13-42.doc.

57 "I want bin Laden's head": Schroen op. cit., p. 38.

57 eighty million Americans: Stanley A. Reshon, "Presidential Address," *Political Psychology*, 2005, p. 592.

57 "a lengthy campaign": George W. Bush, Address to a Joint Session of Congress, Washington, D.C., September 20, 2001, http://georgewbush-whitehouse.archives.gov/news/releases/2001/0 9/20010920-8.html. For a good account of the writing of the speech see Bob Woodward and Dan Balz, "A Presidency Defined in One Speech," *Washington Post*, February 1, 2002.

57 "They hate our freedoms": George W. Bush, Address to a Joint Session of Congress, September 20, 2001, Washington, D.C. http://georgewbush-whitehouse.archives.gov/news/releases/2001/09/20010920-8.html.

57 largely silent about American freedoms: In a review of 24 authentic statements made by bin Laden from 1994 to 2004, 72% of the content of the speeches referred to supposed Western or Jewish aggression against or exploitation of Muslims, while only 1% criticized the American way of life or culture, James L. Payne, Independent Review 2008: http://www.independent.org/publications/tir/article.asp?a=689.

58 What went unsaid: While the United States imports much of its energy from Mexico, Canada, and Venezuela, it is the Gulf countries' enormous oil reserves that allows them to set prices in the world's oil market.

58 "The first, the supreme": Carl von Clausewitz, *On War* (1832).

59 Authorization of the Use of Military Force: U.S. Congress. House of Representatives and Senate. *Authorization of the use of Military Force*. 107th Congress, 1st session. S.J. Res. 23. Washington, GPO: 2001.

59 "combat by all means": United Nations, Security Council, SECURITY COUNCIL CONDEMNS, 'IN STRONGEST TERMS', TERRORIST ATTACKS ON UNITED STATES, Unanimously Adopting Resolution 1368 (2001), Council Calls on All

States to Bring Perpetrators to Justice. September 12, 2001. http://www.un.org/News/Press/docs/2001/SC7143.doc.htm.

59 invoked Article 5: Toby Harden et al, "Nato: massacre an attack on all members," *Telegraph (UK)*, September 13, 2001. http://www.telegraph.co.uk/news/worldnews/1340439/Nato-massacre-an-attack-on-all-members.html.

59 massive American airpower: Woodward op. cit. 2002; some three hundred U.S. Special Forces soldiers: Hank Crumpton, speech at Center for Strategic and International Studies, January 14, 2008. http://csis.org/files/media/csis/press/080114_smart_crumpton.pdf.

59 on the afternoon of September 26: Schroen op. cit., p. 78; Gary Schroen, PBS Frontline, "The Dark Side," January 20, 2006. http://www.pbs.org/wgbh/pages/frontline/darkside/interviews/schroen.html

59 surprise appearance: Osama bin Laden, "Statement," October 7, 2001. Aired on Al Jazeera.

60 linked up with: Schroen op. cit., p. 194.

60 "death ray": PBS Frontline, "Campaign Against Terror," May 7, 2002. http://www.pbs.org/wgbh/pages/frontline/shows/campaign/interviews/595.html.

60 But the American press: R. W. Apple., Jr. "A military quagmire remembered: Afghanistan as Vietnam," *New York Times*, October 31, 2001.

60 "figured they were going to beat us": Gary Berntsen, interview by author, October 27, 2009, Washington, D.C.

60 "The more the merrier": Gary Berntsen, interview.

61 A couple of weeks: Osama bin Laden (Lawrence) op. cit., p. 106; Transcript of bin Laden's October [2002] interview with Al Jazeera's Taysir Allouni, translated by CNN, February 5, 2002. http://archives.cnn.com/2002/WORLD/asiapcf/south/02/05/binladen.transcript/index.html.

61 "America claims": For reasons that Al Jazeera has never convincingly elucidated, the network did not air this interview for a year. At one point Al Jazeera explained that the decision not to broadcast the interview was because it wasn't newsworthy, an explanation which was, to put it politely, ludicrous. If bin Laden had simply read from the phone book during the interview it would have still been news, as this was bin Laden's *only* post-9/11 television interview. In fact, the Al Jazeera interview was both wide-ranging and newsworthy; which only came to light three months later when CNN broadcast the interview without Al Jazeera's permission.

61 "We practice the good terrorism": Allouni, op. cit.

61 "did not intend to kill": Allouni op. cit.

61 summoned to Kabul in early November 2001 to treat Mohammed Atef: Bootie Cosgrove-Mather, "Osama's doc says he was healthy," *Associated Press*, November 27, 2002. http://www.cbsnews.com/stories/2002/11/27/attack/main531070.shtml.

61 "I didn't see anything abnormal": author interview with Ahmed Zaidan, Islamabad, Pakistan, July 2004.

61 "good health": Bakr Atyani, phone interview, Islamabad, Pakistan, August 22, 2005.

61 "were just lined": Bobby, SGT 1st Class, PBS Frontline, "Campaign Against Terror" http://www.pbs.org/wgbh/pages/frontline/shows/campaign/interviews/534.html.

62 "The people were overjoyed": Peter Jouvenal, interview London, UK, August 23, 2005. p. 323 in Bergen 2006.

62 A few days later: Atef was killed sometime between November 14 and November 16, 2001. GlobalSecurity.org, http://www.globalsecurity.org/security/profiles/mohammed_atef.htm.

62 married his son Muhammad to Atef's daughter: Daniel Klaidman, "Bin Laden's poetry of terror," Newsweek, March 26, 2001.

62 a blow to the organization: Feroz Ali Abbasi, Guantánamo Bay Prison Memoirs, 2002–2004; worked around the clock: Author interview with U.S. intelligence officials, Washington, D.C., June 6, 2003.

62 "sow some dissension": Robert Grenier, interview by author, Washington, D.C., February 19, 2010.

62 October 2: Tenet op. cit., pp. 182–183, and interview with Robert Grenier in Washington, D.C. February 19, 2009.

63 a number of Afghanistan's monarchs: Karzai comes from the same tribe, the Popalzai, as the former Afghan king, Mohammad Zahir Shah. BBC, "Hamid Karzai: shrewd statesman," June 14, 2002. http://news.bbc.co.uk/2/hi/south_asia/2043606.stm.

63 a bitter enemy: "Hamid Karzai: a profile," September 21, 2006. CBC, http://www.cbc.ca/news/background/afghanistan/karzai.html.

63 "Those people": Grenier interview.

63 over the Afghan border: Hamid Karzai, PBS Frontline, "Campaign Against Terror," May 7, 2002. http://www.pbs.org/wgbh/pages/frontline/shows/campaign/interviews/karzai.html.

63 "Tell your people to light fires": Hamid Karzai, interview by PBS Frontline, "Campaign Against Terror," May 7, 2002.

63 food and weapons: Tenet op. cit., p. 219.

63 returned to Afghanistan: Tenet op. cit., p. 220.

64 "We were going to build": Jason Amerine, New America Foundation, Washington, D.C., January 19, 2010.

64 containing up to 500 Taliban: U.S. Army, "The U.S. Army in Afghanistan, Operation Enduring Freedom: October 2001–March 2002," CMH Pub 70-83-1.

64 excused himself: Jason Amerine, PBS Frontline, "Campaign Against Terror." http://www.pbs.org/wgbh/pages/frontline/shows/campaign/ground/tarinkowt.html.

64 "The intense bombardment": Vahid Mojdeh, *Afghanistan Under Five Years of Taliban Sovereignty*, translated by Sepideh Khalili and Saeed Gangi (Kabul, 2001).

64 "The Taliban are coming": Amerine, New America Foundation, op. cit. and Jason Amerine, PBS Frontline, "Campaign Against Terror."

65 "Karzai was the lynchpin": Hank Crumpton, interview by author, November 6, 2009, Washington, D.C.

65 the fall of Kabul: For example, see Tony Karon, "What they're saying about the fall of Kabul," TIME, November 16, 2001. http://www.time.com/time/nation/article/0.8599,184766.00.html.

65 gathering the large force: Jason Amerine, PBS Frontline, "Campaign Against Terror." http://www.pbs.org/wgbh/pages/frontline/shows/campaign/ground/tarinkowt.html.

65 James Dobbins: James Dobbins, *After the Taliban: Nation Building in Afghanistan* (Dulles, VA: Potomac Books, Inc, 2008) pp. 2–4; Dobbins op. cit., pp. 49–51.

66 various Afghan factions: Karzai op. cit.

66 Iranian officials: Ahmed Rashid, *Descent into Chaos: The United States and the Failure of Nation Building in Pakistan, Afghanistan, and Central Asia* (New York: Viking Adult, 2008), p. 104.

66 "this was before the Bush administration": James Dobbins, interview by author, Washington, D.C., November 6, 2009.

66 satellite phone: Rashid op. cit., p. 95.

66 "I wasn't aware of the significance of it": Karzai op. cit. Shut out of the Bonn con-

ference were any representatives of the Taliban. This would have serious long term consequences for Afghanistan: "In effect, they are a political party. But they're a political party that Bonn shut out, so no wonder they formed an insurgency," pointed out a senior American official involved in Afghan policy.

66 urge him to start moving: David Fox, PBS Frontline, "Campaign Against Terror," 2002; http://www.pbs.org/wgbh/pages/frontline/shows/campaign/interviews/fox.html.

67 fallen 2 kilometers short: "Bodies of two Green Berets arrive in Germany," CNN.com, December 6, 2001. http://archives.cnn.com/2001/WORLD/asiapcf/central/12/06/ret.bombing.casualties/index.html

67 recalls saying "OK": Karzai, op. cit. and Eric Blehm, *The Only Thing Worth Dying For* (Harper: New York, 2010), p. 297.

67 more than two hundred vehicles: Christopher Buchanan, "Reporter's Notebook: the Karzai Interview," PBS "Campaign Against Terror," May 7, 2002. http://www.pbs.org/wgbh/pages/frontline/shows/campaign/etc/notebook.html.

Chapter 5

68 "So let me be a martyr": Osama bin Laden (Lawrence) op. cit., page xxiii.

68 Jalalabad: Bergen, 2004, and author visits to the Jalalabad compound between 2003 and 2006.

69 more than six months to build: interview by author with Hutaifa Azzam, Amman, Jordan, September 13, 2005.

69 From bin Laden's house: Author observations, Tora Bora, January 2005.

69 "I really feel secure": Abdel Bari Atwan, interview by author, London, UK, June 2005.

69 "My brothers and I": Omar bin Laden, Najwa bin Laden, Jean Sasson, *Growing Up Bin Laden* (New York: St. Martin's Press, 2009), p. 73.

70 chief bodyguard: Ali Soufan, FBI special agent, interview with author, Manhattan, New York, December 17, 2009.

70 during the month of Ramadan: "Moroccan security source views danger of Moroccans released from Guantánamo," *Al Sharq al Awsat*, August 20, 2004.

70 Around the same time: Tim Weiner, "Bin Laden reported spotted in fortified camp in Afghan east," *New York Times*, November 25, 2001.

70 Berntsen had arrived in Kabul: Gary Berntsen, interview by author, Washington, D.C., October, 27, 2009.

70 arrived uneventfully in Jalalabad: Gary Berntsen, email to author, November 24, 2009.

70 "We spent five weeks": Faiza Saleh Ambah, "Out of Guantánamo and Bitter Toward Bin Laden," *Washington Post*, March 24, 2008.

70 decided to split into two groups of four: interview with Berntsen.

71 an elaborate graphic: "Bin Laden's Mountain Fortress," *The Times* of London, November 29, 2001. Available at http://www.edwardjayepstein.com/nether_fictoid3.htm.

71 even the larger ones: author observations Tora Bora, January 2005.

71 Shortly after 9/11: Dalton Fury, *Kill Bin Laden: A Delta Force Commander's Account of the Hunt for the World's Most Wanted Man* (New York: St. Martin's Press, 2008), page xvi and page 92.

71 There Khan was introduced to: Interview by author with Dalton Fury, telephone, December 19, 2008.

71 the small American and allied force: Fury op. cit., p. xx, and email from Fury to author, December 8, 2009.

72 1,110 precision-guided: Fury, op. cit., p. 289.

72 Muhammad Musa: Muhammad Musa, interview by author, Jalalabad, Afghanistan, June, 2003.

72 briefed Bush and Cheney: Ron Suskind, *The One Percent Doctrine: Deep Inside America's Pursuit of its Enemies since 9/11* (New York: Simon & Schuster, 2007), p. '58; Crumpton interview.

72 Tenet remembers: George Tenet, *At the Center of the Storm* (New York: Harper Collins, 2007), p. 227.

73 By the evening of December 3: Gary Berntsen and Ralph Pezzullo, *Jawbreaker: The attack on bin Laden and al-Qaeda: A personal account by the CIA's key field commander* (New York Crown, 2005), p. 299, and author interview with Gary Berntsen, October 27, 2009, Washington, D.C.

73 "I remember the message": Author interview with Hank Crumpton, Washington, D.C., November 6, 2009.

73 General Franks explained his reasoning: Email to author from General Tommy Franks, November, 24 2009.

74 Franks also said: General Franks told PBS' *Frontline*: "I think it was a pretty good determination, to provide support to that operation, and to work with the Pakistanis along the Pakistani border to bring it to conclusion." "Campaign Against Terror," June 12, 2002 http://www.pbs.org/wgbh/pages/frontline/shows/campaign /interviews/franks.html.

74 Fury recommended: Fury op cit., p. 76.

74 al-Qaeda would not expect an attack: Interview by author with Dalton Fury, telephone, December 19, 2008.

74 "for this most important mission": Fury op. cit., p. 209.

74 a motley crew: Jane Corbin, *Al-Qaeda: In Search of the Terror Network that Threatens the World* (New York: Simon & Schuster, 2003), p. 296; author observations; "Hajji Zahir": Mary Anne Weaver, "Lost at Tora Bora," *New York Times Magazine*, September 11, 2005; U.S. Senate Foreign Relations Committee, "Tora Bora revisited," p. 11. Philip Smucker, "How bin Laden got away; A day-by-day account of how Osama bin Laden eluded the world's most powerful military machine," *Christian Science Monitor*, March 4, 2002. And see also the account in U.S. Special Operations Command History (6th edition, 2008) p. 97. http://www.socom.mil/SOCOM Home/Documents/history6thedition.pdf.

74 direct laser beams: Fury op. cit., p. 76.

74 "the latest intelligence": U.S. Special Operations Command History, op. cit., p. 98.

74 locals were reluctant to give: from U.S. official on ground at Tora Bora, interview by author.

75 flying pennants: Author observations, Tora Bora, summer 2003.

75 The al-Qaeda leader sat: "In the Footsteps of bin Laden," CNN documentary, August 23, 2006. http://www.cnn.com/CNN/Programs/presents/bin.laden/.

75 would have had additional resonance: Lacey op. cit., p. 322. Lacey explains that the story of the Battle of Badr is still cherished by Saudis today.

75 snow was falling steadily: weather observations from a personal log kept by a Delta operator on the ground at Tora Bora. Email to author August 6, 2009.

75 seven hundred thousand pounds of ordnance: Tenet op. cit., p. 226.

75 Abu Jaafar al-Kuwaiti recalled: The statement was posted to Al Neda, al-Qaeda's Web site at the time, on September 11, 2002.

75 "I was out of medicine": Andrew Selsky, "Yemeni says bin Laden was at Tora Bora" Associated Press, September 7, 2007.

75 "day and night": Osama bin Laden, "Message to our Brothers in Iraq," Al Jazeera, February 11, 2003 (translated by ABC News).

75 a U.S. bomber dropped: Fury op. cit., p. 149.

76 Berntsen remembers: author interview, Gary Berntsen Washington, D.C., October, 27, 2009.

76 "were awakened": The statement was posted to Al Neda, al-Qaeda's Web site at the time, on September 11, 2002.

76 bin Laden had dreamed about a scorpion: "Global Islamic Media Front publishes profile of usama bin Ladin's personal habits," September 21, 2007. OSC Summary of Jihadist Websites, October 17, 2007, accessed via World News Connection, Dialog File Number 985 Accession Number 251901321.

76 intercept from Tora Bora: Fury op. cit., p 173.

76 Afghan soldiers said: U.S. Special Operations Command History op. cit., p. 99.

76 Later that evening: Fury op. cit., p. 175, and Fury telephone interview with author on December 8, 2008.

76 a ferocious firefight: Fury op. cit., p. 175.

76 made the decision to bail: Dalton Fury, *60 Minutes*, October 5, 2008. http://www.cbsnews.com/stories/2008/10/02/60minutes/main4494937.shtml and interview by author, December 18, 2008.

77 "They talked on the radio": Muhammad Musa, interview by author, Jalalabad, Afghanistan, June, 2003.

77 Strung out on a ridge: Email from Dalton Fury, December 10, 2009.

77 "Essentially I used": Berntsen interview op. cit.

77 U.S. forces only observed: Interview by author with Dalton Fury, telephone, December 8, 2009.

77 "The time is now": Fury email to author, December 8, 2009.

78 One member of Berntsen's team: Berntsen interview.

78 Hubayshi remains bitter: Robert Lacey, *Inside the Kingdom: Kings, Clerics, Modernists, Terrorists, and the Struggle for Saudi Arabia* (New York: Viking Press, 2009), p. 253.

78 according to an interpreter: Interview by author, Tora Bora battle participant.

78 confirmed by the various American radio intercepts: Interview by author, Tora Bora battle participant.

78 especially sacred day: Koranic verses from the Night of Power chapter: "*The Night of Al-Qadr is better than a thousand months.*" [97:3] "*The Angels and the spirit descend thereon by the leave of their Lord with every command.*" [97:4].

78 "A Soviet airplane": Basil Muhammed, *Al Ansar Al Arab fi Afghanistan* ("The Arab Volunteers in Afghanistan"), The Committee for Islamic Benevolence Publications, 1991, p. 307.

78 escape from Tora Bora: Peter Finn, "Bin Laden used Ruse to Flee; Moroccans Say Guard Took Phone at Tora Bora," *Washington Post*, January 21, 2003.

78 the al-Qaeda leader fled: "Moroccan security source views danger of Moroccans released from Guantánamo," *Al Sharq al Awsat*, August 20, 2004.

79 had gone to Afghanistan: Ghanim Abdul Rahman al Harbi, Guantánamo Administrative Review Board hearing round 1 summaries, p. 1.

79 ended up with a group: Ghanim Abdul Rahman al Harbi, Guantánamo Administrative Review Board hearing round 1 summaries, p. 3. http://projects.nytimes.com/Guantánamo/detainees/516-ghanim-abdul-rahman-al-harbi/documents/1/pages/467.

79 estimated that at battle's end: Fury op. cit., pp. 277–278.

79 thousands of the paramilitary constabulary: Berntsen, *Jawbreaker*, p. 305.

79 attack by a group: Indian parliament, http://www.indianembassy.org/new/parliament_dec_13_01.htm.

79 "We had to respond": Moinuddin Haider, interview by author, January 24, 2002, Karachi, Pakistan.

79 up to 240 militants: Pervez Musharraf, *In the Line of Fire* (New York: Free Press, 2006), p. 265.

80 some four hundred American soldiers: Ambassador Hank Crumpton, "Remarks at CSIS Smart Power series," Washington, D.C., January 14, 2008.

80 "The mountains of Tora Bora": Michael Delong, *A General Speaks Out: The Truth About the Wars in Afghanistan and Iraq* (Osceola: Zenith Press, 2007), p 56.

80 not a single American had died in combat: *Chicago Tribune*, March 23, 2003. http://www.globalsecurity.org/org/news/2003/030330-public-opinion01.htm.

80 more journalists had died than U.S. soldiers: Icasualties.org; three soldiers had died: http://www.icasualties.org/OEF/Fatalities.aspx; four journalists had been killed on November 19, 2001. Claire Cozens, *The Guardian,* November 27, 2001. Swedish TV cameraman killed in Afghanistan http://www.guardian.co.uk/media/2001/nov/27/terrorismandthemedia.afghanistan.

80 "stay in the foothills": Fury op. cit., and Fury interview, December 18, 2008.

80 "wants us to look for options in Iraq": Tommy Franks, *American Soldier* (New York: HarperCollins, 2004), p. 315.

81 "I realized": Richard Myers, *Eyes on the Horizon* (New York: Simon & Schuster, 2009), p. 218.

81 seven days a week, sixteen-plus hours a day: Franks op. cit., p. 335.

81 "close to 100 journalists": email to author from Nic Robertson.

81 Could the Pentagon: Drew Brown, "U.S. lost its best chance to decimate al-Qaida in Tora Bora," Knight Ridder Washington Bureau, October 14, 2002. And see also *U.S. Special Operations Command History* (6th edition, 2008), p. 98, which describes a reinforced company of the 10th Mountain being at Bagram and Mazr-e-Sharif. The Senate Foreign Relations Committee report on page 17 explains that it was the 15th and 26th Marine Expeditionary Units; http://foreign.senate.gov/imo/media/doc/Tora_Bora_Report.pdf.

82 asked to send his men into Tora Bora: Mary Anne Weaver, "Lost at Tora Bora," *New York Times Magazine*, September 11, 2005. http://www.nytimes.com/2005/09/11/magazine/11TORABORA.html.

82 three hundred U.S. soldiers: Interview by author with Dalton Fury, December 19, 2008.

82 blackout conditions: *U.S. Special Operations Command History* (6th edition, 2008), pp. 93–94.

82 "unrealistic": "A Different Kind of War," *United States Army in Operation Enduring Freedom, October 2001–September 2005,* Combat Studies Institute Press, June 2009, p. 128.

82 story on November 25: Tim Weiner, "Bin Laden reported spotted in fortified camp in Afghan east," *New York Times*, November 25, 2001.

82 background briefing reported by CNN: "U.S. Officials Believe bin Laden is in Tora Bora," CNN transcript, December 15, 2001.

83 "senior military officer": John Kifner, "Al-Qaeda balks at surrender," *New York Times*, December 12, 2001.

83 "I think he's probably": Dick Cheney, ABC News, November 29, 2001. http://abcnews.go.com/Primetime/story?id=132168&page=1.

83 Two weeks later: Vice President Dick Cheney, *Meet the Press*, December 9, 2001.

83 "We don't have": Paul Wolfowitz, Defense Department Briefing, December 10, 2002.

83 "at one point or another": Robert Burns, "U.S. war commander says search of Tora Bora caves ending with no bin Laden," *Associated Press*, January 7, 2002.

83 official U.S. military history: *U.S. Special Operations Command History* (6th edition, 2008), p. 101.

83 "Did we get him?": Michael Delong, *A General Speaks Out* (Washington, D.C.: Zenith Press, 2004), p. 57.

83 "When we had Osama": John Kerry, Presidential Debate, Coral Gables, FL, September 30, 2004. http://www.debates.org/pages/trans2004a.html

84 "We don't know": General Tommy Franks, "War of Words," *New York Times*, October 19, 2004.

84 "absolute garbage": Cheney was speaking in Ohio on the morning of October 19, 2004.

84 Bush himself weighed in: Dan Froomkin, "Bush buys himself some time," Washingtonpost.com, October 27, 2004. President Bush was speaking on the morning of October 27 at a rally in Lancaster County, PA.

84 suddenly appeared on a videotape: Gilles Kepel and Jean-Pierre Milelli, *Al-Qaeda in its own Words* (Boston: Belknap Press of Harvard University Press, 2008), p. 75.

84 Kerry was quick to point out: Agence France Presse, "Bush rips Kerry's 'shameful' attacks," October 30, 2004.

85 "I am just a poor slave": Osama bin Laden videotape, Al Jazeera, December 27, 2001.

85 "I was in the Gulf region": Abdel Bari Atwan, interview by author, London, June 2005.

85 "As to my children": Osama bin Laden, "The Will of One Seeking the Support of Allah Almighty, Usama Bin Laden." *Al-Majallah* (Saudi magazine), December 14, 2001. http://www.fas.org/irp/world/para/ubl-fbis.pdf, p. 222.

Chapter 6

86 "The tactics took over": Noman Benotman, interview by author, London, UK, August 30, 2005.

86 Omar bin Laden: BBC1, *Mr. and Mrs. Bin Laden*; http://www.dailymail.co.uk/news/article-512463/Mr-Mrs-Bin-Laden-Rockers-Rome-hoping-peace-meeting-Pope.html.

86 part of the small contingent: Khalid al-Hammadi, "Bin Laden's former bodyguard interviewed," *Al Quds al Arabi*, August 3, 2004 and March 20 to April 4, 2005; Omar bin Laden, Najwa bin Laden, Jean Sasson, *Growing Up Bin Laden* (New York: St. Martin's Press, 2009), pp. 136–145.

87 "Those guys are dummies": Hutaifa Azzam, interview by author, Amman, Jordan, September 13, 2005.

87 permanent wedge: Paul Schemm, "Bin Laden son wants to be peace activist," *Associated Press*, January 18, 2008. For more on Omar's life, see *Growing Up Bin Laden* op. cit. (2009).

87 just how demoralized: Letter from 'Abd al-Halim Adl to Mukhtar, June 13, 2002, translated by Combating Terrorism Center at West Point, Harmony collection. www.ctc.usma.edu/aq/pdf/Al_Adl_Letter_Translation.pdf.

87 how precarious life on the run had become: Muhammad al Shafi'i, "A Site Close to al-Qaeda Posts a Poem by bin Laden in which He Responds to His Son Hamzah," *Al Sharq al Awsat*, June 16, 2002.

87 ten thousand to twenty thousand recruits: CIA analytic report, "Afghanistan: An incubator for international terrorism," CTC 01-40004, Mar. 27, 2001; CIA analytic report, "Al-Qa'ida still well positioned to recruit terrorists." 9/11 Commission Report, p. 470, fn. 78.

88 Only around two hundred: Author interview with former FBI Special Agent Daniel Coleman, Washington, D.C., April 26, 2006.

88 oath of allegiance: West Point, Harmony document "Employment contract," AFGP-2002-600045, http://ctc.usma.edu/aq/pdf/AFGP-2002-600045-Trans.pdf.

88 The training camps: See generally Omar Nasiri, *Inside the Jihad* (New York: Basic Books, 2006).

88 L'Houssaine Kherchtou: USA v. Usama bin Laden, testimony of L'Houssaine Kherchtou, February 21 and 27, 2001, quoted in Peter Bergen, *Holy War, Inc.* (New York: Free Press, 2001), p. 93.

88 *Encyclopedia of Jihad:* C. J. Chivers and David Rohde, "Turning out guerrillas and terrorists to wage a holy war," *New York Times*, March 18, 2002.

88 Al-Qaeda's bylaws: translated by West Point's Combating Terrorism Center, April 18, 2002. AFGP-2002-600048, http://ctc.usma.edu/aq/pdf/AFGP-2002-600048-Trans.pdf.

89 "to discuss their issues": Abu Jandal, FD-302, Federal Bureau of Investigation, pages 40–41. Author's collection.

89 as some had portrayed it: Adam Curtis, "The Power of Nightmares," BBC Two, October 2004; and Jason Burke, *Al-Qaeda: The True Story of Radical Islam* (New York: I. B. Tauris and Co., Ltd, 2004).

90 were part of a far-reaching: "Al-Zarqawi: The Second al-Qa'ida Generation," by Fu'ad Husayn, a Jordanian journalist who received information from three people close to al-Zarqawi, including Saif al-Adel, to whom this chapter is attributed. The Arabic-language London-based daily *Al-Quds al-Arabi* serialized the book. This section was published by the newspaper on 21–22 May 2005.

90 painted a grim picture: Abu Musab al-Suri, *The Call for Global Islamic Resistance*, published on jihadist websites, 2004.

91 Suri's bleak assessment was seconded: Hank Crumpton, "Intelligence and War: Afghanistan, 2001–2002," in Jennifer Sims and Burton Gerber, *Transforming U.S. Intelligence* (Washington, D.C.: Georgetown University Press, 2005), p. 162.

91 "Terrorists want a lot of people watching," Terrorism expert Brian Jenkins, "Will terrorists go nuclear?", November 1975, www.rand.org/pubs/papers/2006/P5541.pdf.

91 economic consequences: Osama bin Laden, interview by Taysir Alouni, somewhere near Kabul, Afghanistan, October 20, 2001.

92 disrupting the global economy: Osama bin Laden, Al Jazeera, October 6, 2002. Original date, location unknown. FBIS Report, Compilation of usama bin Laden Statements, 1994-January 2004.

92 "No doubt about that": Osama bin Laden, (Internet) Jihad Online News Network WWW-Text in Arabic 21 Jan 03. FBIS Report op. cit., p. 244.

92 low tens of thousands: "Asian Muslims hold anti-U.S. marches; Pakistan seeks to curb demos," Agence France Presse, October 19, 2001.

93 the way to accomplish this: see generally Fawaz A. Gerges, *The Far Enemy: Why Jihad Went Global* (New York: Cambridge University Press, 2005).

93 an estimated $500 billion: Royal Institute of International Affairs quoted in James Fallows, "Declaring victory," *The Atlantic*, September 2006; an annual output: Budget of the United States Government, GPO Access, Table 10.1, http://www.gpoaccess.gov/usbudget/fy05/hist.html.

93 provoking the world's only superpower: Peter Bergen, "Al-Qaeda at 20: Dead or Alive?" *Washington Post*, August 17, 2008. http://www.newamerica.net/publications/articles/2008/al_qaeda_20_dead_or_alive_7760.

94 ten hijacked planes: 9/11 Commission Report op. cit., p. 154.

Chapter 7

95 "All you need to know": Cofer Black, Joint hearing of the United States House of Representatives Select Intelligence Committee and the United States Senate Select Intelligence Committee, Washington, D.C., September 26, 2002.

95 "A state of war": United States Supreme Court, HAMDI V. RUMSFELD (03-6696) 542 U.S. 507 (2004), Opinion (O'Connor), June 28, 2004. http://www.law.cornell.edu/supct/html/03-6696.ZO.html.

95 "no information to floods": Bumiller op. cit., p. 168.

95 "inaccurate threat reporting possible": Roger Cressey interview by author, Washington, D.C., November 24, 2009.

96 anthrax letters: "U.S. officials declare researcher is anthrax killer," CNN.com, August 6, 2008. http://www.cnn.com/2008/CRIME/08/06/anthrax.case/index.html.

96 "an enormous impact": Scott McClellan, *What Happened: Inside the Bush White House and Washington's Culture of Deception* (New York: Perseus Books, 2008), p. 108.

96 "Dark Winter": Dark Winter Exercise, Center for Strategic and International Studies and University of Pittsburgh Medical Center, June 2001. http://www.upmc-biosecurity.org/website/events/2001_darkwinter/.

96 believed by the participants: Feith op. cit., p. 216.

97 Bush nixed the idea: David E Sanger, *The Inheritance: The World Obama Confronts and the Challenges to American Power* (New York: Harmony, 2009), p. 423.

97 "undisclosed location": Bumiller op. cit., p. xx.

97 consistently believed that a 9/11: Foreign Policy and the Center for American Progress, "Terrorism Index," May 22, 2008. http://www.americanprogress.org/issues/2008/08/pdf/time_series.pdf, p. 9.

97 And none of the senior: Donald Rumsfeld had served as a Navy aviator in peacetime between 1954 and 1957. Department of Defense, "SecDef Histories," http://www.defense.gov/specials/secdef_histories/bios/rumsfeld.htm.

97 vigorously objected: Colin Powell, Memorandum to Counsel to the President, Assistant to the President for National Security Affairs, subject: Draft Decision Memorandum for the President on the Applicability of the Geneva Convention to the Conflict in Afghanistan, January 26, 2002. http://www.gwu.edu/~nsarchiv/NSAEBB/NSAEBB127/02.01.26.pdf.

98 Abu Omar: Author interview with Abu Omar, Alexandria, Egypt, November 24, 2007.

98 "extraordinary rendition": Jane Mayer, "Outsourcing Torture," *The New Yorker*, February 14, 2005. http://www.newyorker.com/archive/2005/02/14/050214fa_fact6.

98 thousands of documents: Tribunale di Milano, Sezione Giudice per le indagini preliminari, "The judge presiding over preliminary investigations," n. 10838/05, n. 1966/05. Author collection; statements by Abu Omar's wife, "Decree for the application of coercive measures," art. 292 c.p.p., n. n. 10838/05, n. 1966/05.

99 "the Americans imposed you on us": Abu Omar interview.

100 "substantial grounds": United Nations Convention Against Torture and Other Cruel, Inhuman, or Degrading Treatment or Punishment, February 4, 1985, http://www.hrweb.org/legal/cat.html.

100 detailed the methods used: United States Department of State, Bureau of Democracy, Human Rights, and Labor. 2003 Country Reports on Human Rights Practices, February 25, 2004. http://www.state.gov/g/drl/rls/hrrpt/2003/27926.htm.

100 "This country does not believe in torture": George W. Bush, Washington, D.C., March 16, 2005.

100 "has not transported anyone": Condoleezza Rice, Andrews Air Force Base, Maryland, December 5, 2005.

100 sped up dramatically: Peter Bergen and Katherine Tiedemann, "Disappearing Act: Rendition by the Numbers," *Mother Jones*, March 3, 2008. http://www.motherjones.com/politics/2008/03/disappearing-act-rendition-numbers.

100 "outsources our crimes": Philip Bobbitt, *Terror and Consent: The Wars for the 21st Century* (New York: Knopf, 2008), p. 368.

101 "there are approaches": Author interview with Brad Garrett, Washington, D.C., 2007.

101 "a real chilling effect": Author interview, Robert Dannenberg, New York, December 17, 2009.

101 professional liability insurance: Michael Scheuer, interview by author, Washington, D.C., December 23, 2009.
102 set back Spataro's probe dramatically: Author interview, Armando Spataro, Milan, Italy, December 3, 2007.
102 more than ten thousand: Armando Spataro, "The kidnapping of Nasr Osama Mustafa Hassan alias Abu Omar," Milan, February 17, 2007.
103 owned by Phillip Morse: John Crewdson and Tom Hundley, "Jet's travels cloaked in mystery," *Chicago Tribune*, March 20, 2005.
103 went to trial in Milan: Italy convicts U.S. agents in CIA kidnap trial," CNN.com, November 4, 2009. http://edition.cnn.com/2009/WORLD/europe/11/04/italy.rendition.verdict/index.html.
104 "engaged in": DeYoung op cit, pp. 365–366.
104 four dozen nations: New York Times, Guantánamo Docket. Citizens of 48 countries have been held at Guantánamo.
104 "What the hell": Mayer op. cit., p. 82.
104 news even: Karen Greenberg, *The Least Worst Place: Guantánamo's First 100 Days* (New York: Oxford University Press, 2009). pp. 16–17.
104 attractive to administration officials: Donald Rumsfeld, Defense Department Briefing, Arlington, VA, December 27, 2001.
104 "The whole theory": Bobbitt op. cit., p. 265.
105 "failed state": Memorandum for the Joint Chiefs of Staff, Subject: status of Taliban and Al-Qaida, January 19, 2002. http://www.gwu.edu/~nsarchiv/NSAEBB/NSAEBB127/02.01.19.pdf. This memo draws on the January 9, 2002 memo from John Yoo.
105 the State Department's response: William Taft IV, United States Department of State Unclassified Memorandum to John C. Yoo, Subject: Your draft memorandum of January 9. January 11, 2002. http://www.cartoonbank.com/newyorker/slideshows/01TaftMemo.pdf.
105 "Like criminals": Bobbitt op. cit., p. 264.
106 "vicious killers": Donald Rumsfeld, Defense Department Briefing, Camp X-Ray, Cuba, January 27, 2002, http://www.defense.gov/news/newsarticle.aspx?id=43817.
106 only some 5 percent: Mark Denbeaux and Joshua Denbeaux, "Report on Guantánamo detainees: A profile of 517 detainees through analysis of Department of Defense data," Seton University School of Law, http://law.shu.edu/aaafinal.pdf, p. 2.
106 they have never in the past: Ken Ballen and Peter Bergen, "The worst of the worst?", *Foreign Policy*, October 2008. http://www.foreignpolicy.com/story/cms.php?story_id=4535.
106 "I never saw anything useful": Author interview with Daniel Coleman, Princeton, New Jersey, December 19, 2009.
106 "don't recall any information": Author interview with Michael Rolince, Washington, D.C., 2007.
106 David Hicks: Raymond Bonner, "Australian detainee's life of wandering ends with plea bargain," *New York Times*, March 28, 2007.
106 Salim Hamdan: Robert Worth, "Bin Laden driver to be sent to Yemen," *New York Times*, November 25, 2008. http://www.nytimes.com/2008/11/26/washington/26gitmo.html.
106 Ali Hamza al-Bahlul: William Glaberson, "Detainee convicted on terrorism charges," *New York Times*, November 3, 2008. http://www.nytimes.com/2008/11/04/washington/04gitmo.html.
107 legal definition of torture: Bob Woodward, "Detainee tortured, says U.S. official," *Washington Post*, January 14, 2009.

107 But he was turned back: Michael Isikoff and Daniel Klaidman, "How the 20th hijacker got turned away," *Newsweek*, January 26, 2004. http://www.newsweek.com/id/52857.

107 "extreme psychological trauma": "Inside the interrogation of Detainee 063," *TIME*, June 12, 2005. http://www.time.com/time/magazine/article/0.9171.1071284-1.00.html.

108 compared it to a gulag: Amnesty International released a report in 2005 calling Guantánamo "the gulag of our time." Richard Norton-Taylor, "Guantánamo is gulag of our time, says Amnesty," *The Guardian*, May 26, 2005.

108 until April 2006: Ben Fox, "Pentagon releases first list of names of Guantánamo detainees," *Associated Press*, April 20, 2006.

108 accused was not able to see all: Department of Defense, "Military Commission Rules of Evidence, Section I," www.defense.gov/pubs/pdfs/Part%20III%20-%20MCREs%20(FINAL).pdf.

108 covered by the Article 3: Hamdan v. Rumsfeld, Secretary of Defense, et al, Supreme Court of the United States, October 2005. Argued March 28, 2006, decided June 29, 2006. http://www.supremecourtus.gov/opinions/05pdf/05-184.pdf.

108 "accompanying serious physical injury": John C. Yoo, Memorandum to Alberto Gonzales, United States Department of Justice, Office of Legal Counsel, August 1, 2002. http://media.mcclatchydc.com/smedia/2008/06/04/14/Tab-L.source.prod_affiliate.91.pdf; Dana Priest and R. Jeffrey Smith, "Memo offered justification for the use of torture," *Washington Post*, June 8, 2004.

109 hit all of them: Tenet op. cit., p. 241. Scott Shane, "Inside the interrogation of a 9/11 mastermind," *New York Times*, June 22, 2008.

109 Abu Zubaydah was captured: John F. Burns, "In Pakistan's Interior, A Troubling Victory In Hunt for Al-Qaeda," *New York Times*, April 9, 2002; "losing a testicle": Author interview with Ali Soufan, New York, December 17, 2009.

109 CIA arranged for a leading surgeon: Tenet op. cit., p. 241.

110 located in Thailand: Scott Shane and Mark Mazzetti, "In Adopting Harsh Tactics, No Look at Past Use," *New York Times*, April 22, 2009.

110 calling him "Hani": Soufan interview.

110 some sort of a plan: Osama bin Laden, December 13, 2001. Transcript available from CNN, translated by Department of Defense. http://archives.cnn.com/2001/U.S./12/13/tape.transcript/.

110 "Who is Mukhtar?": Soufan interview.

110 his central role: A longtime CIA al-Qaeda expert said that in early March 2002 the Agency had first learned that 'KSM' was behind 9/11 following the arrest of a group of militants in Oman who, when they were interrogated, said that someone who went by the alias of 'Mukhtar' was the brains behind the attacks. When they were shown a bunch of photos of al-Qaeda members the arrested militants pointed out KSM to be 'Mukhtar.' The CIA official said this took place some weeks before Abu Zubayadah was ever in American custody. (Author interview with CIA official, Washington, D.C., 2006).

110 "highest ranking members": U.S. Department of Justice, Office of Legal Counsel, Memorandum for John A. Rizzo, "Interrogation of al-Qaida operative," August 1, 2002. http://www.fas.org/irp/agency/doj/olc/zubaydah.pdf.

110 "al-Qaeda's chief of operations": George W. Bush, Washington, D.C., June 6, 2002. http://georgewbush-whitehouse.archives.gov/news/releases/2002/06/20020606-8.html; "travel agent": Daniel Coleman, interview by author, Princeton, New Jersey, December 19, 2009.

111 White House lawyers authorized: U.S. Department of Justice, Office of Legal Counsel, Memorandum for John A. Rizzo, May 10, 2005.

111 James E. Mitchell: Senate Armed Services Committee op. cit., p. xiv.

111 had never conducted a real interrogation: Scott Shane and Mark Mazzetti, "In Adopting Harsh Tactics, No Look at Past Use," *New York Times*, April 22, 2009.

111 "Enhanced Interrogation Techniques": Central Intelligence Agency, Inspector General, Counterterrorism Detention and Interrogation Activities, May 7, 2004, pp. 13–15.

111 a total of twenty-eight detainees in American custody: Stephen G. Bradbury, "Memorandum Re: Application of United States Obligations Under Article 16 of the Convention Against Torture to Certain techniques that May Be used in the Interrogation of High Value al-Qaeda Detainees", 30 May 2005 (footnote, p. 5), http://luxmedia.vo.llnwd.net/o10/clients/aclu/olc_05302005_bradbury.pdf.

111 "Only one person and one person only": Author interview with Ali Soufan.

112 allowed to resume their questioning: Ali Soufan, testimony before Senate Judiciary Committee, Washington, D.C., May 13, 2009, http://judiciary.senate.gov/hearings/testimony.cfm?id=3842&wit_id=7906; and Michael Isikoff and Mark Hosenball, "Fresh questions about the CIA's interrogation tapes," *Newsweek*, May 2, 2009.

112 jibed with Jose Padilla: author interview with Ali Soufan, Manhattan, New York, December 17, 2009.

112 form of simulated drowning: the number of waterboardings on Abu Zubaydah comes from page 37 of the U.S. Department of Justice, Office of Legal Counsel, Memorandum for John A. Rizzo, May 30, 2005. http://www.fas.org/irp/agency/doj/olc/article16.pdf. United States Senate, Committee on Armed Services. Inquiry into the treatment of detainees in U.S. custody, November 20, 2008, http://armed-services.senate.gov/Publications/Detainee%20Report%20Final_April%2022%202009.pdf.

112 did yield information: Scott Shane, "Waterboarding used 266 times on 2 suspects," *New York Times*, April 20, 2009. http://www.nytimes.com/2009/04/20/world/20detain.html "subject of a front page story"; David Johnston and Philip Shenon, "Man held since August is charged with a role in Sept. 11 terror plot," *New York Times*, December 12, 2001.

112 no specific leads: Peter Finn and Joby Warrick, "Detainee's harsh interrogation foiled no plots," *Washington Post*, March 29, 2009.

112 Dozens of videotapes: Mark Mazzetti, "U.S. says CIA destroyed 92 tapes of interrogations," *New York Times*, March 2, 2009, http://www.nytimes.com/2009/03/03/washington/03web-intel.html.

113 had ended, in any event, in 2003: Joby Warrick and Dan Eggen, "Hill briefed on waterboarding in 2002," *Washington Post*, December 9, 2007.

113 held in jails in Poland and Romania: Council of Europe, Committee on Legal Affairs and Human Rights, "Secret detentions and illegal transfers of detainees involving Council of Europe Member States," June 7, 2007. http://news.bbc.co.uk/1/shared/bsp/hi/pdfs/marty_08_06_07.pdf.

113 "constituted torture": Mark Danner, "U.S. torture: voices from the black sites," *New York Review of Books*, April 9, 2009. http://www.nybooks.com/articles/22530?email.

114 "Informed Interrogator" approach: Ali Soufan interview by author December 17, 2009, New York.

114 "dozens and dozens of people": Ali Soufan interview by author December 17, 2009, New York.

114 picked out eight: Ali Soufan interview by author December 17, 2009, New York. Abu Jandal, FD-302, Federal Bureau of Investigation, pp. 59–63 and 74–81. http://judiciary.senate.gov/press/upload/302-Abu-Jandal-Interview-Unclassified-Part-3. (Since removed)

114 waterboarded 183 times: The number of waterboardings on KSM comes from page 37 of Memorandum to John Rizzo, May 30, 2005 op. cit.

114 prosecuted a group of police officers: The case in question is U.S. v. Lee, No. 83-2675, United States Court of Appeals Fifth Circuit, October 12, 1984, described at length by Professor David Luban before the Senate Judiciary Committee, Subcommittee on Administrative Oversight and the Courts, on May 13, 2009.

114 2002 interview with Yosri Fouda: Yosri Fouda, interview by author, London 2002.

114 183 times: Scott Shane, "Waterboarding used 266 times on 2 suspects," *New York Times*, April 19, 2009, http://www.nytimes.com/2009/04/20/world/20detain.html; Shane 2008 op. cit., and Tenet op. cit., pp. 253–255, and CIA IG Report op. cit., p. 91.

115 would be killed: Central Intelligence Agency, Inspector General Report, "Counterterrorism Detention and Interrogation Activities," May 7, 2004. http://media.washingtonpost.com/wp-srv/nation/documents/cia_report.pdf, p. 43.

115 "used to take great pride": Author interview with former senior CIA official Robert Dannenberg, December 17, 2009, New York City.

115 "If it hadn't been": John F. Harris et al, "Cheney warns of new attacks," Politico.com, February 4, 2009. http://www.politico.com/news/stories/0209/18390.html.

116 "In top secret meetings": Dick Cheney, Washington, D.C., May 21, 2009. http://www.aei.org/docLib/Vice%20President%20Cheney%20Remarks%205%2021%2009.pdf

116 "reporting from KSM has greatly": "Khalid Shaykh Mohamed: Preeminent Source On Al-Qa'ida," July 13, 2004. http://ccrjustice.org/files/CIA%20KSM%20Preeminent%20Source.pdf.

116 program was a dud: Joby Warrick, "Suspect and a setback in al-Qaeda anthrax case," *Washington Post*, October 31, 2006.

117 Hambali was the mastermind: Department of Defense, Detainee Biographies, Hambali. http://www.defenselink.mil/pdf/detaineebiographies1.pdf, p. 3.

117 "like a white collar criminal": Tenet op. cit., pp. 254–255.

117 "more than a dozen": Peter Bergen, "Cheney's Jihad," ForeignPolicy.com, August 26, 2009. http://www.foreignpolicy.com/articles/2009/08/26/cheneys_jihad.

117 "Second Wave": Memorandum to John Rizzo op. cit.

117 "KSM launched several plots": Khalid Sheikh Mohammed Biography, Director of National Intelligence, http://www.defenselink.mil/pdf/detaineebiographies1.pdf.

118 "back burner": Substitution for the Testimony of Khalid Sheikh Mohammed, Department of Justice, http://www.law.umkc.edu/faculty/projects/FTRIALS/moussaoui/sheikhstmt.pdf, pp. 39–40.

118 "did not uncover any evidence": CIA IG Report op. cit.

118 someone that the feds had already identified: New York Times topic page, Ali Saleh Kahlah al Marri, updated May 1, 2009, http:/topics.nytimes.com/topics/reference/timestopics/people/m/ali_saleh_kahlah_al_marri/index.html; and Soufan interview op. cit.

118 only four days after: Combatant Status Review Tribunal Summary, Majid Khan, March 28, 2007, p. 12. http://projects.nytimes.com/Guantánamo/detainees/10020-majid-khan/documents/7/pages/203.

118 many computers and cell phones: NBC Nightly News, Tom Brokaw, March 3, 2003.

119 "I don't believe": David Rose, "Tortured reasoning," *Vanity Fair*, December 16, 2008. http://www.vanityfair.com/magazine/2008/12/torture200812?currentPage=1; "difficult to determine": CIA IG Report op. cit.

119 "These techniques have hurt our image": Joby Warrick, "Intelligence chief says methods hurt U.S.," *Washington Post*, April 22, 2009. http://www.washingtonpost.com/wp-dyn/content/article/2009/04/21/AR2009042104334_pf.html.

119 "Clean Team": Josh White, Dan Eggen, and Joby Warrick, "U.S. to try 6 on capital charges over 9/11 attacks," *Washington Post*, February 12, 2008. http://www.washingtonpost.com/wp-dyn/content/story/2008/02/11/ST2008021101227.html.

119 most well-informed American official: Coleman interview. BBC survey: BBC World Service Poll, "World view of U.S. goes from bad to worse," January 23, 2007. http://news.bbc.co.uk/2/shared/bsp/hi/pdfs/23_01_07_U.S._poll.pdf.

120 poll the same year: Pew Global Attitudes Project, "Global unease with major world powers," June 26, 2007. http://pewglobal.org/reports/pdf/256.pdf.

Chapter 8

121 "One by one": George W. Bush, Camp David, September 14, 2002.

121 ankle-high hiking boots: United States of America v. Richard Colvin Reid, United States District Court of Massachusetts, Crim. No. 02-10013-WGY, Government's Sentencing Memorandum, January 17, 2003.

122 "don't be angry": Sentencing memorandum, USA v. Richard Colvin Reid, U.S. District Court, District of Massachusetts. http://www.investigativeproject.org/documents/case_docs/864.pdf.

122 Three hours into the flight: Sentencing memorandum op. cit.

122 at least 1,200: David Schanzer, Charles Kurzman, Ebrahim Moosa, "Anti-terror lessons of Muslim-Americans," Triangle Center on Terrorism and Homeland Security, p. 7. http://sanford.duke.edu/centers/tcths/documents/Anti-TerrorLessonsfinal.pdf.

122 "far exceeds the interest": Classified declaration of Mr. Jeffery Rapp, Director, Joint Intelligence Task Force for Combating Terrorism from September 9, 2004, declassified on April 5, 2006.

123 "He was using a payphone": Ali Soufan, interview by author, December 17, 2009, New York.

123 plea agreement: USA vs Ali Saleh Khalah al-Marri, Plea Agreement, filed April 3 2009 District Court for the Central District of Illinois, Peoria Division NO. 09-CR-10030.

123 Ohio trucker: "Ohio trucker joined al-Qaeda jihad," CNN.com, June 19, 2003; USA vs. Iyman Faris, United States District Court, Eastern District of Virginia, Alexandria Division, Statement of Facts. http://news.findlaw.com/cnn/docs/faris/usfaris603sof.pdf. Christopher Dickey, *Securing the City* op. cit., pp. 85–87.

123 Always dreaming up: Kevin Mayhood, "Man linked to al-Qaeda wants to void plea deal," *Columbus Dispatch*, February 27, 2005. February 2003: Andrew Welsh-Huggins, *Material Support: A Midwest Al-Qaida Case and the U.S. War on Homegrown Terror* (Ohio University Press, 2011).

124 three North African Muslim men: David Johnston and Paul Zielbauer, "3 held in Detroit after aircraft diagrams are found," *New York Times*, September 20, 2001. http://www.nytimes.com/2001/09/20/U.S./nation-challenged-investigation-3-held-detroit-after-aircraft-diagrams-are-found.html; "suspected of having knowledge": John Ashcroft, October 31, 2001, Department of Justice, Washington, D.C.

124 known con man: Bennett L. Gershman, "How Juries Get it Wrong—Anatomy of the Detroit Terror Case," *Washburn Law Journal*, Vol. 44, 2005. http://ssrn.com/abstract=1292894. "Ex-cabbie to help in terrorism case," *Chicago Tribune*, April 5, 2003. http://articles.chicagotribune.com/2003-04-05/news/0304050295_1_terrorism-case-youssef-hmimssa-terrorists.

124 "What a lovely view!": Danny Hakim, "Final Arguments Start in Trial Of 4 Arabs in Terrorism Case," *New York Times*, May 20, 2003.

124 "just like a tourist tape": Ron Hansen quoted in Adam Curtis, *The Power of Nightmares*, BBC, October 20–November 3, 2004.

124 Yemen's minister of defense: This section is based on Bennett L. Gershman, "How Juries Get it Wrong—Anatomy of the Detroit Terror Case" (October 31, 2008). *Washburn Law Journal,* Vol. 44, 2005. Available at SSRN: http://ssrn.com/abstract =1292894.

125 the supposed al-Qaeda spy at Guantánamo: Laura Parker, "The ordeal of Chaplain Yee," *USA Today*, May 16, 2004. http://www.usatoday.com/news/nation/2004-05-16-yee-cover_x.htm.

125 his son's homework: "FBI apologizes to lawyer held in Madrid bombings," Associated Press, May 25, 2004. http://www.msnbc.msn.com/id/5053007/.

125 "American Taliban": CNN, "People in the news," Profile of John Walker Lindh, http://www.cnn.com/CNN/Programs/people/shows/walker/profile.html.

125 tried for treason: Evan Thomas, "A long, strange trip to the Taliban," *Newsweek*, December 17, 2001. http://www.newsweek.com/id/75261.

125 enough to convict: Jane Mayer, "Lost in the Jihad," *New Yorker*, March 10, 2003. http://www.newyorker.com/archive/2003/03/10/030310fa_fact2.

126 Lackawanna: For more details on the Lackawanna case, see Ravi Satkalmi, "Material Support: The United States v. the Lackawanna Six," *Studies in Conflict and Terrorism*, Vol. 28 issue 3, May/June 2005, and "The Al-Qaeda Documents," Intel-Center ed. Ben Venzke (Tempest Publishing, 2002), p. 160.

126 married a high school cheerleader: Ian Brown, "And justice for all," *Globe and Mail*, September 6, 2003.

126 fueled by pizza: Dina Temple-Raston, *The Jihad Next Door* (New York: Public Affairs, 2007), pp. 30–39.

126 spring and summer of 2001: PBS Frontline, "Chasing the sleeper cell: chronology: the Lackawanna investigation," http://www.pbs.org/wgbh/pages/frontline/shows/sleeper/inside/cron.html.

126 "We don't even think": Matthew Purdy and Lowell Bergman, "Unclear danger," *New York Times*, October 12, 2003, is an authoritative account of the Lackawanna case.

126 faked an ankle injury: Temple-Raston op. cit., p. 120; kept their training a secret: Temple-Raston op. cit., pp. 184–185. washed out: Mitchell Silber and Arvin Bhatt, "Radicalization in the West," New York Police Department, http://www.nypdshield.org/public/SiteFiles/documents/NYPD_Report-Radicalization_in_the_West.pdf, p. 62.

126 "for recruiting the Yemenite youth": Temple-Raston op. cit., p. 24.

127 "Big Meal": Purdy and Bergman op. cit.

127 tender caresses: Purdy and Bergman op. cit.

127 recently broken up in Buffalo: George W. Bush, State of the Union, Washington, D.C., January 28, 2003. "There was never any evidence": Silber et al. op. cit., p. 62.

127 between seven and ten years: Dina Temple-Raston, "Member of Lackawanna Six released from prison," NPR, May 6, 2008. http://www.npr.org/templates/story/story.php?storyId=90235086.

127 Derwish was incinerated: James Risen, "Man believed slain in Yemen tied by U.S. to Buffalo cell," *New York Times*, November 10, 2003. http://www.nytimes.com/2002/11/10/international/middleeast/10YEME.html.

128 Portland Six: USA v. Jeffrey Leon Battle et al, United States District Court of Oregon, No. CR 02-399HA, Indictment. http://www.investigativeproject.org/documents/case_docs/131.pdf. Dhiren Barot: USA vs Dhiren Barot, Southern District of New York 05 Crim. 311 sealed indictment. http://www.washingtonpost.com/wp-srv/articles/hindi.pdf.

128 as an instructor: Esa Al Hindi, *Army of Madinah in Kashmir* (Birmingham: Maktabah al Ansar Birmingham, 1999), p. 152, Author collection.

128 bin Laden tasked Barot: *New York Times*, People: Khalid Sheikh Mohammed, December 8, 2008. http://topics.nytimes.com/top/reference/timestopics/people/m/khalid_shaikh_mohammed/index.html?inline=nyt-per.

128 targets included: United States of America v. Dhiren Barot, United States District Court, Southern District of New York, Sealed Indictment, Crim. No. 05CRIM 311.

128 discovered in an al-Qaeda safe house: Dickey, *Securing the City*, pp. 181–182.

129 "I'll never forget": Frances Townsend, interview by author, Washington, D.C., December 7, 2009.

129 "little more than a graduate school report": Michael Sheehan, *Crush the Cell* (New York: Three Rivers Press, 2009), p. 216.

129 "the real deal": Michael Sheehan, interview by author, Manhattan, New York, November 21, 2009.

129 from going public: "8 men charged with terror offenses," CNN.com, August 17, 2004.

129 "flabbergasted": Sheehan interview op. cit., and this account draws on Sheehan's *Crush the Cell* pages 216–218.

130 "not get blindsided": Townsend interview op. cit.

130 The alert was only lowered: During the Bush administration's two terms the threat alert was raised and lowered 16 times on the following dates: March 12, 2002—Introduction of Homeland Security Advisory System At Yellow; September 10, 2002—Raised from Yellow to Orange; September 24, 2002—Lowered from Orange to Yellow; February 7, 2003—Raised from Yellow to Orange; February 27, 2003—Lowered from Orange to Yellow; March 17, 2003—Raised from Yellow to Orange; April 16, 2003—Lowered from Orange to Yellow; May 20, 2003—Raised from Yellow to Orange; May 30, 2003—Lowered from Orange to Yellow; December 21, 2003—Raised from Yellow to Orange; January 9, 2004—Lowered from Orange to Yellow; August 1, 2004—Raised from Yellow to Orange, specifically for the financial services sectors in New York City, Northern New Jersey, and Washington, D.C.; November 10, 2004—Lowered from Orange to Yellow, for the financial services sectors in New York City, Northern New Jersey, and Washington, D.C.; July 7, 2005—Raised from Yellow to Orange for mass transit; August 12, 2005—Lowered from Orange to Yellow for mass transit; August 10, 2006—Raised from Yellow to Red for flights originating in the United Kingdom bound for the United States; raised to Orange for all commercial aviation operating in or destined for the United States; August 13, 2006—Lowered from Red to Orange for flights originating in the United Kingdom bound for the United States; it remains today at Orange for all domestic and international flights. Department of Homeland Security, "Chronology of changes to the Homeland Security Advisory System," accessed January 7, 2010. http://www.dhs.gov/xabout/history/editorial_0844.shtm.

Chapter 9

131 "How are nations ruled": Karl Kraus, quoted in *Censored 2004: The Top 25 Censored Stories* (New York: Seven Stories Press, 2003), p. 238.

131 "You are entitled": Patrick Moynihan, quoted in Timothy J. Penny, "Facts are Facts," *National Review*, September 4, 2003. http://www.nationalreview.com/nrof_comment/comment-penny090403.asp.

132 By September 2003: Washington Post Poll, Saddam and the Sept. 11 attacks, September 3, 2003. http://www.washingtonpost.com/wp-srv/politics/polls/vault/stories/data082303.htm.

132 Even five years later: CBS News Poll, March 15–18, 2008. http://www.pollingreport.com/iraq.htm.

132 "bulletproof" evidence: Eric Schmitt, "Rumsfeld Says U.S. Has 'Bulletproof' Evidence of Iraq's Links to Al-Qaeda," *New York Times*, September 28, 2002.

132 "protects terrorists": George W. Bush, Cincinnati, OH, October 7, 2002. George W. Bush, Washington, D.C., January 29, 2003. State of the Union Address. http://www.cnn.com/2003/ALLPOLITICS/01/28/sotu.transcript/.

133 "A year before": Osama bin Laden, interview by Peter Arnett and author for CNN, aired May 10, 1997.

133 "can never be trusted": Author interview with Khaled Batarfi, Jeddah, Saudi Arabia, September 5, 2005.

133 volunteered the services: Peter Bergen, *Holy War Inc.* (New York: Free Press, 2001), pp. 77–78.

133 "The land of the Arab world": Hamid Mir, interview by author, Islamabad, Pakistan, March 2005.

133 "I'm personally aware": Author interview with Cofer Black, Washington, D.C., February 6, 2003.

134 "never deemed credible": Author interview Roger Cressey, Arlington, Virginia, May 14, 2004. Cressey made the same kinds of comments in a follow up interview in Washington, D.C., November 24, 2009.

134 "solid reporting": Walter Pincus and Dana Milbank, "Al-Qaeda-Hussein link is dismissed," *Washington Post*, June 17, 2004. http://www.washingtonpost.com/wp-dyn/articles/A47812-2004Jun16.html.

134 no Iraqi connection: Pincus and Milbank op. cit.; Harry A. Weber, "Judge: airlines can't question FBI in 9/11 suits," Associated Press, July 17, 2009. http://www.usatoday.com/travel/flights/2009-07-17-9-11-victims-sue-airlines_N.htm.

134 "no evidence": George W. Bush, Washington, D.C., September 17, 2003. http://georgewbush-whitehouse.archives.gov/news/releases/2003/09/20030917-7.html.

135 Mylroie laid out her case: Laurie Mylroie, *Study of Revenge: Saddam Hussein's Unfinished War with America* (Washington, D.C.: AEI Press, 2001).

135 "generous and timely assistance": ibid., pp. ix–x. Bizarrely, the Pentagon continued to employ Mylroie on an ad hoc basis up till 2007 despite the fact that all of her theories about Iraq had been comprehensively disproven years before. In 2005 Mylroie even prepared a history of al-Qaeda for the Pentagon's Office of Net Assessment that ran some 300 pages. In it she recycled her long-discredited theories that Ramzi Yousef and his uncle Khaled Sheikh Mohammed, the operational commander of 9/11, were "the trained agents of a terrorist state." Mylroie's post-9/11 work for the Pentagon is described in Justin Elliott, "Saddam-Qaeda conspiracy theorist surfaces writing Iraq reports for the Pentagon," *Talking Points Memo,* January 29, 2009. http://tpmmuckraker.talkingpointsmemo.com/2009/01/saddam-qaeda_conspiracy_theorist_surfaces_writing.php.

135 Bush cabinet's reaction: Peter Bergen, "Armchair Provocateur," *Washington Monthly,* December 2003; United States Department of State, Patterns of Global Terrorism (2000), Overview of state-sponsored terrorism. http://www.state.gov/s/ct/rls/crt/2000/2441.htm.

136 an Iraqi intelligence agent: Mylroie 2003 op. cit. chapter 5, Appendix A and B, pp. 261–276.

136 had all found no evidence: Bergen 2003 op. cit. based on phone interviews with Mary Jo White, Kenneth Pollack, Vincent Cannistraro, and Neil Herman in 2003.

137 "enemy combatant": Michael Isikoff, "Terror Watch: The Enemy Within," *Newsweek*, April 21, 2004. http://www.newsweek.com/id/53536?tid=relatedcl.

137 constantly being tasked: Interview by author, Washington, D.C., March 21, 2007.

137 "expert witness": Laurie Mylroie, Testimony before the 9/11 Commission, July 9,

2003. Washington, D.C., http://govinfo.library.unt.edu/911/archive/hearing3/9-11Commission_Hearing_2003-07-09.htm#panel_two.

137 "I take satisfaction": Mark Hosenball, Michael Isikoff, and Evan Thomas, "Cheney's long path to war," *Newsweek*, November 17, 2003. http://www.newsweek.com/id/60579/page/4.

138 close ties to the Israeli right: Marc Perelman, "Cheney taps Syria hawk as adviser on Mideast," *The Forward*, October 31, 2003. http://www.forward.com/articles/6945/; Douglas Feith op. cit., p. 116; and Michael Maloof, interview by PBS *Frontline,* January 10, 2006. http://www.pbs.org/wgbh/pages/frontline/darkside/interviews/maloof.html.

138 a position paper: "A Clean Break: A New Strategy for Securing the Realm," *Institute for Advanced Strategic and Political Studies,* 1996. http://www.iasps.org/strat1.htm

138 Saddam's fortunes had revived: David Wurmser, *Tyranny's Ally: America's Failure to Defeat Saddam Hussein* (Washington, D.C.: AEI Press, 1999).

138 "We did not leave any dot unconnected": Michael Maloof, interview by author, Washington, D.C., June 3, 2004.

138 150-page slide presentation: Author interview with Michael Maloof op. cit. and Maloof 2006 op. cit.

139 led a review of nineteen thousand: Interview by author with Michael Scheuer, Washington, D.C., December 23, 2009.

139 "you are not going to get it": Interview by author with Daniel Coleman, Princeton, New Jersey December 19, 2009.

139 two new researchers: Bryan Burrough, Evgenia Peretz, and David Rose, "The Path to War: The Rush to Invade Iraq," *Vanity Fair*, May 2004.

139 "mature, symbiotic relationship": Tenet op. cit., p. 347.

139 "Feith-based analysis": Tenet op. cit., pp. 346–347.

139 "Iraq and al-Qa'ida": Kenneth R. Timmerman, *Shadow Warriors: the Untold Story of Traitors, Saboteurs, and the Party of Surrender* (New York: Crown Forum, 2007), p. 330.

140 "more akin to activity": United States. Senate. Select Committee on Intelligence. *Whether public statements regarding Iraq by U.S. government officials were substantiated by intelligence information*. 110th Congress, 2nd session. June 2008. intelligence.senate.gov/080605/phase2a.pdf.

140 In January 2003: Tenet op. cit., p. 358.

140 "turned over every rock": Author interview with John McLaughlin, Washington, D.C. December 7, 2009.

140 "smuggled conventional weapons": Jeffrey Goldberg, "The Great Terror," *New Yorker*, March 25, 2002.

140 was lying about his Kandahar trip: Jason Burke, "The missing link?" *The Guardian*, February 9, 2003. http://www.guardian.co.uk/world/2003/feb/09/alqaida.afghanistan.

141 "to hijack aircraft with knives": David Rose, "An Inconvenient Iraqi," *Vanity Fair*, January 2003; and David Rose, "Inside Saddam's Deadly Aresnal," *Vanity Fair*, May 2002.

141 how to hijack planes: "Iraqi defector offers talks of terrorist training camps," Agence France Press, November 12, 2001.

141 *New York Times* similarly quoted: Patrick E. Tyler and John Tagliabue, "Czechs Confirm Iraqi Agent Met With Terror Ringleader," *New York Times*, October 27, 2001.

141 "intelligence officer": Jonathan Manthorpe, "Is Iraq, not bin Laden, real force behind terror?" *Vancouver Sun,* November 9, 2001.

141 "former Iraqi army officer": Nicholas Rufford, "Mock attack on British bus," *Sunday Times* (London), July 14, 2002.

141 White House "white paper": Michael Isikoff and David Corn, *Hubris: The Inside Story of Spin, Scandal, and the Selling of the Iraq War* (New York: Crown Publishing Group, 2006), pp. 54–55.

141 "non-Iraqi Arabs": Jonathan Schanzer, "Saddam's ambassador to al-Qaeda," *Weekly Standard*, March 1, 2004. http://www.weeklystandard.com/content/public/articles/000/000/003/768rwsbj.asp?pg=2.

141 no "credible reports": United States. Senate. Select Committee on Intelligence. "Postwar findings about Iraq's WMD programs and links to terrorism and how they compare with prewar assessments," September 8, 2006, p. 108.

141 "so much of this crap": Author interview with Vincent Cannistraro, Washington, D.C., 2004.

141 tens of millions of dollars: This was first reported by Jonathan Landay and Tish Wells of Knight Ridder Newspapers. According to Thomas E. Ricks, *Fiasco: The American Military Adventure in* Iraq (New York: Penguin Press, 2006), p. 57, total US Government payments to the INC from 2001 to 2003 were $36 million.

142 more than a hundred stories: James Risen, "Data from Iraqi exiles under scrutiny," *New York Times*, February 12, 2004. http://query.nytimes.com/gst/fullpage.html?res=9804E7D8133AF931A25751C0A9629C8B63.

142 before flying to the United States: 9/11 Commission Report op. cit., p. 228.

142 "still working to confirm or deny": United States. Central Intelligence Agency. George J. Tenet, Testimony Before the Joint Inquiry into Terrorist Attacks Against the United States, Washington, D.C., June 18, 2002. https://www.cia.gov/news-information/speeches-testimony/2002/dci_testimony_06182002.html.

142 as many as four times: Woodward 2004 op. cit., p. 292.

142 "every kitchen sink": Richard Armitage, PBS *Frontline*, "Bush's War," December 18, 2007. http://www.pbs.org/wgbh/pages/frontline/bushswar/interviews/armitage.html

142 "we are increasingly skeptical": Senate Intelligence Committee September 8, 2006, op. cit., p. 110.

143 "all sorts of garbage": John McLaughlin, interview by author, Washington, D.C., December 7, 2009.

143 "unfortunately the substance didn't hold up": Tenet op. cit., p. 375.

144 told investigators: From the German indictment of Shadi Abdalla (alias Emad Abdelhadie), May 14, 2003. There are also excerpts from his interviews with German authorities that occurred between April 2002 (when he was arrested) and May 2003.

144 founded a training camp: Hutaifa Azzam, interview by author, Amman, Jordan, September 13, 2005.

144 "Someone could legitimately say": Donald Rumsfeld, Defense Department Briefing, Arlington, VA, June 17, 2004.

144 blistering critique of Saddam: Abu Musab al-Zarqawi, June 23, 2004. SITE Institute, Washington, D.C. www.siteintelgroup.org/terrorismlibrary/communique/communique_1103219979.pdf.

144 "the best evidence": Nic Robertson, "Bush stands by al-Qaeda, Saddam link," CNN.com, June 15, 2004, http://www.cnn.com/2004/WORLD/meast/06/15/bush.alqaeda/index.html.

144 "the regime did not a have a relationship": Senate Select Committee on Intelligence, September 8, 2006, op. cit., p. 92. I wrote a piece before the Iraq War explaining why such a relationship made no sense. I found it hard to get it published in an American newspaper, but it was published in *The Guardian* on January 30, 2003.

144 hardly meant that he had control: In January 2004 Powell distanced himself from his U.N. presentation saying of al-Qaeda's supposed ties to Iraq, "I have not seen smoking-gun, concrete evidence about the connection, but I think the possibility

of such connections did exist and it was prudent to consider them at the time that we did."

145 "I will be more than happy": Charles Faddis, interview by author, Washington, D.C. January 20, 2010.

145 "wholly unimpressive place": C. J. Chivers, "Islamists in Iraq offer a tour of 'poison factory' cited by Powell," *New York Times*, February 9, 2003. http://query.nytimes.com/gst/fullpage.html?res=9D04E3D6133BF93AA35751C0A9659C8B63.

145 "derail the plans": Faddis interview.

145 Two days after: "Preparations for possible attacks gear up," CNN.com, February 8, 2003; Tom Ridge, Department of Homeland Security, Press Release, February 7, 2003, http://www.dhs.gov/xnews/speeches/speech_0088.shtm; David Johnston, "Ridge says warning levels might be lowered in days," *New York Times*, February 17, 2003. http://www.nytimes.com/2003/02/17/world/threats-responses-intelligence-ridge-says-warning-levels-might-be-lowered-days.html.

146 detailed advice: Philip Shenon, "Administration gives advice on how to prepare for a terrorist attack," *New York Times*, February 10, 2003. http://www.nytimes.com/2003/02/11/U.S./threats-responses-precautions-administration-gives-advice-prepare-for-terrorist.html.

146 surge in sales of plastic: Jeanne Meserve, "Duct tape sales rise amid terror fears," CNN.com, February 11, 2003. http://www.cnn.com/2003/U.S./02/11/emergency.supplies/.

146 "provided training in poisons and gases": United States. Senate. Senate Armed Services Committee, 108th Congress. Washington, D.C., February 12, 2003.

146 "advise al-Libi of his rights": Jack Cloonan, interview by author, New York, December 17, 2009.

147 about Richard Reid: Cloonan interview op. cit.

147 Albert burst into: This episode was first described in Jane Mayer's important book, *The Dark Side*, pp. 104–106, and also in Cloonan interview.

147 the CIA then rendered Libi: Tenet op. cit., pp. 353–354, p. 269.

147 "canisters containing nuclear materials into New York": Tenet op. cit., p. 269.

147 "Iraq has trained al-Qaeda members": George W. Bush, October 7, 2002, Cincinnati, OH. http://levin.senate.gov/newsroom/supporting/2005/adminstmts.CBW.110605.pdf

147 Libi recanted: Michael Isikoff and David Corn, *Hubris: The Inside Story of Spin, Scandal, and the Selling of the Iraq War* (New York: Three Rivers Press, 2007), pp. 120–121 and 9/11 Commission Report op. cit., p. 470 fn. 76.

147 "fabricated" his tale: Senate Select Committee on Intelligence, September 8, 2006, op. cit., p. 72.

147 "lacks specific details": Senate Select Committee on Intelligence, September 8, 2006, op. cit., p. 66.

148 "geographic base": Vice President Dick Cheney, *Meet the Press with Tim Russert*, MSNBC, September 14, 2003. http://www.msnbc.msn.com/id/3080244/.

148 multiple times: 9/11 Commission Report op. cit., pp. 228–229.

148 "We have never": Dick Cheney, interview with Gloria Borger, CNBC News, June 17, 2004.

149 "Hijackers Timeline": United States. Federal Bureau of Investigation. "Hijackers Timeline." February 1, 2007, pp. 132–133.

149 denied ever meeting him: James Risen, "Iraqi agent denies he met 9/11 hijacker in Prague before attacks on the U.S.," *New York Times*, December 13, 2003. http://www.nytimes.com/2003/12/13/international/europe/13INQU.html.

149 "there was a relationship": "Bush insists Iraq, al-Qaeda had 'relationship,'" CNN.com, June 17, 2004. http://www.cnn.com/2004/ALLPOLITICS/06/17/Bush.alqaeda/.

150 home-baked cookies: Alina Cho, CNN American Morning, January 28, 2008. http://transcripts.cnn.com/TRANSCRIPTS/0801/28/ltm.01.html; George Piro, CBS News, *60 Minutes*, January 27, 2008. http://www.cbsnews.com/stories/2008/01/24/60minutes/main3749494.shtml.

150 elicited the real story: Piro op. cit. and author discussions with George Piro in 2008. "Saddam Hussein talks to the FBI," National Security Archive Electronic Briefing Book No. 279, July 1, 2009. George Washington University. http://www.gwu.edu/~nsarchiv/NSAEBB/NSAEBB279/index.htm.

150 "No weapons over there": "Bush's WMD joke draws criticism," AP, March 26, 2004. http://www.msnbc.msn.com/id/4608166/.

150 "We were all wrong": United States. Senate. Armed Services Committee. "Hearing on the subject of Iraqi weapons of mass destruction programs," Washington, D.C., January 28, 2004.

150 "We haven't really had": Dick Cheney interview with M.E. Sprengelmeyer, *Rocky Mountain News*, January 9, 2004.

151 34 million pages of documents: Senate Select Committee on Intelligence, September 8, 2006, op. cit.

151 no "smoking gun": Institute for Defense Analyses, "Iraqi Perspectives Project: Saddam and Terrorism: Emerging Insights from Captured Iraqi Documents," September 2007. http://abcnews.go.com/images/Politics/Saddam%20and%Terrorism%20Redaction%20EXSUM%20Extract.pdf.

151 Gulbuddin Hekmatyar: Hekmatyar had a longtime talent for extracting money from a variety of patrons. By a conservative estimate he received 600 million dollars of U.S. aid via the Pakistani intelligence service, ISI, during the 1980s war against the Soviets.

151 discover a memo: This was a detailed note by the *Mukhabarat*. Document dated August 18, 2002, Operation Iraqi Freedom, documents collected at U.S. Army Foreign Military Studies Office, document number iISGZ02004-019920.

151 no "cooperative relationship": United States. Senate. Select Committee on Intelligence. Report on whether public statements regarding Iraq by U.S. government officials were substantiated by intelligence information together with additional and minority views. Report 110–345. 110th Congress, 2nd session. June 2008. http://intelligence.senate.gov/pdfs/110345.pdf, p. 72.

152 broadcast the speeches: Senate Select Committee on Intelligence September 8, 2006 op. cit., p. 72. http://intelligence.senate.gov/phaseiiaccuracy.pdf.

Chapter 10

153 "There is always an easy": Henry Louis Mencken: quoted in Bartleby's, *Respectfully Quoted: A Dictionary of Quotations* (Washington, D.C.: Library of Congress, 1989).

153 "I will not wait": George W. Bush, Washington, D.C., January 29, 2002. http://georgewbush-whitehouse.archives.gov/news/releases/2002/01/20020129-11.html.

154 "If we wait for threats": George W. Bush, Address at West Point, NY, June 1, 2002. http://georgewbush-whitehouse.archives.gov/news/releases/2002/06/20020601-3.html.

154 A few weeks later: Tenet op. cit., p. 309; Bumiller op. cit., p. 185; and Richard Haass, *War of Necessity, War of Choice* (New York: Simon & Schuster, 2009), p. 213.

154 "He doesn't get it": Rand Beers interview with author, December 24, 2009, Washington, D.C.

155 "What we did after 9/11": Douglas Feith on *60 Minutes*, CBS News, April 6, 2008. http://www.cbsnews.com/stories/2008/04/03/60minutes/main3992653.shtml.

155 tendered his resignation: Two months after the invasion of Iraq, Beers would start working for Democratic presidential candidate John Kerry as his foreign policy advisor, his first foray into politics after more than three decades of government service.

155 Bush issued the order: George W. Bush, quoted in Patrick E. Tyler, "U.S. and British troops push into Iraq as missiles strike Baghdad compound," *New York Times*, March 21, 2003. http://query.nytimes.com/gst/fullpage.html?res=9D06E6DC1E31F932A15750C0A9659C8B63.

155 privatizing state industries: Steven R. Weisman, "Kurdish region in Iraq will get to keep special status," *New York Times*, January 5, 2004; James Dobbins, Seth Jones, Benjamin Runkle, Siddarth Mohandas, *Occupying Iraq: A History of the Coalition Provisional Authority* (RAND: Santa Monica, 2009), p. 217; introducing a flat tax: Dana Milbank and Walter Pincus, "Flat tax system imposed on Iraq," *Washington Post*, November 1, 2003. On this point generally see Rajiv Chandrasekaran, *Imperial Life in the Emerald City: Life Inside Iraq's Green Zone* (New York: Knopf, 2006).

156 mandated the removal: CPA orders 1 and 2 from Ali Allawi, *The Occupation of Iraq: Winning the War, Losing the Peace* (New York: Yale University Press, 2007), pp. 150–157; Ricks op. cit., pp. 159–162. Ricks gives a higher number than Allawi's 400,000, positing 385,000 members of the armed forces and 285,000 in the Interior Ministry and 50,000 in the presidential security units (p. 162).

156 "flipped the social": Donald P. Wright and COL Timothy R. Reese, *On Point II: Transition to the New Campaign: The United States Army in Operation IRAQI FREEDOM, May 2003–January 2005* (CSI Press: Washington, D.C., 2008), p. 92.

156 did not secure the massive weapons caches: Raymond Bonner, "Iraqi arms caches cited in attacks," *New York Times*, October 14, 2003; and Ricardo S. Sanchez and Donald T. Phillips, *Wiser in Battle: A Soldier's Story* (New York: Harper Collins, 2008), p. 173.

156 "open-air bazaars": Sanchez and Phillips op. cit., pp. 173–174.

156 "imbalance was staggering": James Dobbins, et al, *Occupying Iraq* (RAND: Santa Monica, CA, 2009), p. 99.

157 "the searching of homes": Allawi op. cit., p. 186.

157 "more philosophical than practical": Sanchez op. cit., p. 238.

157 the CPA's hostility: Tenet op. cit., pp. 441–442.

157 drifted over the four hundred mark: ICasualties.org, U.S. Deaths by Month/Year: January–November 2003: 446 deaths. http://icasualties.org/Iraq/usByYear.aspx

157 "the Expanding Insurgency in Iraq": Linda Robinson, *Tell Me How This Ends: General David Petraeus and the Search for a Way Out of Iraq* (New York: Perseus Books, 2008), p. 7; and James Risen, *State of War: The Secret History of the CIA and the Bush Administration* (New York: Free Press, 2006), pp. 145–146.

157 would rise to two thousand: Ricks op. cit., p. 408.

158 just one of a long series of jihads: Tenet op. cit., pp. 437–438.

158 "We're not calling it an insurgency": Robert Grenier, interview with author Washington, D.C., January 19, 2010.

158 "pockets of dead enders": Donald Rumsfeld, Defense Department Operational Update Briefing, Arlington, VA, June 18, 2003; "the more desperate": George W. Bush, Remarks with L. Paul Bremer, Washington, D.C., October 27, 2003.

158 "not an insurgency": Paul Wolfowitz, MSNBC Hardball with Campbell Brown, June 23, 2004; "last throes": Dick Cheney, CNN Larry King Live, May 30, 2005; "state of desperation": Dick Cheney, CBS Face the Nation, March 19, 2006.

159 at least ninety thousand Iraqis: Iraq Body Count, Monthly Table, 2003–2008. Accessed Feb. 5, 2009. http://www.iraqbodycount.org/database/.

159 4.7 million Iraqis: United Nations High Commissioner on Refugees, Iraq Country Page. http://www.unhcr.org/iraq.html; "largest single movement": Jennifer Pagonis, United Nations High Commissioner on Refugees, Geneva, April 8, 2008; http://www.aims.org.af/services/sectoral/emergency_assistance/refugee/unhcr_summaries/jul_08/summary1.pdf.

159 "seem not to make the press": Donald Rumsfeld, Washingon, D.C., August 9, 2004. http://www.defenselink.mil/transcripts/transcript.aspx?transcriptid=2547.

159 "terrible ecosystem": Dexter Filkins, *The Forever War* (New York: Random House, 2008), p. 294; ribbon cuttings: Filkins op. cit., p.171.

159 Some 130 journalists: "Kurdish journalists under assault in Iraq," Reuters, August 26, 2008. http://www.reuters.com/article/worldNews/idUSLQ27271020080827.

159 more than double: 63 journalists were killed in Vietnam from 1955–1975: Reporters Without Borders, "Three years of slaughter in Iraq," March 20, 2006. http://www.rsf.org/article.php3?id_article=16793.

159 morphed into a fortress: Filkins op. cit., p. 223.

160 one hundred civilians were dying every day: Unclassified total; from coalition and Iraqi reports, Department of Defense document, author collection.

160 Abu Musab al-Zarqawi: For a good profile see Jeffrey Gettleman and Abu Romman, "Zarqawi's Journey: From Dropout to Prisoner to an Insurgent Leader in Iraq," *New York Times*, July 13, 2004.

160 whiled away his youth: David S. Cloud, "Elusive Enemy: Long in U.S. Sights, A Young Terrorist Builds Grim Resume," *Wall Street Journal*, February 10, 2004.

160 "he wasn't that smart": Betsy Pisik, "Mother denies suspect is terrorist," *Washington Times*, February 24, 2003.

161 "He can fight an army alone": Hutaifa Azzam, interview by author, Amman, Jordan, September 13, 2005.

161 worked out manically: Loretta Napoleoni, *Insurgent Iraq: Al Zarqawi and the New Generation* (New York: Seven Stories Press, 2005), pp. 61–70; Fuad Hussein, *Al Zarqawi: The Second Al-Qaeda Generation*, serialized in *Al Quds al Arabi*, May 15, 2005, and June 8 to July 15, 2005.

161 gave an amnesty: BBC News, "Jordan: King endorses general amnesty law," March 23, 1999.

161 plotted to blow up a Radisson hotel: Jonathan Finer and Craig Whitlock, "Zarqawi's network asserts it launched attacks in Amman," *Washington Post*, November 11, 2005. http://www.washingtonpost.com/wp-dyn/content/article/2005/11/10/AR2005111002074_pf.html.

161 did succeed in killing Laurence Foley: "U.S. diplomat killed in Jordan," CNN, October 28, 2002. http://archives.cnn.com/2002/WORLD/meast/10/28/jordan.shooting/.

161 set up a training camp: Fuad Hussein, *Al Zarqawi: The Second al-Qaeda Generation*, serialized in *Al Quds al Arabi*, May 15, 2005 and June 8 to July 15, 2005. "Jihadist Biography of the Slaughtering Leader Abu Mus'ab al Zarqawi" by Saif al-Adel, military commander of al-Qaeda which surfaced on a jihadist website on June 20, 2009 and was translated by World News Connection on August 17, 2009. File Number 985 Accession Number 285351362.

162 Gulbuddin Hekmatyar: ibid.

162 complexion and accents: Fuad Hussein op. cit.

162 arrive in Kurdish Iraq: Fuad Hussein op. cit.

162 Zarqawi traveled: Bundeskriminalarnt (BKA) Intelligence Report, Abu Musab al-Zarqawi, April 2002, translated by Steven Arons. Author's collection.

162 bombed the United Nations' headquarters: Ricks op. cit., p. 216; "bombed the Jordanian embassy": BBC News, "Jordan embassy blast inquiry." August 8, 2003. http://news.bbc.co.uk/2/hi/middle_east/3134145.stm; "25 killed in Iraq blast,"

The Guardian, November 12, 2003. http://www.guardian.co.uk/world/2003/nov/12/iraq.italy.

163 viewed millions of times: Garry Barker, "A war of pictures," *The Age (Australia)*, May 16, 2004. http://www.theage.com.au/articles/2004/05/16/1084646070652.html.

163 on the tape Berg is: BBC News, "Zarqawi beheaded U.S. man in Iraq." May 13, 2004. http://news.bbc.co.uk/2/hi/middle_east/3712421.stm.

163 two other Americans: "Video shows American hostage beheaded," CNN.com, September 20, 2004. http://edition.cnn.com/2004/WORLD/meast/09/20/iraq.beheading/ and Edward Wong, "Iraqi video shows beheading of man said to be American," *New York Times*, September 21, 2004. http://www.nytimes.com/2004/09/21/international/middleeast/21iraq.html; Jason Burke, "Theatre of terror," *The Guardian*, November 21, 2004. http://www.guardian.co.uk/theobserver/2004/nov/21/features.review7.

163 living under some form of arrest: U.S. counterterrorism officials, interview by author, Washington, D.C., June 6, 2003.

163 beloved Syrian mother: *Growing Up Bin Laden* op. cit., pp. 8–9 and 166.

164 snakes and scorpions: Abu Musab al Zarqawi's letter to Osama bin Laden, Coalition Provisional Authority, February 12, 2004.

164 Zarqawi's father-in-law: Mary Anne Weaver, "The short, violent life of Abu Musab al-Zarqawi," *The Atlantic*, July/August 2006. http://www.theatlantic.com/doc/200607/zarqawi/4. "Najaf bombing kills Shiite leader," CNN.com, August 30, 2003, http://edition.cnn.com/2003/WORLD/meast/08/29/sprj.irq.najaf/.

164 the Golden Mosque in Samarra: Fuad Hussein op. cit.; Knickmeyer, Ellen and Ibrahim, K.I., "Bombing shatters mosque in Iraq." *Washington Post*, February 23, 2006. http://www.washingtonpost.com/wp-dyn/content/article/2006/02/22/AR2006022200454.html.

164 in Anbar province: Cloud and Jaffe op. cit., p. 188.

164 Shia death squads: BBC News, Iraq 'death squad caught in act," February 16, 2006. http://news.bbc.co.uk/2/hi/middle_east/4719252.stm.

164 soldiers of the 82nd Airborne: "U.S. Troops Fire Back at Iraqi Protesters," Associated Press, April 29, 2003; and Human Rights Watch, "Violent Response," June 16, 2003. http://www.hrw.org/en/node/12318/section/4; four American security contractors: PBS *Frontline*, "The High Risk Contracting Business," June 21, 2005. http://www.pbs.org/wgbh/pages/frontline/shows/warriors/contractors/highrisk.html.

165 halted by Bremer on April 9: "Marines half offensive operations in Fallujah for negotiations," Associated Press, April 9, 2004.

165 was a turning point: Sanchez op. cit., pp. 350–351.

165 on November 7, 2004: Global Security.org, Operation al-Fajr (Dawn). November 8, 2004. http://www.globalsecurity.org/military/ops/oif-phantom-fury-fallujah.htm.

165 thousands of jihadist insurgents: Dexter Filkins and James Glanz, "With airpower and armor, troops enter rebel-held city," *New York Times*, November 8, 2004.

165 since the battle of Hue: Jim Garamone, "ScanEagle proves worth in Fallujah fight," DefenseLink, January 11, 2005. http://www.defenselink.mil/news/newsarticle.aspx?id=24397.

165 thousands of the city's buildings were destroyed and hundreds of thousands of its inhabitants fled: Ann Scott Tyson, "Increase security in Fallujah slows efforts to rebuild," *Washington Post*, April 19, 2005. http://www.washingtonpost.com/wp-dyn/articles/A64292-2005Apr18.html.

165 "Bring 'em on": George W. Bush, Washington, D.C., July 2, 2003, http://georgewbush-whitehouse.archives.gov/news/releases/2003/07/20030702-3.html.

166 "a terrorist magnet": Ricardo Sanchez, CNN's Late Edition with Wolf Blitzer, July 27, 2003. http://www.defenselink.mil/transcripts/transcript.aspx?transcriptid=2904; George W. Bush, Greeley, Colorado, October 25, 2004.

166 "Seems like the reverse": Interview by author with Art Keller, Albuquerque, New Mexico, February 13, 2007.

166 National Intelligence Estimate: Declassified Key Judgments of the National Intelligence Estimate "Trends in Global Terrorism: Implications for the United States," dated April 2006. http://www.dni.gov/press_releases/Declassified_NIE_Key_Judgments.pdf.

166 "plunge into the ocean": Jeffrey Pool (translator), "Zarqawi's pledge of allegiance to al-Qaeda." Jamestown Foundation, Terrorism Monitor, December 16, 2004. http://www.jamestown.org/terrorism/news/article.php?articleid=2369020; "Mujahid brother": CRS Report for Congress, "Al-Qaeda: Evolving Statements and Ideology," January 26, 2006; and Osama bin Laden, audiotape, Al Jazeera, December 27, 2004.

166 exercise more restraint: Ayman al Zawahiri, letter to Abu Musab al Zarqawi, July 9, 2005. www.rjchq.org/media/pdf/zawahiriletter.pdf.

166 thirteen hundred foreign fighters: Michael Gordon and Mark Mazzetti, "General Warns of Risks in Iraq if G.I.'s are Cut." *New York Times,* November 16, 2006. http://www.nytimes.com/2006/11/16/world/middleeast/16policy.html?_r=2&ref=todayspaper&oref=slogin&oref=slogin.

166 90 percent Iraqis: Edward Gistaro, Statement for the Record House Permanent Select Committee on Intelligence and House Armed Services Committee. Director of National Intelligence, July 25, 2007. http://www.dni.gov/testimonies/20070725_testimony.pdf.

166 more than ten thousand Iraqis: Mohamed Hafez, email to author December 14, 2009.

166 combined since 1981: Assaf Moghadam *Globalization of Martyrdom* (Baltimore, MD: Johns Hopkins University Press, 2008), p. 251.

166 up to 90 percent: Jim Michaels, "Foreign fighters leaving Iraq, military says," *USA Today*, March 21, 2008. http://www.usatoday.com/news/world/iraq/2008-03-20-fighters_N.htm.

166 of the 139 "known" suicide bombers: Author correspondence with Mohammed Hafez, December 14, 2009; and see generally Mohammed Hafez, *Suicide Bombers in Iraq* (Washington, D.C.: USIP Press, 2007).

167 61 percent were Saudi: Reuven Paz quoted in Susan Glasser, "'Martyrs' in Iraq mostly Saudis," *Washington Post*, May 15, 2005.

167 Of the 606 foreign fighters: West Point, Combating Terrorism Center. "Al-Qaida's Foreign Fighters in Iraq: a First Look at the Sinjar Records." December 19, 2007. http://www.ctc.usma.edu/harmony/pdf/CTCForeignFighter.19.Dec07.pdf

168 "as my wedding party": Will and Testament of a Suicide Bomber, NMEC-2007-637872, Combating Terrorism Center at West Point.

168 killing sixty: Hassan Fattah and Michael Slackman, "3 Hotels Bombed in Jordan; At Least 57 Die." *New York Times*. November 10, 2005. http://www.nytimes.com/2005/11/10/international/middleeast/10jordan.html; "Israeli spies": PBS Newshour, "Analyzing the Jordan bombings," November 11, 2005. http://www.pbs.org/newshour/bb/terrorism/july-dec05/jordan_11-11.html.

168 highly bureaucratized group: West Point, Combating Terrorism Center, "Al-Qaida's Foreign Fighters in Iraq," 2007 op. cit.

169 eighty executions: Michael Ware, "Papers give peek inside al-Qaeda in Iraq," CNN.com, June 11, 2008. http://www.cnn.com/2008/WORLD/meast/06/11al.qaeda.iraq/index.html.

169 AQI was well financed: Ayman al-Zawahiri, letter to Abu Musab al-Zarqawi, July 9, 2005. www.rjchq.org/media/pdf/zawahiriletter.pdf.

169 recorded income of $386,000: West Point, Combating Terrorism Center. *Bombers, Bank Accounts, and Bleedout: Al-Qaida's Road in and out of Iraq,* ed. Brian Fishman. http://ctc.usma.edu/harmony/pdf/CTCForeignFighter.19.Dec07.pdf.

169 double suicide attacks: Edward Wong, "Mosque attacks kill 70 in Iraq; hotel is hit too," *New York Times,* November 19, 2005. http://www.nytimes.com/2005/11/19/international/19iraq.html.

169 Diyala: Martin Chulov, "Violent province's 27 female suicide bombers who set out to destroy Iraqi hopes of peace," *The Guardian,* November 12, 2008. http://www.guardian.co.uk/world/2008/nov/12/iraq-gender-suicide-bombers-diyala.

169 husband-wife suicide teams: BBC News, "Journey of a Belgian female 'bomber.'" December 2, 2005. http://news.bbc.co.uk/2/hi/europe/4491334.stm; baker's assistant: Anthony Browne and Rory Watson, "The girl who went from baker's assistant to Baghdad bomber," *Times of London,* December 2, 2005. http://www.timesonline.co.uk/tol/news/world/iraq/article744833.ece; "walked into a wedding reception": "Jordan failed bomber confesses on TV," CNN.com, November 14, 2005. http://www.cnn.com/2005/WORLD/meast/11/13/jordan.blasts/index.html. Full confession available from *The Independent,* "Words of a would-be killer," November 14, 2005. http://www.independent.co.uk/news/world/middle-east/sajida-mubarak-atrous-alrishawi-words-of-a-wouldbe-killer-515256.html.

169 Al-Qaeda also deployed children: Ben Morgan, "Iraq story: meeting the suicide bomber child." Agence France Press blog, September 4, 2008. http://blogs.afp.com/?post/2008/09/04/Puzzling-over-the-motives-of-a-suicide-bomb-child.

170 mentally unstable: David Leppard and Abul Taher, "MI5 fears jihadis will use mentally ill as suicide bombers," *The Times (London),* May 25, 2008. http://www.timesonline.co.uk/tol/news/uk/article3999058.ece; killed around 100: "U.S. raids Iraqi psychiatric hospital over attacks," Reuters, February 10, 2008, http://www.reuters.com/article/idusL10400113.

170 the use of chlorine in bombs: BBC News, " 'Chlorine bomb' hits Iraq village." May 16, 2007. http://news.bbc.co.uk/2/hi/middle_east/6660585.stm. See also chapter 13 of this book for a more detailed account of the chlorine attacks.

170 responded to an IED: Clarence Williams, "Life of normalcy rests in his palm," *Washington Post,* November 28, 2005; Katherine Heerbrandt, "Soldier's wife comforts wounded," Gazette.net, October 13, 2005. http://www.gazette.net/stories/101305/frednew192331_31892.shtml and Brian Doyne, interview by author, Virginia 2007.

170 wrapped in a steel case: Discovery Channel, "Mission Ops: Assignment IEDs." Originally aired May 15, 2007. Directed by Carsten Oblaender and author interview with Sidney Alford, Somerset, England, September 5, 2007.

170 3 percent: Robert Bryce, "Man vs. Mine," *The Atlantic,* January/February 2006. http://www.theatlantic.com/doc/200601/explosives; "one in ten": Rick Atkinson, "The IED problem is getting out of control. We've got to stop the bleeding," *Washington Post,* September 30, 2007. http://www.washingtonpost.com/wp-dyn/tent/article/2007/09/29/AR2007092900751.html.

171 "an integral part": United States Marines. State of the Insurgency in al-Anbar. August 17, 2006. http://media.washingtonpost.com/wp-srv/nation/documents/marines_iraq_document_020707.pdf.

171 millions of dollars: John Burns and Kirk Semple, "U.S. finds Iraq insurgency has funds to sustain itself," *New York Times,* November 26, 2006, http://www.nytimes.com/2006/11/26/world/middleeast/26insurgency.html?pagewanted=print.

171 "I wouldn't say": John Negroponte. United States Senate. 2007, January 11. Select Committee on Intelligence. *Current and projected national security threats.* 110th

Congress, 1st session. increased sevenfold: Peter Bergen and Paul Cruickshank, "The Iraq Effect," *Mother Jones*, March 1, 2007. http://www.motherjones.com/news/featurex/2007/03/iraq_effect_1.html.

172 undermined America's place in the world: Pew Global Attitudes Project, "A Year After Iraq War," March 16, 2004. http://pewglobal.org/reports/pdf/206.pdf.p._1; "Pew Global Attitudes Project, "Views of a Changing World 2003: War with Iraq further divides global publics," June 3, 2003. http://pewglobal.org/reports/pdf/185.pdf.

172 On May 1, 2003: George W. Bush, Aboard the USS *Abraham Lincoln*, May 1, 2003. http://www.cnn.com/2003/U.S./05/01/bush.transcript/.

172 was not the case: See the January 2003 paper by the CIA that is referenced in chapter 9, and is described in George Tenet's autobiography, *At the Center of the Storm*, on page 358.

Chapter 11

174 "It is very important": Paul Wolfowitz, Department of Defense News Briefing, December 10, 2001. http://www.defenselink.mil/transcripts/transcript.aspx?transcriptid=2628.

175 back into the Middle Ages: Author observations and interviews, Kabul, Afghanistan, December 1999.

175 The moneychangers down by the Kabul River: These impressions are based on my visits to Kabul in 1999 and 2002.

175 almost two million Afghans came home: United Nations High Commissioner on Refugees, Operational Information—Monthly Summary Report, July 2008, p. ii. http://www.aims.org.af/services/sectoral/emergency_assistance/refugee/unhcr_summaries/jul_08/summary1.pdf.

175 firmly in the grip of the United States: Author observations in Kandahar in 2004.

175 forty-eight U.S. servicemen being killed: CNN.com, Enduring Freedom Casualties—Special Reports, 2003. http://www.cnn.com/SPECIALS/2004/oef.casualties/2003.12.html; "disarming almost all": United Nations Office for the Coordination of Humanitarian Affairs, "Afghanistan: Where Rule by the Gun Continues," IRIN News, May 2006. http://www.irinnews.org/InDepthMain.aspx?InDepthId=8&ReportId=34289&Country=Yes. On this point also see page 297 of "A Different Kind of War," The U.S. Army's official history of the war in Afghanistan from October 2001 to September 2005.

176 consolation prize: Amin Tarzi, "Karzai turns warlord into potential ally," *Radio Free Europe/Radio Liberty*, January 19, 2005. http://www.rferl.org/content/article/1056955.html.

176 fancy title but no real power: CanWest News Service, "Former Afghan warlord says he can defeat the Taliban," May 10, 2007. http://www.canada.com/topics/news/world/story.html?id=1acb5330-dfe8-4f0e-8a1b-4f581478244f&k=44800&p=1.

176 dropped Mohammad Fahim: Carlotta Gall, "Defense chief backs Karzai's rival," *New York Times*, August 5, 2004.

176 "warlord-led militias," *The Economist*, January 1, 2005.

176 Ten million Afghans registered: BBC News, "Afghanistan's election challenge," September 6, 2004. http://news.bbc.co.uk/2/hi/south_asia/3631920.stm.

176 turnout was heavy: Author observations in Gardez on the day of the election, October 9, 2004.

176 Eight million Afghans voted: Kenneth Katzman, "Afghanistan: Elections, Constitution, and Government," Congressional Research Service, August 8, 2006. http://fpc.state.gov/documents/organization/71864.pdf.

176 70 percent: Carlotta Gall and Stephen Farrell, "Afghan election called a suc-

cess despite attacks," *New York Times*, August 20, 2009, http://www.nytimes.com/2009/08/21/world/asia/21afghan.html; "since 1900": Peter F. Nardulli, Jon K. Dalager and Donald E. Greco, "Voter Turnout in U.S. Presidential Elections: An Historical View and Some Speculation," *Political Science and Politics*, September 1996.

176 Eighty-three percent: "Afghans' criticism of U.S. efforts rises; in the southwest, Taliban support grows," BBC/ABC News Poll, December 3, 2007; "less than one in five Iraqis": "Poll finds broad optimism in Iraq, but also deep divisions among groups," ABC News poll, December 12, 2005.

177 There were many grim statistics: World Health Organization, Afghanistan and Iran, 2006. http://www.who.int/countries/afg/en/ and http://www.who.int/countries/irn/en/.

177 ubiquitous street kids: Author interview with Muzghan and her family, Kabul, Afghanistan September 2006.

178 "Me no speak English": Author reporting, Kabul Afghanistan, September 2006. Peter Bergen, "Waltzing with warlords," *Nation*, January 1, 2007.

179 shot the guards: Nick Meo, "Foreigners in Afghanistan now key targets for Taleban's suicide bombers," *The Times (London)*, January 16, 2008 and author observations over the course of multiple trips to Afghanistan after 9/11.

179 Graeme Smith: Graeme Smith, "Talking to the Taliban," *Globe and Mail*, 2008. http://v1.theglobeandmail.com/talkingtothetaliban/. Pashtun Ghilzai tribes played a prominent role in the leadership of the Taliban, in particular Mullah Omar's Hotaki sub-branch of the Ghilzai. This was an undervalued point in helping to understand the Taliban insurgency, which could, at least in part, be understood as a movement of Ghilzai Pashtuns, rural tribes long on the outs in Afghanistan, fighting for power against the Durrani Pashtuns who have traditionally ruled the country since the mid-18th century. See Thomas Johnson and M. Chris Mason, "Understanding the Taliban and insurgency in Afghanistan," *Foreign Policy Research Institute*, winter 2007. A survey commissioned by the British government of some two hundred members of the Taliban and others who supported them found a range of reasons for joining or supporting the insurgency, including the perception that the central government was corrupt, the failure of the state to provide security and justice, and the behavior of foreign forces, particularly house searches at night. Sarah Ladbury, "Testing hypotheses of radicalization in Afghanistan: why do men join the Taliban and Hezb-i-Islami? How much do local communities support them?" Department of International Development, August 14, 2009.

179 The Taliban also benefited: Michael R. Gordon, "Bush would stop U.S. peacekeeping in Balkan fights," *New York Times*, October 21, 2000; "a disagreement": George W. Bush, Boston, Massachusetts, October 4, 2000; "not our key strategic goal": Memo from Douglas J. Feith to Donald Rumsfeld, October 11, 2001. Originally from www.dougfeith.com. It was removed from the site at some point in 2009.

180 "We don't want to repeat the Soviets' mistakes": Franks op. cit., p. 324.

180 Marshall Plan to Afghanistan: George W. Bush, Lexington, VA, April 17, 2002, http://georgewbush-whitehouse.archives.gov/news/releases/2002/04/20020417-1.html and David Rohde and David Sanger, "How a 'good war' in Afghanistan went bad," *New York Times*, August 12, 2007. http://www.nytimes.com/2007/08/12/world/asia/12afghan.html; "low input": James Dobbins, *After the Taliban: Nation-Building in Afghanistan* (Dulles, VA: Potomac Books Inc, 2008), pp. 144–145.

180 Aid per capita to Bosnians: James Dobbins, John G. McGinn, Keith Crane, Seth G. Jones, Rollie Lal, Andrew Rathmell, Rachel M. Swanger, Anga R. Timilsina, America's Role in Nation Building From Germany to Iraq (RAND,: Santa Monica, 2003), p. 146.

180 "low levels of security": James Dobbins quoted in Elizabeth Rubin, "Taking the fight to the Taliban," *New York Times Magazine,* October 29, 2006.

180 "economy of force": Michael Mullen, Washington, D.C., July 2, 2008 http://www.defenselink.mil/transcripts/transcript.aspx?transcriptid=4256; "least amount of resources": James Dobbins, Testimony before the United States Senate Foreign Relations Committee, March 8, 2007. foreign.senate.gov/testimony/2007/Dobbins Testimony070308.pdf, p. 3.

181 meeting in the White House Situation Room: James Dobbins, *After the Taliban: Nation-Building in Afghanistan* (Dulles, VA: Potomac Books Inc, 2008), pp. 114–116. "the strong antipathy": "A Different Kind of War" op. cit., p. 327. "under enormous pressure": "A Different Kind of War" op. cit., p. 246.

181 slowed the formation: Pamela Constable, "Key security initiatives founder in Afghanistan; Taliban resurgent in as development, reforms lag," *Washington Post,* September 19, 2003. four times more soldiers and policemen: Peter Bergen and Katherine Tiedemann, "Obama's War," *Washington Post,* February 15, 2009.

181 couldn't hold many of: Sean Rayment, "British troops hunt the Taliban in Afghanistan," *The Daily Telegraph,* September 4, 2007. http://www.telegraph.co.uk/news/uknews/1561956/British-troops-hunt-the-Taliban-in-Afghanistan.html.

181 "mowing the lawn": author interview with western diplomat, Kabul, Afghanistan, July 2008.

182 traveled to Kuwait City: Author interview with Robert Grenier, Washington, D.C., February 18, 2009.

182 five times more U.S. funding: Amy Belasco, "The Cost of Iraq, Afghanistan, and other global war on terror operations since 9/11," Congressional Research Service, May 15, 2009. www.fas.org/sgp/crs/natsec/RL33110.pdf.

182 "way too committed to Iraq": David Gordon, interview by author, Washington, D.C. October 15, 2009.

182 Rumsfeld ordered: Rashid op. cit., p. 353.

182 "Tragically, I believe that": David Barno, Testimony before the United States House of Representatives, Committee on Foreign Affairs, February 15, 2007. foreign affairs.house.gov/110/33319.pdf.

182 "Where the road ends": Karl Eikenberry interview by author, Kabul, Afghanistan, September 2006.

183 Afghans hadn't seen much: Yuma Turabi and Lorenzo Delegates, "Afghanistan: Bringing Accountability Back In From Subjects of Aid to Citizens of the State," Integrity Watch Afghanistan Report, June 2008. http://www.iwaweb.org/Bringing Accountabilitybackin.pdf.

183 funneled back: Matt Waldman, "Falling Short: Aid Effectiveness in Afghanistan," Oxfam Research Report, May 2008. http://www.oxfamamerica.org/files/ACBARAidEffectivenessPaper.pd]; Jon Hemming, "Afghan Aid ineffective, Inefficient, Watchdog Says," *Reuters,* June 9, 2008. http://uk.reuters.com/article/id UKISL1120120080609; "local Afghan projects": A report by the Peace Dividend Trust in 2007 states only 15% of aid used Afghan resources.

183 Too often: Oxfam International, "Falling Short: Aid Effectiveness in Afghanistan," by Matt Waldman. March 2008. http://www.oxfam.org/files/ACBAR_aid_effective ness_paper_0803.pdf.

183 typical of suicide bombers in Afghanistan: Christine Fair, "Suicide attacks in Afghanistan, 2001–2007," United Nations Assistance Mission in Afghanistan, September 9, 2007.

184 chat with a failed suicide bomber: Author interview with Imdadullah, April 2007, Kabul, Afghanistan.

184 Eight of every ten: Human Rights Watch, "The Human Cost," April 15, 2007. http://www.hrw.org/en/reports/2007/04/15/human-cost-0.

184 Taliban were back with a vengeance: Christine Fair op. cit.; "IED attacks doubled": "IED attacks up in Afghanistan, down in Iraq," November 15, 2007. http://www.armytimes.com/news/2007/11/gns_ied_071115/; highest levels: CNN OEF casualties database op. cit.

185 brought more attacks into Afghanistan: Jason Dye, Anderson Cooper 360, CNN, July 5, 2007. http://transcripts.cnn.com/TRANSCRIPTS/0707/05/acd.02.html. and author's observations at the Bermel base in eastern Afghanistan, September 11–14 2006; "signed a peace deal": BBC News, "Pakistan Taleban in peace deal," September 5, 2006. http://news.bbc.co.uk/2/hi/south_asia/5315564.stm.

185 unwilling or incapable: Author interview with U.S. military officials Kabul, Afghanistan, September 2006. Amir Haqqani: Frank Sturek, interview by author, Zabul, Afghanistan, July 2006.

185 "generally accepted": James Jones, testimony before the United States Senate Foreign Relations Committee, Washington, D.C., September 21, 2006.

185 "down to a particular section of Quetta": Peter Bergen and Charlie Moore, "Source: Mullah Omar in Pakistan," CNN.com, September 9, 2006. http://www.cnn.com/2006/WORLD/asiapcf/09/09/pakistan.mullahomar/index.html.

186 "They were calling from Pakistan": Author interview, Abdul Haq Hanif, Kabul, Afghanistan, April 2007.

186 "We would not have got him": Author interview, U.S. military official, Kabul, Afghanistan, April 2007.

186 at some 40 million: CIA World Factbook, Afghanistan and Pakistan, February 10, 2009. https://www.cia.gov/library/publications/the-world-factbook/geos/af.html; BBC/ABC/ARD, "their view of the Taliban": Afghanistan poll by BBC/ABC, January 2009. http://news.bbc.co.uk/2/shared/bsp/hi/pdfs/05_02_09afghan_poll_2009.pdf, p. 20; high as 27%: International Council on Security and Development, "On a knife edge: southern and eastern Afghanistan," May 2007. http://icosgroup.net/modules/reports/Knife_Edge_Report.

187 between 7,000 and 10,000: Author interview U.S. military official, Kabul, Afghanistan, September 2006.

187 some 12,000 fighters: BBC News, "Afghanistan: Taleban second coming," June 2, 2006. http://news.bbc.co.uk/2/hi/south_asia/5029190.stm; "in contact with his top aides": CBS News, CBS Evening News with Katie Couric, December 29, 2006.

187 "They won't be taken": Author interview with U.S. military official, Kabul, Afghanistan, September 2006.

187 "The Arabs taught us": Sami Yousafzai and Ron Moreau, "The Taliban in their own words," *Newsweek*, September 26, 2009, http://www.newsweek.com/id/216235/page/1. This section draws on Peter Bergen, "The Front," *The New Republic*, October 19, 2009.

187 bin Laden himself had supervised: Carlotta Gall, "A mile from Cheney, Afghan bomber kills at least 23," *New York Times*, February 28, 2007; "Al Libi was behind the operation": Alisa Tang, "Libyan blamed for bomb at Cheney visit," *Associated Press*, May 3, 2007. http://www.washingtonpost.com/wp-dyn/content/article/2007/05/03/AR2007050300963.html.

187 Hassan Gul: "U.S. reveals al-Qaeda Iraq plot," BBC, February 9, 2004, http://news.bbc.co.uk/2/hi/middle_east/3473881.stm; "the case of Omar Al Farouk": Justin Huggler, "The last stand of Al Qaida's Houdini," *The Independent (London)*, September 27, 2006.

188 "trained in Iraq": Author interview with Hamid Mir, Islamabad, Pakistan, May, 2007.

188 "We are on a good and strong relationship": Mustafa Abu al-Yazid's interview with Al Jazeera, June 22, 2009, translated by NEFA Foundation. www.nefafoundation.org/miscellaneous/ . . . /nefa_yazidqa0609.pdf.

188 a piece of red-hot coal: Pamela Constable, "Tales of the Taliban: Part tragedy, part farce," *Washington Post*, February 28, 2004.

188 their cell phone numbers: Daniel Kimmage, "Al-Qaeda Central and the Internet," New America Foundation, February 2010.

188 Hundreds of dollars: Author interview with U.S. military official in Afghanistan, September 2006.

189 scores of tapes like this: Selection of Taliban propaganda tapes, IntelCenter, Washington, D.C., 2005–2009.

189 two dozen law courts: Yochi Dreazen and Siobhan Gorman, "Taliban regains power, influence in Afghanistan," *Wall Street Journal*, November 20, 2008. http://online.wsj.com/article/SB122713845685342447.html.

189 fourteen pages of "national caveats": Author interview with senior NATO commander, Kabul, Afghanistan, December 2005; "only a handful of countries": Author interview with U.S. military official, Kabul, Afghanistan, April 2007.

189 German forces: "A Different Kind of War" op. cit., p. 298.

190 the summer of 2008: Carlotta Gall, "Afghan border concerns NATO's force leader," *New York Times*, June 5, 2008. http://www.nytimes.com/2008/06/05/world/asia/05afghan.html.

190 $100 or more a month: Peter Bergen, "The Taliban, regrouped and rearmed," *Washington Post*, September 10, 2006; "$70 salary of an Afghan policeman": Farah Stockman, "On the streets of Kabul, a scramble for money," *New York Times*, April 11, 2007. http://www.nytimes.com/2007/04/11/world/asia/11iht-afghan.5226639.html.

190 millions of dollars: author interview with Abdul Haq Hanif, Kabul, Afghanistan, April 2007.

190 a drug cartel: author interview with Abdul Haq Hanif, Kabul, Afghanistan, April 2007.

190 from April 2007 to January 2009: Embassy of Afghanistan, History. http://www.embassyofafghanistan.org/history.html; "preference for aerial eradication": Kirk Semple and Tim Golden, "Afghans pressed by U.S. on plan to spray poppies," *New York Times*, October 8, 2007. http://www.nytimes.com/2007/10/08/world/asia/08spray.html.

191 jump into a fifty-five-gallon drum: Author interview with U.S. official then involved in Afghan policy, Washington, D.C.

191 General Mohammed Daud: Two years later Canada's *Globe and Mail* newspaper would identify General Daud as someone who himself profited from the drug trade, a charge he denied. "a very dangerous place": Author interview with Afghan counternarcotics official, Uruzgan, Afghanistan, April 2007.

191 fifth-largest poppy harvest: United Nations Office on Drugs and Crimes, Afghanistan Opium Survey 2008, http://www.unodc.org/documents/crop-monitoring/Afghanistan_Opiu m_Survey_2008.pdf, p. 171.

192 DynCorp guys were easy to spot: Author observation of the Afghan Eradication Force in Uruzgan province, April 2007.

192 Afghan support for poppy cultivation: ABC/BBC/ARD News poll, "Afghans' criticism of U.S. efforts rises; in the southwest, Taliban support grows," December 3, 2007. abcnews.go.com/images/PollingUnit/1049a1Afghanistan-WhereThingsStand.pdf.

192 put up to three million people out of work: Vanda Felbab-Brown, *Shooting Up* (Washington, D.C.: Brookings Press, 2009), p. 135.

192 twelve dollars a day: Felbab-Brown op. cit., p. 134.

192 successful counternarcotics policy: Lt. Gen. David Barno, observation to author, Washington, D.C. 2007.

193 one of the most corrupt countries: Transparency International, "Corruption Perceptions Index 2008," http://www.transparency.org/policy_research/surveys_indices/cpi/2008/cpi_2008_table.

193 nine tons: William Grimes, "Afghan struggle to change poppy fields into roads," *New York Times*, November 7, 2007. http://www.nytimes.com/2007/11/07/books/07grim.html?fta=y.

193 profiting from the drug business: James Risen, "Reports link Karzai's brother to heroin trade," *International Herald Tribune*, October 4, 2008. http://www.iht.com/articles/2008/10/04/asia/05afghan.php.

193 instituted a review: Meghan O'Sullivan interview. Washington, D.C., November 6, 2009 and email to author, June 11, 2011.

193 "There were many discussions": U.S. national security official Washington, D.C., January 2009.

193 everything was fine: Author interview with former U.S. official, Washington, D.C., December 2009.

193 "from their bubble": Author interview with U.S. official, Washington, D.C., January 2009.

193 "the shura": David Kilcullen, author interview, New York; November 20, 2009, "in May 2007": Associated Press, "Bush Taps Lt. Gen. Douglas Lute as 'War Czar' for Iraq, Afghanistan," May 15, 2007; "the green shrinking": Eliot Cohen, author interview, December 10, 2009, Washington, D.C.

194 "There is a point": Douglas E. Lute, interview by author, Washington, D.C., January 8, 2010.

194 soup-to-nuts: Lute interview.

194 "all Iraq all the time": Kilcullen interview.

194 "I don't want a written report": Kilcullen ibid.

194 private polling: Author interview with former U.S. official Washington, D.C., January 2009.

195 "We gave them a briefing": Kilcullen interview, Washington, D.C. January 19, 2010.

195 "leave it for us": Hadley op. cit.

195 "unpublicized Bush review": Lute, Hadley, Kilcullen interviews.

195 adjusting their tactics: Julian Barnes, "U.S. general seeks to curb Afghan civilian deaths," *Los Angeles Times*, September 17, 2008. http://articles.latimes.com/2008/sep/17/world/fg-afghan17.

195 four hundred tribes: Author interview with U.S. intelligence official, 2008.

195 pilot program: Dexter Filkins, "Afghan and U.S. plan to recruit local militias," *New York Times*, December 23, 2008. http://www.nytimes.com/2008/12/24/world/asia/24afghan.html.

195 requested more than 20,000: Tom Vanden Brook, "Commander sees 'tough fight' in Afghan war," *USA Today*, December 8, 2008. http://www.usatoday.com/news/military/2008-12-07-afghantroops_N.htm. See also Stephen J. Hadley in the *Washington Post*, "How Obama's surge can stabilize Afghanistan," December 11, 2009. http://www.washingtonpost.com/wp-dyn/content/article/2009/12/10/AR2009121003439.html.

196 Taliban had a permanent presence: International Council on Security and Development, "Struggle for Kabul: The Taliban Advance," London, UK, December 2008, p. 9.

196 by 2008 more American: iCasualties.org; compare U.S. casualties in Iraq in June 2008 (29) to Afghanistan (46). http://icasualties.org/oef/.

196 "*not* part of the formula": David Barno quoted in Peter Bergen, "How Osama bin Laden beat George W. Bush," *The New Republic*, October 15, 2007. http://www.lawandsecurity.org/get_article/?id=82; and David Barno, "Fighting the other war," *Military Review*, September/October 2007. http://usacac.leavenworth.army.mil/CAC/milreview/English/SepOct07/barnoengseptoct07.pdf.

Chapter 12

197 "God has bestowed": Al Jazeera, "Al-Qaeda's Afghan head named," May 24, 2007. http://english.aljazeera.net/news/asia/2007/05/20085251431519301.html.

197 "We are at war": Mohammed Siddique Khan, al Jazeera, released September 2, 2005. http://www.telegraph.co.uk/news/worldnews/middleeast/1497473/We-are-at-war-I-am-a-soldier.html.

197 "The plague bacillus": Albert Camus, *The Plague* (1947).

197 happy, even euphoric: U.K. House of Commons Home Office Narrative of 7 July 2005 Bombings, news.bbc.co.uk/2/shared/bsp/hi/pdfs/11_05_06_narrative.pdf.

198 an unremarkable bunch: United Kingdom, House of Commons, Report of the Official Account of the Bombings in London on 7th July 2005; a keen cricketer: Ian Herbert and Arifa Akbar, "He was proud to be British," *The Independent,* July 14, 2005, http://www.independent.co.uk/news/uk/crime/shahzad-tanweer-i-cannot-begin-to-explain-this-he-was-proud-to-be-british-498754.html; "red Mercedes": London Investigation Update, PBS, July 13, 2005. http://www.pbs.org/newshour/bb/europe/july-dec05/london_7–13.html.

198 They seemed utterly ordinary: Milan Ray, *7-7: The London Bombings, Islam, and the Iraq War* (London: Pluto Press, 2006), p. 10; buy jihadi videos: Richard Watson, "Rise of the British Jihad," *Granta 103,* http://www.granta.com/Magazine/Granta-103, p. 49.

198 link up there with militant groups: Home Office Report op. cit.

198 a farewell video: Watson op. cit., p. 74; and Lee Glendinning, "Look after mummy," *Guardian*, April 25, 2008. http://www.guardian.co.uk/uk/2008/apr/25/july7.uksecurity.

199 Typical of this view: David Leppard and Robert Winnett, "Blair's extremism proposals attacked as the hunt continues for terror's new breed," *The Sunday Times* (London), August 7, 2005. http://www.timesonline.co.uk/tol/news/uk/article552690.ece.

199 videotape of Khan: London bomber: text in full, BBC News, September 1, 2005. http://news.bbc.co.uk/2/hi/uk_news/4206800.stm.

199 Zawahiri himself made an appearance: "CIA: bomber tape 'appears genuine,'" CNN.com, September 2, 2005. http://www.cnn.com/2005/WORLD/europe/09/02/london.tape.cia/index.html; and Alan Cowell, "Al Jazeera video links London bombings to al-Qaeda," *New York Times*, September 2, 2005. http://www.nytimes.com/2005/09/02/international/europe/02london.html.

199 martyrdom video: BBC News, "Video of 7 July bomber released," July 6, 2006. http://news.bbc.co.uk/2/hi/uk_news/5154714.stm.

199 Khan returned to England: House of Commons Report op. cit., p. 20; noticed that their plants were wilting: Silber et al op. cit, p. 49; bleach their hair: Watson op. cit., p. 52; commercial grade refrigerator: Christopher Dickey, *Securing the City: Inside America's Best Counterterror Force—the NYPD* (New York: Simon & Schuster, 2009), p. 212.

200 cost around £8,000: House of Commons report op. cit., p. 23.

200 to watch videos: Sarah Lyall, "In Britain, migrants took a new path: to terrorism," *New York Times*, July 28, 2005.

200 black burqa: Steve Bird, "21/7 leader Yassin Omar's fiancée is jailed for disguising him in burka," *The Times (London)*, July 12, 2008. http://www.timesonline.co.uk/tol/news/uk/crime/article4319160.ece.

200 Prosecutors said: Alison Pargeter, *The New Frontiers of Jihad: Radical Islam in Europe* (Philadelphia: University of Pennsylvania, 2008), p. 159; BBC News, "Four guilty over 21/7 bomb plot," July 10, 2007. http://news.bbc.co.uk/2/hi/uk_news/6284350.stm.

200 "to do jihad", "convicted Ibrahim": Pargeter op. cit., p. 159; BBC News, "Four guilty over 21/7 bomb plot," July 10, 2007. http://news.bbc.co.uk/2/hi/uk_news/6284350.stm.

201 popped up: For instance, two tapes from bin Laden were released on May 15, 2008 and May 18, 2008.

201 "on the run": George W. Bush quoted in Mark Mazzetti and David Rohde, "Signs of al-Qaeda resurgence," *New York Times*, February 19, 2007, http://www.iht.com/articles/2007/02/19/africa/web.0219intel.php?page=2.

201 "We Won": James Fallows, "Declaring victory," *The Atlantic*, September 2006.

201 "Al-Qaeda is operationally dead": Marlena Telvick, "Al-Qaeda's New Front," PBS *Frontline*, http://www.pbs.org/wgbh/pages/frontline/shows/front/etc/today.html.

201 "the present threat": Marc Sageman, *Leaderless Jihad* (Philadelphia: University of Pennsylvania Press, 2008), p. viii.

201 "main terrorist threat": Marc Sageman, "The homegrown young radicals of next-gen jihad," *Washington Post*, June 8, 2008.

202 "a fundamental misreading": Bruce Hoffman, "The myth of grass-roots terrorism," *Foreign Affairs*, May/June 2008.

202 "the go-to guy": Elaine Sciolino and Eric Schmitt, "A not very private feud over terrorism," *New York Times*, June 8, 2008.

202 "a typical pyramid organization": Louis Beam, "Leaderless resistance," *The Seditionist*, February 1992. http://www.louisbeam.com/leaderless.htm.

202 set up his own training camp: Brynjar Lia, *Architect of Global Jihad: The life of al-Qaeda strategist Abu Musab al-Suri* (New York: Columbia University Press, 2008), p. 230.

203 Videotapes recovered: Key sections of the tapes were translated by Mohannad Hage Ali, who reports on al-Qaeda for *Al Hayat* in London, material that was translated for *The Osama bin Laden I Know* (New York: Free Press, 2006).

203 "nizam la tanzim": Lia op. cit., p. 421.

203 assassination of Theo van Gogh: "Gunman kills Dutch film director," BBC, November 2, 2004. http://news.bbc.co.uk/2/hi/europe/3974179.stm.

204 dead man's chest: For an excellent account of the van Gogh assassination see Ian Buruma, *Murder in Amsterdam* (New York: Penguin, 2006).

204 There had been some discussion: Gabriel Weimann, *Terror on the Internet* (Washington, D.C.: USIP Press, 2006), p. 133.

204 Spain a potential target: Osama bin Laden audiotape, "A message to the Americans," aired on Al Jazeera, October 18, 2003.

204 the Madrid attacks: Spanish police calculated the attacks cost between 41,000 and 54,000 Euros. Javier Jordan, Fernando M. Manas, Nicola Horsburgh, "Strengths and Weaknesses of Grassroot Jihadist Networks in the West," *Studies in Conflict and Terrorism*, 31:1, January 2008.

204 a known jihadist organization: Fernando Reinares, "Jihadist radicalization and the 2004 Madrid bombing network," CTC *Sentinel*, November 2009.

204 "many groups without links": Author interview with Armando Spataro, Florence, Italy, May 22, 2008.

204 "a fundamental reference point": Author interview with Baltasar Garzon, Florence, Italy, May 23, 2008.

204 was resurging: "Terrorist Threat to the U.S. homeland," National Intelligence Estimate, July 2007.

204 Jonathan Evans: Jonathan Evans, address to the Society of Editors, November 5, 2007, Manchester, England. https://www.mi5.gov.uk/output/intelligence-counter-terrorism-and-trust.html.

205 "a dime a dozen": Author interview with Michael Sheehan, Florence, Italy, May 22, 2008.

205 "almost mathematical increase": Author interview with Philip Mudd, Florence, Italy, May 23, 2008.

205 "We have seen an influx": Prepared Testimony of Director of National Intelligence Michael McConnell to the United States Senate Select Committee on Intelligence, Washington, D.C., February 5, 2008.

206 were directed by al-Qaeda: "Bin Laden allegedly planned attack in Turkey," *Associated Press*, December 17, 2003. http://www.msnbc.msn.com/id/3735645/.

206 he lectured into the camera: BBC News, "Suicide videos: what they said," April 4, 2008. http://news.bbc.co.uk/2/hi/uk_news/7330367.stm.

206 On July 4: Emails from Ali's trial that British prosecutors obtained from the American email service Yahoo! and published, in part, by the *Wall Street Journal* September 7, 2009. Original email trial exhibits in author collection.

206 "a couple of weeks": Duncan Gardham, "Airline bomb plot: one of the biggest since WW2," *Telegraph*, September 8, 2009. http://www.telegraph.co.uk/news/uknews/terrorism-in-the-uk/6152185/Airline-bomb-plot-investigation-one-of-biggest-since-WW2.html

207 "We've got our virgins": Greenberg et al. op. cit.

207 began to chair meetings: Michele Malvesti, interview by author, Washington, D.C., January 7, 2010.

207 "They had a bomb-making factory": Author interview with Frances Fragos Townsend, by author, Washington, D.C., December 7, 2009.

207 When Ali was arrested: Nico Hines, "Terror mastermind Abdullah Ahmed Ali guilty of bombing plot," *Times of London,* September 8, 2008. http://www.timesonline.co.uk/tol/news/uk/crime/article4707468.ece; "time taken": David Byers, "Terror gang plotted to blow up transatlantic airlines," *Times of London*, April 3, 2008. http://www.timesonline.co.uk/tol/news/uk/crime/article3674413.ece. Most of the details of the case are taken from the opening statement of Mr. Wright, the prosecutor in the case. Author collection.

208 HMTD: traces of hexamine: Sciolino op. cit.

208 some fifteen hundred passengers would have died: Richard Greenberg, Paul Cruickshank, and Chris Hansen, "Inside the plot that rivaled 9/11," Dateline NBC, September 14, 2009. http://www.msnbc.msn.com/id/26726987/.

208 "get a move on": Henry Chu and Sebastian Rotella, "Three Britons convicted of plot to blow up planes," *Los Angeles Times*, September 8, 2009, http://articles.latimes.com/2009/sep/08/world/fg-britain-verdict8?pg=3.

208 twenty-nine bottles: Agence France Press, "Terror charges dropped against alleged UK terror mastermind," December 13, 2006.

208 "Who are these people?" Bruce Riedel, interview by author, Washington, D.C., November 23, 2009.

208 affiliate in Kenya almost succeeded: "Al-Qaeda claims Kenya attacks," BBC, December 3, 2003.

209 struck by a missile as it took off: Agence France Presse, "Civilian plane hit by missile over Baghdad," November 23, 2003.

209 The same year militants: "British Airways suspends flights to Saudi Arabia after threats," *New York Times*, August 14, 2003.

209 initially planned to attack Incirlik: *Associated Press*, May 31, 2004; and Jarret Brachman, *Global Jihadism: Theory and Practice* (Routledge: 2008), pp. 17–18.

209 "Every dollar": "Bin Laden: goal is to bankrupt U.S.," CNN.com, November 1, 2004. http://www.cnn.com/2004/WORLD/meast/11/01/binladen.tape/.

209 launched an attack: Dan Murphy, "What other al-Qaeda linked attacks have involved Yemen?" *Christian Science Monitor*, December 29, 2009.

209 In Yanbu: "Gunmen kill at least six in Saudi Arabia," Associated Press, May 1, 2004. http://www.usatoday.com/news/world/2004-05-01-saudi-attack_x.htm.

209 Four weeks later: Abdul Hameed Bakier, "Lessons from al-Qaeda's attack on the Khobar compound," *Terrorism Monitor*, August 11, 2006. http://www.usatoday.com/news/world/2004-05-01-saudi-attack_x.htm.

210 bin Laden drew attention: Osama bin Laden, "Statement," December 16, 2004, posted on the internet (translated by BBC monitoring); perhaps the most important": Chris Zambelis, "Attacks in Yemen reflect al-Qaeda's global oil strategy," *Terrorism Monitor*, September 4, 2008; "10%": Hassan M. Fatah, "Attack on Saudi oil facility thwarted," *New York Times*, February 24, 2006.

210 Grand Hyatt, Radisson, and Days Inn: Scott Macleod, "Behind the Amman hotel attack," *Time*, November 10, 2005. http://www.time.com/time/world/article/0,8599,1128209,00.html.

210 According to Spanish prosecutors: interview by author Florence, Italy, May 27, 2009.

210 "were under pledge": Anne Stenersen, "Are the Afghan Taliban involved in international terrorism?" CTC *Sentinel*, September 2009.

211 The suicide bomber: Joby Warrick and Pamela Constable, "CIA base attacked in Afghanistan supported airstrikes against al-Qaeda, Taliban," *Washington Post*, January 1, 2010; "Bomber Fooled CIA, Family, Jordanian Intelligence," Associated Press, January 6, 2010.

211 how he planned to attack the group: "An interview with the Shaheed Abu Dujaanah al Khorshani (Humam Khalil Abu-Mulal al-Balawi)," February 28, 2010, NEFA Foundation.

211 "avenge our good martyrs": Mustafa Abu al-Yazid, "Infiltrating the American Fortresses," December 31, 2009, NEFA Foundation. http://www.nefafoundation.org/miscellaneous/nefaAbul-Yazid0110.pdf.

211 was revenge: Stephen Farrell, "Video links Taliban to CIA attack," *New York Times*, January 9, 2010. http://www.nytimes.com/2010/01/10/world/middleeast/10balawi.html.

211 Armed with that training and $8,000 in cash: *United States of America v. Faisal Shahzad*, Plea agreement, Southern District of New York, June 21, 2010.

211 "only organization qualified": Quoted in Peter Bergen, "Where you bin?" *The New Republic*, January 29, 2006.

211 the green light: Author interview with Saudi official, February 25, 2008, Riyadh, Saudi Arabia.

211 battle is conducted in the media: See for instance his letter to Mullah Mohammed Omar, the leader of the Afghan Taliban, in West Point's Harmony documents, February 14, 2006. AFGP-2002-600321.

211 nearly one hundred: IntelCenter Breakout of as-Sahab audio/video, 2002-26 February 2009. Email from Ben Venzke, February 26, 2009.

211 2 percent: In 2007, 1.8% of Afghans and .01% of Pakistanis were Internet users, according to the International Telecommunications Union, "Information Society Statistical Profiles—Asia and the Pacific, 2009." http://www.itu.int/publ/D-IND-RPM.AP-2009/en; "1%": In 2008, 1% of Iraqis were Internet users, according to the International Telecommunications Union, "Information Society Statistical Profiles—Arab states, 2009," http://www.itu.int/publ/D-IND-RPM.AR-2009/en.

Chapter 13

214 "Acquiring nuclear": Rahimullah Yusufzai, "Osama bin Laden lashes out against the West," *Time*, January 11, 1999. http://www.time.com/time/asia/asia/magazine/1999/990111/osama1.html.

214 "I wish to declare": Hamid Mir, "Osama claims he has nukes," *Dawn*, November 10, 2001. http://www.dawn.com/2001/11/10/top1.htm.

215 "I asked this question": Hamid Mir, interview by author, Islamabad, Pakistan, May 11, 2002.

215 in a pre-9/11 memo: Roland Jacquard, *L'Archive Secretès d'al Qaida*, (Paris: Jean Picollec, 2002), p. 291.

215 For that information: Peter Baker, "Pakistani Scientist Who Met Bin Laden Failed Polygraphs, Renewing Suspicions," *Washington Post*, March 3, 2002.

215 al-Qaeda's leaders turned to: Graham Allison, *Nuclear Terrorism* (New York: Henry Holt, 2004), pp. 20–22.

215 "a rather strange man": author interview with Pervez Hoodbhoy, May 11, 2002, Islamabad, Pakistan.

215 spent part of his retirement: Baker op. cit.

216 charity aimed to establish: David Albright and Holly Higgins, "Pakistani Nuclear Scientists: How Much Nuclear Assistance to Al-Qaeda?" Washington, D.C.: Institute for Science and International Security. August 30, 2002.

216 reporters found: Albright and Higgins op. cit.

216 failed polygraph tests: Peter Baker, "Pakistani Scientist Who Met Bin Laden Failed Polygraphs, Renewing Suspicions," *Washington Post*, March 3, 2002.

216 Mahmood had provided information: Albright and Higgins op. cit.

216 "wouldn't you tell him": Charles Faddis, interview by author, Washington, D.C., January 20, 2010.

217 told his interrogators: Henry Schuster, "Walker Lindh: Al-Qaeda spoke of more attacks," CNN.com, October 4, 2002. http://archives.cnn.com/2002/LAW/10/03/walker.lindh.documents/index.html; "told al Jazeera": BBC News, "Al-Qaeda 'plotted nuclear attacks,'" September 8, 2002. http://news.bbc.co.uk/2/hi/middle_east/2244146.stm.

217 crop-dusting planes: Transcript from Johnelle Bryant interview by Brian Ross, ABC News, June 6, 2002. http://abcnews.go.com/WNT/story?id=130304&page=1.

217 wrote an essay: The essay was posted on Al Neda and translated by MEMRI. Suleiman Abu Ghaith, "In the Shadow of the Lances," The Middle East Research Institute, Special Dispatch Series—No. 338, June 12, 2002.

217 the fatwa of a Saudi cleric: Nasir bin Hamad al-Fahd, "A treatise on the legal status of using weapons of mass destruction against infidels," May 2003. http://www.carnegieendowment.org/static/npp/fatwa.pdf.

218 first known atomic thief: PBS *Frontline,* "Loose Nukes," 1996. http://www.pbs.org/wgbh/pages/frontline/shows/nukes/interviews/smirnov.html.

218 "I was the shift leader": Author interview with Leonid Smirnov, Podolsk, Russia, April 28, 2002; Blinding Horizon, National Geographic, 2003. http://channel.nationalgeographic.com/episode/blinding-horizon-1337/Overview.

219 strictly an amateur affair: Abu Walid al-Masri, *The history of the Arab Afghans from the time of their arrival in Afghanistan until their departure with the Taliban*, serialized in *Al Sharq al Awsat*, December 8–14, 2004.

219 issued a statement: Osama bin Laden statement, "Dangers and Signs of the Indian Nuclear Explosions," May 14, 1998, author collection.

219 al-Masri: Abu Walid al-Masri, *The history of the Arab Afghans from the time of their arrival in Afghanistan until their departure with the Taliban*, serialized in *Al Sharq al Awsat*, December 8–14, 2004.

219 Zawahiri wrote to Mohamed Atef: Alan Cullison and Andrew Higgins, "A computer in Kabul reveals thinking behind four years of al-Qaeda doings," *Wall Street Journal*, December 31, 2001.

220 \$2,000–\$4,000: Anne Stenersen, *Al-Qaida's Quest for Weapons of Mass Destruction: The History behind the Hype* (Saarbrücken: VDM Verlag, 2009), p. 35.

220 "refused to voice": Al-Masri op. cit.

220 Fadl said: *USA vs. Usama bin Laden*, Testimony of Jamal al-Fadl, February 7 and 20, 2001.

220 stockpiled a considerable quantity: Al-Masri op. cit.

220 advised the Taliban leader: Charles J. Hanley, "Taliban naïve of nuclear arms," Associated Press, July 1, 2002.

220 underground facility near Kandahar airport: Drew Brown, "U.S. finds materials for dirty bombs," Knight Ridder, December 22, 2001.

221 "some forms": Peter Zimmerman and Cheryl Loeb, "Dirty bombs: the threat revisited," National Defense University, *Defense Horizons*, No. 38. January 2004. http://www.ndu.edu/inss/DefHor/DH38/dh38.htm.

221 In 1996: International Atomic Energy Agency, "Combating illicit trafficking in nuclear and other radioactive material," Technical Guidance Reference Manual (Vienna: IAEA, 2007), p. 127.

221 one hundred times above normal levels: The information about the Gisht-Kuprik incident comes from the author's 2002 visit to the Uzbek-Kazakh border, interviews with U.S. Customs officials William Lambert and Richard Melton and Colonel Sadritdin Jalilov of Uzbek Customs, and National Geographic's *Blinding Horizon* documentary, op. cit.

222 virtually impossible: David Albright, Kathyrn Buehler, and Holly Higgins, "Bin Laden and the bomb," *Bulletin of the Atomic Scientists*, January/February 2002. http://www.isis-online.org/publications/terrorism/binladenandbomb.pdf.

222 U.S government analysts: Thom Shanker, "U.S. analysts find no sign bin Laden had nuclear arms," *New York Times*, February 26, 2002.

222 crude chemical weapons: Barton Gellman, "Al-Qaeda nears biological, chemical arms production," *Washington Post*, March 23, 2003.

222 al-Qaeda videotape from this period: Nic Robertson, "Tapes shed new light on bin Laden's network," CNN.com, August 19, 2002. CNN videotape collection.

222 were ignored: Omar bin Laden, Najwa bin Laden, Jean Sasson, *Growing Up bin Laden* (2009) p. 230.

222 seven-thousand-page: *Encyclopedia of Jihad*. Author Collection.

222 chemical engineer: West Point, Combating Terrorism Center, "Profile of Abu Khabab," 2007.

222 hundreds of militants: Carlotta Gall and Douglas Jehl, "U.S. raid killed Qaeda leaders, Pakistanis say," *New York Times*, January 19, 2006.

222 "Obtain the liquid": Roland Jacquard, *L'Archive Secretès d'al Qaida*, (Paris: Jean Picollec, 2002), p. 281.

223 American-educated scientists: James Bone and Zahid Hussain, "Al-Qaeda woman Aifia Siddiqui in court on attempted murder charge," *The Times (London)*, August 6, 2008. http://www.timesonline.co.uk/tol/news/world/U.S._and_americas/article4467148.ece.

223 Al-Qaeda recruit with an American science degree: Justine Redman, "Letters detail al-Qaeda's anthrax program," CNN.com, May 23, 2005.

223 biologist working for the Pakistani government:, Rolf Mowatt-Larssen, former official responsible for WMD at the CIA's Counterterrorist Center; author interview, Washington, D.C., December 18, 2009; "looking for anthrax": Joby Warrick, "Suspects and a setback in al-Qaeda anthrax case; scientist with ties to group goes free," *Washington Post*, October 31, 2006.

223 could only weaponize anthrax: Bruce Ivins, *New York Times*, http://topics.nytimes.com/top/reference/timestopics/people/i/bruce_e_ivins/index.html?8qa&scp=1-spot&sq=bruce+ivins&st=nyt.

223 Gary Ackerman: Gary Ackerman, email to author, May 6, 2010.

224 CNN reported this story: "Ricin suspects linked to al-Qaeda," CNN.com, January 16, 2003. http://www.cnn.com/2003/WORLD/europe/01/16/ricin.alqaeda/index.html.

224 gave his speech: Colin Powell, presentation before the United Nations, February 5, 2003, New York City. http://www.globalsecurity.org/wmd/library/news/iraq/2003/iraq-030205-powell-un-17300pf.htm.

224 But two years later: Walter Pincus, "London ricin finding called a false positive," *Washington Post*, April 14, 2005; and Stenersen op. cit. p. 48.

224 "has the potential": Jason Bennetto, "Mass panic was aim of £70,000 dirty bomb," *The Independent (London)*, November 8, 2006. http://www.independent.co.uk/news/uk/crime/mass-panic-was-aim-of-16370000-dirty-bomb-423425.html.

224 "comical": Michael Sheehan, *Crush the Cell; How to Defeat Terrorism without Terrorizing Ourselves* (New York: Crown, 2008), p. 235.

225 sickened hundreds of Iraqis: BBC News, "'Chlorine bomb' hits Iraq village." May 16, 2007. http://news.bbc.co.uk/2/hi/middle_east/6660585.stm; "stopped using": Stenersen op. cit., p. 42.

225 "there was a lot of effort": Charles Faddis interview by author, Washington, D.C. January 20, 2010.

225 "poisons and deadly gases": George W. Bush, Cincinnati, OH, October 7, 2002. http://georgewbush-whitehouse.archives.gov/news/releases/2002/10/20021007-8.html.

225 trotted out the dubious tales: Paul Williams, *Osama's Revenge: The Next 9/11: What the Media and the Government Haven't Told You* (Amherst, NY: Prometheus Books, 2004), pp. 46–47.

225 hyperbolic reporting: Ron Suskind, *The One Percent Doctrine: Deep Inside America's Pursuit of Its Enemies Since 9/11* (New York: Simon & Schuster, 2006), pp. 193–197 and 218.

226 Milton Leitenberg of the University of Maryland: Global Security Newswire, June 26, 2006. http://www.nti.org/d_newswire/issues/2006/6/26/017198a4-bb95-40d5-9738-817ce4a469bb.html.

226 credited with discovering: Ron Suskind, "How an Al-Qaeda cell planned a poison-gas attack on the NY subway," TIME Magazine, June 17, 2006. http://www.time.com/time/nation/article/0,8599,1205309,00.html.

226 according to Michael Sheehan: Michael Sheehan interview, New York City, November 21, 2009.

226 "We built a model of it": John McLaughlin, interview by author, December 7, 2009, Washington, D.C.

227 "on the current path": Graham Allison, *Nuclear Terrorism: the Ultimate Preventable Catastrophe* (New York: Times Books, 2004), p. 15.

227 issued a report in December 2008: Commission on the Prevention of Weapons of Mass Destruction Proliferation and Terrorism. (New York: Vintage Books, 2008). http://www.preventwmd.gov/report/.

227 Joe Biden was briefed: Change.gov, Vice President-elect Joe Biden to be briefed on prevention of WMD and terrorism. http://change.gov/newsroom/entry/vice_president_elect_joe_biden_to_be_briefed_on_prevention_of_wmd_and_terro/.

227 The total of all the known thefts of HEU: IAEA Combating Trafficking op. cit., pp. 129–130. http://www-pub.iaea.org/MTCD/publications/PDF/Pub1309_web.pdf.

228 are not about to hand over: Brian Michael Jenkins, *Will Terrorists Go Nuclear?* (Amherst, NY: Prometheus Books, 2008), p. 143.

228 distinctive signatures: Daniel Chivers and Jonathan Snider, "International nuclear forensics regime," Security for a New Century Study Group Report, February 2, 2007.

228 $100 million: Thom Shanker and David Sanger, "Pakistan is rapidly adding nuclear arms, U.S. says," *New York Times*, May 17, 2009. http://www.nytimes.com/2009/05/18/world/asia/18nuke.html.

228 Defense has assessed: Department of Defense, "Proliferation Threat and Response," January 2001. http://www.dod.mil/pubs/ptr20010110.pdf, p. 27.

228 stored unassembled: Carnegie Endowment for International Peace, "Nuclear weapons status 2005," http://www.carnegieendowment.org/images/npp/nuke.jpg.

228 one layer of protection: Paul Kerr and Mary Beth Nikitin, "Pakistan's nuclear weapons: proliferation and security issues," Congressional Research Service, June 12, 2009. http://www.fas.org/sgp/crs/nuke/RL34248.pdf.

228 PAL: Kerr and Nikitin op. cit; Peter Crail, "Pakistan nuclear stocks safe, officials say," *Arms Control Today*, June 2009, http://www.armscontrol.org/act/2009_6/Pakistan.

228 "important steps": Michael Maples, U.S. Senate. Armed Services Committee. The current and future worldwide threats to the national security of the United States. March 10, 2009.

228 "a high probability": *Hardball with Chris Matthews*, MSNBC, February 5, 2009. http://www.msnbc.msn.com/id/29034366/.

229 After obtaining his PhD in Belgium; traveled to Holland; made centrifuges suitable; steal the blueprints: Michael Laufer, "A.Q. Khan nuclear chronology," Proliferation Review, Carnegie Endowment for International Peace. http://www.carnegieendowment.org/publications/index.cfm?fa=view&id=17420.

229 placed under house arrest: Victoria Schofield and David Wastell, "Scientist who sold nuclear secrets 'can keep his money,'" *Sunday Telegraph*, February 8, 2004. http://www.telegraph.co.uk/news/worldnews/asia/pakistan/1453785/Scientist-who-sold-atomic-secrets-can-keep-his-money.html.

229 Sultan Bashiruddin Mahmood: Gordon Corera, *Shopping for Bombs: Nuclear Proliferation, Global Insecurity, and the Rise and Fall of the AQ Khan Network* (London: Oxford University Press, 2006), p. 29 and generally pp. 9–30.

Chapter 14

233 "Although we have": National Intelligence Council, National Intelligence Assessment, "The terrorist threat to the U.S. homeland," July 2007. http://www.dni.gov/press_releases/20070717_release.pdf.

234 "had a lot of girl friends": This section draws on Peter Bergen, "The Front," *The New Republic*, October 19, 2009. http://www.tnr.com/article/world/the-front. Also USA v. Najibullah Zazi, Eastern District of New York, Indictment. http://www.investigativeproject.org/documents/case_docs/1063.pdf; and Michael Wilson, "From smiling coffee vendor to terror suspect," *New York Times*, September 25, 2009. http://www.nytimes.com/2009/09/26/nyregion/26profile.html.

234 three or four a day: Anne Kornblut, "Obama team says Zazi case illustrates balanced approach to terror threat," *Washington Post*, October 6, 2009. http://www.washingtonpost.com/wp-dyn/content/article/2009/10/05/AR2009100503989.html.

234 "subway lines in Manhattan": John Marzulli, "Najibullah Zazi pleads guilty to plotting NYC terror attack, supporting al Qaeda," *New York Daily News*, February 22, 2010.

234 pages of handwritten notes: USA v. Najibullah Zazi, Eastern District of New York, 09-CR-663 Memorandum of law in support of the government's motion for a permanent order of detention (Via IntelWire).

235 traveled to Pakistan's tribal areas: USA vs Bryant Neal Vinas, Eastern District Court of New York 08-CR-823. http://intelfiles.egoplex.com/2009-07-22-Bryant-Neal-Vinas-Court-Docs.pdf. He pled guilty on January 28, 2009 to the charges against him.

235 Long Island Rail Road: William K. Rashbaum and Souad Mekhennet, "L.I. man helped al-Qaeda, then informed," *New York Times*, July 22, 2009. http://www.nytimes.com/2009/07/23/nyregion/23terror.html

235 Californian convert: USA v. Adam Gadahn, Central District Court of California, SA CR 05-254 A Superseding Indictment.

235 charged with treason: Raffi Khatchadourian, "Azzam the American," *New Yorker*, January 22, 2007.

235 David Headley: Headley information comes from United States vs. David C. Headley, Northern District of Illinois, Eastern Division, Affidavit in Support of Criminal Complaint. http://media1.suntimes.com/multimedia/headley%20complaint.pdf_20091027_09_57_00_15.imageContent.

235 cartoons as a "catastrophe": Inal Ersan, "Bin Laden warns EU over Prophet cartoons," Reuters, March 20, 2008, http://www.reuters.com/article/idusN19338241200803201.

236 killing six: Jane Perlez and Pir Zubair Shah, "Blast near Danish embassy in Pakistan kills six," *New York Times*, June 2, 2008, http://www.nytimes.com/2008/06/02/world/asia/02iht-pakistan.2.13391102.html.

236 key role in LeT's massacre in Mumbai: USA v. David Coleman Headley U.S. District Court Northern District of Illinois Eastern Division Case No. 09 CR 830.

237 some three dozen American citizens or residents: New York University Center on Law and Security 2009 op. cit.

237 formally pledged allegiance: "Somalia's Shabab proclaim allegiance to bin Laden," Agence France Press, September 22, 2009.

237 his own imprimatur: Osama bin Laden tape, translated by NEFA Foundation, March 19, 2009. http://www.nefafoundation.org/miscellaneous/nefaubl0309-2.pdf

237 some measure of stability: "Islamist Control of Mogadishu Raises Concern of Extremist Future for Somalia," June 8, 2006.

238 Ahmed drove a truck: Spencer Hsu and Carrie Johnson, "Somali Americans recruited by extremists," *Washington Post*, March 11, 2009. http://www.washingtonpost.com/wp-dyn/content/article/2009/03/10/AR2009031003901.html.

238 matched Ahmed's finger: USA vs Cabdulaahi Ahmed Faarax, Abdeiweli Yassin Isse, criminal complaint filed October 8, 2009 in U.S. District Court Minnesota. http://graphics8.nytimes.com/packages/pdf/U.S./20091124_TERROR_DOCS/faarax.pdf.

238 The FBI suspected: "FBI investigating Seattleite in suicide bombing," Associated Press, September 25, 2009. http://www.msnbc.msn.com/id/33025395/ns/world_news-terrorism/.

238 "How dare you": NEFA Foundation, transcript of al Shabab video from Abu Mansoor al Amiriki, "A response to Barack Obama's speech in Cairo," July 9, 2009; http://www.nefafoundation.org/miscellaneous/FeaturedDocs/nefa_abumansoor0709.pdf;: Andrea Elliott, "The jihadist next door," *New York Times Magazine*, January 31, 2010.

238 six other Somali-Americans: Spencer Hsu, "Concern grows over recruitment of Somali Americans by Islamists," *Washington Post*, October 4, 2009. http://www.washingtonpost.com/wp-dyn/content/article/2009/10/03/AR2009100302901.html.

239 outside an Army barracks: Emma Brockes, "British man named as bomber who killed 10," *The Guardian*, December 28, 2000. http://www.guardian.co.uk/uk/2000/dec/28/india.kashmir.

239 not be much of a concern: Peter Bergen, "The terrorists among us," *ForeignPolicy.com*, November 19, 2009.

239 American-born cleric: "Sudarsan Raghavan, "Cleric says he was confidant to Hasan," *Washington Post*, November 16, 2009.

239 "was asking for an edict": Anwar al-Awlaki, interview by Abdelela Haidar Shayie, AlJazeera.net, December 23, 2009. Translation by Middle East Media Research Institute, http://www.memrijttm.org/content/en/report.htm?report=3859%26param=GJN.

239 strippers: Joseph Rhee, "Accused Fort Hood shooter was a regular at shooting range, strip club," ABC News, November 16, 2009. http://abcnews.go.com/Blotter/accused-fort-hood-shooter-nidal-hasan-visited-strip/story?id=9090116.

239 filmed at a convenience store: Maria Newman and Michael Brick, "Neighbor says Hasan gave belongings away before attack," *New York Times*, November 7, 2009.

http://www.nytimes.com/2009/11/07/U.S./07suspect.html; "the color white": David Cook, *Martyrdom in Islam* (Cambridge University Press, 2007), p. 117.

240 "I am going to do God's work": Scott Shane and James Dao, "Investigators study tangle of clues on Fort Hood suspect," New York Times, November 14, 2009. http://www.nytimes.com/2009/11/15/U.S./15hasan.html.

240 shouted at the top of his lungs: Sanjay Gupta on Anderson Cooper 360, interview with Logan Burnette, November 11, 2009. http://transcripts.cnn.com/TRANSCRIPTS/0911/11/acd.01.html.

240 U.S. military recruiting station: District Court of Little Rock, Arkansas, County of Pulaski, Affidavit for Search and Seizure Warrant. http://www.investigativeproject.org/documents/case_docs/988.pdf.

240 According to federal prosecutors: USA v Daniel Patrick Boyd et al Indictment in U.S. District Court for the Eastern District of North Carolina, filed 7/22/09 http://www.investigativeproject.org/documents/case_docs/1029.pdf; and the superseding indictment in the same case dated September 24, 2009. http://www.investigativeproject.org/documents/case_docs/1075.pdf.

241 told a government informant: NEFA Foundation report, "Fort Dix Plot," January 2008. http://www.nefafoundation.org/miscellaneous/fortdixplot.pdf.

241 an array of automatic weapons: USA vs Mohamad Ibrahim Shnewer, Dritan Duka, Eljvir Duka, Shain Duka, Serdar Tatar U.S. District Court, District of New Jersey, Criminal No 07-459. http://www.investigativeproject.org/documents/case_docs/564.pdf.

241 "exactly what we are looking for": USA vs Mohamad Ibrahim Shnewer Criminal Complaint U.S. District Court, District of New Jersey filed May 7, 2007, p. 11.

241 "Al-Qaeda in California": USA vs Kevin James et al U.S. District Court for the Central District of California Case No. CR 05-214-CJC and exhibits. http://www.investigativeproject.org/documents/case_docs/1089.pdf.

241 James's crew planned: USA vs Kevin James et al op. cit.

242 at least twenty: New York University Center on Law and Security 2009 op. cit., and New American Foundation dataset on domestic jihadist terrorism cases, publication forthcoming.

242 "Homegrown terrorists": "U.S. fears home-grown terror threat," BBC News, June 24, 2006. http://news.bbc.co.uk/2/hi/5112354.stm.

242 smoked a great deal of weed: Abby Goodnough, "Trial starts for men in plot to destroy Sears Tower," *New York Times*, October 3, 2007, http://www.nytimes.com/2007/10/03/U.S./nationalspecial3/03liberty.html.

242 A government informant: Abby Goodnough, "Trial starts for men in plot to destroy Sears Tower," *New York Times*, October 3, 2007. http://www.nytimes.com/2007/10/03/U.S./nationalspecial3/03liberty.html; "three times": "5 convicted in Liberty City terror trial," CNN.com, May 12, 2009. http://www.cnn.com/2009/CRIME/05/12/liberty.seven/index.html.

243 largely ghettoized: Abdirahman Mukhtar, testimony before the Senate Homeland Security and Governmental Affairs Committee, March 11, 2009. http://hsgac.senate.gov/public/index.cfm?FuseAction=Files.View&FileStore_id=c762508c-3694-4894-808a-229fafb1d8d9.

243 truck driver: TIME magazine profile by Claire Suddath, July 24, 2009, http://www.time.com/time/nation/article/0,8599,1912512,00.html; and Michael Powell, "U.S. recruit reveals how Qaeda trains foreigners," *New York Times,* July 23, 2009. http://www.nytimes.com/2009/07/24/nyregion/24terror.html.

243 illegal immigrants: "Fort Dix six allegedly had bomb recipes, made fun of U.S.," ABC News, May 10, 2007. http://abcnews.go.com/GMA/story?id=3160739&page=1.

244 "they are not interested": Joel Roberts, CBS News, June 18, 2006. http://www.cbsnews.com/stories/2006/06/18/terror/main1726666.shtml.

244 as many as two thousand: Michael Evans, "MI5's spymaster Jonathan Evans comes out of the shadows," *Times of London*, January 7, 2009. http://www.timesonline.co.uk/tol/news/uk/article5462528.ece.

245 hiring an additional two thousand intelligence analysts: Federal Bureau of Investigation, "Intelligence" fact sheet, http://www.fbi.gov/aboutus/transformation/intelligence.htm; Federal Bureau of Investigation, "By the numbers" fact sheet, http://www.fbi.gov/page2/september06/numbers090606.htm; just 16 names: Reuters, "U.S. lacked data to put suspect on no-fly list," December 26, 2009. http://www.reuters.com/article/idusN2613148620091227.

245 "multiple terrorist risk factors": Scott Shane and Lowell Bergman, "Adding up the ounces of prevention," *New York Times,* September 10, 2006. http://www.nytimes.com/2006/09/10/weekinreview/10shane.html; "suicide bombing in Hilla": Scott Macleod, "A jihadist's tale," *Time,* March 28, 2005. http://www.time.com/time/magazine/article/0.9171.1042473.00.html; and Charlotte Buchen, "The man turned away," PBS *Frontline,* "The Enemy Within," http://www.pbs.org/wgbh/pages/frontline/enemywithin/reality/al-banna.html.

246 More than a third: Daniel Benjamin and Steven Simon, *The Next Attack* (New York: Macmillan, 2006), p. 119.

Chapter 15

247 "Only jihad": "Profile: Baitullah Mehsud," BBC News, December 28, 2007. http://news.bbc.co.uk/2/hi/south_asia/7163626.stm.

248 military-jihadi complex: Barnett Rubin, an American expert on Afghanistan, uses this term.

248 on the Pakistani side: BBC In Depth, "The Future of Kashmir?" http://news.bbc.co.uk/2/shared/spl/hi/south_asia/03/kashmir_future/html/.

248 several of their leaders: Ahmed Rashid, *Taliban: Militant Islam, Oil & Fundamentalism in Central Asia* (New Haven: Yale University Press, 2001), p. 90.

248 hub of jihadist violence: United States Department of State, Country Reports on Terrorism, Chapter 8: Foreign Terrorist Organizations, April 28, 2006. http://www.state.gov/s/ct/rls/crt/2005/65275.htm; bombing of a Sheraton hotel: BBC News, "Analysis: Pakistan searches for blast leads," June 14, 2002, http://news.bbc.co.uk/2/hi/south_asia/2045045.stm; three separate attacks: BBC News, "Pakistan bomb kills U.S. diplomat," March 2, 2006, http://news.bbc.co.uk/2/hi/south_asia/4765170.stm; CNN.com, "Karachi consulate shooting kills 2," February 28, 2003. http://www.cnn.com/2003/WORLD/asiapcf/south/02/28/karachi.shooting/.; "Karachi riot kills six after suicide attack," *International Herald Tribune*, June 1, 2005. http://www.iht.com/articles/2005/06/01/news/mosque.php.

249 This would make Pearl: Mariane Pearl blames a story by the Pakistani journalist Kamran Khan in *The News* on January 30, 2002 for making public that her husband was Jewish. Mariane Pearl, *A Mighty Heart* (New York: Scribner, 2004), p. 146.

249 reporting on the various Pakistani militant groups: The French intellectual Bernard-Henri Levy published a 2003 book about Pearl's kidnapping titled *Who Killed Daniel Pearl?* In his account Levy advanced the theory that Pearl was killed because he had stumbled upon secrets of Pakistan's nuclear program. There is no convincing evidence for this claim. See Bernard-Henri Levy, *Who Killed Daniel Pearl?* (New York: Melville House, 2003), pp. 440–443.

249 set out to interview Fuqra's founder: Mariane Pearl op. cit., pp. 24–25.

250 "dropped in to talk": Author interview with Jameel Yusuf, Karachi, Pakistan, January 2003. "It was a prepaid telephone card": Author interview with Jameel Yusuf.

250 "National Movement": Mariane Pearl op. cit., pp. 104–106.
250 The FBI also dispatched: Mariane Pearl op. cit., p. 106; murdered by three Arab men, p. 198.
251 surrendered to Brigadier Ejaz Shah: Mariane Pearl op. cit., p. 182.
251 KSM has claimed: BBC News, "Key 9/11 figure 'beheaded Pearl,'" March 15, 2007. http://news.bbc.co.uk/2/hi/americas/6455307.stm.; and author interview with Fouda op. cit.
251 an interview with both KSM and Ramzi Binalshibh: Fouda and Fielding op. cit., p. 72.
251 an unusual offer: Fouda and Fielding op. cit., p. 36; and author interview with Yosri Fouda, London, 2002.
252 "you look familiar": Yosri Fouda interview.
252 "They are right": Yosri Fouda interview.
252 "too many volunteers": Yosri Fouda interview op. cit.
252 "a very old concept": Ramzi Binalshibh in Al Jazeera documentary, "The Road to September 11," September 11, 2002.
252 nuclear power plants: Author interview with Yosri Fouda.
253 On September 11, 2002: David Rohde, "Karachi raid provides hint of Qaeda's rise in Pakistan," *New York Times*, September 14, 2002. http://www.nytimes.com/2002/09/15/world/threats-responses-karachi-karachi-raid-provides-hint-qaeda-s-rise-pakistan.html; "slipped away to Quetta": "Top al-Qaeda operative caught in Pakstan," CNN.com, March 1, 2003, http://www.cnn.com/2003/WORLD/asiapcf/south/03/01/pakistan.arrests/.
253 "What the fuck": Author interview with a Western diplomat, Islamabad, Pakistan, 2003.
253 "I am with KSM": Scott Shane, "Inside a 9/11 mastermind's interrogation," *New York Times*, June 22, 2008. http://www.nytimes.com/2008/06/22/washington/22ksm.html.
253 the CIA gave the Associated Press a photo: Tenet op. cit., p. 252.
253 "personal signature trail": Author interview with senior U.S. intelligence official, Washington, D.C., 2003.
253 a trove of information: Department of Defense, Verbatim Transcript of Combatant Status Review Trial, Khalid Sheikh Mohammed, March 10, 2007. http://www.defenselink.mil/news/transcript_ISN10024.pdf.
254 Pakistan handed over: Pervez Musharraf, *In the Line of Fire: A Memoir* (New York: Free Press, 2008), p. 237.
254 "creative young engineers": Robert Dannenberg, December 17, 2009, Manhattan, New York.
254 And so al-Qaeda: Dannenberg interview op. cit.; decided to leave Karachi: Department of Defense, Detainee Biographies, Ahmed Khalfan Ghailani. http://www.defenselink.mil/pdf/detaineebiographies1.pdf, p. 2.
254 "wild and merciless fanaticism": Winston Churchill, *The Story of the Malakand Field Force* (1898), p. 5.
255 female literacy rate: Jane Perlez, "Aid to Pakistan in tribal areas raises concerns," *New York Times*, July 16, 2007. http://www.nytimes.com/2007/07/16/world/asia/16pakistan.html.
255 the compounds in which they live: Author observations over the course of many trips to FATA since 1983.
255 more than two thousand: Author interview with intelligence official, Washington, D.C., 2008.
255 around 100 to 150 members: Author interview with U.S. intelligence official, Washington, D.C., 2008.

255 Powell was visiting Islamabad: "U.S. has come to stay, Powell tells Afghans: South Waziristan operation praised," *Dawn,* March 18, 2004. http://www.dawn.com/2004/03/18/top13.htm.

255 "high value target": "Pakistani sources: Zawahiri surrounded," CNN.com, March 18, 2004. http://www.cnn.com/2004/WORLD/asiapcf/03/18/pakistan.alqaeda/index.html. And for an account of those operations see Zahid Hussein, *Frontline Pakistan: The Struggle with Militant Islam* (New York: Columbia University Press, 2007), pp. 143–148.

256 filmed their executions: Author observation of Taliban videos by Umar production company; Hayat Ullah Khan, a fixer for PBS's *Frontline* who was killed in the FATA in 2006. "A journalist in the tribal areas," PBS *Frontline,* http://www.pbs.org/wgbh/pages/frontline/taliban/tribal/hayatullah.html.

256 where Mullah Omar: U.S. intelligence officials, multiple interviews by author, 2006–2008.

256 two out of Pakistan's four: Election results can be found at Adam Carr, Election Archive, Legislative Election of 10 October 2002. http://psephos.adam-carr.net/countries/p/pakistan/pakistan2002.txt.

256 power-hungry officer: PBS NewsHour, Gwen Ifill, April 30, 2002. http://www.pbs.org/newshour/bb/middle_east/jan-june02/vote_4-30.html.

256 banned the militant Kashmiri groups: "Musharraf bans Lashkar, Jaish; wants dialogue on Kashmir," Rediff.com, January 12, 2002. http://www.rediff.com/news/2002/jan/12mush.htm.

257 to the brink of war: Steve Coll, "The Stand-off," *The New Yorker*, February 13, 2006, is the best account of this episode.

257 target of their wrath: Musharraf op. cit., pp. 245–256; and Salman Masood, "Pakistani leader escapes attempt at assassination," *New York Times*, December 26, 2003.

257 specifically calling for attacks on Musharraf: "Arab networks air al Qaeda tape," CNN.com, September 29, 2003, http://edition.cnn.com/2003/WORLD/meast/09/28/alzawahiri.tape/index.html.

257 Red Mosque: Peter Bergen, "Red Dawn: Musharraf's enemies close in," *The New Republic*, July 23, 2007. http://www.newamerica.net/publications/articles/2007/musharrafs_enemies_close_5816.

258 "We will resist": Abdul Rashid Ghazi interview with author, Islamabad, Pakistan, May 4, 2007.

258 Ghazi was killed: "Pakistan militant cleric killed," BBC News, July 10, 2007. http://news.bbc.co.uk/2/hi/south_asia/6288704.stm.

258 ambassador intervened: Howard French, "Mosque siege reveals Chinese connection," *International Herald Tribune*, July 12, 2007. http://www.iht.com/articles/2007/07/12/asia/letter.php.

258 rallying cry: Bruce Riedel, "Al-Qaeda's resurgence in Pakistan," West Point, Combating Terrorism Center *Sentinel* (December 2007).

258 filled with comfortable villas: Author observations, Islamabad, Pakistan, 1983–2009.

259 lawyers: "Pakistan judge row sparks arrests," BBC, March 26, 2007, http://news.bbc.co.uk/2/hi/south_asia/6494971.stm; "most prominently Geo Television": *The Times of India,* March 16, 2007, http://www.asiamedia.ucla.edu/article.asp?parentid=65974.

259 "We were showing police": Hamid Mir, interview by author, Islamabad, Pakistan, May 2 2007. And CNN-IBN, March 16, 2007, http://www.newssafety.com/hotspots/countries/pakistan/miscagencies/pakistan160307.htm.

259 to emulate neighboring India: The highest priorities for Pakistanis were free elections, free press and independent judiciary. Terror Free Tomorrow, "Results of a new nationwide public opinion survey before the June 2008 Pakistani

by-elections," June 2008. http://www.terrorfreetomorrow.org/upimagestft/Pakistan PollReportJune08.pdf.

260 a constant barrage of calls: "Rice calls Musharraf over emergency rule," *Agence France Presse*, November 5, 2007; declared emergency rule: Griff Witte, "Musharraf declares emergency rule in Pakistan," *Washington Post*, November 7, 2004.

260 "I admire your courage": George W. Bush, quoted in "Bush unaware of Musharraf's contention," *Associated Press*, September 23, 2006. http://www.usatoday.com/news/washington/2006-09-22-bush-musharraf_x.htm.

260 "We got real concerns about this": Stephen Hadley, interview by author, December 15, 2009, Washington, D.C.

260 "we were getting diddled": Frances Fragos Townsend, interview by author, December 7, 2009, Washington, D.C.

260 local militant leaders: International Crisis Group, "Pakistan's Tribal Areas: Appeasing the Militants," December 11, 2006.

261 200 percent higher: Jim Garamone, "NATO, U.S., Afghan forces battling Taliban in Afghanistan," American Forces Press Service, January 16, 2007. http://www.defenselink.mil/news/NewsArticle.aspx?ID=2708; "a steady pace": Author embed at Bermel base in eastern Afghanistan, September 11, 2006.

261 obvious to the Bush team: Hadley interview.

261 some $11 billion: Congressional Research Service, "Direct Overt U.S. Aid and Military Reimbursements to Pakistan, FY2002-FY2009," http://www.fas.org/sgp/crs/row/pakaid.pdf.

261 "has protected or regenerated": National Intelligence Community. National Intelligence Estimates. "The terrorist threat to the U.S. homeland," July 2007. www.dni.gov/press_releases/20070717_release.pdf.

261 "still in Quetta": Author interview with U.S. military official in Kabul, Afghanistan, April 2007.

261 "target folders": Author interview with U.S. military official in Islamabad, Pakistan, May 1 2007.

261 nixed a proposed attack: Mark Mazzetti, "Rumsfeld called off 2005 plan to capture top al-Qaeda figures," *International Herald Tribune*, http://www.iht.com/articles/2007/07/08/news/qaeda.php.

261 only 11 percent: Adam Carr Election Archive, Legislative election of 10 October 2002, http://psephos.adam-carr.net/countries/p/pakistan2002.txt; "a piffling 2%": Adam Carr Election Archive, Legislative election of 18 February 2008, http://psephos.adam-carr.net/countries/p/pakistan/pakistan2008.txt.

262 dropped the corruption charges: CNN.com, "Bhutto corruption charges dropped," October 5, 2007. http://edition.cnn.com/2007/WORLD/asiapcf/10/05/pakistan.elections/index.html.

262 widely believed to have looted: "Bhutto: corruption charges remain," CNN.com, October 3, 2007.

262 woman who returned: She was born in 1953, elected prime minister in 1988, and returned from exile in 2007.

262 targeted the former prime minister in Karachi: MSNBC, "Blasts aimed at Bhutto kill more than 120," October 19, 2007. http://www.msnbc.msn.com/id/21344367/.

263 "Were they our men?": Translated in Martin Fletcher, "Named: the al-Qaeda chief who 'masterminded murder,'" *Times of London*, December 29, 2007. http://www.timesonline.co.uk/tol/news/world/asia/article3105443.ece; BBC News, "Bhutto's murder: key questions," February 8, 2008. http://news.bbc.co.uk/2/hi/south_asia/7165892.stm.

263 authenticated that it was Mehsud's voice": Author interview Western official, Islamabad, Pakistan, January 2, 2008.

263 press conference: Syed Shoaib Hasan, "Meeting Pakistan's most feared militant," BBC, May 27, 2008, http://news.bbc.co.uk/2/hi/south_asia/7420606.stm.

263 killing about fifty-five: Greg Miller, "Two al-Qaeda suspects believed killed in Pakistan," *Los Angeles Times*, January 9, 2009. http://www.latimes.com/news/nationworld/world/africa/la-fg-terror9-2009jan09.0.4086437.story; and "Pakistan's al-Qaeda leaders 'dead,'" BBC News, January 9, 2009. "http://news.bbc.co.uk/2/hi/south_asia/7819305.stm.

263 masterminded by an al-Qaeda leader: Zahid Hussein, "Usama al-Kini, head of al-Qaeda in Pakistan, killed by U.S. military," *Times of London*, January 9, 2009, http://www.timesonline.co.uk/tol/news/world/asia/article5479455.ece.

264 at the last minute: Elizabeth Palmer, "Arrests made in Pakistan hotel bombing," CBS/AP, September 22, 2008. http://www.cbsnews.com/stories/2008/09/22/terror/main4466838.shtml.

264 support for suicide attacks: Pew Global Attitudes Survey, "Unfavorable views of Jews and Muslims on the increase in Europe," September 17, 2008. http://pewglobal.org/reports/pdf/262.pdf, question 73.

264 nearly 3,000: South Asia Terrorism Portal, Casualties of Terrorist Violence in Pakistan, http://www.satp.org/satporgtp/countries/pakistan/database/casualties.htm; Author email correspondence with Pakistani government official, November 17, 2008; some 1,500: 1,574 coalition casualties 2001–2010: http://icasualties.org/oef/.

265 aided by elements of the ISI: Mark Mazzetti and Eric Schmitt, "Pakistanis aided Kabul attack, U.S. officials say," *New York Times*, August 1, 2008. http://www.nytimes.com/2008/08/01/world/asia/01pstan.html?em.

265 creeping rapprochement: For an account of the back channel Kashmir negotiations, see Steve Coll, "The Back Channel," *New Yorker*, March 2, 2009. http://www.newyorker.com/reporting/2009/03/02/090302fa_fact_coll.

265 fifth-largest country: United Nations, World Population Prospects: The 2006 revision. http://un.org/esa/population/publications/wpp2006/WPP2006_Highlights_rev.pdf. p. 47.

Chapter 16

266 "Just because you invade a country stupidly": Quoted in Thomas Ricks, *The Gamble: General David Petraeus and the American Military Adventure in Iraq, 2006–2008* (New York: Penguin Group, 2009), p. 29.

266 "Security may be ten percent": Quoted in Neil Sheehan, *A Bright Shining Lie: John Paul Vann and America in Vietnam* (New York: Random House, 1988), p. 67.

266 In the summer of 2006: Sterling Jensen, "Lessons from an Anbar sheikh," *Washington Post*, September 29, 2007, http://www.washingtonpost.com/wp-dyn/content/article/2007/09/28/AR2007092801554.html; lanky, intense, 28-year-old Mormon with a talent for languages; author interview with Sterling Jensen, Washington, D.C. November 12, 2008.

267 city of some three hundred thousand: Ann Scott Tyson, "Troops fight to expand foothold in Ramadi," *Washington Post*, August 2, 2006, http://www.washingtonpost.com/wp-dyn/content/article/2006/08/01/AR2006080101733.html; only 100 cops: Tom Bowman, "Sunnis sheikhs join Iraqi police to fight al-Qaida," NPR, February 19, 2007, http://www.npr.org/templates/story/story.php?storyId=7486653.

267 nightmarish mash-up: author interview with Sterling Jensen.

267 dead people with signs: Author interview with Sterling Jensen; author interview with Anbar sheik, May 31, 2008, Anbar Province, Iraq.

267 met with: Jim Michaels, "An Army colonel's gamble pays off in Iraq," *USA Today*, May 1, 2007, http://www.usatoday.com/news/world/iraq/2007-04-30-ramadi-colonel_n.htm.

267 killed his father and three of his brothers: Joshua Partlow, Ann Scott Tyson and Robin Wright, "Bomb kills a key Sunni ally of U.S.," *Washington Post*, September 14, 2007 and Todd Pittman, "Sunni sheikhs join fight vs. insurgency," Associated Press, March 25, 2007.

267 effectively ruled: "State of the insurgency in al Anbar," August 17, 2006. http://media.washingtonpost.com/wp-srv/nation/documents/marines_iraq_document_020707.pdf.

268 "this is awesome": Jensen interview op. cit.

268 "Never interrupt": Napoleon Bonaparte, quoted in James Charlton, *The Military Quotation Book* (New York: Macmillan, 2002), p. 93.

268 an aggressive assault: Jim Michaels op. cit.; http://www.usatoday.com/news/world/iraq/2007-04-30-ramadi-colonel_n.htm

268 live side by side: Jim Michaels op. cit., http://www.usatoday.com/news/world/iraq/2007-04-30-ramadi-colonel_n.htm; "tactic that had worked": George W. Bush, Renaissance Cleveland Hotel, Cleveland, OH, March 20, 2006. http://georgewbush-whitehouse.archives.gov/news/releases/2006/03/20060320-7.html.

268 twenty-nine small outposts: Greg Jaffe and David S. Cloud, *The Fourth Star* (New York: Random House, 2009), p. 206.

268 fifty thousand soldiers: Jaffe and Cloud op. cit., p. 163.

269 little or no understanding: Author observations in Ramadi in June 2008.

269 his face for the first time: Rob Watson, "First Zarqawi video significant," BBC, April 26, 2006. http://news.bbc.co.uk/2/hi/middle_east/4947768.stm.

269 The breakthough: The account of the interrogations that led to the information about Zarqawi can be found in "The Ploy" by Mark Bowden, *The Atlantic,* May 2007, and also in Matthew Alexander, *How to Break a Terrorist* (New York: Free Press, 2008), especially pages 274–275.

270 "shocked by the death": Osama bin Laden, translated by CNN, June 29, 2006, http://transcripts.cnn.com/TRANSCRIPTS/0606/29/acd.02.html.

270 reaching a peak around the New Year of 2007: Department of Defense Multinational Corps-Iraq, Pentagon Press Conference, November 1, 2007, http://www.defense.gov/DODCMSShare/briefingslide/317/071101-D-6570C-001.pdf.

270 "OK, you beat us": 'Matthew Alexander,' interview by author, Washington, D.C. January 18, 2010.

270 changed its name: Stephen Negus, "Call for Sunni State in Iraq." *Financial Times,* October 15, 2006.

270 unsigned oath of allegiance: Combating Terrorism Center at West Point, Sinjar Documents, Harmony NMEC-2007-637854. http://www.ctc.usma.edu/harmony/pdf/Combined%20Orig_Trans/NMEC-2007-637854_comb.pdf.

270 foreign-fighter flow: Joseph Felter and Brian Fishman, "Al-Qaida's Foreign Fighters in Iraq: A First Look at the Sinjar Records," Combating Terrorism Center, December 2007; and Brian Fishman (ed.), "Bombers, Bank Accounts, and Bleedout: al-Qaida's Road in and out of Iraq," Combating Terrorism Center, July 22, 2008.

270 from around 120 a month: Jim Michaels, "Foreign fighters leaving Iraq," *USA Today,* March 21, 2008, http://www.usatoday.com/news/world/iraq/2008-03-20-fighters_N.htm; "around half": Brian Fishman, "Bombers, bank accounts, and bleedout," Combating Terrorism Center at West Point, www.ctc.usma.edu/harmony/pdf/Sinjar_2_July_23.pdf, p. 7; slowed to a dribble: author interview with Emma Sky, senior official on General Raymond Odierno's staff in Iraq on September 29, 2009, Washington, D.C.

270 did little for its poor image: author interview with Emma Sky.

271 "changing course": Harmony MNFT-2007-005648, http://www.ctc.usma.edu/harmony/pdf/Combined%20Orig_Trans/MNFT-2007-005648_comb.pdf.

271 under such pressure: Amit Paley, "Shift in tactics aims to revive struggling insurgency." *Washington Post,* February 8, 2008.

271 a wounded organization: Paley 2008 op. cit.

271 "Beware of division": Text available from the NEFA Foundation, http://www1.nefafoundation.org/miscellaneous/nefabinladen1007.pdf.

271 larger than the size of New England: Area of New England is 62,806 (U.S. Census Bureau, Quick Facts, 2000) and Anbar is 53,000 square miles U.S. Fed News, "Marines end Anbar mission as Army takes lead," January 26, 2010. Al-Qaeda also controlled large swaths of other parts of Sunni Iraq.

271 85 percent: David Kilcullen, "Anatomy of a tribal revolt," *Small Wars Journal,* August 29, 2007. http://smallwarsjournal.com/blog/2007/08/anatomy-of-a-tribal-revolt/

272 100,000 men: Andrew North, "Sons of Iraq move hailed a success," BBC, November 18, 2008, http://news.bbc.co.uk/2/hi/in_depth/7734978.stm

272 "since 2003": author interview with Stephen Hadley, December 15, 2009, Washington, D.C.

272 generally not engaged in sectarian conflict: Vali Nasr, *The Shia Revival* (New York: Norton, 2007), p. 26.

272 her mounting concern: Hadley op. cit.

273 "surgios": Linda Robinson, *Tell Me How This Ends* (New York: Public Affairs, 2008), p. 28, and author interviews with Hadley, Meghan O'Sullivan, November 6, 2009, Washington, D.C., and Brett McGurk, December 15, 2009, Washington, D.C.

273 behind the back of his boss: Ricks op. cit., p. 112.

273 standing down: Author interview with Jack Keane, Washington, D.C., December 16, 2009; and Bing West, *The Strongest Tribe* (New York: Random House, 2009), pp. 108–112.

274 "When you'd sit": McGurk interview.

274 two major offensives: Kimberly Kagan, *The Surge: A Military History* (New York: Encounter Books, 2008), pp. 11–13.

274 was convinced: O'Sullivan op. cit.; "far less capable": David Petraeus, interview by author, Washington, D.C., October 7, 2009.

274 "I told friends": McGurk interview.

275 "communal civil war": Stephen Biddle, "Seeing Baghdad, thinking Saigon," *Foreign Affairs,* March/April 2006.

275 did not feel he made any headway: Keane interview.

275 "*without exception*": O'Sullivan interview.

276 John Nagl: Author interview with John Nagl, Washington, D.C. December 9, 2009.

276 Conrad Crane: Conrad Crane, "Minting COIN," *Air & Space Power Journal,* Winter 2007. http://www.airpower.maxwell.af.mil/airchronicles/apj/apj07/win07/crane.html.

276 David Galula: Nagl op. cit. and Crane op. cit.

276 "The population becomes the objective": David Galula, *Counterinsurgency Warfare: Theory and Practice* (Westport, Connecticut: Praeger, 1964), p. 52.

277 "We had a vetting": Crane comments at a conference hosted by New York University at a panel chaired by the author, November 20, 2009.

277 new ideas: Crane 2007 op. cit.

277 "Sarah's influence": Nagl interview, "FM-324 available in hard copy," *Small Wars Journal,* May 8, 2007. http://smallwarsjournal.com/blog/2007/05/-fm-324-the-new/.

277 a serious review: Richard H. Schultz and Andrea Dew, "Counterinsurgency, by the book," *New York Times,* August 7, 2006. http://www.nytimes.com/2006/08/07/opinion/07shultz.html.

277 The doctrines: FM-324, pp. 1–29. http://www.fas.org/irp/doddir/army/fm3-24.pdf.

277 "Paradoxes": FM-324, pp. 1–27. http://www.fas.org/irp/doddir/army/fm3-24.pdf.

278 "thumping": George W. Bush, November 8, 2006. http://www.cnn.com/2006/POLITICS/11/08/bush.transcript3/index.html.
278 dumped . . . Rumsfeld; installed in his place: "Bush replaces Rumsfeld to get 'fresh perspective,'" CNN.com, November 9, 2006. http://www.cnn.com/2006/POLITICS/11/08/rumsfeld/.
278 "We need to try": McGurk interview.
278 increasingly alarmed: Hadley interview.
279 "tourniquet": Author interview with Fred Kagan, Washington, D.C., November 17, 2009.
279 "force generation" model: Kagan interview; the first of the group's reports is available from AEI, January 5, 2007. http://www.aei.org/docLib/20070111_ChoosingVictoryupdated.pdf.
279 "He is a Sphinx": Kagan interview; December 11: Jack Keane, interview by author, Washington, D.C., December 16, 2009.
280 fundamentally disagreed: Keane interview and author interview with Ray Odierno, Washington, D.C., December 14, 2009.
280 Bush also met privately: Biddle, Cohen and Keane interviews by author.
280 "unbelievably somber": Author interview Stephen Biddle, Washington, D.C. November 9, 2009.
280 "I was very blunt": Author interview with Eliot Cohen, Washington, D.C. December 10, 2009.
281 "We got around": Keane interview; "the knowledge space": Biddle interview.
281 "he was quizzical": Keane interview.
281 Iraq Study Group: United States Institute of Peace, "Iraq Study Group Report," December 6, 2006. http://media.usip.org/reports/iraq_study_group_report.pdf.
282 "If we do this": O'Sullivan interview.
282 On December 13: Bob Woodward, *The War Within* (New York: Simon & Schuster, 2008), pp. 286–289.
282 Hadley recalls: Hadley interview.
283 "we need more troops": O'Sullivan interview and Odierno interview.
283 Around the same time: Woodward, op. cit. p. 295.
283 all five brigades as soon as possible: Odierno interview; "Petraeus agreed": Petraeus interview by author, Washington, D.C., December 18, 2009.
283 "does this guy want to win or not?": McGurk interview.
283 the new surge: Eventually the surge would involve 30,000 soldiers.
283 twenty thousand soldiers: George W. Bush, Washington, D.C., January 10, 2007. http://georgewbush-whitehouse.archives.gov/news/releases/2007/01/20070110-7.html.
283 "I am not persuaded": Barack Obama, interviewed by Keith Olbermann, January 10, 2007.
283 more or less the entire Democratic party: Jonathan Karl, "Troop surge already underway," ABC News, January 10, 2007. http://abcnews.go.com/WNT/IraqCoverage/story?id=2785532
284 "most dangerous foreign policy blunder": Chuck Hagel, hearing of the Senate Foreign Relations Committee, "The administration's plan for Iraq," Washington, D.C., January 11, 2007.
284 A survey: *Foreign Policy* magazine and the Center for American Progress, "The Terrorism Index," August 20, 2007. http://www.americanprogress.org/issues/2007/08/terrorism_index.html; 61 percent: Jon Cohen and Dan Balz, "Poll: most Americans opposed to Bush's Iraq plan," *Washington Post*, January 11, 2007; "Chuck Hagel": "Reid: Iraq war "worst foreign policy mistake in U.S. history," CNN.com, February 18, 2007. http://www.cnn.com/2007/POLITICS/02/18/reid.iraq/index.html.

284 "Give me everything": Petraeus interview with author December 18, 2009.
284 back channel: Odierno and Keane interviews.
284 Emma Sky: A good profile of Emma Sky is by Alissa Rubin, "A civilian voice at Odierno's side in Iraq," *New York Times*, November 21, 2009.
285 "the huge psychological": Sky interview.
285 Initiatives Group: Emma Sky, "Iraq 2007—Moving Beyond Counter-Insurgency Doctrine—a firsthand perspective," Royal United Services Institute, December 1, 2007; and Emma Sky interview by author in September, 29, 2009, Washington, D.C.
285 winter of 2004: Woodward op. cit., pp. 17–26.
285 "The biggest mind-set change": Emma Sky, interview by author.
285 General Petraeus arrived: Peter Baker, "General is front man for Bush's Iraq plan," *Washington Post*, February 7, 2007, http://www.washingtonpost.com/wp-dyn/content/article/2007/02/06/AR2007020601918.html
285 "I just couldn't believe it": Petraeus interview with author, October 7, 2009. Washington D.C.
285 well over two hundred car bombings: slide from October 2009, "Patterns in high profile explosions," published in Anthony Cordesman, "Iraq security trends," Center for Strategic and International Studies, November 19, 2009.
286 more than 1,600 every week: CENTCOM slide from October 2009, "Iraq: Weekly security Incidents."
286 Laughing, he recalls: David Petraeus, interview.
286 Battlefield Update Assessment: Author observations of Petraeus in Baghdad, June 2008.
286 three-page letter: Multi-national Force-Iraq Commander's Counterinsurgency Guidance July 15 2008 http://usacac.leavenworth.army.mil/CAC2/MilitaryReview/Archives/English/MilitaryReview_20081031_art004.pdf.
286 another key role: Sky interview interview.
286 "Where everyone": O'Sullivan interview.
287 "Persisting indefinitely": Richard Lugar, June 25, 2007, Washington, D.C. http://lugar.senate.gov/press/record.cfm?id=277751.
287 "charged beyond belief": David Petraeus, interview by author, Washington, D.C.; December 16, 2009.
287 "suspension of disbelief": Hillary Clinton, before the Senate Armed Services Committee, September 11, 2007.
287 banner headline: MoveOn.org ad available from cdn.moveon.org/pac/content/pac/pdfs/PetraeusNYTad.pdf; "Army of One": Petraeus interview.
288 "twenty-three or twenty-five-mile": David Petraeus, interview by author, Washington, D.C., October 7, 2009.
288 put two brigades: Robinson op. cit., p. 104.
288 deadliest month in two years: Ricks op. cit., p. 179.
288 For those who worked: Sky interview; "the most difficult times": Odierno interview.
288 "Tony Soprano does Iraq": Biddle interview.
289 traveled in January 2007 to Ramadi: Odierno interview.
289 cash payments: Colin Kahl, Michèle A. Flournoy, Shawn Brimley, *Shaping the Iraq Inheritance*, CNAS June 2008, p. 18; and Ricks op. cit., p. 215.
289 "As we were able to": Odierno interview.
290 half the Sunni population: West op. cit., p. 320.
290 efforts to register: Ernesto Londono, "U.S. takes battle against Iraq violence to border," *Washington Post*, October 30, 2008; and author interviews with various U.S. military officers in Iraq June 2008.
290 gated communities: Petraeus interview with author, October 7, 2009, Washington, D.C.

290 number of hours flown by unmanned aerial vehicles: "Military replying more on drones, mostly in Iraq," Associated Press, January 1, 2008, http://www.msnbc.msn.com/id/22463596/. These numbers do not include the large numbers of hours flown by the Pentagon's UAV workhorse the Raven.

290 signals intelligence: author interviews with various U.S. military officers in Iraq, June 2008.

290 "two rounds a night!": David Gordon, interview by author, Washington, D.C., October 15, 2009.

290 IED attacks: Thom Shanker, "Makeshift bombs spread beyond Afghanistan, Iraq," *New York Times*, October 28, 2009. http://www.nytimes.com/2009/10/29/world/29military.html.

290 "So you reverse": Petraeus, interview with author, December 16, 2009.

291 pitched battles: "Iraqi, U.S. forces battle al-Sadr's militia," CNN.com, August 6, 2004, http://www.cnn.com/2004/WORLD/meast/08/05/iraq.main/index.html.

291 sixty thousand men: Tom Ricks and Ann Scott Tyson, "Intensified combat on streets likely," *Washington Post*, January 11, 2007, http://www.washingtonpost.com/wp-dyn/content/article/2007/01/10/AR2007011002581_pf.html.

291 Iraqi civilians: http://www.iraqbodycount.org/database/.

291 sectarian violence: Information from a series of unclassified U.S. military briefing slides from the week of May 31, 2008.

291 six-month truce: Charles Crain, "Iraq militias fighting for supremacy," TIME magazine, August 29, 2007. http://www.time.com/time/world/article/0,8599,1657449,00.html.

292 attack on the city of Basra: "UK halts troop cuts after Iraq clashes," CNN.com, April 1, 2008, http://edition.cnn.com/2008/WORLD/meast/04/01/uk.iraq/index.html.

292 70 percent: CBS News, "UK exit leaves Basra's future in doubt," September 4, 2–7, http://www.cbsnews.com/stories/2007/09/04/america_in_iraq/main3232921.shtml.

292 He barely gave: Stephen Farrell and James Glanz, "More than 1,000 in Iraq's forces quit Basra fight," *New York Times*, April 4, 2008, http://www.nytimes.com/2008/04/04/world/middleeast/04iraq.html?scp=6&sq=basra&st=cse; and author's reporting trip to Basra in June 2008.

292 "arguably impulsive": Petraeus interview with author October 7, 2009, Washington, D.C.

292 "There were all": David Gordon interview.

292 "If he succeeds": Hadley interview.

292 militias were decimated: Author interviews with British and American officers in Baghdad and Basra, Iraq, June 2008.

292 Maliki followed up: Sudarsan Raghavan, "19 tense hours in Sadr City alongside the Mahdi Army," *Washington Post*, March 29, 2008, http://www.washingtonpost.com/wp-dyn/content/article/2008/03/28/AR2008032803810_pf.html

292 Sunni sheikhs: The four sheikhs were Hamid al-Haiys, Jassim Suwaydawi, Abd al-Jabbar and Ali Hatem, interviewed by author in Anbar, Iraq, May 31, 2008.

293 some six hundred thousand Iraqi soldiers and policemen: Peter Bergen and Katherine Tiedemann, "Obama's War," *Washington Post*, February 15, 2009.

293 fired eighteen: Stephen Biddle, Michael E. O'Hanlon, and Kenneth M. Pollack, "How to leave a stable Iraq," *Foreign Affairs*, September/October 2008, http://www.foreignaffairs.com/print/63565; and author interview with Major General Hussein al-Awadi, June 2008, Baghdad, Iraq.

293 a mixed force: Stephen Biddle, Michael O'Hanlon, and Kenneth Pollack, "How to leave a stable Iraq," *Foreign Affairs*, September/October 2008.

293 provincial election law: Sudarsan Raghavan, "Parliament approves elections law in Iraq," *Washington Post*, September 25, 2008, http://www.washingtonpost.

com/wp-dyn/content/article/2008/09/24/AR2008092400752.html; "went largely peacefully": New York Times, "Iraq Elections," http://topics.nytimes.com/topics/news/international/countriesandterritories/iraq/elections/index.html.

293 late November 2008: White House, Text of Strategic Framework Agreement and Security Agreement Between the United States of America and the Republic of Iraq, November 27, 2008, http://georgewbush-whitehouse.archives.gov/news/re leases/2008/11/20081127-2.html.

294 "I just never believed": Sky interview.

000 blood and treasure: CNN, U.S. and coalition casualties, http://www.cnn.com/SPE CIALS/2003/iraq/forces/casualties/index.html; "at least 100,000 Iraqis killed": http://www.washingtonpost.com/wp-dyn/content/article/2008/03/07/AR200 8030702846.html; "increased around the world sevenfold": Peter Bergen and Paul Cruickshank, "The Iraq Effect," *Mother Jones,* March 1, 2007. http://www.mother jones.com/news/featurex/2007/03/iraq_effect_1.html.

294 An alliance: Kevin M. Woods, "Saddam and terrorism: emerging insights from captured Iraqi documents," Institute for Defense Analyses, November 2007.

294 road to Jerusalem: Fouad Ajami, "Iraq and the Arabs' future," *Foreign Affairs*, January/February 2003. http://www.foreignaffairs.org/20030101faessay10218/fouad-ajami/iraq-and-the-arabs-future.html.

295 "finance its own reconstruction": Paul Wolfowitz, before the Defense Subcommittee of the House Appropriations Committee, March 27, 2003.

295 "never been closer to defeat": Adrian Croft, "Al-Qaeda in Iraq never closer to defeat," Reuters, May 24, 2008; "killed hundreds": For example, a series of bombings on August 19, 2009, killed 95 in Baghdad ("95 killed on Iraq's deadliest day since U.S. handover," CNN.com, August 19, 2009), and at least 127 were killed when a series of truck bombs exploded on December 8, 2009 (BBC, "Baghdad car bombs cause carnage," December 8, 2009).

295 "They will really be": Odierno interview.

295 around 30 percent: Bush Job approval ratings, CNN/Opinion Research, January 11, 2007. http://www.pollingreport.com/BushJob.htm.

295 "There's only one guy": Cohen interview.

296 crowed about: Octavia Nasr, "Tape: bin Laden tells Sunnis to fight Shiites in Iraq," CNN.com, July 1, 2006, http://www.cnn.com/2006/WORLD/meast/07/01/bin-laden.message/index.html.

Chapter 17

297 "Striking the World Trade:" Frapper l'immeuble du 'World Trade Center,' je considere cela comme criminel. From an interview with *Al Arabiya* in 2005, translated into French; http://www.recherches-sur-leterrorisme.com/Documentsterrorisme/abdallah-anas.html

297 "history's unmarked grave": George W. Bush, Address to a Joint Session of Congress and the American People, September 20, 2001, Washington, D.C. http://georgewbush-whitehouse.archives.gov/news/releases/2001/09/20010920-8 .html.

297 "stupid and will be punished": Mohamed Tantawi, quoted in Douglas Jehl, "More extremists find basis for rebellion in Islam," *New York Times*, September 22, 2001.

298 "a grave sin": Yusaf al-Qaradawi, quoted in Caryle Murphy, "Muslim leaders speak out," *Washington Post*, October 13, 2001.

298 "greatest of sins": "The Mufti of Saudi Arabia on the recent terrorist attacks in the USA," *The Muslim Creed*, September 2001 (9:9), p. 4.

298 "will not force the United States": Interview with Muhammad al-Shafi'I, "Abdallah Anas, the son-in-law of Abdallah Azzam, tells *Al-Sharq al-Awsat:* Al-Zarqawi's

banner is illegitimate and the AL-Qa'ida trials have no credibility; the bombings in London are criminal deeds." February 9, 2006. Open Source Center via World News Connection.

298 "My brother Osama": Quoted in Turki al-Saheil, "Reaction to Salman al-Awdah's bin Laden letter," *Al-Sharq al-Awsat*, September 18, 2007. http://www.aawsat.com/english/news.asp?section=1&id=10241.

299 "message to his followers": Author interview with Salman al-wdah, Riyadh, Saudi Arabia, February 25, 2008.

299 one of the reasons: I was the producer of the CNN interview, which aired on May 10, 1997, and was conducted somewhere in eastern Afghanistan.

299 twenty-six Saudi clerics: Toby Jones, "Saudi Arabia: reform or ruin?," *Daily Star*, December 18, 2004.

299 withdrew his support: Ellen Knickmeyer, "Egyptian extremist rewriting rationale for armed struggle," *Washington Post*, July 15, 2007. http://www.washingtonpost.com/wp-dyn/content/article/2007/07/14/AR2007071401182_pf.html. This section draws on Peter Bergen and Paul Cruickshank, "The Unraveling," *The New Republic*, June 11, 2008.

299 terrorism against civilians: Abdul Hameed Bakier, "Imprisoned leader of Egypt's Islamic Jihad challenges al-Qaeda," *Terrorism Monitor*, Jamestown Foundation, December 10, 2007.

299 "extremely immoral": Middle East Media Research Institute, "Major Jihadi Cleric and Author of Al-Qaeda's Shari'a Guide to Jihad: 9/11 Was a Sin; A Shari'a Court Should Be Set Up to Hold Bin Laden and Al-Zawahiri Accountable; There Are Only Two Kinds of People in Al-Qaeda—The Ignorant and Those Who Seek Worldly Gain," December 14, 2007, Dispatch No. 1785.

299 turned against al-Qaeda: Paul Cruickshank and Nic Robertson, "New jihadi code threatens al-Qaeda," CNN, November 10, 2009. http://edition.cnn.com/2009/WORLD/africa/11/09/libya.jihadi .code/.

299 mainstream Islamic theology: "Whoever judges that someone is no longer a Muslim, it is they who have deviated from Islam and transgressed God's will because they have judged another's faith," explains Hasan al Hudaybi, the leader of Egypt's Muslim Brotherhood from 1949 to 1973.

300 dramatically in Iraq: Mohammed Hafez's book *Suicide Bombers in Iraq: The Strategy and Ideology of Martyrdom* (Washington, D.C.: USIP Press, 2007) describes this phenomenon.

300 claimed to be defending Muslims: Tom Chivers, "Al-Qaeda doesn't kill the innocent," *Daily Telegraph*, April 3, 2008.

300 over the Internet: Selected Questions and Answers from Dr. Ayman al-Zawahiri, April 17, 2008, translated by NEFA Foundation.

300 The Q&A did not go well: The Open Meeting with Shayk Ayman al Zawahiri, *As Sahab*, 1429, pages 2, 4, and 13.

300 "not the intended targets": Osama bin Laden, "The way to frustrate the conspiracies," December 29, 2007, translated by NEFA Foundation. http://www1.nefafoundation.org/miscellaneous/nefabinladen1207.pdf.

301 only 10 percent of Saudis: Terror Free Tomorrow, Saudi Arabia, December 2007. http://www.terrorfreetomorrow.org/upimagestft/TFT%20Saudi%20Arabia%20Survey.pdf.

301 2005 letter sent by Zawahiri: Ayman al-Zawahiri, letter to Abu Musab al Zarqawi, July 9, 2005. www.rjchq.org/media/pdf/zawahiriletter.pdf.

302 favorable view of bin Laden: Pew Global Attitudes Project op. cit., p. 84.

302 quite negative attitude toward the United States: Pew Global Attitudes Project op. cit., p. 1.

302 subsequently arrested: "Saudi Arabia announces al-Qaeda arrests," CNN.com, August 19, 2009, http://www.cnn.com/2009/WORLD/meast/08/19/saudi.alqaeda.arrests/index.html.

302 leaders in jail or dead: Aside from a bombing in July 2009, there were no JI-related incidents in Indonesia since 2005, and many of the group's leaders were arrested or executed. (*New York Times*, Times Topics, "Jemaah Islamiyah," July 19, 2009). The leader of a JI splinter group, Noordin Top, was killed in September 2009 (Tom Allard, "Terror kingpin Noordin shot dead," *The Age*, September 18, 2009.

302 popular legitimacy: In 2009, only 13 percent of Indonesians surveyed said suicide bombings could be justified, down from 26 percent in 2002, and 24 percent had confidence in bin Laden to "do the right thing regarding world affairs," down from 57 percent in the spring of 2003. Pew Global Attitudes Project, "Confidence in Obama lifts U.S. image around the world," July 23, 2009. http://pewglobal.org/reports/pdf/264.pdf.

302 "without achieving this goal": Zawahiri, *Knights Under the Banner of the Prophet* (2001).

Chapter 18

303 "I've noticed": Anderson Cooper 360, February 3, 2010, Washington, D.C. http://transcripts.cnn.com/TRANSCRIPTS/0902/03/acd.01.html.

304 largest massacre: *New York Times,* Times Topics, Irish Republican Army, March 10, 2009. http://topics.nytimes.com/topics/reference/timestopics/organizations/i/irish_republican_army/index.html.

304 "al-Qaeda and its allies": Barack Obama, "Remarks by the president on a new strategy for Afghanistan and Pakistan," March 27, 2009, Washington, D.C. http://www.whitehouse.gov/the-press-office/remarks-president-a-new-strategy-afghanistan-and-pakistan.

304 On Christmas Day: Anahad O'Connor and Eric Schmitt, "Terror attempt seen as man tries to ignore device on jet," *New York Times*, December 26, 2009; "80 grams of PETN", prominent Nigerian family: Carrie Johnson, "Explosive in Detroit terror case could have blown hole in airplane, sources say," *Washington Post*, December 29, 2009; recently graduated: "Bomb suspect Umar Farouk Abdulmutallab on UK watch-list," BBC, December 29, 2009; originally flown from: "Key dates surrounded the Christmas Day attack," *Associated Press*, December 30, 2009, http://www.wtop.com/?nid=116&sid=1851004; carried a syringe: Richard Esposito and Brian Ross, "Photos of the Northwest Airlines Flight 253 bomb," ABC News, December 28, 2009. http://abcnews.go.com/print?id=9436297.

304 acquired in Yemen; "Yemen can carry out airstrikes against al-Qaeda," CNN.com, December 30, 2009. http://www.cnn.com/2009/WORLD/meast/12/30/U.S..yemen.strikes/index.html.

304 On August 28: Peter Bergen, "Similar explosive used in Saudi attack," CNN.com, December27,2009.http://www.cnn.com/2009/U.S./12/27/bergen.terror.plot/index.html.

305 traditionally a time of repentance: Peter Bergen, "Saudi investigation: would-be assassin hid bomb in underwear," CNN.com, September 30, 2009. http://edition.cnn.com/2009/WORLD/meast/09/30/saudi.arabia.attack/index.html.

305 hundred-gram device: Bergen, September 2009, op. cit; "rare": author interview with senior U.S. counterterrorism official, December 27, 2009.

305 "try it": Author interview with top Saudi counterterrorism official, October, 2009.

306 White House's own review: Summary of the White House Review of the December 25, 2009 Attempted Terrorist Attack, p. 2. http://www.whitehouse.gov/the-press-office/white-house-review-summary-regarding-12252009-attempted-terrorist-attack.

306 assassination attempt: John Brennan, White House press conference, Washington, D.C., January 7, 2010. http://www.whitehouse.gov/the-press-office/briefing-homeland-security-secretary-napolitano-assistant-president-counterterrorism.
306 "dodged a bullet": Jake Tapper, Karen Travers, and Huma Khan, "Obama: system failed in a potentially disastrous way," ABC News, January 5, 2010. http://abcnews.go.com/print?id=9484260.
306 On January 21: Scott Shane, Mark Mazzetti, Helene Cooper, "Obama reverses key Bush security policies," *New York Times*, January 22, 2009; http://www.nytimes.com/2009/01/23/U.S./politics/23obama.html; "reject as false": Barack Obama, Washington, D.C., January 20, 2009.
306 six-month review: Mark Mazzetti and William Glaberson, "Obama issues directive to shut down Guantánamo," *New York Times*, January 21, 2009. http://www.nytimes.com/2009/01/22/U.S./politics/22gitmo.html.
307 Sixty had already been cleared for release: Richard Lister, "What next for Guantánamo inmates?" BBC News, January 23, 2009, http://news.bbc.co.uk/2/hi/7846203.stm; "flown to the island nation of Bermuda": Erik Eckholm, "Out of Guantánamo, Uighurs bask in Bermuda," *New York Times*, June 14, 2009. http://www.nytimes.com/2009/06/15/world/americas/15uighur.html.
307 some one hundred Yemenis: Adam Levine, "U.S. may hand over Yemeni detainees at Gitmo to Saudis," CNN.com, March 13, 2009, http://www.cnn.com/2009/WORLD/meast/03/13/Guantánamo.saudis.yemen/index.html.
307 two jailbreaks: Ahmed Al-Haj, "U.S., Yemenis meet about Guantánamo detainees," ABC News/ Associated Press, July 3, 2008. http://abcnews.go.com/International/wireStory?id=5301764.
307 released in November 2007: Robert Worth, "Freed by the U.S., Saudi becomes al Qaeda chief," *New York Times*, January 22, 2009. http://www.nytimes.com/2009/01/23/world/middleeast/23yemen.html.
307 became the deputy leader: Worth op. cit.
307 chart his changing character: Rajiv Chandrasekaran, "From captive to suicide bomber," *Washington Post*, February 22, 2009. http://www.washingtonpost.com/wp-dyn/content/article/2009/02/21/AR2009022101234.html.
307 "hostile, hardened individual": Chandrasekaran op. cit.
307 Pentagon fact sheet: The list, entitled "Former Guantánamo Detainee Terrorism Trends," is available from http://abcnews.go.com/images/Politics/Guantánamo_recidivism_list_090526.pdf as of January 6, 2010.
308 "One in seven": Dick Cheney, Washington, D.C., May 21, 2009. http://www.nytimes.com/2009/06/07/opinion/07pubed.html
308 the true rate: Peter Bergen and Katherine Tiedemann, "Who really returned to the battlefield?" New America Foundation, July 20, 2009. http://counterterrorism.newamerica.net/publications/policy/Guantánamo_who_really_returned_battlefield.
308 some fifty: Peter Finn, "Justice task force recommends about 50 Guantánamo detainees be held indefinitely," *Washington Post*, January 22, 2010.
308 Obama backed away: Jane Mayer, "The trial," *New Yorker*, February 15, 2010.
308 ended in 2003: Michael V. Hayden, hearing of the House of Representatives Select Committee on Intelligence, "Worldwide threats," February 7, 2008, Washington, D.C.
308 dramatically increased: Peter Bergen and Katherine Tiedemann, The New America Foundation, "The Year of the Drone," February 24, 2010, www.newamerica.net/drones.

Chapter 19

309 "The Taliban regime": Agence France Presse, "Cheney declares death of Taliban as alliance mops up in Afghanistan," March 13, 2002.

309 "[The Taliban] have a": Admiral Mike Mullen, House of Representatives, Hearing of the Foreign Affairs Committee, "U.S. strategy in Afghanistan," Washington, D.C., December 2, 2009.

309 "central front": Barack Obama, Remarks to State Department Employees, Washington, D.C., January 22, 2009.

309 Obama announced: Obama 2009 op. cit.

310 Just as Holbrooke: Richard Oppel, "Obama's special envoy arrives in Afghanistan," *New York Times*, February 12, 2009. http://www.nytimes.com/2009/02/13/world/asia/13afghan.html?emc=eta1.

310 threat assessment map: Afghan National Security Forces/United Nations maps, April 2009, described in Peter Bergen and Katherine Tiedemann, "More troops needed for Afghan war," CNN.com, August 4, 2009. http://www.cnn.com/2009/POLITICS/08/04/bergen.afghanistan/index.html.

310 "take over in one hour": Author interview with former senior Afghan cabinet member, September 2006, Kabul.

310 U.S. military slide: Afghanistan: Security Incidents CENTCOM slide as of October 4, 2009. Author collection.

310 "inner shura": Maj. Gen. Michael Flynn, ISAF briefing slides December 2009, Peter Bergen, "U.S. intelligence briefing: Taliban increasingly effective," CNN.com, January 25, 2010. http://www.cnn.com/2010/WORLD/asiapcf/01/25/afghanistan.taliban/index.html.

311 "going around and around in circles": Dinner participant, interview by author; "this dinner is over": Dexter Filkins, "Former favorite, Karzai slips in U.S. eyes," *New York Times*, February 8, 2009.

311 "ten different answers": Tony Blinken, interview by author, Washington, D.C., December 18, 2009.

311 had helped to pull Pakistan and India back: Bruce Riedel, "American diplomacy and the 1999 Kargil Summit at Blair House," Center for the Advanced Study of India, 2002.

311 "Hi, Bruce, it's Barack": Bruce Riedel, interview by author, Washington, D.C., November 23, 2009.

312 "closely linked; not a monolith": Bruce Riedel interview op. cit.

312 Pashtun ethic group: 42 percent of Afghans are Pashtun. CIA World Factbook, Afghanistan, 2009. https://www.cia.gov/library/publications/the-world-factbook/geos/af.html.

312 "not going to recruit": Riedel interview op. cit.

313 Afghan army and police: Stephen Hadley, "How Obama's surge in Afghanistan can stabilize the region," *Washington Post*, December 11, 2009; 10,000: Riedel interview op. cit.; 12,000: Blinken op. cit. and Douglas Lute, interview by author, January 8, 2010, Washington, D.C.

313 strong outlier: Riedel interview.

313 "killer argument against": Riedel interview.

313 "does not want to be the Hubert Humphrey": Riedel interview.

313 twenty-five thousand Taliban full-time fighters, "quadrupled in size": Adam Entous, "Taliban growth weighs on Obama strategy review," Reuters, October 9, 2009. http://uk.reuters.com/article/idUKN09496447.

314 *every four days:* This section draws on Peter Bergen, "Winning the good war," *Washington Monthly*, July/August 2009, http://www.washingtonmonthly.com/features/2009/0907.bergen.html.

314 holding pattern: Riedel interview.

314 21,000 more: Richard Wolf, "Obama: Afghanistan a 'joint problem,'" *USA Today*, April 3, 2009. http://www.usatoday.com/news/world/2009-04-03-obama-town-hall-meeting_N.htm.

314 "I want to see the impact": Senior U.S. national security official, interview by author, Washington, D.C.

314 "There's no guarantee": Riedel interview op. cit.

315 Recommendation number one: White House, "White Paper of the Interagency Policy Group's Report on U.S. Policy toward Afghanistan and Pakistan," March 27, 2009. http://www.whitehouse.gov/assets/documents/afghanistan_pakistan_white_paper_final.pdf.

315 some additional four thousand trainers: Ann Scott Tyson, "Military wants more troops for Afghan war," *Washington Post*, April 2, 2009. http://www.washingtonpost.com/wp-dyn/content/article/2009/04/01/AR2009040102652.html.

315 voted against: Perry Bacon Jr., "House passes war funds as 51 Democrats dissent," *Washington Post*, May 15, 2009, http://www.washingtonpost.com/wp-dyn/content/article/2009/05/14/AR2009051403480.html.

315 move to turn off the money spigot: "U.S. House committee approves Iraq, Afghanistan war funding," Voice of America, May 7, 2009, http://www.voanews.com/english/2009-05-07-voa49.cfm.

315 the war was a mistake: Tom Vanden Brook, "Poll: more view Afghan war as a mistake," *USA Today*, March 16, 2009, http://www.usatoday.com/news/world/2009-03-16-poll_N.htm.

315 57 percent: CNN Opinion Research Poll, August 28–31, 2009. http://i2.cdn.turner.com/cnn/2009/images/09/01/rel12a.pdf.

315 a cover story: Evan Thomas and John Barry, "Obama's Vietnam," *Newsweek*, February 9, 2009, http://www.newsweek.com/id/182650

315 "Fearing another Quagmire": Helene Cooper, "Fearing another quagmire in Afghanistan," *New York Times*, January 24, 2009, http://www.nytimes.com/2009/01/25/weekinreview/25cooper.html; "isn't worth fighting": Rory Stewart, "The good war isn't worth fighting," *New York Times*, November 22, 2008, http://www.nytimes.com/2008/11/23/opinion/23stewart.html.

316 have won military victories: Peter Bergen, "Graveyard myths," *New York Times*, March 28, 2009, http://www.nytimes.com/2009/03/28/opinion/28bergen.html.

316 2005 poll by ABC/BBC: ABC News Poll: Life in Afghanistan, December 7, 2005, http://abcnews.go.com/images/Politics/998a1Afghanistan.pdf.

316 less than one in five Iraqis: ABC News Poll: Iraq—Where Things Stand, December 12, 2005, http://abcnews.go.com/images/Politics/1000a1IraqWhereThingsStand.pdf.

316 same poll taken in Afghanistan in 2009: ABC/BBC Poll: Life in Afghanistan, February 9, 2009, http://news.bbc.co.uk/2/shared/bsp/hi/pdfs/05_02_09afghan_poll_2009.pdf.

316 continued to approve: 62 percent of Afghans surveyed in December 2009 supported the presence of NATO forces in Afghanistan. ABC/BBC Poll: Life in Afghanistan, December 11-23, 2009, http://news.bbc.co.uk/2/shared/bsp/hi/pdfs/11_01_10_afghanpoll.pdf.

316 In 2008 more than two thousand Afghan civilians died: United Nations, "Number of Afghan civilian deaths in 2008 highest since Taliban ouster, says UN," February 17, 2009, http://www.un.org/apps/news/story.asp?NewsID=29918&Cr=Afghan&Cr1=civilian+rights;

316 less than a fourth: According to the Iraq Body Count database, more than 9,200 civilians were killed in 2008 in Iraq. http://www.iraqbodycount.org/database/.

316 more than three thousand civilians were dying every *month*: Iraq Body Count database, between July 2006 and July 2007, http://www.iraqbodycount.org/database/.

317 closed the U.S. Embassy: The Embassy was closed on January 30, 1989. Embassy of the United States—Kabul, Afghanistan, "About the Embassy." http://kabul.usembassy.gov/about_the_embassy.html.

317 zeroed out aid: Roy Gutman, *How We Missed the Story: Osama bin Laden, the Taliban, and the Hijacking of Afghanistan* (Washington, D.C.: United States Institute of Peace Press, 2008), p. 55.

317 puny size of the Afghan Army: Ann Scott Tyson, "More recruits, U.S. arms planned for Afghan military," *Washington Post,* December 5, 2007, http://www.washingtonpost.com/wp-dyn/content/article/2007/12/04/AR2007120402086.html.

318 "It was a very close-hold": David Petraeus interview with author, Washington, D.C., December 18, 20009.

318 was retiring on May 11: Ann Scott Tyson, "Top U.S. commander in Afghanistan is fired," *Washington Post,* May 12, 2009, http://www.washingtonpost.com/wp-dyn/content/article/2009/05/11/AR2009051101864_pf.html.

318 "the bottom fell out": Riedel interview.

318 "if we'd said no?": Stephen Biddle, interview by author, November 9, 2009, Washington, D.C.

319 "what shocked me": Andrew Exum, interview by author, Washington, D.C., December 9, 2009.

319 "centrality of Kandahar": Fred Kagan, interview by author, Washington, D.C., November 17, 2009.

319 "discover that the Taliban controlled Kandahar": Fred Kagan, interview by author.

319 where ten thousand Marines: Richard Oppel, "U.S. Marines try to retake Afghan valley from Taliban," *New York Times,* July 1, 2009, http://www.nytimes.com/2009/07/02/world/asia/02afghan.html.

319 "ten thousand fucking Marines": White House official, interview by author.

320 had already signed off: David Kilcullen, interview by author, Washington, D.C., January 19, 2010.

320 Nearly 60 percent: Bergen and Tiedemann, July 2009, op. cit.

320 "on their arse, literally": senior U.S. Marine officer, interview by author, September 10, 2009, Helmand, Afghanistan.

320 During the summer of 2009: Author observations, Nawa, Helmand, Afghanistan, summer of 2009.

320 80 percent of the U.S. casualties in Helmand: Michael Flynn, ISAF intelligence briefing, cited in Peter Bergen, "U.S. intelligence briefing: Taliban increasingly effective," CNN.com, January 25, 2010.

320 The assessment: COMISAF's Initial Assessment, Memo from Gen. Stanley McChrystal to Robert Gates, August 30, 2009, obtained by the *Washington Post,* September 21, 2009, http://www.washingtonpost.com/wp-dyn/content/article/2009/09/21/AR2009092100110.html.

321 "McChrystal: More Forces or 'Mission Failure'": Bob Woodward, "McChrystal: More Forces or 'Mission Failure," *Washington Post*, September 21, 2009. http://www.washingtonpost.com/wp-dyn/content/article/2009/09/20/AR2009092002920.html.

321 multiple and credible: Sabrina Tavernise and Abdul Waheed Wafa, "U.N. Official Acknowledges 'Widespread Fraud' in Afghan Election," *New York Times*, October 11, 2009, http://www.nytimes.com/2009/10/12/world/asia/12afghan.html.

321 "supposing no one gets fifty percent": Richard Holbrooke, interview by author, February 3, 2010, Washington, D.C.

321 almost a quarter: "Audit finds almost a quarter of Afghan vote is fraudulent," *New York Times*, October 20, 2009. http://www.nytimes.com/interactive/2009/10/20/world/asia/1020-afghan-recount-analysis.html.

321 first meeting of his war cabinet: Sunlen Miller, "A Look at the President's Meetings on Afghanistan and Pakistan," ABC News, November 10, 2009, http://blogs.abcnews.com/politicalpunch/2009/11/a-look-at-the-presidents-meetings-on-afghanistan-and-pakistan.html.

322 eight years ago to the day: See chapter 4 for an account of that meeting.
322 "exploded like a piñata": senior administration official, interview by author.
322 "resourcing is thirty to one: senior administration official, interview by author.
322 long pushed for legislation: Enhanced Partnership with Pakistan Act, Fact Sheet: Biden-Lugar Pakistan Legislation, July 15, 2008, http://lugar.senate.gov/record.cfm?id=300696.
323 On October 1: Sunlen op. cit.; gave a speech: Gen. Stanley McChrystal, Address, International Institute for Strategic Studies, London, UK, October 1, 2009, www.iiss.org/EasySiteWeb/GatewayLink.aspx?alId=31537.
323 third Afghan review meeting: Sunlen op. cit; "sounds kind of reasonable": Participant, interview by author, Washington, D.C.
323 There was another: Sunlen op. cit.; "throwaways": senior military officer, interview by author.
324 "we'll know if this is working": White House official, interview by author, Washington, D.C.
324 "Where are those fuckers?": White House official, interview by author, Washington, D.C.
324 $55 billion: Amy Belasco, "The cost of Iraq, Afghanistan, and other global war on terror operations since 9/11," Congressional Research Service, September 28, 2009, Table 1; "saying versions of": White House official, interview by author, Washington, D.C.; could ill afford: White House official, interview by author.
324 only two of its 105 units: Government Accountability Office, "Afghanistan Security: Further Congressional action may be needed to ensure completion of a detailed plan to develop and sustain capable Afghan National Security Forces," June 2008.
325 "There was a whole debate": White House official, interview by author.
325 "a bit of a rush job": National security official, interview by author.
325 "political capital was included": political appointee, interview by author.
325 "There was a point": national security official, interview by author.
325 "not in the cards": national security official, interview by author, Washington, D.C.
326 "Several folks argued": White House official, interview by author.
326 "bitten off more than we needed to chew": White House official, interview by author.
326 "OK, here's what I've taken": White House official, interview by author.
326 "stop dithering": Dick Cheney, Center for Security Policy, October 22, 2009, Washington, D.C. http://www.guardian.co.uk/world/feedarticle/8767329.
326 fifty-nine had died: ICasualties.org, Fatalities by year and month, U.S., Operation Enduring Freedom. http://www.icasualties.org/OEF/ByMonth.aspx.
326 visited Dover Air Force Base; 18 American servicemen: Jeff Zeleny, "Obama visits air base to honor returning dead," *New York Times*, October 29, 2009. http://www.nytimes.com/2009/10/30/U.S./30obama.html.
326 president was silent: Kenneth T. Walsh, "Critics say Obama lacks emotion," *U.S. News and World Report*, December 24, 2009.
327 "He admitted": National security official, interview by author.
327 "Option 2A": Peter Baker, "How Obama came to plan for 'surge' in Afghanistan," *New York Times*, December 5, 2009.
327 "I don't know how": Anne Kornblut, Scott Wilson, Karen DeYoung, "Obama pressed for faster surge," *Washington Post*, December 6, 2009.
327 "Wait a second, Stan": interview by author, White House official.
327 came up with a compromise: interview by author, White House official.
327 "Obama, at the end of the day": National security official, interview by author.
328 49 percent of the vote: Afghanistan Independent Elections Commission, Final Certified Presidential Results, October 21, 2009, http://www.iec.org.af/results/leadingCandidate.html.

328 Karzai refused to do this: John Kerry, interview by author, Washington, D.C., December 7, 2009.
328 "it would turn him": Holbrooke interview.
328 "I think we were able": Kerry interview.
328 standing down on November 1: BBC News, "Abdullah pulls out of Afghan vote," November 1, 2009. http://news.bbc.co.uk/2/hi/south_asia/8336388.stm.
328 "not an adequate strategic partner": Gen. Karl Eikenberry, "COIN strategy: civilian concerns," November 6, 2009, published by the *New York Times*, http://documents.nytimes.com/eikenberry-s-memos-on-the-strategy-in-afghanistan#document/p3.
329 In his next cable: Gen. Karl Eikenberry, "Looking beyond counterinsurgency in Afghanistan," November 9, 2009, published by the *New York Times*, http://documents.nytimes.com/eikenberry-s-memos-on-the-strategy-in-afghanistan#document/p6.
329 came as a surprise: Peter Baker, "How Obama Came to Plan for 'Surge' in Afghanistan," *New York Times*, December 6, 2009.
329 penultimate meeting, on November 23: Tom Bowman and Melissa Beck, "Obama to announce Afghan strategy," NPR, November 23, 2009; "Hillary Clinton was the most forceful advocate": Author interview with White House official.
329 final meeting took place: Peter Baker, Eric Schmitt, and David Sanger, "Obama's speech on Afghanistan to envision exit," *New York Times*, November 29, 2009.
329 appears to have made his decision the day before: author interview with White House official.
329 the greatest threat: BBC/ABC poll, op. cit. http://news.bbc.co.uk/2/shared/bsp/hi/pdfs/05_02_09afghan_poll_2009.pdf.
330 going in the right direction: BBC/ABC poll, op. cit.
330 paid by the Pakistanis: senior Obama national security official, interview by author, Washington, D.C., January 2010.
330 In February 2009: Zahid Hussain and Matthew Rosenberg, "Peace deal wavers in Swat Valley," *Wall Street Journal*, April 10, 2009, http://online.wsj.com/article/SB123929350855705481.html; "ski lift operator": Mukhtar Khan, "The Return of Shari'a Law to Pakistan's Swat Region," Jamestown Foundation, *Terrorism Monitor*, March 3, 2009.
330 just sixty miles: "Buner falls into the hands of the Swat Taliban," *Dawn*, April 22, 2009. http://www.dawn.com/wps/wcm/connect/dawn-content-library/dawn/news/pakistan/nwfp/buner-falls-to-swat-taliban—bi.
330 had grown exponentially: Pak Institute for Peace Studies, Security Report, 2009.
331 strike in three different places: Jane Perlez and Pir Zubair Shah, "Day of suicide attacks displays strength of Pakistani Taliban," *New York Times*, April 5, 2009. http://www.nytimes.com/2009/04/06/world/asia/06pstan.html.
331 twenty-hour Taliban attack: "10 dead in attack on Pakistani military HQ," CBS/AP, October 10, 2009, http://www.cbsnews.com/stories/2009/10/10/world/main5375901.shtml.
331 "foreign area": *Ilaqa ghair* is often used in Urdu to refer to the FATA, meaning generally "no-go area." I. A. Rehman, "FATA priorities," *Dawn*, June 25, 2009.
331 more than a million: Declan Walsh, "Pakistan claims 700 Taliban killed in Swat valley strikes," *The Guardian*, May 11, 2009, http://www.guardian.co.uk/world/2009/may/11/pakistan-swat-taliban-army-refugees.
331 at least thirty thousand troops: Karin Bruillard, "Pakistan launches full-scale offensive," *Washington Post*, October 18, 2009, http://www.washingtonpost.com/wp-dyn/content/article/2009/10/17/AR2009101700673.html.
331 previous military operations: For an account of those operations see Sameer Lalwani, "The Pakistani military's adaptation to counterinsurgency in 2009," *CTC*

Sentinel, January 2010, and for Pakistani public support of these operations see "Military action in Waziristan: opinion poll," Gilani Poll/Gallup Pakistan, November 3, 2009. www.gallup.com.pk/Polls/03-11-09.pdf.

331 fifty-one American drone strikes in Pakistan in 2009 alone: Bergen and Tiedemann 2010 op. cit.; receiving a leg massage: Agence France Presse, "Mehsud killed while getting leg massage," August 10, 2009; Jane Mayer, "The Predator war," *New Yorker*, October 26, 2009, http://www.newyorker.com/reporting/2009/10/26/091026fa_fact_mayer.

332 lead headline: "Good riddance, killer Baitullah," *Dawn*, August 8, 2009.

332 record eighty-seven suicide attacks: Pak Institute for Peace Studies 2009 Security Report.

332 nearly 6,000 Afghan civilians: United States Assistance Mission to Afghanistan, Annual Report on the Protection of Civilians in Armed Conflict, 2009. http://www.foreignpolicy.com/images/100113_Protection_20of_20Civilian_202009_20report_20English.pdf

332 Around 100 to 150: Lolita C. Baldor, "Terror Training Camps Smaller, Harder to Target," Associated Press, November 9, 2009. http://abcnews.go.com/print?id=9031020.

332 held by the Haqqani Taliban network: "David Rohde, Times Reporter, Escapes Taliban After 7 Months," *New York Times*, June 20, 2009. http://www.nytimes.com/2009/06/21/world/asia/21taliban.html

332 "terrifying presence": David Rohde, "Held by the Taliban, Part Four—A Drone Strike and Dwindling Hope," *New York Times*, October 20, 2009, http://www.nytimes.com/2009/10/21/world/asia/21hostage.html?pagewanted=print; Jason Burke, "On the front line in war on Pakistan's Taliban," *The Guardian*, November 16, 2008. http://www.guardian.co.uk/world/2008/nov/16/pakistan-afghanistan taliban.

332 suspected "spies": "Taliban kill seven 'U.S. spies' in North Waziristan," *Dawn*, January 24, 2010.," http://www.dawn.com/wps/wcm/connect/dawn-content-library/dawn/news/pakistan/04-taliban-kill-six-nwaziristan-qs-06; "Taliban kill two U.S. 'spies' in Miranshah," *Daily Times*, January 31, 2010. http://www.dailytimes.com.pk/default.asp?page=2010\01\31\story_31-1-2010_pg1_3.

333 A December 2009: Michael Flynn briefing, described in Bergen, "U.S. intelligence briefing," 2010.

333 "That was probably": Barack Obama, interview by Steve Kroft, *60 Minutes*, December 7, 2009, http://www.cbsnews.com/stories/2009/12/13/60minutes/main5975421.shtml.

333 "I make this decision": Barack Obama, "Remarks by the President in Address to the Nation on the Way Forward in Afghanistan and Pakistan," West Point, NY, December 1, 2009, http://www.whitehouse.gov/the-press-office/remarks-president-address-nation-way-forward-afghanistan-and-pakistan.

333 And at the time: Author briefing White House officials, December 1, 2009.

Chapter 20

335 "So my Lord": Osama bin Laden, "Exposing the new crusader war," February 2003.

335 "I have an excellent idea": Timothy J. Burger, "10 questions for Porter Goss," *Time*, June 27, 2005. http://www.time.com/time/magazine/article/0.9171.1074112.00.html.

335 "a person who's now been marginalized": George W. Bush, March 13, 2002, Washington, D.C. http://georgewbush-whitehouse.archives.gov/news/releases/2002/03/20020313-8.html. "CIA even closed Alec Station": Mark Mazzetti, "CIA closes unit focused on capture of bin Laden," *New York Times*, July 4, 2006. http://www.

nytimes.com/2006/07/04/washington/04intel.html. Since 9/11 bin Laden has issued: The tapes have not only: IntelCenter, a U.S. government contractor that tracks jihadist publications, says bin Laden released 33 tapes in the eight years between 9/11 and January 2010. IntelCenter Breakout of as-Sahab audio/video, 2002–26 February 2010. Email from Ben Venzke, February 26, 2010.

336 The tapes have not only: "Istanbul rocked by double bombing," BBC News, November 20, 2003, http://news.bbc.co.uk/2/hi/europe/3222608.stm; Craig Whitlock and Susan Glasser, "On tape, bin Laden tries new approach," *Washington Post*, December 17, 2004. http://www.washingtonpost.com/wp-dyn/articles/A3927-2004Dec16.html; Abqaia facility: Joel Roberts, "Al Qaeda threatens more oil attacks," CBS News, February 25, 2006, http://www.cbsnews.com/stories/2006/02/27/world/main1346541_page2.shtml; "Bin Laden tape encourages Pakistanis to rebel," Associated Press, September 20, 2007, http://www.usatoday.com/news/world/2007-09-20-al Qaeda-video_N.htm.

336 a private study: Author discussions with Saudi officials, Riyadh, Saudi Arabia, February 26, 2008.

337 "heroes": London bomber: text in full, BBC News, September 1, 2005. http://news.bbc.co.uk/2/hi/uk_news/4206800.stm.

337 "Now the time has come": Cahal Milmo, " 'You will be destroyed': bombers of Heathrow plot," *The Independent*, September 9, 2008. http://www.independent.co.uk/news/uk/crime/you-will-be-destroyed-bombers-convicted-of-heathrow-plot-923467.html.

337 "Leave our lands": "Bomber's message of hate," *The Plymouth Herald (U.K.)*, November 21, 2008. http://www.thisisplymouth.co.uk/news/Bomber-s-sentence-adjourned/article-492697-detail/article.html.

337 "There is very limited": Author interview with U.S. counterterrorism official, Washington, D.C., 2006.

337 thousands of matchboxes: interview Norine MacDonald, Kabul, Afghanistan, April 10, 2007, and Senlis Council, "The Return of the Taliban," Spring/summer 2006. http://www.icosgroup.net/documents/Afghanistan_5_Years_Later.pdf.

338 Ninety-eight percent: According to the World Bank, in 2007 Afghanistan had 500,000 Internet users and a population of 26.2 million. World Bank: World Development Indicators Online.

338 Annapolis: "New Usama bin Laden tape slams Palestinian negotiations, urges holy war for liberation," Associated Press, March 20, 2008. http://www.foxnews.com/story/0,2933,340016.00.html; recent Israeli invasion of Gaza: "Bin Laden 'tape' calls Israel offensive in Gaza a holocaust," *The Guardian*, March 14, 2009. http://www.guardian.co.uk/world/2009/mar/14/osama-bin-laden-gaza-israel.

338 "sent by the heroes," Osama bin Laden, "From usama to Obama," January 24, 2010, translated by NEFA Foundation.

338 Musharraf said: "Pakistan's Musharraf: Bin Laden probably dead," CNN, January 18, 2002. http://edition.cnn.com/2002/WORLD/asiapcf/south/01/18/gen.musharraf.binladen/.

338 painful kidney stones: Laden, Laden, Sasson, op. cit., p. 172.

338 coordinated by Ali Mohamed: United States of America v. Ali Mohamed, United States Southern District, New York. S(7) 98 Cr. 1023 (LBS), October 24, 2000.

339 only fifteen: Lawrence Wright, The man behind bin Laden," *New Yorker*, September 16, 2002.

339 In 1997: Author observations, near Jalalabad, Afghanistan, March 1997.

339 Arthur Keller: Author interview with Art Keller, Albuquerque, New Mexico, February 13, 2007; Admiral William J. Fallon: Author interview with William J. Fallon, Florence, Italy, May 23, 2008.

340 Pew poll: "A Year After Iraq War," *The Pew Global Attitudes Project*, March 16, 2004. http://people-press.org/reports/pdf/206.pdf.

340 His son Omar recalled: *Growing Up Bin Laden* op. cit., p. 99.

340 "Bin Laden pushed: *Growing Up Bin Laden* op. cit., p. 115, and Khaled al-Fauwaz, interview by author, London, April 1, 1997.

340 "He wanted his followers": Khalid al-Hammadi, "Bin Laden's former bodyguard interviewed," *Al-Quds al-Arabi*, March 20–April 4, 2005.

340 dinner consisted of: Abdel Bari Atwan, interview by author, London, UK, June 2005.

340 to drink cold water: Zaynab Khadr, interview by Terrence McKenna, Islamabad, Pakistan. "Al Qaeda Family," CBC, "Maha Elsammah and Zaynab Khadr," February 22, 2004.

341 "You should learn": Noman Benotman, interview by author, London, UK, August 30, 2005.

341 "hermit on the hilltop": Author interview with Cofer Black, Washington, D.C., February 6, 2003.

341 "It was November 2002": Ahmed Zaidan, interview by author, Islamabad, Pakistan, March 2005.

341 On the audiotape: "Bin Laden's message," Al Jazeera, November 12, 2002, translated by BBC Monitoring, http://news.bbc.co.uk/2/hi/middle_east/2455845.stm.

341 Rice called: Joanna McGeary, "Why can't we find bin Laden?" *Time,* November 17, 2002. http://www.time.com/time/covers/1101021125/story.html.

342 varied the media outlets: author interview with Ahmed Zaidan, Islamabad, Pakistan, July 2004; more than 100: IntelCenter breakout of *Al-Sahab* audio/video, 2002-September 1, 2009; around $50 billion: Reuters, "U.S. says 2008 intelligence budget was $47.5 billion," October 28, 2008. http://www.reuters.com/article/idus TRE49R8DO20081028.

342 Pentagon officials were not surprised: CNN correspondent Barbara Starr discussed the bin Laden tape on CNN's *Wolf Blitzer Reports*, October 29, 2004.

342 "why did we not attack Sweden?": Osama bin Laden, "Message to the American people," quoted in Gilles Kepel, *Al Qaeda in its Own Words* (Boston: Belknap Press, 2008), p. 71.

342 Kerry later said: "Exclusive: Kerry says UBL tape cost him election," FOX News, November 21, 2004. http://www.foxnews.com/story/02933,139060,00.html.

342 "profound impact": John Kerry interview by author, Washington, D.C., December 7, 2010.

342 It was clear: *Agence France Press,* May 31, 2005; *Agence France Press*, March 15, 2003; *Sunday Times* (London), September 29, 2002; National Public Radio *Morning Edition*, April 2, 2002; curtains: Linda Frum, "Peter Bergen Talks to Linda Frum," *Maclean's*, January 30, 2006. Author observations of multiple videos by Zawahiri.

343 read a story about a goat: Al Jazeera, "Full transcript of bin Laden's speech," October 29, 2004. http://english.aljazeera.net/archive/2004/11/200849163336457223.html; BBC, "Text: Bin Laden Tape," January 19, 2006. http://news.bbc.co.uk/2/hi/middle_east/4628932.stm; arcane debate: BBC, "Bin Laden Tape: Text," February 12, 2003. http://news.bbc.co.uk/2/hi/middle_east/2751019.stm; ban Muslim headscarves: "Bin Laden deputy slams scarf ban." CNN.com, February 24, 2004. http://edition.cnn.com/2004/WORLD/meast/02/24/qaeda.headscarves/. favorably mentioned the work of Chomsky: SITE Group translation, September 11, 2007. http://counterter rorismblog.org/site-resources/images/SITE-OBL-transcript.pdf.

343 Chitral: Author interview with U.S. military intelligence official, July 2006.

343 cash rewards: PBS Online Newshour, "Facing justice," June 18, 1997. http://www.pbs.org/newshour/bb/law/june97/cia_6-18.html; "$25 million": AP, Pro-

file: Khalid Sheikh Mohammed, March 1, 2003, http://www.foxnews.com/story/0,2933,79989,00.html; played a role: Tenet op. cit., p. 253.

344 explained what methods had worked: Author interview, Brad Garrett, Washington, D.C., 2004. Some of this section draws on the Afterword of *The Osama bin Laden I Know* (Bergen, 2006) and "The Long Hunt for Osama," *Atlantic*, Peter Bergen, October 2004.

344 looking for "anomalies": Robert Grenier, Testimony before the House of Representatives Permanent Select Committee on Intelligence, April 9, 2008. http://intelligence.house.gov/Media/PDFS/Grenier040908b.pdf.

344 thoroughbred horses: Khaled Batarfi, interviews by author, Jeddah, Saudi Arabia, September 5 and 9, 2005.

344 seventy kilometers a day: Al Jazeera interview, "Osama bin Laden," 1998 (undated).

344 five wives and some twenty kids: *Growing Up Bin Laden* op. cit., Appendix A and Bergen 2006, Appendix C: "Osama bin Laden's immediate family."

344 Zawahiri have done: Ismail Khan, "Zawahiri was not here," *Dawn*, January 15, 2006. http://www.dawn.com/2006/01/15/top3.htm. "some of his own": Anne Stenersen, "Al-Qaeda's Allies: Explaining the Relationship between al-Qaeda and Various Factions of the Taliban after 2001," New America Foundation, April 19, 2010. http://counterterrorism.newamerica.net/publications/policy/al_qaeda_s_allies.

345 lack of HUMINT: author interview, Pat Lang, Washington, D.C., 2004.

345 It's possible: Kevin Fedarko et al., "Escobar's dead end," *Time*, December 13, 1993. http://www.time.com/time/printout/0,8816,979803,00.html. "has quit any kind of device": Author interview with U.S. intelligence officials, June 6, 2003.

345 "We have hit couriers": Senior U.S. military official, interview by author, July 2006.

345 Zawahiri: Carlotta Gall et al., "Airstrike by U.S. draws protests from Pakistanis," *New York Times*, January 15, 2006; "more operational and is moving more": author interview with U.S. military official, July 2006: "death of five militants": Carlotta Gall and Douglas Jehl, "U.S. raid killed Qaeda leaders, officials say," *New York Times*, January 19, 2006; "thumbing his nose": Hassan Fattah, "Qaeda deputy taunts Bush for 'failure' in airstrike," *New York Times*, January 31, 2006.

345 expand its attacks: There were six drone strikes reported in Pakistan between January and June 2008, and 28 between July and December, according to the New America Foundation's drones database, www.newamerica.net/drones; "45 minutes": Jay Solomon, Siobhan Gorman, Matthew Rosenberg, "U.S. plans new drone attacks in Pakistan," *Wall Street Journal*, March 26, 2010. http://online.wsj.com/article/SB123803414843244161.html; author interview with former Bush administration official, February 2009, Washington, D.C.

346 fivefold increase: Peter Bergen and Katherine Tiedemann, "Obama's War," *Washington Post*, February 15, 2009.

346 killed dozens: Peter Bergen and Katherine Tiedemann, "Revenge of the Drones," New America Foundation, October 19, 2009. http://counterterrorism.newamerica.net/publications/policy/revenge_of_the_drones; Amir Mir, "60 drone hits kill 14 al-Qaeda men, 687 civilians," *The News*, April 10, 2009; http://www.thenews.com.pk/top_story_detail.asp?Id=21440.

346 Other militants: Peter Bergen and Katherine Tiedemann, "The Drone War," *The New Republic*, June 3, 2009.

346 "We've got a few days": Dick Cheney, Late Edition with Wolf Blitzer, January 9, 2009. http://georgewbush-whitehouse.archives.gov/news/releases/2009/01/20090111.html; "brought to justice": George W. Bush, Larry King Live, January 15, 2009, http://www.cnn.com/2009/POLITICS/01/14/1kl.bush/index.html.

346 "keep al-Qaeda guessing": Michael Hayden, Remarks at the Atlantic Council, Washington, D.C., November 13, 2008.

347 number of "spies": author interview with former Bush administration official, Washington, D.C., February, 2009.

347 dropped by half in 2008: IntelCenter Breakout of as Sahab audio/video, 2002–26 February 2010. Email from Ben Venzke to author, February 26, 2010.

347 taken into Iranian custody: Author interviews with U.S. intelligence officials, Washington, D.C., June 6, 2003.

348 "As long as": Ahmed Zaidan, interview by author, Islamabad, Pakistan, July 2004.

348 "close the 9/11 chapter": Roger Cressey interview; "death would signal": Author interview with Robert Grenier; "other advantages": John McLaughlin, interview by author, December 7, 2009, Washington, D.C.

348 seen as a divisive force: Jamal Ismail, interview by author, July 29, 2004, Islamabad, Pakistan.

348 Americans being taken hostage: author interview with U.S. official; and Michael Scheuer, former head of the CIA's bin Laden unit, interview with author, Washington, D.C. December 23, 2009.

348 His former bodyguard: Khalid al-Hammadi, "Bin Laden's former 'bodyguard' interviewed," *Al-Quds al-Arabi*, August 3, 2004 and March 20 to April 4, 2004.

348 "I have sworn": *The Guardian* Website has a useful chronology of statements by bin Laden and Zawahiri at http://www.guardian.co.uk/alqaida/page/0,,839823,00.html, where bin Laden's February 20, 2006, statement can be found.

349 size twelve shoes: Author interview with Julie Sirrs, Washington, D.C. 2003.

349 Saad bin Laden: Mary Louise Kelly, "Bin Laden son reported killed in Pakistan," NPR, July 22, 2009, http://www.npr.org/templates/story/story.php?storyId=106903109.

349 "his blood": Al-Hammadi op. cit.

349 2008 survey of opinion: Pew Global Attitudes Project, "Global public opinion in the Bush years," December 18, 2008. http://pewglobal.org/reports/display.php?ReportID=263.

349 "mission is accomplished": author interview with Michael Scheuer, Washington, D.C., December 23, 2009.

Bibliography

Selected Books

Feroz Ali Abbasi, Guantánamo Bay Prison Memoirs, 2002–2004. Author's collection.

Gary Ackerman and Jeremy Tamsett (eds.), *Jihadists and Weapons of Mass Destruction* (Boca Raton, FL: CRC Press, 2009).

Matthew Alexander, *How to Break a Terrorist: The U.S. Interrogators Who used Brains, Not Brutality, to Take Down the Deadliest Man in Iraq* (New York: Free Press, 2008).

Ali Allawi, *The Occupation of Iraq: Winning the War, Losing the Peace* (New York: Yale University Press, 2007).

Graham Allison, *Nuclear Terrorism: The Ultimate Preventable Catastrophe* (New York: Henry Holt, 2004).

Anonymous (Michael Scheuer). *Through Our Enemies' Eyes: Osama bin Laden, Radical Islam, and the Future of America* (Washington, D.C.: Brassey's Inc., 2003).

Abdullah Azzam, *Defense of Muslim Lands, The Most Important Personal Duty* (published in booklet form by Modern Mission Library, Amman, 1984).

James Bamford, *A Pretext for War: 9/11, Iraq, and the Abuse of America's Intelligence Agencies* (New York: Doubleday, 2004).

Moazzam Begg. *Enemy Combatant: A British Muslim's Journey to Guantánamo and Back* (London: Free Press, 2006).

Daniel Benjamin and Steven Simon, *Age of Sacred Terror: Radical Islam's War Against America* (New York: Random House, 2002).

Daniel Benjamin and Steven Simon, *The Next Attack: The Failure of the War on Terror and a Strategy for Getting it Right* (New York: Macmillan, 2006).

Gina Bennett, *National Security Mom: Why "Going Soft" Will Make America Strong* (Deadwood, Oregon: Wyatt-MacKenzie Publishing, 2009).

Owen Bennett-Jones. *Pakistan: Eye of the Storm* (New Haven, CT: Yale, 2002).

Peter Bergen, *Holy War, Inc.: Inside the Secret World of Osama bin Laden* (New York: Free Press, 2001).

Peter Bergen, *The Osama bin Laden I Know: An Oral History of al-Qaeda's Leader* (New York: Free Press, 2006).

Paul Berman, *Terror and Liberalism* (New York: Norton, 2003).

Gary Berntsen and Ralph Pezzullo, *Jawbreaker: The Attack on bin Laden and al-Qaeda: A Personal Account by the CIA's Key Field Commander* (New York: Crown, 2005).

Eric Blehm, *The Only Thing Worth Dying For: How Eleven Green Berets Forged a New Afghanistan* (New York: Harper, 2010).

Philip Bobbitt, *Terror and Consent: The Wars for the 21st Century* (New York: Knopf, 2008).

Mark Bowden, *Black Hawk Down: A Story of Modern War* (New York: Penguin, 2000).

Jarret Brachman, *Global Jihadism: Theory and Practice* (New York: Routledge, 2008).

John R. Bradley, *Inside Egypt: The Land of the Pharaohs on the Brink of a Revolution* (New York: Palgrave Macmillan, 2008).

Elizabeth Bumiller, *Condoleezza Rice: An American Life* (New York: Random House, 2007).

Jason Burke, *Al-Qaeda: The True Story of Radical Islam* (New York: I. B. Tauris and Co., Ltd, 2004).

Michael Burleigh. *Blood and Rage: A Cultural History of Terrorism* (London: HarperPress, 2008).

Ian Buruma, *Murder in Amsterdam: The Death of Theo van Gogh and the Limits of Tolerance* (London: Penguin Press, 2006).

Daniel Byman, *The Five Front War: The Better Way to Fight Global Jihad* (Hoboken, NJ: Wiley, 2008).

Christopher Caldwell, *Reflections on the Revolution in Europe: Can Europe be the Same with Different People in It?* (London: Allen Lane, 2009).

Rajiv Chandrasekaran, *Imperial Life in the Emerald City: Life Inside Iraq's Green Zone* (New York: Knopf, 2006).

Sarah Chayes, *The Punishment of Virtue: Inside Afghanistan After the Taliban* (New York: Penguin, 2006).

Winston Churchill, *The Story of the Malakand Field Force* (1898).

Richard Clarke, *Against All Enemies: Inside America's War on Terror* (New York: Free Press, 2004).

Rickard Clarke (ed). *The Annals: Terrorism: What the Next President Will Face* (Thousand Oaks: Sage, 2008).

David Cloud and Greg Jaffe, *The Fourth Star: Four Generals and the Epic Struggle for the Future of the United States Army* (New York: Crown, 2009).

Andrew Cockburn, *Rumsfeld: His Rise, Fall, and Catastrophic Legacy* (New York: Simon & Schuster, 2007).

Stephen Cohen, *The Idea of Pakistan* (Washington, D.C.: Brookings, 2005).

Steve Coll, *The Bin Ladens: An Arabian Family in the American Century* (New York: Penguin, 2008).

Steve Coll, *Ghost Wars: The Secret History of the CIA, Afghanistan and Bin Laden, From the Soviet Invasion to September 10, 2001* (New York: Penguin, 2004).

Aukai Collins, *My Jihad: The True Story of An American Mujahid's Amazing Journey from Osama Bin Laden's Training Camps to Counterterrorism with the FBI and CIA* (Guilford, CO: Lyons Press, 2002).

David Cook, *Understanding Jihad* (Los Angeles: University of California Press, 2005).

David Cook, *Martyrdom in Islam: Themes in Islamic History* (New York: Cambridge University Press, 2007).

Jane Corbin, *Al-Qaeda: In Search of the Terror Network that Threatens the World* (London: Simon & Schuster, 2003).

Anthony H. Cordesman, *The Lessons of Afghanistan: War Fighting, Intelligence, and Force Transformation* (Washington, D.C.: CSIS, 2002).

Gordon Corera, *Shopping for Bombs: Nuclear Proliferation, Global Insecurity, and the Rise and Fall of the AQ Khan Network* (London: Oxford University Press, 2006).

Audrey Kurth Cronin, *Ending Terrorism: Lessons for Defeating al-Qaeda* (London: IISS, 2008).

N. J. Dawood, *The Koran: Translated with Notes* (New York: Penguin Books, 1997).

Michael Delong, *A General Speaks Out: The Truth About the Wars in Afghanistan and Iraq* (Osceola: Zenith Press, 2007).

Karen DeYoung, *Soldier: The Life of Colin Powell* (New York: Vintage, 2007).

John Diamond. *The CIA and the Culture of Failure* (Stanford: Stanford University Press, 2008).

Christopher Dickey, *Securing the City: Inside America's Best Counterterror Force—the NYPD* (New York: Simon & Schuster, 2009).

James Dobbins, *After the Taliban: Nation Building in Afghanistan* (Dulles, VA: Potomac Books, Inc, 2008).

Michael Scott Doran. "Somebody Else's Civil War." In *How Did This Happen? Terrorism and the New War*. Eds. James F. Hoge Jr. and Gideon Rose (New York: Public Affairs, 2010).

Gilles Dorronsoro, *Revolution Unending: Afghanistan, 1979 to the Present* (New York: Columbia University Press, 2005).

John Esposito and Dalia Mogahed, *Who Speaks for Islam? What a Billion Muslims Really Think* (New York: Gallup Press, 2007).

Gregory Feifer. *The Great Gamble: The Soviet War in Afghanistan* (New York: HarperCollins, 2009).

Douglas J. Feith, *War and Decision: Inside the Pentagon at the Dawn of the War on Terrorism* (New York: HarperCollins, 2008).

Vanda Felbab-Brown, *Shooting Up: Counterinsurgency and the War on Drugs* (Wahington, D.C.: Brookings Press, 2009).

Reuven Firestone, *Jihad: The Origin of Holy War in Islam* (New York: Oxford University Press, 1999).

Yosri Fouda and Nick Fielding, *Masterminds of Terror: The Truth Behind the Most Devastating Attack The World Has Ever Seen* (New York: Arcade Publishing, 2003).

Tommy Franks, *American Soldier* (New York: Harper Collins, 2004).

Dalton Fury, *Kill Bin Laden: A Delta Force Commander's Account of the Hunt for the World's Most Wanted Man* (New York: St. Martin's Press, 2008).

David Galula, *Counterinsurgency Warfare: Theory and Practice* (Westport, CT: Praeger, 1964).

Barton Gellman, *Angler: The Cheney Vice Presidency* (New York: Penguin, 2008).

Joshua Alexander Geltzer, *U.S. Counter-Terrorism Strategy and al-Qaeda: Signalling and the Terrorist World-view* (New York: Routledge, 2010).

Fawaz A. Gerges, *The Far Enemy: Why Jihad Went Global* (New York: Cambridge University Press, 2005).

Antonio Giustozzi, *Koran, Kalashnikov, and Laptop: The Neo-Taliban Insurgency in Afghanistan* (New York: Columbia University Press, 2008).

Antonio Giustozzi (ed.), *Decoding the New Taliban: Insights from the Afghan Field* (New York: Columbia University Press, 2009).

Michael R. Gordon and Bernard E. Trainor, *COBRA II: The Inside Story of the Invasion and Occupation of Iraq* (New York: Vintage, 2006).

Bradley Graham, *By His Own Rules: The Ambitions, Successes, and Ultimate Failures of Donald Rumsfeld* (New York: Public Affairs, 2009).

Karen Greenberg, *The Least Worst Place: Guantánamo's First 100 Days* (New York: Oxford University Press, 2009).

Karen Greenberg (ed.), *Al-Qaeda Now: Understanding Today's Terrorists* (New York: Cambridge, 2005).

Stephen Grey, *Ghost Plane: The True Story of the CIA Torture Program* (New York: St. Martins, 2006).

Stephen Grey, *Operation Snake Bite: The Explosive True Story of An Afghan Desert Siege* (New York: Viking, 2009).

Roy Gutman, *How We Missed the Story: Osama Bin Laden, the Taliban and the Hijacking of Afghanistan* (Washington, D.C.: USIP, 2008).

Richard Haass, *War of Necessity, War of Choice: A Memoir of Two Iraq Wars* (New York: Simon & Schuster, 2009).

Mohammed Hafez, *Suicide Bombers in Iraq: The Strategy and Ideology of Martyrdom* (Washington, D.C.: USIP Press, 2007).

Stephen F. Hayes, *The Connection: How al-Qaeda's Collaboration with Saddam Hussein Has Endangered America* (New York: HarperCollins, 2004).

Thomas Hegghammer, *Jihad in Saudi Arabia: Violence and Pan-Islamism Since 1979* (New York: Cambridge University Press, 2010).

Steve Hendricks, *A Kidnapping in Milan: The CIA on Trial* (New York: Norton, 2010).

Esa Al-Hindi, *Army of Madinah in Kashmir* (Birmingham: Maktabah al Ansar, 1999).

Bruce Hoffman, *Inside Terrorism* (New York: Columbia Univ. Press, 1998).

James F. Hoge Jr. and Gideon Rose (eds.), *How Did This Happen? Terrorism and the New War* (New York: Public Affairs, 2001).

Mark Huband, *Warriors of the Prophet: The Struggle for Islam* (Boulder, Colorado: Westview Press, 1998).

Rex Hudson, *The Sociology and Psychology of Terrorism: Who Becomes a Terrorist and Why* (Guilford, CT: Lyons Press, 1999).

Ed Husain, *The Islamist: Why I Became an Islamic Fundamentalist, What I Saw Inside, and Why I Left* (New York: Penguin, 2009).

Fu'ad Husayn, *Al-Zarqawi: The Second al-Qa'ida Generation.* Serialized in *Al-Quds al-Arabi* May 21–22, 2005.

Zahid Hussein, *Frontline Pakistan: The Struggle with Militant Islam* (New York: Columbia University Press, 2007).

Raymond Ibrahim, *The al-Qaeda Reader* (New York: Broadway Books, 2007).

Michael Isikoff and David Corn, *Hubris: The Inside Story of Spin, Scandal, and the Selling of the Iraq War* (New York: Crown Publishing Group, 2006).

Roland Jacquard, *L'Archive Secretès d'al Qaida* (Paris: Jean Picollec, 2002).

Brian Michael Jenkins, *Will Terrorists Go Nuclear?* (Amherst, NY: Prometheus Books, 2008).

Seth G. Jones, *In the Graveyard of Empires: America's War in Afghanistan* (New York: W. W. Norton and Company, 2009).

Kimberly Kagan, *The Surge: A Military History* (New York: Encounter Books, 2008).

Stanley Karnow, *Vietnam: A History* (New York: Penguin, 1990).

Gilles Kepel, *The War for Muslim Minds: Islam and the West* (Cambridge, MA: Belknap Press, 2004).

Gilles Kepel and Jean-Pierre Milelli, *Al-Qaeda in its own Words* (Cambridge, MA: Belknap Press of Harvard University Press, 2008).

Hans G. Kippenberg and Tilman Seidensticker, *The 9/11 Handbook* (London: Equinox Publishing, 2007).

Alan Krueger, *What Makes a Terrorist: Economics and the Roots of Terrorism* (Princeton, NJ: Princeton University Press, 2007).

Mark Kukis, *My Heart Became Attached: The Strange Journey of John Walker Lindh* (Washington, D.C.: Brasseys, 2003).

Robert Lacey, *Inside the Kingdom: Kings, Clerics, Modernists, Terrorists, and the Struggle for Saudi Arabia* (New York: Viking Press, 2009).

Omar bin Laden, Najwa bin Laden, Jean Sasson, *Growing Up Bin Laden: Osama's Wife and Son Take Us Inside Their Secret World* (New York: St. Martin's Press, 2009).

William Langewiesche, *The Atomic Bazaar: The Rise of the Nuclear Poor* (New York: Farrar, Straus, and Giroux, 2007).

Bruce Lawrence, *Messages to the World: The Statements of Osama bin Laden* (New York: Verso, 2005).

Bernard-Henri Lévy, *Who Killed Daniel Pearl?* (Hoboken: Melville House Publishing, 2003).

Bernard Lewis, *The Crisis of Islam: Holy War and Unholy Terror* (New York: The Modern Library, 2003).

Bernard Lewis, *What Went Wrong?: The Clash Between Islam and Modernity in the Middle East* (New York: Perennial, 2002).

Brynjar Lia, *Architect of Global Jihad: The life of al-Qaeda strategist Abu Musab al-Suri* (New York: Columbia University Press, 2008).

David Loyn, *In Afghanistan: Two Hundred Years of British, Russian and American Occupation* (New York: Palgrave Macmillan, 2009).

Marc Lynch, *Voices of the New Arab Public: Iraq, al-Jazeera, and Middle East Politics Today* (New York: Columbia University Press, 2006).

William Maley, *Rescuing Afghanistan: Briefings* (Sydney: UNSW Press, 2007).

James Mann, *The Rise of the Vulcans: The History of Bush's War Cabinet* (New York: Penguin, 2004).

Abu Walid al-Masri, *The History of the Arab Afghans from the Time of their Arrival in Afghanistan until their Departure with the Taliban*. Serialized in *Al Sharq al Awsat*, December 8–14, 2004.

Jane Mayer, *The Dark Side: The Inside Story of How the War on Terror Turned into a War on American Ideals* (New York: Doubleday, 2008).

Scott McClellan, *What Happened: Inside the Bush White House and Washington's Culture of Deception* (New York: Perseus Books, 2008).

Terry McDermott, *Perfect Soldiers: The 9/11 Hijackers: Who They Were, Why They Did It* (New York: HarperCollins, 2005).

Hugh Miles, *Al-Jazeera: The Inside Story of the Arab News Channel That is Challenging the West* (London: Abacus, 2005).

Assaf Moghadam, *Globalization of Martyrdom: Al-Qaeda, Salafi Jihad, and the Diffusion of Suicide Attacks* (Baltimore, MD: The Johns Hopkins University Press, 2008).

Vahid Mojdeh, *Afghanistan under Five Years of Taliban Sovereignty*, translated by Sepideh Khalili and Saeed Gangi (Kabul, 2001).

John Mueller, *Overblown: How Politicians and the Terrorism Industry Inflate National Security Threats and Why We Believe Them* (New York: Free Press, 2006).

Basil Muhammed, *Al Ansar Al Arab fi Afghanistan* (The Arab Volunteers in Afghanistan). The Committee for Islamic Benevolence Publications, 1991.

Craig M. Mullaney, *The Unforgiving Minute: A Soldier's Education* (New York: The Penguin Press, 2009).

Pervez Musharraf, *In the Line of Fire: A Memoir* (New York: Free Press, 2006).

Richard Myers, *Eyes on the Horizon: Serving on the Front Lines of National Security* (New York: Simon & Schuster, 2009).

Laurie Mylroie, *Bush vs. The Beltway: The Inside Battle over War in Iraq* (New York: Regan Books, 2003).

Laurie Mylroie, *Study of Revenge: Saddam Hussein's Unfinished War with America* (Washington, D.C.: AEI Press, 2001).

Laurie Mylroie, *War Against America: Saddam Hussein And The World Trade Center Attacks* (New York: Regan Books, 2001).

Malcolm W. Nance, *The Terrorists of Iraq: Inside the Strategy and Tactics of the Iraq Insurgency* (BookSurge Publishing, 2007).

Loretta Napoleoni, *Insurgent Iraq: Al Zarqawi and the New Generation* (New York: Seven Stories Press, 2005).

Omar Nasiri, *Inside the Jihad: My Life with Al-Qaeda* (New York: Basic Books, 2006).

Vali Nasr, *The Shia Revival: How Conflicts within Islam Will Shape the Future* (New York: Norton, 2007).

Sean Naylor, *Not a Good Day to Die: The Untold Story of Operation Anaconda* (New York: Berkeley Publishing Group, 2005).

George Packer, *The Assassins' Gate: America in Iraq* (New York: Farrar, Straus and Giroux, 2005).

Robert Pape, *Dying to Win: The Strategic Logic of Suicide Terrorism* (New York: Random House, 2005).

Alison Pargeter, *The New Frontiers of Jihad: Radical Islam in Europe* (Philadelphia: University of Pennsylvania Press, 2008).

Mariane Pearl, *A Mighty Heart: The Brave Life and Death of My Husband, Danny Pearl* (New York: Scribner, 2004).

David Petraeus et al., *The U.S. Army Marine Corps Counterinsurgency Field Manual* (Chicago: University of Chicago Press, 2006).

Kenneth M. Pollack, *A Path Out of the Desert: A Grand Strategy for America in the Middle East* (New York: Random House, 2008).

Syed Qutb, *Milestones* (Mumbai: Bilal Books, 1998 edition).

Ahmed Rashid, *Descent into Chaos: The United States and the Failure of Nation Building in Pakistan, Afghanistan, and Central Asia* (New York: Viking Adult, 2008).

Ahmed Rashid, *Taliban: Militant Islam, Oil & Fundamentalism in Central Asia* (New Haven: Yale University Press, 2001).

Milan Ray, *7-7: The London Bombings, Islam, and the Iraq War* (London: Pluto Press, 2006).

Maria A. Ressa, *Seeds of Terror: An Eyewitness Account of Al-Qaeda's Newest Center of Operations in Southeast Asia* (New York: Free Press, 2003).

Louise Richardson, *What Terrorists Want: Understanding the Enemy, Containing the Threat* (New York: Random House 2007).

Thomas E. Ricks, *Fiasco: The American Military Adventure in Iraq* (New York: Penguin Press, 2006).

Thomas Ricks, *The Gamble: General David Petraeus and the American Military Adventure in Iraq, 2006–2008* (New York: Penguin Group, 2009).

James Risen, *State of War: The Secret History of the CIA and the Bush Administration* (New York: Free Press, 2006).

Linda Robinson, *Tell Me How This Ends: General David Petraeus and the Search for a Way Out of Iraq* (New York: Perseus Books, 2008).

Malise Ruthven, *A Fury for God: The Islamist Attack on America* (New York: Granta Books, 2002).

Malise Ruthven, *Islam in the World* (London: Oxford University Press, 1983).

Marc Sageman, *Leaderless Jihad: Terror Networks in the Twenty-First Century* (Philadelphia: University of Pennsylvania Press, 2008).

Marc Sageman, *Understanding Terror Networks* (Philadelphia: University of Pennsylvania Press, 2004).

Ricardo S. Sanchez and Donald T. Phillips, *Wiser in Battle: A Soldier's Story* (New York: HarperCollins, 2008).

David E. Sanger, *The Inheritance: The World Obama Confronts and the Challenges to American Power* (New York: Harmony, 2009).

Gary Schroen, *First In: An Insider's Account of How the CIA Spearheaded the War on Terror in Afghanistan* (New York: Presidio Press, 2005).

Neil Sheehan, *A Bright Shining Lie: John Paul Vann and America in Vietnam* (New York: Random House, 1988).

Michael Sheehan, *Crush the Cell: How to Defeat Terrorism without Terrorizing Ourselves* (New York: Random House, 2006).

Philip Shenon, *The Commission: the Uncensored History of the 9/11 Investigation* (New York: Hachette Book Group, 2008).

Jennifer Sims and Burton Gerber (eds.), *Transforming U.S. Intelligence* (Washington, D.C.: Georgetown University Press, 2005).

Clive Stafford Smith. *Eight O'clock Ferry to the Windward Side: Seeking Justice in Guantánamo Bay* (New York: Nation Books, 2007).

Anne Stenersen, *Al-Qaida's Quest for Weapons of Mass Destruction: The History Behind the Hype* (Saarbrücken: VDM Verlag, 2009).

Hew Strachan, *Carl von Clausewitz's On War: A Biography* (London: Atlantic Books, 2007).

Abu Musab al-Suri, *The Call for Global Islamic Resistance*, published on jihadist websites, 2004.

Ron Suskind, *The One Percent Doctrine: Deep Inside America's Pursuit of its Enemies since 9/11* (New York: Simon & Schuster, 2007).

Dina Temple-Raston, *The Jihad Next Door: The Lackawanna Six and Rough Justice in an Age of Terror* (New York: PublicAffairs, 2007).

George Tenet, *At the Center of the Storm: My Years at the CIA* (New York: Harper Collins, 2007).

Kenneth R. Timmerman, *Shadow Warriors: The Untold Story of Traitors, Saboteurs, and the Party of Surrender* (New York: Crown Forum, 2007).

Mark Urban, *War In Afghanistan* (London: Macmillan, 1988).

Ibrahim Warde, *The Price of Fear: The Truth behind the Financial War on Terror* (Los Angeles: University of California Press, 2007).

W. Montgomery Watt, *Muhammad: Prophet and Statesman* (New York: Oxford University Press, 1974).

Gabriel Weimann, *Terror on the Internet: The New Arena, the New Challenges* (Washington, D.C.: USIP Press, 2006).

Andrew Welsh-Huggins, *Material Support: A Midwest Al-Qaida Case and the U.S. War on Homegrown Terror* (Ohio University Press, forthcoming).

Bing West, *The Strongest Tribe: War, Politics, and the Endgame in Iraq* (New York: Random House, 2008).

Paul Williams, *Osama's Revenge: The Next 9/11: What the Media and the Government Haven't Told You* (Amherst, NY: Prometheus Books, 2004).

Roberta Wohlstetter, *Pearl Harbor: Warning and Decision* (Stanford: Stanford University Press, 2003).

Bob Woodward, *Bush At War* (New York: Simon & Schuster, 2003).

Bob Woodward, *Plan of Attack: The Definitive Account of the Decision to Invade Iraq* (New York: Simon & Schuster, 2004).

Bob Woodward, *The War Within: A Secret White House History 2006–2008* (New York: Simon & Schuster, 2008).

Andy Worthington, *The Guantánamo Files: The Stories of the 774 Detainees in America's Illegal Prison* (Ann Arbor: Pluto 2007).

Lawrence Wright, *The Looming Tower: Al-Qaeda and the Road to 9/11* (New York: Vintage, 2007).

David Wurmser, *Tyranny's Ally: America's Failure to Defeat Saddam Hussein* (Washington, D.C.: AEI Press, 1999).

Mohammad Yousaf and Mark Adkin, *The Bear Trap: The Defeat of a Superpower* (London: Leo Cooper, 1992).

Rahimullah Yusufzai, *Most Wanted: Profiles of Terror* (New Delhi: Lotus/Roli, 2002).

Abdul Salam Zaeef, *My Life with the Taliban* (New York: Columbia University Press, 2010).

Mariam Abou Zahab and Olivier Roy, *Islamist Networks: The Afghan-Pakistan Connection* (New York: Columbia University Press, 2004).

Ayman al-Zawahiri. *Knights Under the Banner of the Prophet*, excerpts published by *Al Sharq al Awsat*, December 2001.

Montasser al-Zayyat. *The Road to al-Qaeda: The Story of Bin Laden's Right Hand Man* (Sterling, VA: Pluto Press, 2004).

Amy Zegart, *Spying Blind: The CIA, the FBI and the Origins of 9/11* (Princeton: Princeton University Press, 2007).

Selected Congressional hearings and reports

United States. House of Representatives. International Relations Committee, Subcommittee on Oversight and Investigations. *Prepared Testimony of Andrew Kohut,*

How the United States is Perceived in the Arab and Muslim Worlds. November 10, 2005.

United States. Senate. Select Committee on Intelligence. *Prewar Intelligence Assessments About Postwar Iraq*. 110th Congress, 1st session. http://intelligence.senate.gov/prewar.pdf.

United States. Senate. *Report of the Select Committee on Intelligence on Postwar findings about Iraq's WMD programs and links to terrorism and how they compare with prewar assessments*. September 8, 2006. http://www.fas.org/irp/congress/2006_rpt/srpt109-331.pdf

United States. House of Representatives. Foreign Affairs Committee. *Prepared testimony of Peter Bergen*. February 15, 2007.

United States. House of Representatives. Foreign Affairs Committee. Hearing on *Extraordinary Rendition in U.S. Counterterrorism Policy: The Impact on Transatlantic Relations*. April 17, 2007.

United States. Senate. Committee on the Homeland Security and Governmental Affairs. *Hearing on Prison Radicalization: are terrorist cells forming in U.S. cell blocks?* 109th Congress, 2nd session.

United States. Senate. Foreign Relations Committee. *Prepared testimony of James Dobbins: Ending Afghanistan's Civil War*. March 8, 2007.

U.S. Congress. House of Representatives and Senate. *Authorization of the use of Military Force*. 107th Congress, 1st session. S.J. Res. 23. Washington, GPO: 2001.

U.S. Congress. Senate. *Tora Bora Revisited: How We Failed to Get Bin Laden and Why It Matters Today*. 111th Congress, 1st session. S. Prt. 110. Washington, GPO: 2009.

U.S. Congress. House of Representatives and Senate. *Joint hearing of the United States House of Representatives Select Intelligence Committee and the United States Senate Select Intelligence Committee*. Washington, D.C., September 26, 2002.

U.S. Congress. Senate. Homeland Security and Governmental Affairs Committee. *Testimony of Abdirahman Mukhtar*. March 11, 2009.

U.S. Congress. House of Representatives. Permanent Select Committee on Intelligence. *Testimony of Robert Grenier*. April 9, 2008.

U.S. Congress. Senate. Committee on Armed Services. *Inquiry into the treatment of detainees in U.S. custody*. November 20, 2008.

U.S. Congress. Senate. Select Committee on Intelligence. *Prepared Testimony of Director of National Intelligence Michael McConnell*. February 5, 2008.

U.S. Congress. Senate. Select Committee on Intelligence. *Whether public statements regarding Iraq by U.S. government officials were substantiated by intelligence information*. 110th Congress, 2nd session. June 2008.

U.S. Congress. Senate. Select Committee on Intelligence. *Postwar findings about Iraq's WMD programs and links to terrorism and how they compare with prewar assessments*. September 8, 2006.

U.S. Congress. Senate. Armed Services Committee. *Hearing on the subject of Iraqi weapons of mass destruction programs*. Washington, D.C., January 28, 2004.

U.S. Congress. Senate. Select Committee on Intelligence. *Report on whether public statements regarding Iraq by U.S. government officials were substantiated by intelligence information together with additional and minority views*. Report 110–345. 110th Congress, 2nd session. June 2008.

U.S. Congress. Senate. Select Committee on Intelligence. *Current and projected national security threats*. 110th Congress, 1st session. January 11, 2007.

U.S. Congress. Senate. Foreign Relations Committee. *Confronting al-Qaeda: Understanding the threat in Afghanistan and beyond*. 111th Congress, 1st session. October 2009.

U.S. Senate. Armed Services Committee. *The current and future worldwide threats to the national security of the United States*. 111th Congress, 1st session. March 10, 2009.

Selected speeches by Western government officials

Jason Amerine, New America Foundation, Washington, D.C., January 19, 2010.

John Ashcroft, October 31, 2001, Department of Justice, Washington, D.C.

John Brennan, White House press conference, Washington, D.C., January 7, 2010. http://www.whitehouse.gov/the-press-office/briefing-homeland-security-secretary-napolitano-assistant-president-counterterrorism.

George W. Bush, Address to a Joint Session of Congress, Washington, D.C., September 20, 2001.

George W. Bush, Washington, D.C., January 29, 2002.

George W. Bush, March 13, 2002, Washington, D.C.

George W. Bush, Address at West Point, NY, June 1, 2002.

George W. Bush, Washington, D.C., June 6, 2002.

George W. Bush, Cincinnati, OH, October 7, 2002.

George W. Bush, State of the Union, Washington, D.C., January 28, 2003.

George W. Bush, Aboard the USS *Abraham Lincoln*, May 1, 2003.

George W. Bush, Washington, D.C., September 17, 2003.

George W. Bush, Remarks with L. Paul Bremer, Washington, D.C., October 27, 2003.

George W. Bush, Greeley, Colorado, October 25, 2004.

George W. Bush, Washington, D.C., March 16, 2005.

George W. Bush, Renaissance Cleveland Hotel, Cleveland, OH, March 20, 2006.

George W. Bush, Washington, D.C., January 10, 2007.

Dick Cheney, Washington, D.C., May 21, 2009.

Dick Cheney, Center for Security Policy, October 22, 2009, Washington, D.C.

Hank Crumpton, speech at Center for Strategic and International Studies, January 14, 2008. http://csis.org/files/media/csis/press/080114_smart_crumpton.pdf.

Jonathan Evans, address to the Society of Editors, November 5, 2007, Manchester, England. https://www.mi5.gov.uk/output/intelligence-counter-terrorism-and-trust.html.

Michael Hayden, Remarks at the Atlantic Council, Washington, D.C., November 13, 2008.

Gen. Stanley McChrystal, Address, International Institute for Strategic Studies, London, UK, October 1, 2009, www.iiss.org/EasySiteWeb/GatewayLink.aspx?alId=31537.

Barack Obama, "Remarks by the president on a new strategy for Afghanistan and Pakistan," March 27, 2009, Washington, D.C.

Barack Obama, "Remarks by the President in Address to the Nation on the Way Forward in Afghanistan and Pakistan," West Point, NY, December 1, 2009.

Jennifer Pagonis, United Nations High Commissioner on Refugees, Geneva, April 8, 2008.

Colin Powell, presentation before the United Nations, February 5, 2003, New York City. http://www.globalsecurity.org/wmd/library/news/iraq/2003/iraq-030205-powell-un-17300pf.htm.

Condoleezza Rice, Andrews Air Force Base, Maryland, December 5, 2005.

Donald Rumsfeld, Defense Department Briefing, Arlington, VA, December 27, 2001.

Donald Rumsfeld, Defense Department Briefing, Camp X-Ray, Cuba, January 27, 2002.

Donald Rumsfeld, Defense Department Operational Update Briefing, Arlington, VA, June 18, 2003.

Donald Rumsfeld, Defense Department Briefing, Arlington, VA, June 17, 2004.

Donald Rumsfeld, "New Realities in the Media Age," Council on Foreign Relations, February 16, 2006. http://www.cfr.org/publication/9900/.

Selected statements by al-Qaeda leaders and other allied militants

Abu Mansoor al-Amriki. NEFA Foundation, transcript of al Shabab video from Abu Mansoor al-Amiriki, "A response to Barack Obama's speech in Cairo," July 9, 2009; http://www.nefafoundation.org/miscellaneous/FeaturedDocs/nefa_abumansoor0709.pdf.

Osama bin Laden, "Declaration of war against the Americans occupying the land of the two holy places," published in *Al Quds al Arabi*, August 1996. http://www.pbs.org/newshour/terrorism/international/fatwa_1996.html.

Osama bin Laden statement, "Dangers and Signs of the Indian Nuclear Explosions," May 14, 1998, author collection.

Osama bin Laden, December 13, 2001. Transcript available from CNN, translated by Department of Defense. http://archives.cnn.com/2001/US/12/13/tape.transcript/.

Osama bin Laden, "The Will of One Seeking the Support of Allah Almighty, Usama Bin Laden." *Al-Majallah* (a Saudi magazine), December 14, 2001. http://www.fas.org/irp/world/para/ubl-fbis.pdf, p. 222.

Osama bin Laden, videotape released to Al Jazeera after Battle of Tora Bora. December 27, 2001.

Osama bin Laden, "To the Americans." 2002. Posted to Islamist websites and quoted in *Messages to the World: The Statements of Osama bin Laden*. Ed. Bruce Lawrence. London: Verso, 2005, p. 165.

Osama bin Laden, "Message to our Brothers in Iraq," Al Jazeera, February 11, 2003 (translated by ABC News).

Osama bin Laden audiotape, "A Message to the Americans," aired on Al Jazeera, October 18, 2003.

Osama bin Laden, "Message to the American People," October 2004. Quoted in Gilles Kepel, *Al-Qaeda in its Own Words* (Boston: Belknap Press, 2008).

Osama bin Laden. Al Jazeera, "Full transcript of bin Laden's speech," October 29, 2004. http://english.aljazeera.net/archive/2004/11/200849163336457223.html.

Osama bin Laden, "Statement," December 16, 2004, posted on the Internet (translated by BBC monitoring).

Osama bin Laden. *The Guardian* Website has a useful chronology of statements by bin Laden and Zawahiri at http://www.guardian.co.uk/alqaida/page/0,,839823,00.html where bin Laden's February 20, 2006 statement can be found.

Osama bin Laden, translated by CNN, June 29, 2006, http://transcripts.cnn.com/TRANSCRIPTS/0606/29/acd.02.html

Osama bin Laden, "The Way to Frustrate the Conspiracies," December 29, 2007, translated by NEFA Foundation. http://www1.nefafoundation.org/miscellaneous/nefabinladen1207.pdf.

Osama bin Laden, "From Usama to Obama," January 24, 2010, released to Internet, translated by NEFA Foundation.

Omar Abdel-Rahman, Will. Distributed by his sons at a press conference organized by bin Laden on May 26, 1998. The card was translated into English for the first time in Peter Bergen, *The Osama bin Laden I Know*, pp. 204–205.

Abu Musab al-Suri, *The Call for Global Islamic Resistance*, published on jihadist websites, 2004.

Abu Musab al-Zarqawi, "Letter to Osama bin Laden," Coalition Provisional Authority, February 12, 2004.

Abu Musab al-Zarqawi, June 23, 2004. SITE Institute, Washington, D.C. www.siteintelgroup.org/terrorismlibrary/communique/communique_1103219979.pdf.

Abu Musab al-Zarqawi. Pool, Jeffrey (translator). "Zarqawi's pledge of allegiance to al-Qaeda." Jamestown Foundation, Terrorism Monitor, December 16, 2004. http://www.jamestown.org/terrorism/news/article.php?articleid=2369020.

Ayman al-Zawahiri, "Letter to Abu Musab al Zarqawi," July 9, 2005. www.rjchq.org/media/pdf/zawahiriletter.pdf.

Ayman al-Zawahiri. "The Open Meeting with Shaykh Ayman al Zawahiri," *Al Sahab*, 2008.

Selected U.S. government documents

Central Intelligence Agency, Inspector General, Counterterrorism Detention and Interrogation Activities, May 7, 2004.

Central Intelligence Agency, "Khalid Shaykh Mohamed: Preeminent Source On Al-Qa'ida," July 13, 2004.

Central Intelligence Agency, Office of the Inspector General, "Report on CIA Accountability With Respect to the 9/11 Attacks," released August 2007. http://www.fas.org/irp/cia/product/oig-911.pdf

City of New York. Police Department. Mitchell Silber and Arvin Bhatt, "Radicalization in the West," http://www.nypdshield.org/public/SiteFiles/documents/NYPD_Report-Radicalization_in_the_West.pdf.

Colin Powell, Memorandum to Counsel to the President, Assistant to the President for National Security Affairs, subject: Draft Decision Memorandum for the President on the Applicability of the Geneva Convention to the Conflict in Afghanistan, January 26, 2002.

Declassified Key Judgments of the National Intelligence Estimate "Trends in Global Terrorism: Implications for the United States," dated April 2006.

Department of Defense, Detainee Biographies.

Department of Defense, Verbatim Transcript of Combatant Status Review Trial, Khalid Sheikh Mohammed, March 10, 2007. http://www.defenselink.mil/news/transcript_ISN10024.pdf.

Department of Homeland Security, "Strategic Sector Assessment: U.S. Aviation." May 18, 2006.

FBI Affidavit on Ali Mohamed, submitted by Special Agent Daniel Coleman, September 1998.

FBI Report, Abu Jandal, FD-302.

FBI Report, "Interview of John Philip Walker Lindh," December 9–10, 2001.

United States. Federal Bureau of Investigation. "Hijackers Timeline." February 1, 2007.

FBIS Report, Compilation of Usama bin Laden Statements, 1994–January 2004.

Government Accountability Office, "Afghanistan Security: Further Congressional action may be needed to ensure completion of a detailed plan to develop and sustain capable Afghan National Security Forces," June 2008.

John C. Yoo, Memorandum to Alberto Gonzales, United States Department of Justice, Office of Legal Counsel, August 1, 2002.

National Commission on Terrorist Attacks Upon the United States Final Report (Washington, D.C., 2004) ("9/11 Commission Report.")

National Intelligence Council, National Intelligence Assessment, "The terrorist threat to the U.S. homeland," July 2007. http://www.dni.gov/press_releases/20070717_release.pdf.

New York City Police Department, "Al-Qaeda Plots in the West: Assessment of Operations 1988–2008."

State Department, Bureau of Democracy, Human Rights, and Labor, Human Rights Report.

State Department, Patterns of Global Terrorism.

U.S. Army, "The U.S. Army in Afghanistan, Operation Enduring Freedom: October 2001–March 2002," CMH Pub 70-83-1.

U.S. Army, "A Different Kind of War," United States Army in Operation Enduring Freedom, October 2001–September 2005, Combat Studies Institute Press, June 2009.

U.S. Department of Justice, Office of Legal Counsel, Memorandum for John A. Rizzo, "Interrogation of al-Qaida operative," August 1, 2002.

U.S. Department of Justice, Office of Legal Counsel, Memorandum for John A. Rizzo, May 10, 2005.

White House, Text of Strategic Framework Agreement and Security Agreement Between the United States of America and the Republic of Iraq, November 27, 2008, http://georgewbush-whitehouse.archives.gov/news/releases/2008/11/20081127-2.html.

White House, "White Paper of the Interagency Policy Group's Report on U.S. Policy toward Afghanistan and Pakistan," March 27, 2009. http://www.whitehouse.gov/assets/documents/afghanistan_pakistan_white_paper_final.pdf.

Summary of the White House Review of the December 25, 2009 Attempted Terrorist Attack, p. 2. http://www.whitehouse.gov/the-press-office/white-house-review-summary-regarding-12252009-attempted-terrorist-attack.

Donald P. Wright and Colonel Timothy R. Reese, *On Point II: Transition to the New Campaign: The United States Army in Operation IRAQI FREEDOM, May 2003–January 2005* (Washington, D.C.: CSI Press, 2008).

Selected document sets and reports

"A Clean Break: A New Strategy for Securing the Realm," *Institute for Advanced Strategic and Political Studies*, 1996. http://www.iasps.org/strat1.htm.

Amy Belasco, "The Cost of Iraq, Afghanistan, and other global war on terror operations since 9/11," Congressional Research Service, May 15, 2009. www.fas.org/sgp/crs/natsec/RL33110.pdf.

"Battle for Pakistan," multiple papers and authors, New America Foundation, 2010.

Combating Terrorism Center at West Point, *Al-Qa'ida's Foreign Fighters in Iraq: A First Look at the Sinjar Records*, December 19, 2007.

Commission on the Prevention of Weapons of Mass Destruction Proliferation and Terrorism (New York: Vintage Books, 2008). http://www.preventwmd.gov/report/.

Congressional Research Service, "Direct Overt U.S. Aid and Military Reimbursements to Pakistan, FY2002-FY2009," http://www.fas.org/sgp/crs/row/pakaid.pdf.

Council of Europe, Committee on Legal Affairs and Human Rights, "Secret detentions and illegal transfers of detainees involving Council of Europe Member States," June 7, 2007. http://news.bbc.co.uk/1/shared/bsp/hi/pdfs/marty_08_06_07.pdf.

Sara Daly, John Parachini, and William Rosenau. "Aum Shinrikyo, Al-Qaeda, and the Kinshasa Reactor: Implications of Three Case Studies for Combating Nuclear Terrorism." RAND Project AIR FORCE 2005. RAND Corporation. http://www.rand.org/pubs/documented_briefings/2005/RAND_DB458.pdf

Mark Denbeaux and Joshua Denbeaux, "Report on Guantánamo detainees: A profile of 517 detainees through analysis of Department of Defense data," Seton University School of Law, http://law.shu.edu/aaafinal.pdf.

James Dobbins, Seth Jones, Benjamin Runkle, Siddarth Mohandas, *Occupying Iraq: A History of the Coalition Provisional Authority* (Santa Monica: RAND, 2009).

James Dobbins, John G. McGinn, Keith Crane, Seth G. Jones, Rollie Lal, Andrew Rathmell, Rachel M. Swanger, Anga R. Timilsina, *America's Role in Nation Building From Germany to Iraq* (Santa Monica: RAND, 2003).

Gilles Dorronsoro, "The Taliban's Winning Strategy in Afghanistan." Carnegie Endowment for International Peace, 2009.

Christine Fair, "Suicide attacks in Afghanistan, 2001–2007," United Nations Assistance Mission in Afghanistan, September 9, 2007.

George Washington University. National Security Archive.

Government of India, Final Report on Mumbai Attacks, 26–28 November, 2008.

Nancy Kay Hayden. "Terrifying Landscapes: a study of scientific research into understanding motivations of non-state actors to acquire and/or use weapons of mass destruction." Defense Threat Reduction Agency. June 22, 2007. http://www.dtra.mil/documents/asco/publications/pdf/Terrifying_Landscapes.pdf.

Scott Helfstein, Nassir Abdullah, Muhammad al-Obaidi. "Deadly Vanguards: a Study of al-Qa'ida's Violence against Muslims." Combating Terrorism Center at West Point, December 2009.

Scott Helfstein. "Making the Grade?: Assessing al-Qa'ida's Learning and Adaptation." Combating Terrorism Center at West Point, May 2009.

Human Rights Watch, "The Human Cost," April 15, 2007. http://www.hrw.org/en/reports/2007/04/15/human-cost-0.

Institute for Defense Analyses, "Iraqi Perspectives Project: Saddam and Terrorism: Emerging Insights from Captured Iraqi Documents," September 2007.

International Atomic Energy Agency, "Combating illicit trafficking in nuclear and other radioactive material," Technical Guidance Reference Manual (IAEA: Vienna, 2007).

International Crisis Group. "Afghanistan's Endangered Compact." Policy Briefing, January 29, 2007. http://www.crisisgroup.org/library/documents/asia/south_asia/b59_afghanistans_endangered_compact.pdf.

International Crisis Group. "Countering Afghanistan's insurgency: no quick fixes." Asia Report, November 2, 2006. http://www.crisisgroup.org/home/index.cfm?id=4485.

International Crisis Group. "In Their Own Words: Reading the Iraqi Insurgency." Middle East Report No. 50. February 15, 2006. http://www.crisisgroup.org/home/index.cfm?id=3953.

IntelCenter. "The Al-Qaeda Documents," Ben Venzke (Tempest Publishing, 2002).

IntelCenter Breakout of as-Sahab audio/video.

International Crisis Group, "Pakistan's Tribal Areas: Appeasing the Militants," December 11, 2006.

Colin Kahl, Michèle A. Flournoy, Shawn Brimley, "Shaping the Iraq Inheritance," CNAS, June 2008.

Hekmat Karzai, "Strategic and Operational Measures to Curb the Growing Threat of Suicide Terrorism in Afghanistan." Centre for Conflict and Peace Studies, Kabul, Afghanistan.

Kenneth Katzman, "Afghanistan: Elections, Constitution, and Government," Congressional Research Service, August 8, 2006. http://fpc.state.gov/documents/organization/71864.pdf.

Kenneth Katzman. "Afghanistan: post-war governance, security, and U.S. policy." CRS Report for Congress, September 10, 2007. http://www.fas.org/sgp/crs/row/RL30588.pdf

Sarah Ladbury, "Testing hypotheses of radicalization in Afghanistan: why do men join the Taliban and Hezb-i-Islami? How much do local communities support them?" Department of International Development, August 14, 2009.

Sameer Lalwani, "Pakistani Capabilities for a Counterinsurgency Campaign: A Net Assessment," New America Foundation, September 2009.

Robert S. Leiken, "Bearers of global jihad?" The Nixon Center, March 2004.

Daniel Markey, "Securing Pakistan's Tribal Belt," Council on Foreign Relations, 2008.

Pew Global Attitudes Survey, "Unfavorable views of Jews and Muslims on the increase in Europe," September 17, 2008. http://pewglobal.org/reports/pdf/262.pdf

Pew Global Attitudes Project, "Global public opinion in the Bush years," December 18, 2008. http://pewglobal.org/reports/display.php?ReportID=263.

Terror Free Tomorrow, "Results of a new nationwide public opinion survey before the June 2008 Pakistani by-elections," June 2008. http://www.terrorfreetomorrow.org/upimagestft/PakistanPollReportJune08.pdf.

Terror Free Tomorrow, "Pakistanis reject U.S. military action against al-Qaeda; more support bin Laden than President Musharraf," September 2007. http://www.terrorfreetomorrow.org/upimagestft/Pakistan%20Poll%20Report.pdf.

David Schanzer, Charles Kurzman, Ebrahim Moosa, "Anti-terror lessons of Muslim-Americans," Triangle Center on Terrorism and Homeland Security, p. 7. http://sanford.duke.edu/centers/tcths/documents/Anti-TerrorLessonsfinal.pdf.

Senlis Council, "The Return of the Taliban," Spring/summer 2006. http://www.icosgroup.net/documents/Afghanistan_5_Years_Later.pdf.

Yuma Turabi and Lorenzo Delegates, "Afghanistan: Bringing Accountability Back In From Subjects of Aid to Citizens of the State," Integrity Watch Afghanistan Report, June 2008.

New York University Center on Law and Security, "Terrorist Trial Report Card, U.S. edition," September 11, 2006, http://www.lawandsecurity.org/publications/TTRC Complete.pdf.

United Kingdom. Home Office. "Report of the Official Account of the Bombings in London on 7th July 2005." http://www.homeoffice.gov.uk/documents/7-july-report.pdf?view=Binary.

United Nations Assistance Mission to Afghanistan. "Suicide attacks in Afghanistan." September 1, 2007.

United Nations Commission of Inquiry into the Facts and Circumstances of the Assassination of Former Prime Minister Benazir Bhutto, April 15, 2010.

United States Institute of Peace, "Iraq Study Group Report," December 6, 2006. http://media.usip.org/reports/iraq_study_group_report.pdf.

Matt Waldman, "Falling Short: Aid Effectiveness in Afghanistan," Oxfam Research Report, May 2008.

West Point. Combating Terrorism Center. Harmony collection.

West Point, Combating Terrorism Center. *Bombers, Bank Accounts, and Bleedout: Al-Qaeda's Road in and out of Iraq,* ed. Brian Fishman.

Joshua T. White, "Pakistan's Islamist Frontier: Islamic Politics and U.S. Policy in Pakistan's North-West Frontier." Center on Faith and International Affairs, 2008).

Andrew Wilder and Andrew Reynolds, "Free, fair or flawed?" Afghanistan Research Evaluation Unit, September 2004, http://www.cmi.no/pdf/?file=/afghanistan/doc/AfghanElections-FreeFairorFlawed.pdf.

World Health Organization, Afghanistan and Iran, 2006.

Zroona Zehnoona. "An assessment of the hearts and minds campaign in southern Afghanistan." Senlis Council, autumn 2006. http://www.senliscouncil.net/modules/publications/017_publication

Selected court documents

Bundeskriminalamt, "Auswertebericht ze Ahmad Fadil Nazal Al Khalayleh alias Abu Musab al-Zarqawi," July 22, 2005.

United States of America v. Adam Gadahn, Central District Court of California, SA CR 05-254 A Superseding Indictment.

United States of America v. Ali Hamza Ahmad Sulayman al Bahlul.

United States of America v. Ali Mohamed, United States Southern District, New York. S(7) 98 Cr. 1023 (LBS), October 24, 2000.

United States of America v. Bryant Neal Vinas, Eastern District Court of New York 08-CR-823.

United States of America v. Cabdulaahi Ahmed Faarax, Abdeiweli Yassin Isse, criminal complaint filed October 8, 2009 in U.S. District Court Minnesota.

United States of America v. Daniel Patrick Boyd et al.; Indictment in U.S. District Court for the Eastern District of North Carolina, filed 7/22/09.

United States of America v. David C. Headley, Northern District of Illinois, Eastern Division, Case No. 09 CR 830. Affidavit in Support of Criminal Complaint.

United States of America v. Dhiren Barot, Southern District of New York 05 Crim. 311 sealed indictment.

United States of America v. Enaam Arnaout, No. 02-CR-892 (North District of Illinois, filed January 6, 2003).

United States of America v. Hassan Abujihaad, a/k/a "Paul R. Hall,' District Court of Connecticut, March 1, 2007.

United States of America v. Iyman Faris, United States District Court, Eastern District of Virginia, Alexandria Division, Statement of Facts.

United States of America v. Jeffrey Leon Battle et al, United States District Court of Oregon, No. CR 02-399HA, Indictment.

United States of America v. John Phillip Walker Lindh, United States District Court, Eastern District of Virginia, Crim. No. 02-37-A, "Proffer of facts in support of defendant's suppression motions."

United States of America v. Kevin James et al U.S. District Court for the Central District of California Case No. CR 05-214-CJC and exhibits.

United States of America v. Mohamad Ibrahim Shnewer, Dritan Duka, Eljvir Duka, Shain Duka, Serdar Tatar, U.S. District Court, District of New Jersey, Criminal No 07-459.

United States of America v. Richard Colvin Reid, United States District Court of Massachusetts, Crim. No. 02-10013-WGY, Government's Sentencing Memorandum, January 17, 2003.

United States of America v. Najibullah Zazi, Eastern District of New York. Indictment. 09-CR-663: Memorandum of law in support of the government's motion for a permanent order of detention.

United States of America v. Ali Saleh Khalah al-Marri, Plea Agreement, filed April 3, 2009, District Court for the Central District of Illinois, Peoria Division N0. 09-CR-10030.

United States of America v. Usama bin Laden, et al. S(7) 98 Cr. 1023 (LBS). United States District Court, Southern District of New York.

United States of America v. Zacarias Moussaoui, Crim. No. 01-455-A (Eastern District of Virginia, Alexandria division).

United States Supreme Court, HAMDI V. RUMSFELD (03-6696) 542 U.S. 507 (2004), Opinion (O'Connor), June 28, 2004.

District Court of Little Rock, Arkansas, County of Pulaski, Affidavit for Search and Seizure Warrant. Carlos Leon Bleds.

Mohammed Abdullah Warsame, Affidavit in support of pre-trial detention," filed by Special Agent Kiann Vandenover, U.S. District Court of Minnesota, Crim. 04-29 (JRT/FLN), February 6, 2004.

Tribunale di Milano, Sezione Giudice per le indagini preliminari, "The judge presiding over preliminary investigations," n. 10838/05, n. 1966/05. "Decree for the application of coercive measures," art. 292 c.p.p., n. n. 10838/05, n. 1966/05.

Newspapers, magazines, journals, news agencies and broadcast news

Newspapers: The Age, Al-Quds al-Arabi, Al-Sharq al-Awsat, Arab News, Chicago Tribune, Christian Science Monitor, Columbus Dispatch, Daily Telegraph, Daily Times (Pakistan), *Dawn* (Pakistan), *Der Spiegel, Financial Times, The Forward, Globe and Mail, The Guardian, Al-Hayat, Independent, Los Angeles Times, New York Daily News, New York Times, The News* (Pakistan), *Philadelphia Inquirer, Plymouth Herald, Sunday Mail, Times of India, Times of London, U.S. News and World Report, USA Today, Vancouver Sun, Wall Street Journal, Washington Post, Washington Times*

Magazines: Al Majallah, American Interest, Arms Control Today, Atlantic Monthly, Bulletin of the Atomic Scientists, Commentary, Defense Horizons, Granta, Foreign Policy, Friday Times, Jihad, Middle East Media Research Institute Special Dispatch Series, Mother Jones, The Nation, National Interest, National Review, New Scientist, The New Republic, New York Review of Books, New York Times Magazine, The New Yorker, Newsweek, Politico, Prospect, Talking Points Memo, Time, Vanity Fair, Washington Monthly, The Weekly Standard

Journals: Air & Space Power Journal, CTC Sentinel, Current History, Democracy, Foreign Affairs, Foreign Policy Research Institute, Georgetown Journal of International Affairs, International Security, Jane's Intelligence Review, Journal of Democracy, Journal of Strategic Studies, Middle East Policy, Middle East Quarterly, Middle East Review of International Affairs, Nonproliferation Review, RAND Paper Series, Military Review, Political Psychology, Political Science and Politics, Political Science Quarterly,

Quarterly Journal of Military History, Review of Politics, Studies in Conflict & Terrorism, Terrorism and Political Violence, Terrorism Monitor (Jamestown Foundation), *Washburn Law Journal, Washington Quarterly, World Policy Journal*

News agencies: Agence France Presse, American Forces Press Service, Associated Press, CanWest News, Global Security Newswire, Reuters

Broadcast news and radio: ABC, Al Arabiya, Al Jazeera, BBC, CBC, CBS News, CNN, Fox News, Geo, MBC, NBC, NPR, Radio Free Europe/Radio Liberty, PBS, Voice of America

Documentaries

Adam Curtis, "The Power of Nightmares," BBC Two, October 2004.

CNN, "In the Footsteps of bin Laden." Aired August 23, 2006.

CNN, "Terror Nation", January 1994.

Discovery/Times Channel, "Mission Ops: Assignment IEDs." Aired May 15, 2007. Story House Productions.

Discovery/Times Channel, "Al-Qaeda 2.0." Aired March 25, 2003. Story House Productions.

Yosri Fouda. "Top Secret: The Road to September 11." Al-Jazeera (Qatar). Aired September 11, 2002.

Home Box Office, "The Journalist and the Jihadi: The Murder of Daniel Pearl," 2006.

National Geographic, "Holy War, Inc." Story House Productions, 2001.

National Geographic, "Blinding Horizon: Osama Bin Laden's Quest for the Bomb." Story House Productions, 2003.

PBS Frontline, "Obama's War" (2009); "Bush's War" (2007); "The Dark Side" (2006); "Chasing the Sleeper Cell" (2003); "Campaign Against Terror" (2002); "Gunning for Saddam" (2001); "Loose Nukes" (1996).

Acknowledgments

No book is an island, and this one certainly wasn't. Katherine Tiedemann worked on all phases of this book: performing and organizing research, making important editorial suggestions, fact-checking and footnoting all of the material, and doing photo research. It was my good fortune to have found someone as smart and well-organized as Katherine to work on this book and to have worked with every day for the past three years at the New America Foundation. Katherine is going on to do her Ph.D. in political science at George Washington University and has a very bright future ahead of her.

The New America Foundation in Washington, D.C., has been my home for almost a decade and I'm grateful to Steve Clemons for bringing me on board. And I am especially lucky to work there with Steve Coll, who read a draft of this book and made some typically acute suggestions about how to improve it significantly. It is a privilege to work with Steve whose smarts and self-effacement are legendary in a town that rarely sees much of those qualities in combination. Thanks also to my other New America colleagues: Brian Fishman, who had helpful feedback on the manuscript, and Patrick Doherty, whom I work with every day on some of the issues that are discussed in this book. And thanks to Simone Frank, Danielle Maxwell, Andrew Lebovich, Matt Caris, and Christina Satkowski.

Ken Ballen, a leading pollster in the Muslim world, read the manuscript not once but twice and had many important suggestions about how to improve it. Similarly, the security expert Andy Marshall made key editorial observations about how to conceptualize the book. The financial historian Liaquat Ahamed and his wife, Meena, also made helpful suggestions about the manuscript. Karen Greenberg at New York University's Center on Law and Security had useful ideas about improvements to the book and has been a great supporter. Karen's annual counterterrorism conference at La Pietra in Florence is a constant source of new ideas and connections. Thanks also to Stephen Holmes at NYU.

Some of the reporting for this book first appeared in *The New Republic*. I am grateful to editor Franklin Foer for that opportunity. The magazine's executive editor, Richard

Just, made my pieces much better and had some excellent ideas about improvements to this book. Meaghan Rady Pesavento, a former student of mine at Harvard, took time out of her busy life to read the manuscript and had a host of ideas about ways to sharpen the manuscript.

Thanks to Jane Mayer, Lawrence Wright, and James Risen who looked over the manuscript and whose work in the field, along with Steve Coll's, has been foundational. Thomas Hegghammer, a leading scholar of jihadism, reviewed the manuscript as did Stephen Tankel, an expert on jihadist groups. Gary Ackerman, an authority on the intersection between terrorists and weapons of mass destruction, reviewed the chapter on WMD. I'm very grateful to all of you, while any errors of fact and interpretation remain, of course, my own.

Some of the reporting and ideas for the book took shape while collaborating with other writers, in particular Paul Cruickshank and Katherine Tiedemann, and also Laurence Footer, Michael Lind, Swati Pandey, Alec Reynolds, and Sameer Lalwani. Thanks to you all. Additional thanks to Richard Clarke, who solicited two papers on terrorism for the July 2008 Annals of the American Academy of Political and Social Science, and to Brian Fishman—then at West Point's Combating Terrorism Center—for commissioning a chapter in the 2008 publication *Bombers, Bank Accounts, and Bleedout: Al-Qa'ida's Road In and Out of Iraq*.

Thanks also to all those who agreed to be interviewed for the book. Some of those who were interviewed are leading writers, scholars, and practitioners in the field whose work has been influential on mine, and many of whom have helped me in a myriad of other ways. Their names can be found in the list of interviewees on pages 353–356.

Thanks to Joel Rayburn and Emma Sky for your hospitality and insights in Iraq. In Afghanistan, thanks to Khalid Mafton, Yusuf Masoud, Hamid Hamidullah, May Ying Welsh and the staff at Gandamack Lodge and in particular to Peter and Hassina Jouvenal. Peter and Richard Mackenzie were my guides on my first trip to Afghanistan in 1993; thanks to you both for almost two decades of friendship. In Pakistan, thanks for repeated help over the years to Rahimullah Yusufzai, Ismail Khan, Jamal Ismail, Imtiaz Ali, and Declan Walsh. Thanks for the hospitable welcome and insights I was given in Saudi Arabia by Khaled Batarfi and Saad al-Jabri. In Egypt thanks to Reem Nada for your help on and off over the past decade. In Milan, thanks to Leo Sisti for your sage advice, and in London to Mohammed al-Shafey for your help.

I have worked at CNN in one capacity or another since 1990 and am grateful to continue to work there today with so many of its excellent reporters, executives, producers, and editors—in particular, David Doss, Kathy Slobogin, Cliff Hackel, Ken Shiffman, Pamela Sellars, Rick Davis, Richard Galant, Steve Turnham, Penny Manis, Kerry Rubin, Jill Chappell, Stephanie Kotuby, and Kay Jones. A special thanks to Charlie Moore, Anderson Cooper, and Phil Littleton for the various trips to Afghanistan and Pakistan we have taken in the past several years. Thanks also to Henry Schuster, now at CBS's *60 Minutes*, who has been a friend and colleague for a decade and a half.

Thanks to Carsten Oblaender of Storyhouse Productions with whom I have worked on four intellectually stimulating documentaries about various aspects of the "war on terror." And thanks to producer Simon Epstein who helped me to better understand the world of IEDs. And at Discovery thanks to Bill Smee, Ed Hersh, and Ron Simon. Some of the reporting for this book first took shape in a number of different magazines and newspapers. Thanks to Cullen Murphy at the *Atlantic*, Paul Glastris at *Washington Monthly*, Adam Katz at *The Nation*, Gideon Rose at *Foreign Affairs*, Marie Arana, Warren Bass, and Jonathan Pomfret at *The Washington Post*, David Shipley and Tobin Harshaw at *The New York Times*, Bobby Ghosh at *Time*, David Goodhart at *Prospect*, Will Dana at *Rolling Stone*, and Monika Bauerlein at *Mother Jones*. At *Vanity Fair*, thanks to Graydon Carter, Chris Garrett, Wayne Lawson, and Cullen Murphy for taking a continuing interest in my work on al-Qaeda.

In addition to those reporters acknowledged elsewhere in this book, the work of the following was especially helpful in reconstructing the events of the "war on terror"—at the *New York Times*: Mark Mazzetti, Scott Shane, Eric Schmitt, Pir Zubair Shah, Jane Perlez, Peter Baker, Carlotta Gall, C.J. Chivers, Dexter Filkins, Alissa Rubin, Jeffrey Gettleman, and David Rohde, and at the *Washington Post*: Craig Whitlock, Joby Warrick, Sudarsan Raghavan, Karen DeYoung, Rajiv Chandrasekaran, Peter Finn, Barton Gellman, Walter Pincus, Dana Priest, and Bob Woodward. Also Jason Burke at *The Observer*.

Teaching graduate students at Harvard and at Johns Hopkins University has been instrumental in helping to form my thinking about the "war on terror." Thanks to Juliette Kayyem for introducing me to Ash Carter at Harvard's Kennedy School and to Ash for hiring me to teach a class there in 2008. A particular thank you is due to teaching assistant Hope LeBeau without whom I could not have taught the class. Thanks also to all the students in that class. Also thanks to Sunil Khilnani, who hired me to teach at the School of Advanced International Studies at Johns Hopkins in 2003, and to the students I have taught there over the years.

Thanks to Bruce Hoffman for involving me in his scholarly journal, *Studies in Conflict & Terrorism* and for our work together for the National Security Preparedness Group, and to its co-chairs Lee Hamilton and Thomas Kean, and director Michael Allen. And thanks to Susan Glasser, Blake Hounshell, and Rebecca Frankel of *Foreign Policy* for their collaboration on the AfPak Channel. And thanks to Katherine Tiedemann for her key work on that project. Thanks also to Marin Strmecki of the Smith Richardson foundation, Nancy Chang of the Open Society Institute, and Barmak Pazhwak of the United States Institute of Peace for their funding of our counterterrorism work at the New America Foundation.

Thanks to Chris Clifford of Keppler Speakers, Clark Forcey, and Steve Sadicario of NS Bienstock for their advice and help over the years. Thanks also to Shaun Waterman, Eason Jordan, Walter Purdy, Gregory Saathoff, Brent Stirton, Tim Hetherington, Scott Wallace, Richard Parry, Gina Bennett, George P. Luczko, Oubai Shahbandar, Thomas W. Collins, and Erroll Southers.

Thanks to Martha Levin and Dominick Anfuso of Free Press for commissioning and publishing my work since 1999. The contract for this book was signed in 2004. Martha and Dominick have waited patiently since then for the appearance of this book. In between came another book, *The Osama bin Laden I Know*, which mushroomed into a much larger project than was initially conceived. Thanks to Dominick, who edited both books and had a number of valuable ideas about how this book should be shaped. Maura O'Brien, Dominick's assistant, was a great help. Thanks to Carol de Onís for overseeing the complicated copy edit, Tom Pitoniak for his excellent work on that copy edit, Elisa Rivlin for her legal review, Carisa Hays for her always sage advice, and big thanks to Jill Siegel. Thanks also to Gene Thorp for the handsome maps and to Keith Sinzinger, Stine Smemo, and Rumana Haider.

My agent Tina Bennett of Janklow & Nesbit has been a joy to work with since 2001, both as a friend and as an intellectual sounding board. Also at Janklow, thanks to Svetlana Katz.

Thanks to my family: Tom Bergen—who died before he could read this—Sarah Bergen, Katherine Bergen, and Con Coughlin—in whose house some of this book was written—Margaret Bergen and the McCanns: Charlotte (who helped to organize some of my research), Isabel and Brendan. Thanks also to all the Mabile family: Clebert and Alberta Mabile; Donnovan, Denise, Ahsly, Mia, and Reese Mabile; Heidi, Clay, Andrew, and Bella Gould—in whose house I wrote some of this book—and Daphane, George, and Ian Takacs.

Above all, thanks to my wife, Tresha Mabile. I apologize for all the missed weekends and vacations and promise to make it up. Thanks for reading this book many times over and constantly steering me away from the trivial to focus on the important, as you have done in the widest sense possible in all spheres of life. This book is dedicated to you with admiration and with love.

Index

About the Author

Peter Bergen is the author of *Holy War, Inc.*, which has been translated into eighteen languages, and *The Osama bin Laden I Know*. They were both named among the best nonfiction books of the year by *The Washington Post* and documentaries based on the books were both nominated for Emmys. Bergen is CNN's national security analyst, a director at the New America Foundation and a fellow at New York University's Center on Law & Security. He is a contributing editor at *The New Republic* and has worked as a correspondent for National Geographic television, Discovery, and CNN. He has held teaching positions at the Kennedy School of Government at Harvard University and at the School of Advanced International Studies at Johns Hopkins University. His writing has appeared in the *New York Times, Washington Post, Wall Street Journal, Foreign Affairs, Atlantic, Rolling Stone, Time, Vanity Fair*, and many other newspapers and magazines around the world. He is a member of the National Security Preparedness Group, a successor to the 9/11 Commission, and is the editor of the AfPak Channel, which can be found at www.foreignpolicy.com/afpak. He has testified before several congressional committees about Afghanistan, Pakistan, and al-Qaeda. Bergen holds a M.A. in modern history from New College, Oxford University. He is married to the documentary director Tresha Mabile. They live in Washington, D.C.

For more information visit www.peterbergen.com.